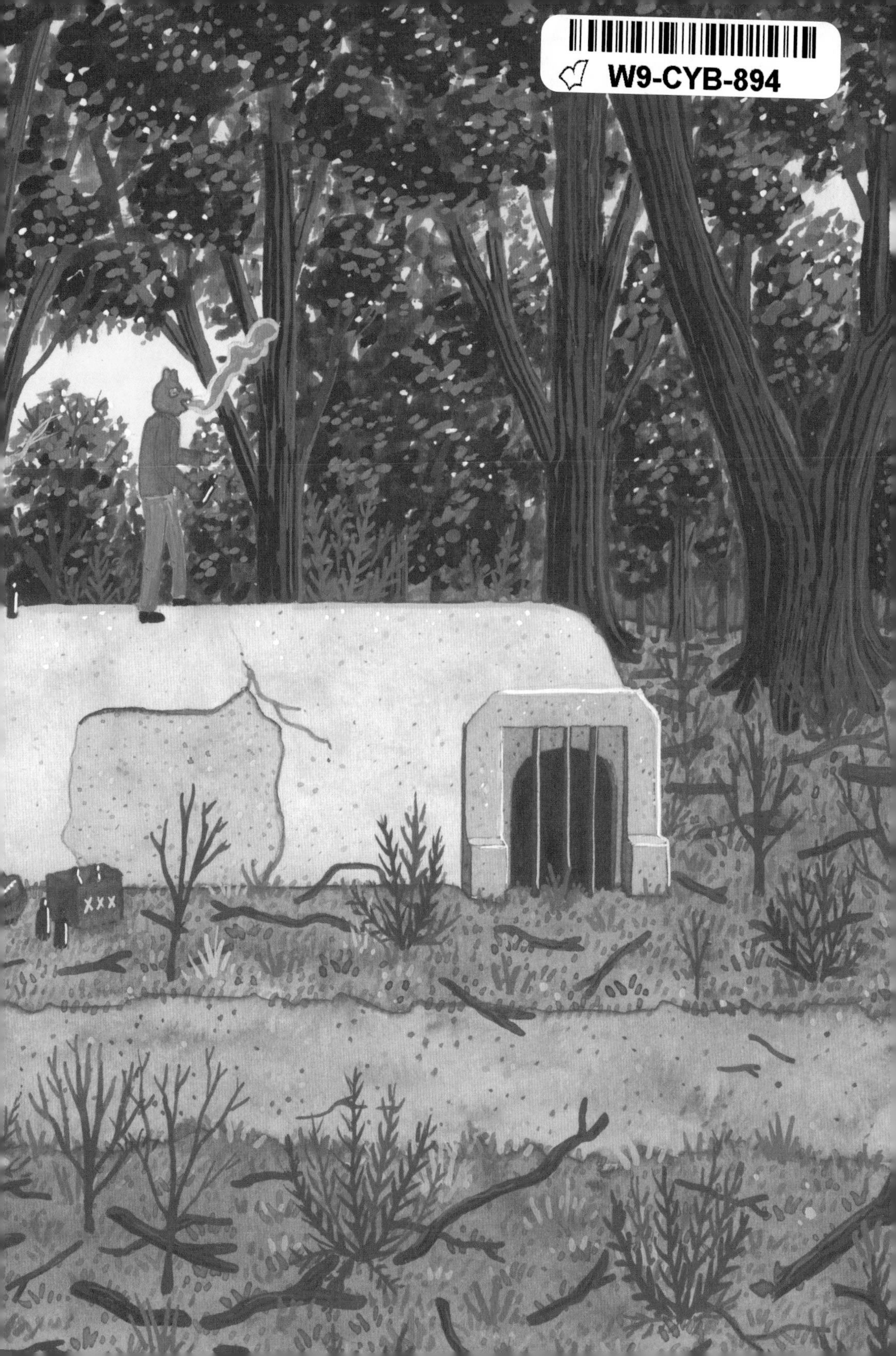
XXX

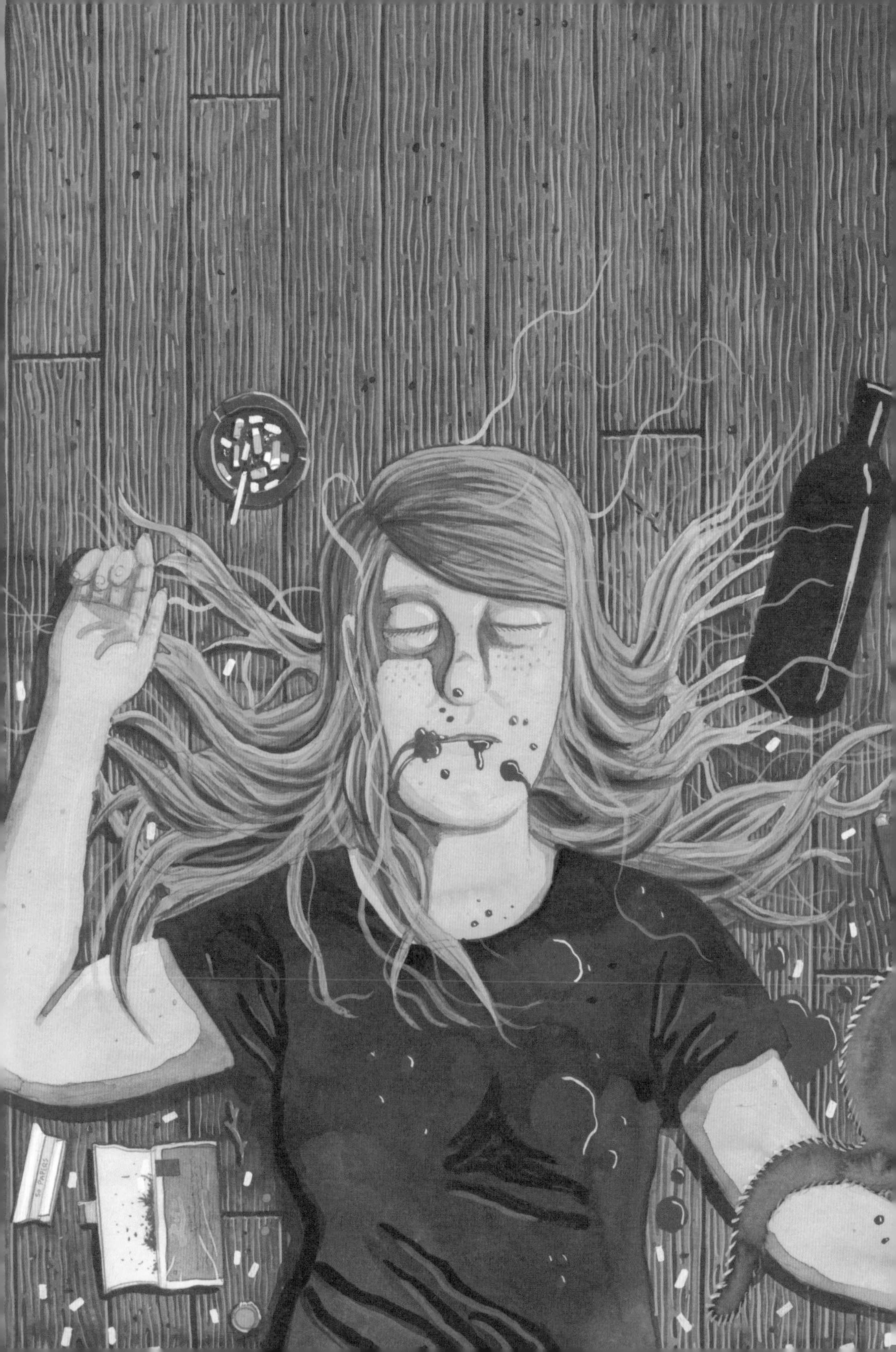
50 PAPERS

ONE MORE YEAR

SH FB

CONTENTS, CAST OF CHARACTERS, INDICIA:

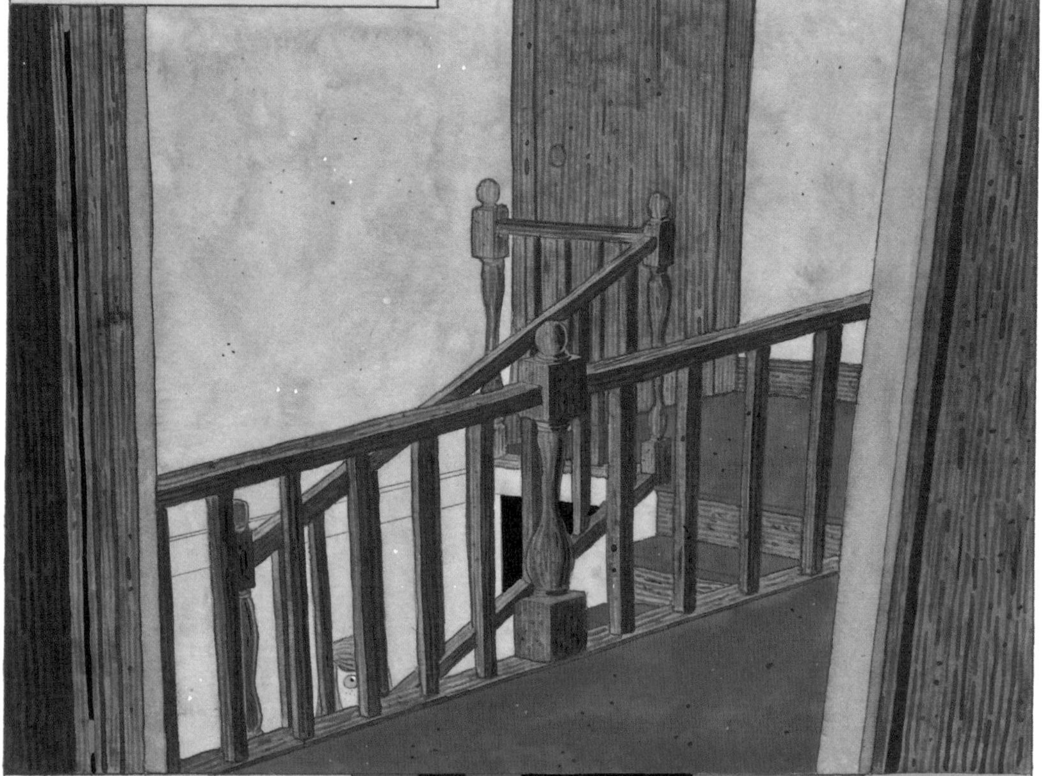

CHRONOLOGY NOTE: THESE EPISODES TAKE PLACE DURING OR BEFORE THE END OF "MEGAHEX".

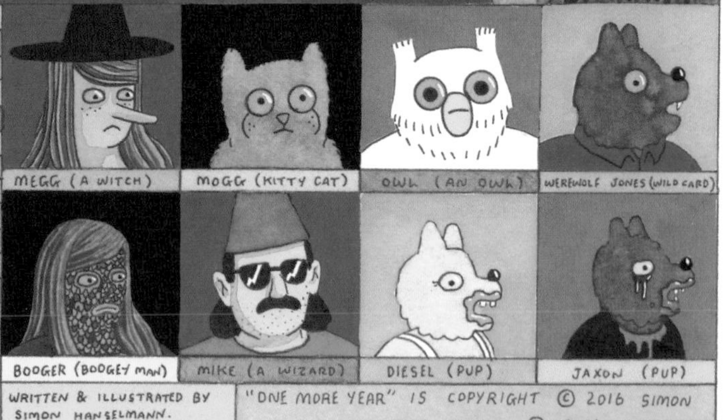

MEGG (A WITCH) · MOGG (KITTY CAT) · OWL (AN OWL) · WEREWOLF JONES (WILD CARD)

BOOGER (BOOGEY MAN) · MIKE (A WIZARD) · DIESEL (PUP) · JAXON (PUP)

WRITTEN & ILLUSTRATED BY SIMON HANSELMANN.

EDITOR & ASSOCIATE PUBLISHER: ERIC REYNOLDS.

BOOK DESIGN: SIMON HANSELMANN.

PRODUCTION: PAUL BARESH.

PUBLISHER: GARY GROTH.

FANTAGRAPHICS BOOKS INC.
7563 LAKE CITY WAY NE
SEATTLE, WASHINGTON
UNITED STATES 98115

ISBN: 978-1-60699-997-4

LIBRARY OF CONGRESS CONTROL NUMBER: 2016911485

FIRST PRINTING. MAY 2017. PRINTED IN KOREA.

FANTAGRAPHICS BOOKS

FOR KARL VON BAMBERGER & ALVIN BUENAVENTURA.

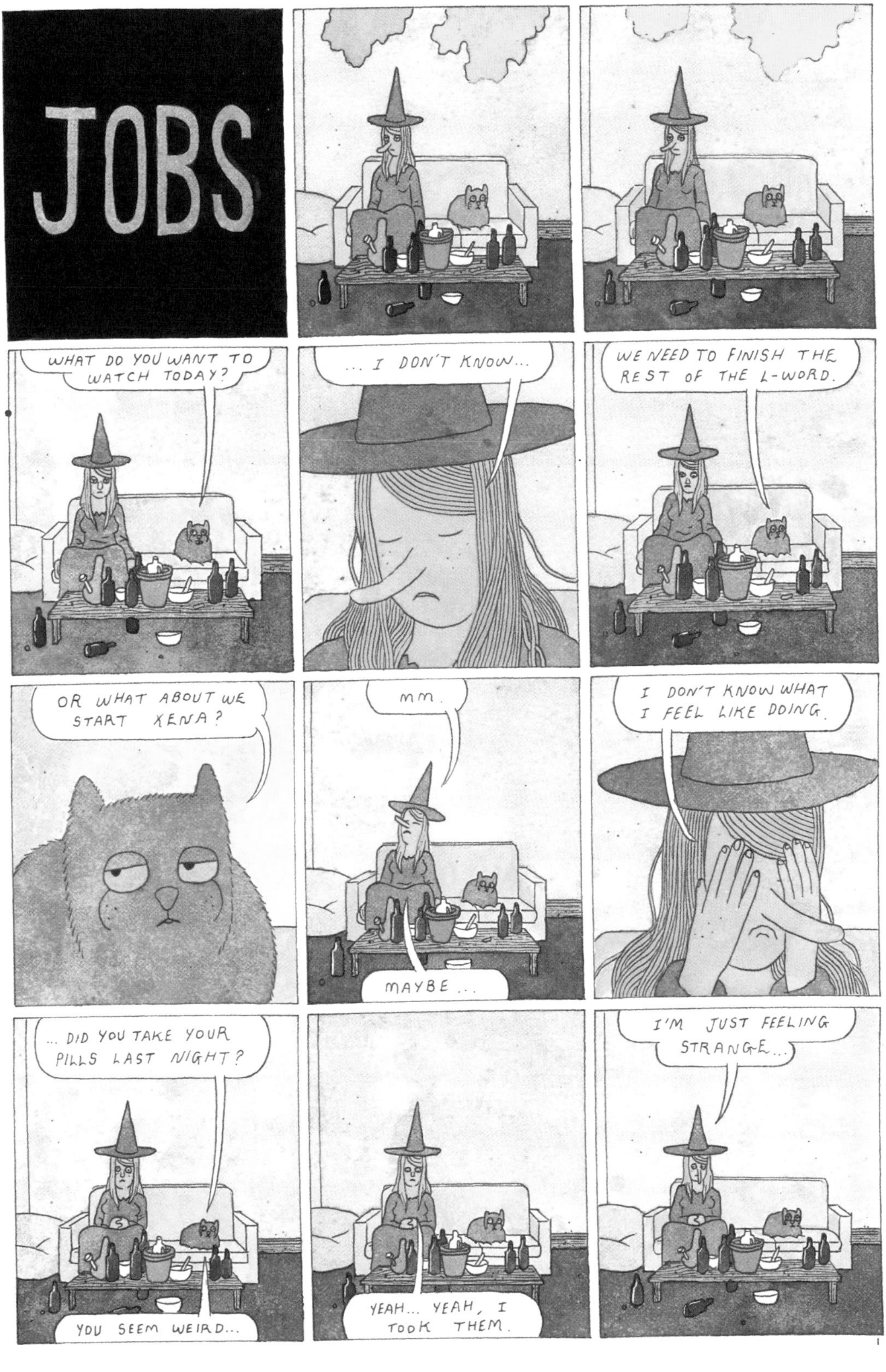
JOBS
WHAT DO YOU WANT TO WATCH TODAY?
... I DON'T KNOW...
WE NEED TO FINISH THE REST OF THE L-WORD.
OR WHAT ABOUT WE START XENA?
MM.
MAYBE...
I DON'T KNOW WHAT I FEEL LIKE DOING.
... DID YOU TAKE YOUR PILLS LAST NIGHT?
YOU SEEM WEIRD...
YEAH... YEAH, I TOOK THEM.
I'M JUST FEELING STRANGE...

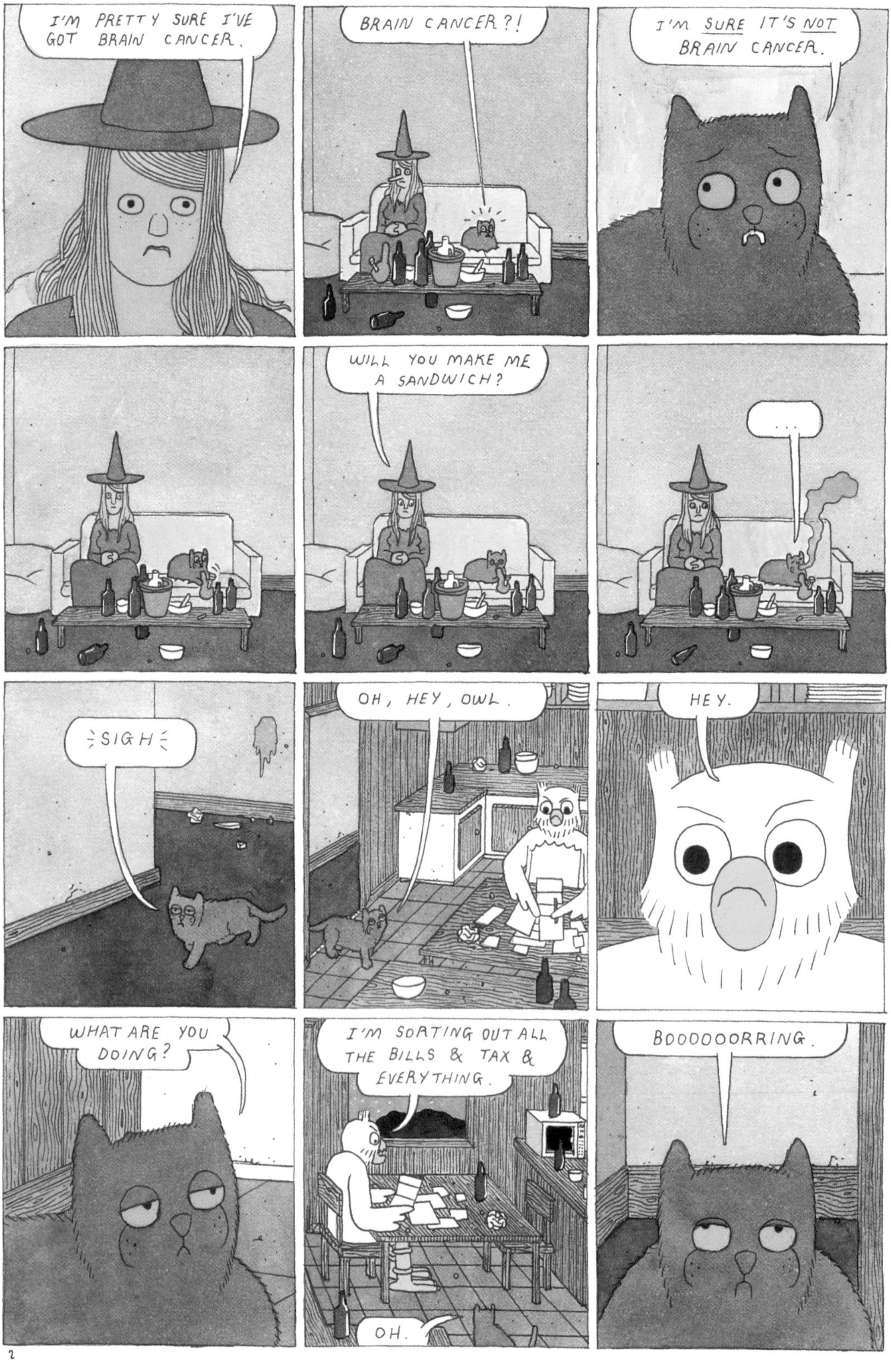
I'M PRETTY SURE I'VE GOT BRAIN CANCER.
BRAIN CANCER?!
I'M SURE IT'S NOT BRAIN CANCER.
WILL YOU MAKE ME A SANDWICH?
...
SIGH
OH, HEY, OWL.
HEY.
WHAT ARE YOU DOING?
I'M SORTING OUT ALL THE BILLS & TAX & EVERYTHING.
OH.
BOOOOOORRING.

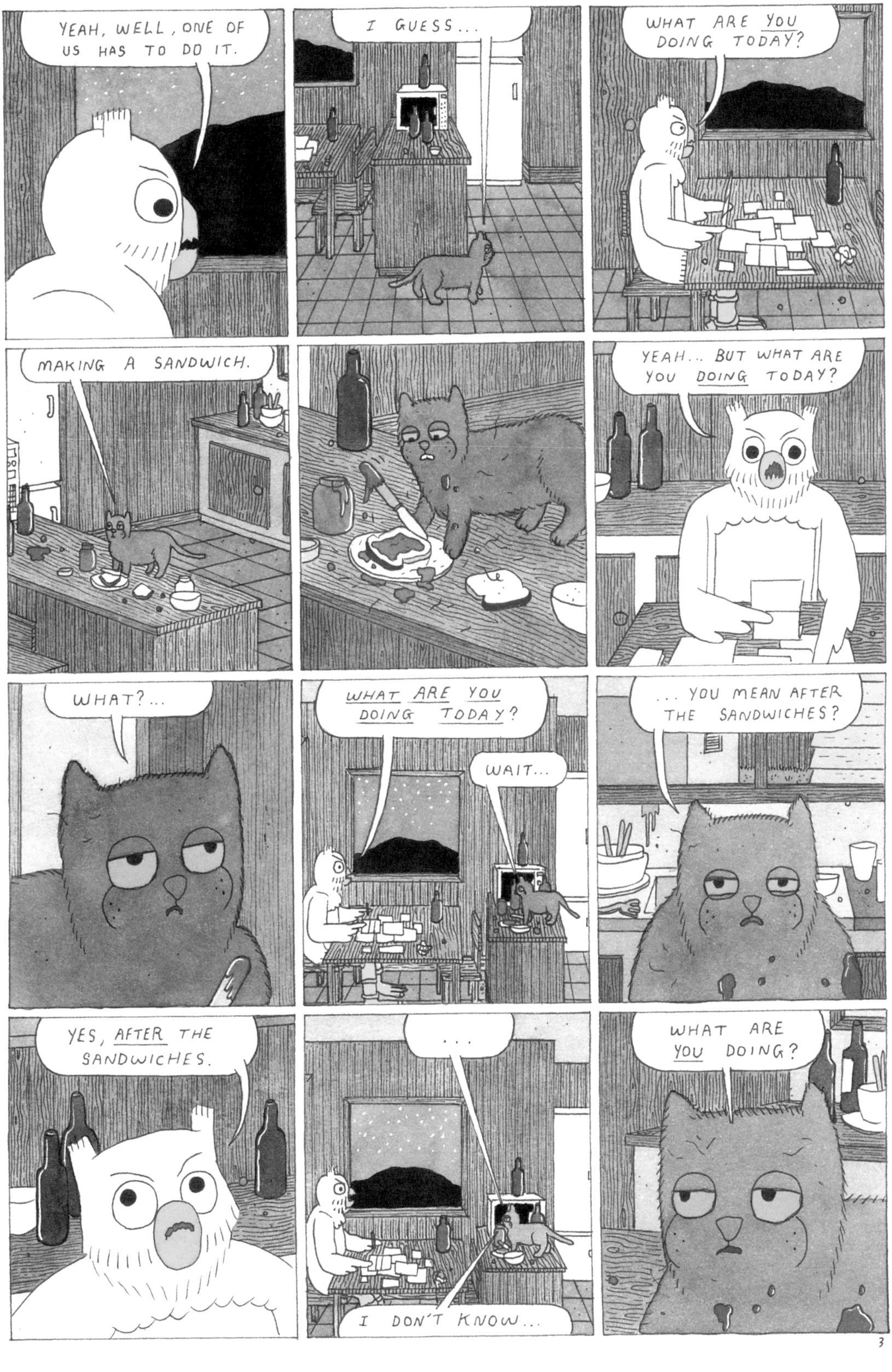

YEAH, WELL, ONE OF US HAS TO DO IT.
I GUESS...
WHAT ARE YOU DOING TODAY?
MAKING A SANDWICH.
YEAH... BUT WHAT ARE YOU DOING TODAY?
WHAT?...
WHAT ARE YOU DOING TODAY?
WAIT...
... YOU MEAN AFTER THE SANDWICHES?
YES, AFTER THE SANDWICHES.
...
I DON'T KNOW...
WHAT ARE YOU DOING?

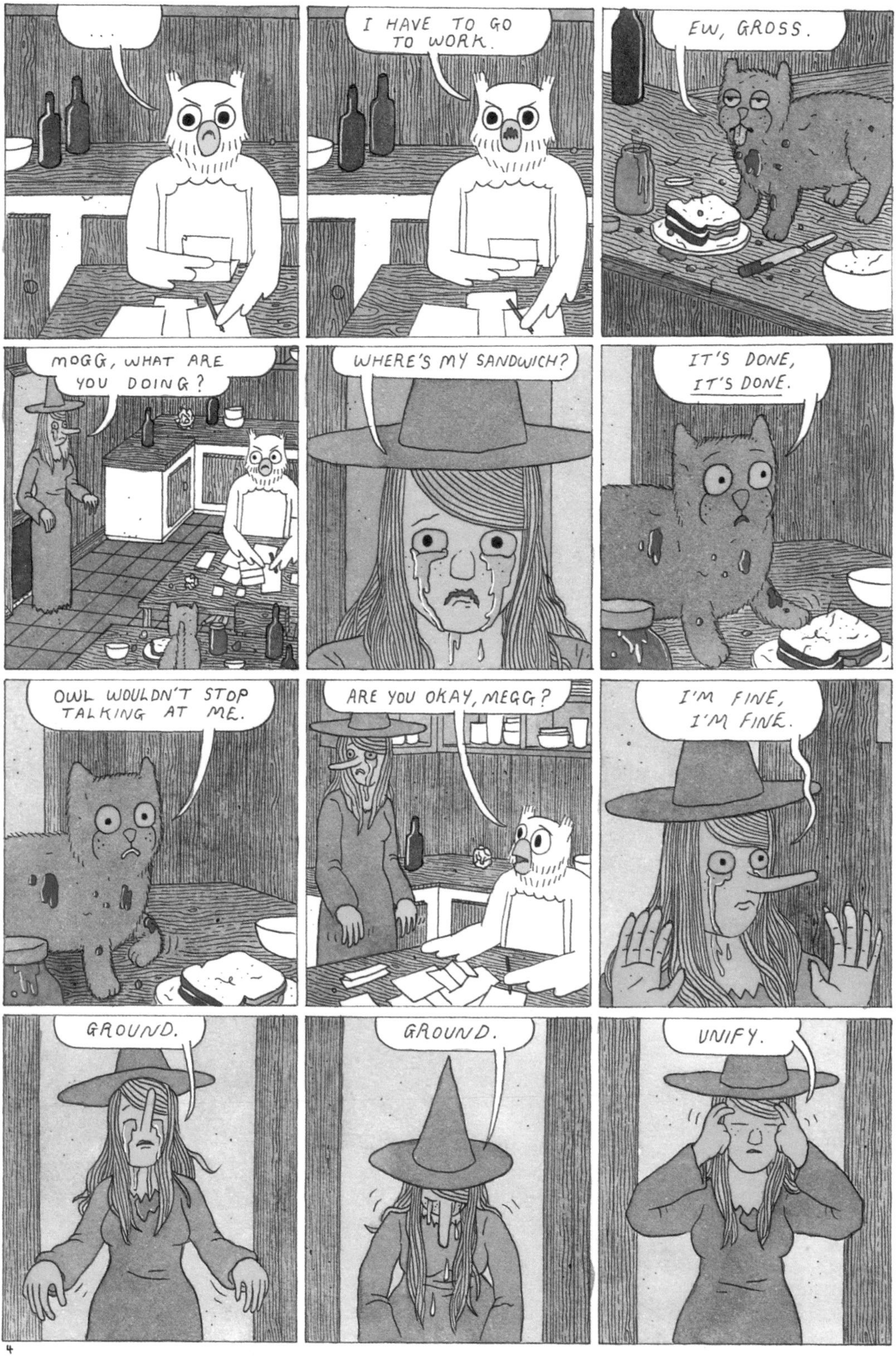
...
I HAVE TO GO TO WORK.
EW, GROSS.
MOGG, WHAT ARE YOU DOING?
WHERE'S MY SANDWICH?
IT'S DONE, IT'S DONE.
OWL WOULDN'T STOP TALKING AT ME.
ARE YOU OKAY, MEGG?
I'M FINE, I'M FINE.
GROUND.
GROUND.
UNIFY.

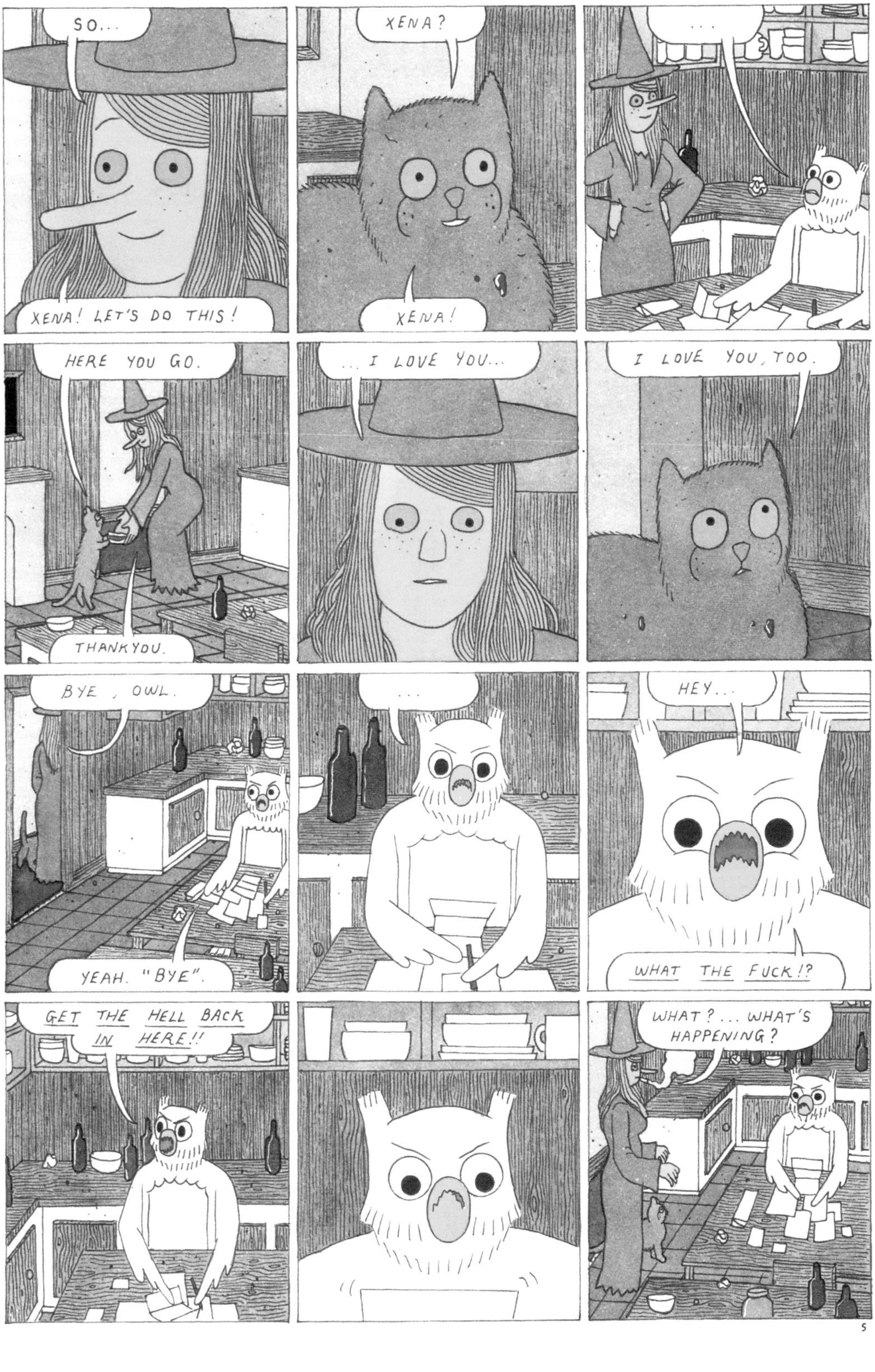
SO...
XENA! LET'S DO THIS!
XENA?
XENA!
...
HERE YOU GO.
THANKYOU.
... I LOVE YOU...
I LOVE YOU, TOO.
BYE, OWL.
YEAH. "BYE".
...
HEY...
WHAT THE FUCK!?
GET THE HELL BACK IN HERE!!
WHAT?... WHAT'S HAPPENING?

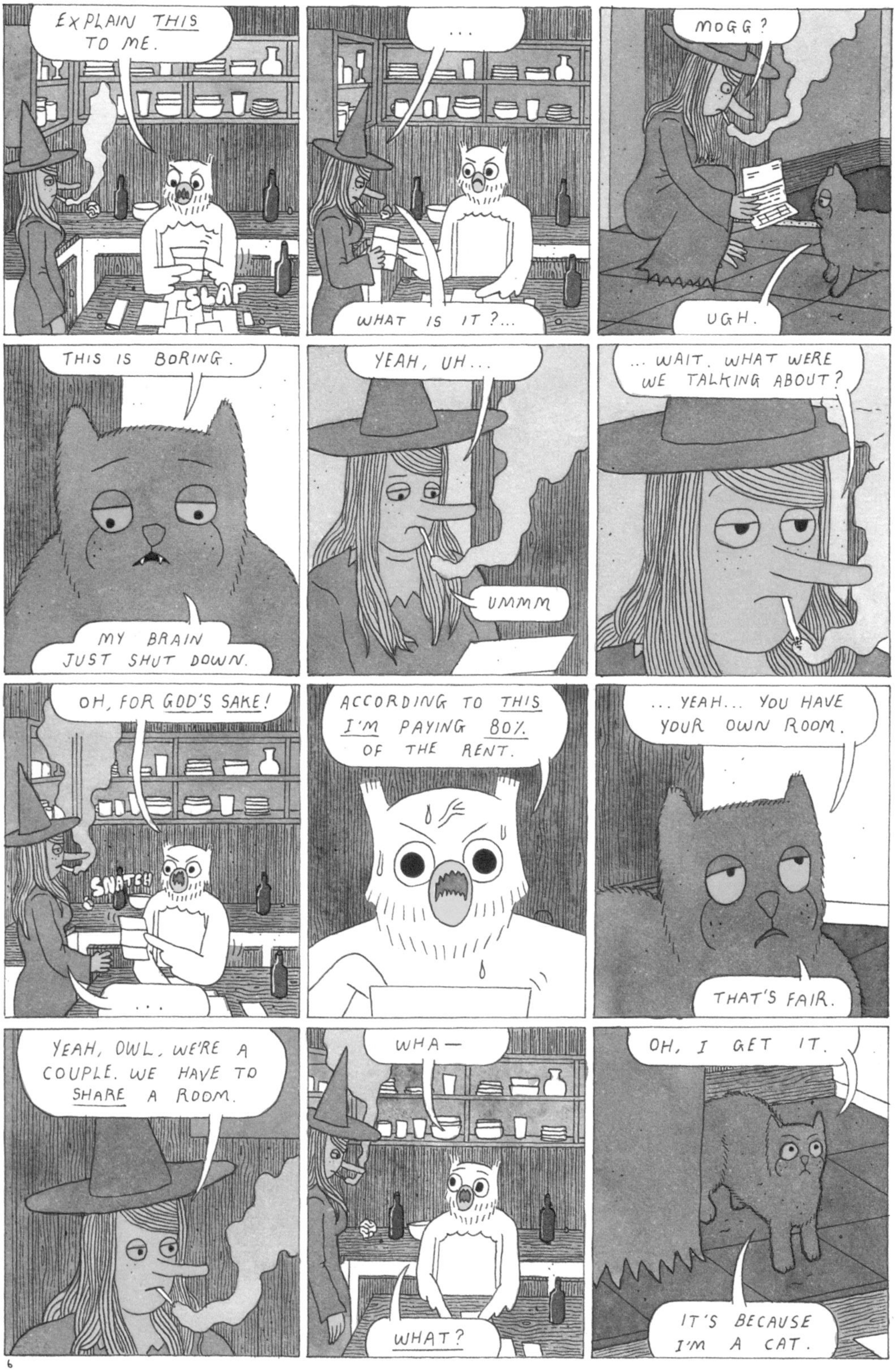
EXPLAIN THIS TO ME.
SLAP
...
WHAT IS IT?...
MOGG?
UGH.
THIS IS BORING.
MY BRAIN JUST SHUT DOWN.
YEAH, UH...
UMMM
...WAIT. WHAT WERE WE TALKING ABOUT?
OH, FOR GOD'S SAKE!
SNATCH
...
ACCORDING TO THIS I'M PAYING 80% OF THE RENT.
...YEAH... YOU HAVE YOUR OWN ROOM.
THAT'S FAIR.
YEAH, OWL, WE'RE A COUPLE. WE HAVE TO SHARE A ROOM.
WHA—
WHAT?
OH, I GET IT.
IT'S BECAUSE I'M A CAT.

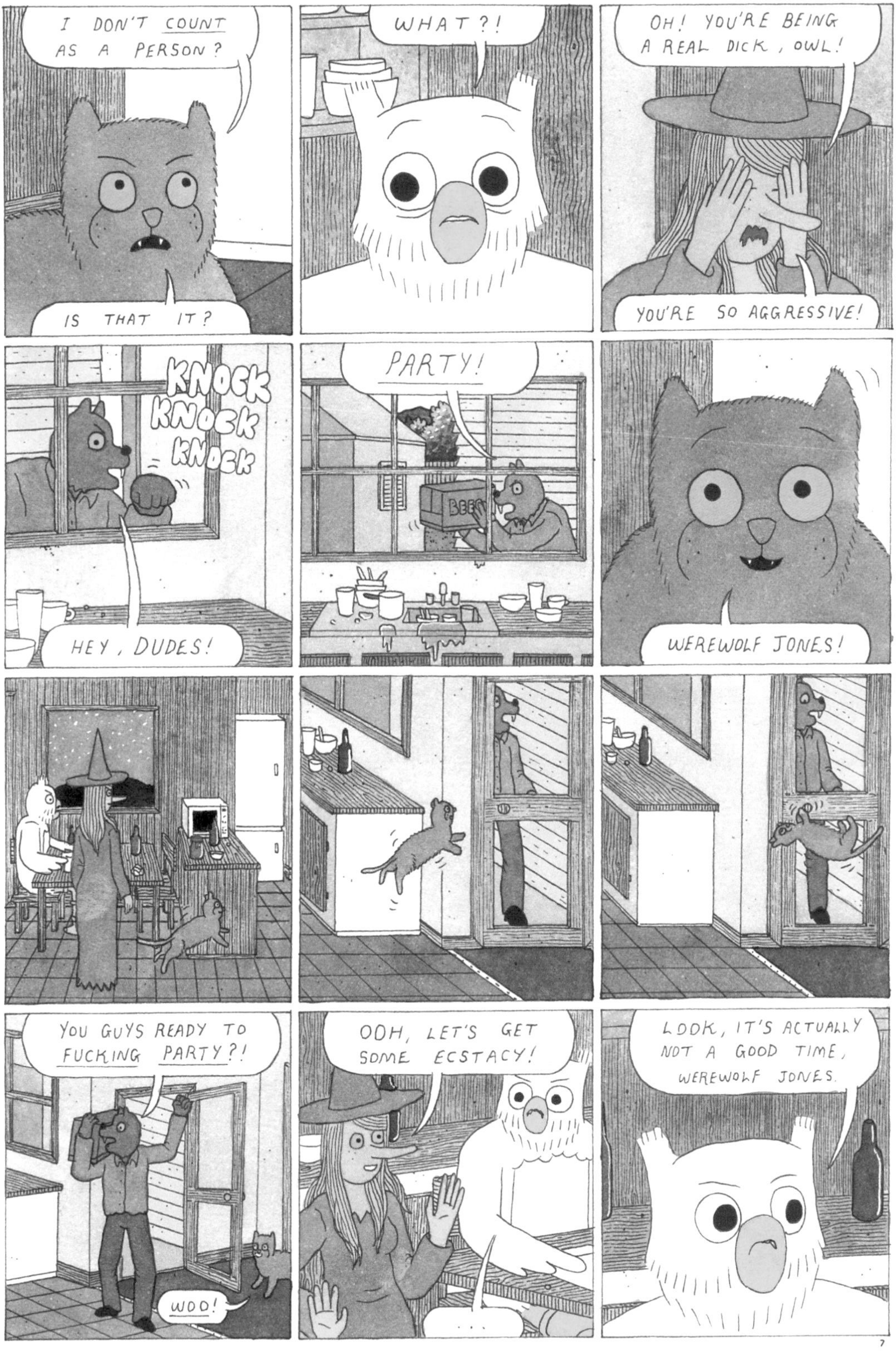
I DON'T COUNT AS A PERSON?
IS THAT IT?
WHAT?!
OH! YOU'RE BEING A REAL DICK, OWL!
YOU'RE SO AGGRESSIVE!
KNOCK KNOCK KNOCK
HEY, DUDES!
PARTY!
WEREWOLF JONES!
YOU GUYS READY TO FUCKING PARTY?!
WOO!
OOH, LET'S GET SOME ECSTACY!
. . .
LOOK, IT'S ACTUALLY NOT A GOOD TIME, WEREWOLF JONES.

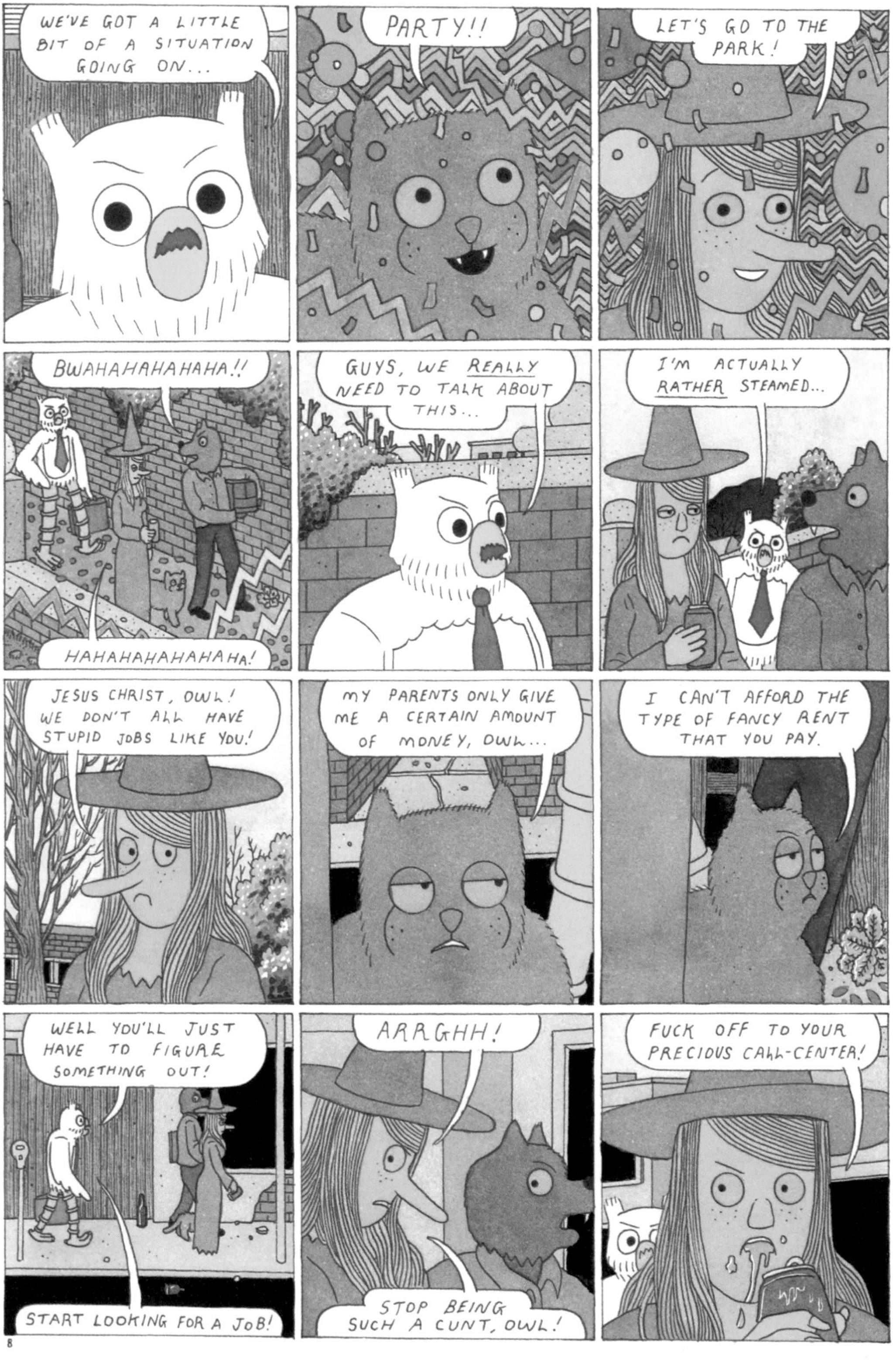
WE'VE GOT A LITTLE BIT OF A SITUATION GOING ON...
PARTY!!
LET'S GO TO THE PARK!
BWAHAHAHAHAHA!!
HAHAHAHAHAHAHA!
GUYS, WE REALLY NEED TO TALK ABOUT THIS...
I'M ACTUALLY RATHER STEAMED...
JESUS CHRIST, OWL! WE DON'T ALL HAVE STUPID JOBS LIKE YOU!
MY PARENTS ONLY GIVE ME A CERTAIN AMOUNT OF MONEY, OWL...
I CAN'T AFFORD THE TYPE OF FANCY RENT THAT YOU PAY.
WELL YOU'LL JUST HAVE TO FIGURE SOMETHING OUT!
START LOOKING FOR A JOB!
ARRGHH!
STOP BEING SUCH A CUNT, OWL!
FUCK OFF TO YOUR PRECIOUS CALL-CENTER!

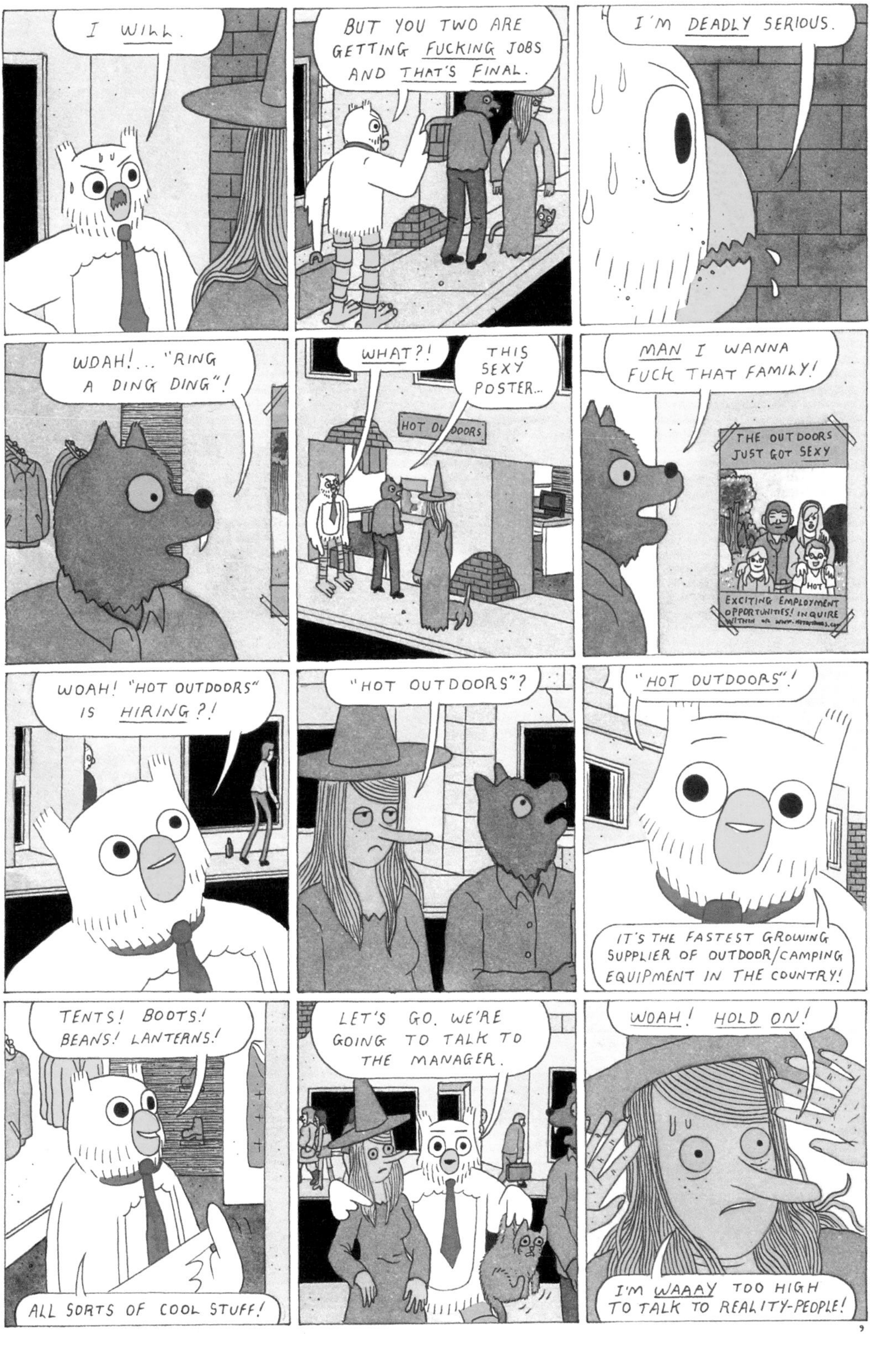
I WILL.
BUT YOU TWO ARE GETTING FUCKING JOBS AND THAT'S FINAL.
I'M DEADLY SERIOUS.
WOAH!... "RING A DING DING"!
WHAT?!
THIS SEXY POSTER...
MAN I WANNA FUCK THAT FAMILY!
THE OUTDOORS JUST GOT SEXY
HOT
EXCITING EMPLOYMENT OPPORTUNITIES! INQUIRE WITHIN
WOAH! "HOT OUTDOORS" IS HIRING?!
"HOT OUTDOORS"?
"HOT OUTDOORS"!
IT'S THE FASTEST GROWING SUPPLIER OF OUTDOOR/CAMPING EQUIPMENT IN THE COUNTRY!
TENTS! BOOTS! BEANS! LANTERNS!
ALL SORTS OF COOL STUFF!
LET'S GO. WE'RE GOING TO TALK TO THE MANAGER.
WOAH! HOLD ON!
I'M WAAAY TOO HIGH TO TALK TO REALITY-PEOPLE!

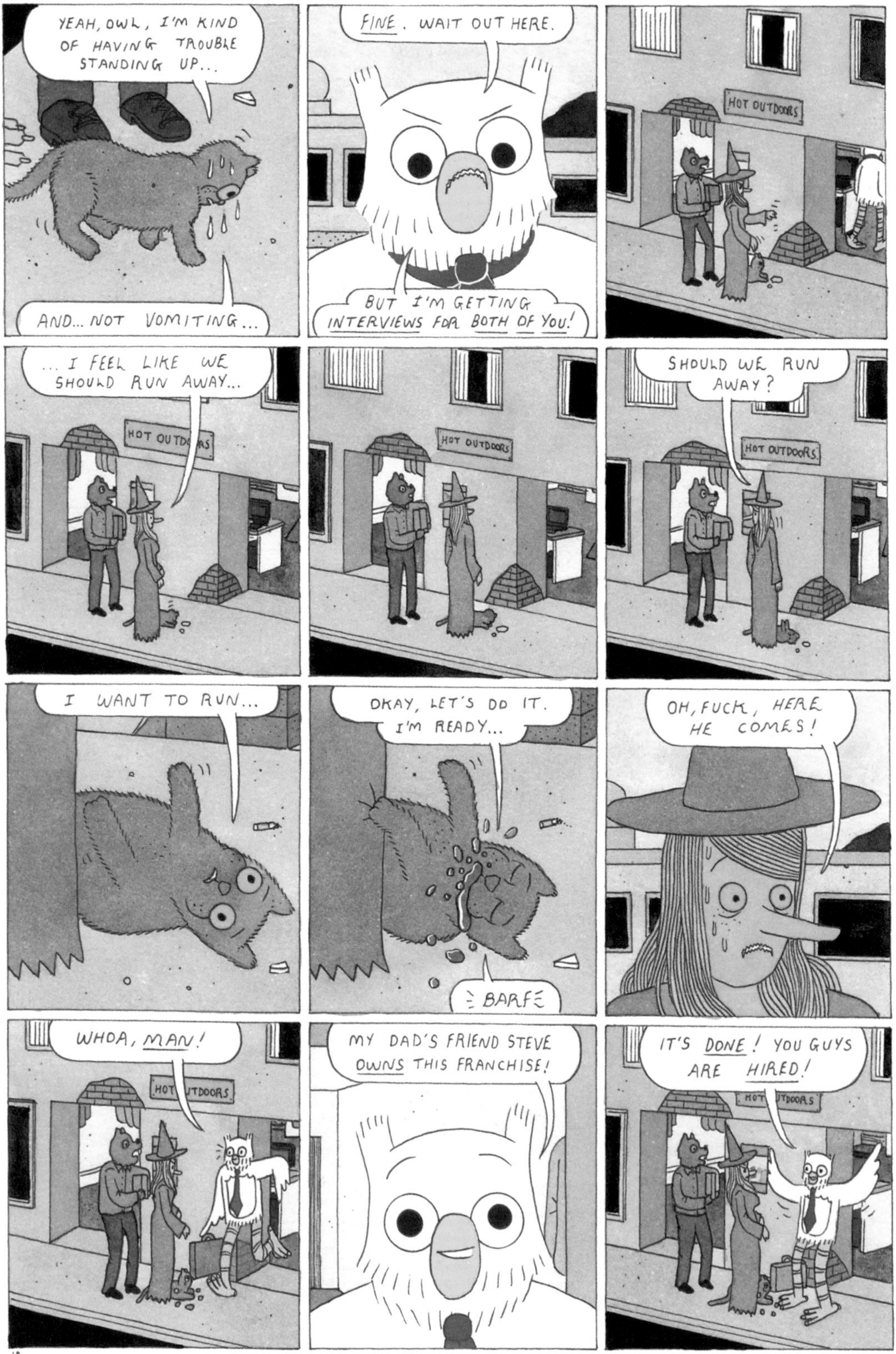
YEAH, OWL, I'M KIND OF HAVING TROUBLE STANDING UP...
AND... NOT VOMITING...
FINE. WAIT OUT HERE.
BUT I'M GETTING INTERVIEWS FOR BOTH OF YOU!
HOT OUTDOORS
... I FEEL LIKE WE SHOULD RUN AWAY...
HOT OUTDOORS
HOT OUTDOORS
SHOULD WE RUN AWAY?
HOT OUTDOORS
I WANT TO RUN...
OKAY, LET'S DO IT. I'M READY...
BARF
OH, FUCK, HERE HE COMES!
WHOA, MAN!
MY DAD'S FRIEND STEVE OWNS THIS FRANCHISE!
IT'S DONE! YOU GUYS ARE HIRED!

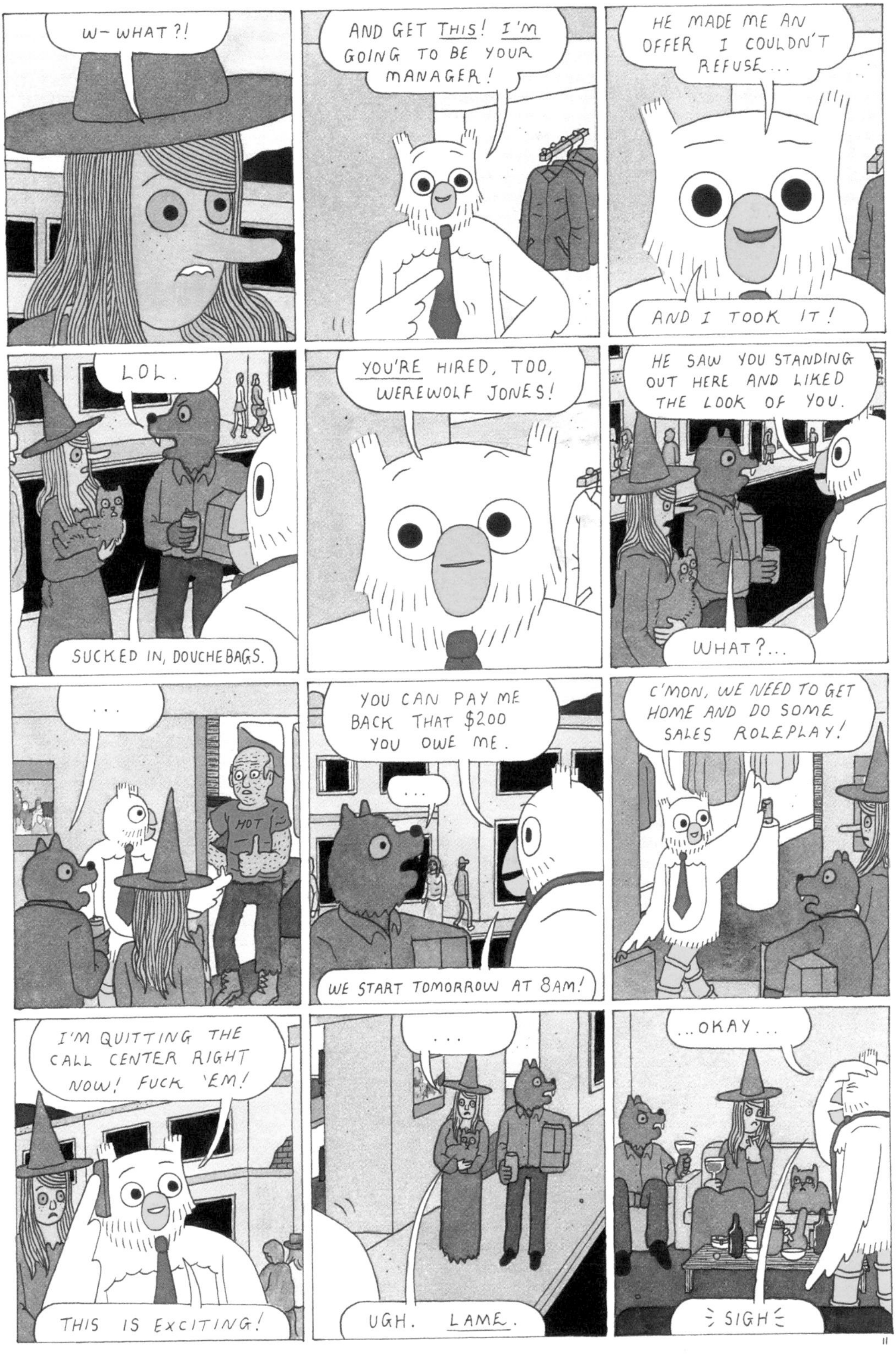
W-WHAT?!
AND GET THIS! I'M GOING TO BE YOUR MANAGER!
HE MADE ME AN OFFER I COULDN'T REFUSE...
AND I TOOK IT!
LOL.
SUCKED IN, DOUCHEBAGS.
YOU'RE HIRED, TOO, WEREWOLF JONES!
HE SAW YOU STANDING OUT HERE AND LIKED THE LOOK OF YOU.
WHAT?...
...
HOT
YOU CAN PAY ME BACK THAT $200 YOU OWE ME.
...
WE START TOMORROW AT 8AM!
C'MON, WE NEED TO GET HOME AND DO SOME SALES ROLEPLAY!
I'M QUITTING THE CALL CENTER RIGHT NOW! FUCK 'EM!
THIS IS EXCITING!
...
UGH. LAME.
...OKAY...
SIGH

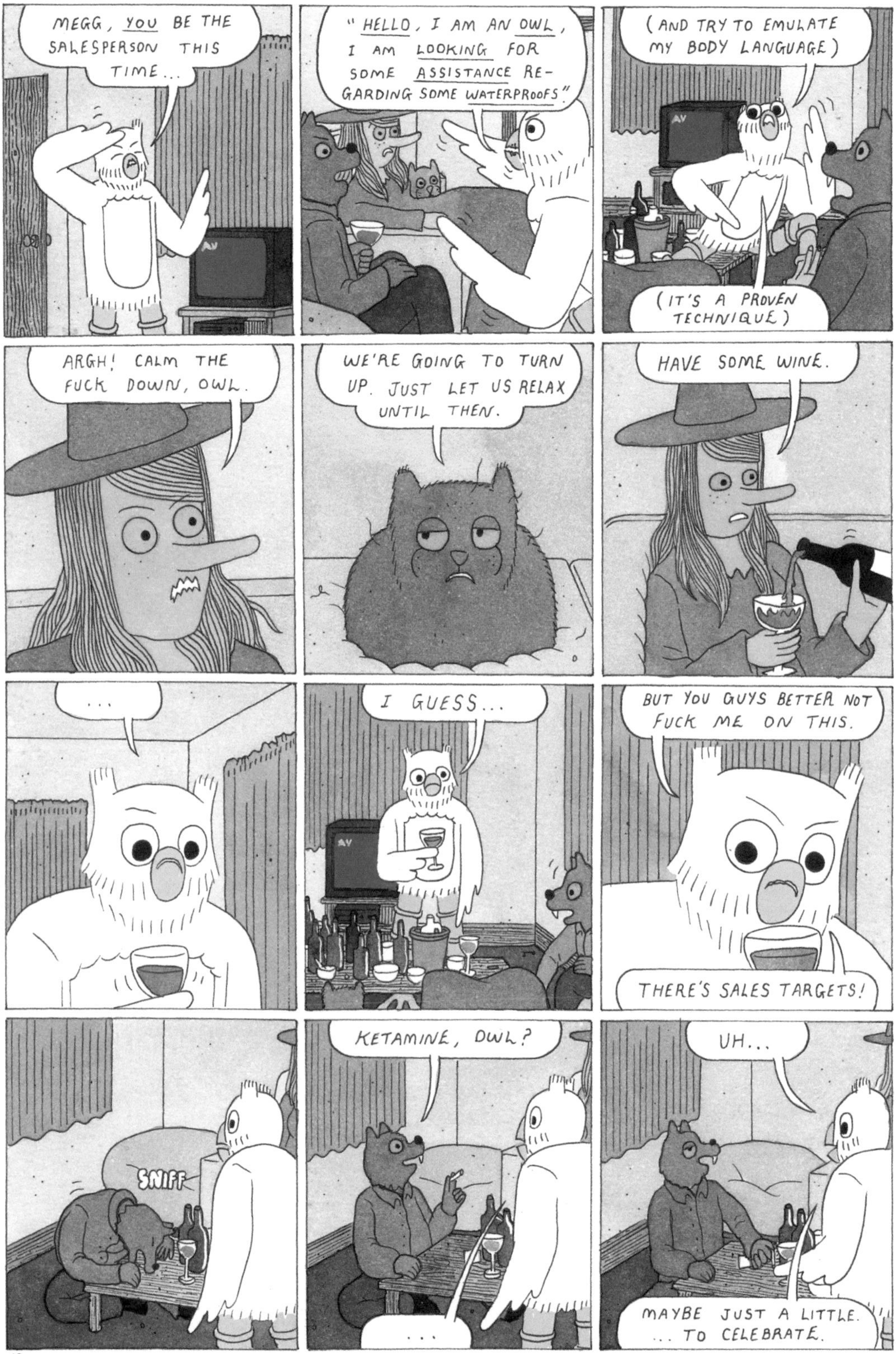
MEGG, YOU BE THE SALESPERSON THIS TIME...
"HELLO, I AM AN OWL, I AM LOOKING FOR SOME ASSISTANCE REGARDING SOME WATERPROOFS"
(AND TRY TO EMULATE MY BODY LANGUAGE)
(IT'S A PROVEN TECHNIQUE)
ARGH! CALM THE FUCK DOWN, OWL.
WE'RE GOING TO TURN UP. JUST LET US RELAX UNTIL THEN.
HAVE SOME WINE.
...
I GUESS...
BUT YOU GUYS BETTER NOT FUCK ME ON THIS.
THERE'S SALES TARGETS!
SNIFF
KETAMINE, OWL?
...
UH...
MAYBE JUST A LITTLE. ... TO CELEBRATE.

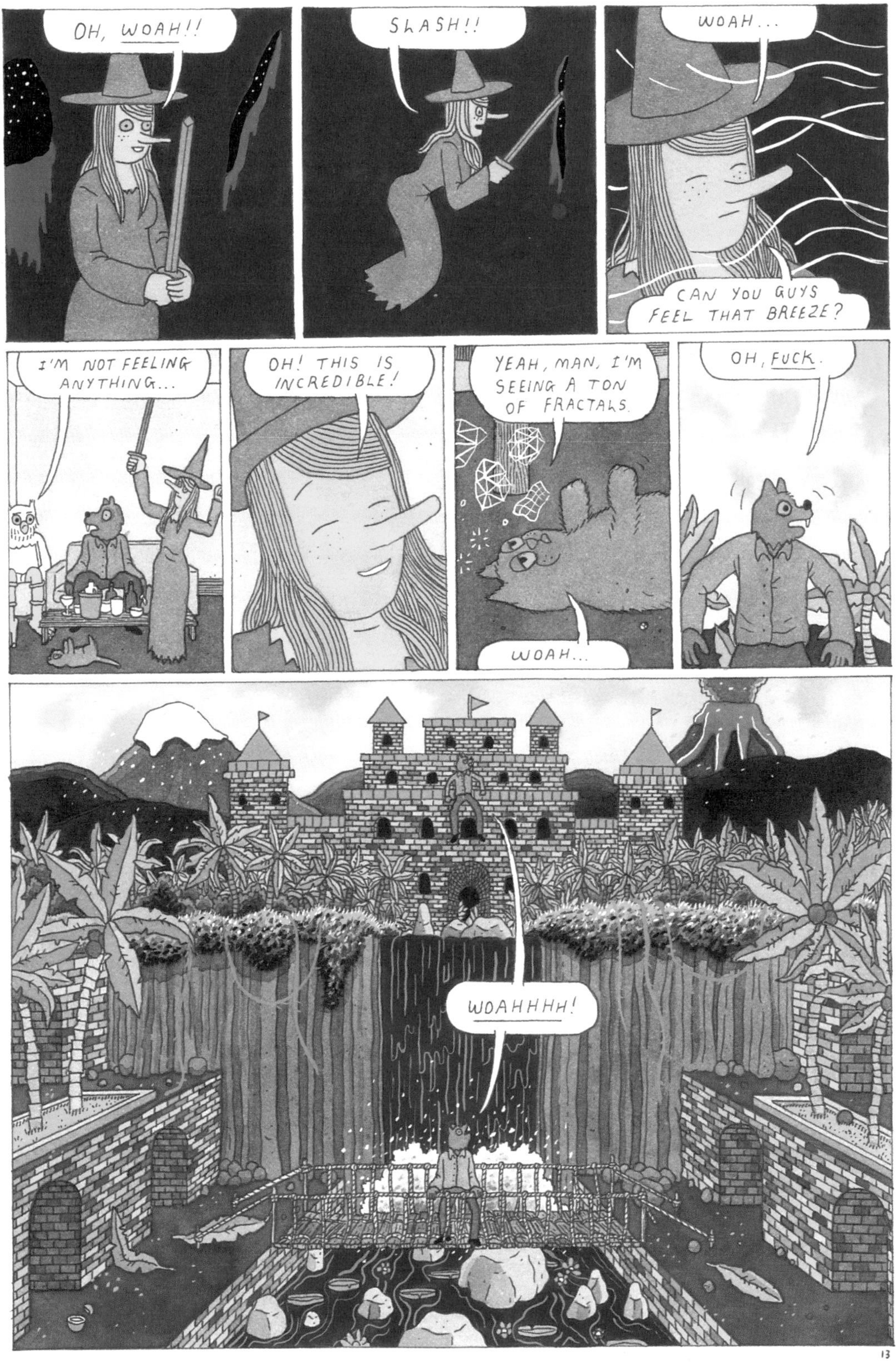
OH, WOAH!!
SLASH!!
WOAH...
CAN YOU GUYS FEEL THAT BREEZE?
I'M NOT FEELING ANYTHING...
OH! THIS IS INCREDIBLE!
YEAH, MAN, I'M SEEING A TON OF FRACTALS.
WOAH...
OH, FUCK.
WOAHHHH!

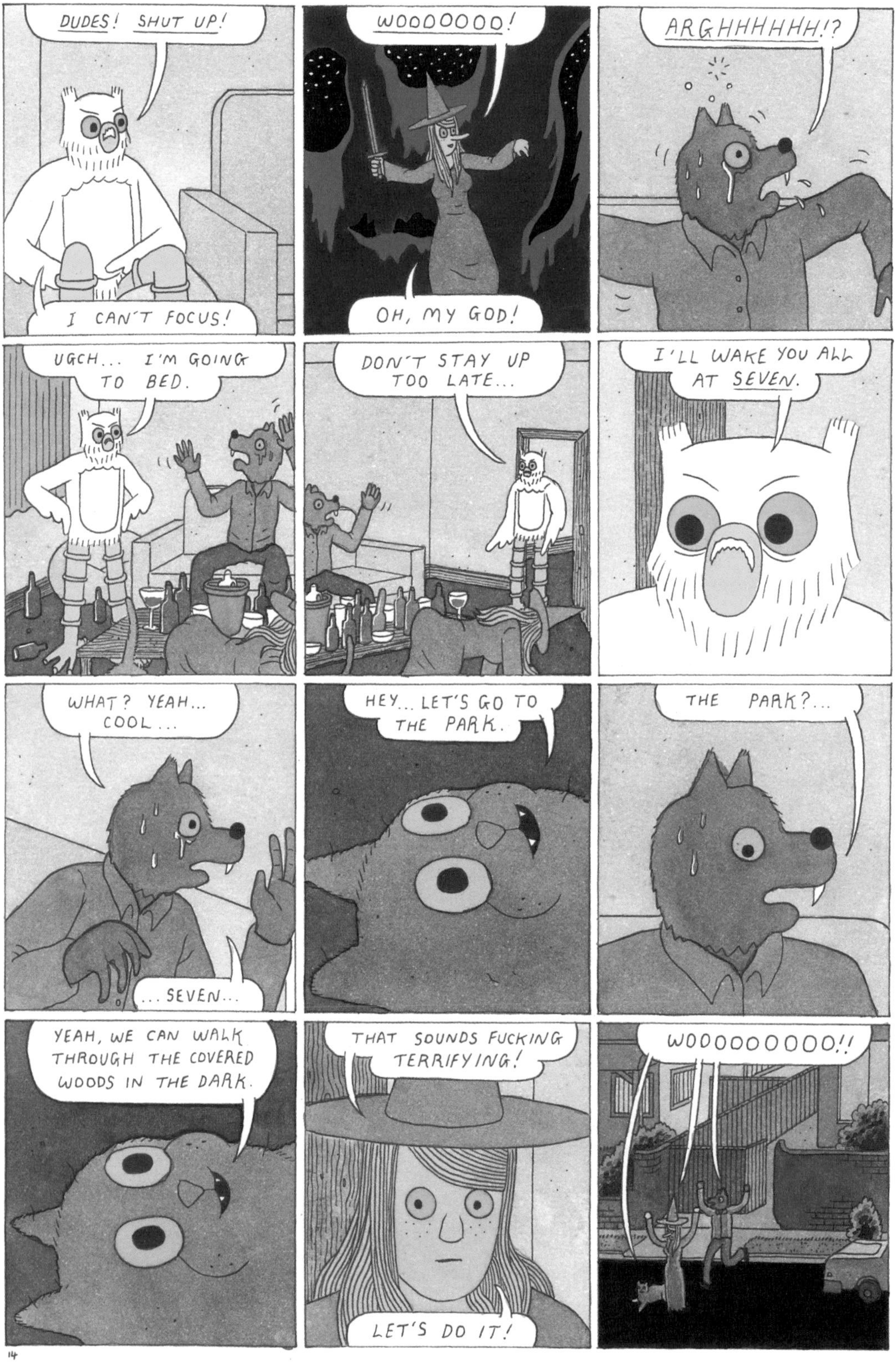
DUDES! SHUT UP!
I CAN'T FOCUS!
WOOOOOOO!
OH, MY GOD!
ARGHHHHHH!?
UGCH... I'M GOING TO BED.
DON'T STAY UP TOO LATE...
I'LL WAKE YOU ALL AT SEVEN.
WHAT? YEAH... COOL...
...SEVEN...
HEY... LET'S GO TO THE PARK.
THE PARK?...
YEAH, WE CAN WALK THROUGH THE COVERED WOODS IN THE DARK.
THAT SOUNDS FUCKING TERRIFYING!
LET'S DO IT!
WOOOOOOOOO!!

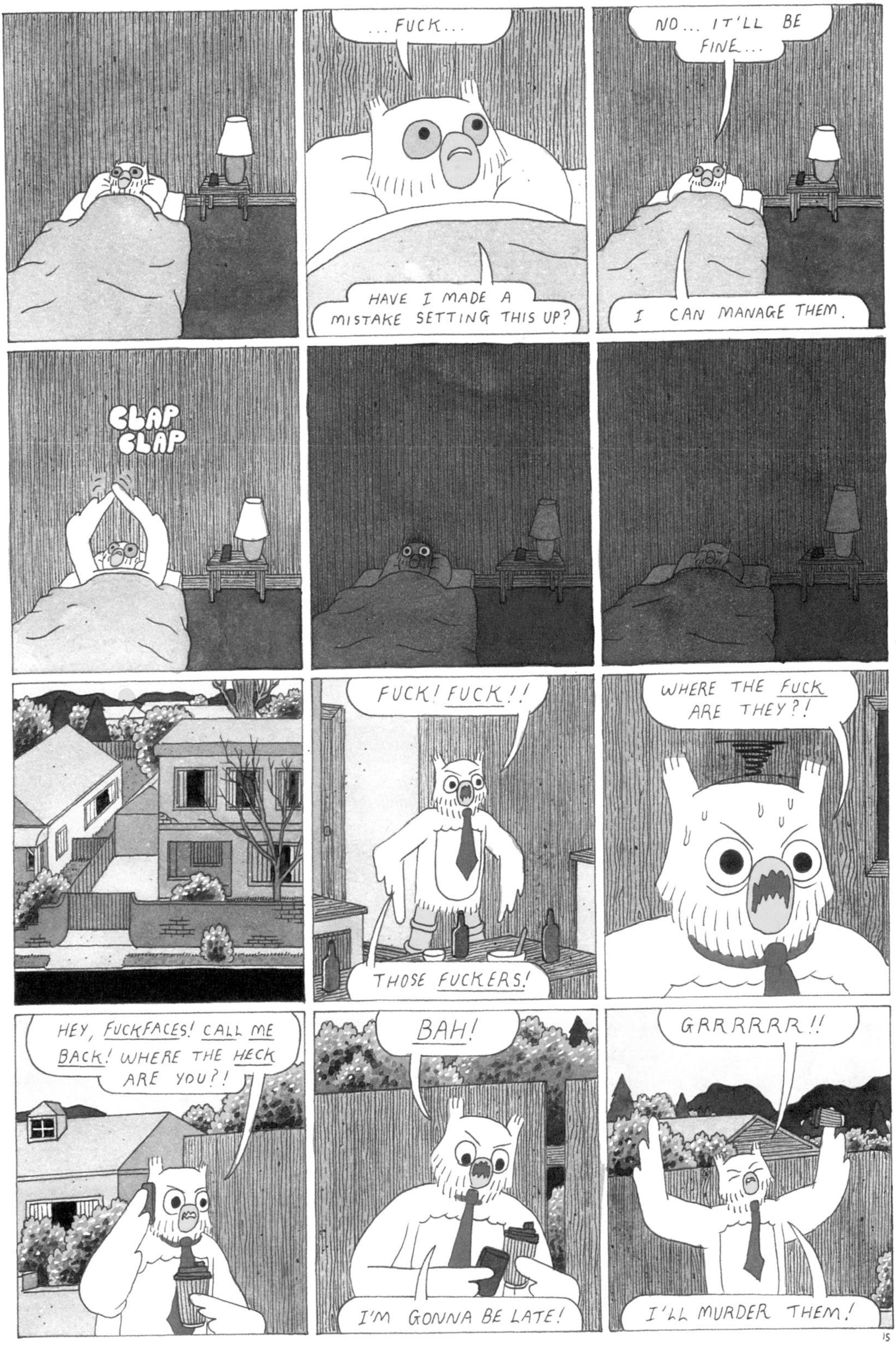
...FUCK...
HAVE I MADE A MISTAKE SETTING THIS UP?
NO... IT'LL BE FINE...
I CAN MANAGE THEM.
CLAP CLAP
FUCK! FUCK!!
THOSE FUCKERS!
WHERE THE FUCK ARE THEY?!
HEY, FUCKFACES! CALL ME BACK! WHERE THE HECK ARE YOU?!
BAH!
I'M GONNA BE LATE!
GRRRRRR!!
I'LL MURDER THEM!

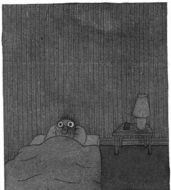

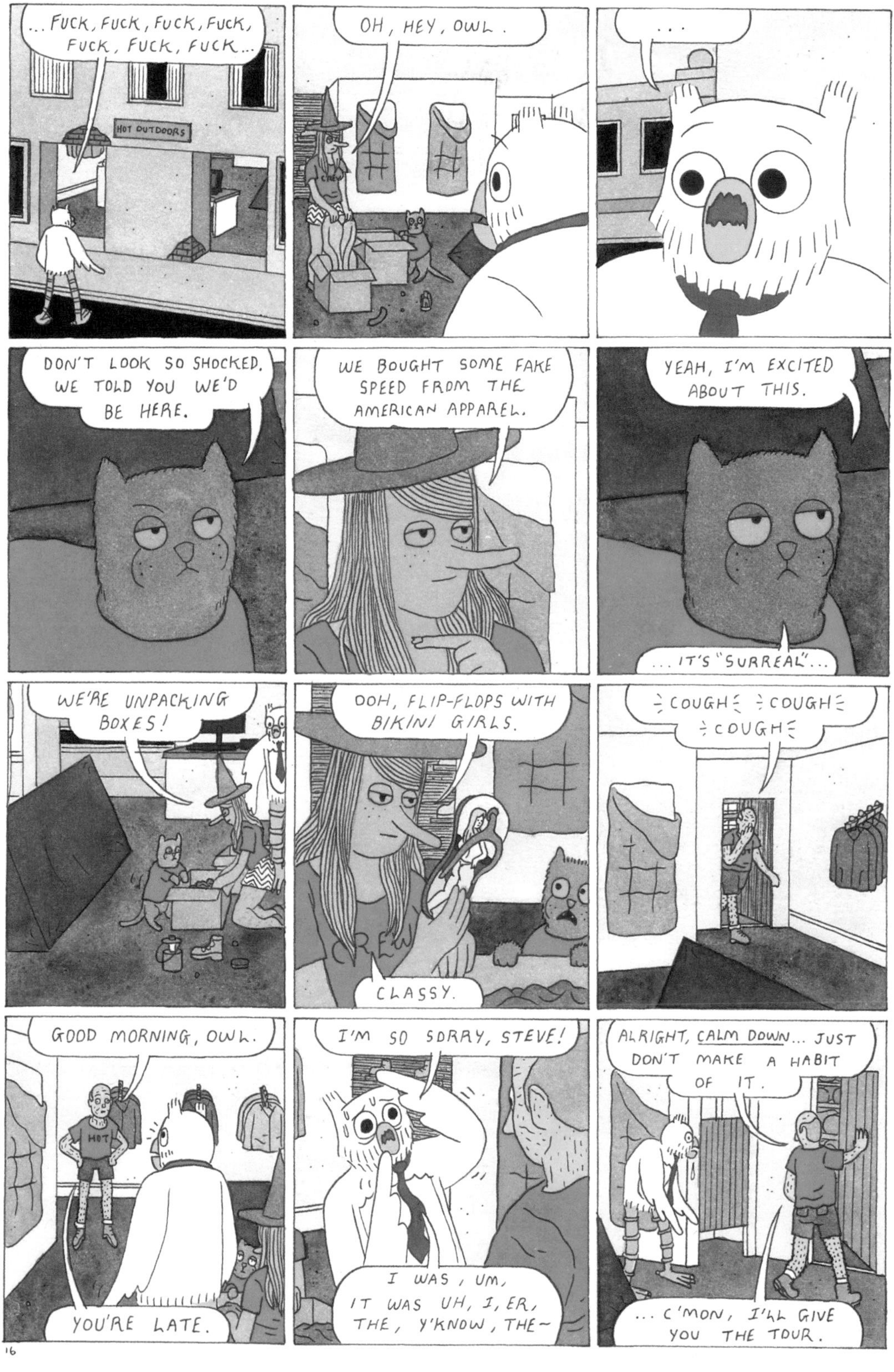
... FUCK, FUCK, FUCK, FUCK, FUCK, FUCK, FUCK...
HOT OUTDOORS
OH, HEY, OWL.
...
DON'T LOOK SO SHOCKED. WE TOLD YOU WE'D BE HERE.
WE BOUGHT SOME FAKE SPEED FROM THE AMERICAN APPAREL.
YEAH, I'M EXCITED ABOUT THIS.
... IT'S "SURREAL"...
WE'RE UNPACKING BOXES!
OOH, FLIP-FLOPS WITH BIKINI GIRLS.
CLASSY.
COUGH COUGH COUGH
GOOD MORNING, OWL.
HOT
YOU'RE LATE.
I'M SO SORRY, STEVE!
I WAS, UM, IT WAS UH, I, ER, THE, Y'KNOW, THE~
ALRIGHT, CALM DOWN... JUST DON'T MAKE A HABIT OF IT.
... C'MON, I'LL GIVE YOU THE TOUR.

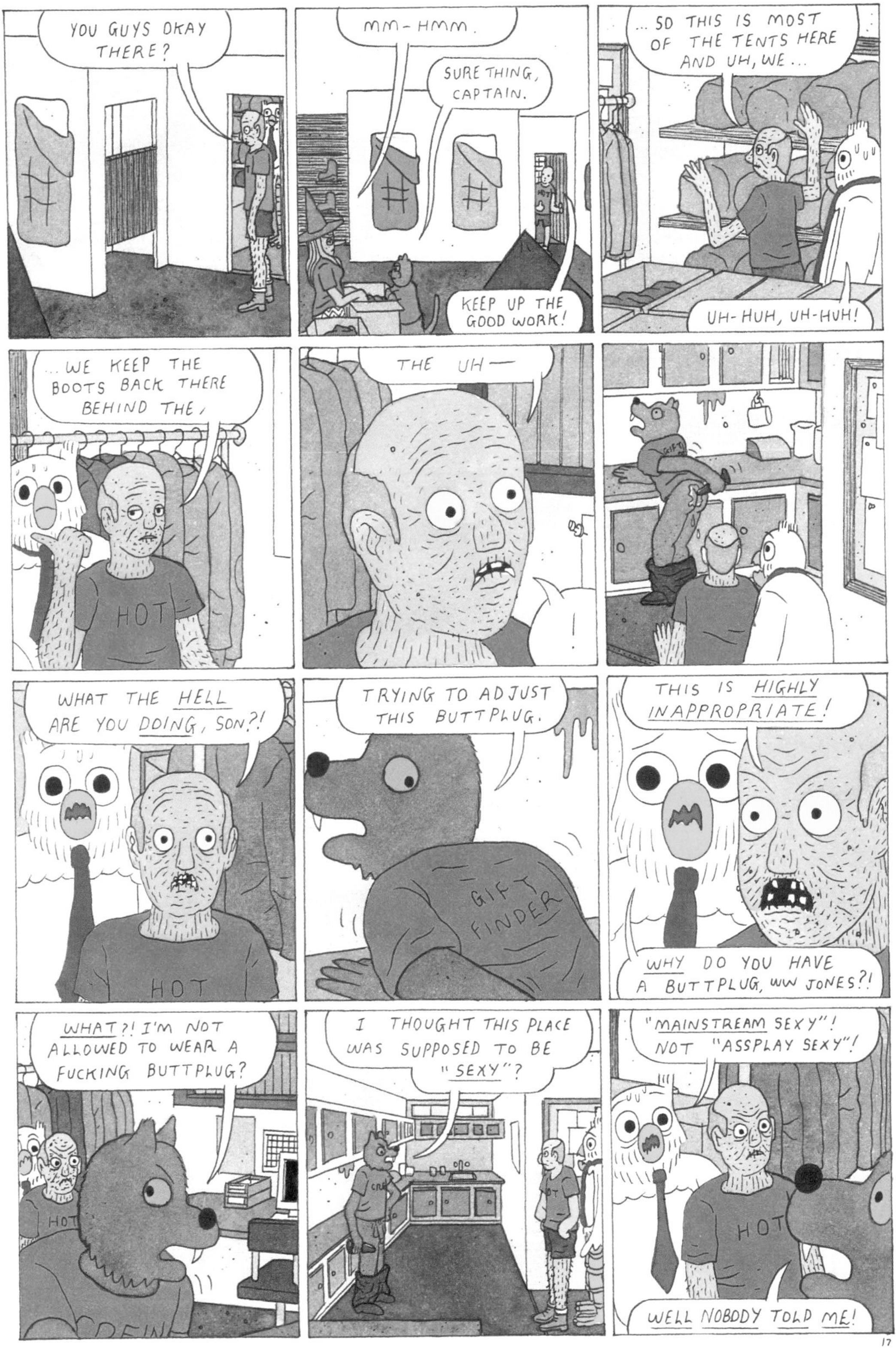

YOU GUYS OKAY THERE?
MM-HMM.
SURE THING, CAPTAIN.
KEEP UP THE GOOD WORK!
...SO THIS IS MOST OF THE TENTS HERE AND UH, WE...
UH-HUH, UH-HUH!
...WE KEEP THE BOOTS BACK THERE BEHIND THE,
THE UH—
WHAT THE HELL ARE YOU DOING, SON?!
TRYING TO ADJUST THIS BUTTPLUG.
GIFT FINDER
THIS IS HIGHLY INAPPROPRIATE!
WHY DO YOU HAVE A BUTTPLUG, WW JONES?!
WHAT?! I'M NOT ALLOWED TO WEAR A FUCKING BUTTPLUG?
HOT
I THOUGHT THIS PLACE WAS SUPPOSED TO BE "SEXY"?
"MAINSTREAM SEXY"! NOT "ASSPLAY SEXY"!
HOT
WELL NOBODY TOLD ME!

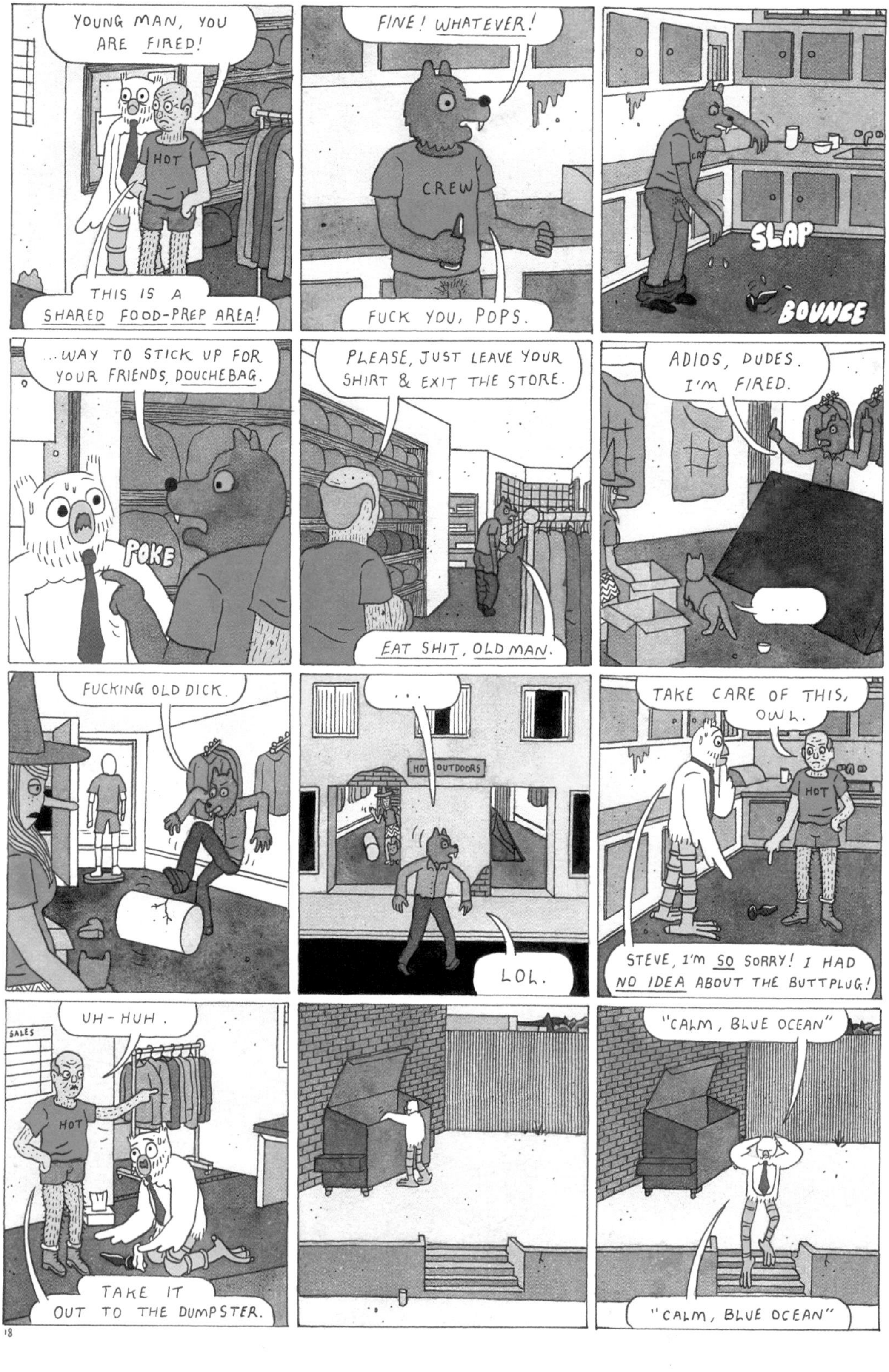
YOUNG MAN, YOU ARE FIRED!
THIS IS A SHARED FOOD-PREP AREA!
FINE! WHATEVER!
FUCK YOU, POPS.
SLAP
BOUNCE
...WAY TO STICK UP FOR YOUR FRIENDS, DOUCHEBAG.
POKE
PLEASE, JUST LEAVE YOUR SHIRT & EXIT THE STORE.
EAT SHIT, OLD MAN.
ADIOS, DUDES. I'M FIRED.
. . .
FUCKING OLD DICK.
. . .
HOT OUTDOORS
LOL.
TAKE CARE OF THIS, OWL.
STEVE, I'M SO SORRY! I HAD NO IDEA ABOUT THE BUTTPLUG!
UH-HUH.
SALES
HOT
TAKE IT OUT TO THE DUMPSTER.
"CALM, BLUE OCEAN"
"CALM, BLUE OCEAN"

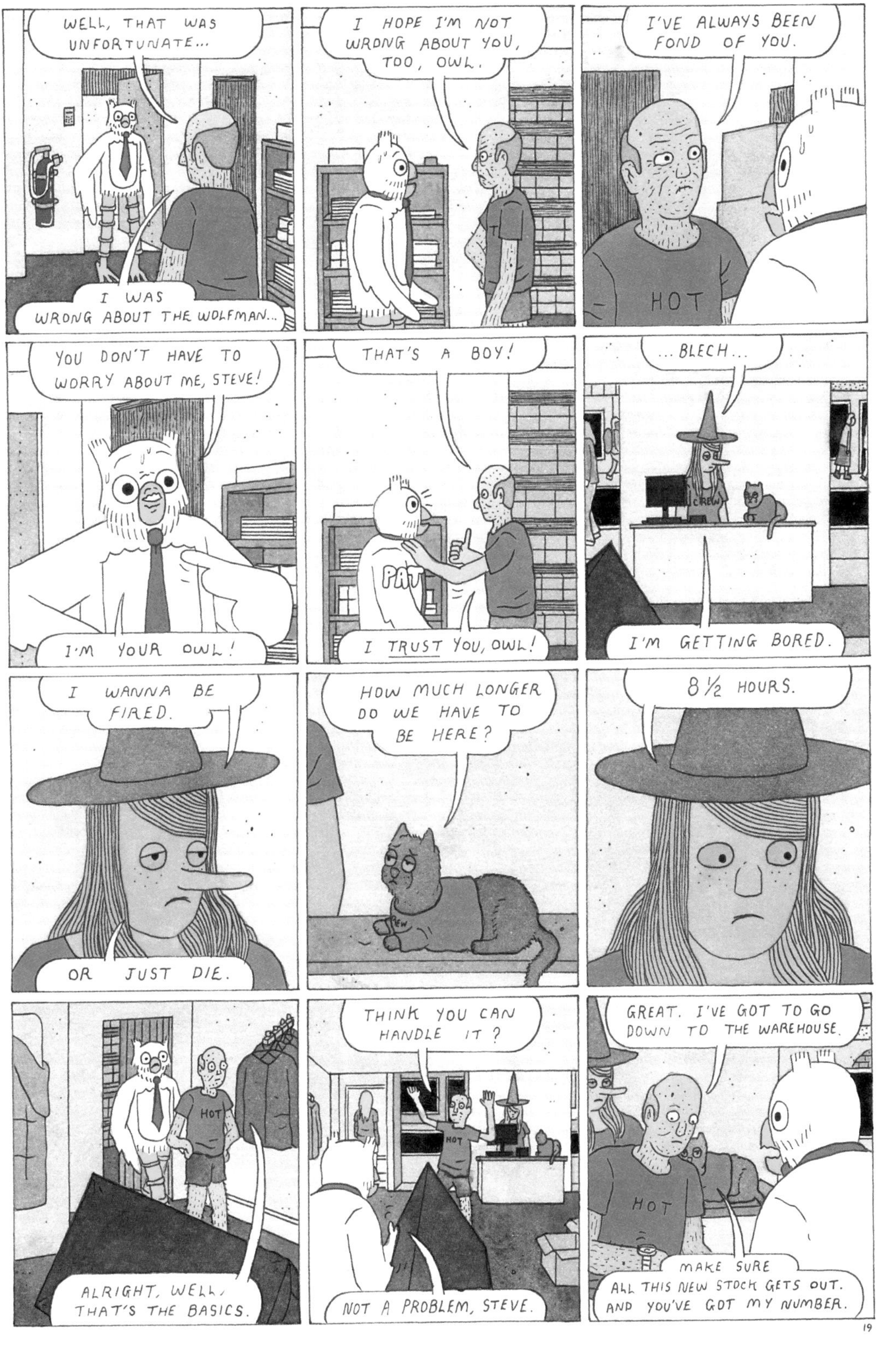
WELL, THAT WAS UNFORTUNATE...
I WAS WRONG ABOUT THE WOLFMAN...
I HOPE I'M NOT WRONG ABOUT YOU, TOO, OWL.
I'VE ALWAYS BEEN FOND OF YOU.
HOT
YOU DON'T HAVE TO WORRY ABOUT ME, STEVE!
I'M YOUR OWL!
THAT'S A BOY!
PAT
I TRUST YOU, OWL!
...BLECH...
CREW
I'M GETTING BORED.
I WANNA BE FIRED.
OR JUST DIE.
HOW MUCH LONGER DO WE HAVE TO BE HERE?
CREW
8 1/2 HOURS.
HOT
ALRIGHT, WELL, THAT'S THE BASICS.
THINK YOU CAN HANDLE IT?
HOT
NOT A PROBLEM, STEVE.
GREAT. I'VE GOT TO GO DOWN TO THE WAREHOUSE.
HOT
MAKE SURE ALL THIS NEW STOCK GETS OUT. AND YOU'VE GOT MY NUMBER.

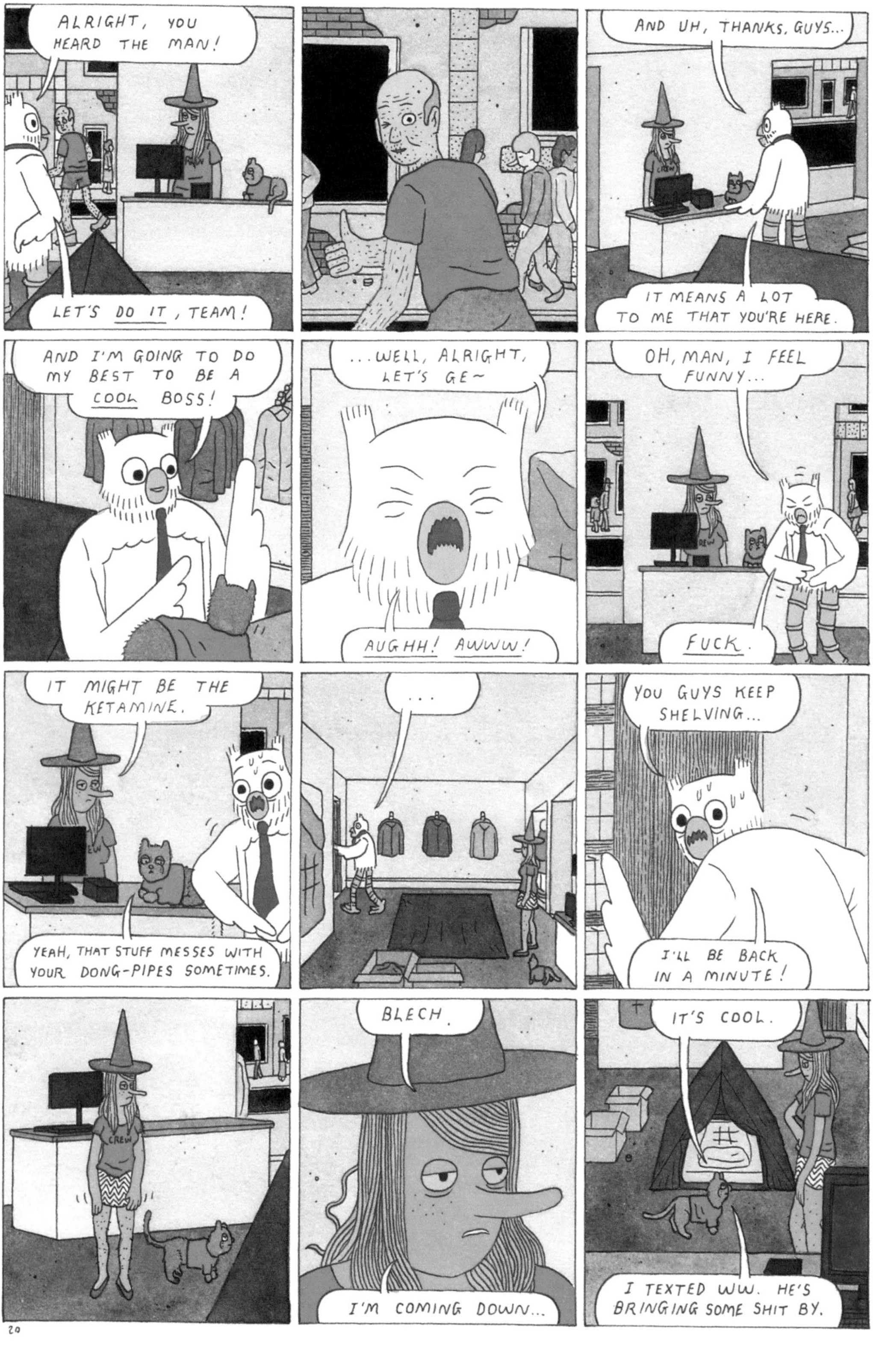
ALRIGHT, YOU HEARD THE MAN!
LET'S DO IT, TEAM!
AND UH, THANKS, GUYS...
IT MEANS A LOT TO ME THAT YOU'RE HERE.
AND I'M GOING TO DO MY BEST TO BE A COOL BOSS!
...WELL, ALRIGHT, LET'S GE~
AUGHH! AWWW!
OH, MAN, I FEEL FUNNY...
FUCK.
IT MIGHT BE THE KETAMINE.
YEAH, THAT STUFF MESSES WITH YOUR DONG-PIPES SOMETIMES.
...
YOU GUYS KEEP SHELVING...
I'LL BE BACK IN A MINUTE!
BLECH.
I'M COMING DOWN...
IT'S COOL.
I TEXTED WW. HE'S BRINGING SOME SHIT BY.

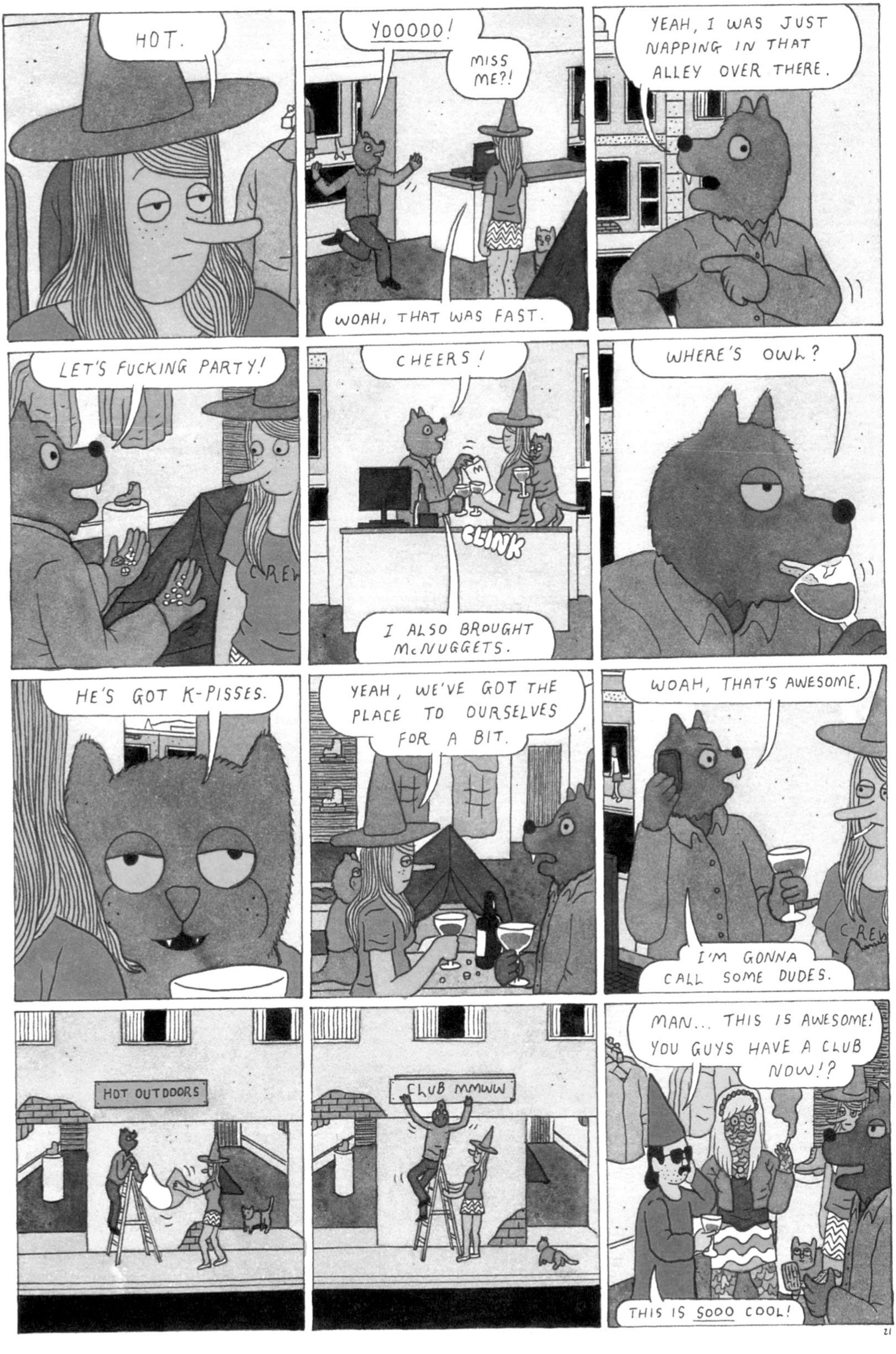
HOT.
YOOOOO!
MISS ME?!
WOAH, THAT WAS FAST.
YEAH, I WAS JUST NAPPING IN THAT ALLEY OVER THERE.
LET'S FUCKING PARTY!
CHEERS!
CLINK
I ALSO BROUGHT McNUGGETS.
WHERE'S OWL?
HE'S GOT K-PISSES.
YEAH, WE'VE GOT THE PLACE TO OURSELVES FOR A BIT.
WOAH, THAT'S AWESOME.
I'M GONNA CALL SOME DUDES.
HOT OUTDOORS
CLUB MMWW
MAN... THIS IS AWESOME! YOU GUYS HAVE A CLUB NOW!?
THIS IS SOOO COOL!

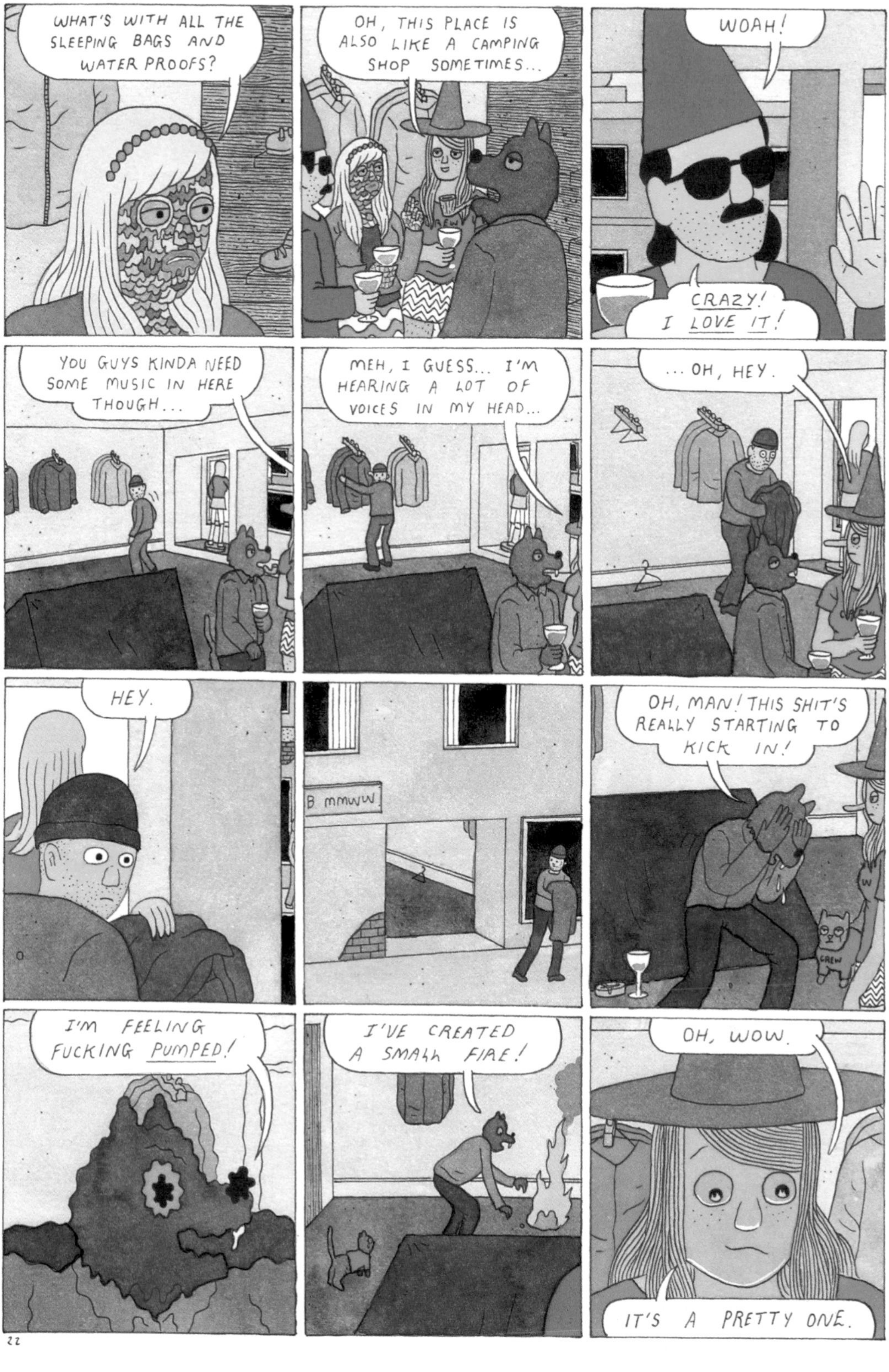
WHAT'S WITH ALL THE SLEEPING BAGS AND WATER PROOFS?
OH, THIS PLACE IS ALSO LIKE A CAMPING SHOP SOMETIMES...
WOAH!
CRAZY! I LOVE IT!
YOU GUYS KINDA NEED SOME MUSIC IN HERE THOUGH...
MEH, I GUESS... I'M HEARING A LOT OF VOICES IN MY HEAD...
...OH, HEY.
HEY.
OH, MAN! THIS SHIT'S REALLY STARTING TO KICK IN!
I'M FEELING FUCKING PUMPED!
I'VE CREATED A SMALL FIRE!
OH, WOW.
IT'S A PRETTY ONE.

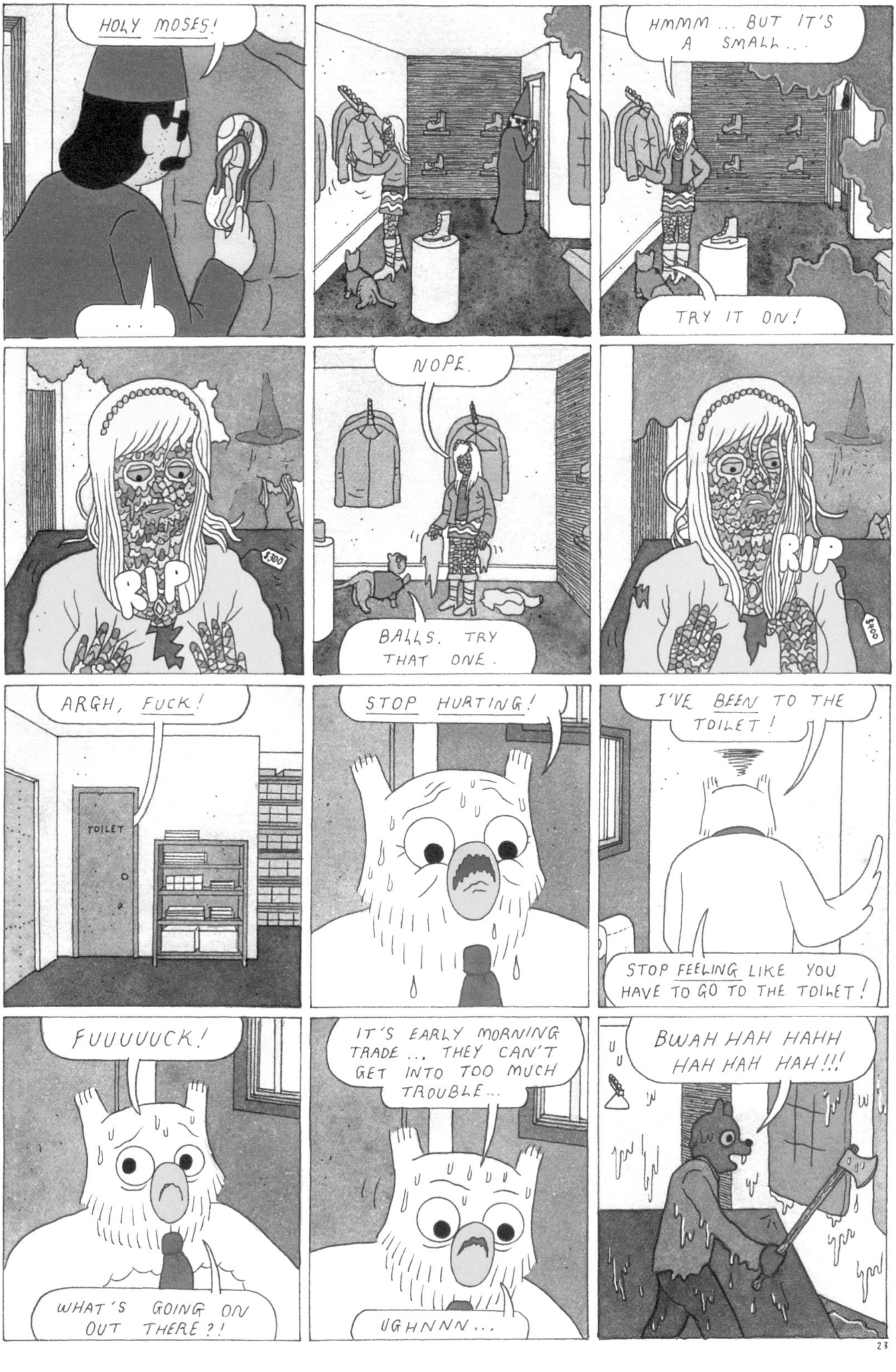
HOLY MOSES!
...
HMMM ... BUT IT'S A SMALL...
TRY IT ON!
$300
NOPE.
BALLS. TRY THAT ONE.
$300
ARGH, FUCK!
TOILET
STOP HURTING!
I'VE BEEN TO THE TOILET!
STOP FEELING LIKE YOU HAVE TO GO TO THE TOILET!
FUUUUUCK!
WHAT'S GOING ON OUT THERE?!
IT'S EARLY MORNING TRADE ... THEY CAN'T GET INTO TOO MUCH TROUBLE...
UGHNNN...
BWAH HAH HAHH HAH HAH HAH!!!

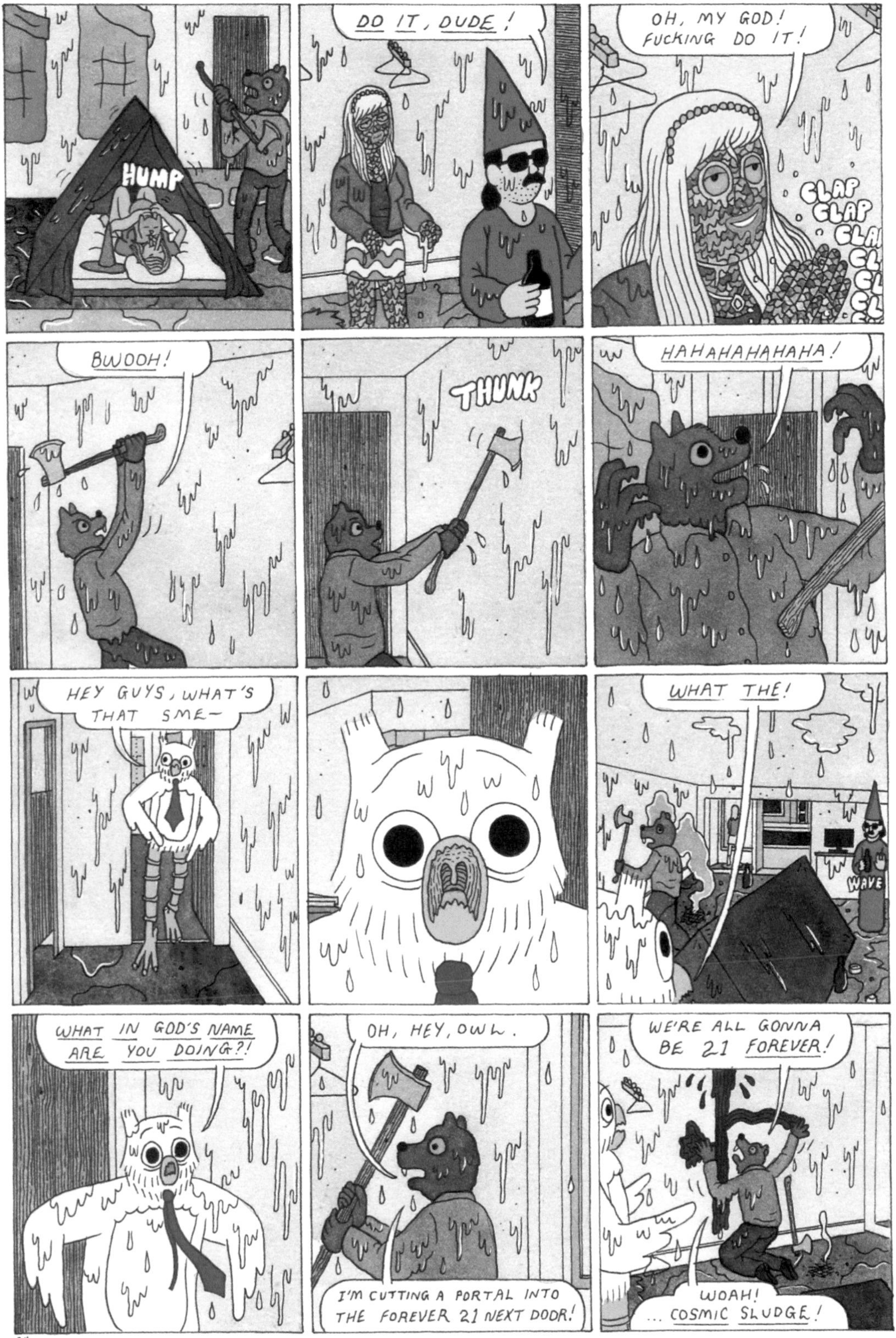
HUMP
DO IT, DUDE!
OH, MY GOD! FUCKING DO IT!
CLAP CLAP CLAP
BWOOH!
THUNK
HAHAHAHAHAHA!
HEY GUYS, WHAT'S THAT SME—
WHAT THE!
WAVE
WHAT IN GOD'S NAME ARE YOU DOING?!
OH, HEY, OWL.
I'M CUTTING A PORTAL INTO THE FOREVER 21 NEXT DOOR!
WE'RE ALL GONNA BE 21 FOREVER!
WOAH! ...COSMIC SLUDGE!

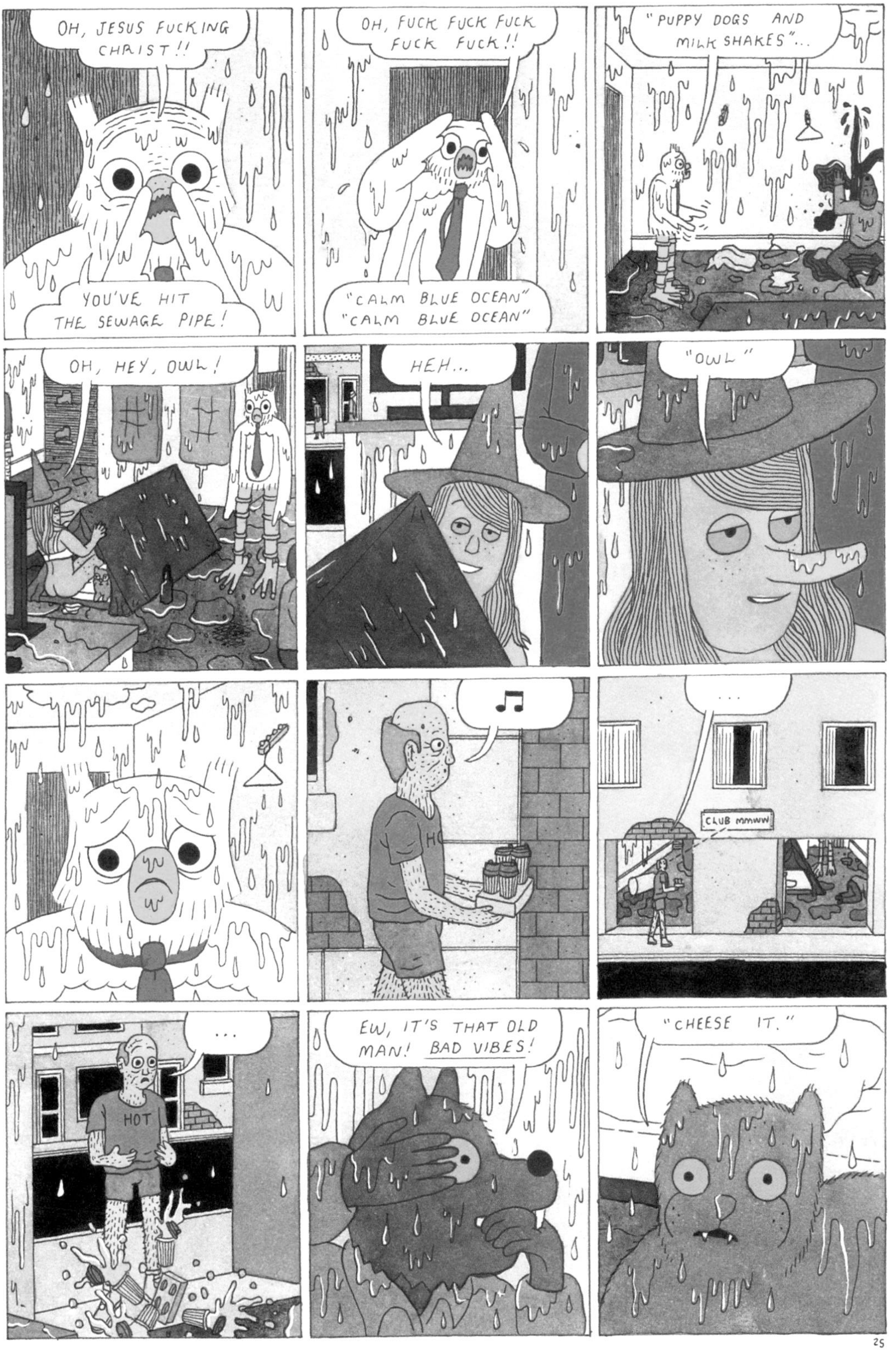
OH, JESUS FUCKING CHRIST!!
YOU'VE HIT THE SEWAGE PIPE!
OH, FUCK FUCK FUCK FUCK FUCK!!
"CALM BLUE OCEAN" "CALM BLUE OCEAN"
"PUPPY DOGS AND MILK SHAKES"...
OH, HEY, OWL!
HEH...
"OWL"
HO
...
CLUB MMWW
...
HOT
EW, IT'S THAT OLD MAN! BAD VIBES!
"CHEESE IT."

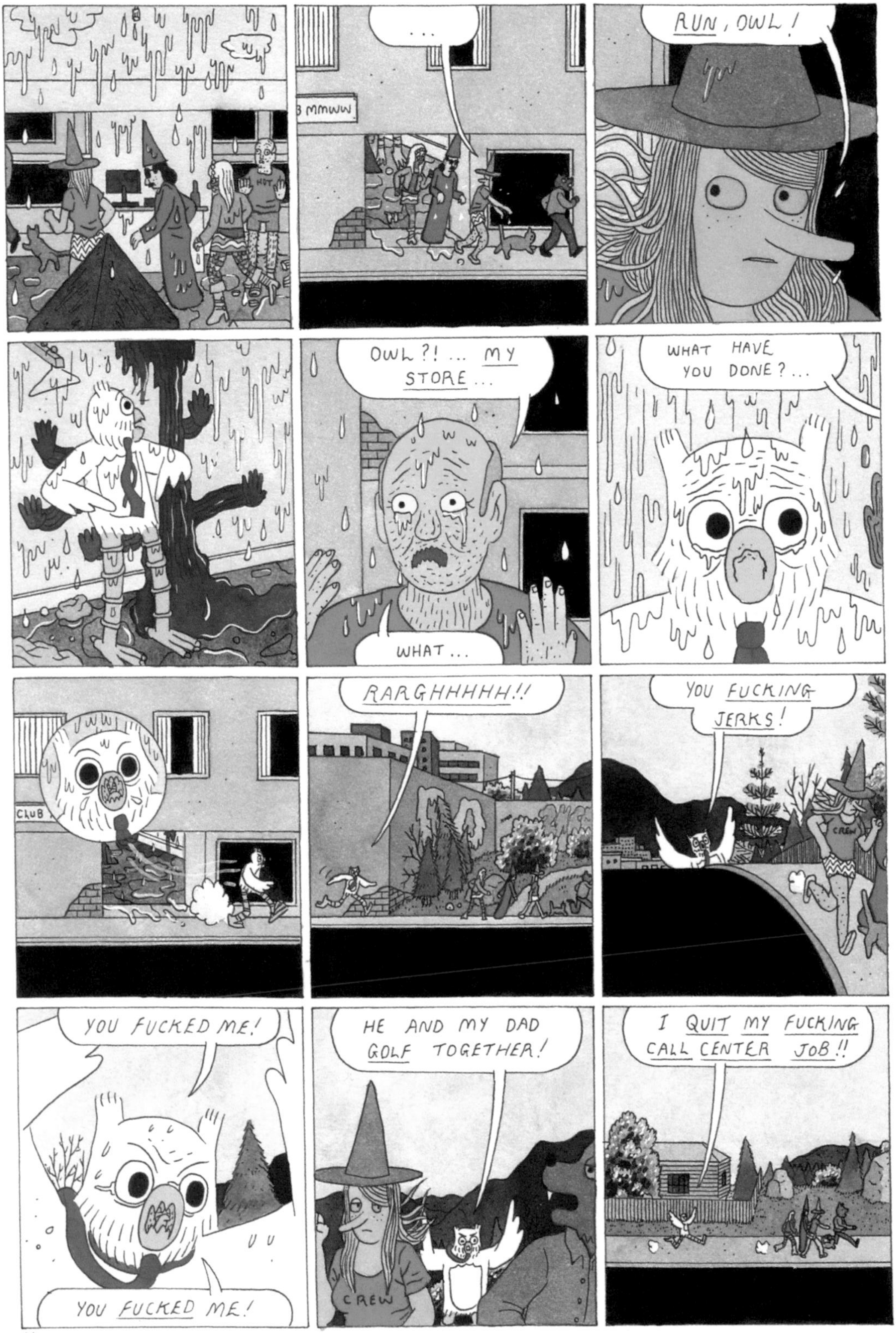
B MMWW
...
RUN, OWL!
OWL?! ... MY STORE ...
WHAT ...
WHAT HAVE YOU DONE? ...
CLUB
RARGHHHHH!!
YOU FUCKING JERKS!
CREW
YOU FUCKED ME!
YOU FUCKED ME!
HE AND MY DAD GOLF TOGETHER!
CREW
I QUIT MY FUCKING CALL CENTER JOB!!

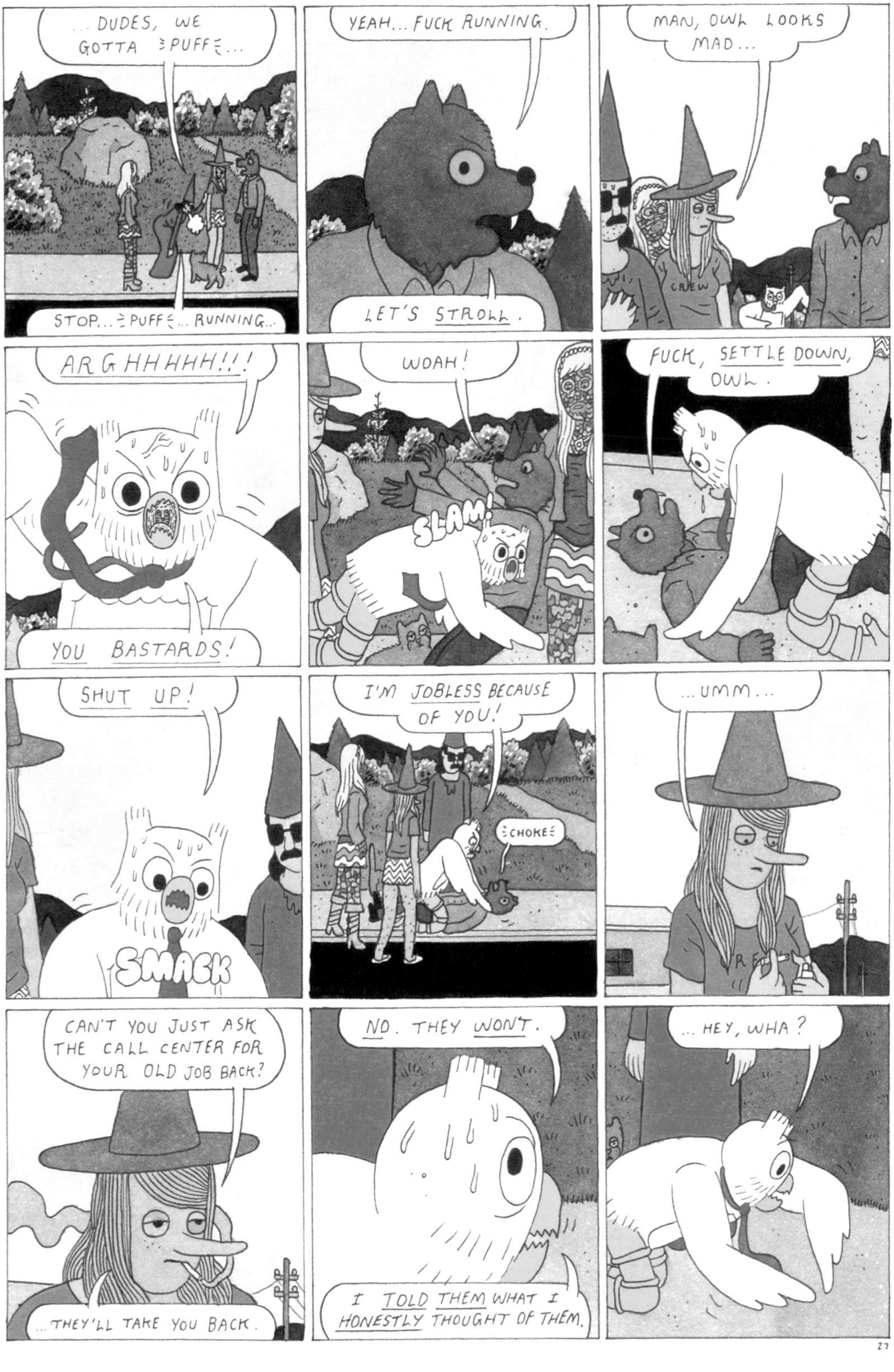

...DUDES, WE GOTTA PUFF...
STOP... PUFF... RUNNING...
YEAH... FUCK RUNNING.
LET'S STROLL.
MAN, OWL LOOKS MAD...
CREW
ARGHHHHH!!!
YOU BASTARDS!
WOAH!
SLAM!
FUCK, SETTLE DOWN, OWL.
SHUT UP!
SMACK
I'M JOBLESS BECAUSE OF YOU!
CHOKE
...UMM...
CAN'T YOU JUST ASK THE CALL CENTER FOR YOUR OLD JOB BACK?
...THEY'LL TAKE YOU BACK.
NO. THEY WON'T.
I TOLD THEM WHAT I HONESTLY THOUGHT OF THEM.
...HEY, WHA?

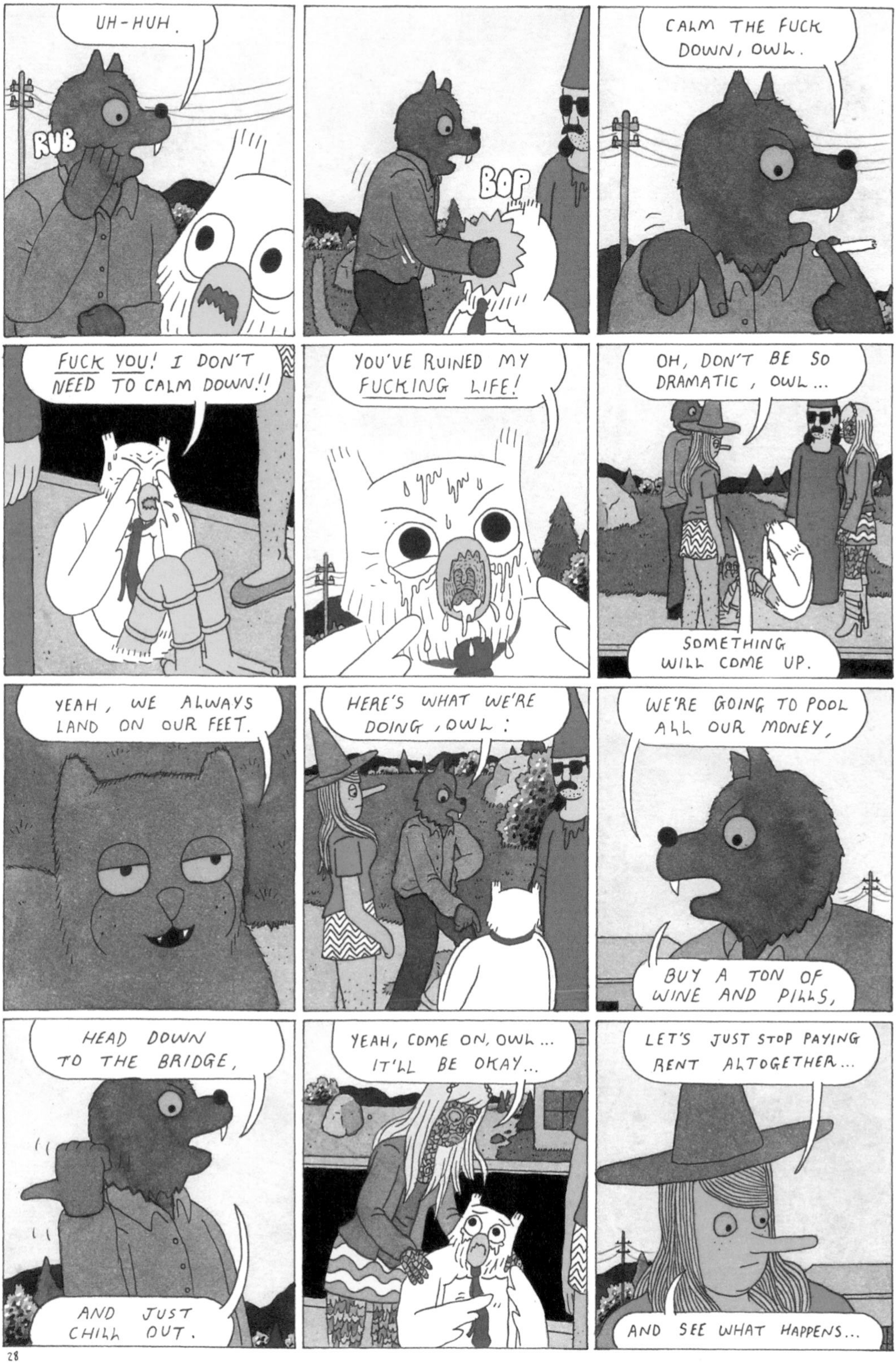
UH-HUH.
RUB
BOP
CALM THE FUCK DOWN, OWL.
FUCK YOU! I DON'T NEED TO CALM DOWN!!
YOU'VE RUINED MY FUCKING LIFE!
OH, DON'T BE SO DRAMATIC, OWL...
SOMETHING WILL COME UP.
YEAH, WE ALWAYS LAND ON OUR FEET.
HERE'S WHAT WE'RE DOING, OWL:
WE'RE GOING TO POOL ALL OUR MONEY,
BUY A TON OF WINE AND PILLS,
HEAD DOWN TO THE BRIDGE,
AND JUST CHILL OUT.
YEAH, COME ON, OWL... IT'LL BE OKAY...
LET'S JUST STOP PAYING RENT ALTOGETHER...
AND SEE WHAT HAPPENS...

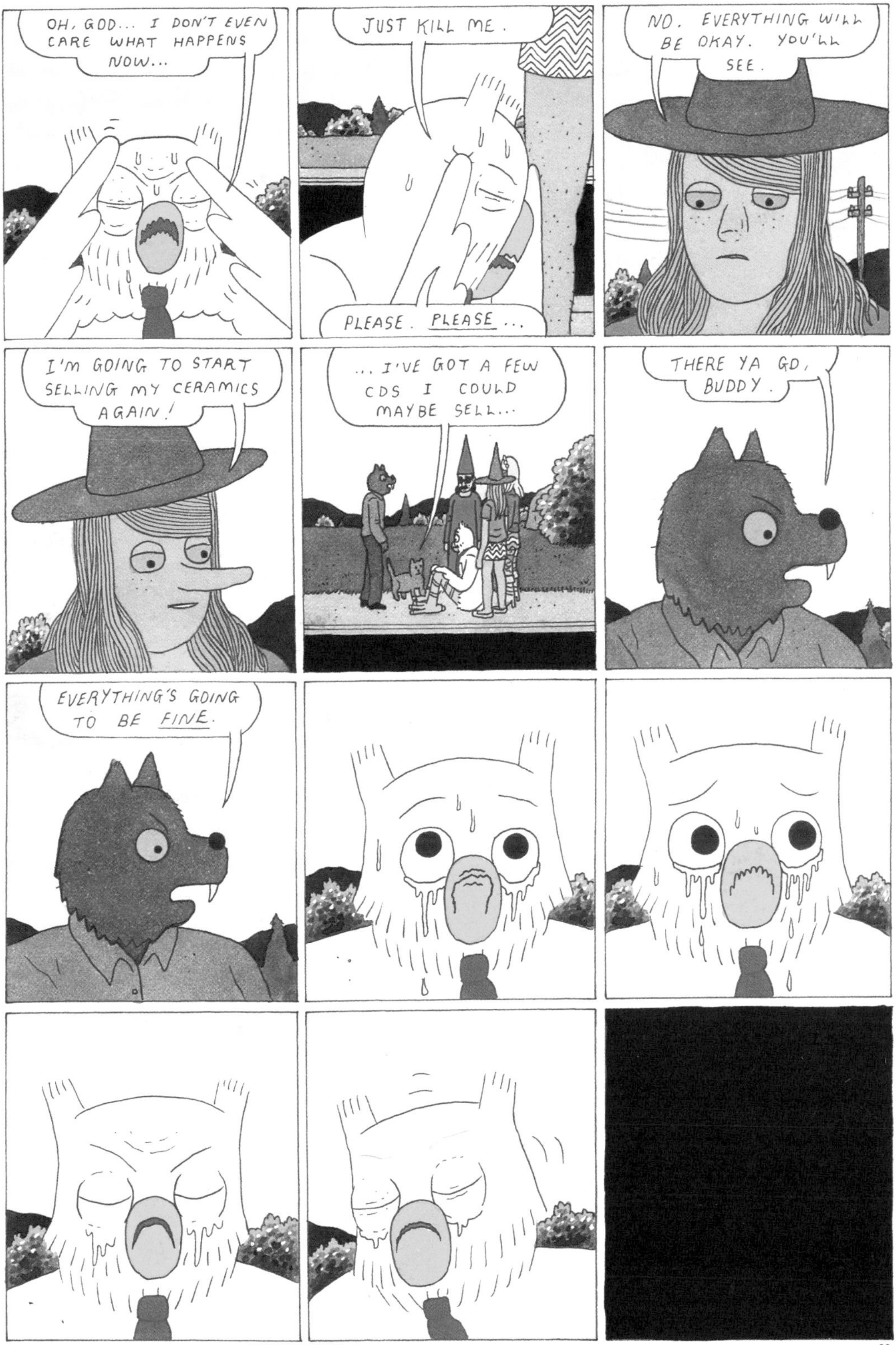
OH, GOD... I DON'T EVEN CARE WHAT HAPPENS NOW...
JUST KILL ME.
PLEASE. PLEASE...
NO. EVERYTHING WILL BE OKAY. YOU'LL SEE.
I'M GOING TO START SELLING MY CERAMICS AGAIN!
...I'VE GOT A FEW CDS I COULD MAYBE SELL...
THERE YA GO, BUDDY.
EVERYTHING'S GOING TO BE FINE.

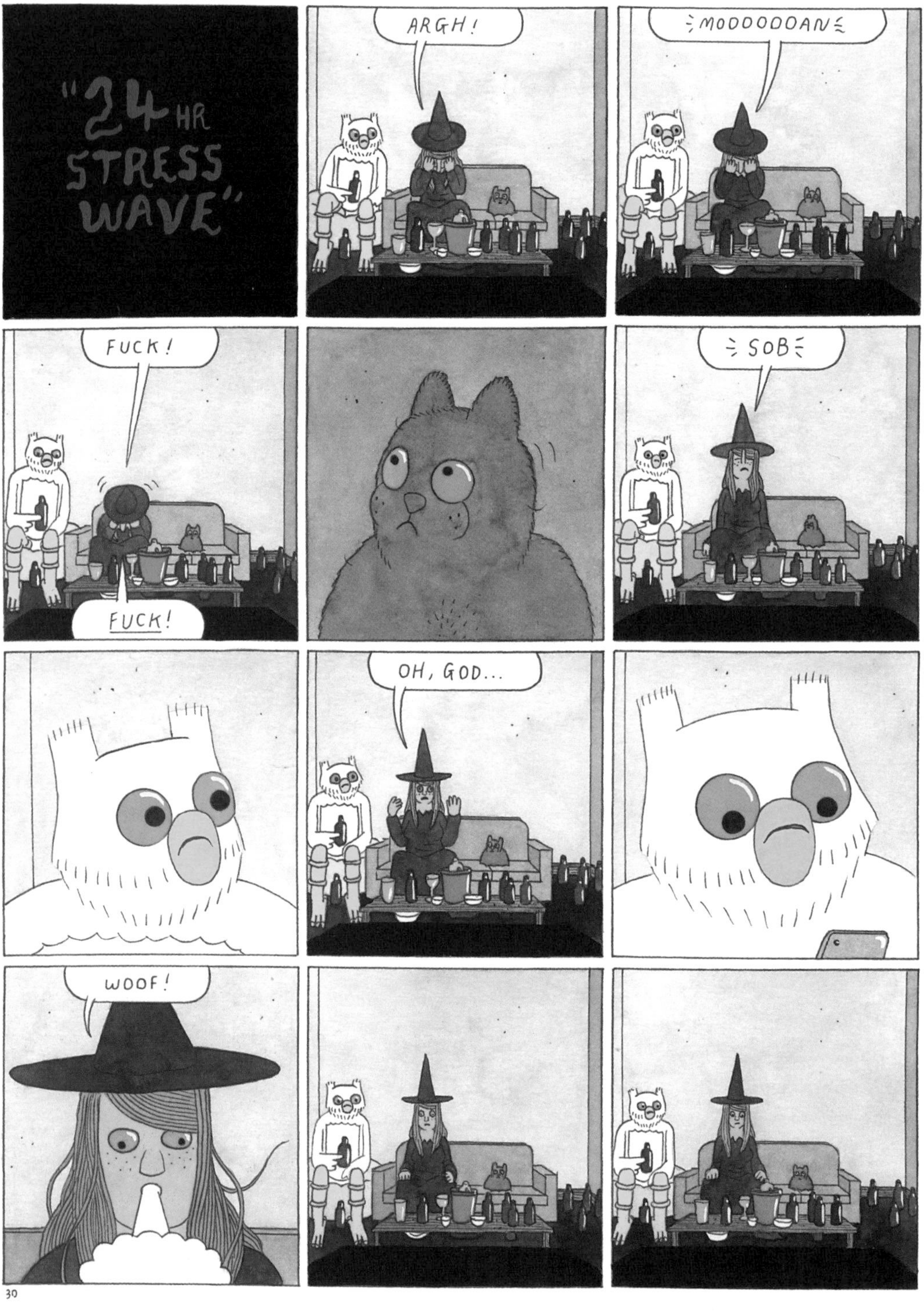
"24 HR STRESS WAVE"
ARGH!
MOOOOOOAN
FUCK!
FUCK!
SOB
OH, GOD...
WOOF!

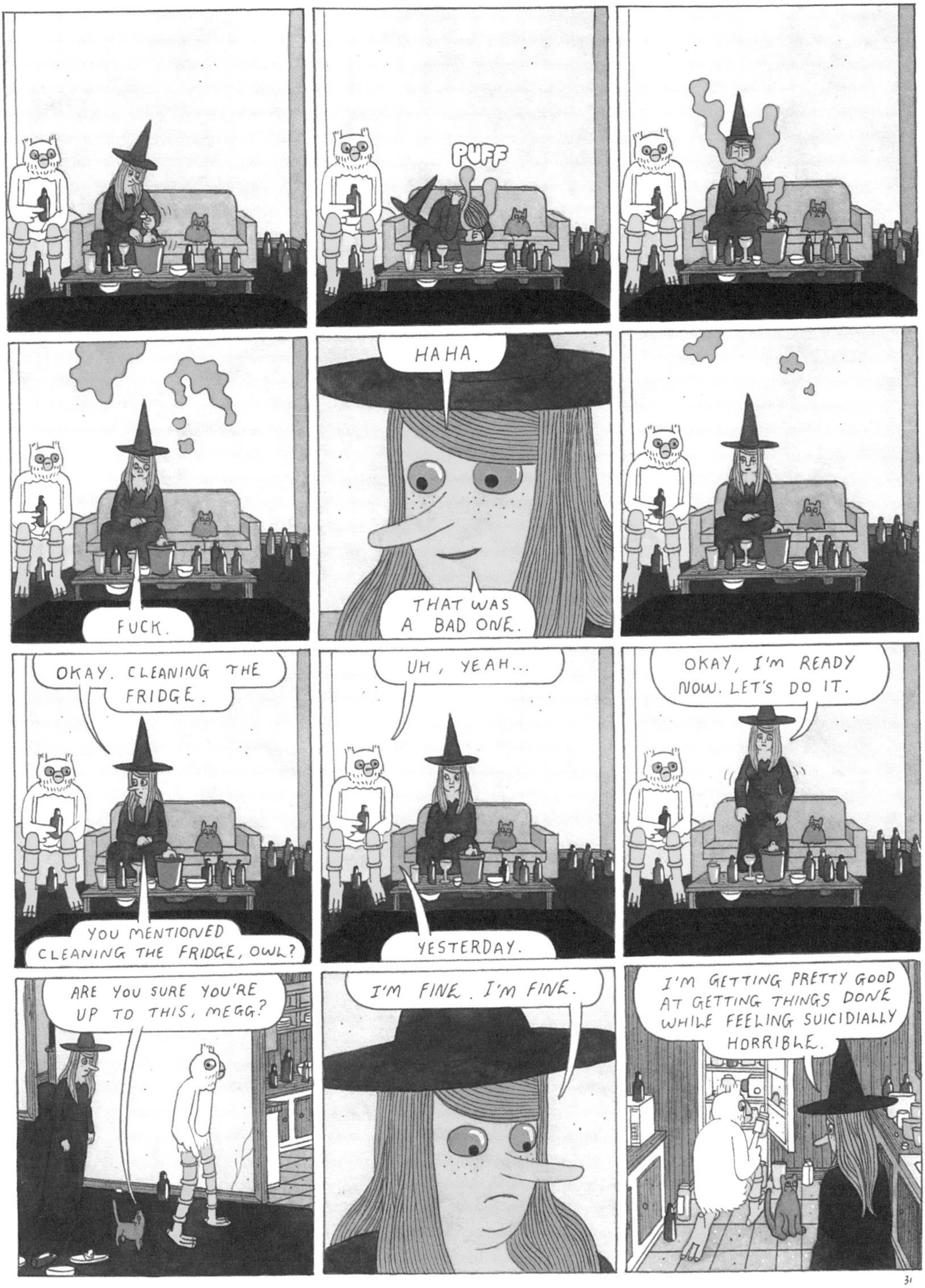
PUFF
FUCK.
HAHA.
THAT WAS A BAD ONE.
OKAY. CLEANING THE FRIDGE.
YOU MENTIONED CLEANING THE FRIDGE, OWL?
UH, YEAH...
YESTERDAY.
OKAY, I'M READY NOW. LET'S DO IT.
ARE YOU SURE YOU'RE UP TO THIS, MEGG?
I'M FINE. I'M FINE.
I'M GETTING PRETTY GOOD AT GETTING THINGS DONE WHILE FEELING SUICIDIALLY HORRIBLE.

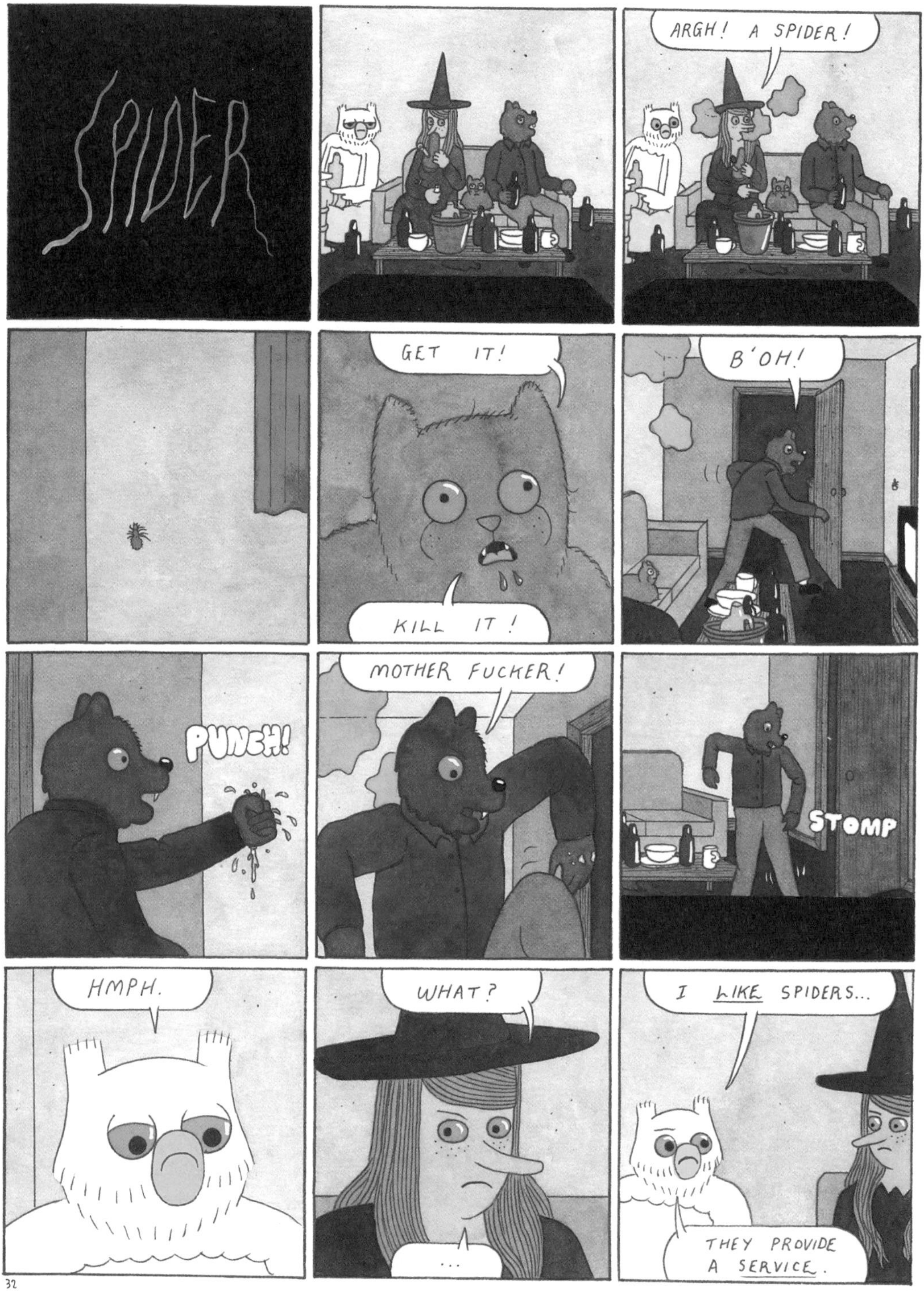
SPIDER
ARGH! A SPIDER!
GET IT!
KILL IT!
B'OH!
PUNCH!
MOTHER FUCKER!
STOMP
HMPH.
WHAT?
...
I LIKE SPIDERS...
THEY PROVIDE A SERVICE.

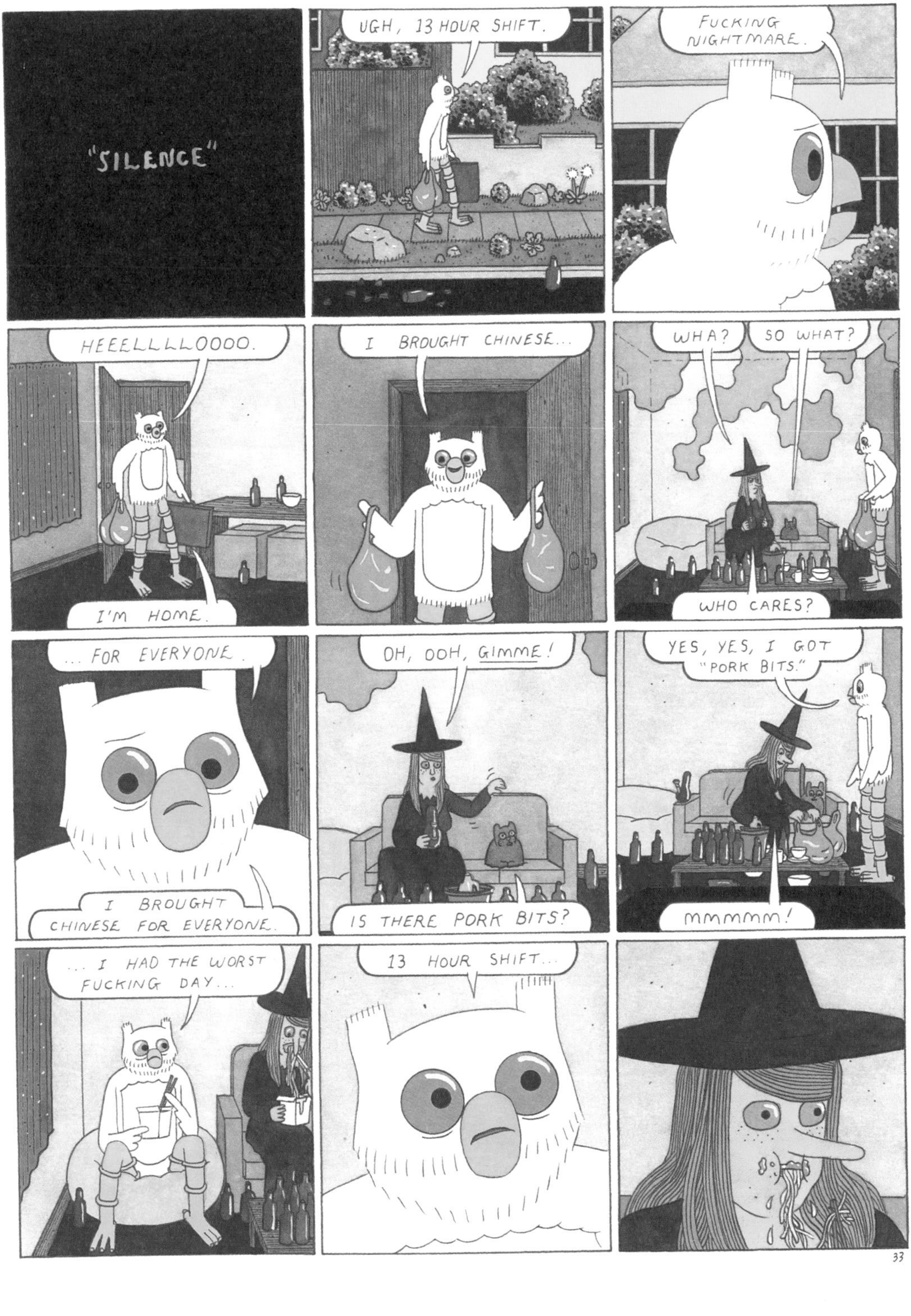
"SILENCE"
UGH, 13 HOUR SHIFT.
FUCKING NIGHTMARE.
HEEELLLLLOOOO.
I'M HOME.
I BROUGHT CHINESE...
WHA?
SO WHAT?
WHO CARES?
... FOR EVERYONE.
I BROUGHT CHINESE FOR EVERYONE.
OH, OOH, GIMME!
IS THERE PORK BITS?
YES, YES, I GOT "PORK BITS."
MMMMM!
... I HAD THE WORST FUCKING DAY...
13 HOUR SHIFT...

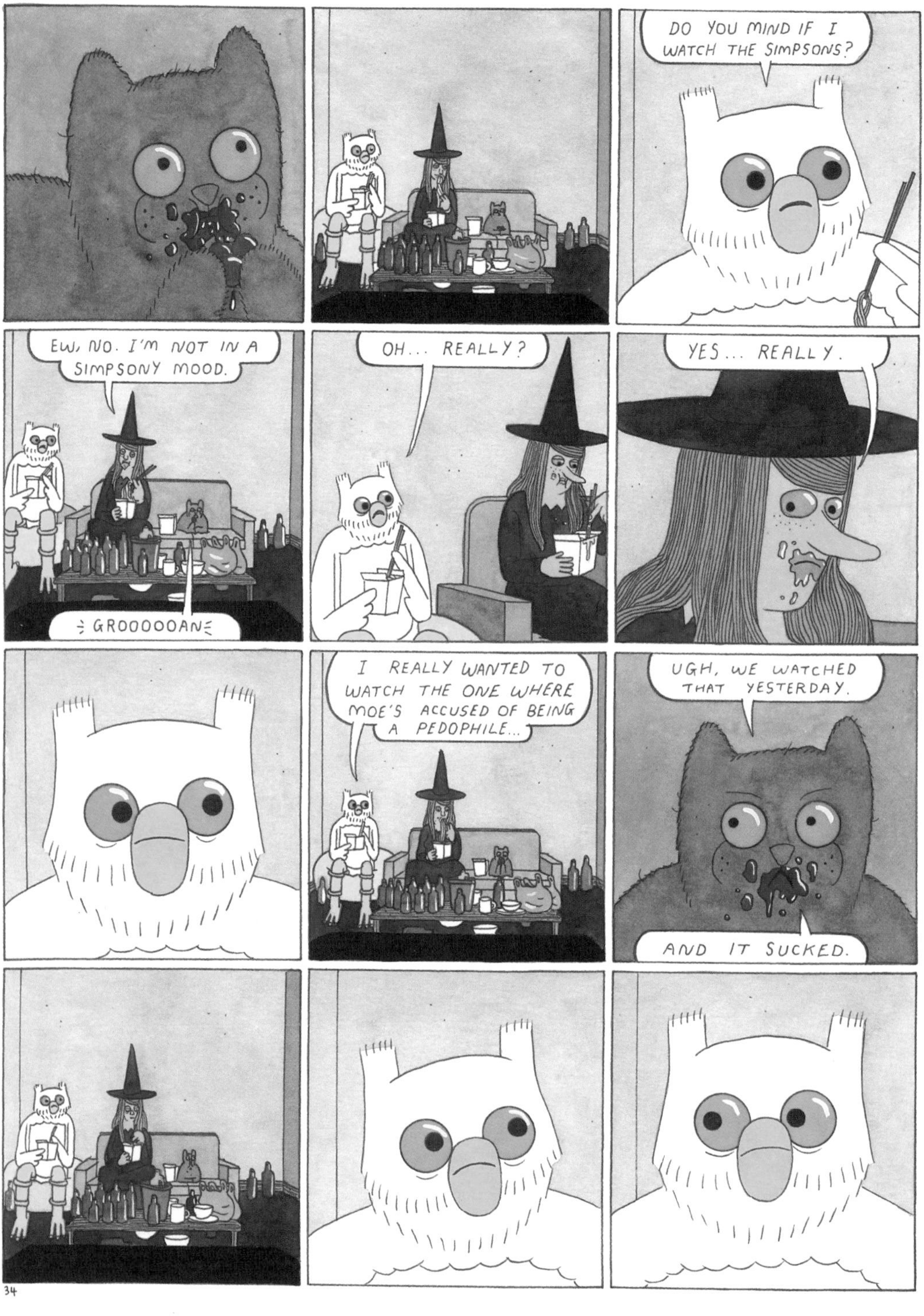
DO YOU MIND IF I WATCH THE SIMPSONS?
EW, NO. I'M NOT IN A SIMPSONY MOOD.
GROOOOOAN
OH... REALLY?
YES... REALLY.
I REALLY WANTED TO WATCH THE ONE WHERE MOE'S ACCUSED OF BEING A PEDOPHILE...
UGH, WE WATCHED THAT YESTERDAY.
AND IT SUCKED.

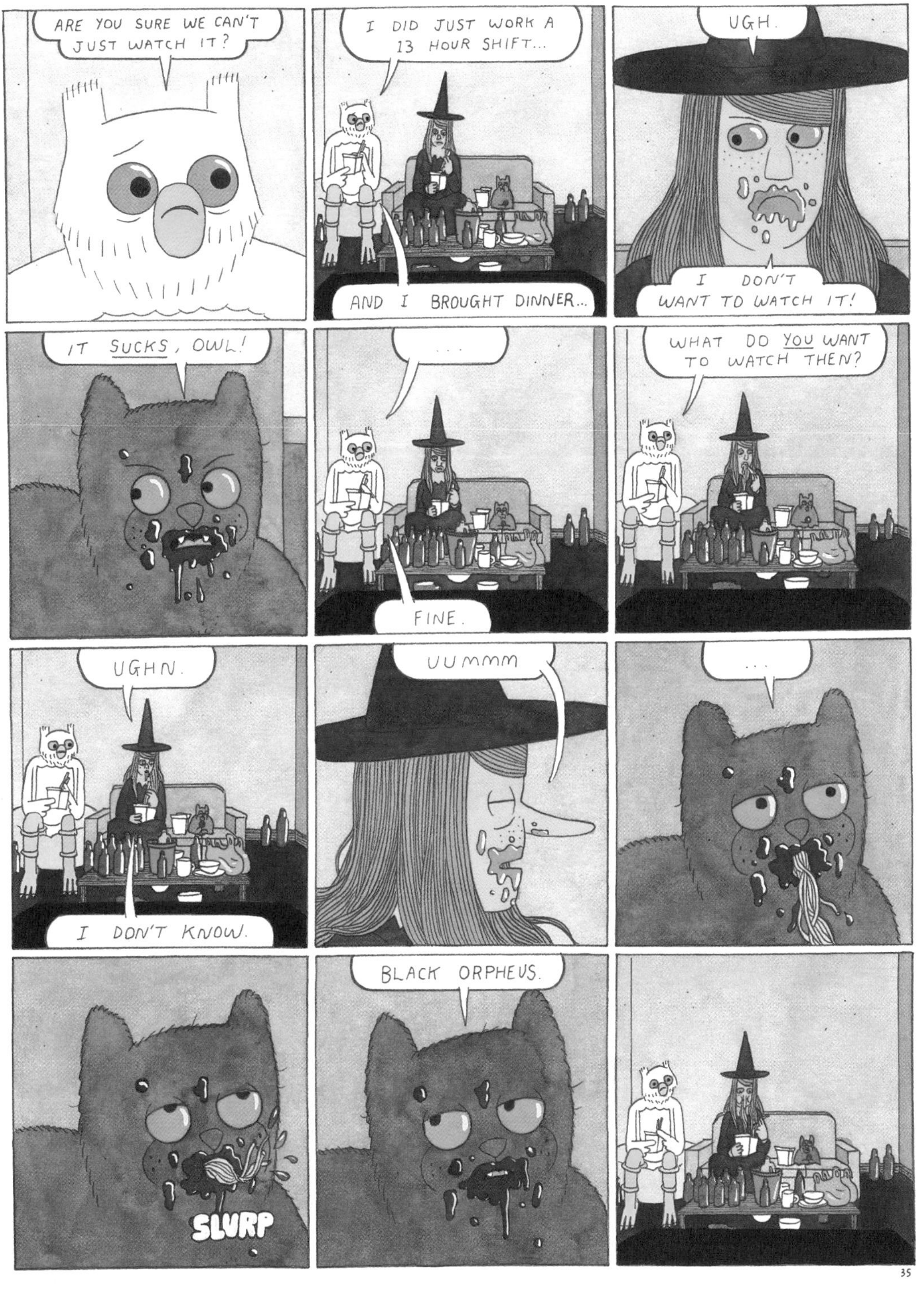
ARE YOU SURE WE CAN'T JUST WATCH IT?
I DID JUST WORK A 13 HOUR SHIFT...
AND I BROUGHT DINNER...
UGH.
I DON'T WANT TO WATCH IT!
IT SUCKS, OWL!
...
FINE.
WHAT DO YOU WANT TO WATCH THEN?
UGHN.
I DON'T KNOW.
UUMMM
...
SLURP
BLACK ORPHEUS.

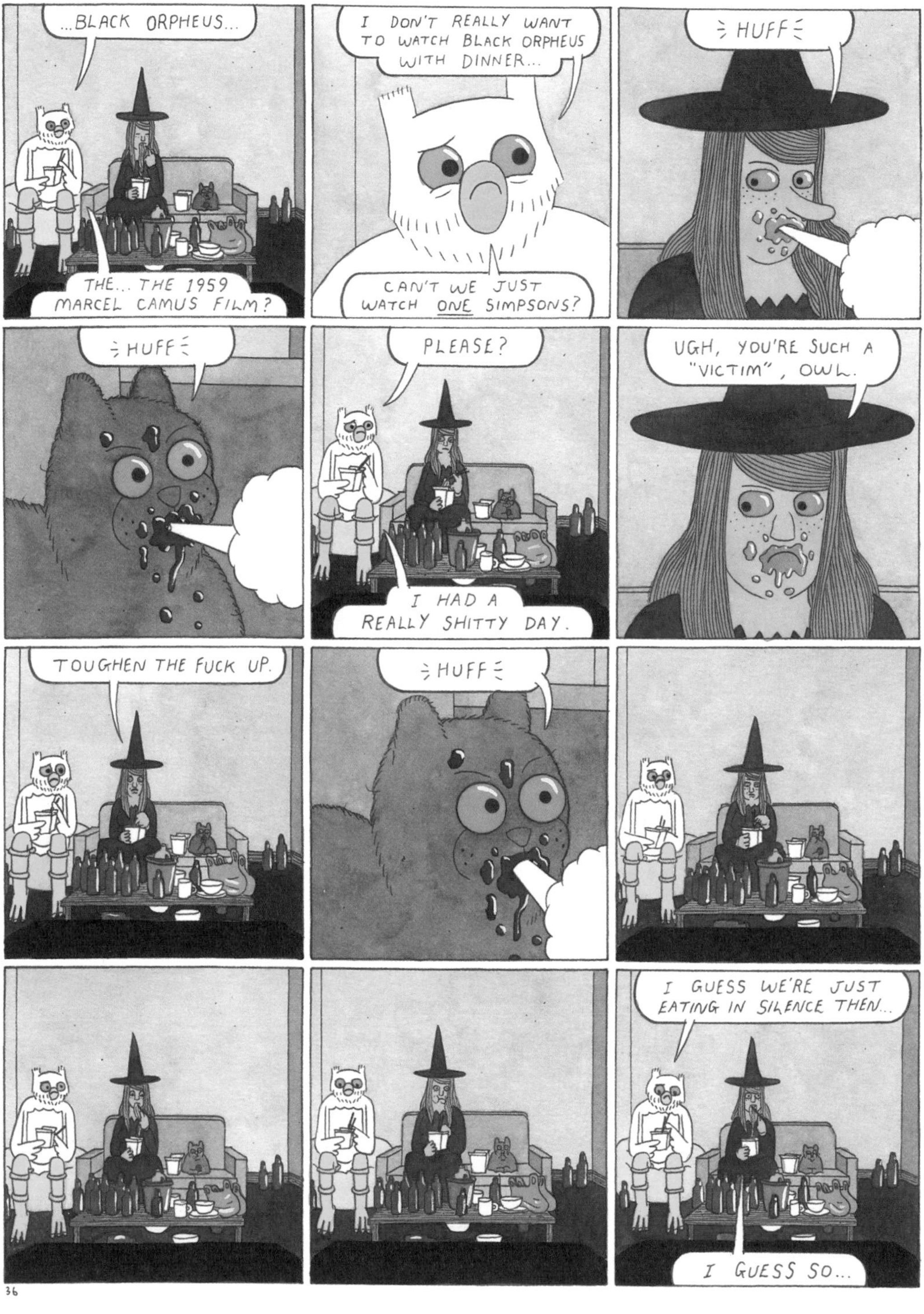
...BLACK ORPHEUS...
THE... THE 1959 MARCEL CAMUS FILM?
I DON'T REALLY WANT TO WATCH BLACK ORPHEUS WITH DINNER...
CAN'T WE JUST WATCH ONE SIMPSONS?
HUFF
HUFF
PLEASE?
I HAD A REALLY SHITTY DAY.
UGH, YOU'RE SUCH A "VICTIM", OWL.
TOUGHEN THE FUCK UP.
HUFF
I GUESS WE'RE JUST EATING IN SILENCE THEN...
I GUESS SO...

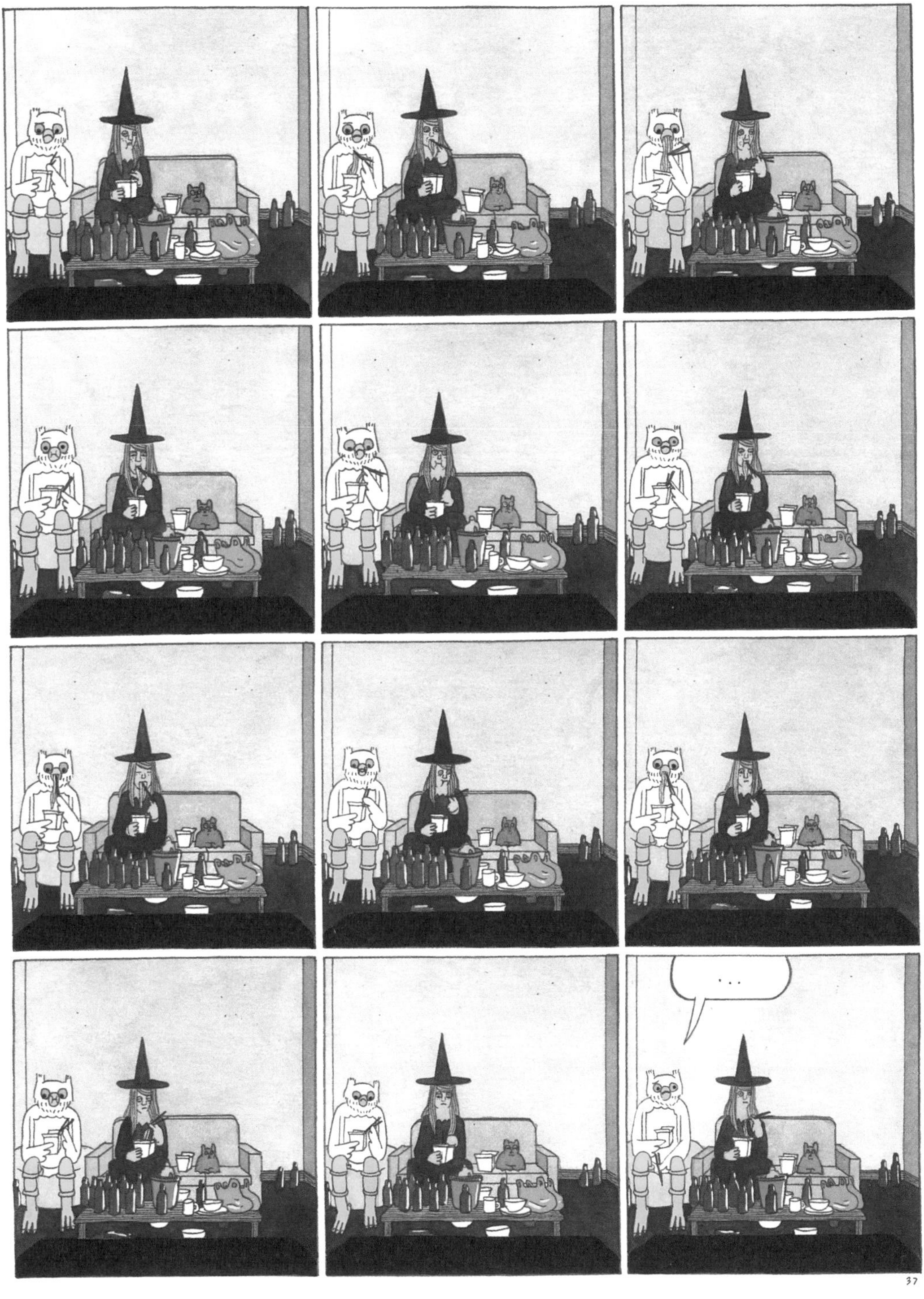
. . .

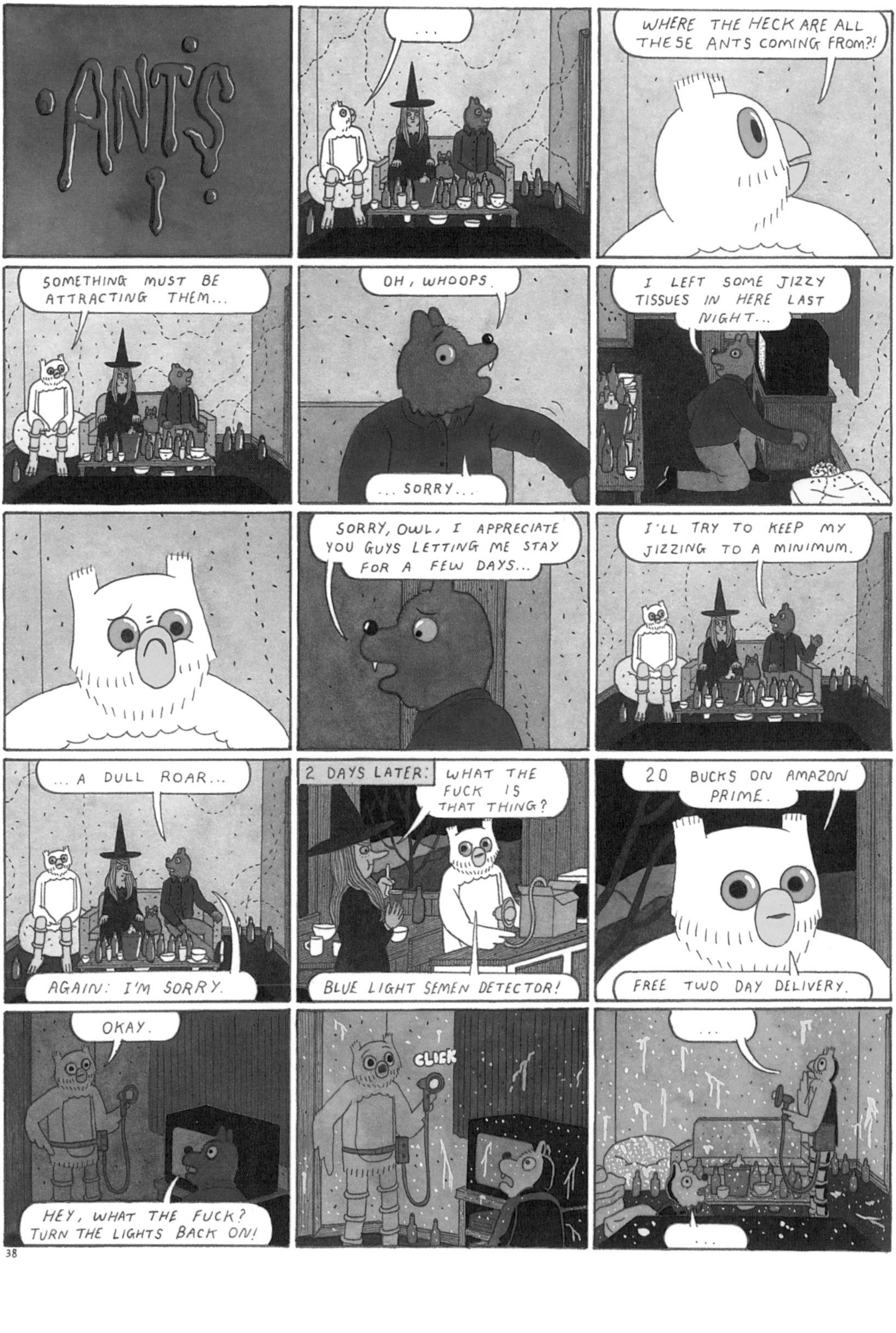
ANTS
...
WHERE THE HECK ARE ALL THESE ANTS COMING FROM?!
SOMETHING MUST BE ATTRACTING THEM...
OH, WHOOPS.
... SORRY...
I LEFT SOME JIZZY TISSUES IN HERE LAST NIGHT...
SORRY, OWL, I APPRECIATE YOU GUYS LETTING ME STAY FOR A FEW DAYS...
I'LL TRY TO KEEP MY JIZZING TO A MINIMUM.
... A DULL ROAR...
AGAIN: I'M SORRY.
2 DAYS LATER:
WHAT THE FUCK IS THAT THING?
BLUE LIGHT SEMEN DETECTOR!
20 BUCKS ON AMAZON PRIME.
FREE TWO DAY DELIVERY.
OKAY.
HEY, WHAT THE FUCK? TURN THE LIGHTS BACK ON!
CLICK
...
...

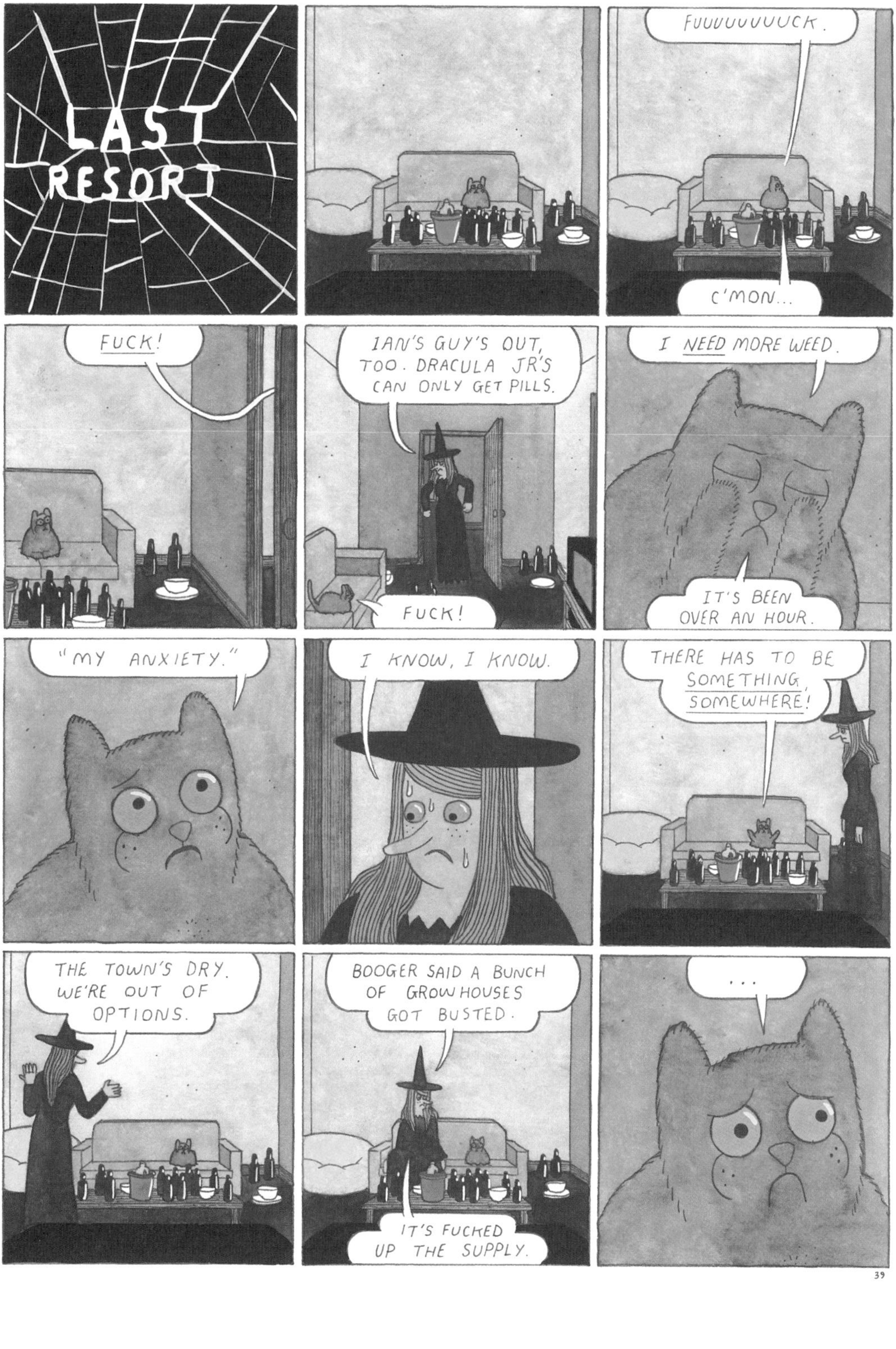
LAST RESORT
FUUUUUUUUCK.
C'MON...
FUCK!
IAN'S GUY'S OUT, TOO. DRACULA JR'S CAN ONLY GET PILLS.
FUCK!
I NEED MORE WEED.
IT'S BEEN OVER AN HOUR.
"MY ANXIETY."
I KNOW, I KNOW.
THERE HAS TO BE SOMETHING, SOMEWHERE!
THE TOWN'S DRY. WE'RE OUT OF OPTIONS.
BOOGER SAID A BUNCH OF GROWHOUSES GOT BUSTED.
IT'S FUCKED UP THE SUPPLY.
...

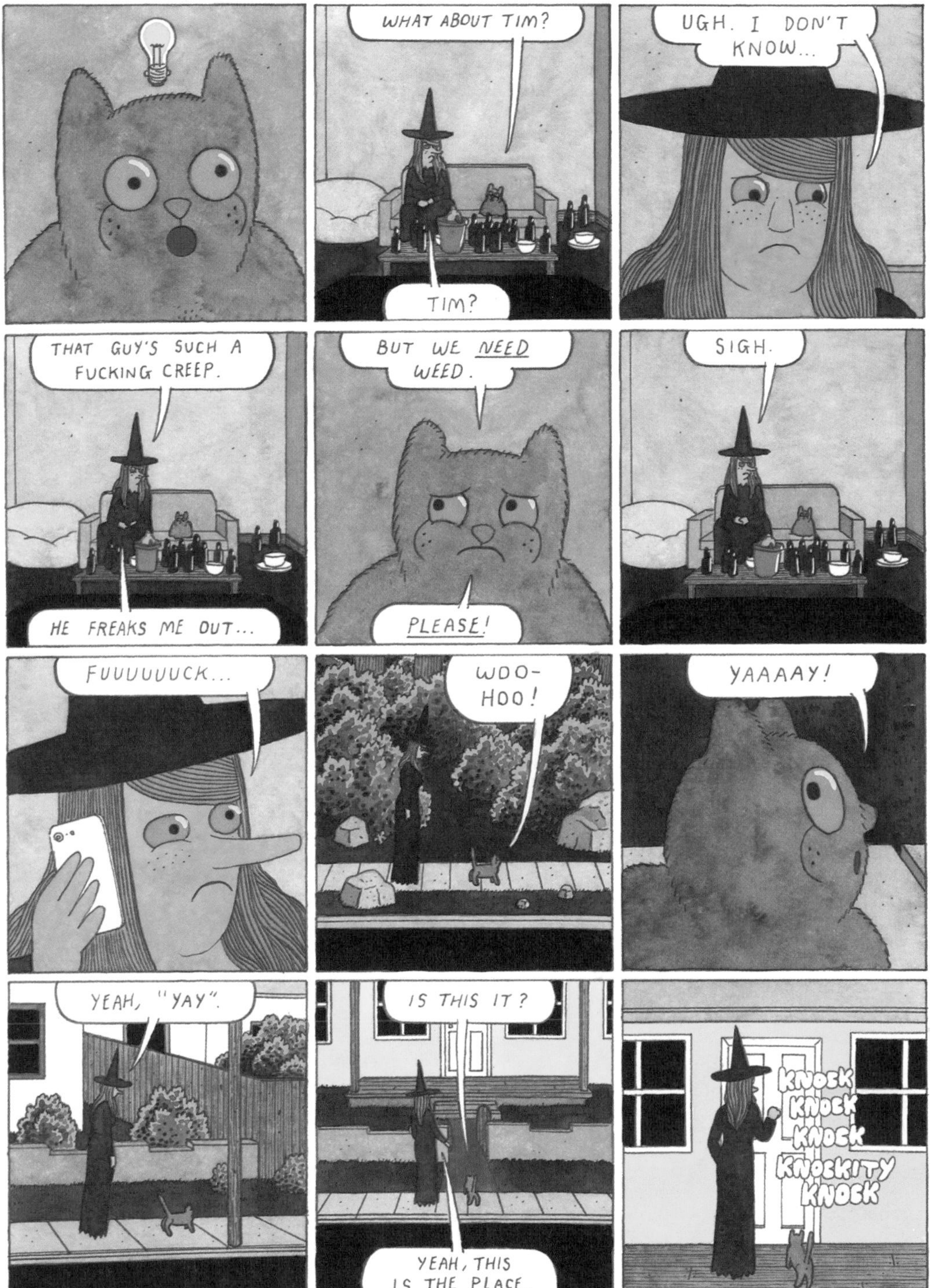
WHAT ABOUT TIM?
TIM?
UGH. I DON'T KNOW...
THAT GUY'S SUCH A FUCKING CREEP.
HE FREAKS ME OUT...
BUT WE NEED WEED.
PLEASE!
SIGH.
FUUUUUUCK...
WOO-HOO!
YAAAAY!
YEAH, "YAY".
IS THIS IT?
YEAH, THIS IS THE PLACE.
KNOCK
KNOCK
KNOCK
KNOCKITY
KNOCK

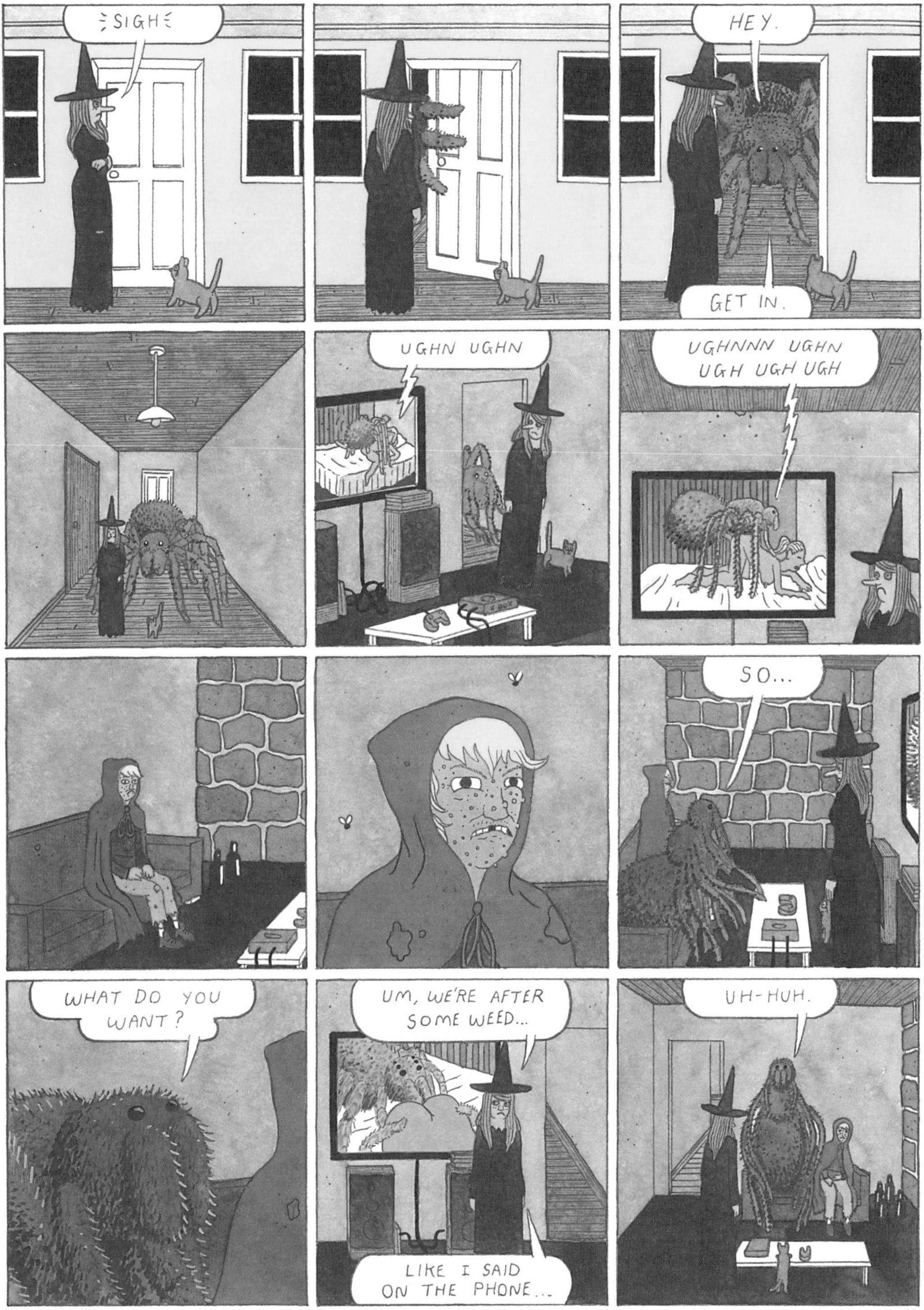
SIGH
HEY.
GET IN.
UGHN UGHN
UGHNNN UGHN UGH UGH UGH
SO...
WHAT DO YOU WANT?
UM, WE'RE AFTER SOME WEED...
LIKE I SAID ON THE PHONE...
UH-HUH.

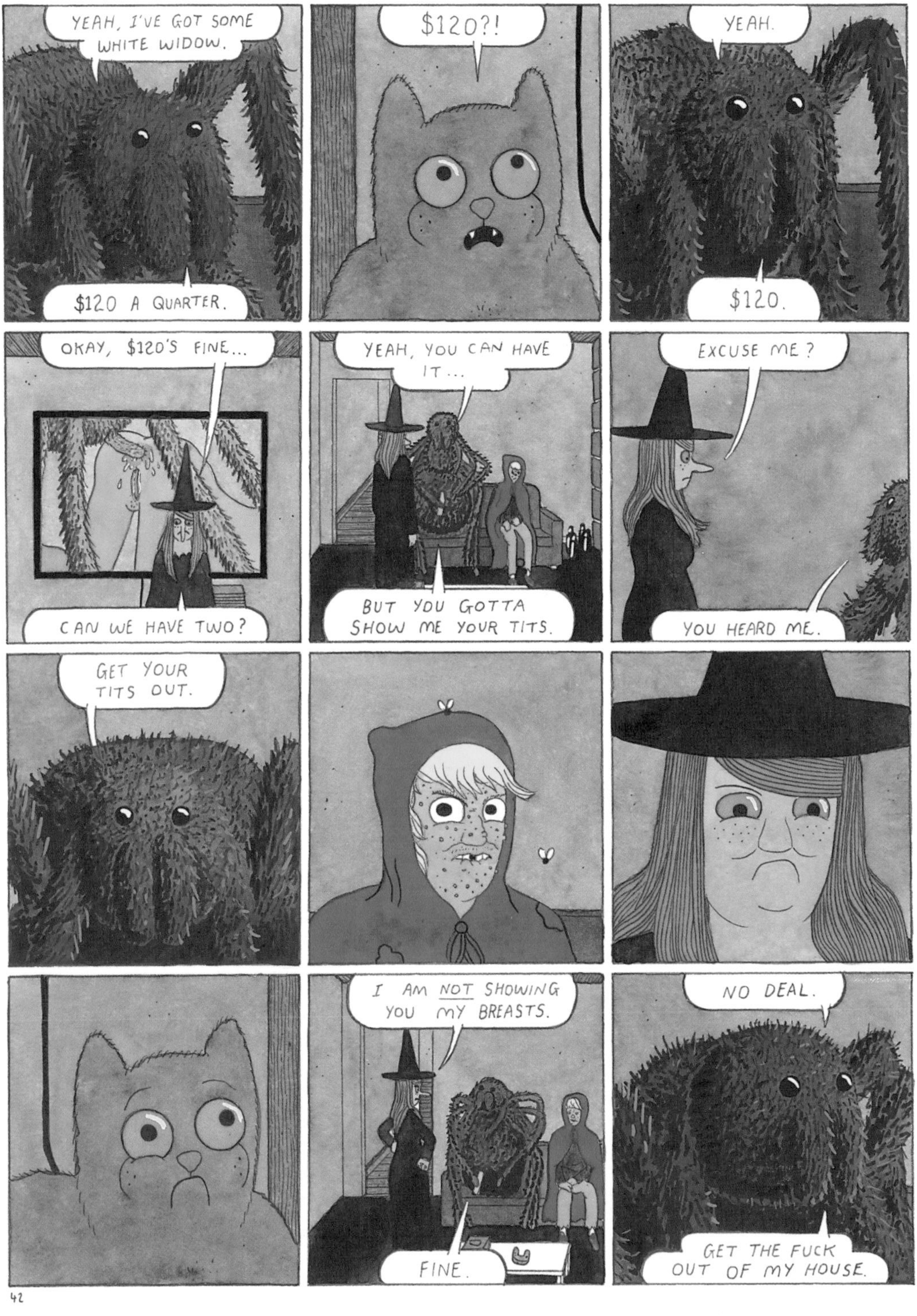
YEAH, I'VE GOT SOME WHITE WIDOW.
$120 A QUARTER.
$120?!
YEAH.
$120.
OKAY, $120'S FINE...
CAN WE HAVE TWO?
YEAH, YOU CAN HAVE IT...
BUT YOU GOTTA SHOW ME YOUR TITS.
EXCUSE ME?
YOU HEARD ME.
GET YOUR TITS OUT.
I AM NOT SHOWING YOU MY BREASTS.
FINE.
NO DEAL.
GET THE FUCK OUT OF MY HOUSE.

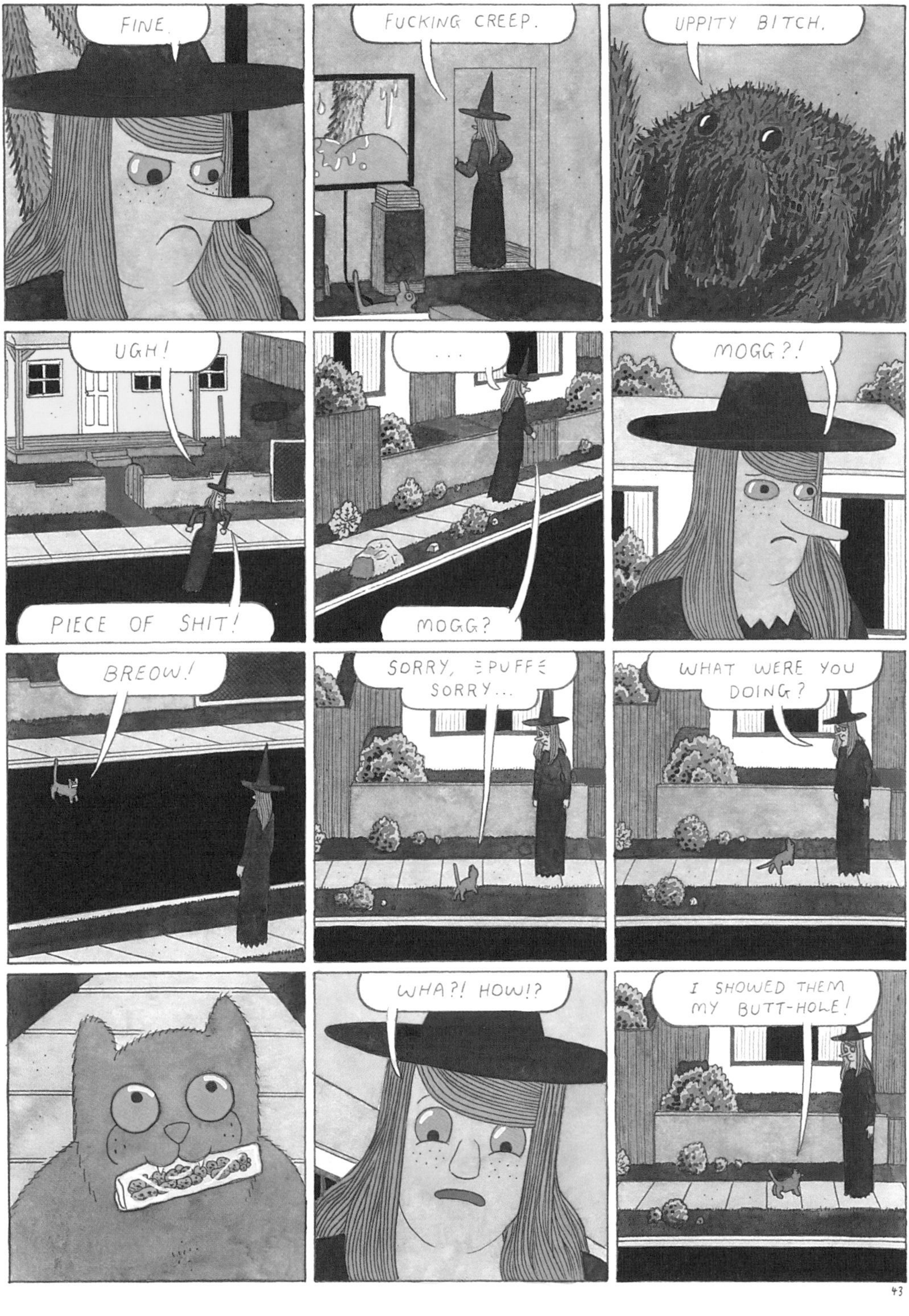
FINE.
FUCKING CREEP.
UPPITY BITCH.
UGH!
PIECE OF SHIT!
...
MOGG?
MOGG?!
BREOW!
SORRY, ≡PUFF≡ SORRY...
WHAT WERE YOU DOING?
WHA?! HOW!?
I SHOWED THEM MY BUTT-HOLE!

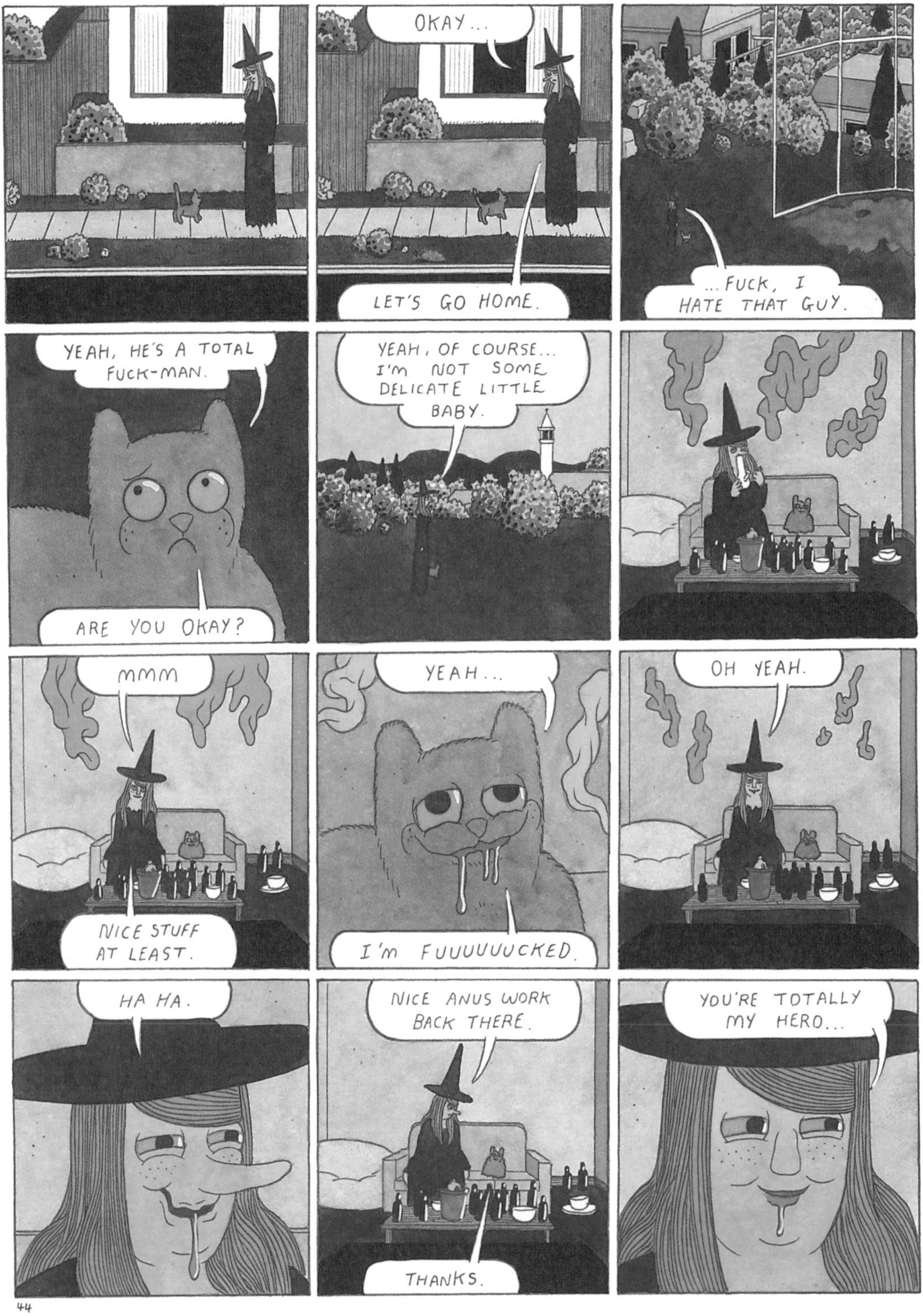
OKAY...
LET'S GO HOME.
...FUCK, I HATE THAT GUY.
YEAH, HE'S A TOTAL FUCK-MAN.
ARE YOU OKAY?
YEAH, OF COURSE... I'M NOT SOME DELICATE LITTLE BABY.
MMM
NICE STUFF AT LEAST.
YEAH...
I'M FUUUUUUCKED.
OH YEAH.
HA HA.
NICE ANUS WORK BACK THERE.
THANKS.
YOU'RE TOTALLY MY HERO...

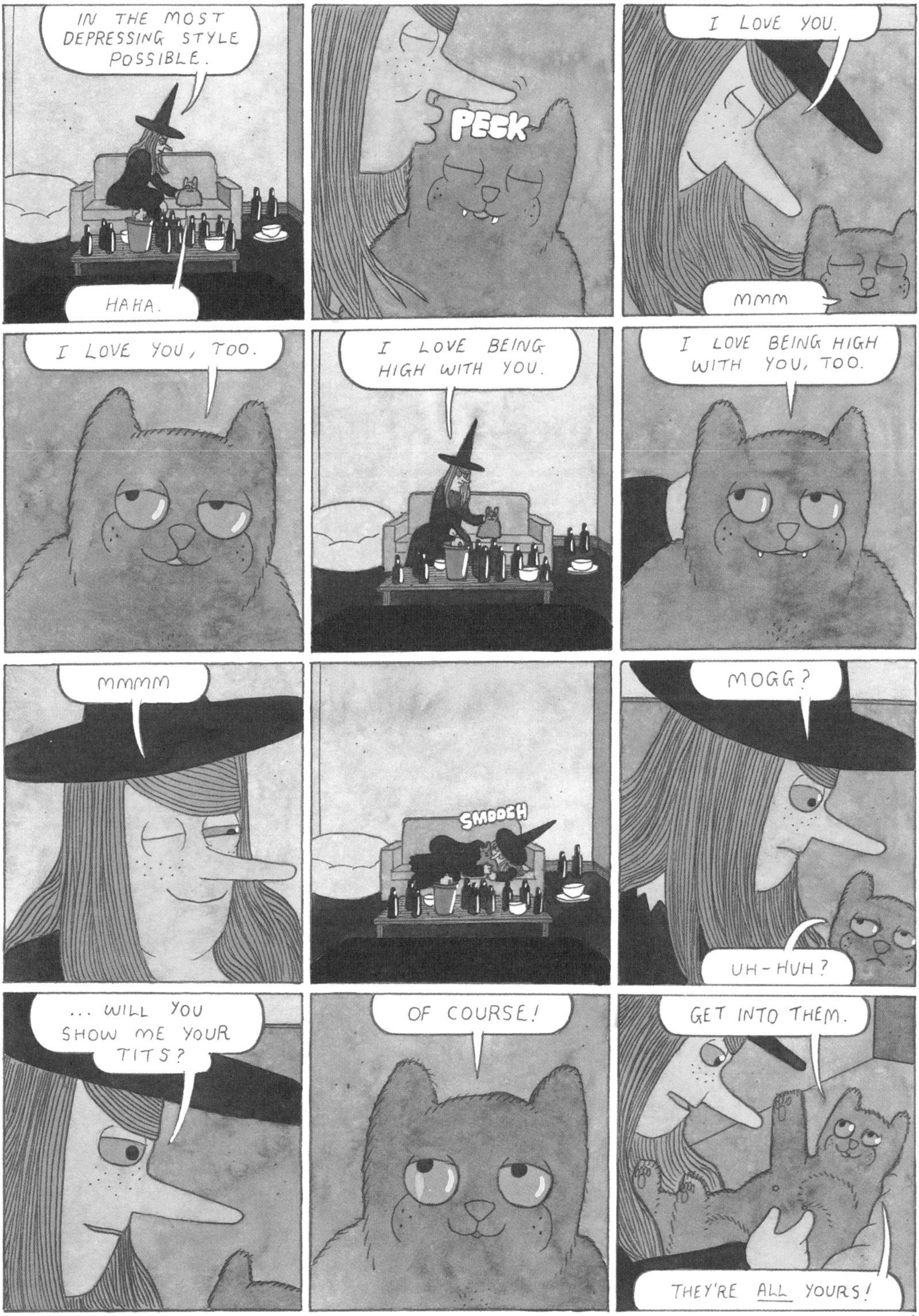
IN THE MOST DEPRESSING STYLE POSSIBLE.
HAHA.
PECK
I LOVE YOU.
MMM
I LOVE YOU, TOO.
I LOVE BEING HIGH WITH YOU.
I LOVE BEING HIGH WITH YOU, TOO.
MMMM
SMOOCH
MOGG?
UH-HUH?
... WILL YOU SHOW ME YOUR TITS?
OF COURSE!
GET INTO THEM.
THEY'RE ALL YOURS!

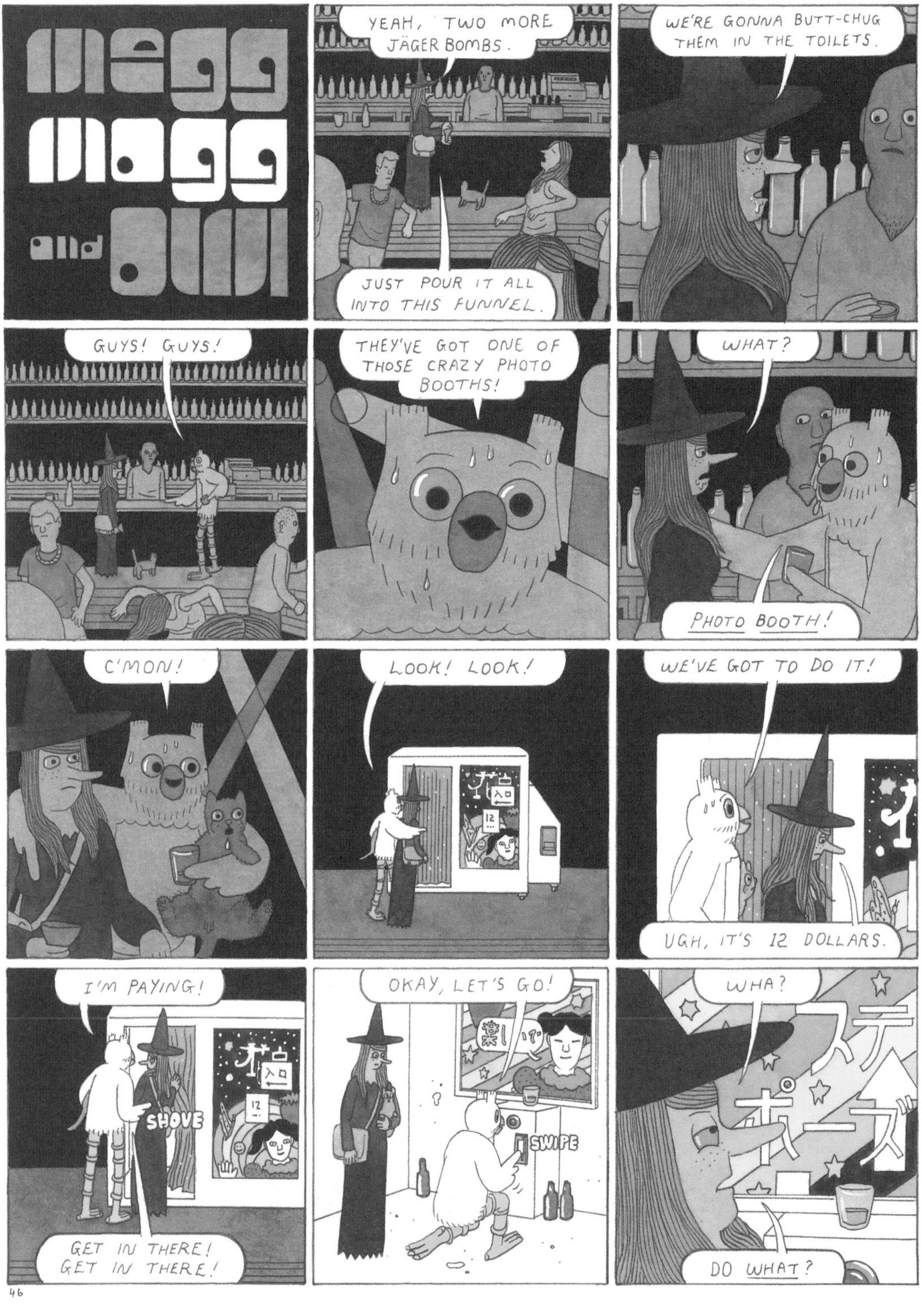
Megg Mogg and Owl
YEAH, TWO MORE JÄGER BOMBS.
JUST POUR IT ALL INTO THIS FUNNEL.
WE'RE GONNA BUTT-CHUG THEM IN THE TOILETS.
GUYS! GUYS!
THEY'VE GOT ONE OF THOSE CRAZY PHOTO BOOTHS!
WHAT?
PHOTO BOOTH!
C'MON!
LOOK! LOOK!
WE'VE GOT TO DO IT!
UGH, IT'S 12 DOLLARS.
I'M PAYING!
SHOVE
GET IN THERE! GET IN THERE!
OKAY, LET'S GO!
楽しい?
SWIPE
WHA?
ステ
ポーズ
DO WHAT?

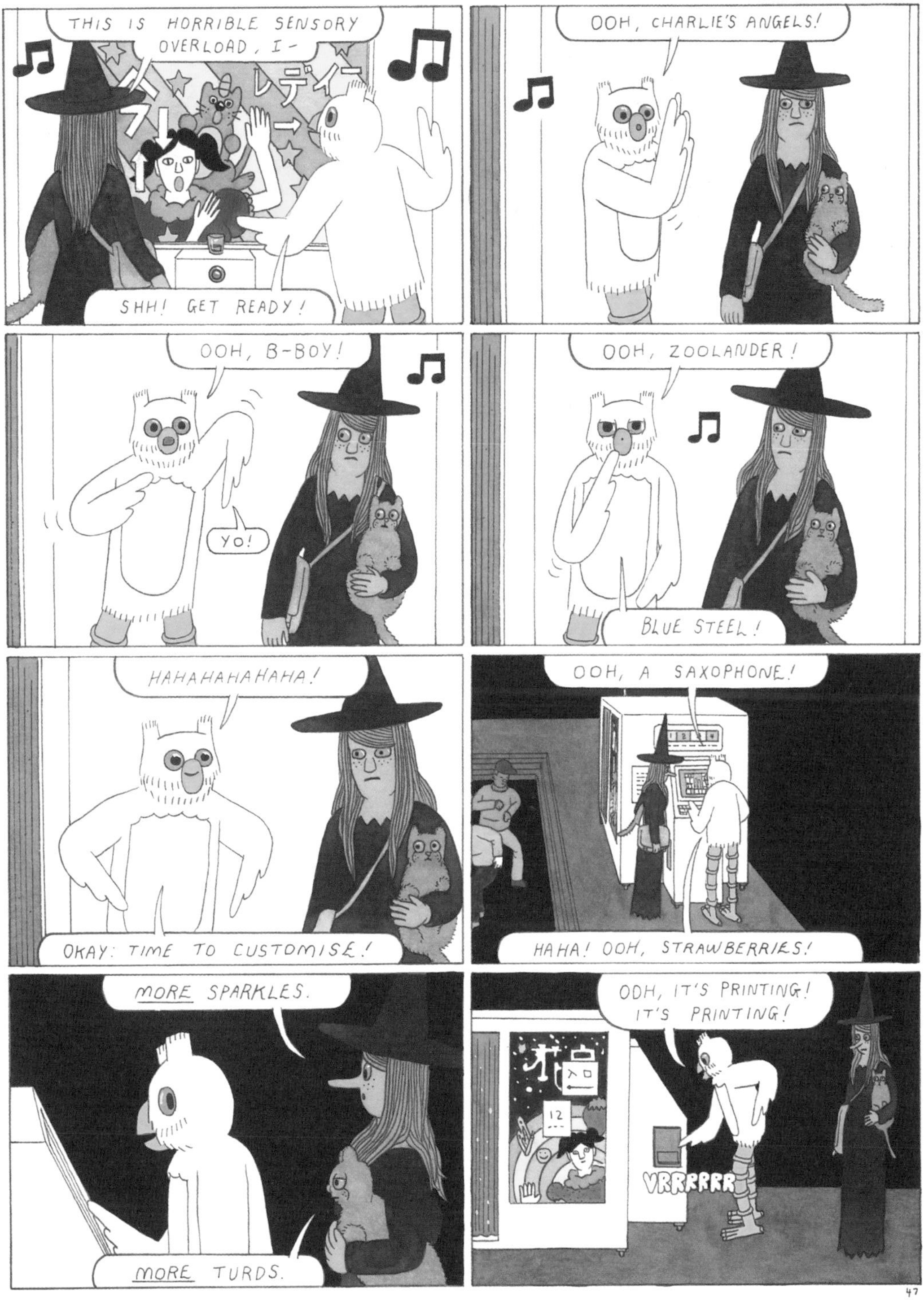

THIS IS HORRIBLE SENSORY OVERLOAD, I-
レディー
SHH! GET READY!
OOH, CHARLIE'S ANGELS!
OOH, B-BOY!
YO!
OOH, ZOOLANDER!
BLUE STEEL!
HAHAHAHAHAHA!
OKAY: TIME TO CUSTOMISE!
OOH, A SAXOPHONE!
HAHA! OOH, STRAWBERRIES!
MORE SPARKLES.
MORE TURDS.
OOH, IT'S PRINTING! IT'S PRINTING!
VRRRRRR

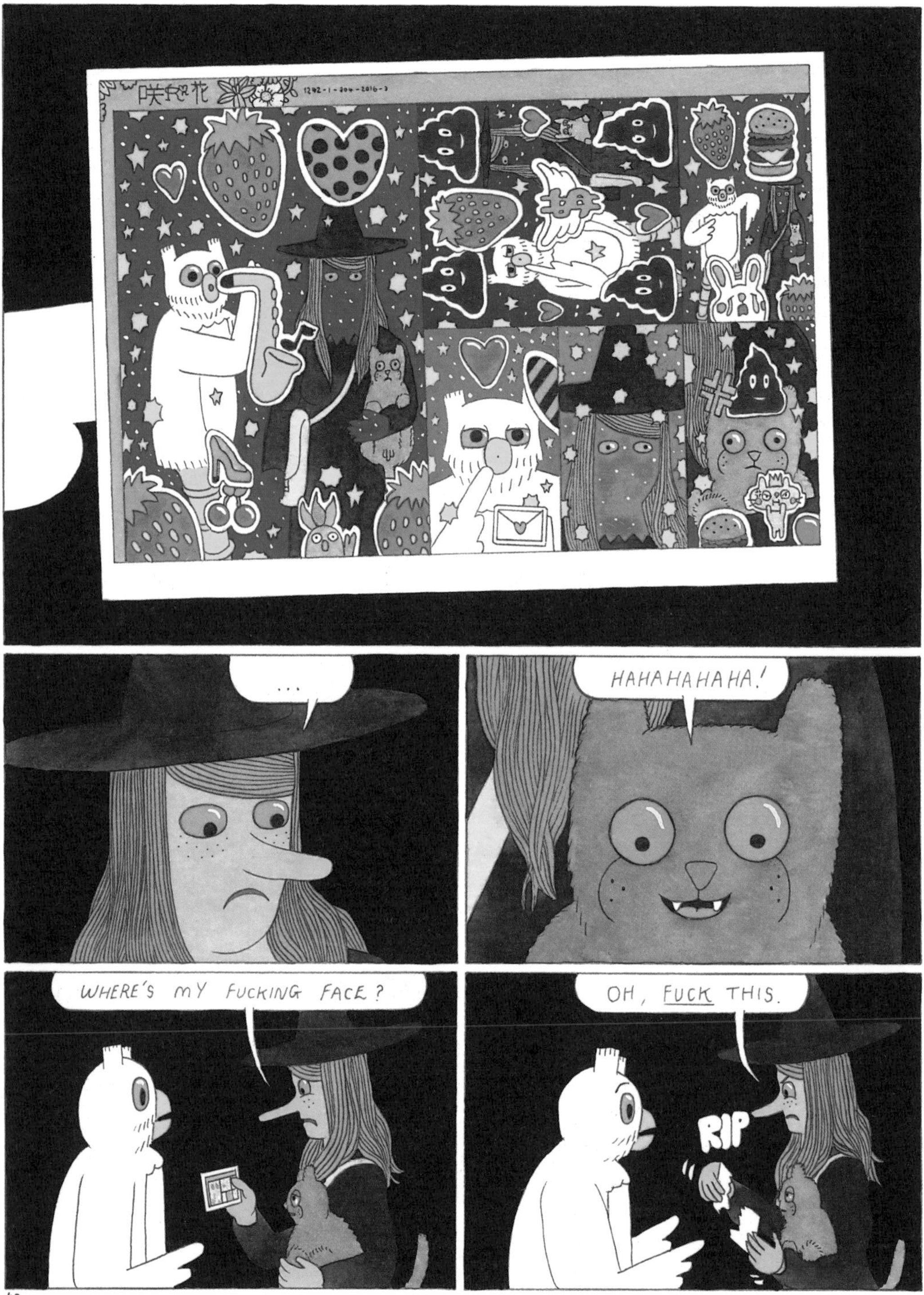

1292-1-204-2016-3
...
HAHAHAHAHA!
WHERE'S MY FUCKING FACE?
OH, FUCK THIS.
RIP

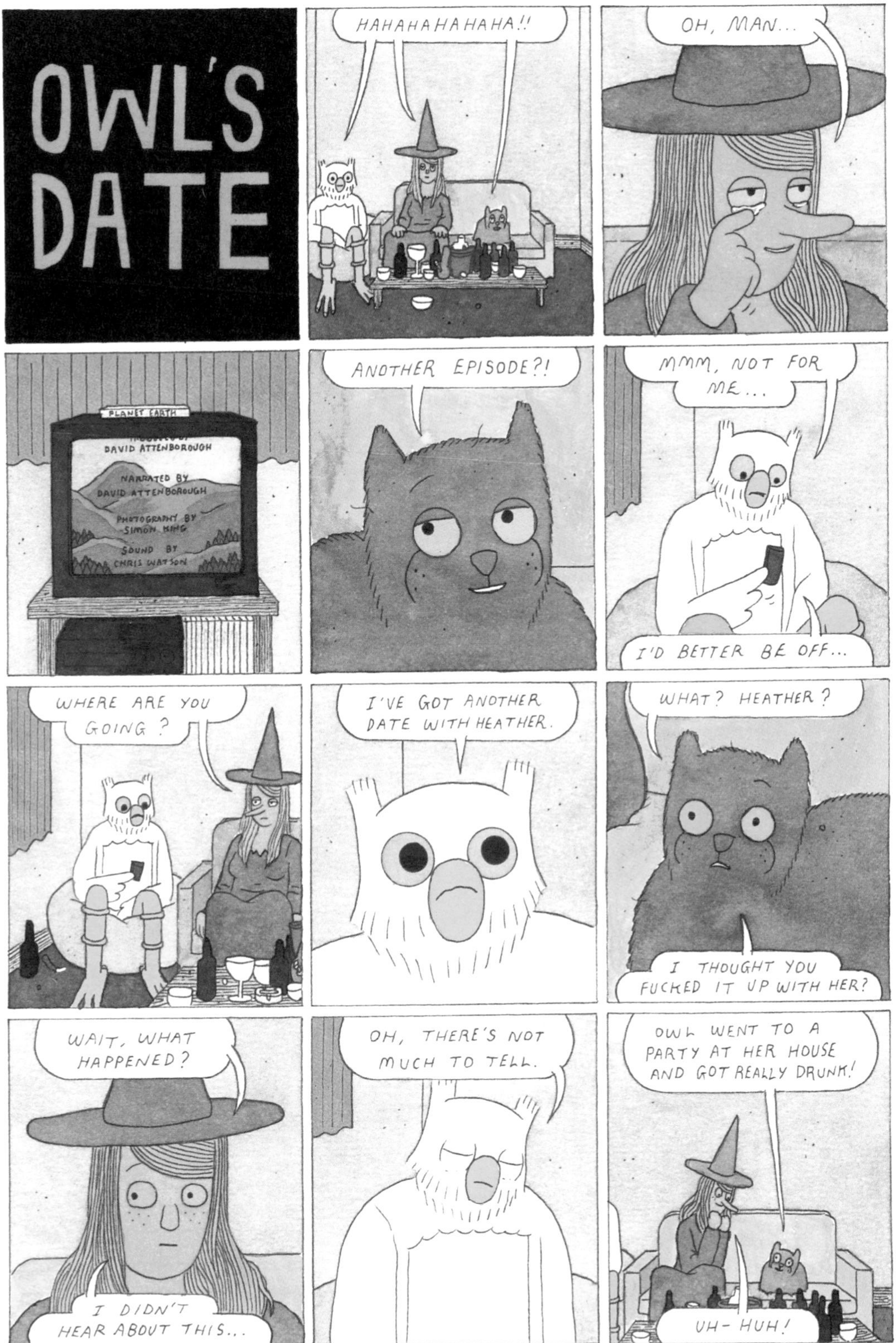
OWL'S DATE
HAHAHAHAHAHA!!
OH, MAN...
PLANET EARTH
DAVID ATTENBOROUGH
NARRATED BY DAVID ATTENBOROUGH
PHOTOGRAPHY BY SIMON KING
SOUND BY CHRIS WATSON
ANOTHER EPISODE?!
MMM, NOT FOR ME...
I'D BETTER BE OFF...
WHERE ARE YOU GOING?
I'VE GOT ANOTHER DATE WITH HEATHER.
WHAT? HEATHER?
I THOUGHT YOU FUCKED IT UP WITH HER?
WAIT, WHAT HAPPENED?
I DIDN'T HEAR ABOUT THIS...
OH, THERE'S NOT MUCH TO TELL.
OWL WENT TO A PARTY AT HER HOUSE AND GOT REALLY DRUNK!
UH-HUH!

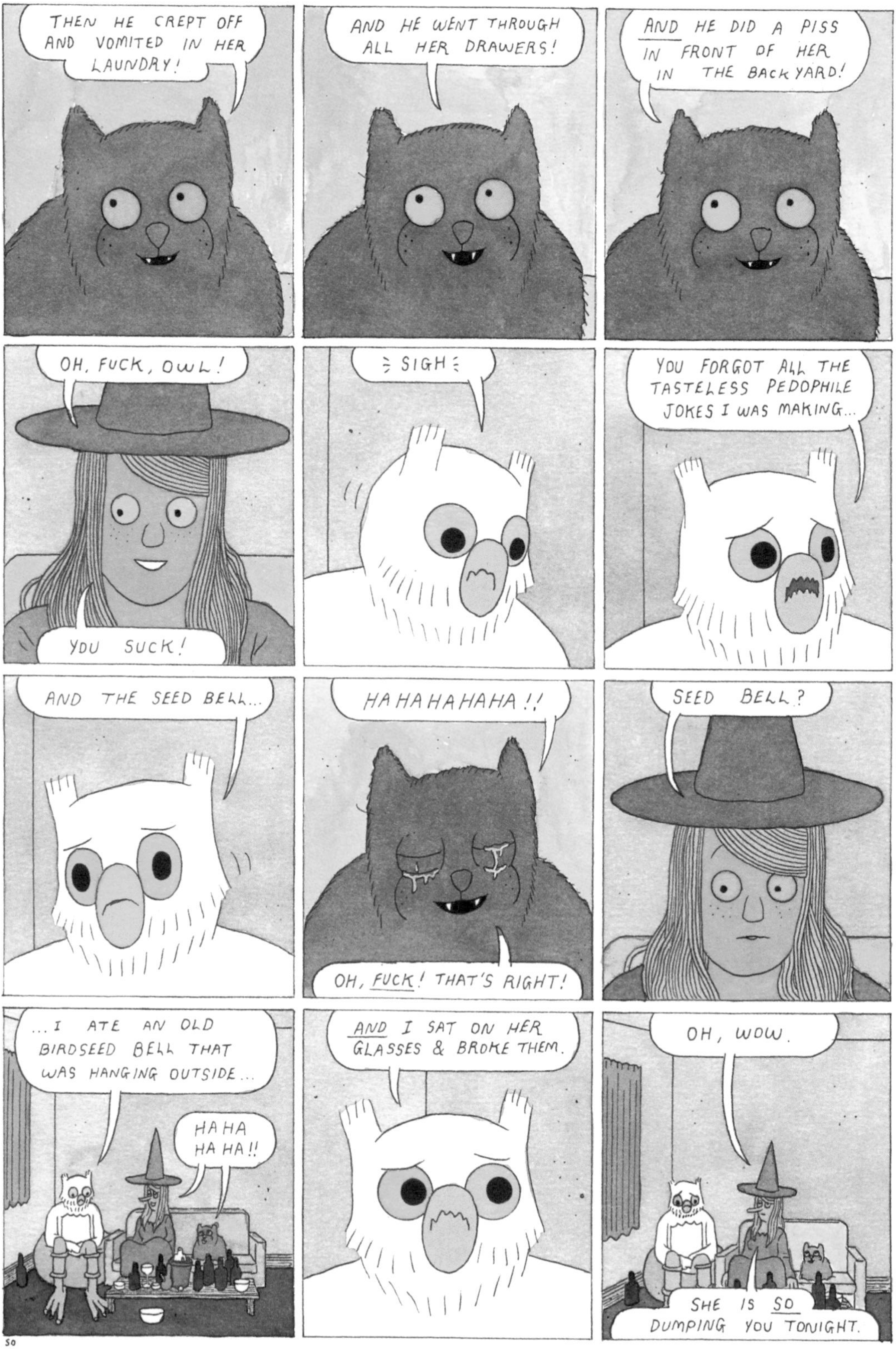
THEN HE CREPT OFF AND VOMITED IN HER LAUNDRY!
AND HE WENT THROUGH ALL HER DRAWERS!
AND HE DID A PISS IN FRONT OF HER IN THE BACK YARD!
OH, FUCK, OWL!
YOU SUCK!
SIGH
YOU FORGOT ALL THE TASTELESS PEDOPHILE JOKES I WAS MAKING...
AND THE SEED BELL...
HAHAHAHAHA!!
OH, FUCK! THAT'S RIGHT!
SEED BELL?
...I ATE AN OLD BIRDSEED BELL THAT WAS HANGING OUTSIDE...
HAHA HAHA!!
AND I SAT ON HER GLASSES & BROKE THEM.
OH, WOW.
SHE IS SO DUMPING YOU TONIGHT.

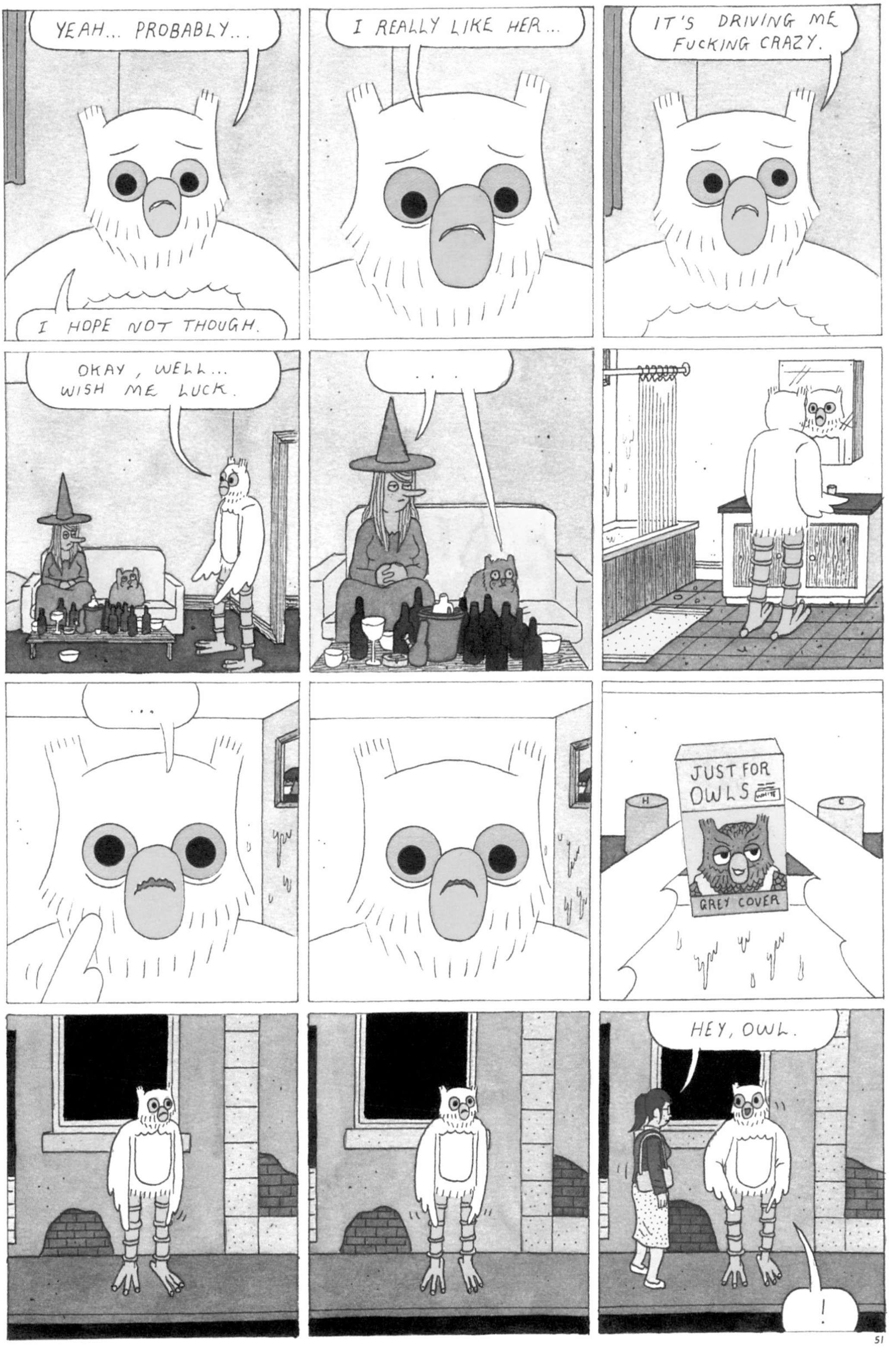

YEAH... PROBABLY...
I HOPE NOT THOUGH.
I REALLY LIKE HER...
IT'S DRIVING ME FUCKING CRAZY.
OKAY, WELL... WISH ME LUCK.
. . .
. . .
JUST FOR OWLS
WHITE
GREY COVER
H
C
HEY, OWL.
!

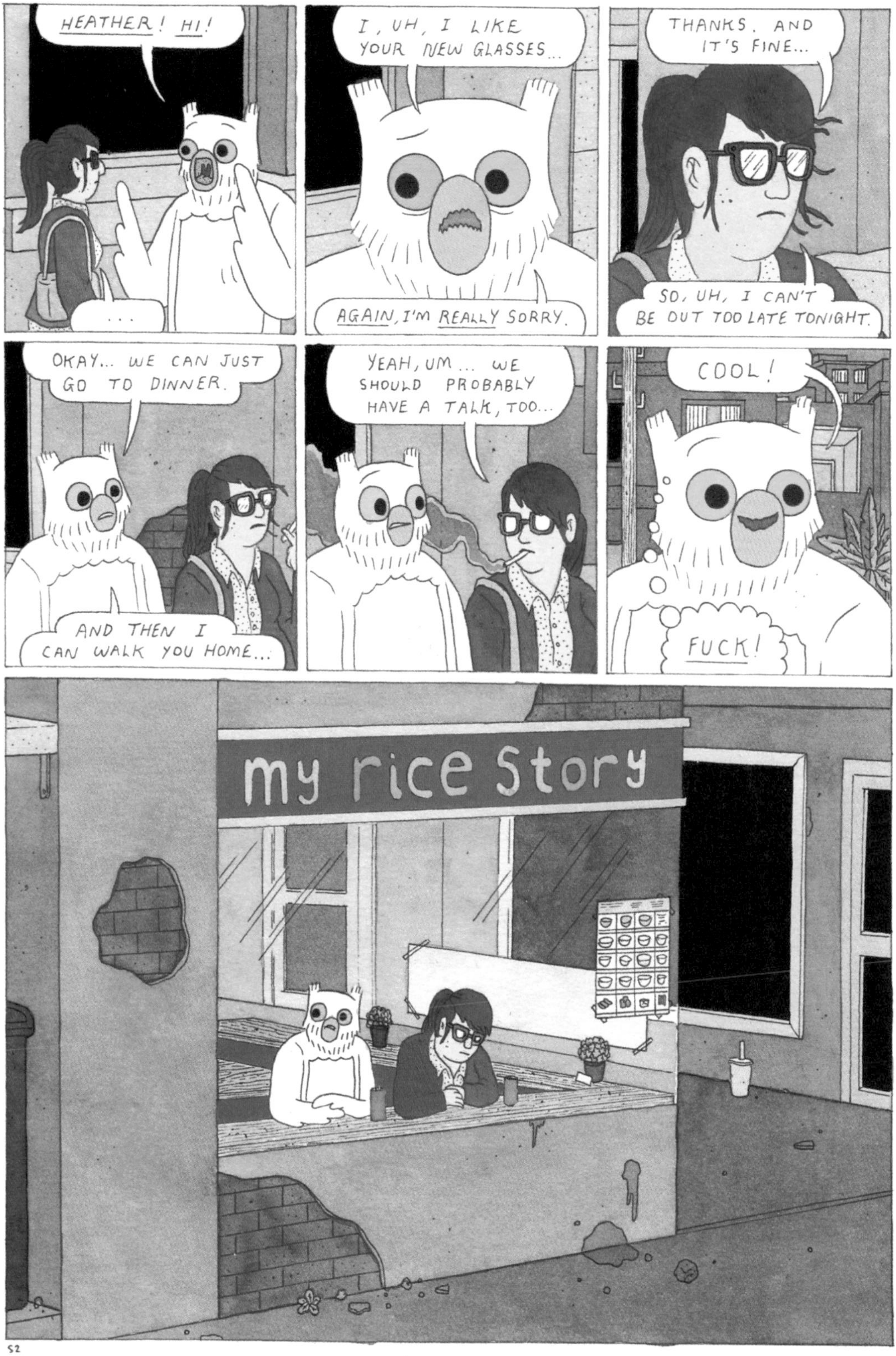
HEATHER! HI!
...
I, UH, I LIKE YOUR NEW GLASSES...
AGAIN, I'M REALLY SORRY.
THANKS. AND IT'S FINE...
SO, UH, I CAN'T BE OUT TOO LATE TONIGHT.
OKAY... WE CAN JUST GO TO DINNER.
AND THEN I CAN WALK YOU HOME...
YEAH, UM... WE SHOULD PROBABLY HAVE A TALK, TOO...
COOL!
FUCK!
my rice Story

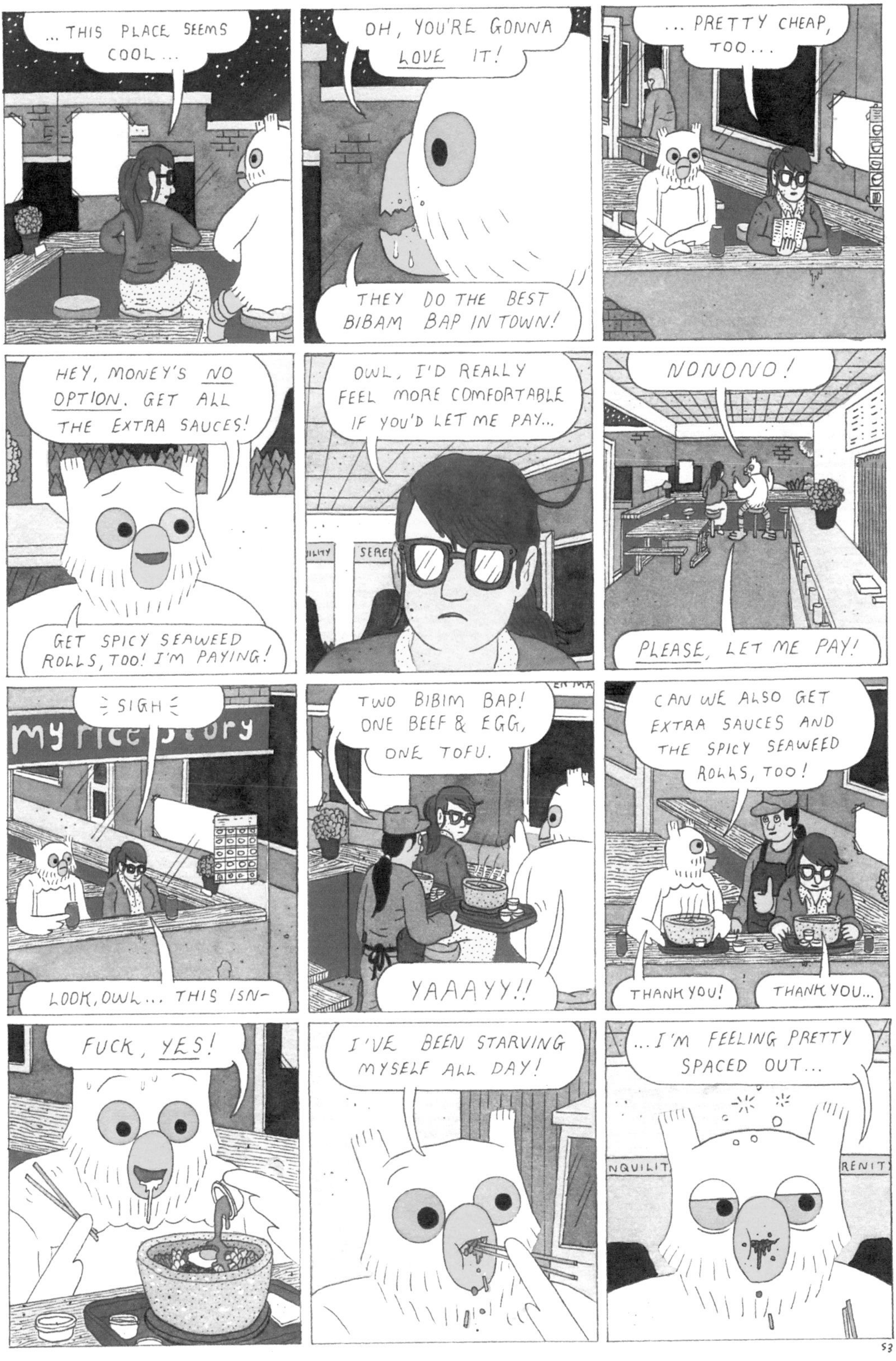
... THIS PLACE SEEMS COOL ...
OH, YOU'RE GONNA LOVE IT!
THEY DO THE BEST BIBAM BAP IN TOWN!
... PRETTY CHEAP, TOO ...
HEY, MONEY'S NO OPTION. GET ALL THE EXTRA SAUCES!
GET SPICY SEAWEED ROLLS, TOO! I'M PAYING!
OWL, I'D REALLY FEEL MORE COMFORTABLE IF YOU'D LET ME PAY...
NONONO!
PLEASE, LET ME PAY!
SIGH
my rice story
LOOK, OWL... THIS ISN-
TWO BIBIM BAP! ONE BEEF & EGG, ONE TOFU.
YAAAYY!!
CAN WE ALSO GET EXTRA SAUCES AND THE SPICY SEAWEED ROLLS, TOO!
THANK YOU!
THANK YOU...
FUCK, YES!
I'VE BEEN STARVING MYSELF ALL DAY!
... I'M FEELING PRETTY SPACED OUT ...

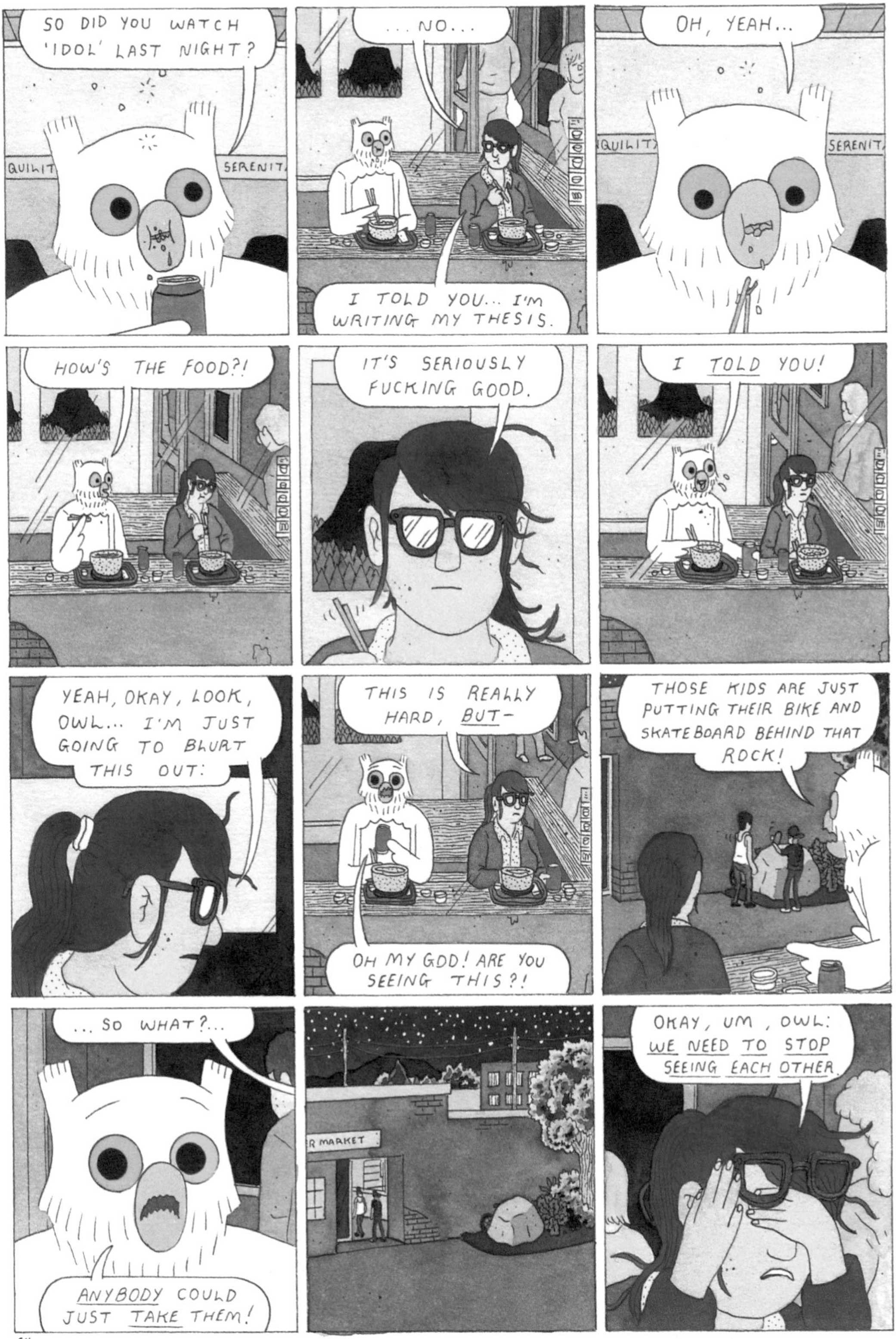
SO DID YOU WATCH 'IDOL' LAST NIGHT?
QUILIT
SERENIT
...NO...
I TOLD YOU... I'M WRITING MY THESIS.
OH, YEAH...
QUILITY
SERENIT
HOW'S THE FOOD?!
IT'S SERIOUSLY FUCKING GOOD.
I TOLD YOU!
YEAH, OKAY, LOOK, OWL... I'M JUST GOING TO BLURT THIS OUT:
THIS IS REALLY HARD, BUT-
OH MY GOD! ARE YOU SEEING THIS?!
THOSE KIDS ARE JUST PUTTING THEIR BIKE AND SKATEBOARD BEHIND THAT ROCK!
...SO WHAT?...
ANYBODY COULD JUST TAKE THEM!
R MARKET
OKAY, UM, OWL: WE NEED TO STOP SEEING EACH OTHER.

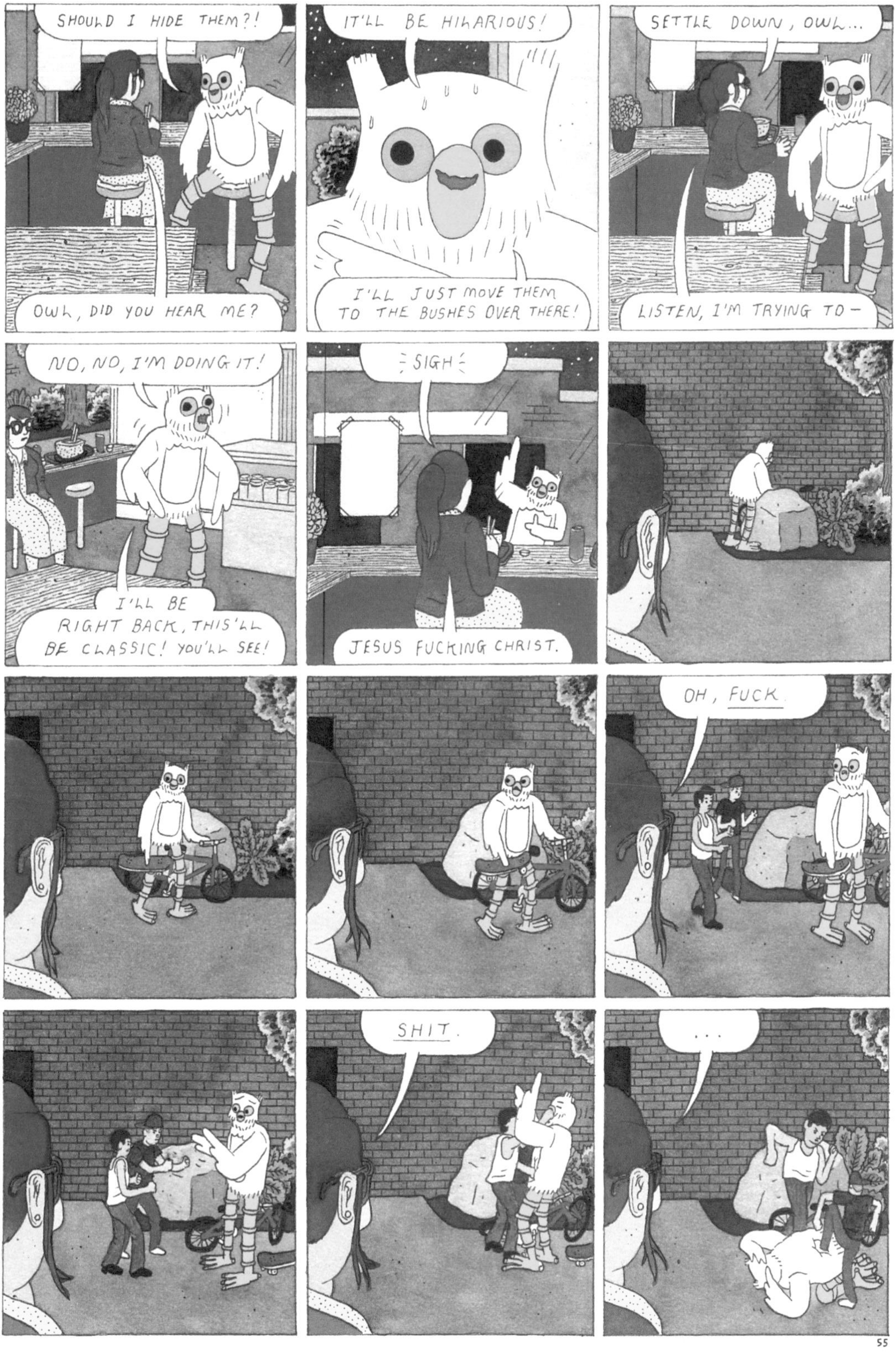
SHOULD I HIDE THEM?!
OWL, DID YOU HEAR ME?
IT'LL BE HILARIOUS!
I'LL JUST MOVE THEM TO THE BUSHES OVER THERE!
SETTLE DOWN, OWL...
LISTEN, I'M TRYING TO—
NO, NO, I'M DOING IT!
I'LL BE RIGHT BACK, THIS'LL BE CLASSIC! YOU'LL SEE!
SIGH
JESUS FUCKING CHRIST.
OH, FUCK.
SHIT.
...

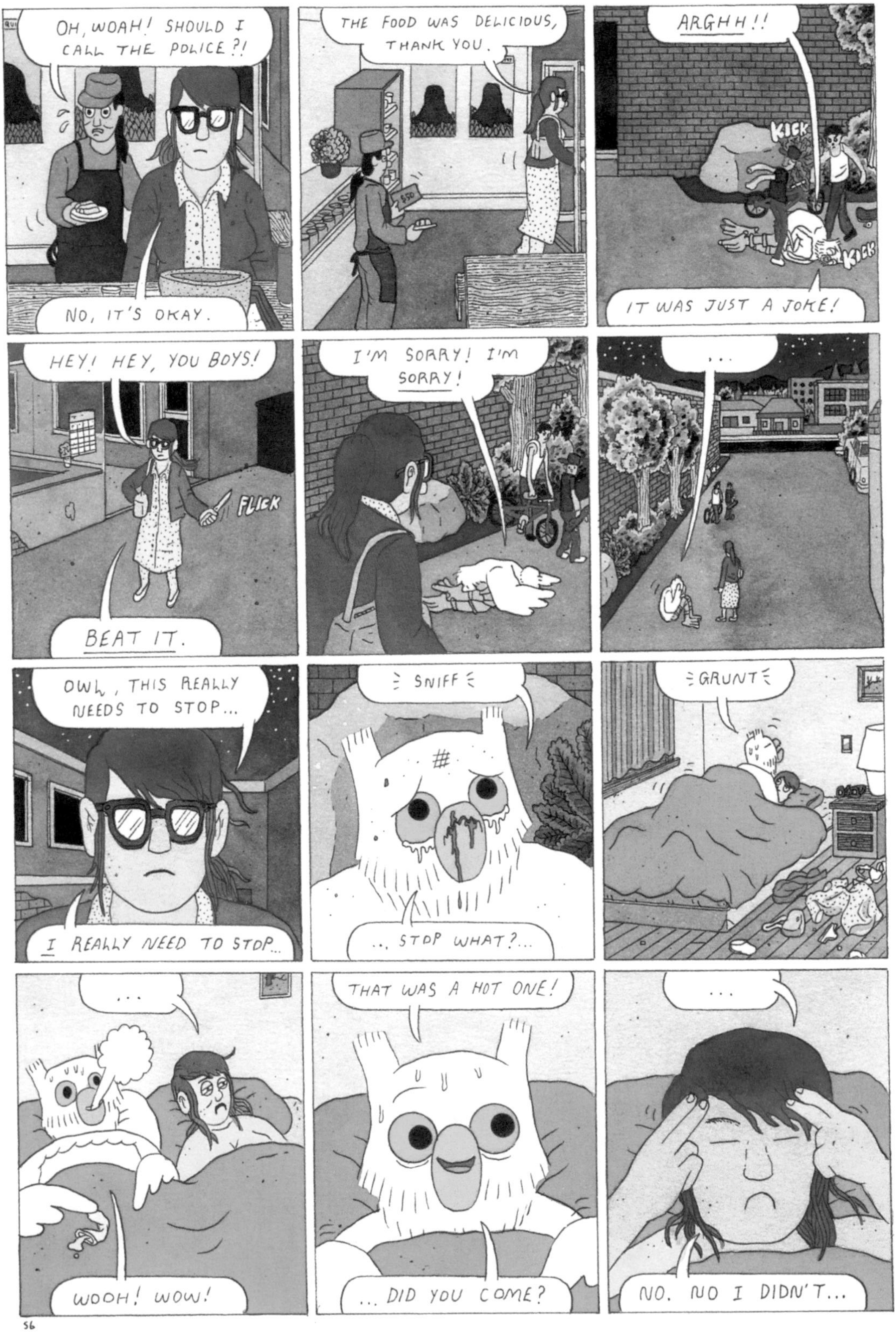
OH, WOAH! SHOULD I CALL THE POLICE?!
NO, IT'S OKAY.
THE FOOD WAS DELICIOUS, THANK YOU.
$50
ARGHH!!
KICK
KICK
IT WAS JUST A JOKE!
HEY! HEY, YOU BOYS!
FLICK
BEAT IT.
I'M SORRY! I'M SORRY!
...
OWW, THIS REALLY NEEDS TO STOP...
I REALLY NEED TO STOP...
SNIFF
..., STOP WHAT?...
GRUNT
...
WOOH! WOW!
THAT WAS A HOT ONE!
... DID YOU COME?
...
NO. NO I DIDN'T...

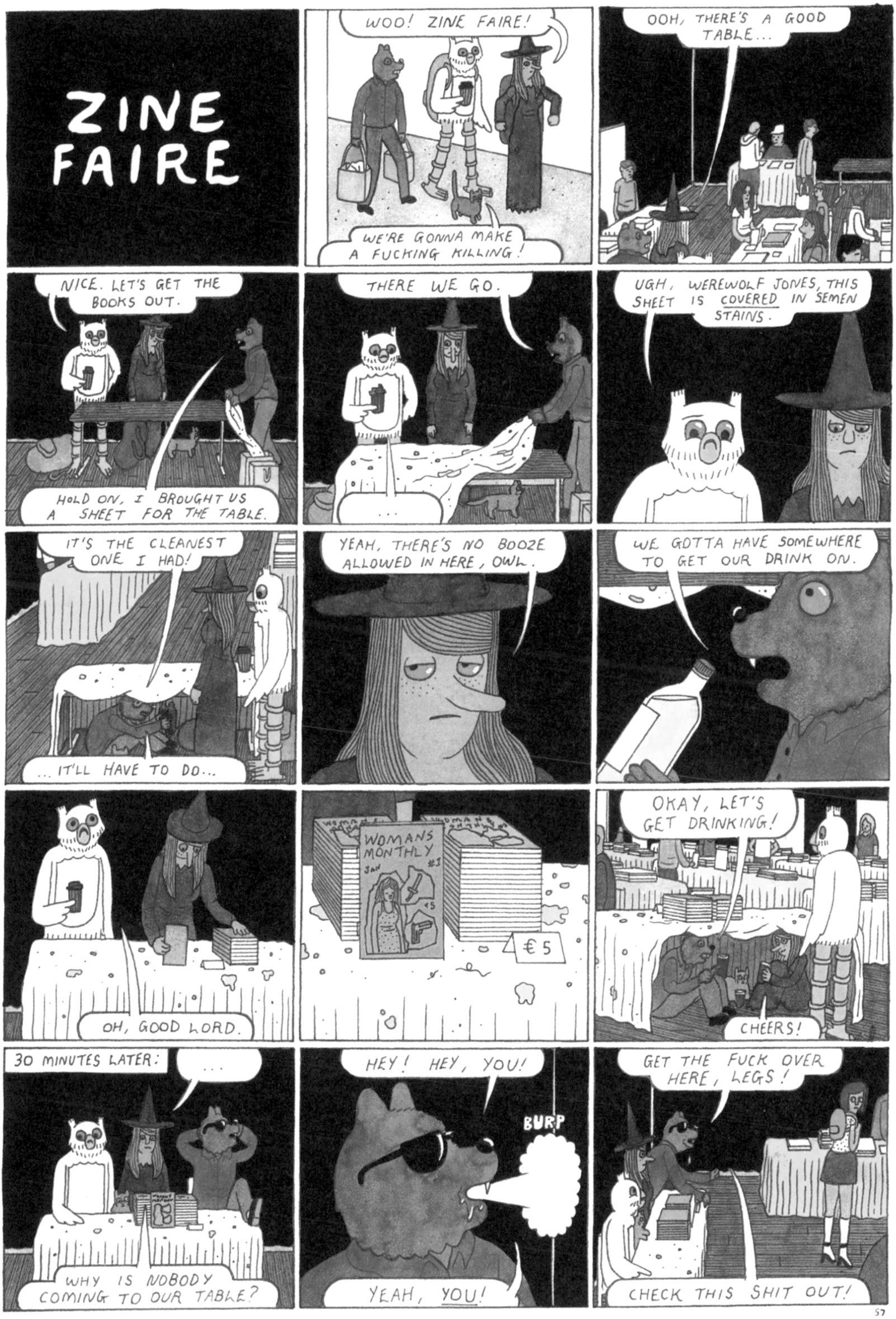
ZINE FAIRE
WOO! ZINE FAIRE!
WE'RE GONNA MAKE A FUCKING KILLING!
OOH, THERE'S A GOOD TABLE...
NICE. LET'S GET THE BOOKS OUT.
HOLD ON, I BROUGHT US A SHEET FOR THE TABLE.
THERE WE GO.
...
UGH, WEREWOLF JONES, THIS SHEET IS COVERED IN SEMEN STAINS.
IT'S THE CLEANEST ONE I HAD!
... IT'LL HAVE TO DO...
YEAH, THERE'S NO BOOZE ALLOWED IN HERE, OWL.
WE GOTTA HAVE SOMEWHERE TO GET OUR DRINK ON.
OH, GOOD LORD.
WOMANS MONTHLY
#1
€5
OKAY, LET'S GET DRINKING!
CHEERS!
30 MINUTES LATER:
...
WHY IS NOBODY COMING TO OUR TABLE?
HEY! HEY, YOU!
BURP
YEAH, YOU!
GET THE FUCK OVER HERE, LEGS!
CHECK THIS SHIT OUT!

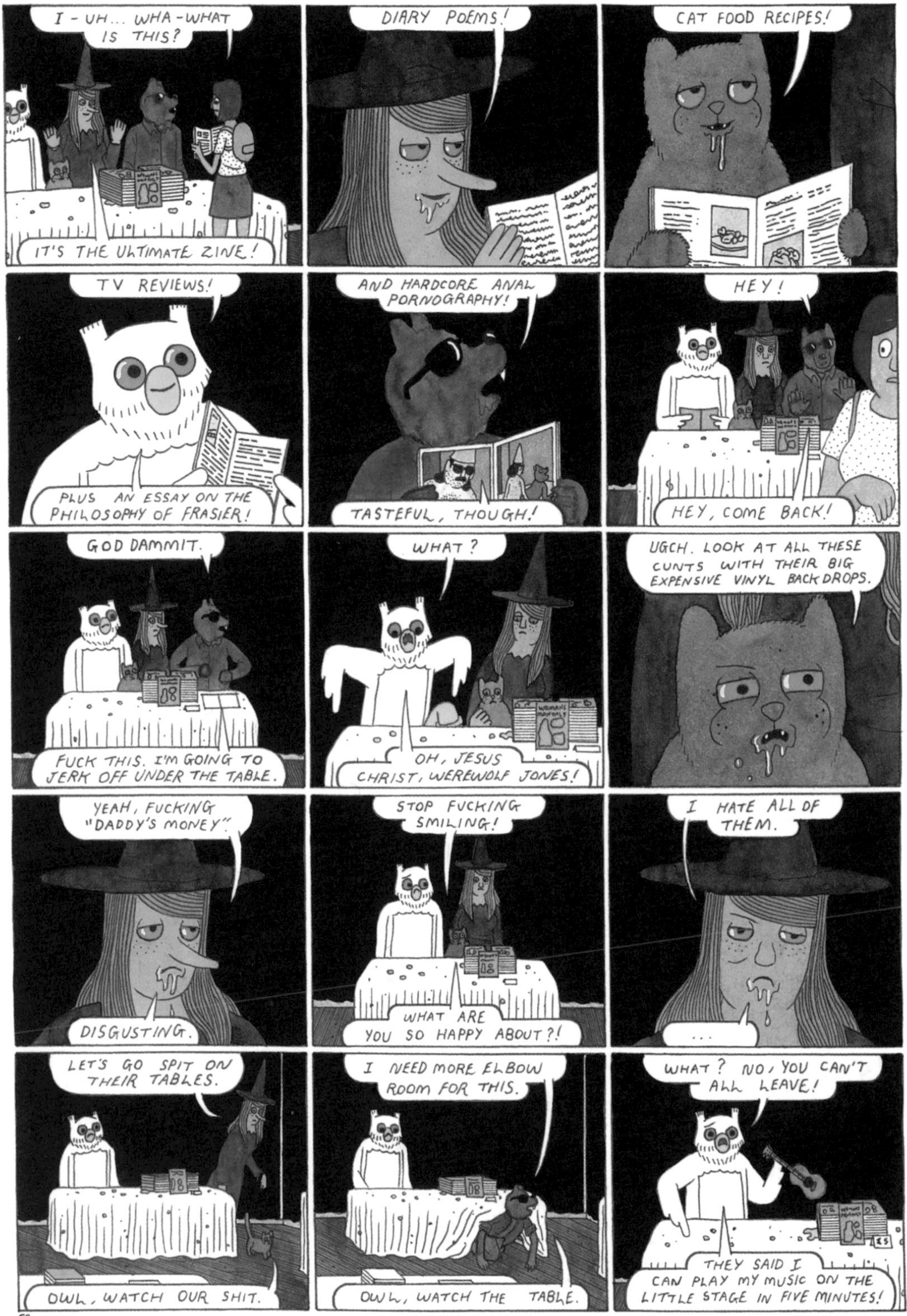
I - UH... WHA - WHAT IS THIS?
IT'S THE ULTIMATE ZINE!
DIARY POEMS!
CAT FOOD RECIPES!
TV REVIEWS!
PLUS AN ESSAY ON THE PHILOSOPHY OF FRASIER!
AND HARDCORE ANAL PORNOGRAPHY!
TASTEFUL, THOUGH!
HEY!
HEY, COME BACK!
GOD DAMMIT.
FUCK THIS. I'M GOING TO JERK OFF UNDER THE TABLE.
WHAT?
OH, JESUS CHRIST, WEREWOLF JONES!
UGCH. LOOK AT ALL THESE CUNTS WITH THEIR BIG EXPENSIVE VINYL BACKDROPS.
YEAH, FUCKING "DADDY'S MONEY".
DISGUSTING.
STOP FUCKING SMILING!
WHAT ARE YOU SO HAPPY ABOUT?!
I HATE ALL OF THEM.
...
LET'S GO SPIT ON THEIR TABLES.
OWL, WATCH OUR SHIT.
I NEED MORE ELBOW ROOM FOR THIS.
OWL, WATCH THE TABLE.
WHAT? NO, YOU CAN'T ALL LEAVE!
THEY SAID I CAN PLAY MY MUSIC ON THE LITTLE STAGE IN FIVE MINUTES!

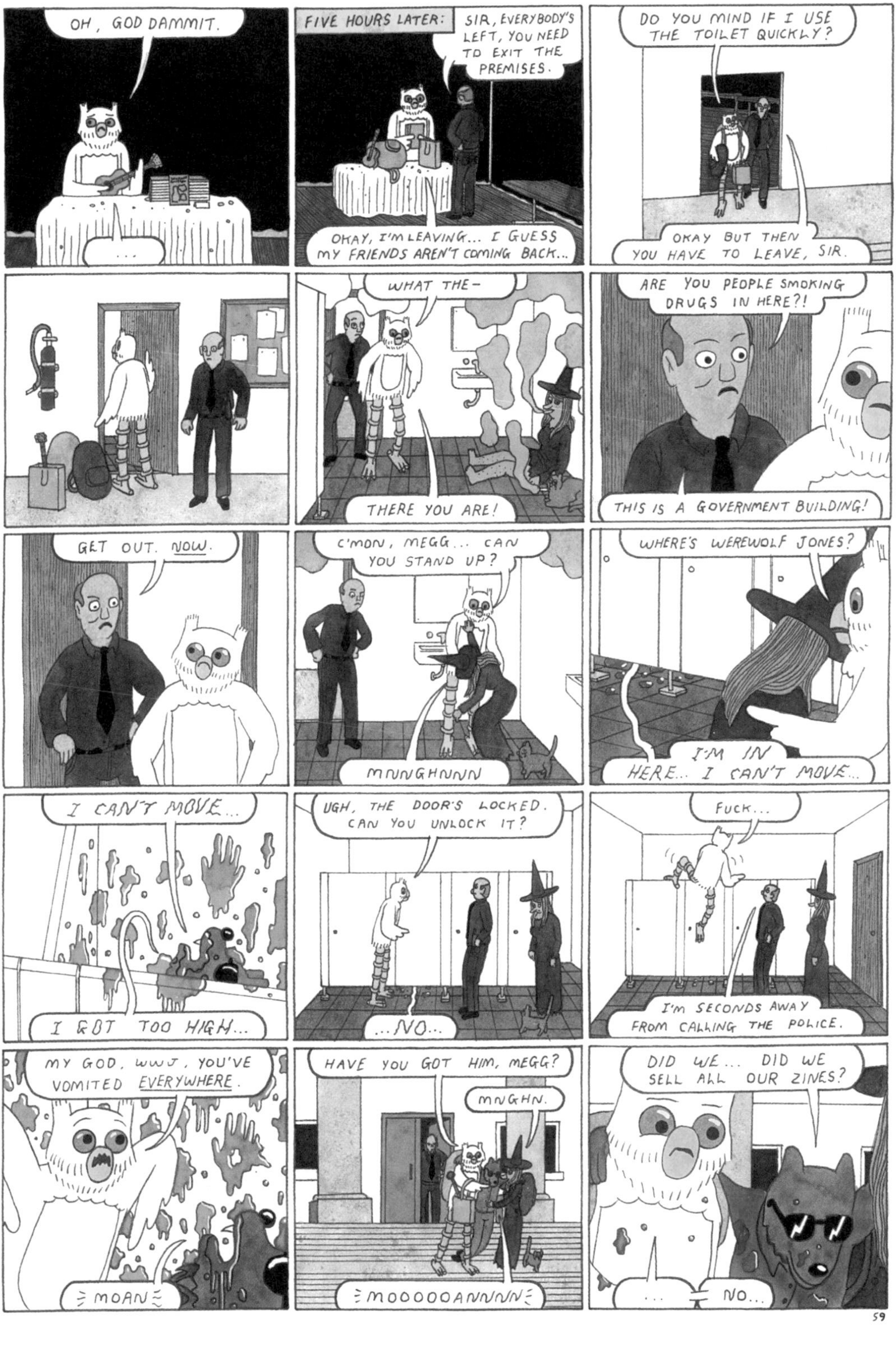
OH, GOD DAMMIT.
...
FIVE HOURS LATER:
SIR, EVERYBODY'S LEFT, YOU NEED TO EXIT THE PREMISES.
OKAY, I'M LEAVING... I GUESS MY FRIENDS AREN'T COMING BACK...
DO YOU MIND IF I USE THE TOILET QUICKLY?
OKAY BUT THEN YOU HAVE TO LEAVE, SIR.
WHAT THE-
THERE YOU ARE!
ARE YOU PEOPLE SMOKING DRUGS IN HERE?!
THIS IS A GOVERNMENT BUILDING!
GET OUT. NOW.
C'MON, MEGG... CAN YOU STAND UP?
MNNGHNNN
WHERE'S WEREWOLF JONES?
I'M IN HERE... I CAN'T MOVE...
I CAN'T MOVE...
I GOT TOO HIGH...
UGH, THE DOOR'S LOCKED. CAN YOU UNLOCK IT?
...NO...
FUCK...
I'M SECONDS AWAY FROM CALLING THE POLICE.
MY GOD, WWJ, YOU'VE VOMITED EVERYWHERE.
MOAN
HAVE YOU GOT HIM, MEGG?
MNGHN.
MOOOOOANNNN
DID WE... DID WE SELL ALL OUR ZINES?
...
NO...

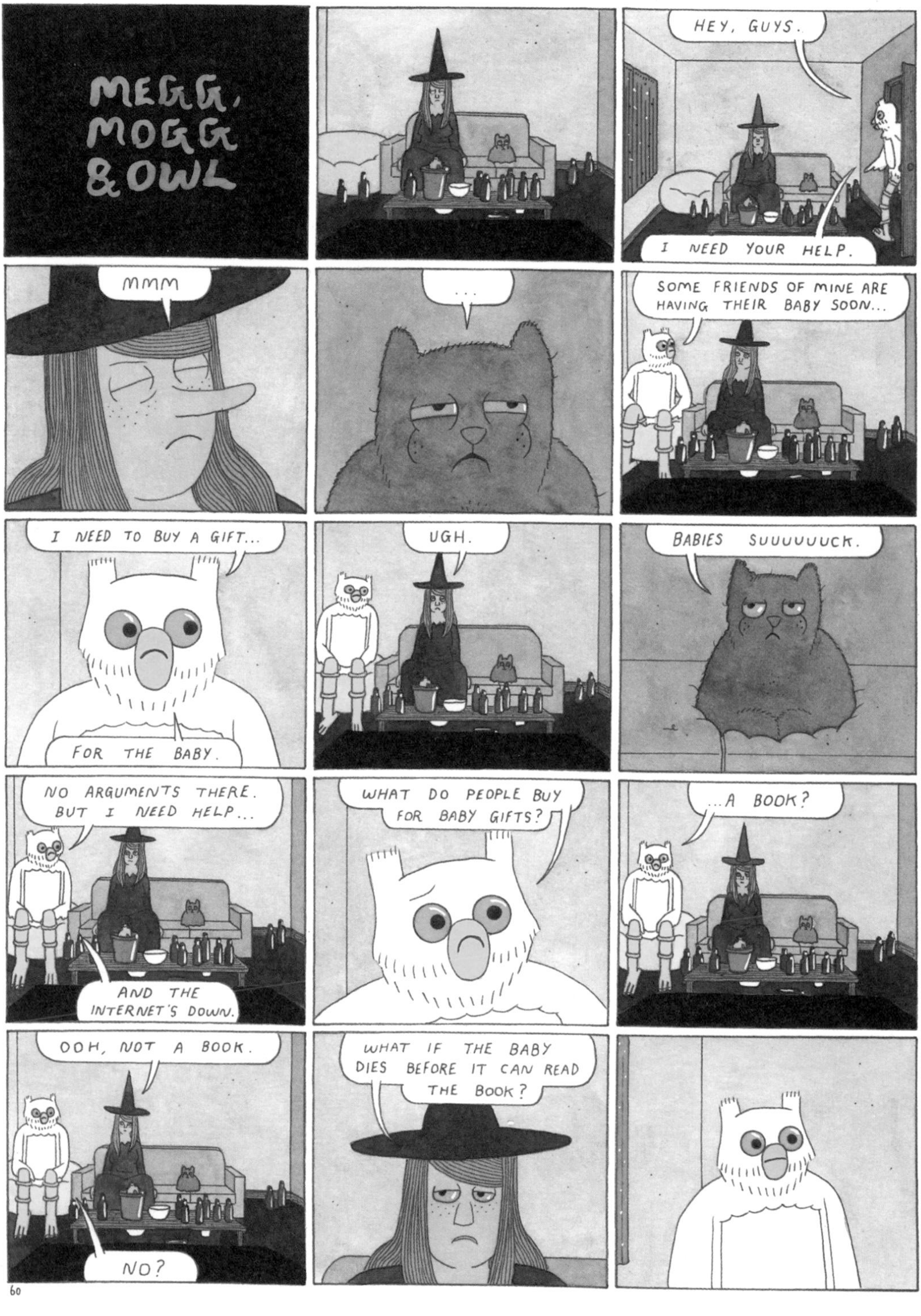
MEGG, MOGG & OWL
HEY, GUYS.
I NEED YOUR HELP.
MMM
...
SOME FRIENDS OF MINE ARE HAVING THEIR BABY SOON...
I NEED TO BUY A GIFT...
FOR THE BABY.
UGH.
BABIES SUUUUUUCK.
NO ARGUMENTS THERE. BUT I NEED HELP...
AND THE INTERNET'S DOWN.
WHAT DO PEOPLE BUY FOR BABY GIFTS?
...A BOOK?
OOH, NOT A BOOK.
NO?
WHAT IF THE BABY DIES BEFORE IT CAN READ THE BOOK?

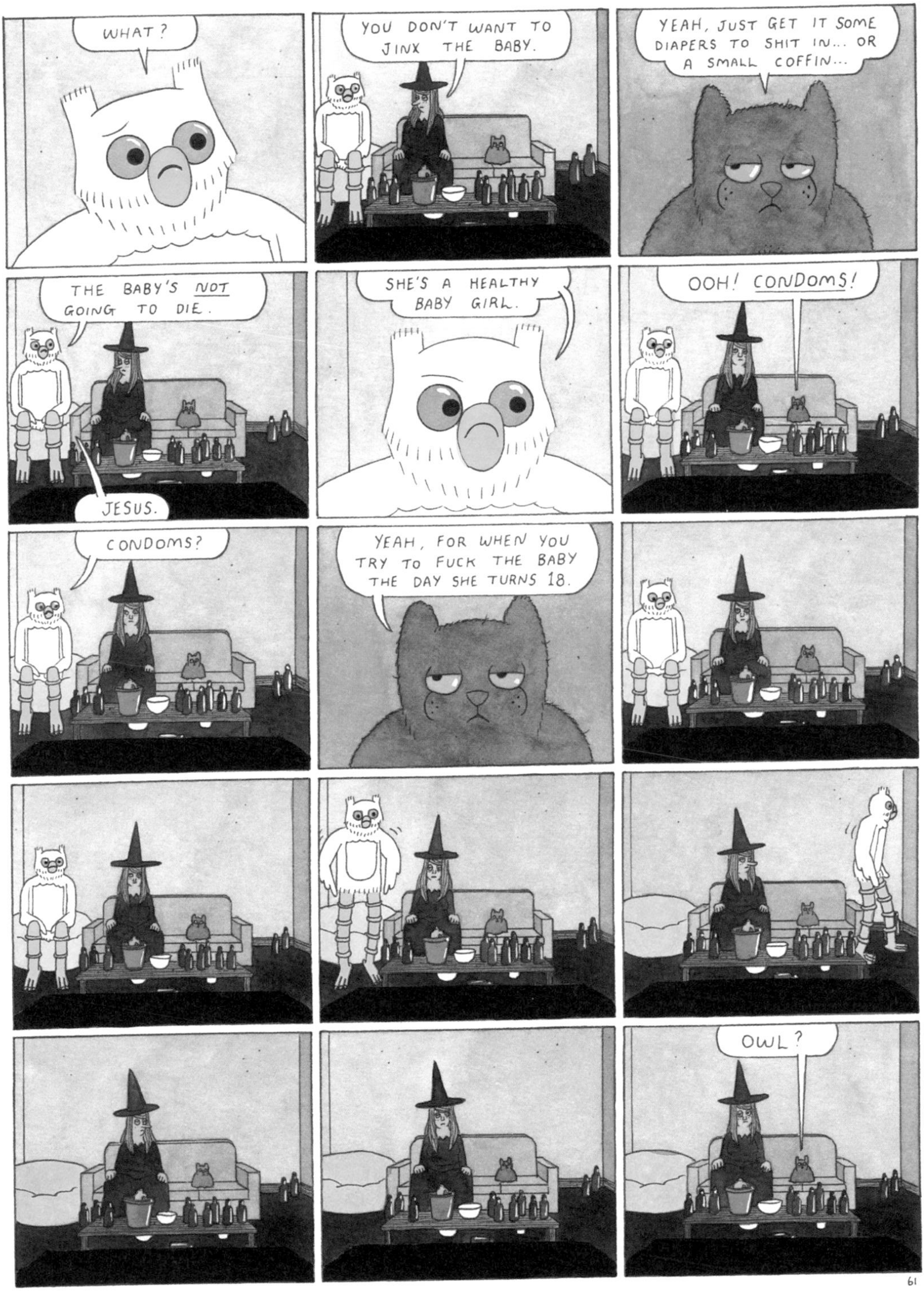
WHAT?
YOU DON'T WANT TO JINX THE BABY.
YEAH, JUST GET IT SOME DIAPERS TO SHIT IN... OR A SMALL COFFIN...
THE BABY'S NOT GOING TO DIE.
JESUS.
SHE'S A HEALTHY BABY GIRL.
OOH! CONDOMS!
CONDOMS?
YEAH, FOR WHEN YOU TRY TO FUCK THE BABY THE DAY SHE TURNS 18.
OWL?

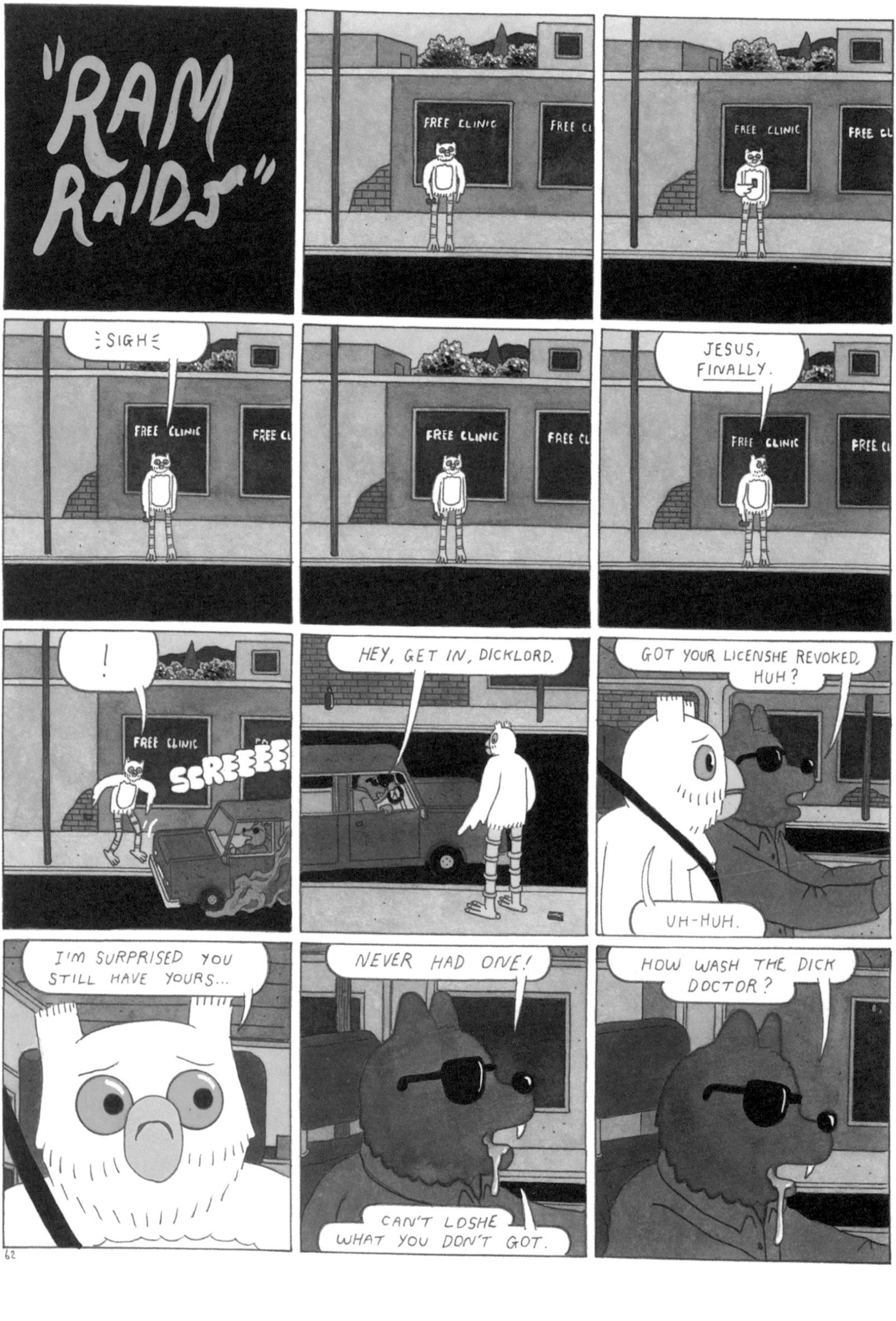
"RAM RAIDS"
FREE CLINIC
FREE CL
FREE CLINIC
FREE CL
SIGH
FREE CLINIC
FREE CL
FREE CLINIC
FREE CL
JESUS, FINALLY.
FREE CLINIC
FREE CL
!
FREE CLINIC
SCREEEEE
HEY, GET IN, DICKLORD.
GOT YOUR LICENSHE REVOKED, HUH?
UH-HUH.
I'M SURPRISED YOU STILL HAVE YOURS...
NEVER HAD ONE!
CAN'T LOSHE WHAT YOU DON'T GOT.
HOW WASH THE DICK DOCTOR?

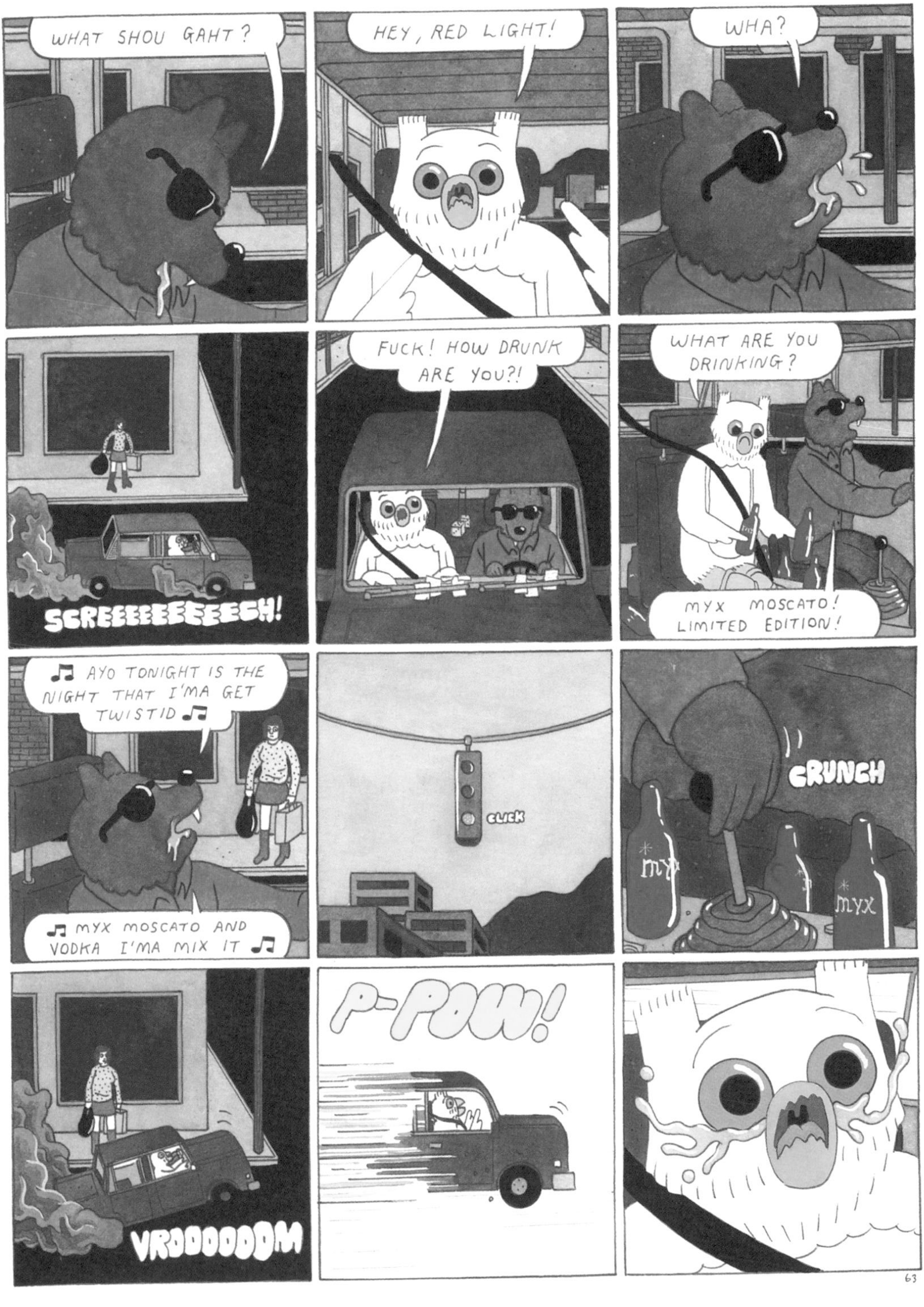
WHAT SHOU GAHT?
HEY, RED LIGHT!
WHA?
SCREEEEEEEEEEECH!
FUCK! HOW DRUNK ARE YOU?!
WHAT ARE YOU DRINKING?
MYX MOSCATO! LIMITED EDITION!
♫ AYO TONIGHT IS THE NIGHT THAT I'MA GET TWISTID ♫
♫ MYX MOSCATO AND VODKA I'MA MIX IT ♫
CLICK
CRUNCH
MYX
MYX
VROOOOOOOM
P-POW!

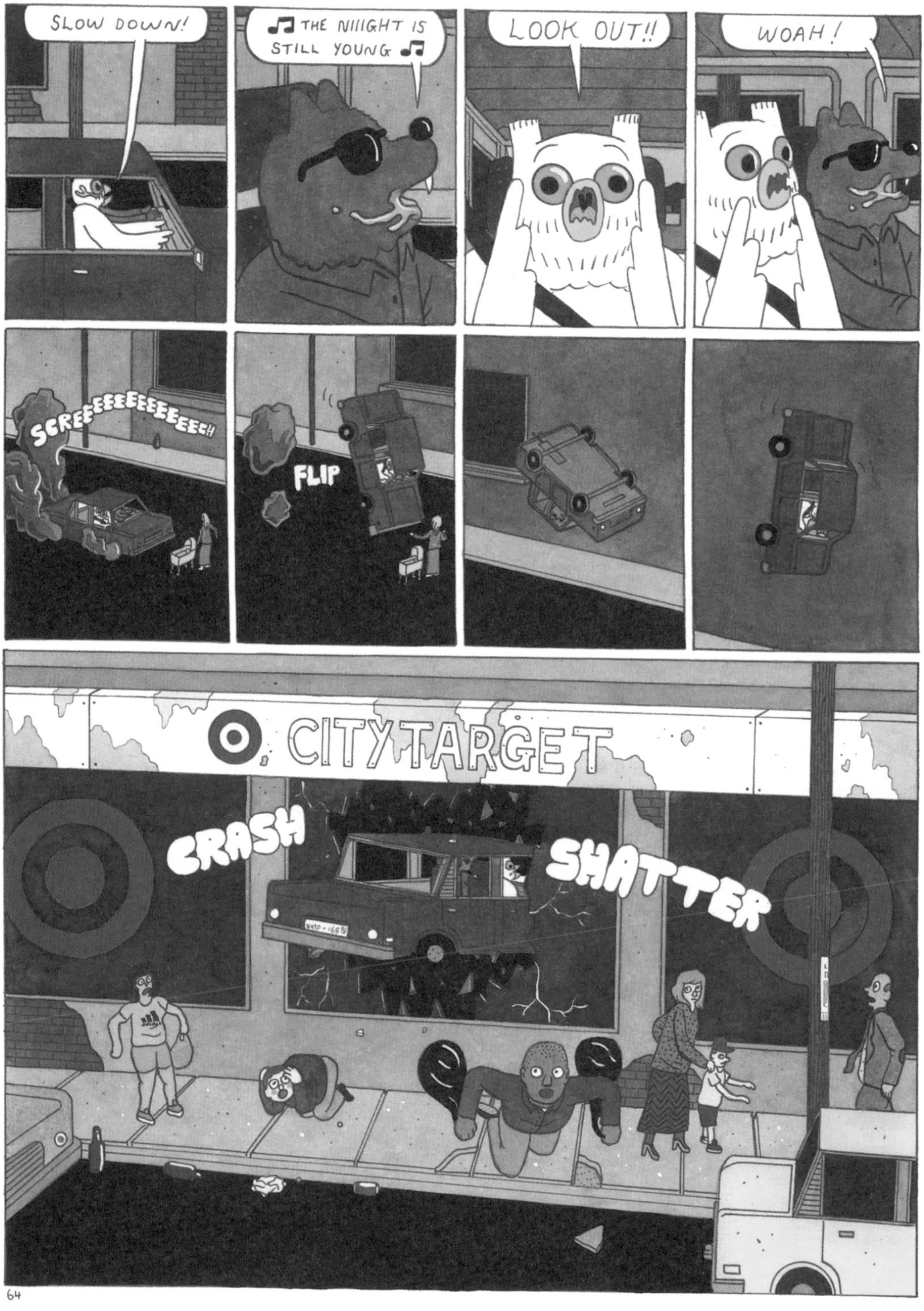
SLOW DOWN!
♫ THE NIIIGHT IS STILL YOUNG ♫
LOOK OUT!!
WOAH!
SCREEEEEEEEEEEEECH
FLIP
CITYTARGET
CRASH
SHATTER

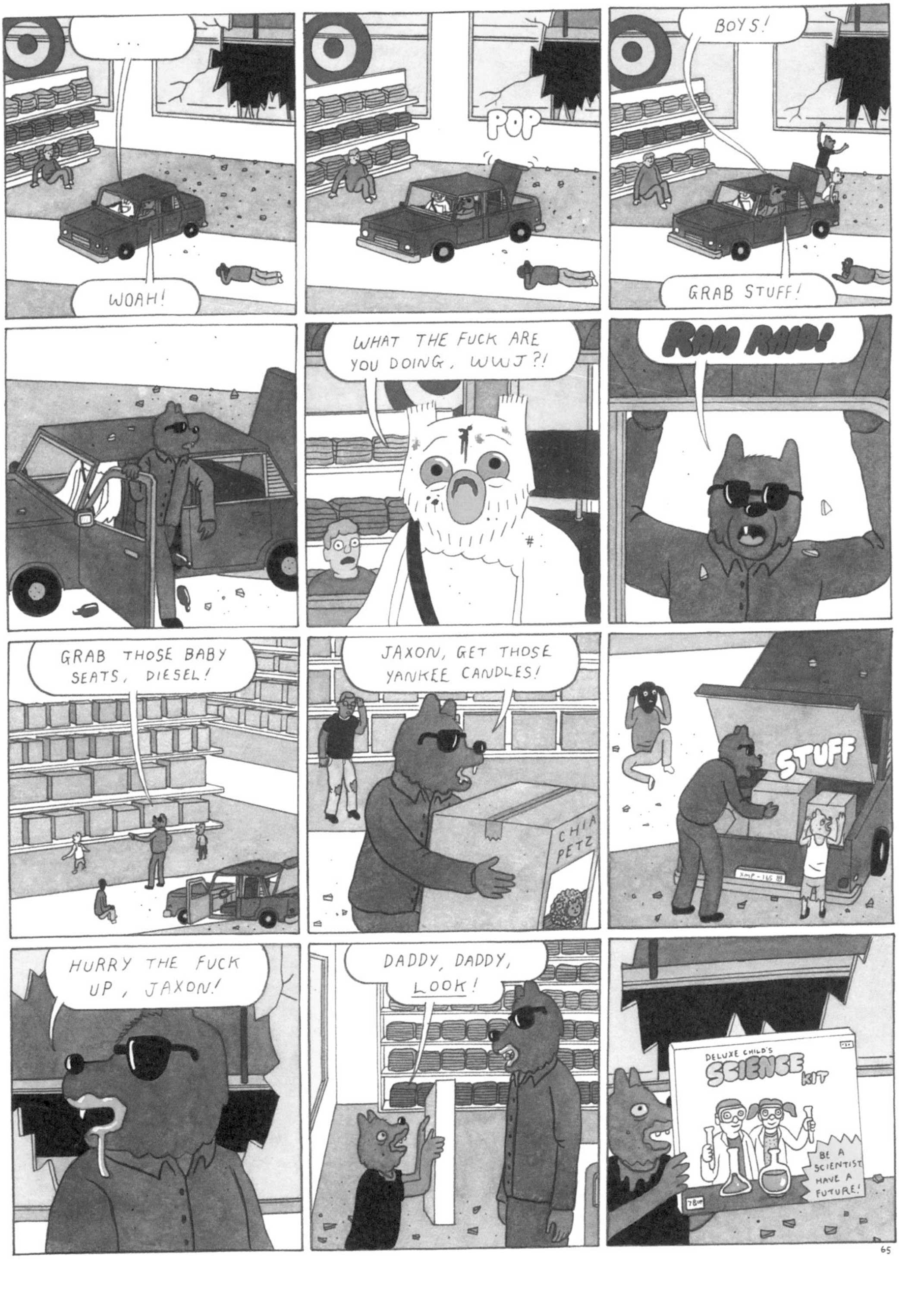

...
WOAH!
POP
BOYS!
GRAB STUFF!
WHAT THE FUCK ARE YOU DOING, WWJ?!
RAM RAID!
GRAB THOSE BABY SEATS, DIESEL!
JAXON, GET THOSE YANKEE CANDLES!
CHIA PETZ
STUFF
HURRY THE FUCK UP, JAXON!
DADDY, DADDY, LOOK!
DELUXE CHILD'S SCIENCE KIT
BE A SCIENTIST HAVE A FUTURE!

CHEM - IST - RY?
TOSS
NO!
LET'S GO!
IN THE BACK, BOYS!
BUCKLE UP, OWL.
DADDY, DADDY!
BOYS, SETTLE THE FUCK DOWN!
DADDY, DADDY!
SHUT THE FUCK UP, JAXON!
SORRY, OWL, I COULDN'T GET A SITTER...
SMASH
I HEAR SIRENS!
OOOHHHH I'M SO SCARED.
KA-CHUNK
VROOOOM
VIN-FUCKING-DIESEL!
R.I.P PAUL WALKER

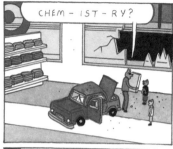

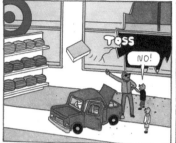

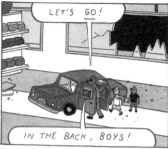

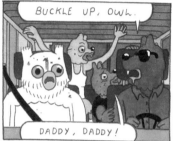

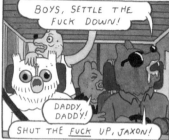

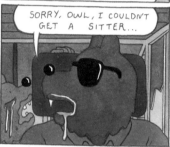

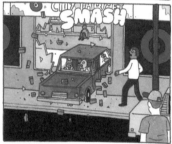

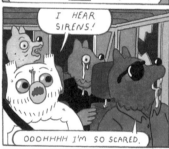

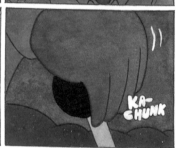

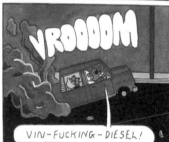

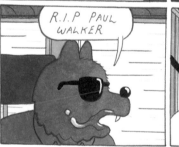

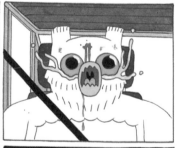

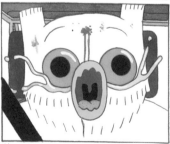

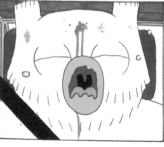

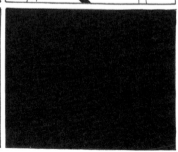

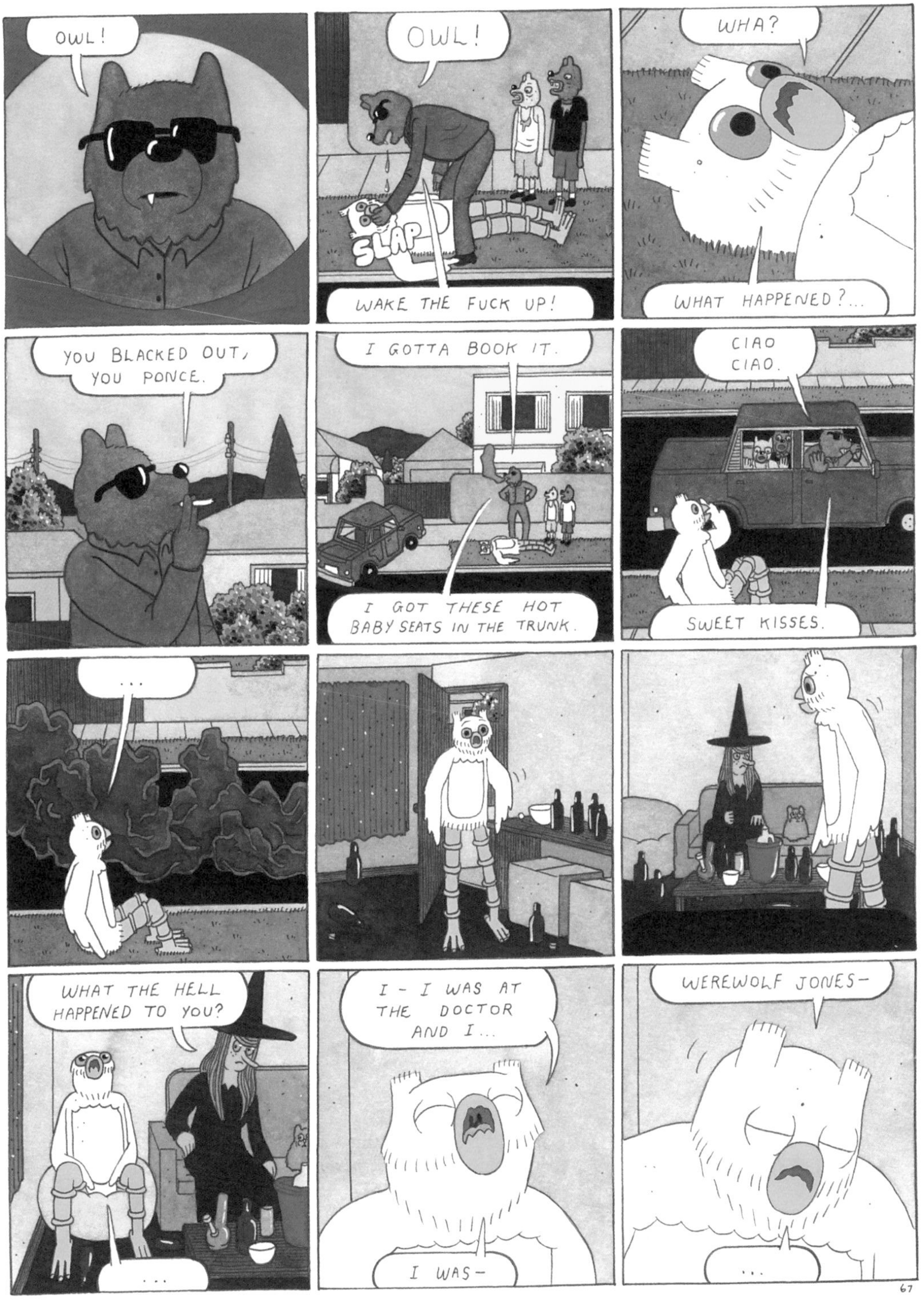
OWL!
OWL!
SLAP
WAKE THE FUCK UP!
WHA?
WHAT HAPPENED?...
YOU BLACKED OUT, YOU PONCE.
I GOTTA BOOK IT.
I GOT THESE HOT BABY SEATS IN THE TRUNK.
CIAO CIAO.
SWEET KISSES.
...
WHAT THE HELL HAPPENED TO YOU?
...
I - I WAS AT THE DOCTOR AND I...
I WAS-
WEREWOLF JONES-
...

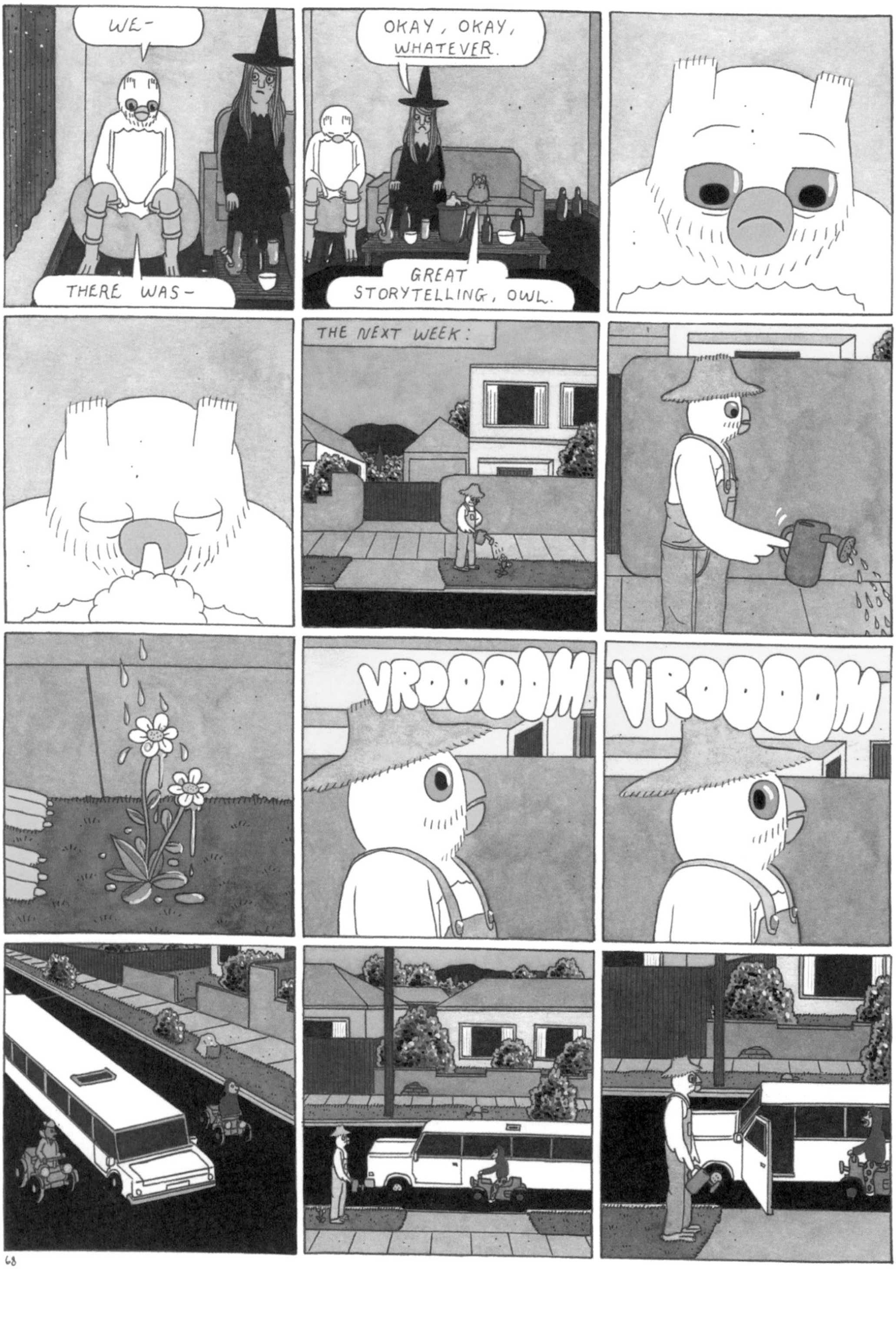
WE-
THERE WAS-
OKAY, OKAY, WHATEVER.
GREAT STORYTELLING, OWL.
THE NEXT WEEK:
VROOOOM
VROOOOOM

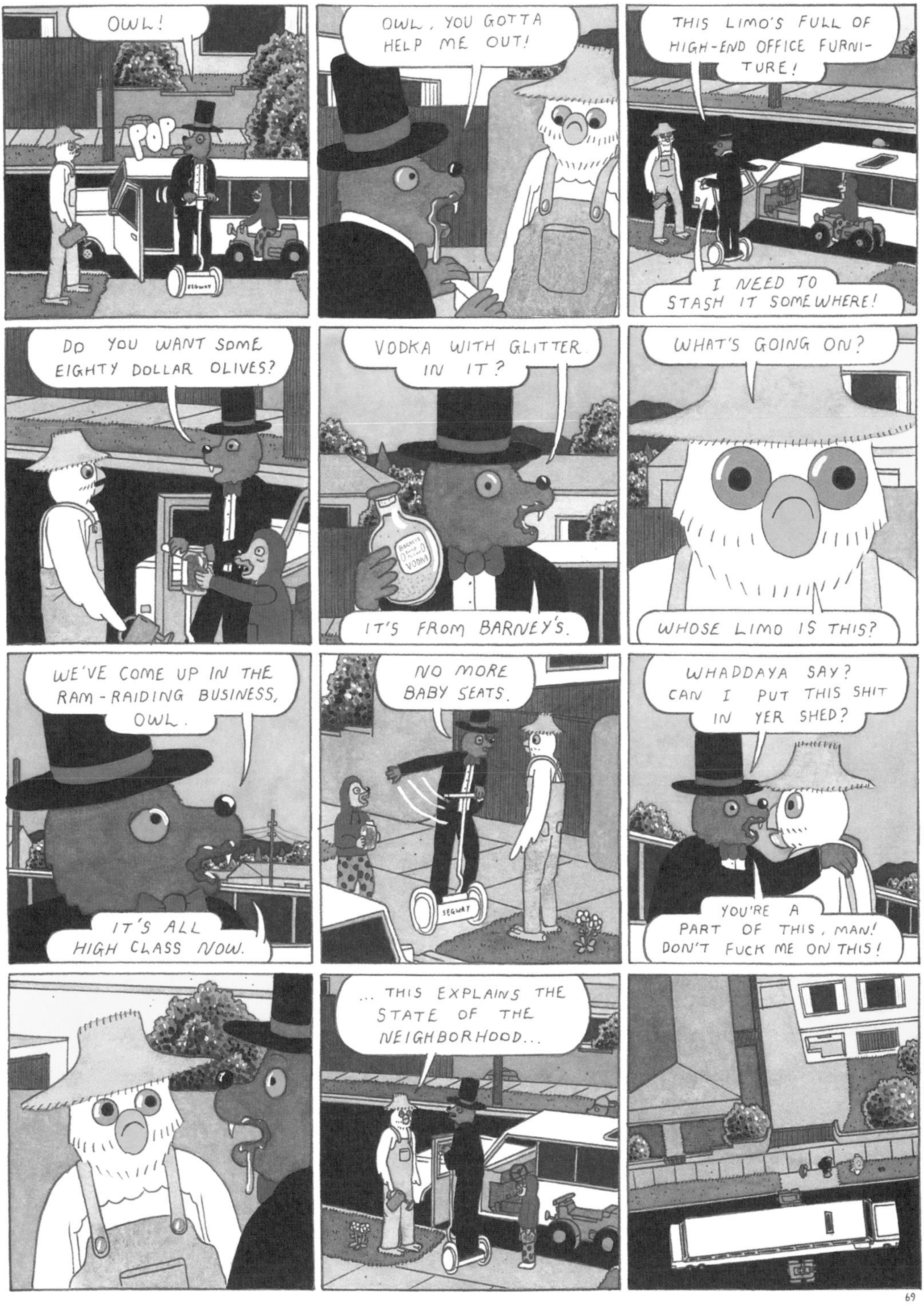
OWL!
POP
SEGWAY
OWL, YOU GOTTA HELP ME OUT!
THIS LIMO'S FULL OF HIGH-END OFFICE FURNITURE!
I NEED TO STASH IT SOMEWHERE!
DO YOU WANT SOME EIGHTY DOLLAR OLIVES?
VODKA WITH GLITTER IN IT?
VODKA
IT'S FROM BARNEY'S.
WHAT'S GOING ON?
WHOSE LIMO IS THIS?
WE'VE COME UP IN THE RAM-RAIDING BUSINESS, OWL.
IT'S ALL HIGH CLASS NOW.
NO MORE BABY SEATS.
SEGWAY
WHADDAYA SAY? CAN I PUT THIS SHIT IN YER SHED?
YOU'RE A PART OF THIS, MAN! DON'T FUCK ME ON THIS!
... THIS EXPLAINS THE STATE OF THE NEIGHBORHOOD...

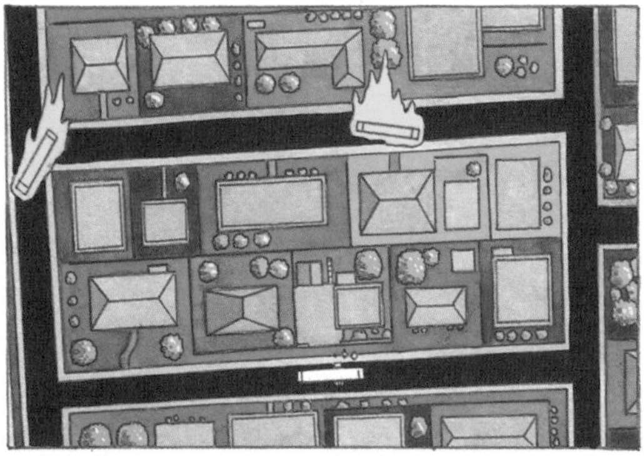

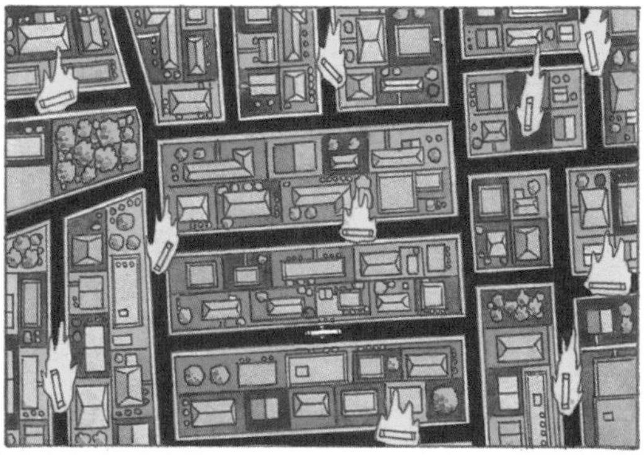

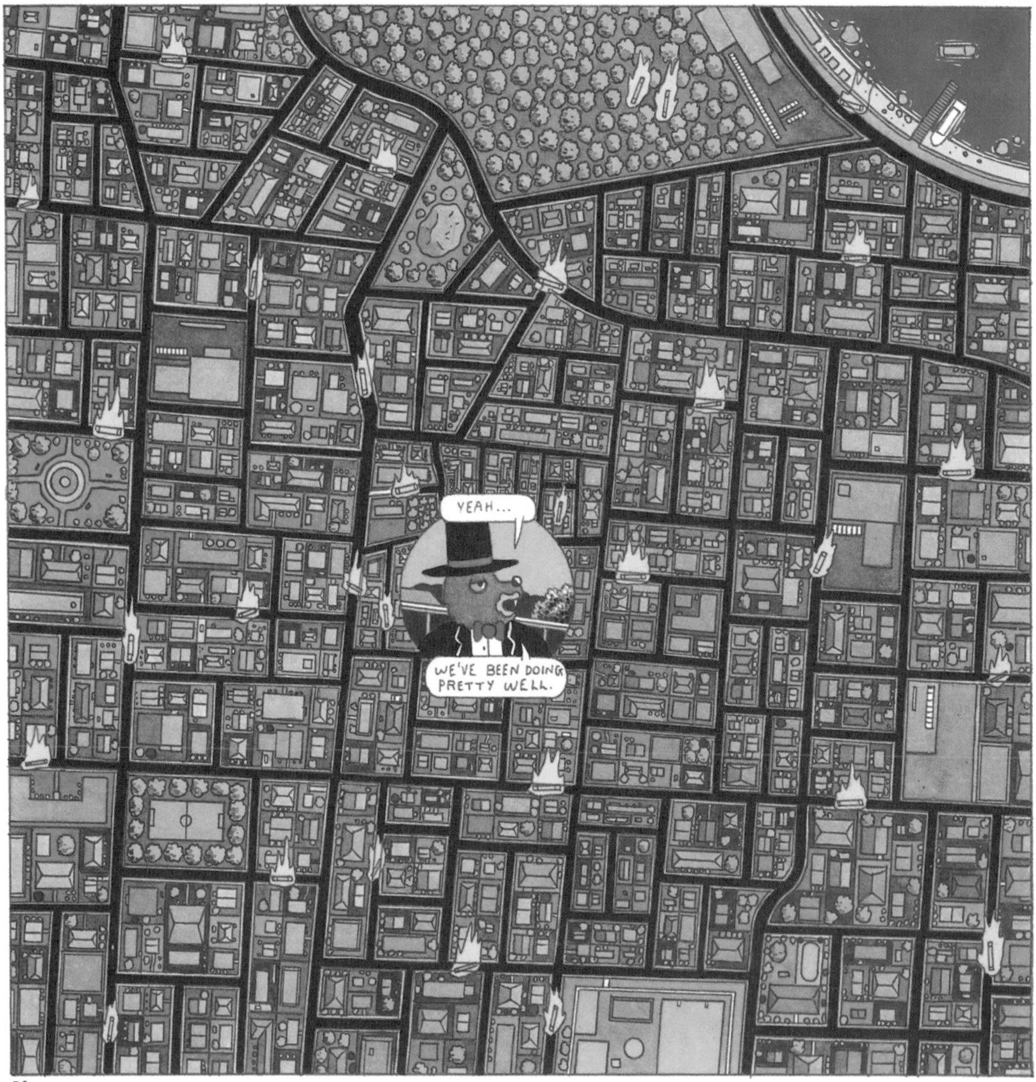
YEAH...
WE'VE BEEN DOING PRETTY WELL.

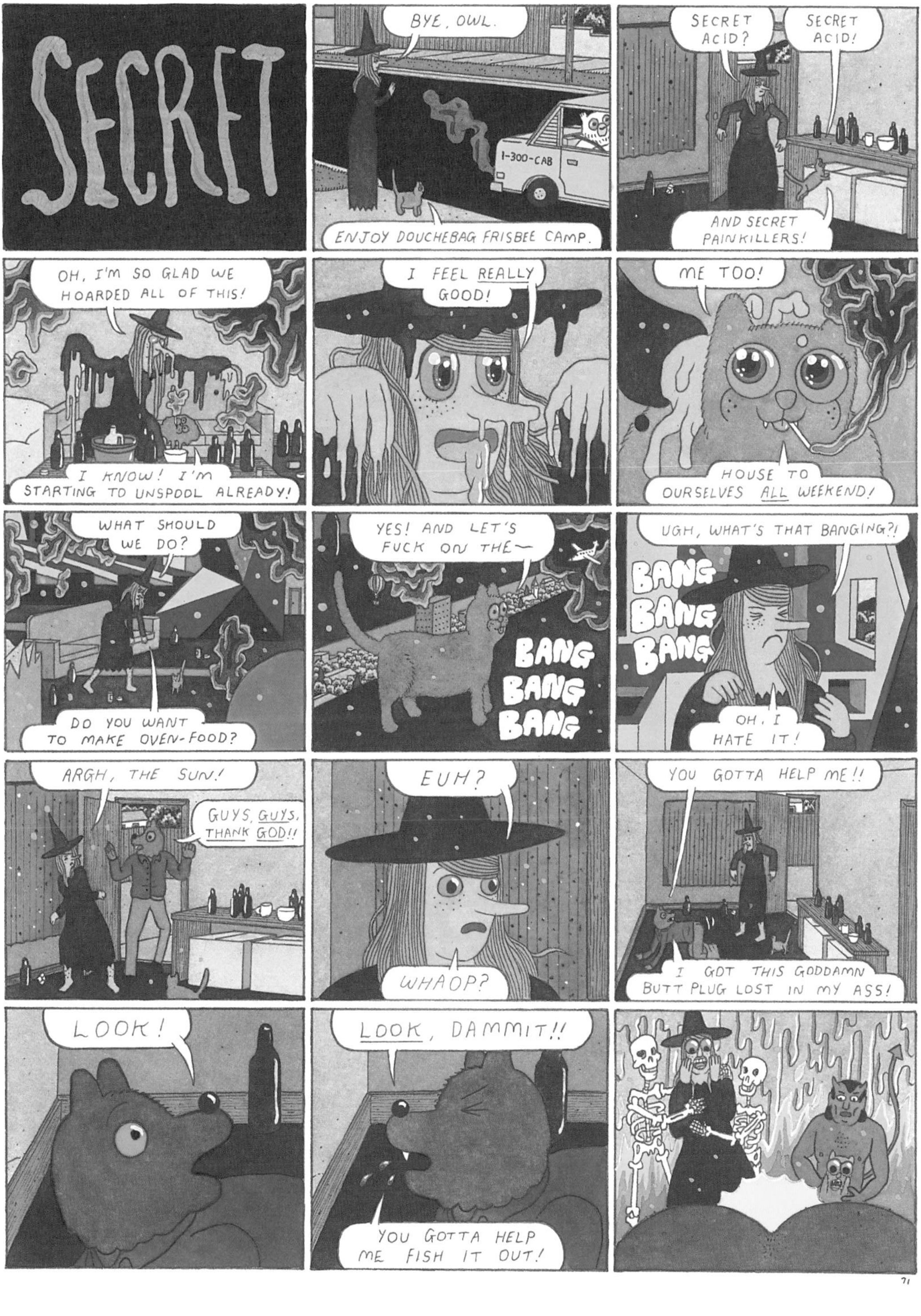
SECRET
BYE, OWL.
1-300-CAB
ENJOY DOUCHEBAG FRISBEE CAMP.
SECRET ACID?
SECRET ACID!
AND SECRET PAINKILLERS!
OH, I'M SO GLAD WE HOARDED ALL OF THIS!
I KNOW! I'M STARTING TO UNSPOOL ALREADY!
I FEEL REALLY GOOD!
ME TOO!
HOUSE TO OURSELVES ALL WEEKEND!
WHAT SHOULD WE DO?
DO YOU WANT TO MAKE OVEN-FOOD?
YES! AND LET'S FUCK ON THE~
BANG BANG BANG
UGH, WHAT'S THAT BANGING?!
BANG BANG BANG
OH, I HATE IT!
ARGH, THE SUN!
GUYS, GUYS, THANK GOD!!
EUH?
WHAOP?
YOU GOTTA HELP ME!!
I GOT THIS GODDAMN BUTT PLUG LOST IN MY ASS!
LOOK!
LOOK, DAMMIT!!
YOU GOTTA HELP ME FISH IT OUT!

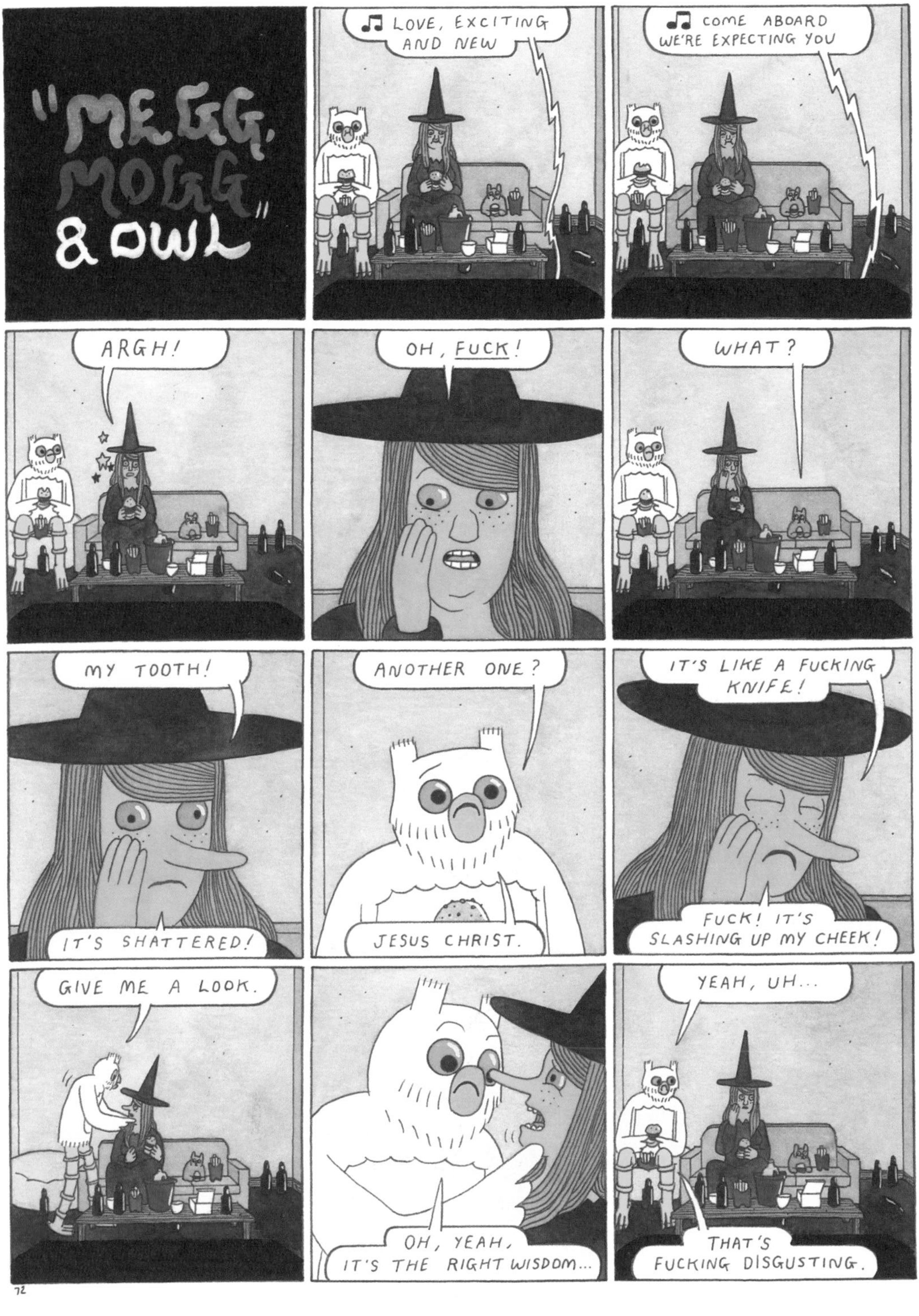
"MEGG, MOGG & OWL"
♫ LOVE, EXCITING AND NEW
♫ COME ABOARD WE'RE EXPECTING YOU
ARGH!
OH, FUCK!
WHAT?
MY TOOTH!
IT'S SHATTERED!
ANOTHER ONE?
JESUS CHRIST.
IT'S LIKE A FUCKING KNIFE!
FUCK! IT'S SLASHING UP MY CHEEK!
GIVE ME A LOOK.
OH, YEAH, IT'S THE RIGHT WISDOM...
YEAH, UH...
THAT'S FUCKING DISGUSTING.

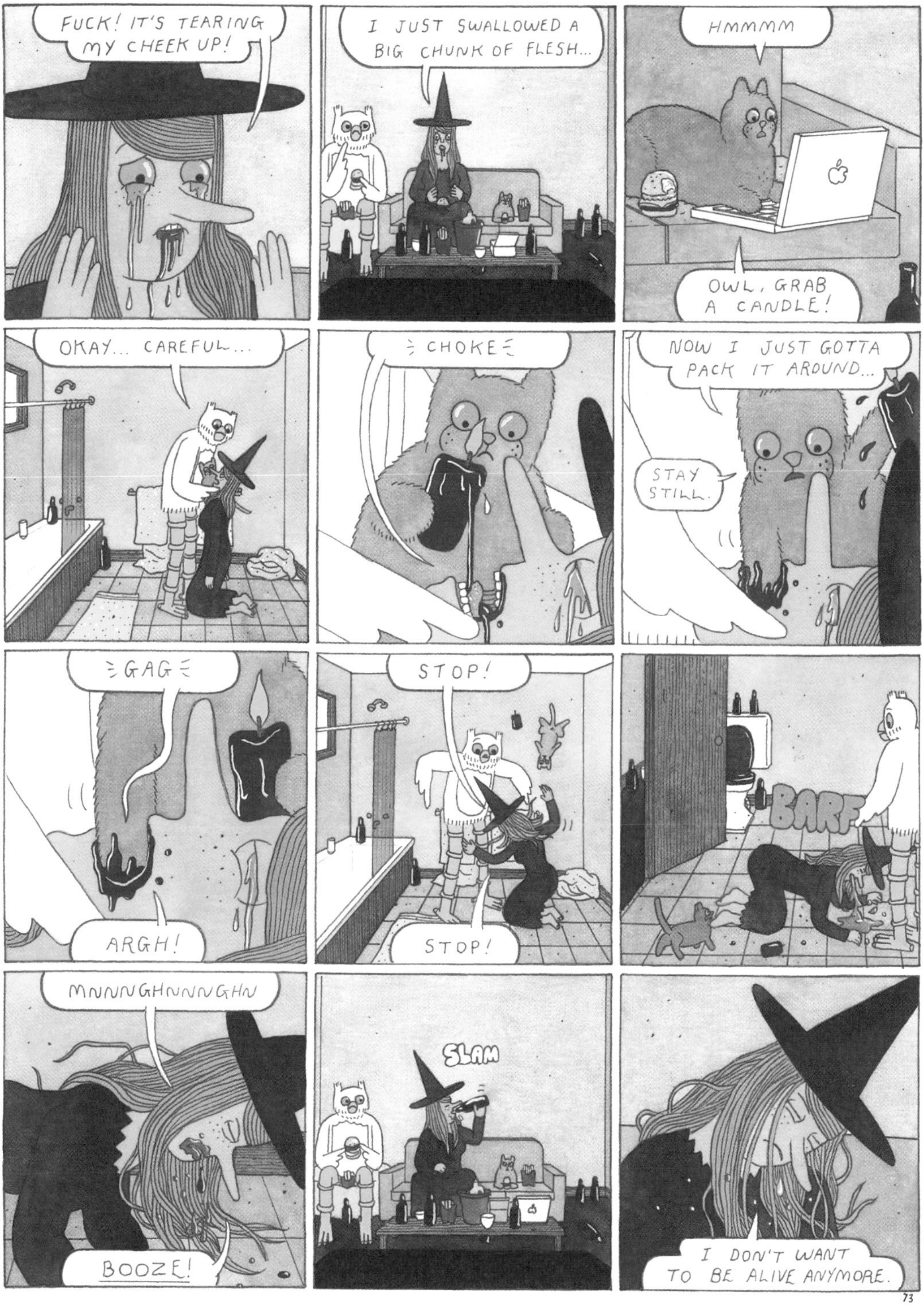
FUCK! IT'S TEARING MY CHEEK UP!
I JUST SWALLOWED A BIG CHUNK OF FLESH...
HMMMM
OWL, GRAB A CANDLE!
OKAY... CAREFUL...
CHOKE
NOW I JUST GOTTA PACK IT AROUND...
STAY STILL.
GAG
ARGH!
STOP!
STOP!
BARF
MNNNGHNNNGHN
BOOZE!
SLAM
I DON'T WANT TO BE ALIVE ANYMORE.

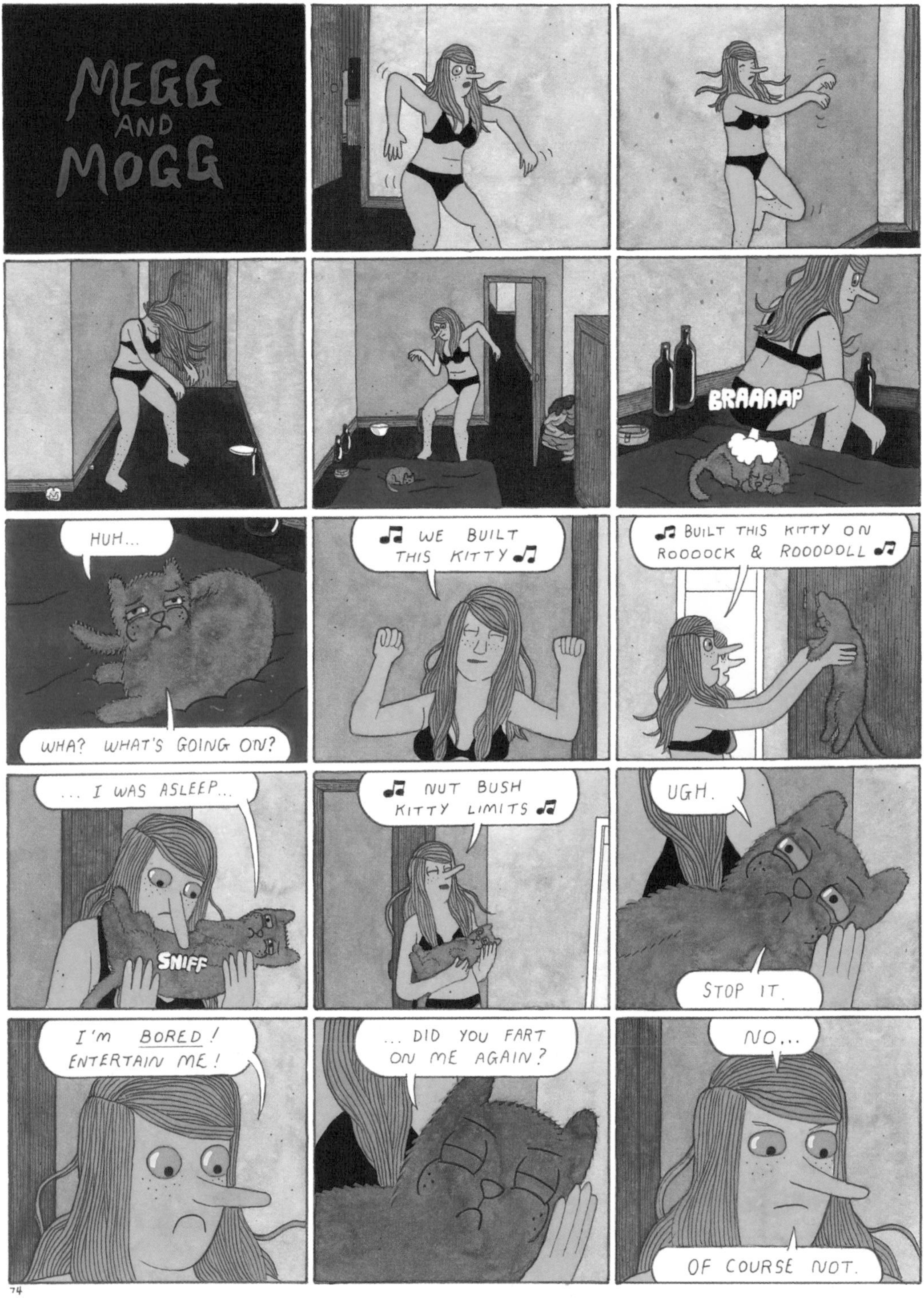
MEGG AND MOGG
BRAAAAP
HUH...
WHA? WHAT'S GOING ON?
WE BUILT THIS KITTY
BUILT THIS KITTY ON ROOOOCK & ROOOOOLL
... I WAS ASLEEP...
SNIFF
NUT BUSH KITTY LIMITS
UGH.
STOP IT.
I'M BORED! ENTERTAIN ME!
... DID YOU FART ON ME AGAIN?
NO...
OF COURSE NOT.

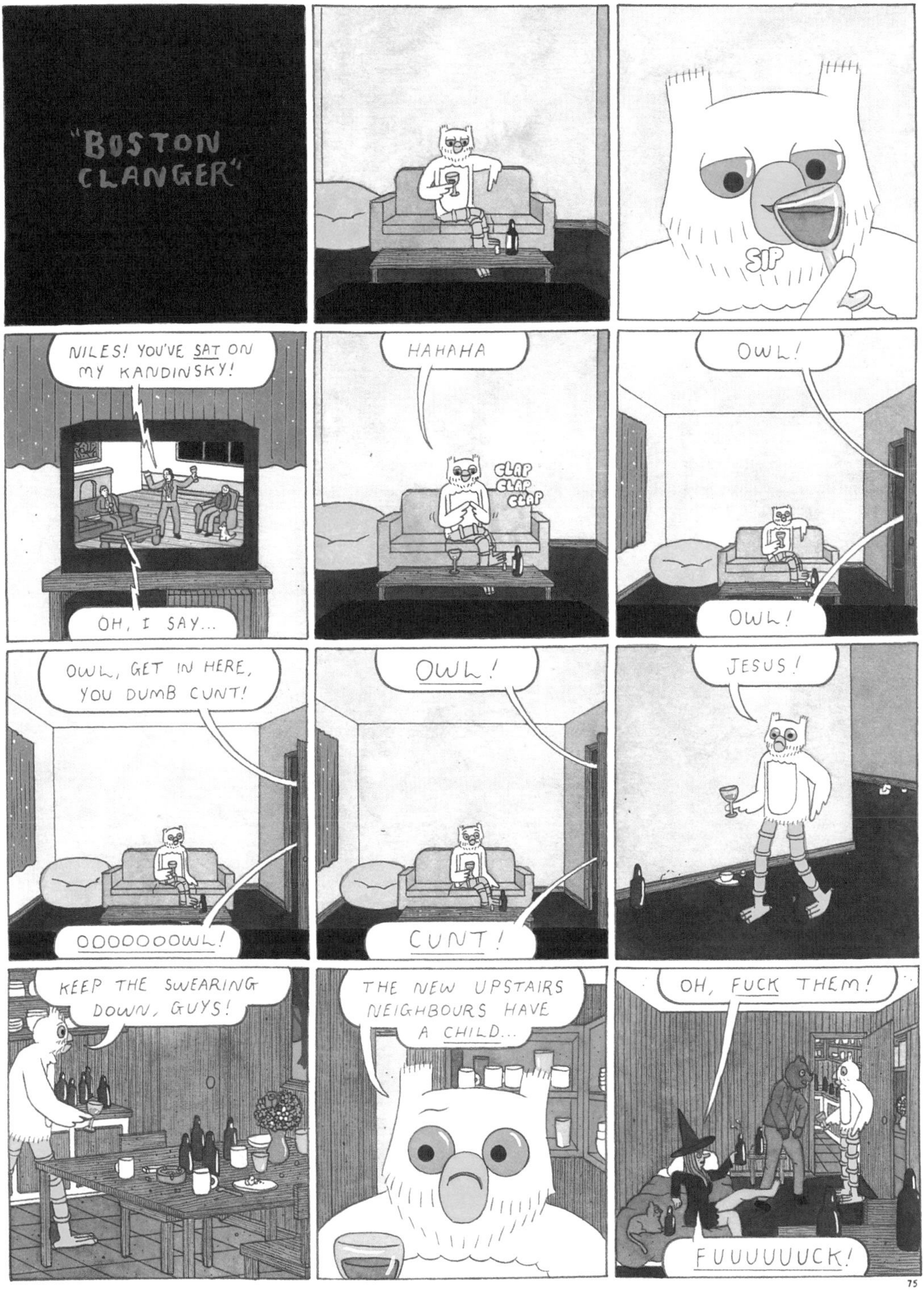
"BOSTON CLANGER"
SIP
NILES! YOU'VE SAT ON MY KANDINSKY!
OH, I SAY...
HAHAHA
CLAP CLAP CLAP
OWL!
OWL!
OWL, GET IN HERE, YOU DUMB CUNT!
OOOOOOOWL!
OWL!
CUNT!
JESUS!
KEEP THE SWEARING DOWN, GUYS!
THE NEW UPSTAIRS NEIGHBOURS HAVE A CHILD...
OH, FUCK THEM!
FUUUUUUCK!

WHAT ARE YOU ALL DOING IN MY ROOM?
HOW DRUNK ARE YOU?
IT'S MY BIRTHDAY, OWL!
OH.
OH, UH...
..."HAPPY BIRTHDAY"...
THANKS!
YEAH, AND I'M DRUNK...
DRUNK ASH FUCK...
... IN ANSWER TO YOUR QUESHTION.
... OKAY...
EVERYBODY OUT OF MY ROOM THEN.

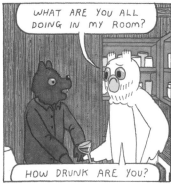

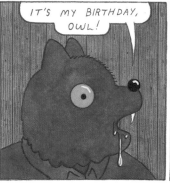

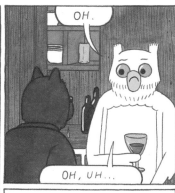

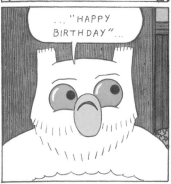

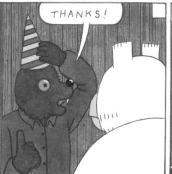

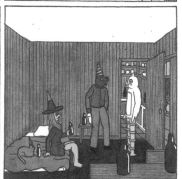

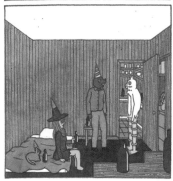

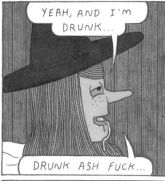

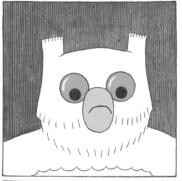

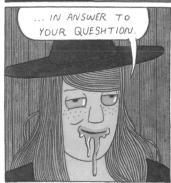

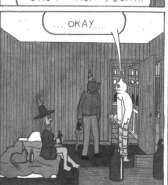

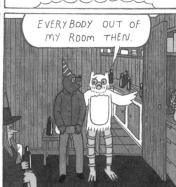

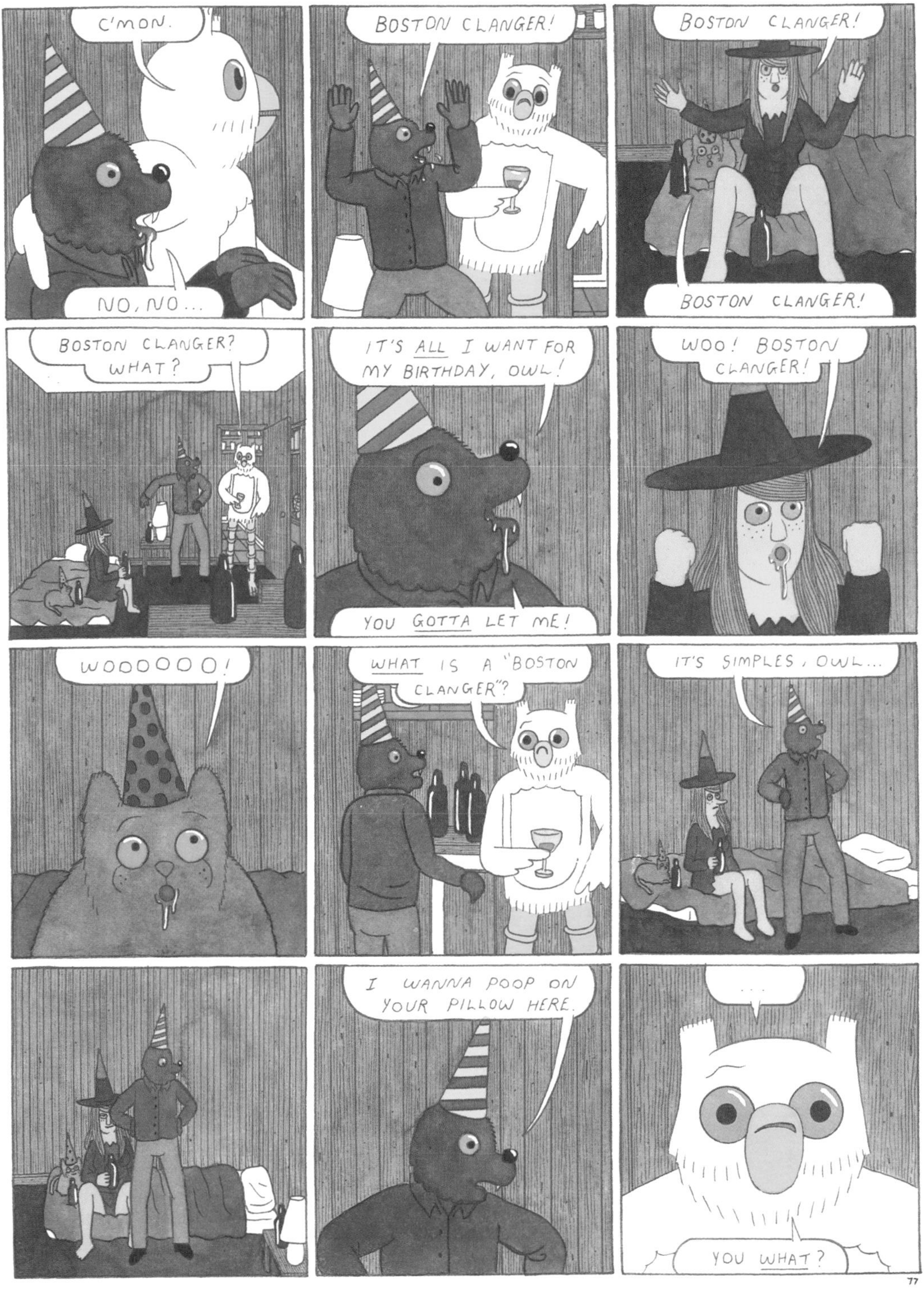
C'MON.
NO, NO...
BOSTON CLANGER!
BOSTON CLANGER!
BOSTON CLANGER!
BOSTON CLANGER? WHAT?
IT'S ALL I WANT FOR MY BIRTHDAY, OWL!
YOU GOTTA LET ME!
WOO! BOSTON CLANGER!
WOOOOOO!
WHAT IS A "BOSTON CLANGER"?
IT'S SIMPLES, OWL...
I WANNA POOP ON YOUR PILLOW HERE.
...
YOU WHAT?

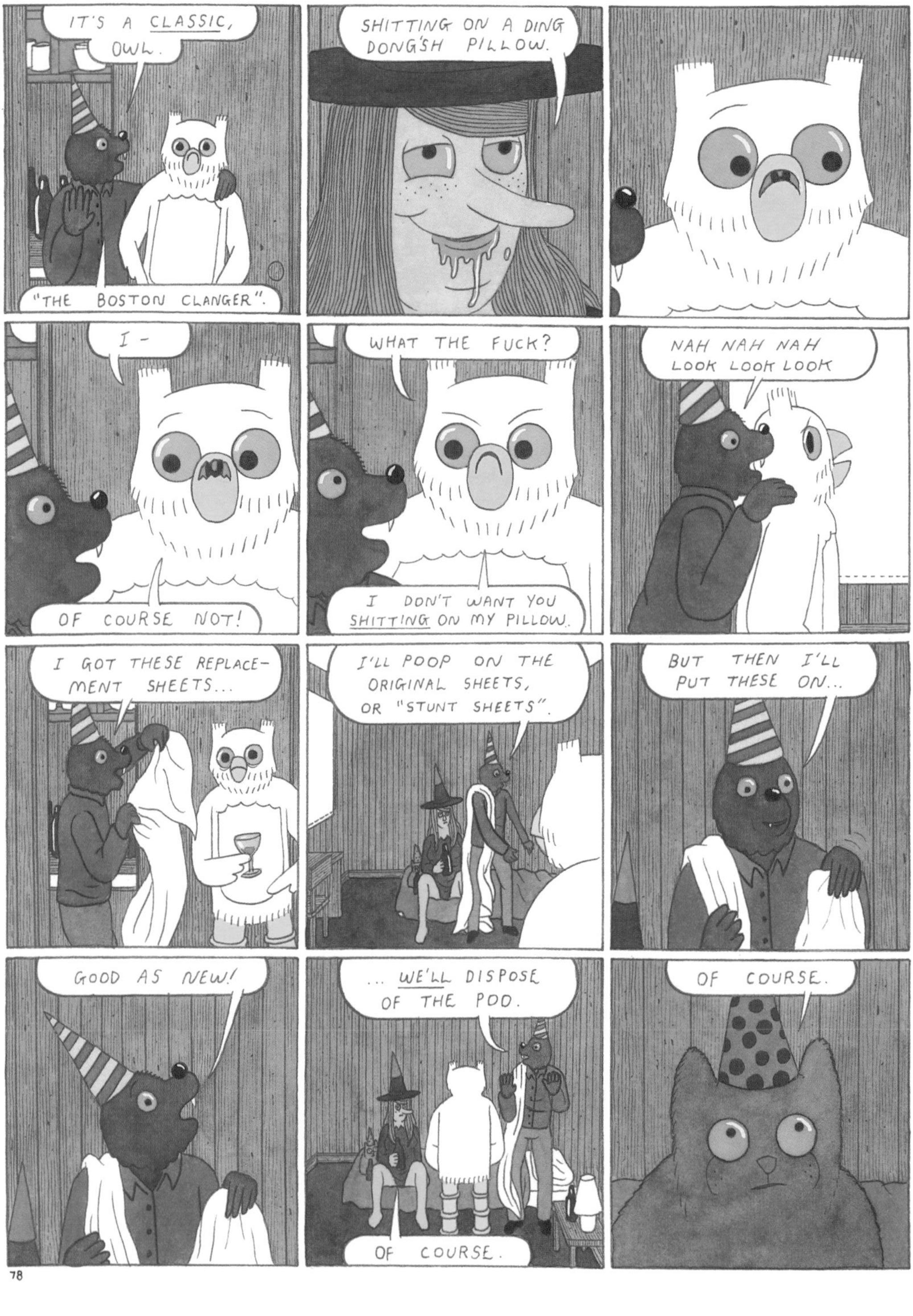
IT'S A CLASSIC, OWL.
"THE BOSTON CLANGER".
SHITTING ON A DING DONG'SH PILLOW.
I -
OF COURSE NOT!
WHAT THE FUCK?
I DON'T WANT YOU SHITTING ON MY PILLOW.
NAH NAH NAH LOOK LOOK LOOK
I GOT THESE REPLACE-MENT SHEETS...
I'LL POOP ON THE ORIGINAL SHEETS, OR "STUNT SHEETS".
BUT THEN I'LL PUT THESE ON...
GOOD AS NEW!
... WE'LL DISPOSE OF THE POO.
OF COURSE.
OF COURSE.

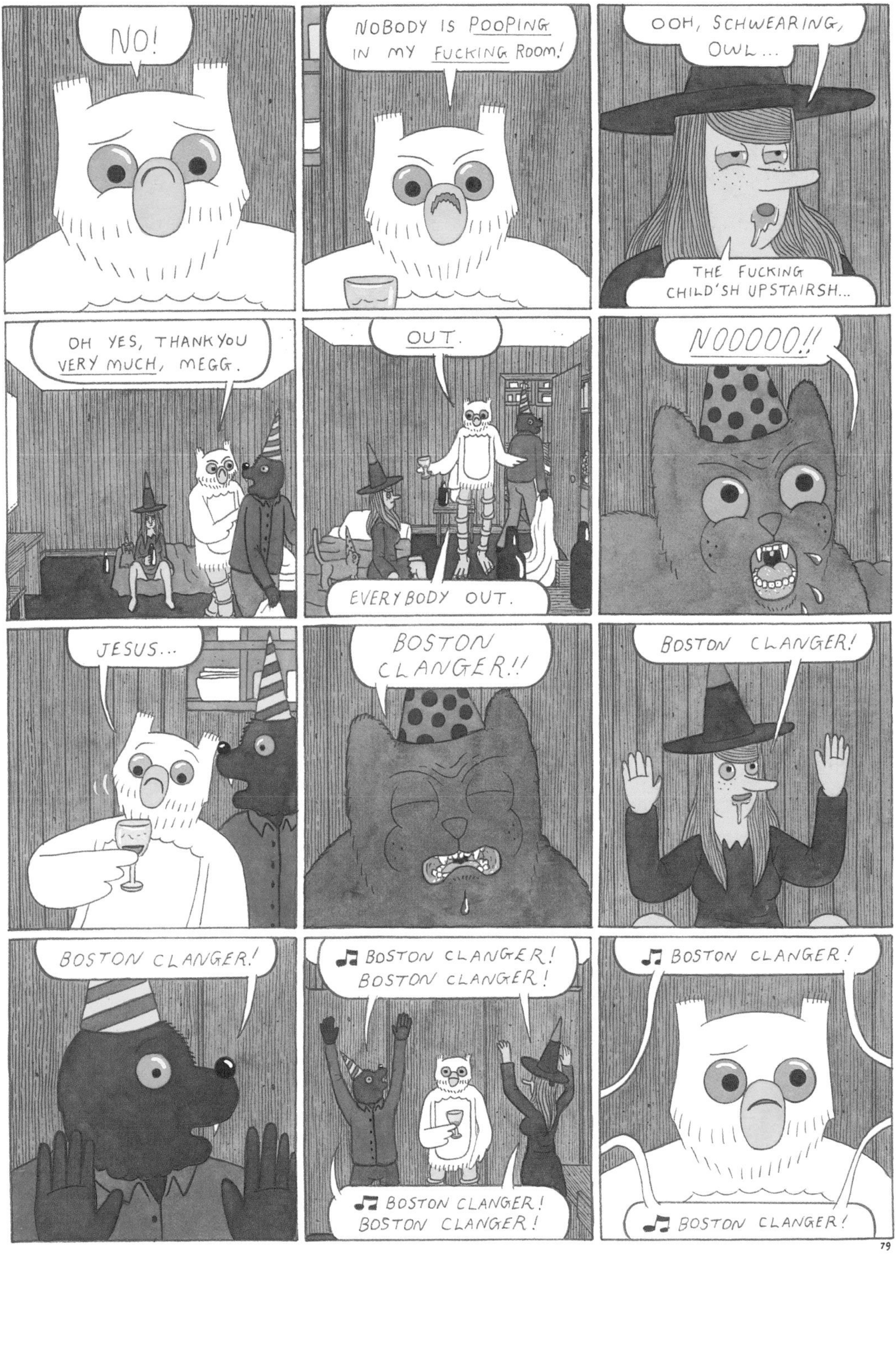
NO!
NOBODY IS POOPING IN MY FUCKING ROOM!
OOH, SCHWEARING, OWL...
THE FUCKING CHILD'SH UPSTAIRSH...
OH YES, THANK YOU VERY MUCH, MEGG.
OUT.
EVERYBODY OUT.
NOOOOO!!
JESUS...
BOSTON CLANGER!!
BOSTON CLANGER!
BOSTON CLANGER!
BOSTON CLANGER! BOSTON CLANGER!
BOSTON CLANGER! BOSTON CLANGER!
BOSTON CLANGER!
BOSTON CLANGER!

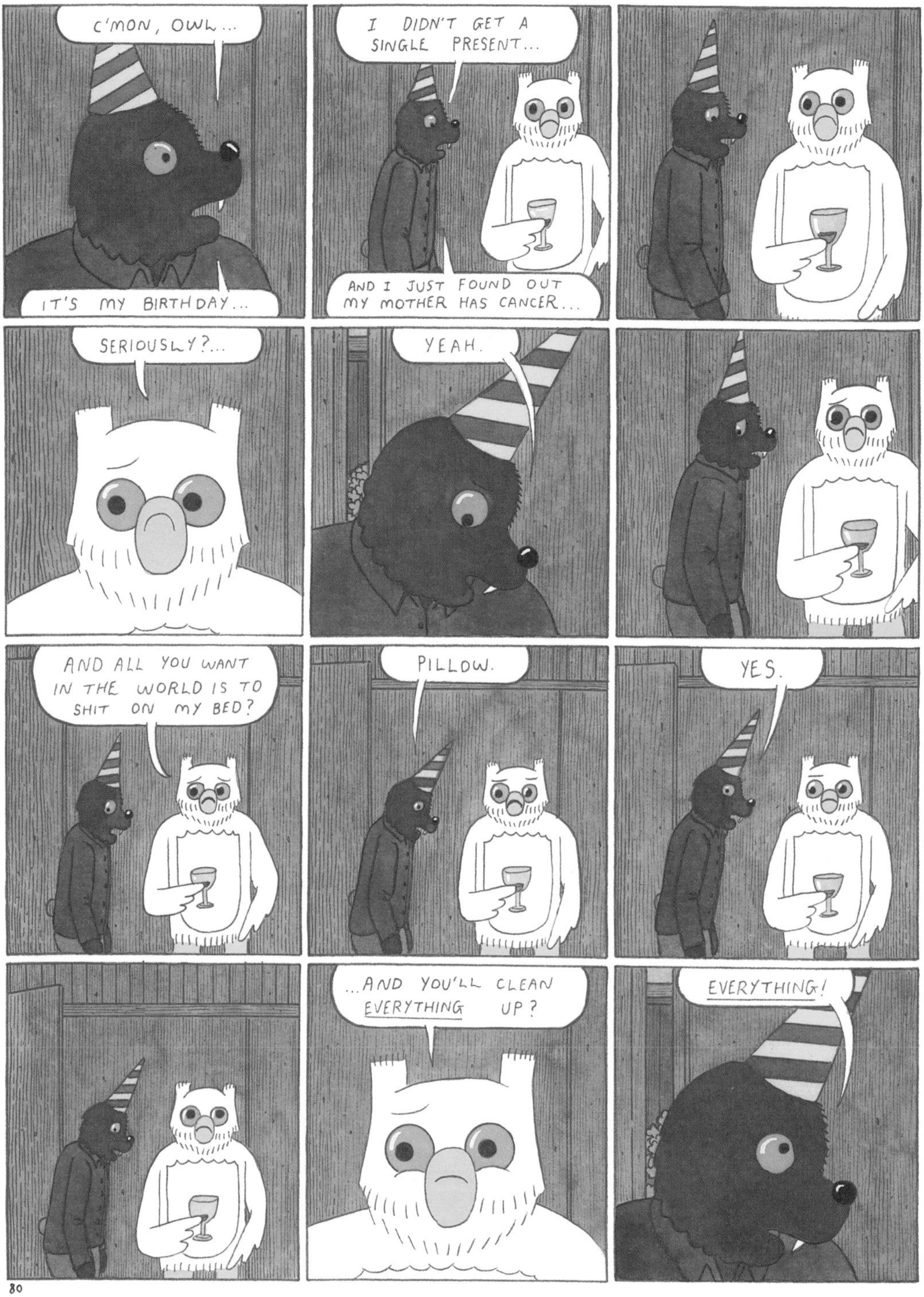
C'MON, OWL...
IT'S MY BIRTHDAY...
I DIDN'T GET A SINGLE PRESENT...
AND I JUST FOUND OUT MY MOTHER HAS CANCER...
SERIOUSLY?...
YEAH.
AND ALL YOU WANT IN THE WORLD IS TO SHIT ON MY BED?
PILLOW.
YES.
...AND YOU'LL CLEAN EVERYTHING UP?
EVERYTHING!

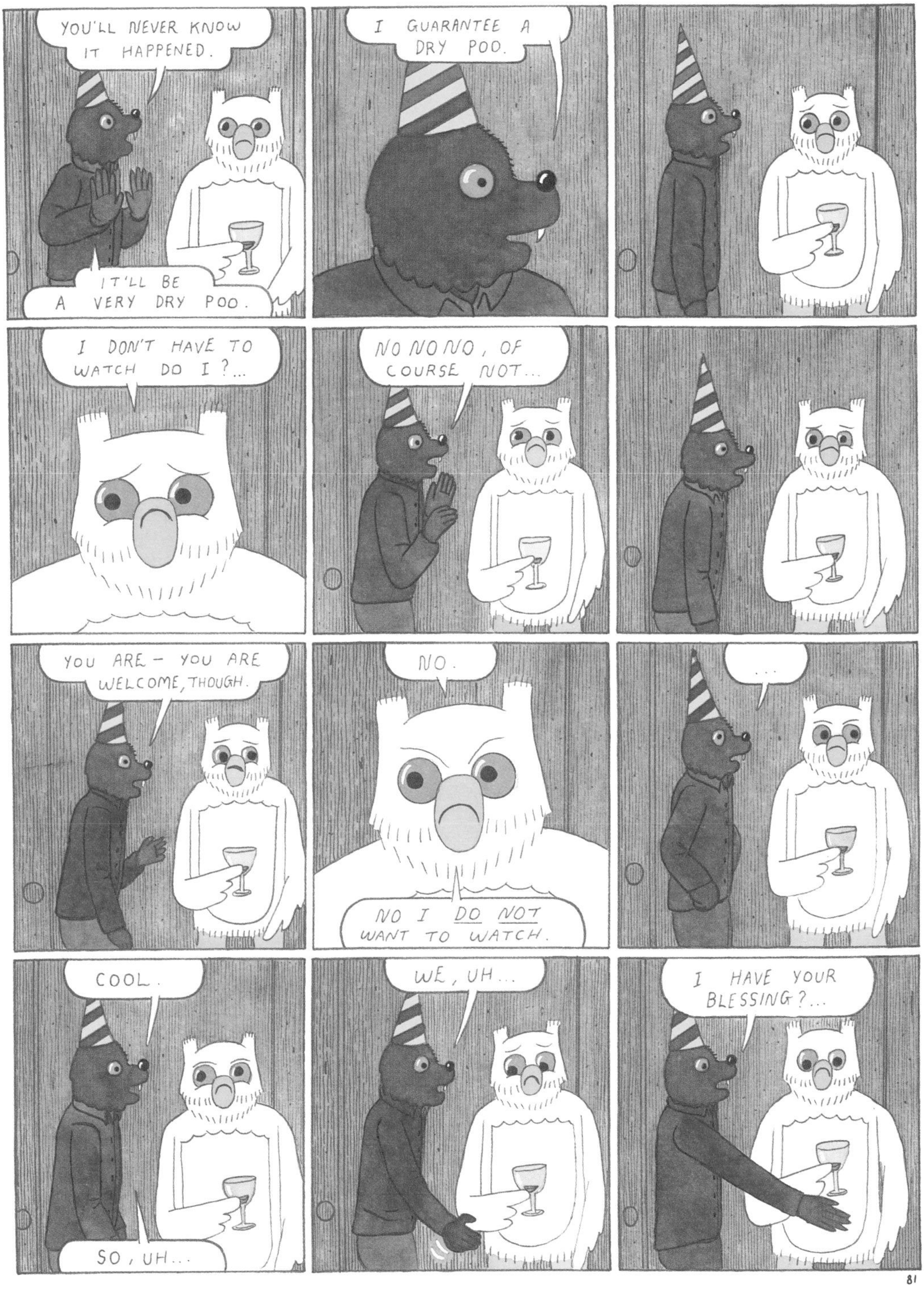
YOU'LL NEVER KNOW IT HAPPENED.
IT'LL BE A VERY DRY POO.
I GUARANTEE A DRY POO.
I DON'T HAVE TO WATCH DO I?...
NO NO NO, OF COURSE NOT...
YOU ARE- YOU ARE WELCOME, THOUGH.
NO.
NO I DO NOT WANT TO WATCH.
...
COOL.
SO, UH...
WE, UH...
I HAVE YOUR BLESSING?...

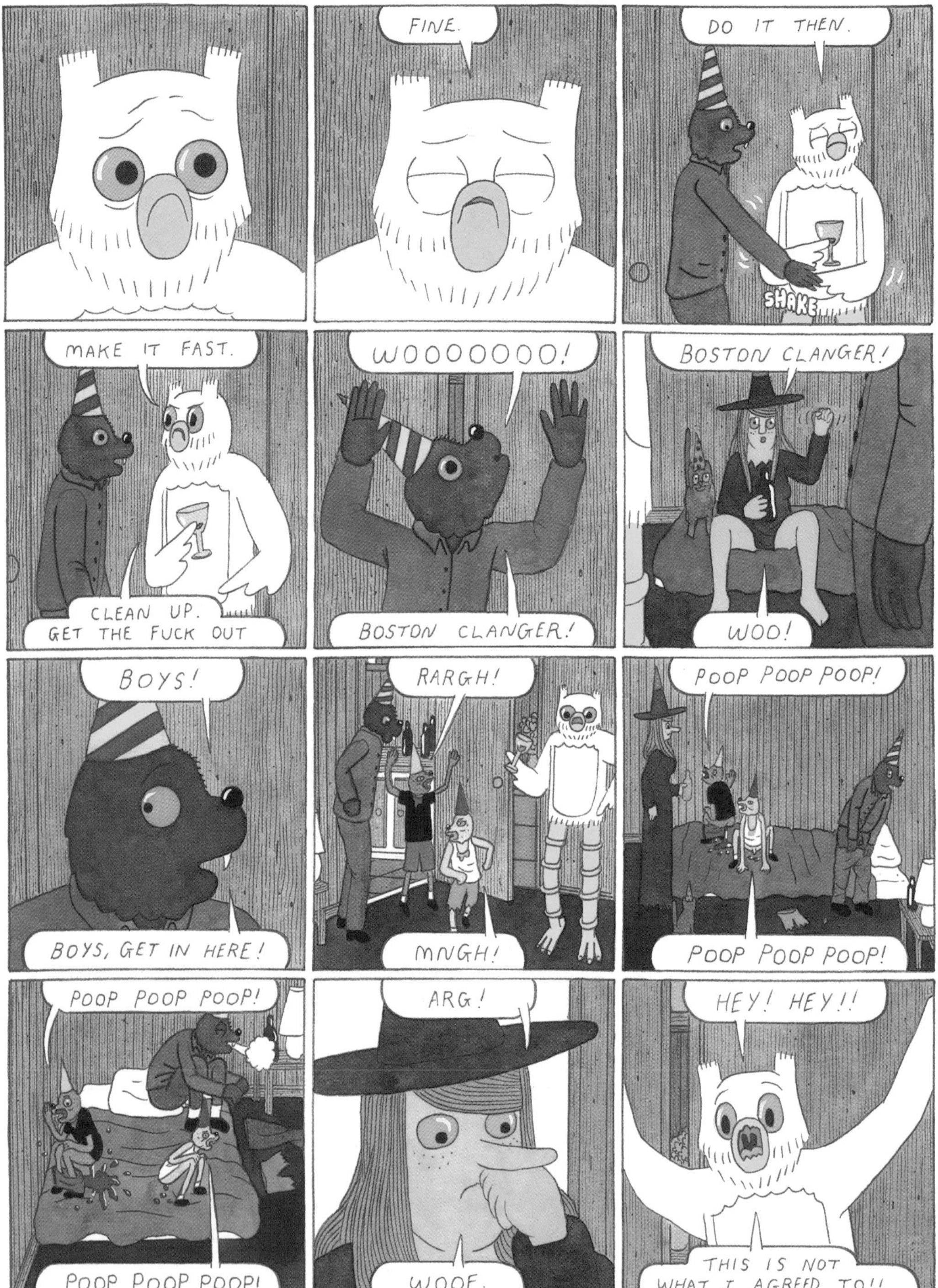
FINE.
DO IT THEN.
SHAKE
MAKE IT FAST.
CLEAN UP.
GET THE FUCK OUT
WOOOOOOO!
BOSTON CLANGER!
BOSTON CLANGER!
WOO!
BOYS!
BOYS, GET IN HERE!
RARGH!
MNGH!
POOP POOP POOP!
POOP POOP POOP!
POOP POOP POOP!
POOP POOP POOP!
ARG!
WOOF.
HEY! HEY!!
THIS IS NOT
WHAT I AGREED TO!!

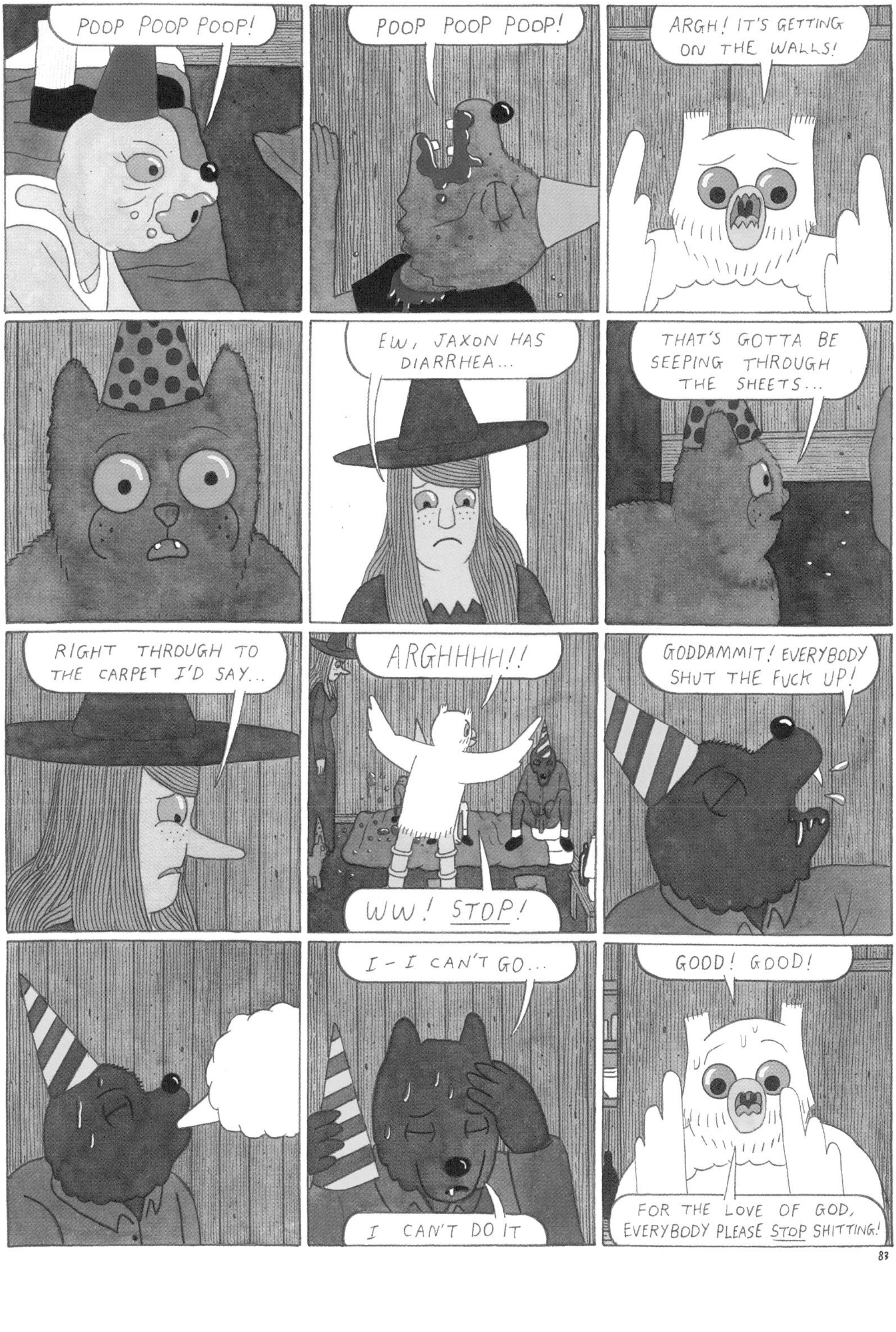
POOP POOP POOP!
POOP POOP POOP!
ARGH! IT'S GETTING ON THE WALLS!
EW, JAXON HAS DIARRHEA...
THAT'S GOTTA BE SEEPING THROUGH THE SHEETS...
RIGHT THROUGH TO THE CARPET I'D SAY...
ARGHHHH!!
WW! STOP!
GODDAMMIT! EVERYBODY SHUT THE FUCK UP!
I-I CAN'T GO...
I CAN'T DO IT
GOOD! GOOD!
FOR THE LOVE OF GOD, EVERYBODY PLEASE STOP SHITTING!

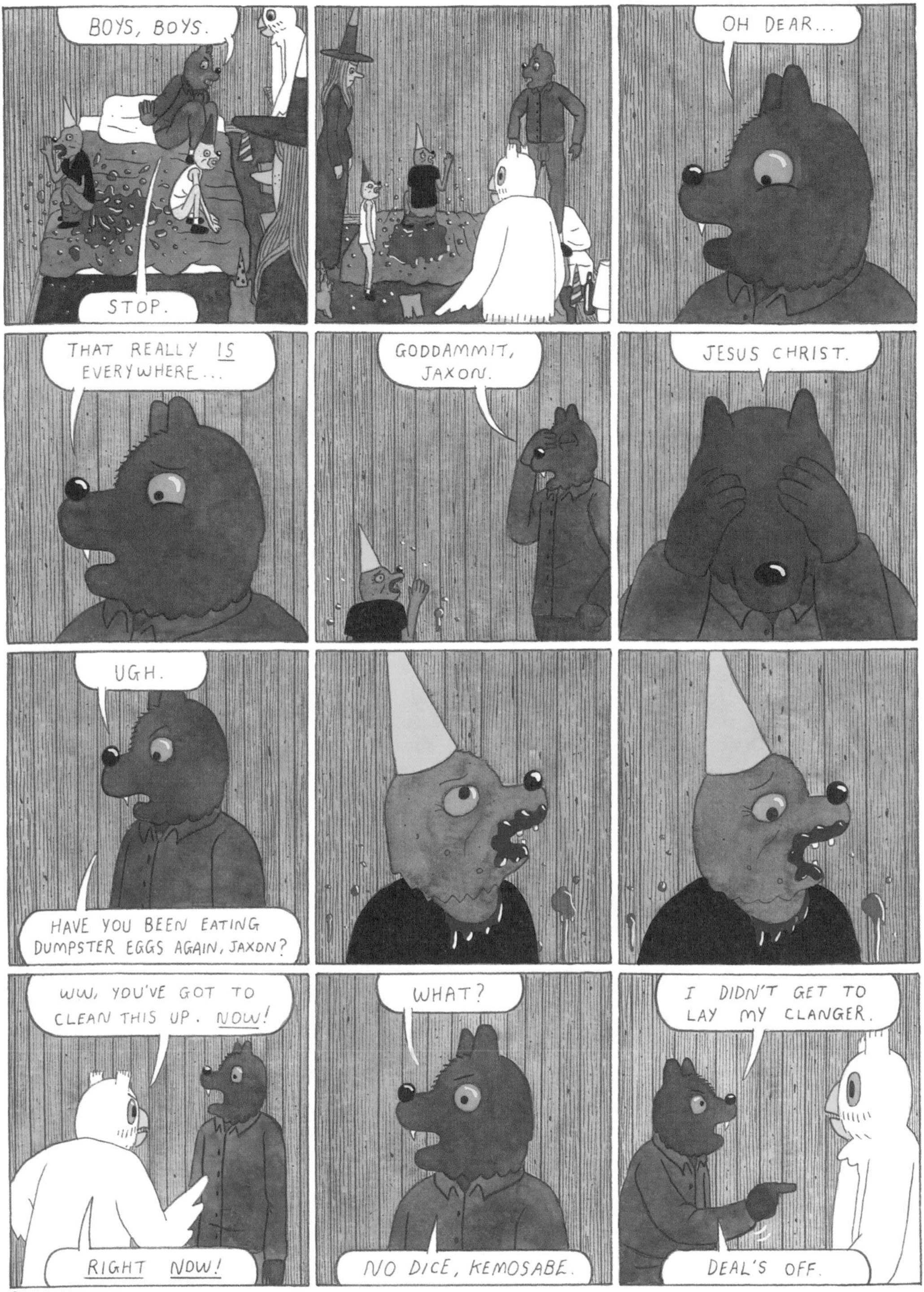
BOYS, BOYS.
STOP.
OH DEAR...
THAT REALLY IS EVERYWHERE...
GODDAMMIT, JAXON.
JESUS CHRIST.
UGH.
HAVE YOU BEEN EATING DUMPSTER EGGS AGAIN, JAXON?
WW, YOU'VE GOT TO CLEAN THIS UP. NOW!
RIGHT NOW!
WHAT?
NO DICE, KEMOSABE.
I DIDN'T GET TO LAY MY CLANGER.
DEAL'S OFF.

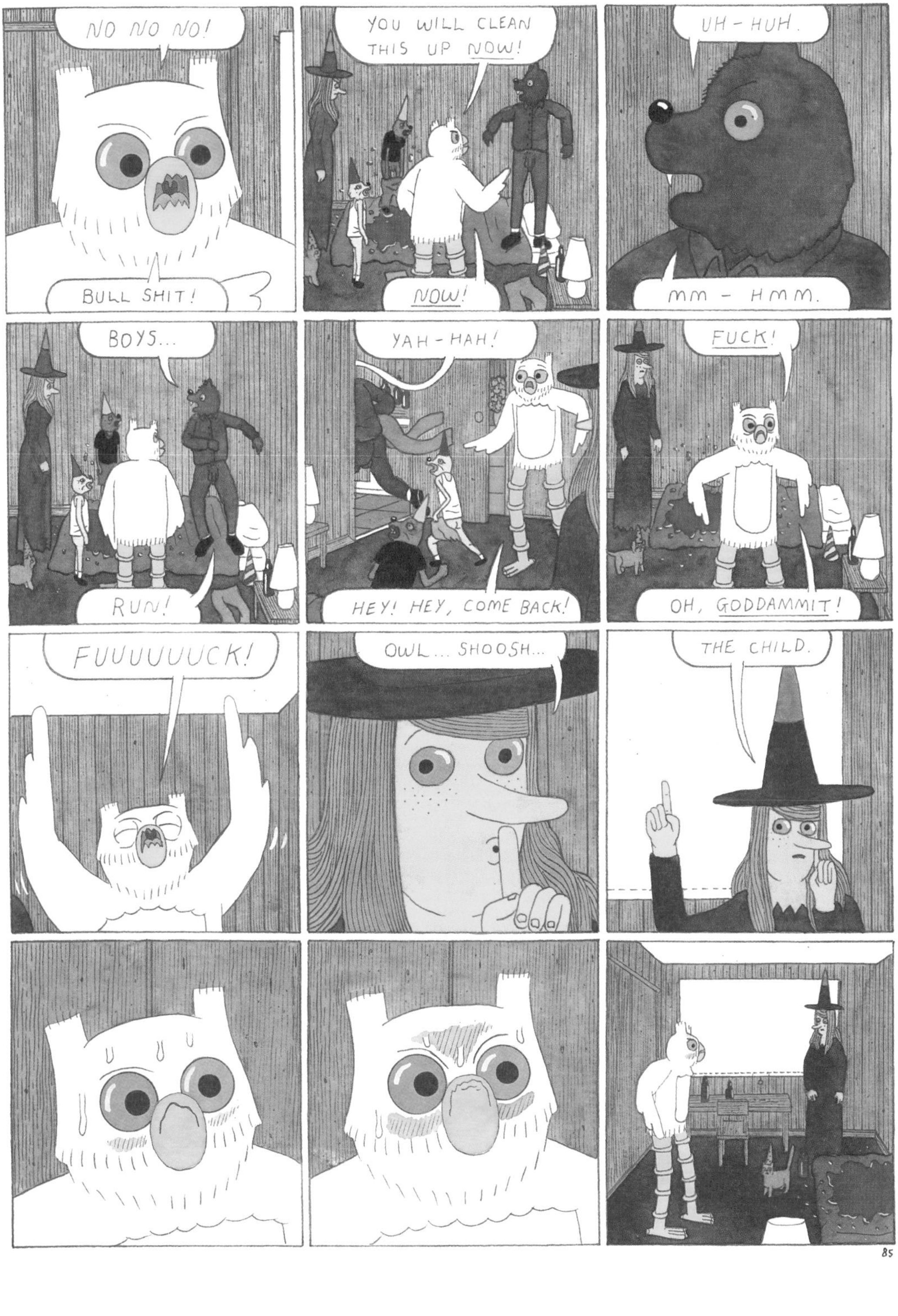
NO NO NO!
BULL SHIT!
YOU WILL CLEAN THIS UP NOW!
NOW!
UH-HUH.
MM-HMM.
BOYS...
RUN!
YAH-HAH!
HEY! HEY, COME BACK!
FUCK!
OH, GODDAMMIT!
FUUUUUUCK!
OWL... SHOOSH...
THE CHILD.

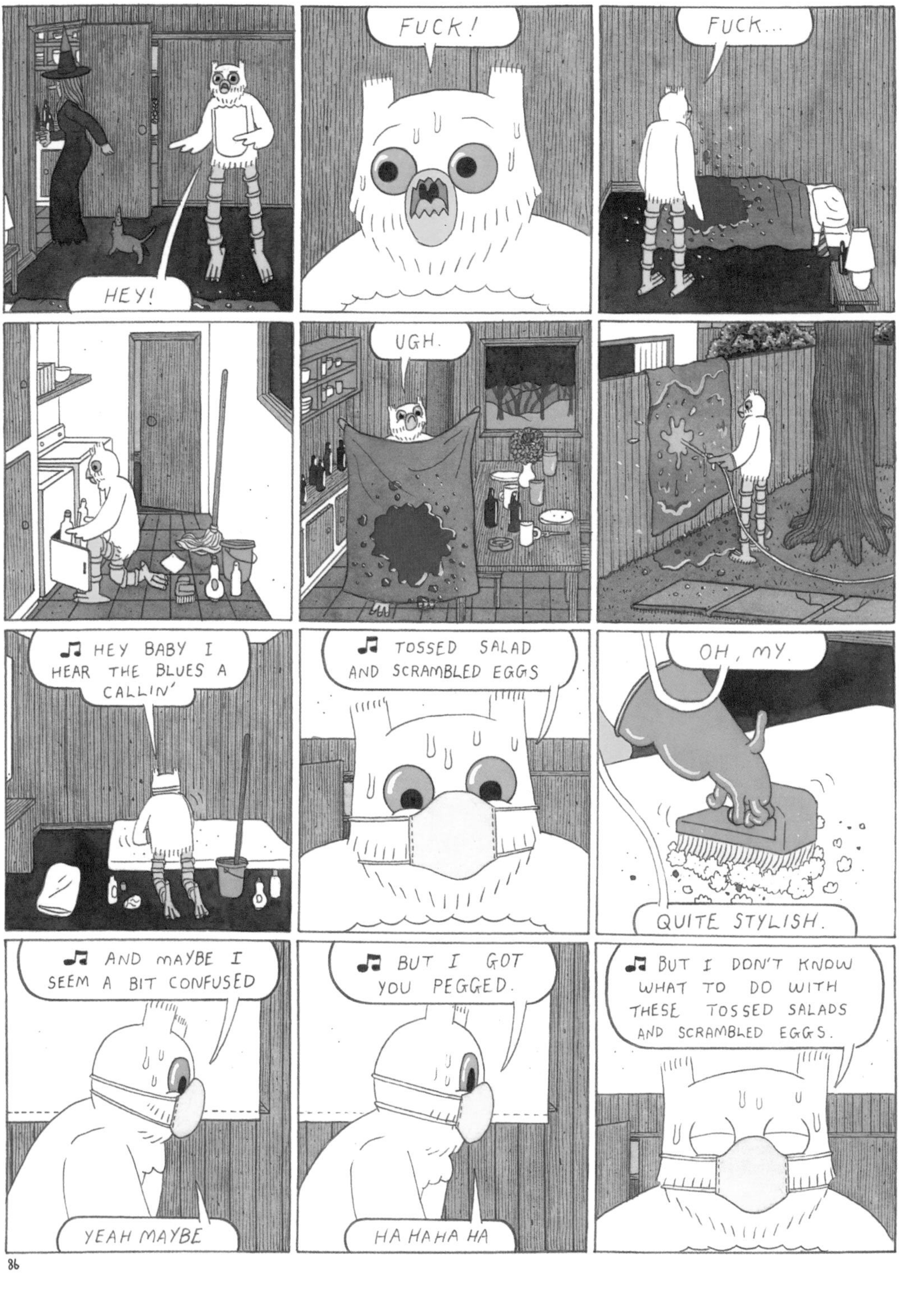
HEY!
FUCK!
FUCK...
UGH.
♫ HEY BABY I HEAR THE BLUES A CALLIN'
♫ TOSSED SALAD AND SCRAMBLED EGGS
OH, MY.
QUITE STYLISH.
♫ AND MAYBE I SEEM A BIT CONFUSED
YEAH MAYBE
♫ BUT I GOT YOU PEGGED.
HA HAHAHA HA
♫ BUT I DON'T KNOW WHAT TO DO WITH THESE TOSSED SALADS AND SCRAMBLED EGGS.

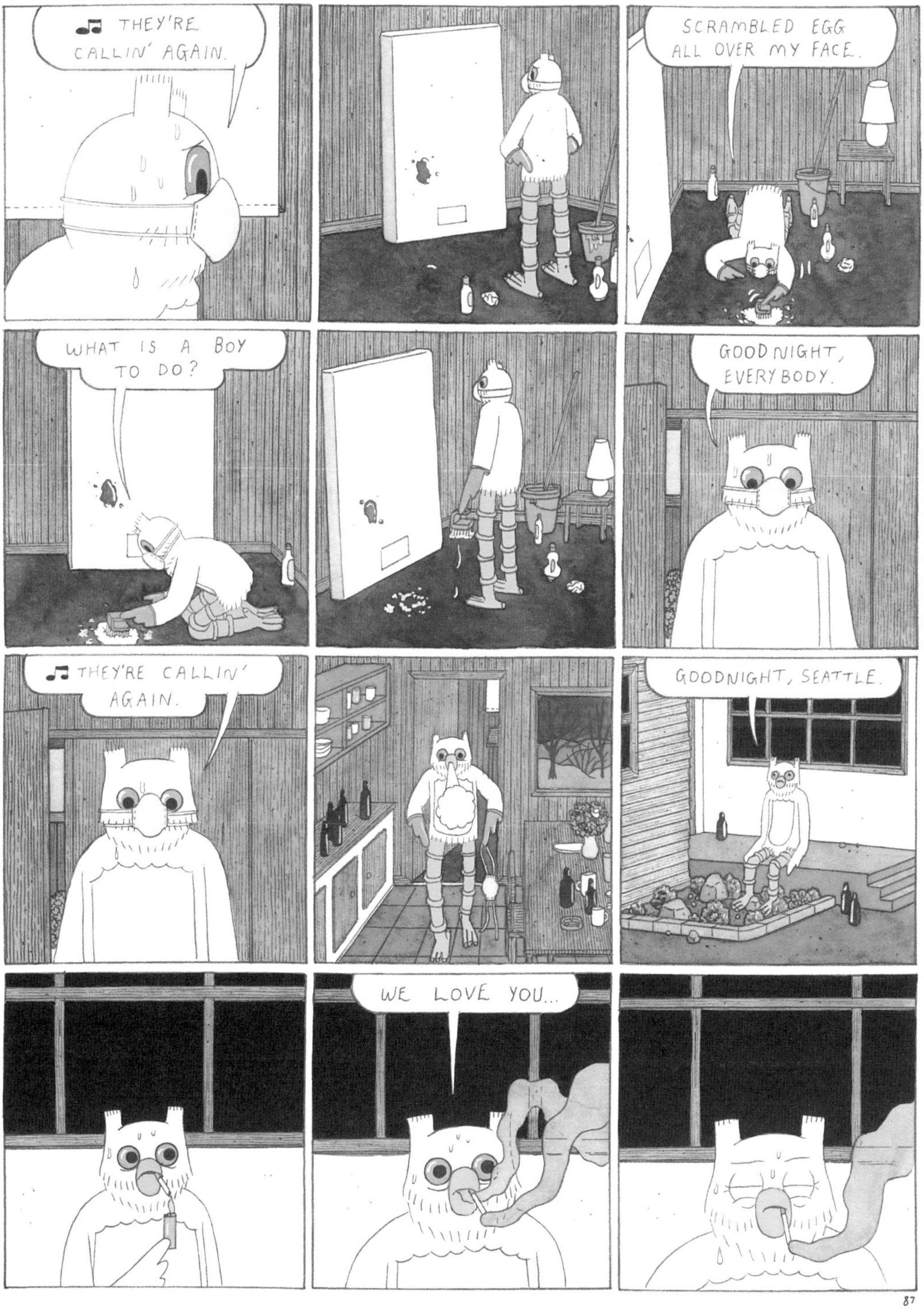
♫ THEY'RE CALLIN' AGAIN.
SCRAMBLED EGG ALL OVER MY FACE.
WHAT IS A BOY TO DO?
GOODNIGHT, EVERYBODY.
♫ THEY'RE CALLIN' AGAIN.
GOODNIGHT, SEATTLE.
WE LOVE YOU...

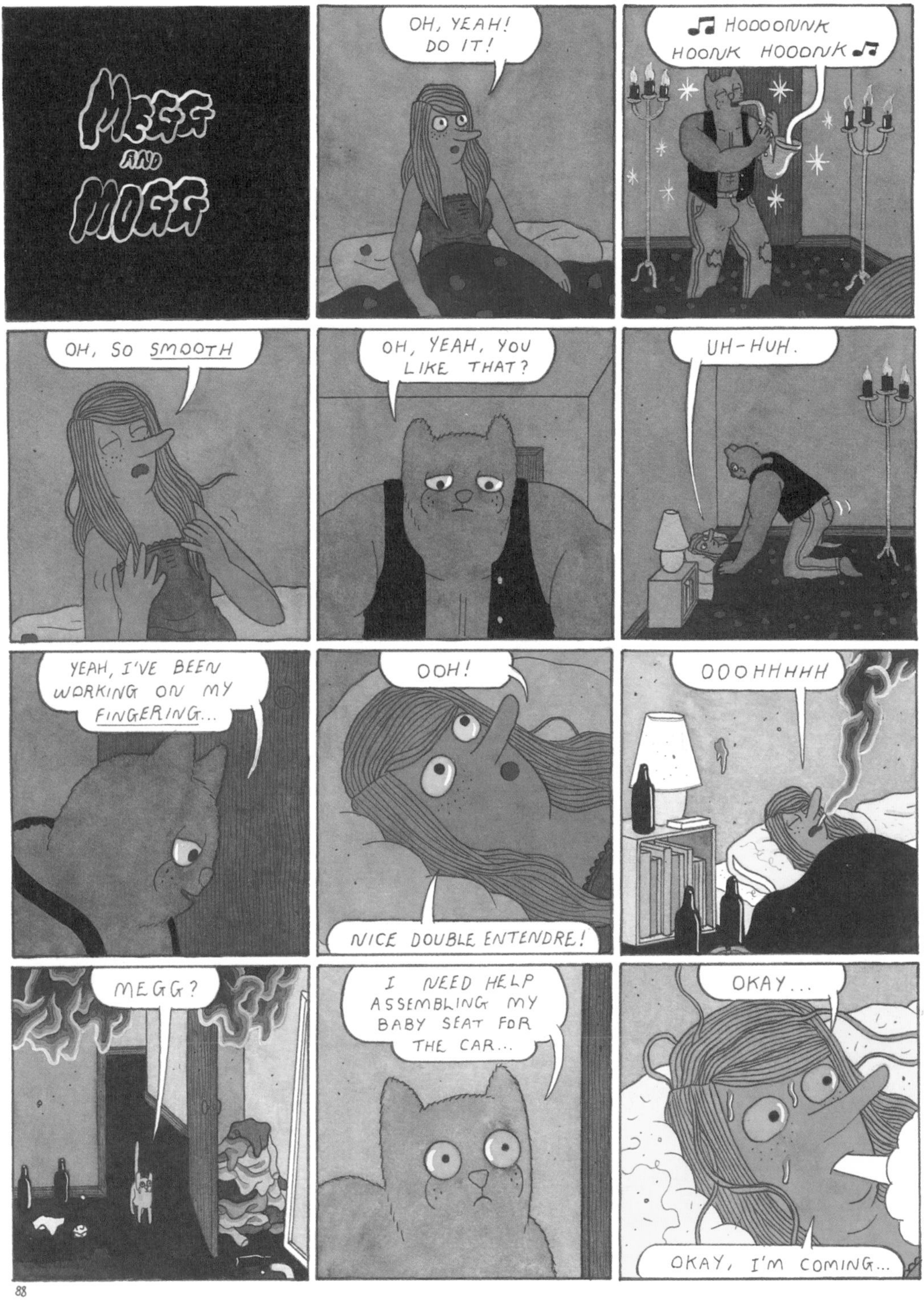
MEGG AND MOGG
OH, YEAH! DO IT!
HOOOONNK HOONK HOOONK
OH, SO SMOOTH
OH, YEAH, YOU LIKE THAT?
UH-HUH.
YEAH, I'VE BEEN WORKING ON MY FINGERING...
OOH!
NICE DOUBLE ENTENDRE!
OOOHHHHH
MEGG?
I NEED HELP ASSEMBLING MY BABY SEAT FOR THE CAR...
OKAY...
OKAY, I'M COMING...

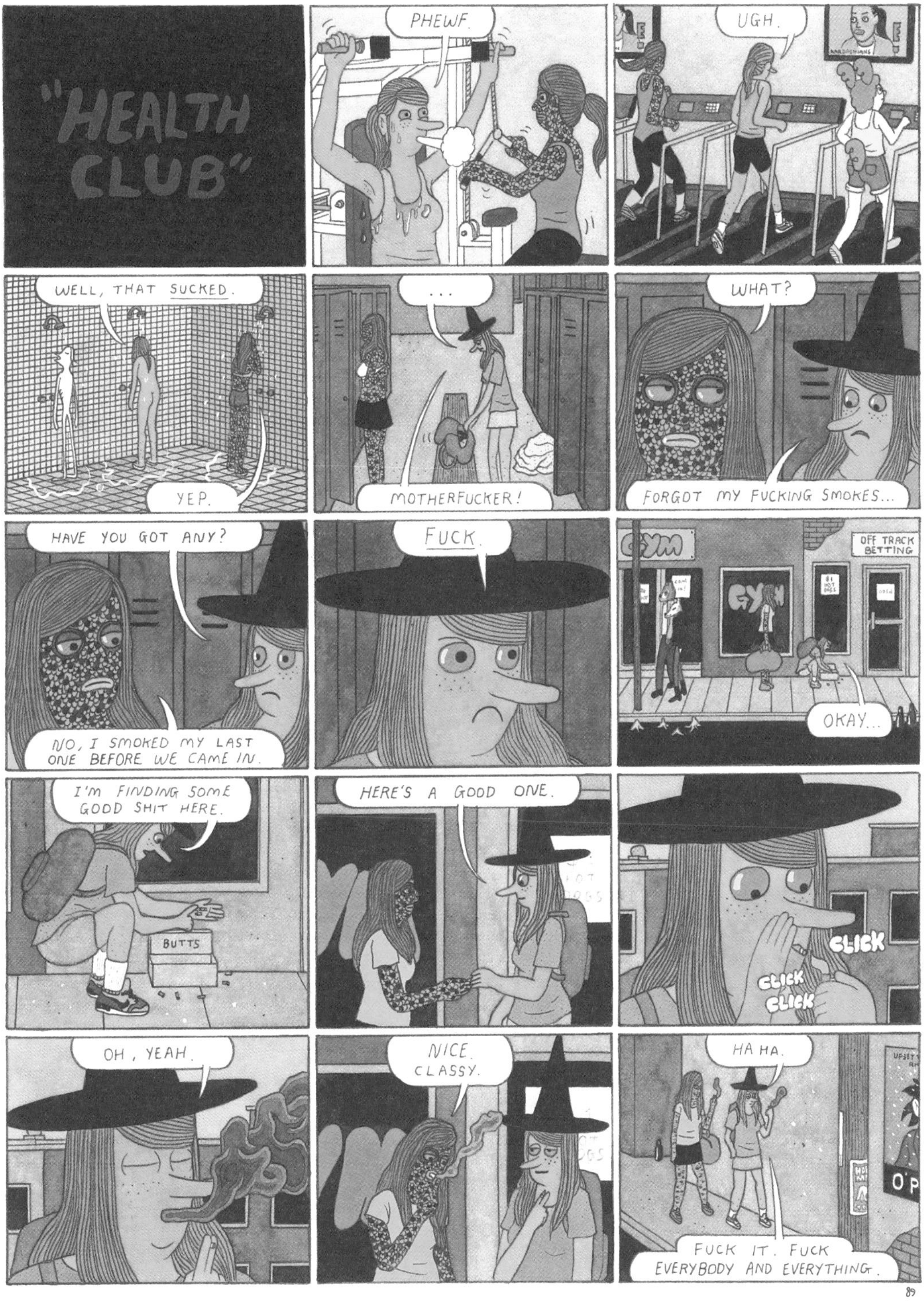
"HEALTH CLUB"
PHEWF.
UGH.
WELL, THAT SUCKED.
YEP.
...
MOTHERFUCKER!
WHAT?
FORGOT MY FUCKING SMOKES...
HAVE YOU GOT ANY?
NO, I SMOKED MY LAST ONE BEFORE WE CAME IN.
FUCK.
GYM
OFF TRACK BETTING
OKAY...
I'M FINDING SOME GOOD SHIT HERE.
BUTTS
HERE'S A GOOD ONE.
CLICK
CLICK
CLICK
OH, YEAH.
NICE. CLASSY.
HA HA.
FUCK IT. FUCK EVERYBODY AND EVERYTHING.

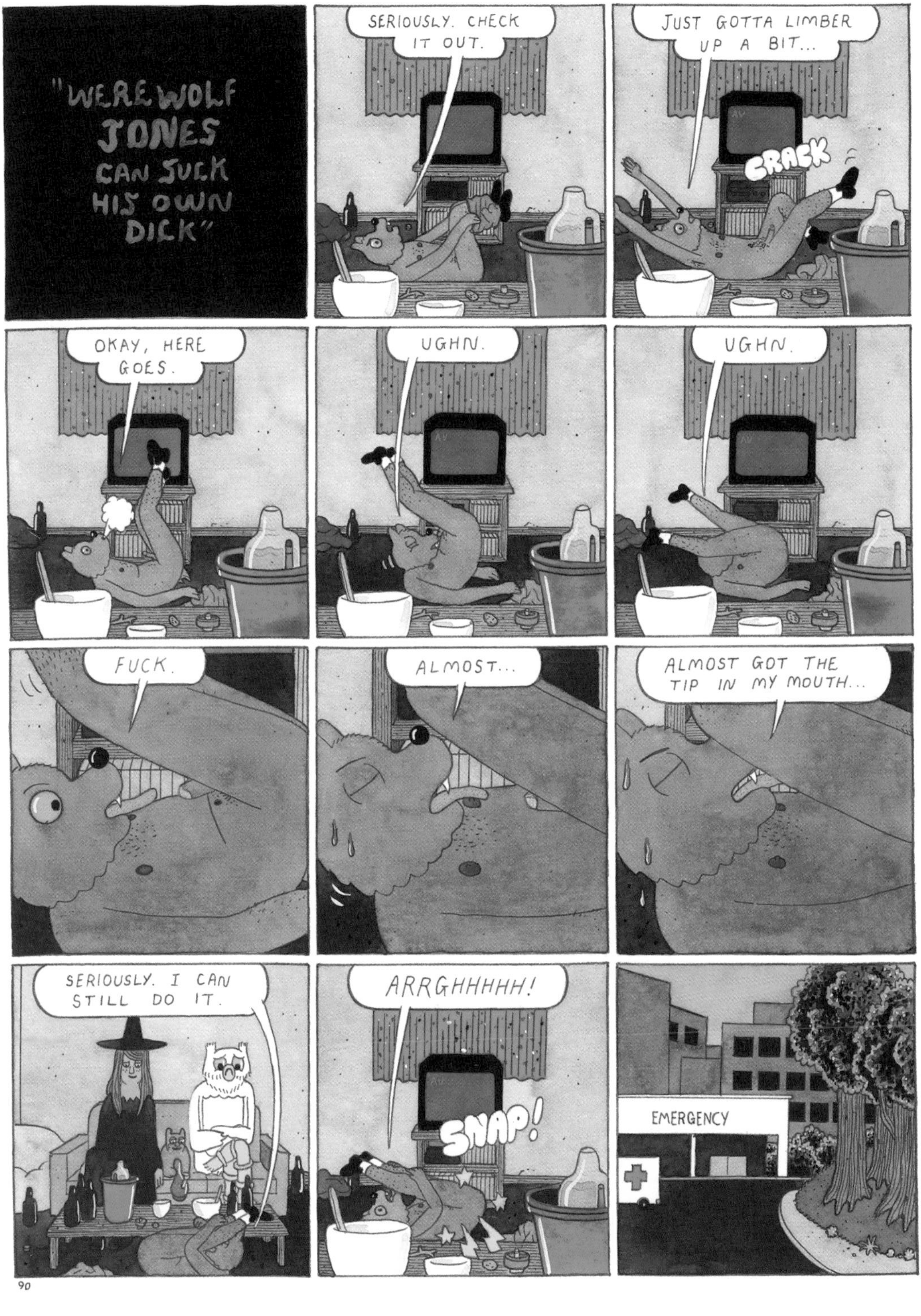
"WEREWOLF JONES CAN SUCK HIS OWN DICK"
SERIOUSLY. CHECK IT OUT.
JUST GOTTA LIMBER UP A BIT...
CRACK
OKAY, HERE GOES.
UGHN.
UGHN.
FUCK.
ALMOST...
ALMOST GOT THE TIP IN MY MOUTH...
SERIOUSLY. I CAN STILL DO IT.
ARRGHHHHH!
SNAP!
EMERGENCY

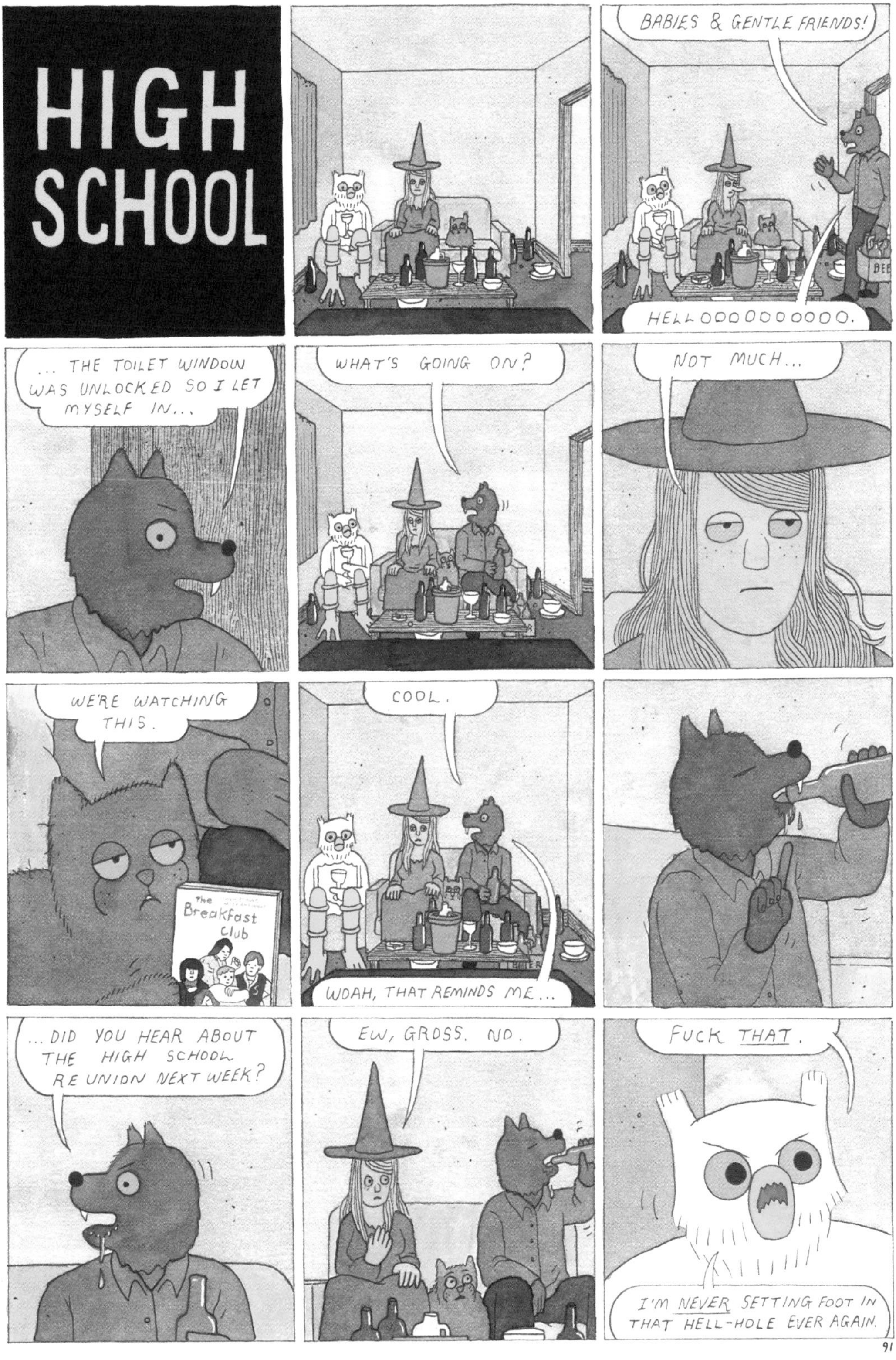
HIGH SCHOOL
BABIES & GENTLE FRIENDS!
HELLOOOOOOOOOO.
... THE TOILET WINDOW WAS UNLOCKED SO I LET MYSELF IN...
WHAT'S GOING ON?
NOT MUCH...
WE'RE WATCHING THIS.
The Breakfast Club
COOL.
WOAH, THAT REMINDS ME...
... DID YOU HEAR ABOUT THE HIGH SCHOOL RE UNION NEXT WEEK?
EW, GROSS. NO.
FUCK THAT.
I'M NEVER SETTING FOOT IN THAT HELL-HOLE EVER AGAIN.

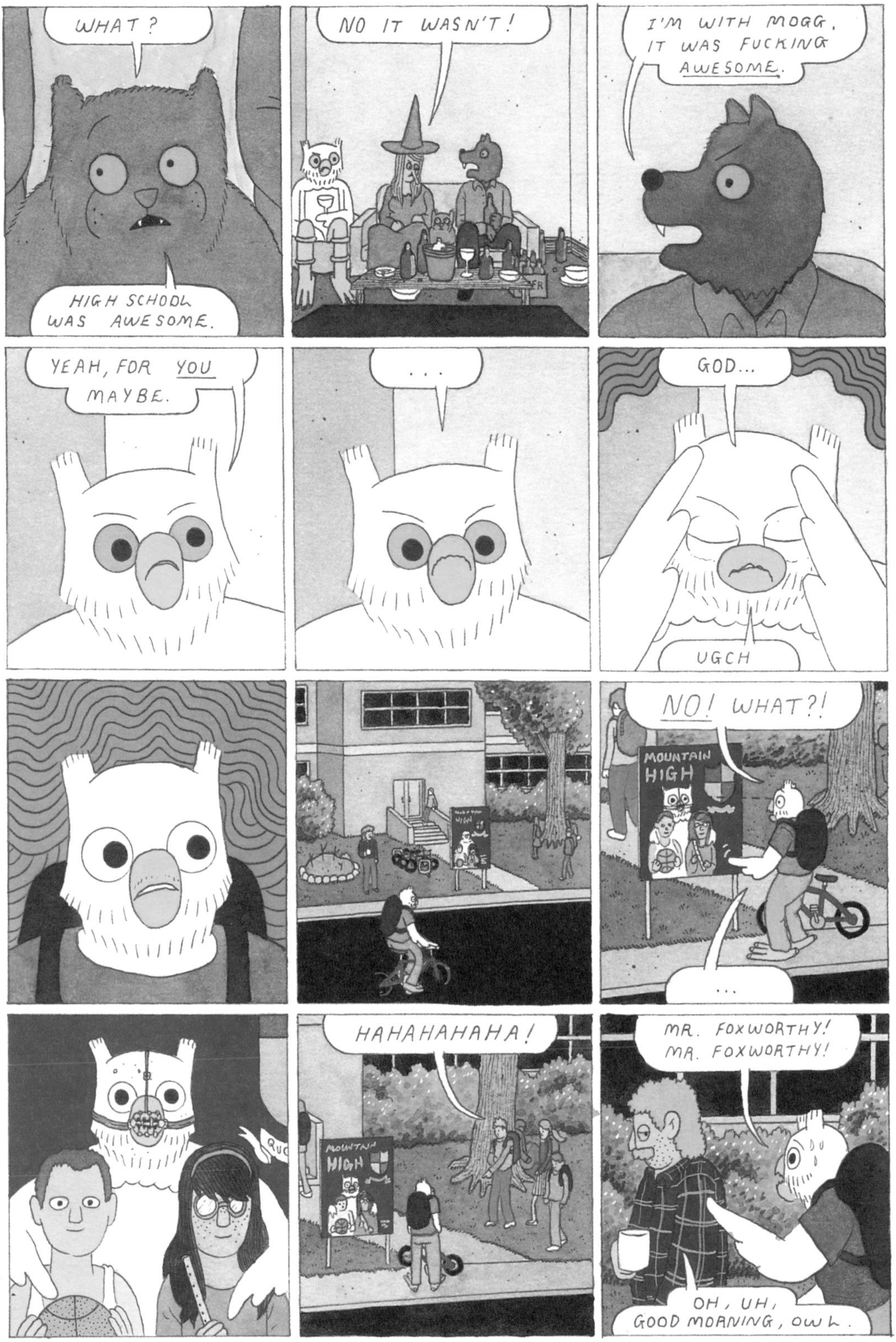
WHAT?
HIGH SCHOOL WAS AWESOME.
NO IT WASN'T!
I'M WITH MOGG. IT WAS FUCKING AWESOME.
YEAH, FOR YOU MAYBE.
...
GOD...
UGCH
MOUNTAIN HIGH
NO! WHAT?!
...
HAHAHAHAHA!
MOUNTAIN HIGH
MR. FOXWORTHY! MR. FOXWORTHY!
OH, UH, GOOD MORNING, OWL.

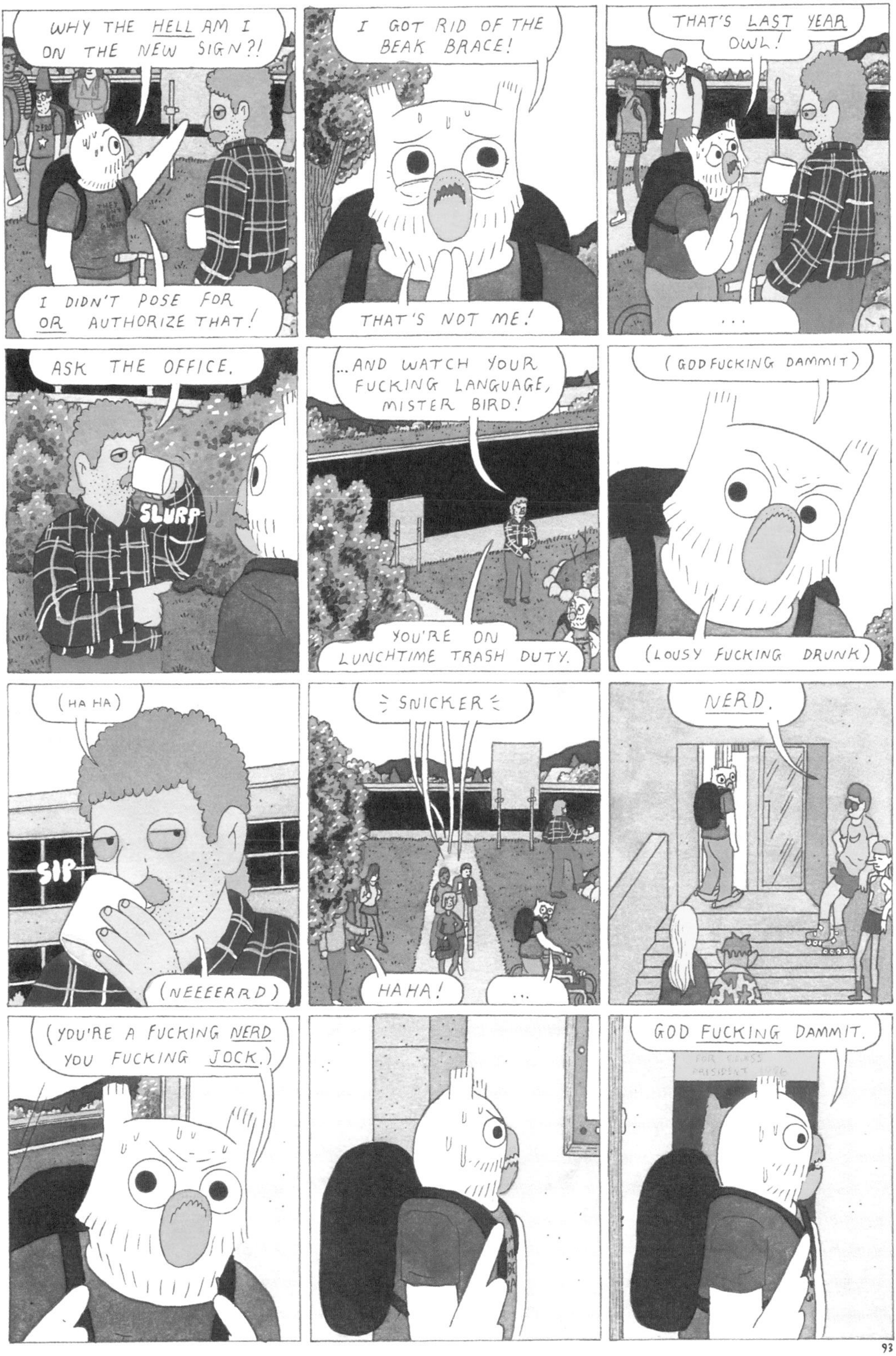
WHY THE HELL AM I ON THE NEW SIGN?!
I DIDN'T POSE FOR OR AUTHORIZE THAT!
I GOT RID OF THE BEAK BRACE!
THAT'S NOT ME!
THAT'S LAST YEAR OWL!
...
ASK THE OFFICE.
SLURP
...AND WATCH YOUR FUCKING LANGUAGE, MISTER BIRD!
YOU'RE ON LUNCHTIME TRASH DUTY.
(GODFUCKING DAMMIT)
(LOUSY FUCKING DRUNK)
(HA HA)
SIP
(NEEEERRD)
SNICKER
HAHA!
...
NERD.
(YOU'RE A FUCKING NERD YOU FUCKING JOCK.)
GOD FUCKING DAMMIT.

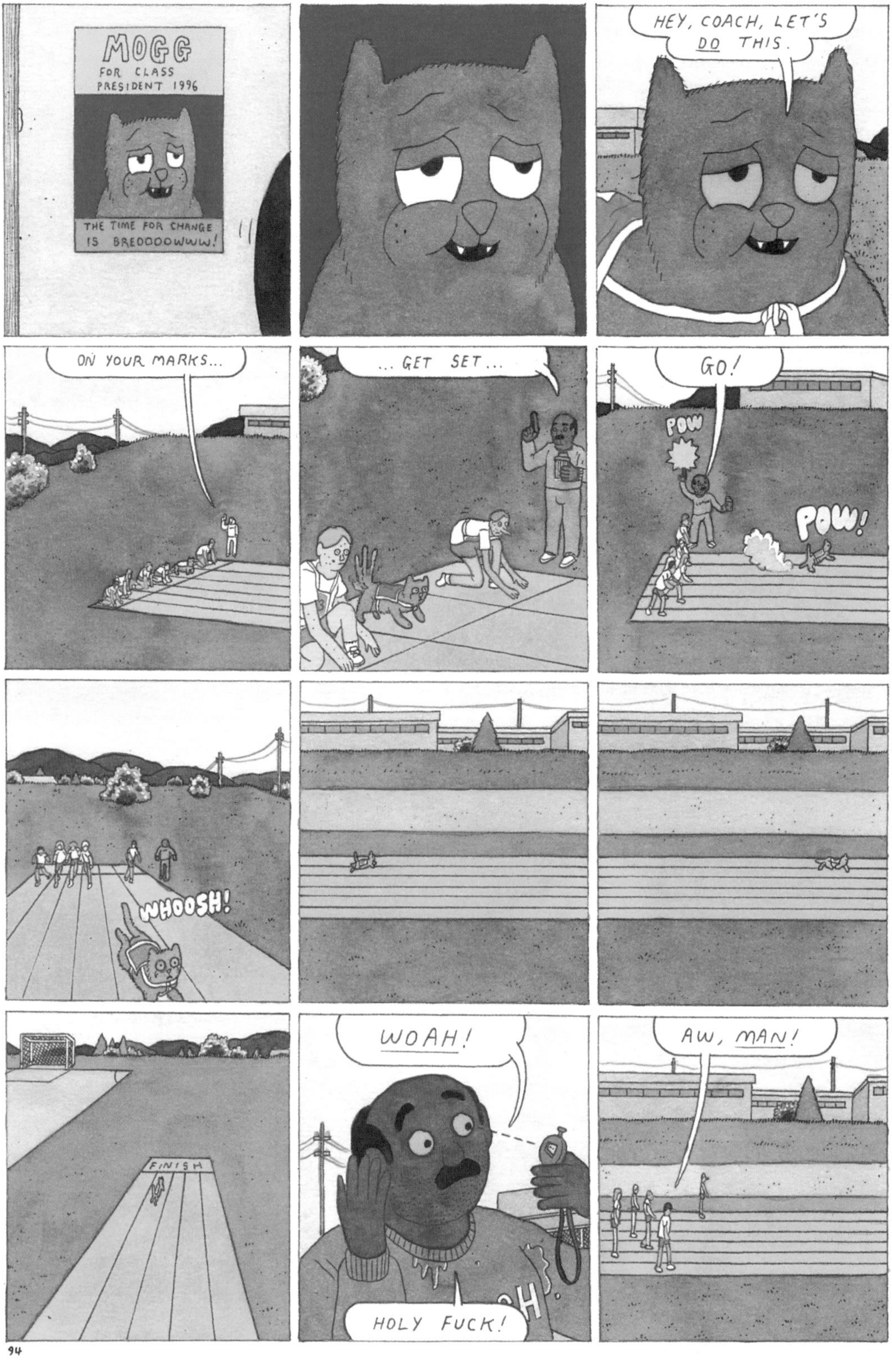
MOGG
FOR CLASS PRESIDENT 1996
THE TIME FOR CHANGE IS BREOOOOWWW!
HEY, COACH, LET'S DO THIS.
ON YOUR MARKS...
...GET SET...
GO!
POW
POW!
WHOOSH!
FINISH
WOAH!
HOLY FUCK!
AW, MAN!

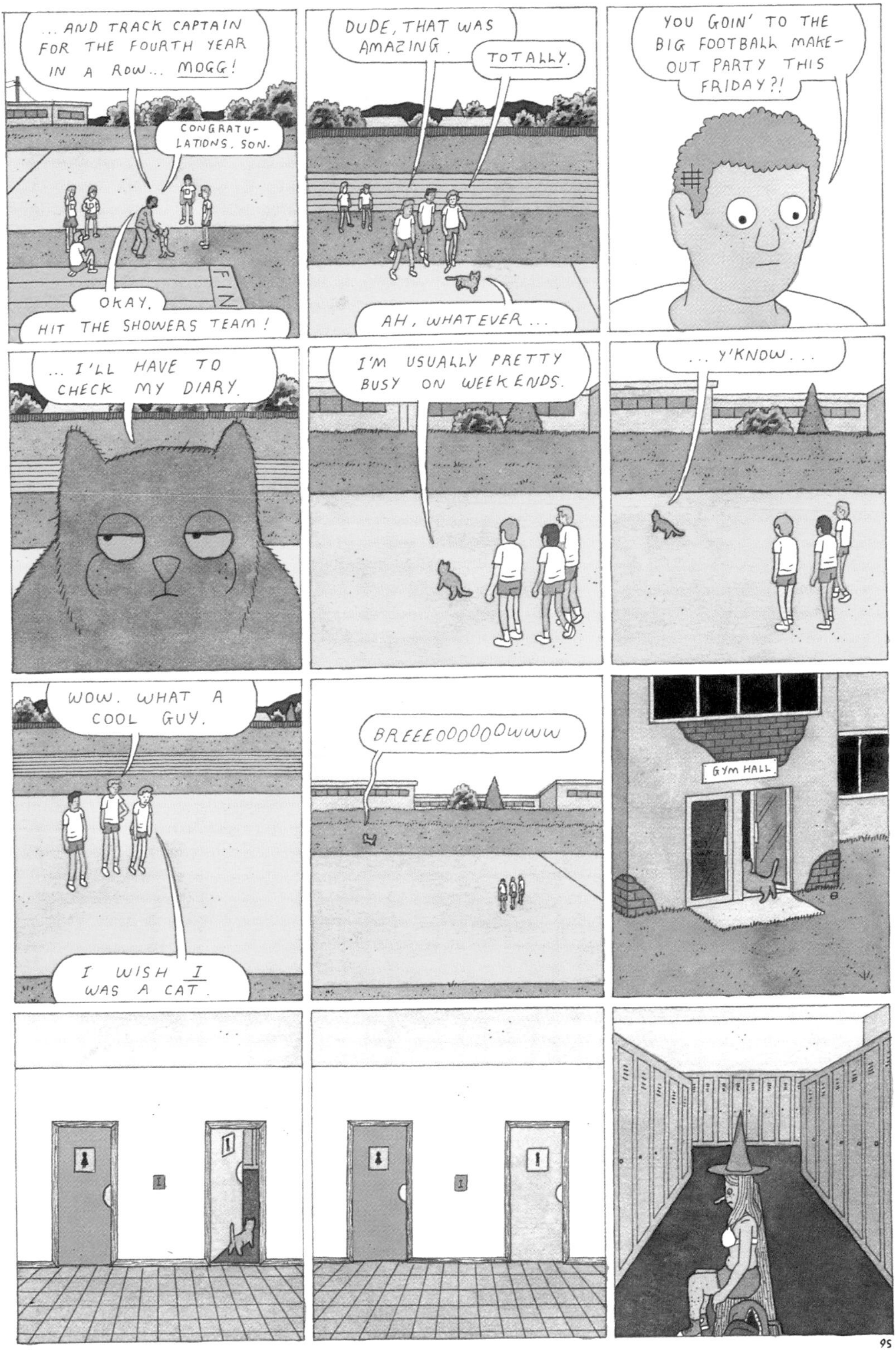
... AND TRACK CAPTAIN FOR THE FOURTH YEAR IN A ROW... MOGG!
CONGRATU-LATIONS, SON.
OKAY. HIT THE SHOWERS TEAM!
FIN
DUDE, THAT WAS AMAZING.
TOTALLY.
AH, WHATEVER...
YOU GOIN' TO THE BIG FOOTBALL MAKE-OUT PARTY THIS FRIDAY?!
... I'LL HAVE TO CHECK MY DIARY.
I'M USUALLY PRETTY BUSY ON WEEKENDS.
... Y'KNOW...
WOW. WHAT A COOL GUY.
I WISH I WAS A CAT.
BREEEOOOOOOWWW
GYM HALL

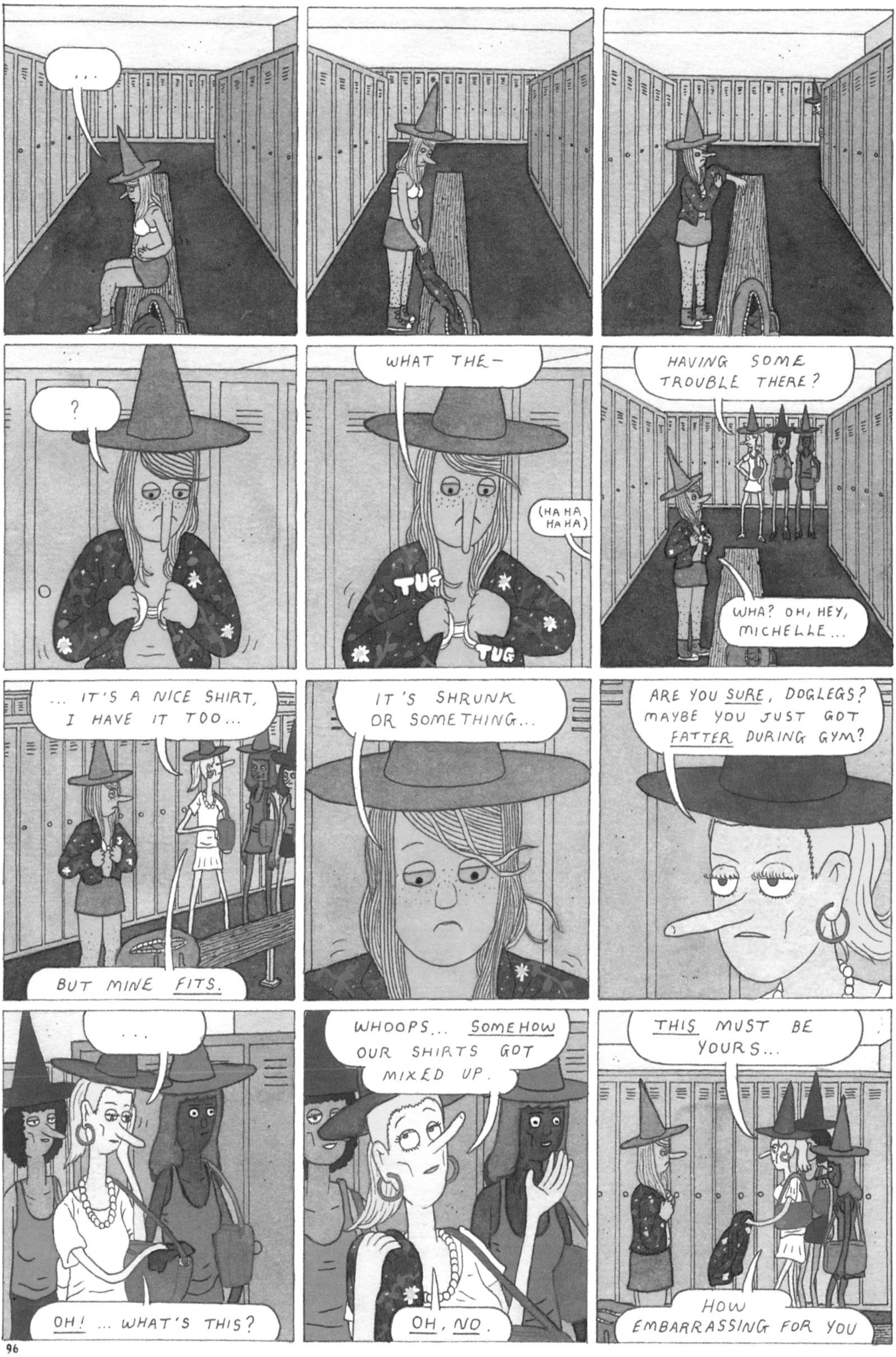
. . .
?
WHAT THE—
(HA HA HA HA)
HAVING SOME TROUBLE THERE?
WHA? OH, HEY, MICHELLE...
... IT'S A NICE SHIRT, I HAVE IT TOO...
BUT MINE FITS.
IT'S SHRUNK OR SOMETHING...
ARE YOU SURE, DOGLEGS? MAYBE YOU JUST GOT FATTER DURING GYM?
. . .
OH! ... WHAT'S THIS?
WHOOPS... SOMEHOW OUR SHIRTS GOT MIXED UP.
OH, NO.
THIS MUST BE YOURS...
HOW EMBARRASSING FOR YOU

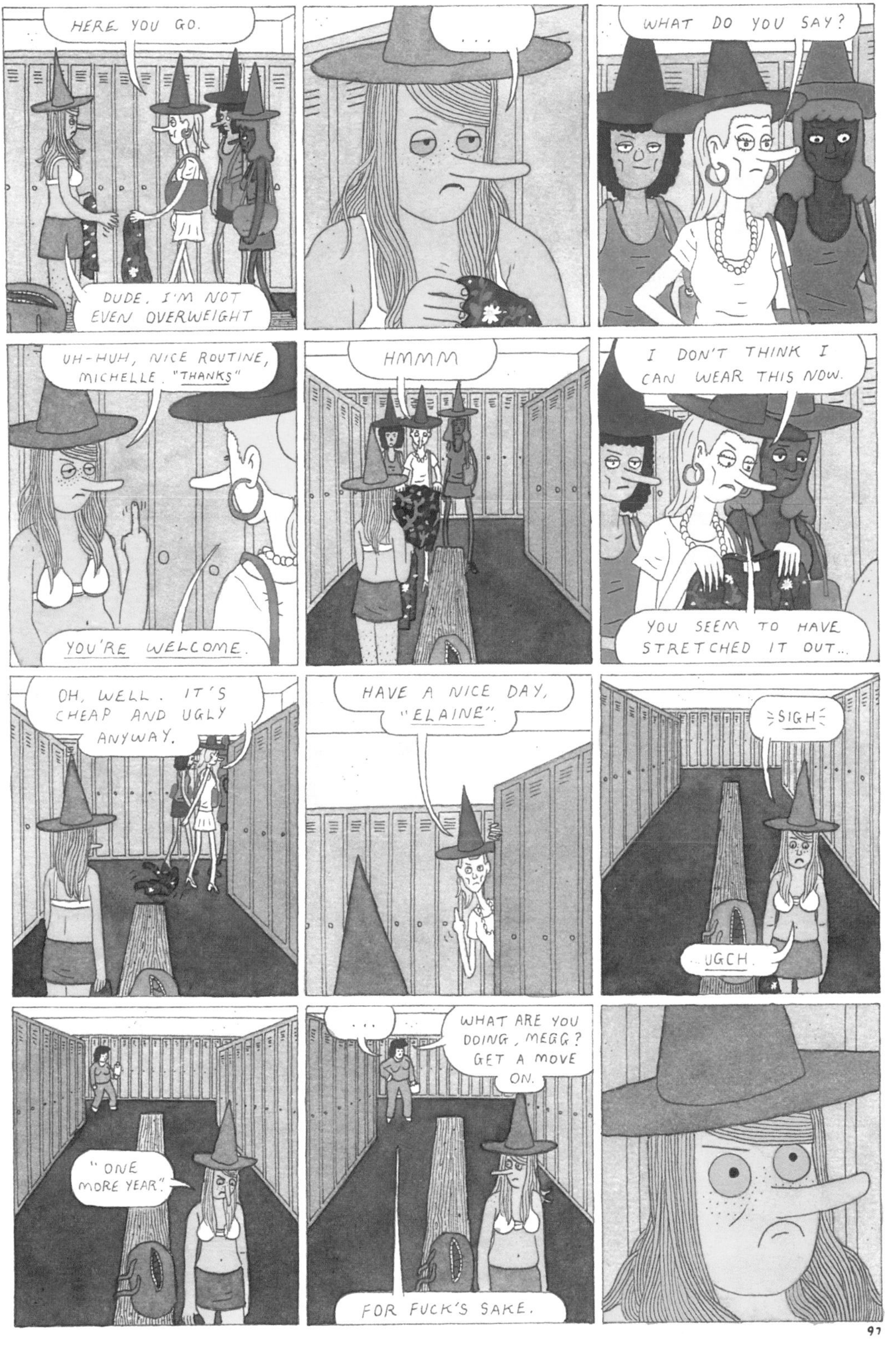
HERE YOU GO.
DUDE. I'M NOT EVEN OVERWEIGHT
...
WHAT DO YOU SAY?
UH-HUH, NICE ROUTINE, MICHELLE. "THANKS"
YOU'RE WELCOME.
HMMM
I DON'T THINK I CAN WEAR THIS NOW.
YOU SEEM TO HAVE STRETCHED IT OUT...
OH, WELL. IT'S CHEAP AND UGLY ANYWAY.
HAVE A NICE DAY, "ELAINE".
SIGH
...UGCH.
"ONE MORE YEAR".
...
WHAT ARE YOU DOING, MEGG? GET A MOVE ON.
FOR FUCK'S SAKE.

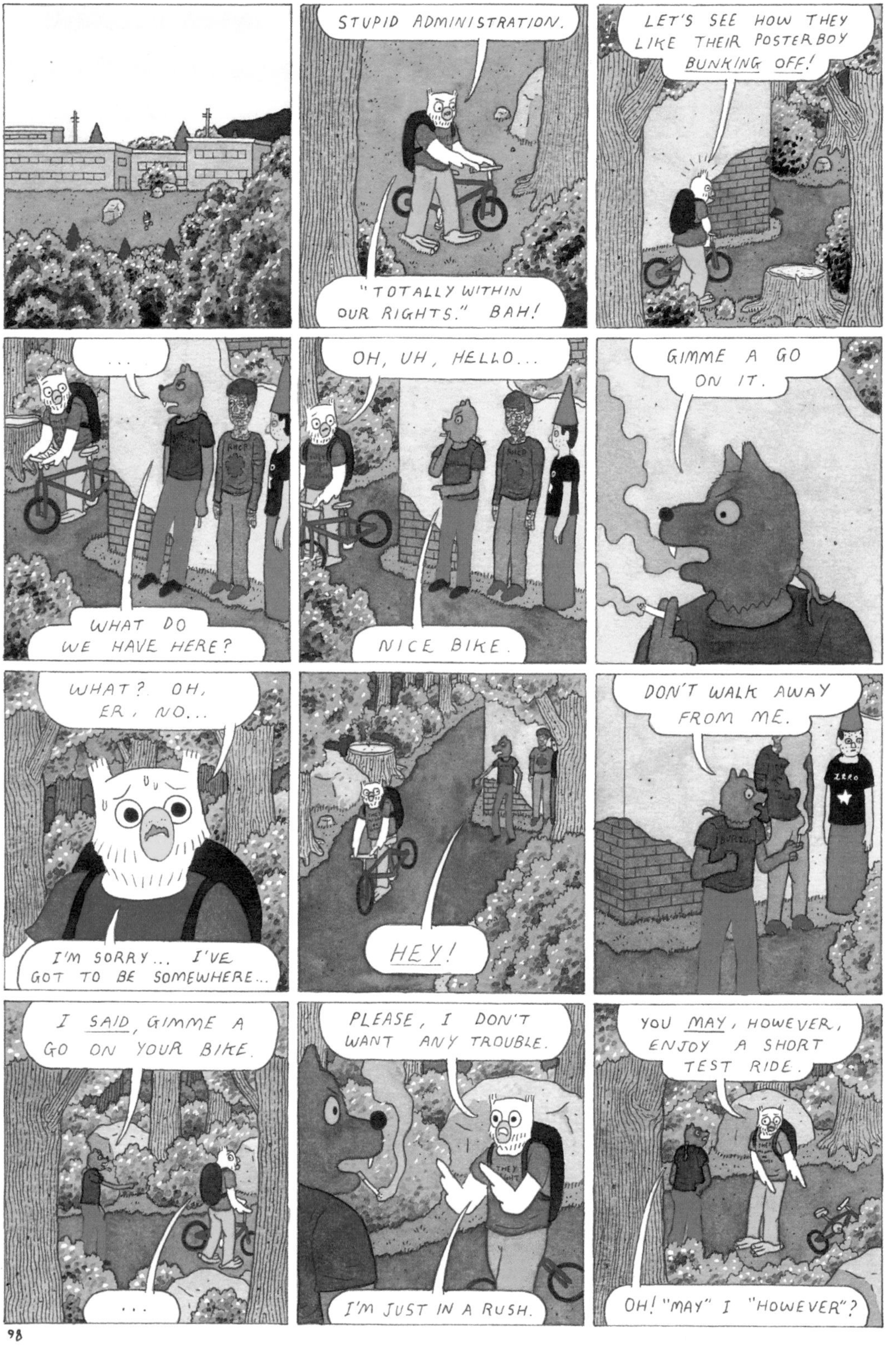
STUPID ADMINISTRATION.
"TOTALLY WITHIN OUR RIGHTS." BAH!
LET'S SEE HOW THEY LIKE THEIR POSTERBOY BUNKING OFF!
...
WHAT DO WE HAVE HERE?
OH, UH, HELLO...
NICE BIKE.
GIMME A GO ON IT.
WHAT? OH, ER, NO...
I'M SORRY... I'VE GOT TO BE SOMEWHERE...
HEY!
DON'T WALK AWAY FROM ME.
ZERO
I SAID, GIMME A GO ON YOUR BIKE.
...
PLEASE, I DON'T WANT ANY TROUBLE.
I'M JUST IN A RUSH.
YOU MAY, HOWEVER, ENJOY A SHORT TEST RIDE.
OH! "MAY" I "HOWEVER"?

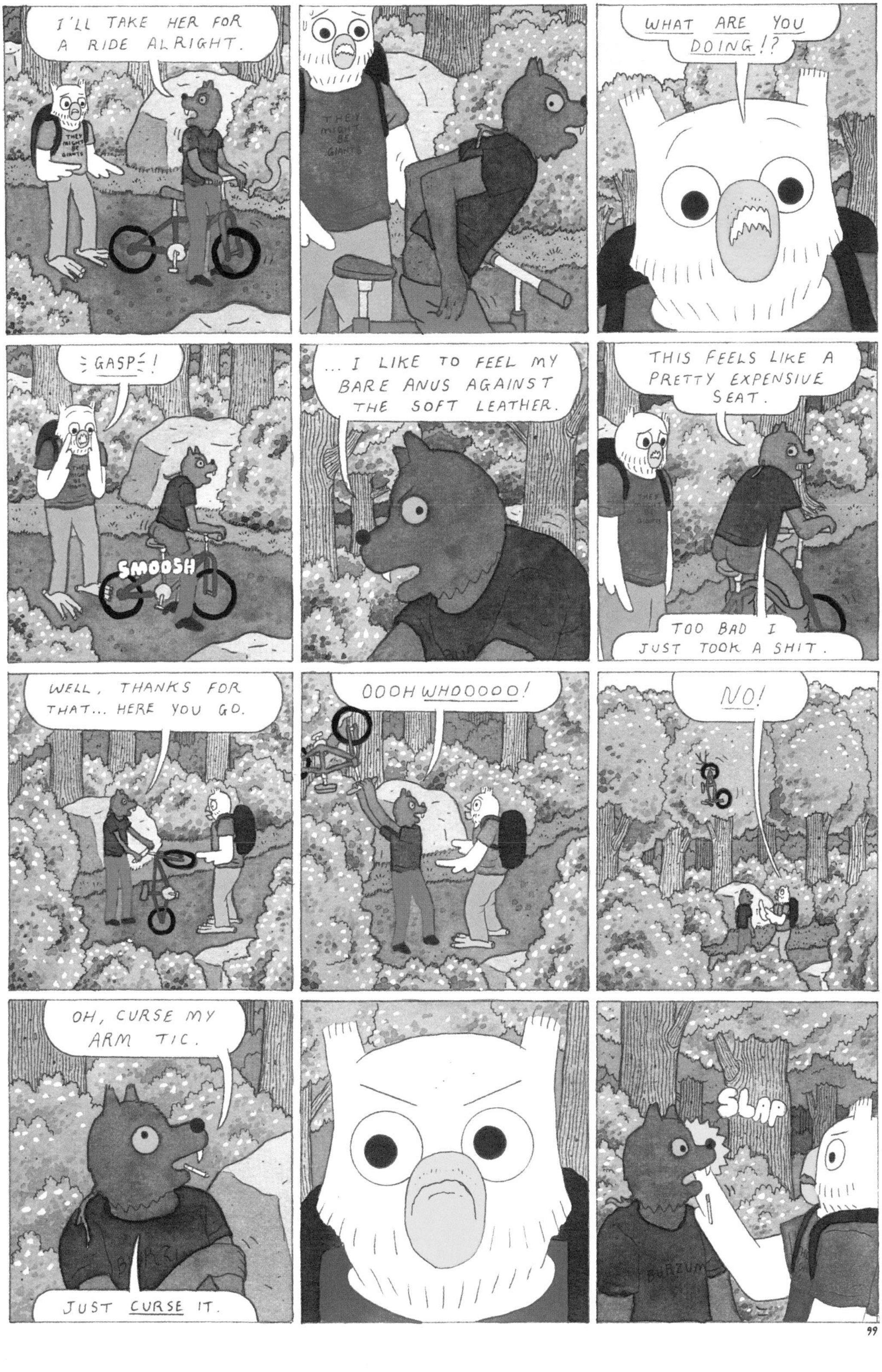
I'LL TAKE HER FOR A RIDE ALRIGHT.
THEY MIGHT BE GIANTS
WHAT ARE YOU DOING!?
GASP!
SMOOSH
...I LIKE TO FEEL MY BARE ANUS AGAINST THE SOFT LEATHER.
THIS FEELS LIKE A PRETTY EXPENSIVE SEAT.
TOO BAD I JUST TOOK A SHIT.
WELL, THANKS FOR THAT... HERE YOU GO.
OOOH WHOOOOO!
NO!
OH, CURSE MY ARM TIC.
JUST CURSE IT.
SLAP
BURZUM

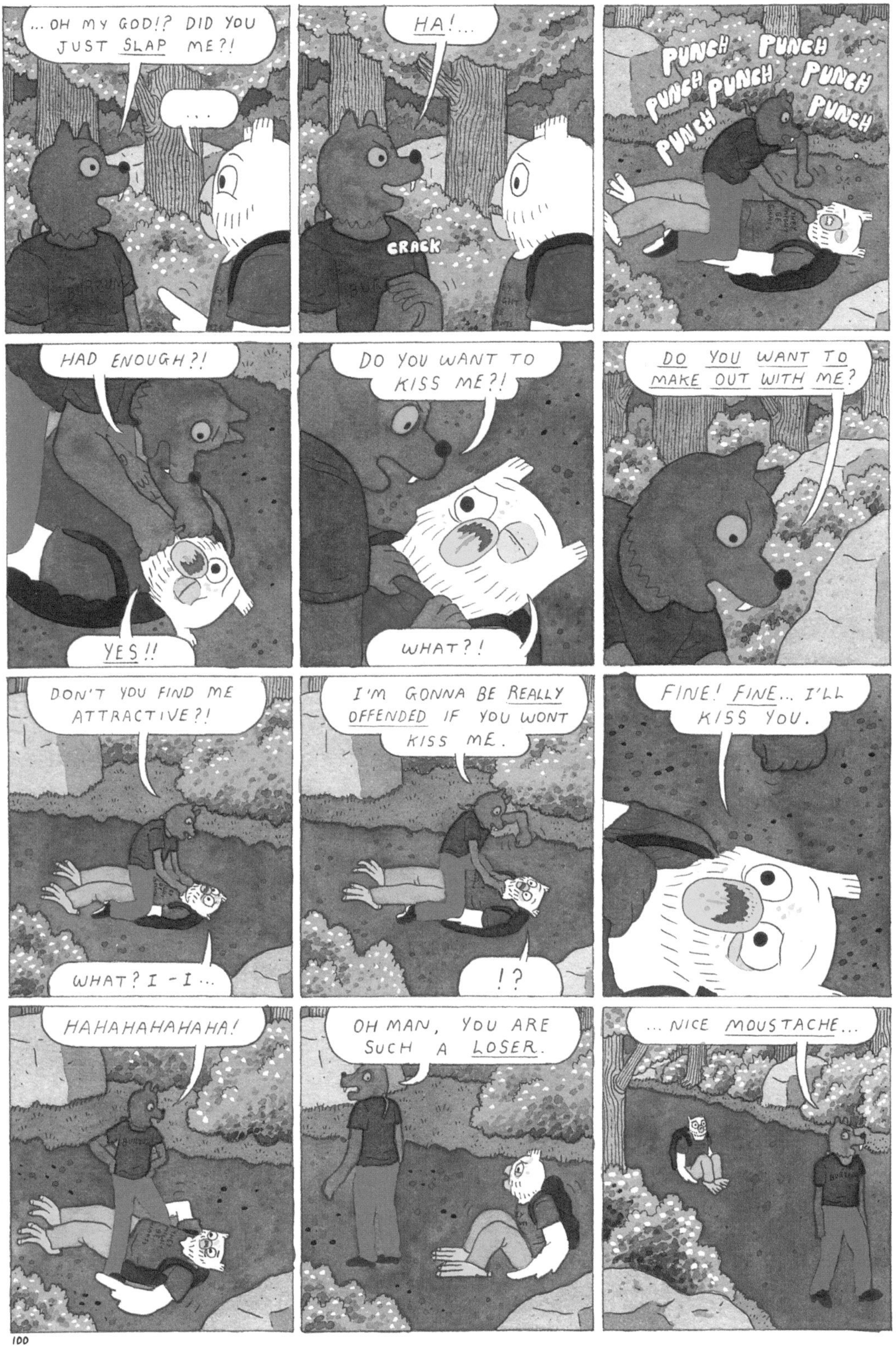
...OH MY GOD!? DID YOU JUST SLAP ME?!
...
HA!...
CRACK
PUNCH PUNCH PUNCH PUNCH PUNCH PUNCH PUNCH PUNCH
HAD ENOUGH?!
YES!!
DO YOU WANT TO KISS ME?!
WHAT?!
DO YOU WANT TO MAKE OUT WITH ME?
DON'T YOU FIND ME ATTRACTIVE?!
WHAT? I-I...
I'M GONNA BE REALLY OFFENDED IF YOU WONT KISS ME.
!?
FINE! FINE... I'LL KISS YOU.
HAHAHAHAHAHA!
OH MAN, YOU ARE SUCH A LOSER.
...NICE MOUSTACHE...

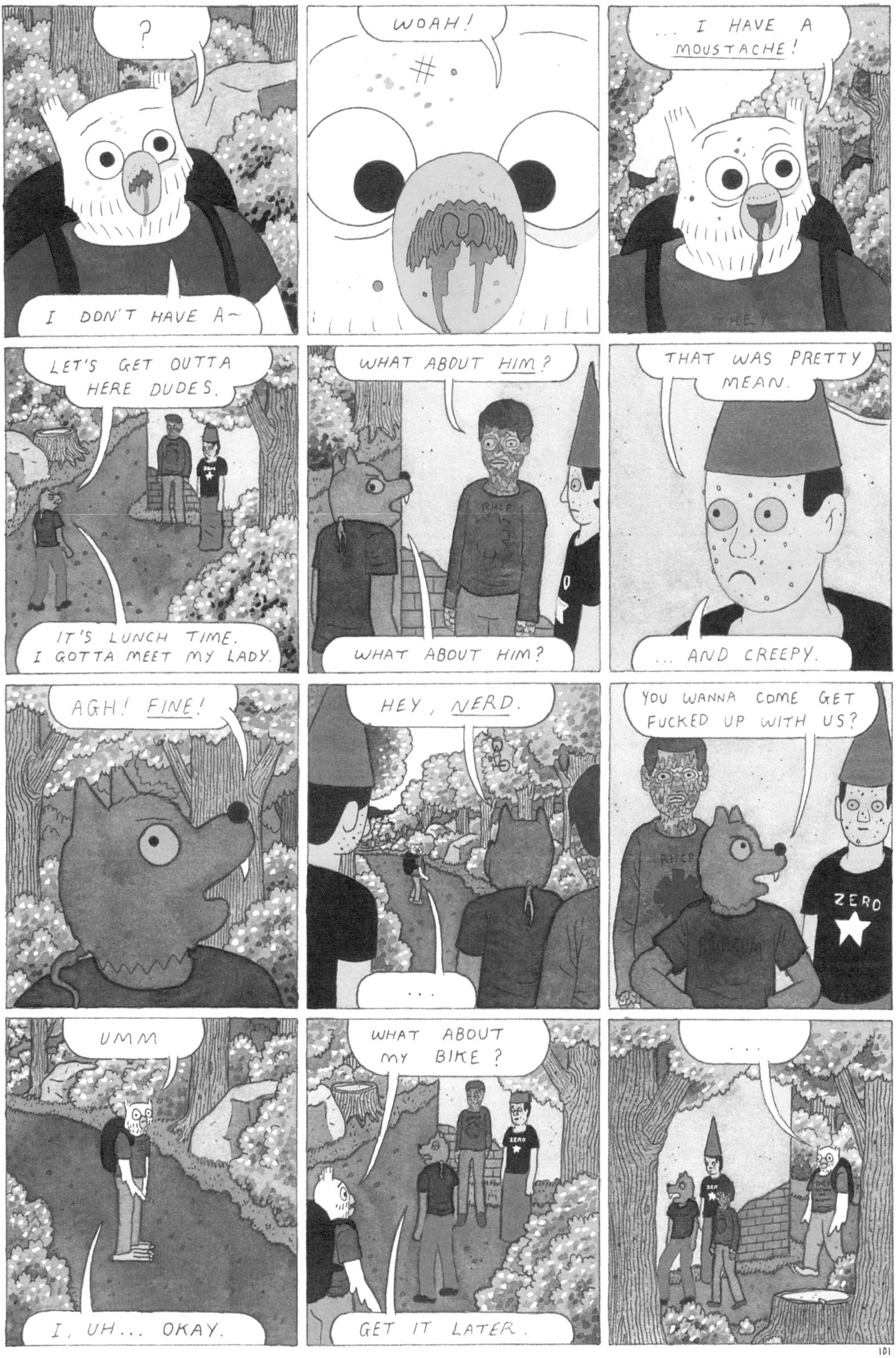
?
I DON'T HAVE A~
WOAH!
... I HAVE A MOUSTACHE!
LET'S GET OUTTA HERE DUDES.
IT'S LUNCH TIME. I GOTTA MEET MY LADY.
WHAT ABOUT HIM?
WHAT ABOUT HIM?
THAT WAS PRETTY MEAN.
... AND CREEPY.
AGH! FINE!
HEY, NERD.
...
YOU WANNA COME GET FUCKED UP WITH US?
ZERO
UMM
I, UH... OKAY.
WHAT ABOUT MY BIKE?
GET IT LATER.
...

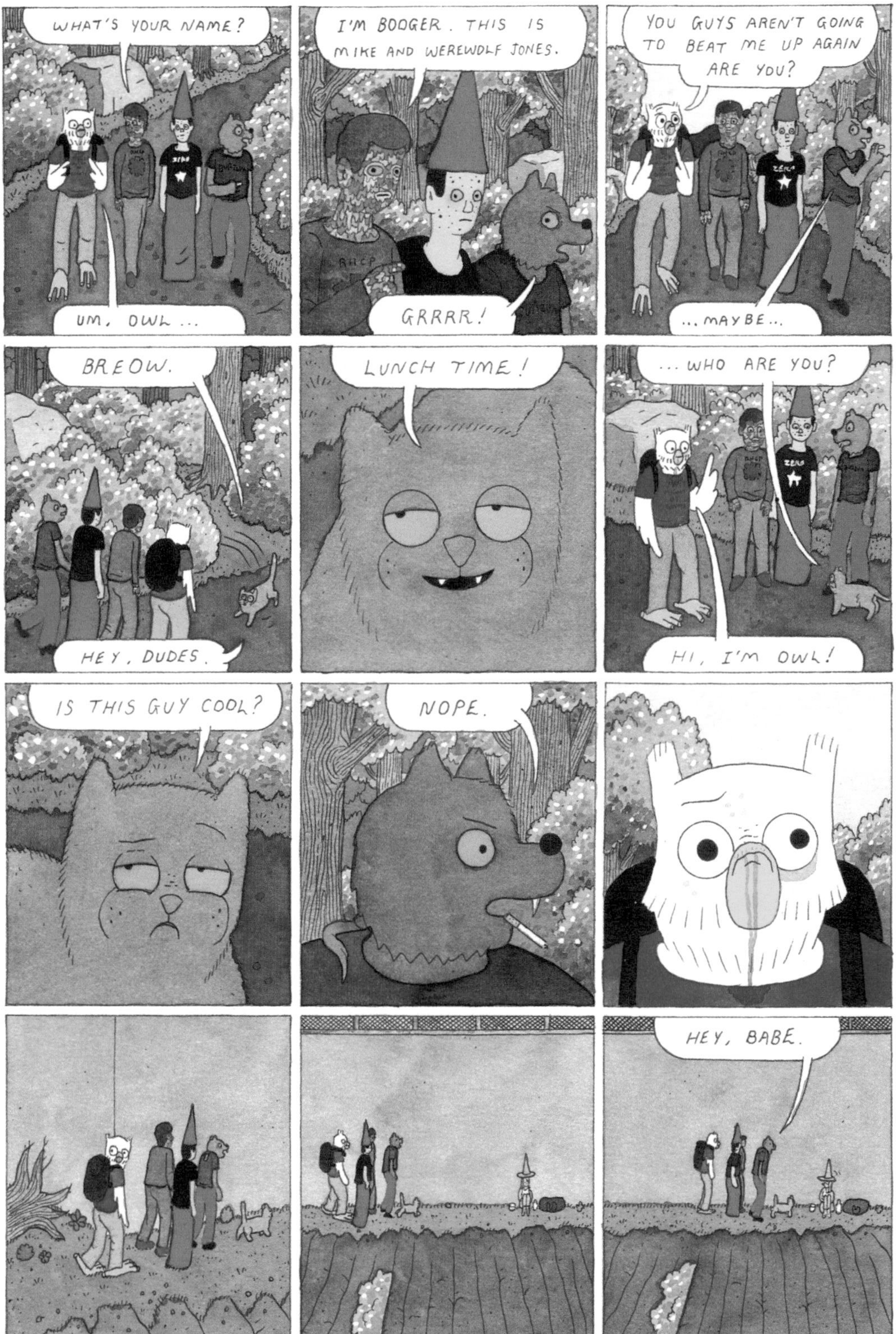
WHAT'S YOUR NAME?
UM, OWL...
I'M BOOGER. THIS IS MIKE AND WEREWOLF JONES.
GRRRR!
YOU GUYS AREN'T GOING TO BEAT ME UP AGAIN ARE YOU?
...MAYBE...
BREOW.
HEY, DUDES.
LUNCH TIME!
...WHO ARE YOU?
HI, I'M OWL!
IS THIS GUY COOL?
NOPE.
HEY, BABE.

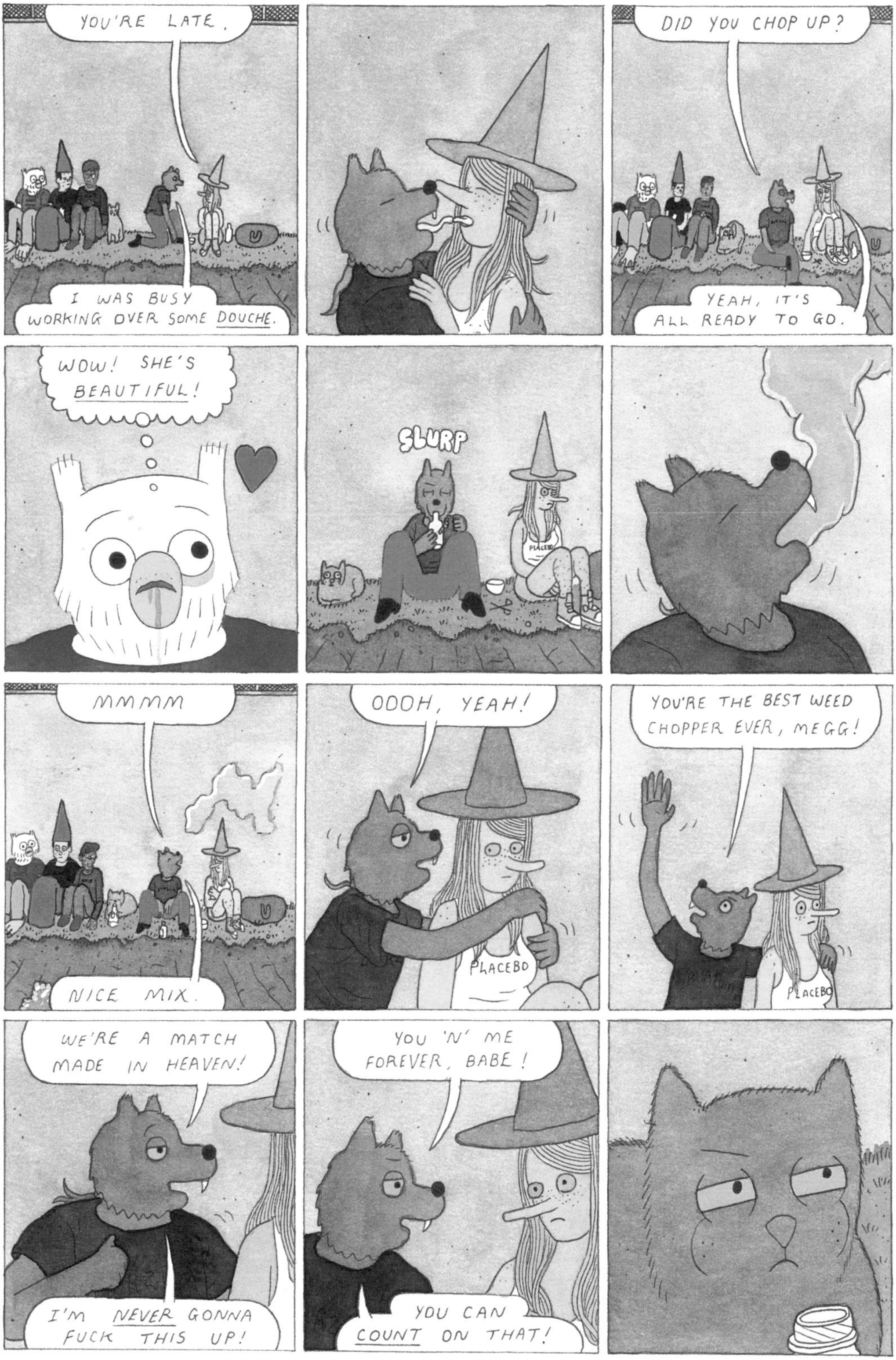
YOU'RE LATE.
I WAS BUSY WORKING OVER SOME DOUCHE.
DID YOU CHOP UP?
YEAH, IT'S ALL READY TO GO.
WOW! SHE'S BEAUTIFUL!
SLURP
MMMM
NICE MIX.
OOOH, YEAH!
YOU'RE THE BEST WEED CHOPPER EVER, MEGG!
PLACEBO
WE'RE A MATCH MADE IN HEAVEN!
I'M NEVER GONNA FUCK THIS UP!
YOU 'N' ME FOREVER, BABE!
YOU CAN COUNT ON THAT!

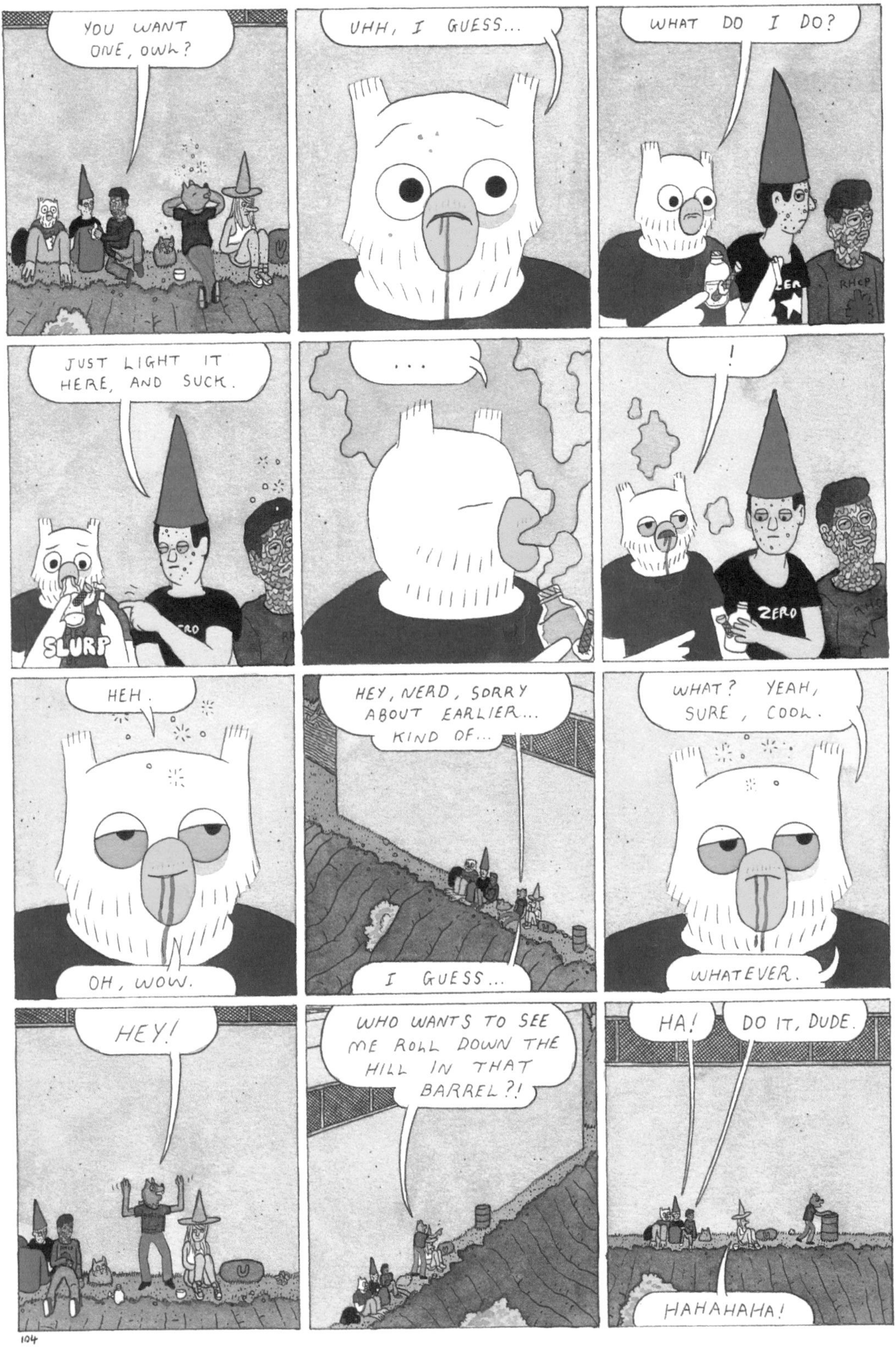
YOU WANT ONE, OWL?
UHH, I GUESS...
WHAT DO I DO?
RHCP
JUST LIGHT IT HERE, AND SUCK.
SLURP
...
!
ZERO
HEH.
OH, WOW.
HEY, NERD, SORRY ABOUT EARLIER... KIND OF...
I GUESS...
WHAT? YEAH, SURE, COOL.
WHATEVER.
HEY!
WHO WANTS TO SEE ME ROLL DOWN THE HILL IN THAT BARREL?!
HA!
DO IT, DUDE.
HAHAHAHA!

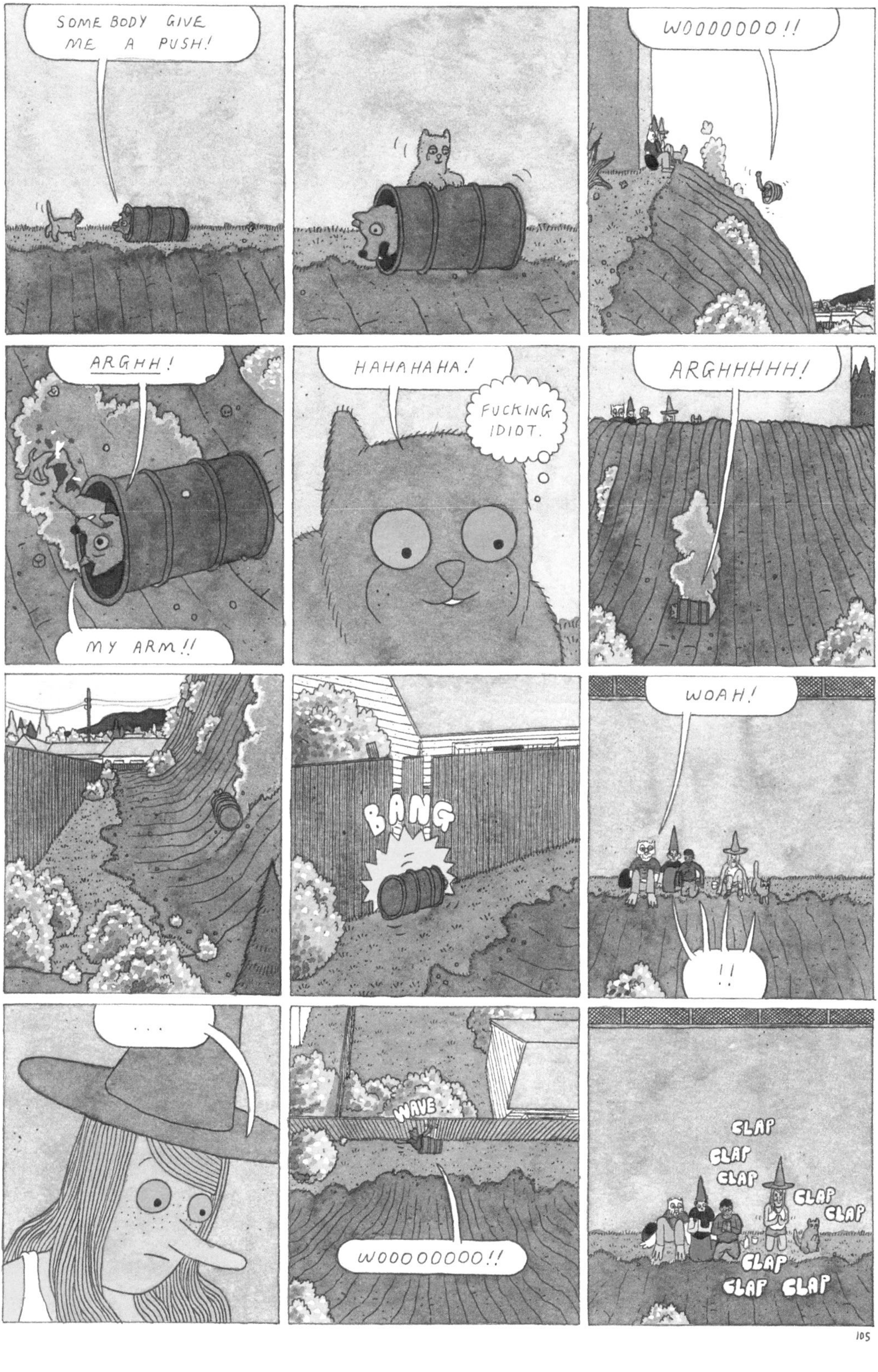
SOMEBODY GIVE ME A PUSH!
WOOOOOOO!!
ARGHH!
MY ARM!!
HAHAHAHA!
FUCKING IDIOT.
ARGHHHHH!
BANG
WOAH!
!!
...
WAVE
WOOOOOOOO!!
CLAP
CLAP
CLAP
CLAP
CLAP
CLAP
CLAP
CLAP

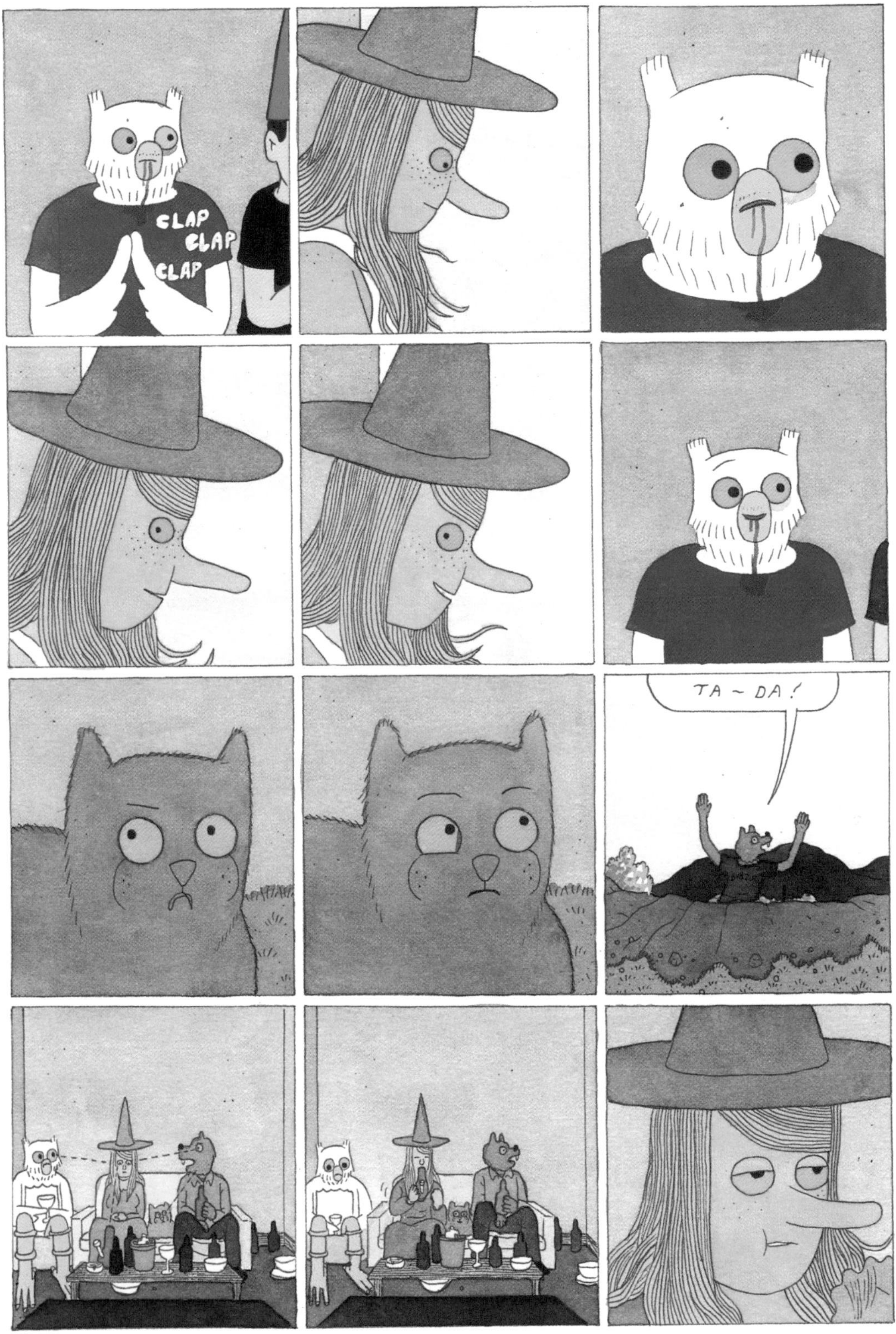
CLAP
CLAP
CLAP
TA ~ DA!

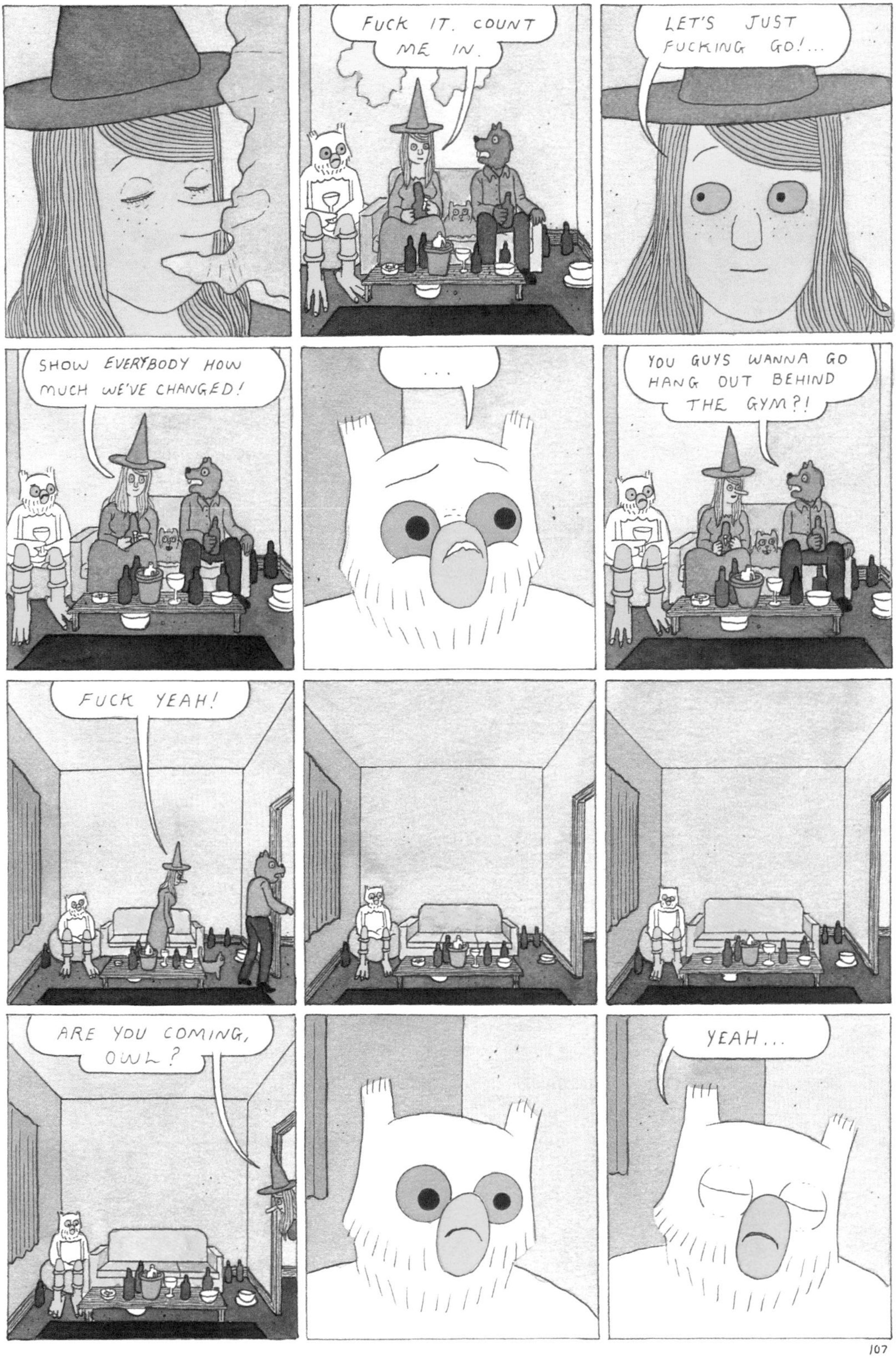
FUCK IT. COUNT ME IN.
LET'S JUST FUCKING GO!...
SHOW EVERYBODY HOW MUCH WE'VE CHANGED!
...
YOU GUYS WANNA GO HANG OUT BEHIND THE GYM?!
FUCK YEAH!
ARE YOU COMING, OWL?
YEAH...

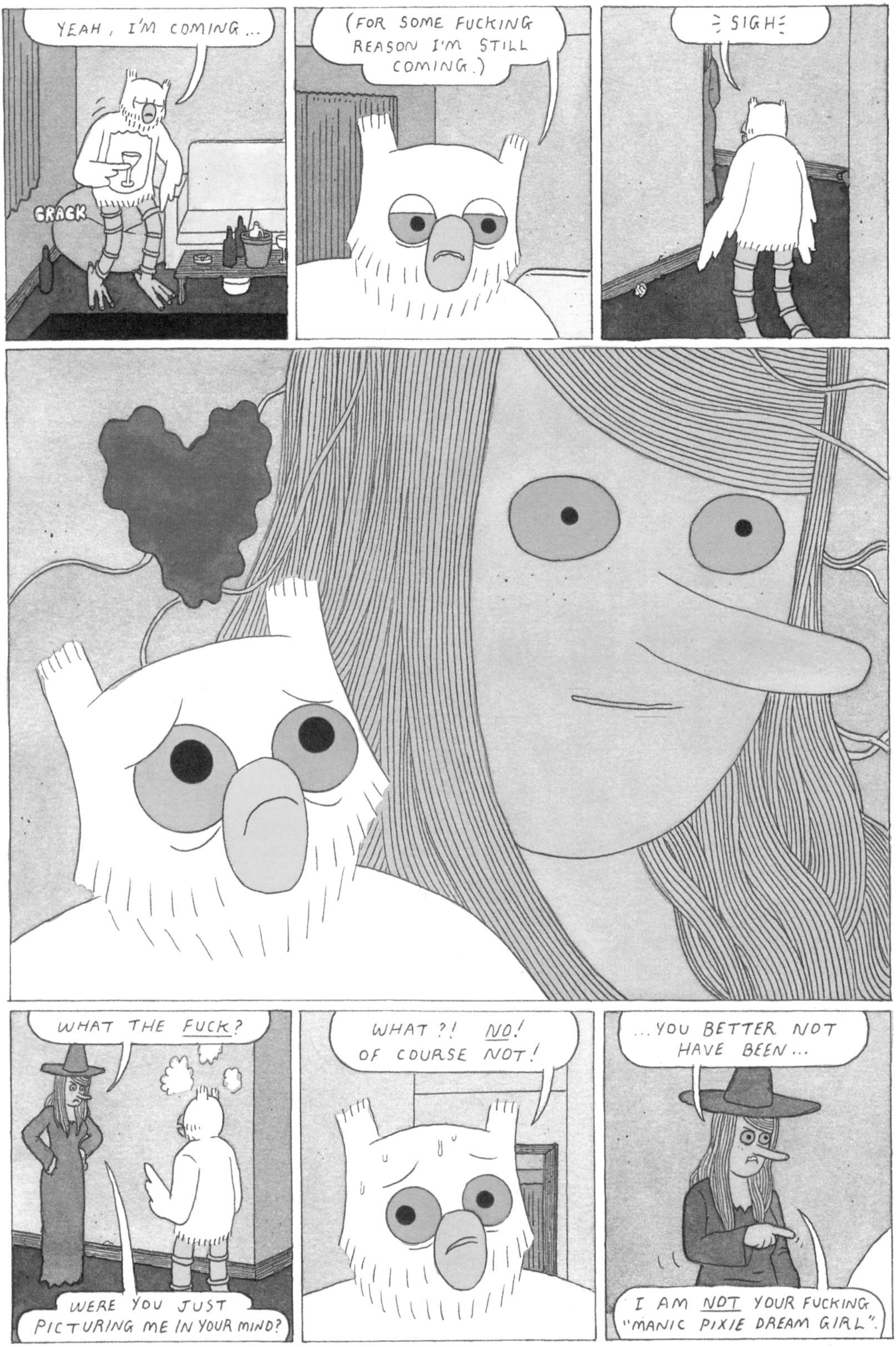
YEAH, I'M COMING...
CRACK
(FOR SOME FUCKING REASON I'M STILL COMING.)
SIGH
WHAT THE FUCK?
WERE YOU JUST PICTURING ME IN YOUR MIND?
WHAT?! NO! OF COURSE NOT!
...YOU BETTER NOT HAVE BEEN...
I AM NOT YOUR FUCKING "MANIC PIXIE DREAM GIRL".

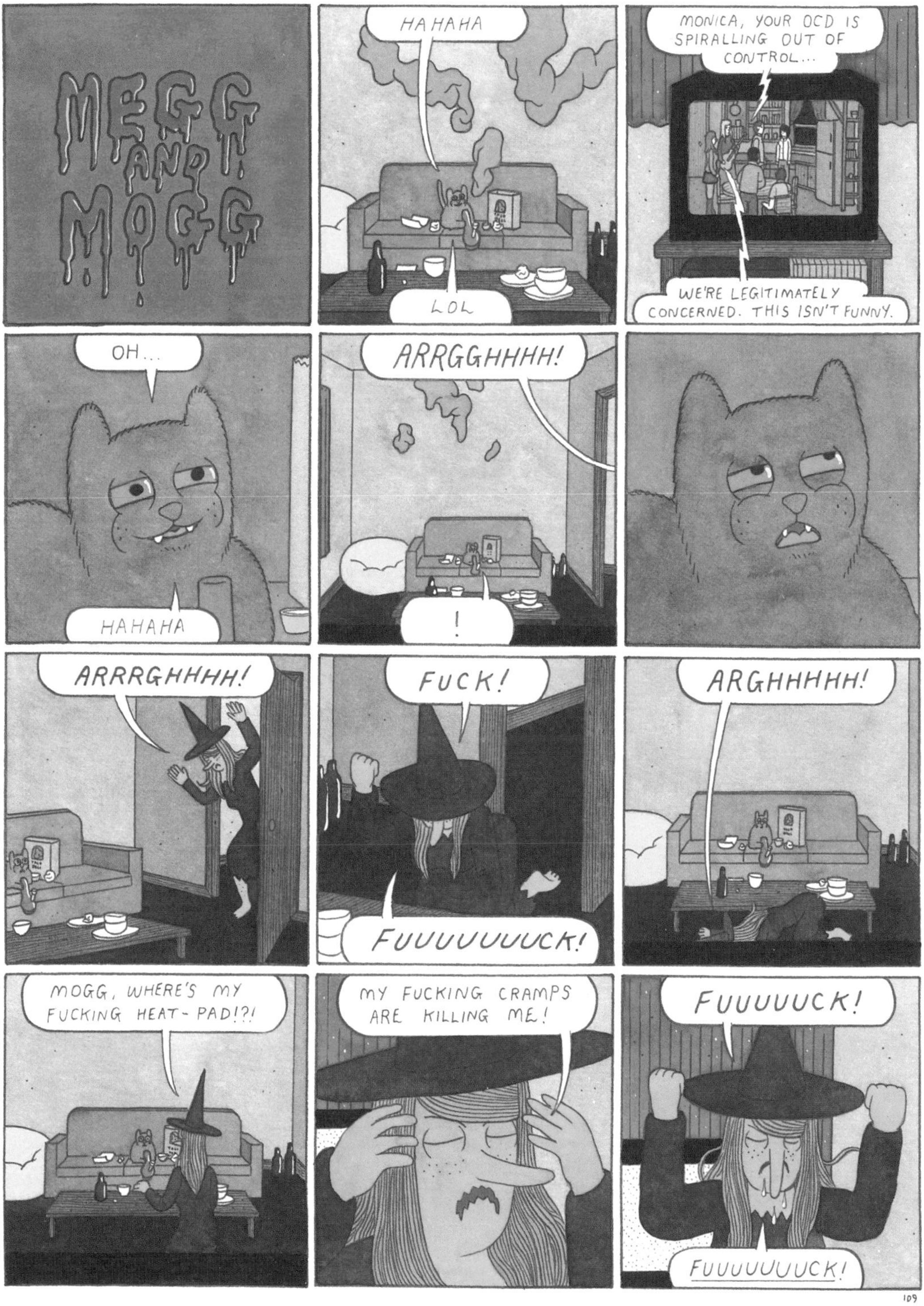
MEGG AND MOGG
HAHAHA
LOL
MONICA, YOUR OCD IS SPIRALLING OUT OF CONTROL...
WE'RE LEGITIMATELY CONCERNED. THIS ISN'T FUNNY.
OH...
HAHAHA
ARRGGHHHH!
!
ARRRGHHHH!
FUCK!
FUUUUUUUCK!
ARGHHHHH!
MOGG, WHERE'S MY FUCKING HEAT-PAD!?!
MY FUCKING CRAMPS ARE KILLING ME!
FUUUUUCK!
FUUUUUUUCK!

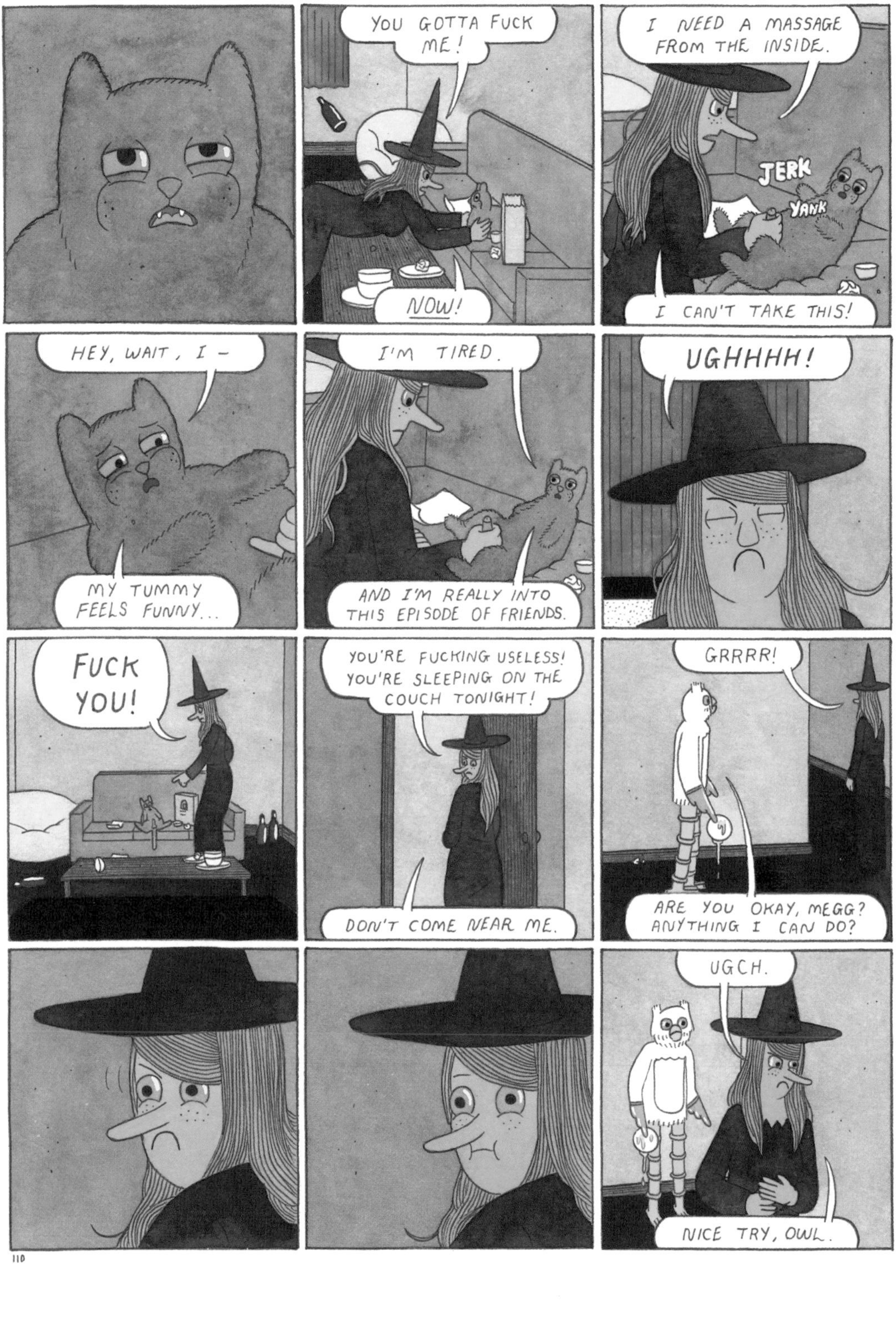
YOU GOTTA FUCK ME!
NOW!
I NEED A MASSAGE FROM THE INSIDE.
JERK
YANK
I CAN'T TAKE THIS!
HEY, WAIT, I –
MY TUMMY FEELS FUNNY...
I'M TIRED.
AND I'M REALLY INTO THIS EPISODE OF FRIENDS.
UGHHHH!
FUCK YOU!
YOU'RE FUCKING USELESS! YOU'RE SLEEPING ON THE COUCH TONIGHT!
DON'T COME NEAR ME.
GRRRR!
ARE YOU OKAY, MEGG? ANYTHING I CAN DO?
UGCH.
NICE TRY, OWL.

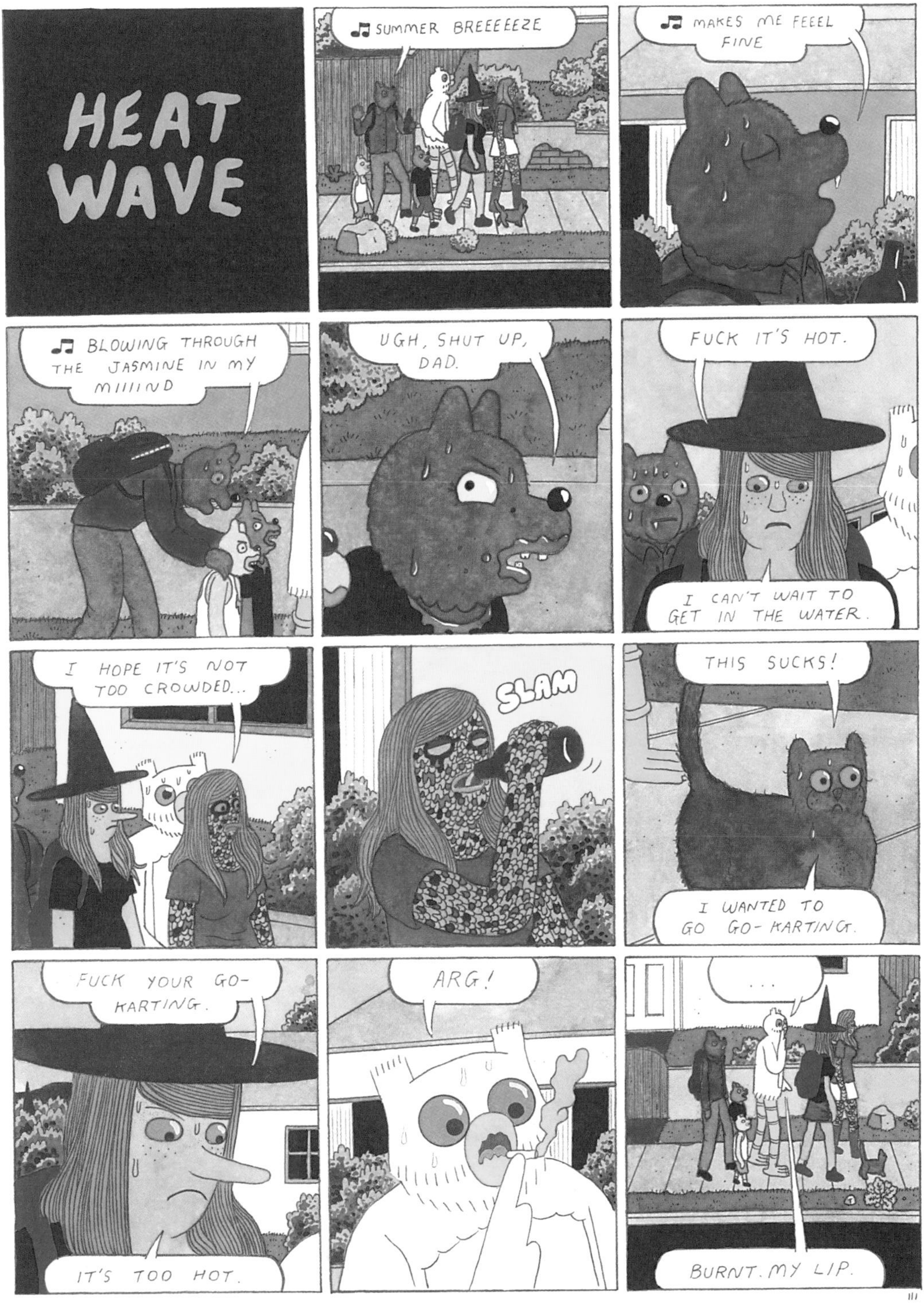
HEAT WAVE
♫ SUMMER BREEEEEZE
♫ MAKES ME FEEEL FINE
♫ BLOWING THROUGH THE JASMINE IN MY MIIIIND
UGH, SHUT UP, DAD.
FUCK IT'S HOT.
I CAN'T WAIT TO GET IN THE WATER.
I HOPE IT'S NOT TOO CROWDED...
SLAM
THIS SUCKS!
I WANTED TO GO GO-KARTING.
FUCK YOUR GO-KARTING.
IT'S TOO HOT.
ARG!
...
BURNT. MY LIP.

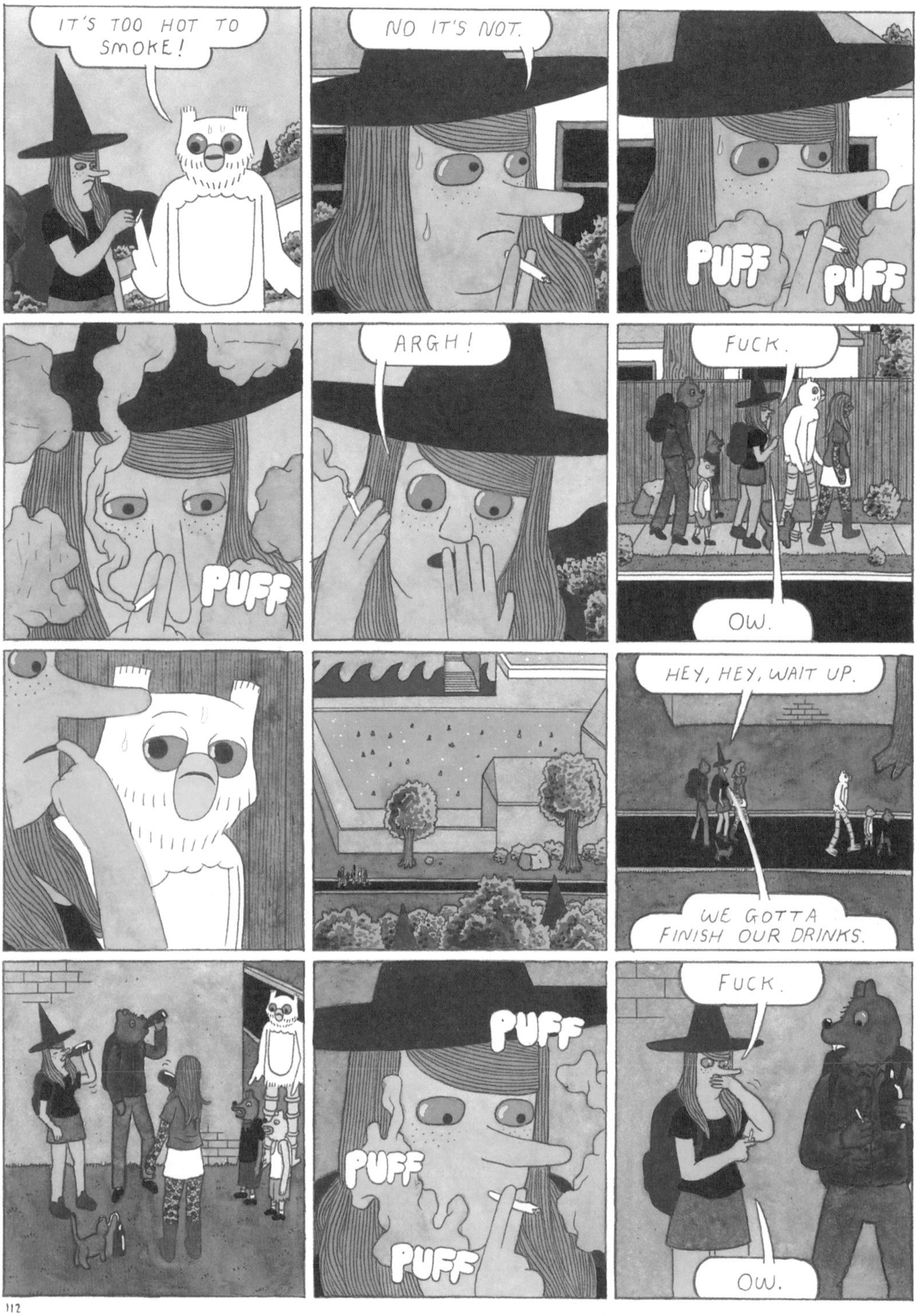
IT'S TOO HOT TO SMOKE!
NO IT'S NOT.
PUFF
PUFF
PUFF
ARGH!
FUCK.
OW.
HEY, HEY, WAIT UP.
WE GOTTA FINISH OUR DRINKS.
PUFF
PUFF
PUFF
FUCK.
OW.

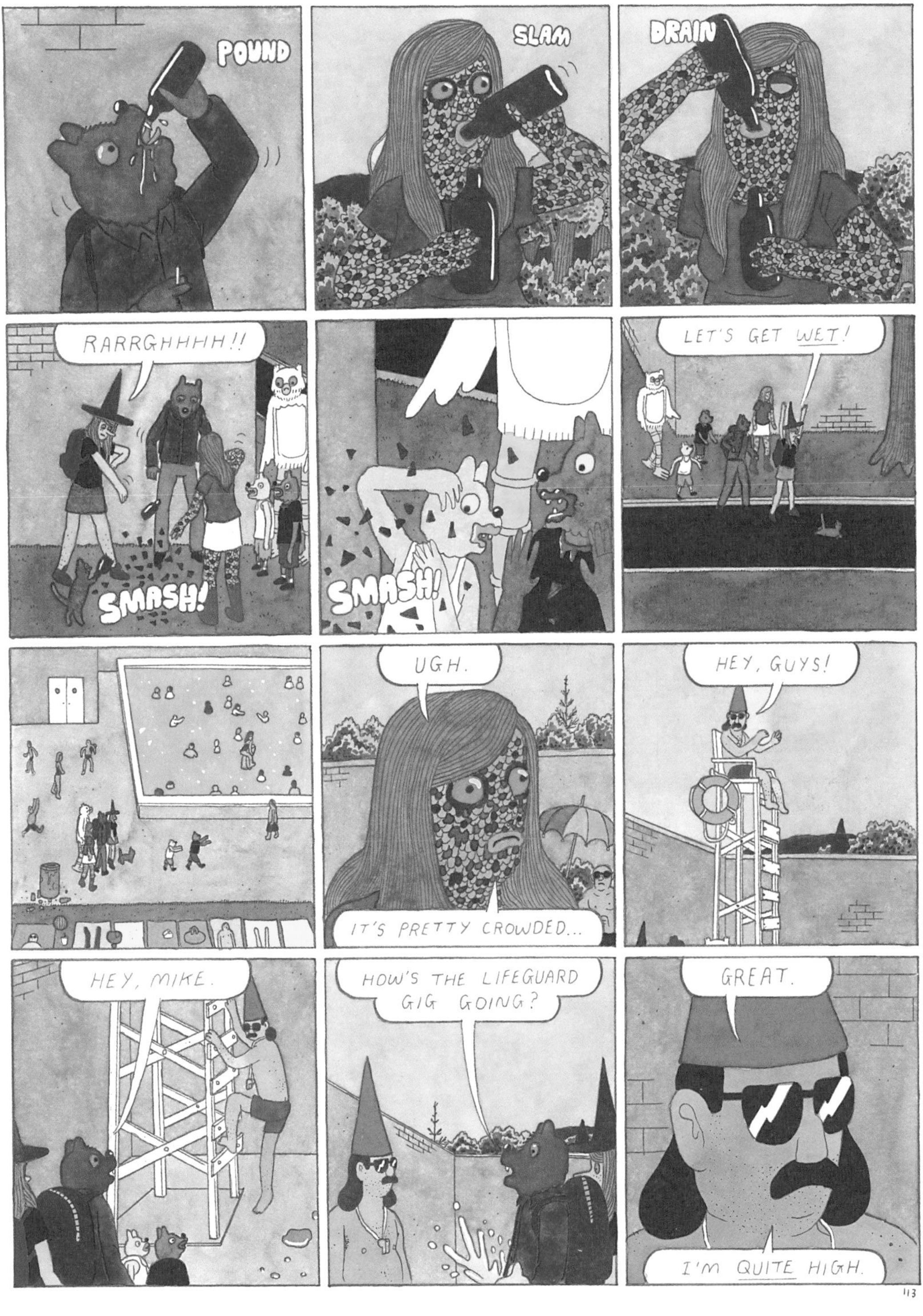
POUND
SLAM
DRAIN
RARRGHHHH!!
SMASH!
SMASH!
LET'S GET WET!
UGH.
IT'S PRETTY CROWDED...
HEY, GUYS!
HEY, MIKE.
HOW'S THE LIFEGUARD GIG GOING?
GREAT.
I'M QUITE HIGH.

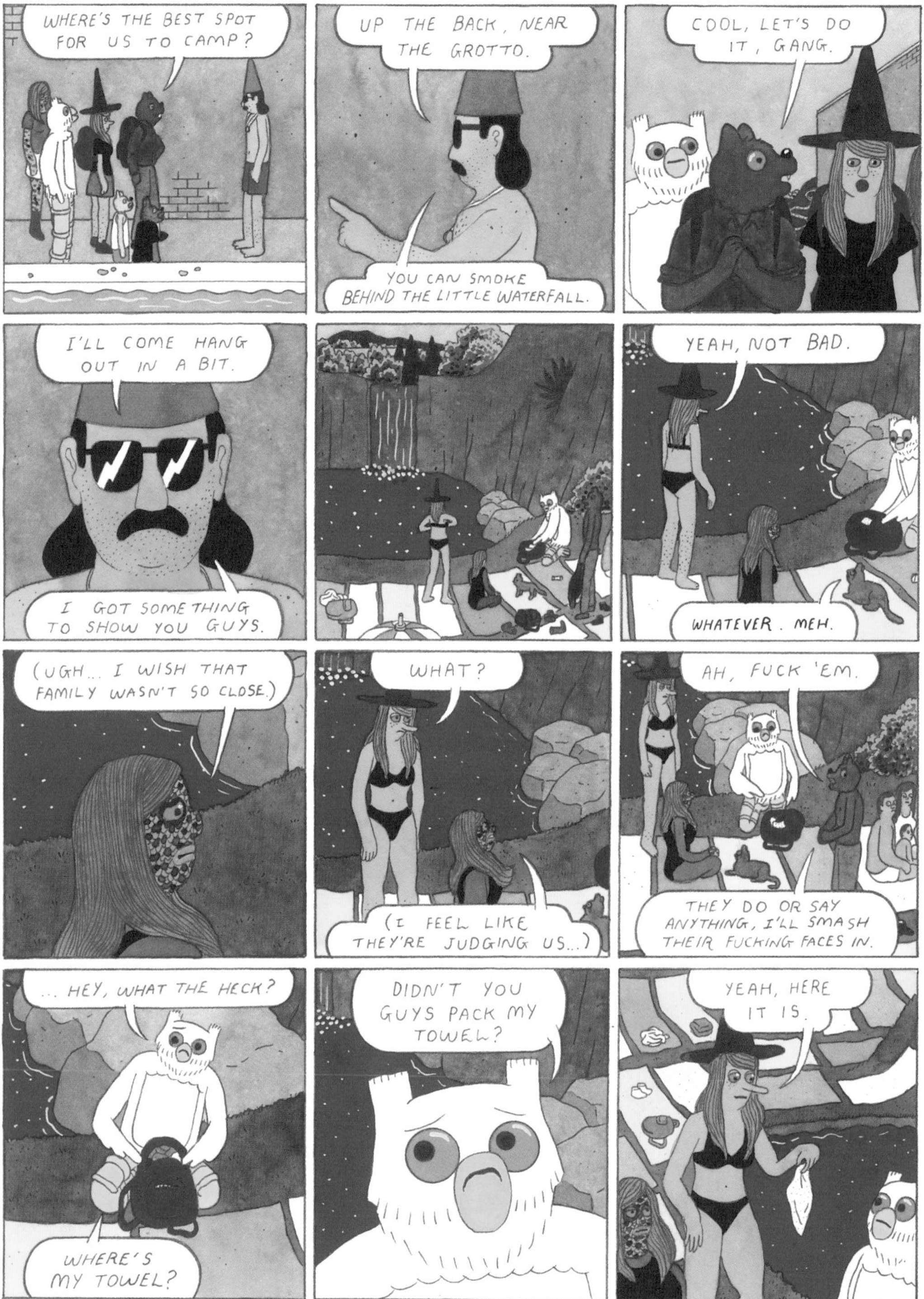
WHERE'S THE BEST SPOT FOR US TO CAMP?
UP THE BACK, NEAR THE GROTTO.
YOU CAN SMOKE BEHIND THE LITTLE WATERFALL.
COOL, LET'S DO IT, GANG.
I'LL COME HANG OUT IN A BIT.
I GOT SOMETHING TO SHOW YOU GUYS.
YEAH, NOT BAD.
WHATEVER. MEH.
(UGH... I WISH THAT FAMILY WASN'T SO CLOSE.)
WHAT?
(I FEEL LIKE THEY'RE JUDGING US...)
AH, FUCK 'EM.
THEY DO OR SAY ANYTHING, I'LL SMASH THEIR FUCKING FACES IN.
... HEY, WHAT THE HECK?
WHERE'S MY TOWEL?
DIDN'T YOU GUYS PACK MY TOWEL?
YEAH, HERE IT IS.

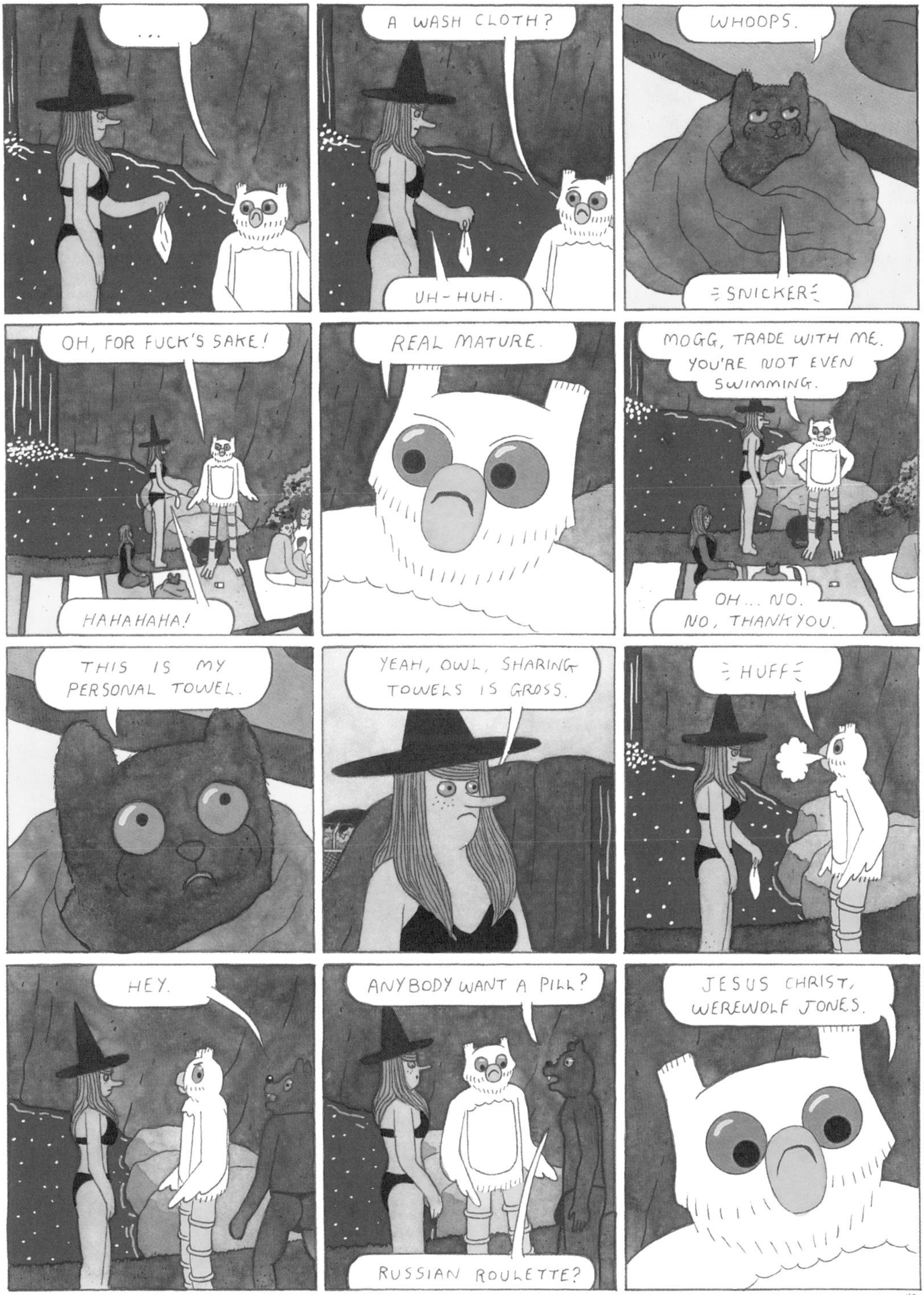
...
A WASH CLOTH?
UH-HUH.
WHOOPS.
SNICKER
OH, FOR FUCK'S SAKE!
HAHAHAHA!
REAL MATURE.
MOGG, TRADE WITH ME. YOU'RE NOT EVEN SWIMMING.
OH... NO. NO, THANK YOU.
THIS IS MY PERSONAL TOWEL.
YEAH, OWL, SHARING TOWELS IS GROSS.
HUFF
HEY.
ANYBODY WANT A PILL?
RUSSIAN ROULETTE?
JESUS CHRIST, WEREWOLF JONES.

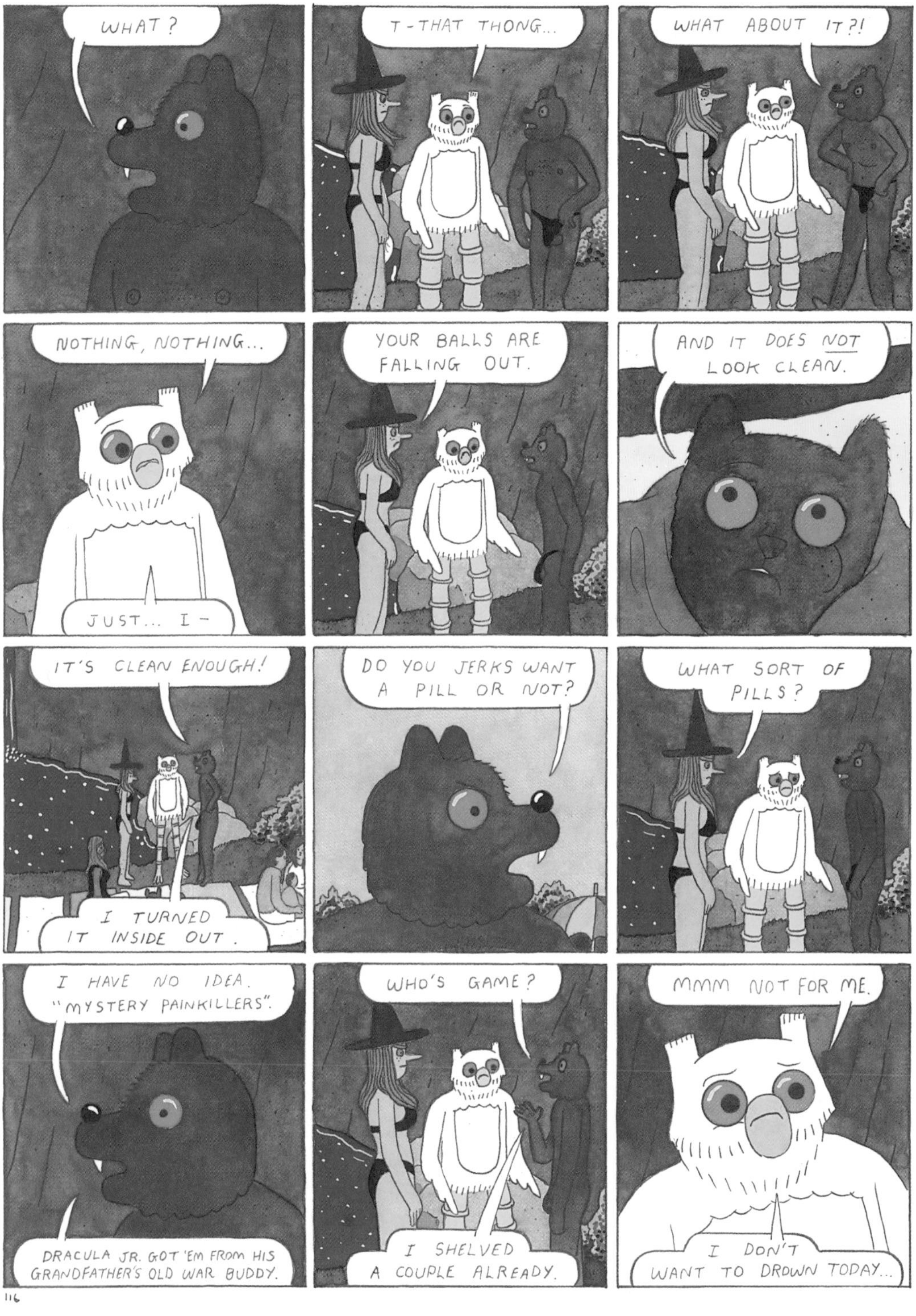
WHAT?
T-THAT THONG...
WHAT ABOUT IT?!
NOTHING, NOTHING...
JUST... I-
YOUR BALLS ARE FALLING OUT.
AND IT DOES NOT LOOK CLEAN.
IT'S CLEAN ENOUGH!
I TURNED IT INSIDE OUT.
DO YOU JERKS WANT A PILL OR NOT?
WHAT SORT OF PILLS?
I HAVE NO IDEA. "MYSTERY PAINKILLERS".
DRACULA JR. GOT 'EM FROM HIS GRANDFATHER'S OLD WAR BUDDY.
WHO'S GAME?
I SHELVED A COUPLE ALREADY.
MMM NOT FOR ME.
I DON'T WANT TO DROWN TODAY...

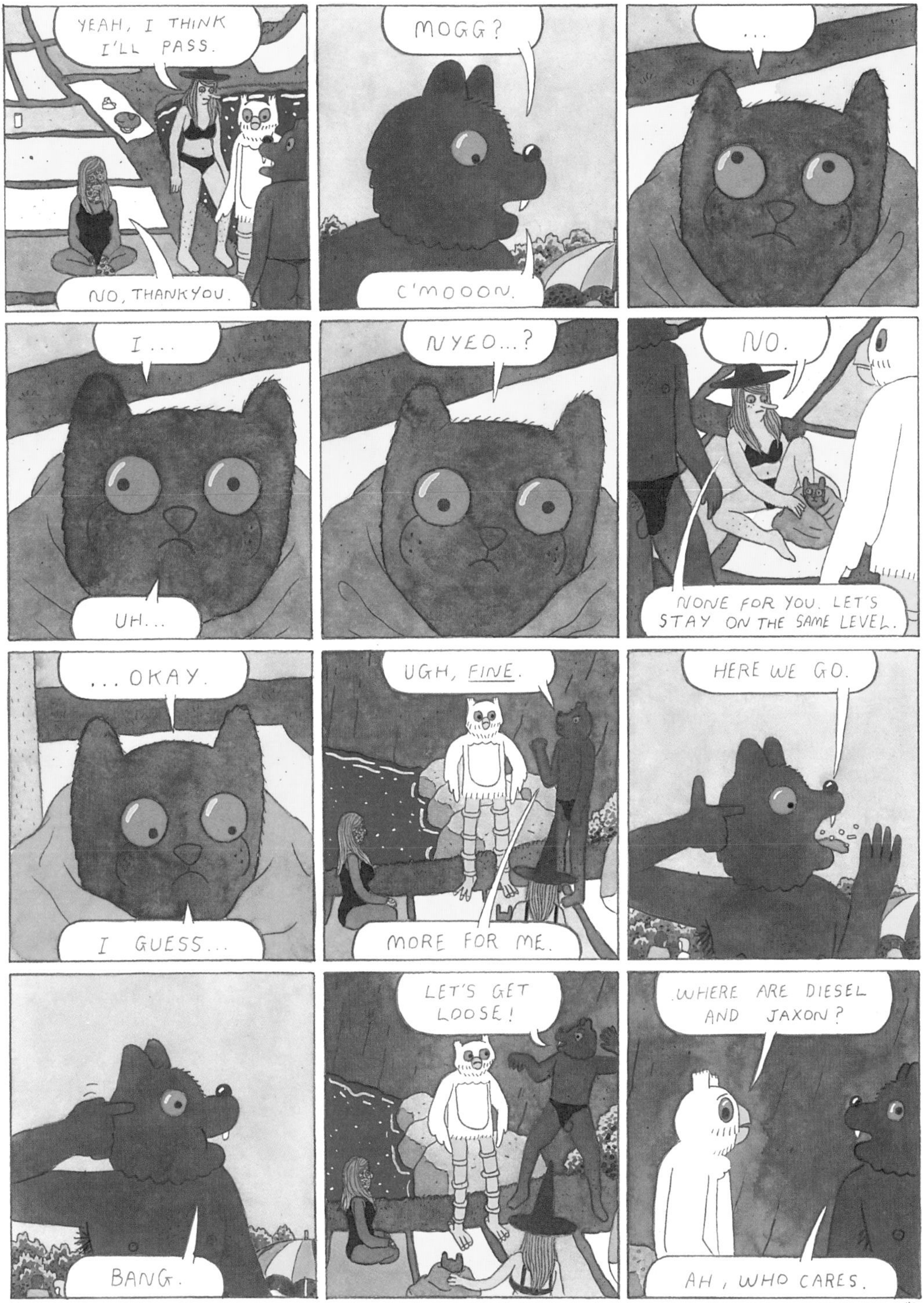
YEAH, I THINK I'LL PASS.
NO, THANKYOU.
MOGG?
C'MOOON.
...
I...
UH...
NYEO...?
NO.
NONE FOR YOU. LET'S STAY ON THE SAME LEVEL.
...OKAY.
I GUESS...
UGH, FINE.
MORE FOR ME.
HERE WE GO.
BANG.
LET'S GET LOOSE!
WHERE ARE DIESEL AND JAXON?
AH, WHO CARES.

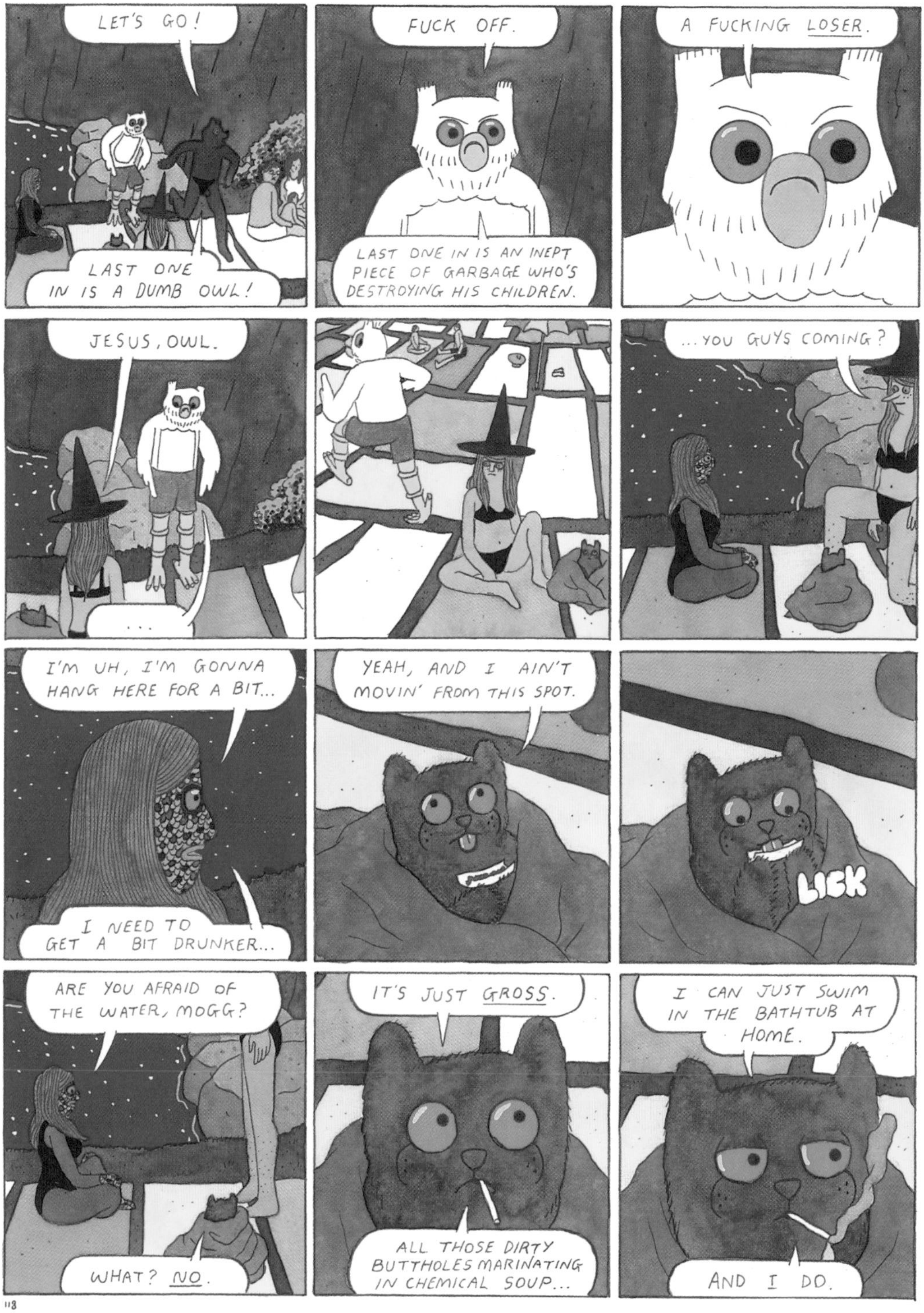
LET'S GO!
LAST ONE IN IS A DUMB OWL!
FUCK OFF.
LAST ONE IN IS AN INEPT PIECE OF GARBAGE WHO'S DESTROYING HIS CHILDREN.
A FUCKING LOSER.
JESUS, OWL.
...
...YOU GUYS COMING?
I'M UH, I'M GONNA HANG HERE FOR A BIT...
I NEED TO GET A BIT DRUNKER...
YEAH, AND I AIN'T MOVIN' FROM THIS SPOT.
LICK
ARE YOU AFRAID OF THE WATER, MOGG?
WHAT? NO.
IT'S JUST GROSS.
ALL THOSE DIRTY BUTTHOLES MARINATING IN CHEMICAL SOUP...
I CAN JUST SWIM IN THE BATHTUB AT HOME.
AND I DO.

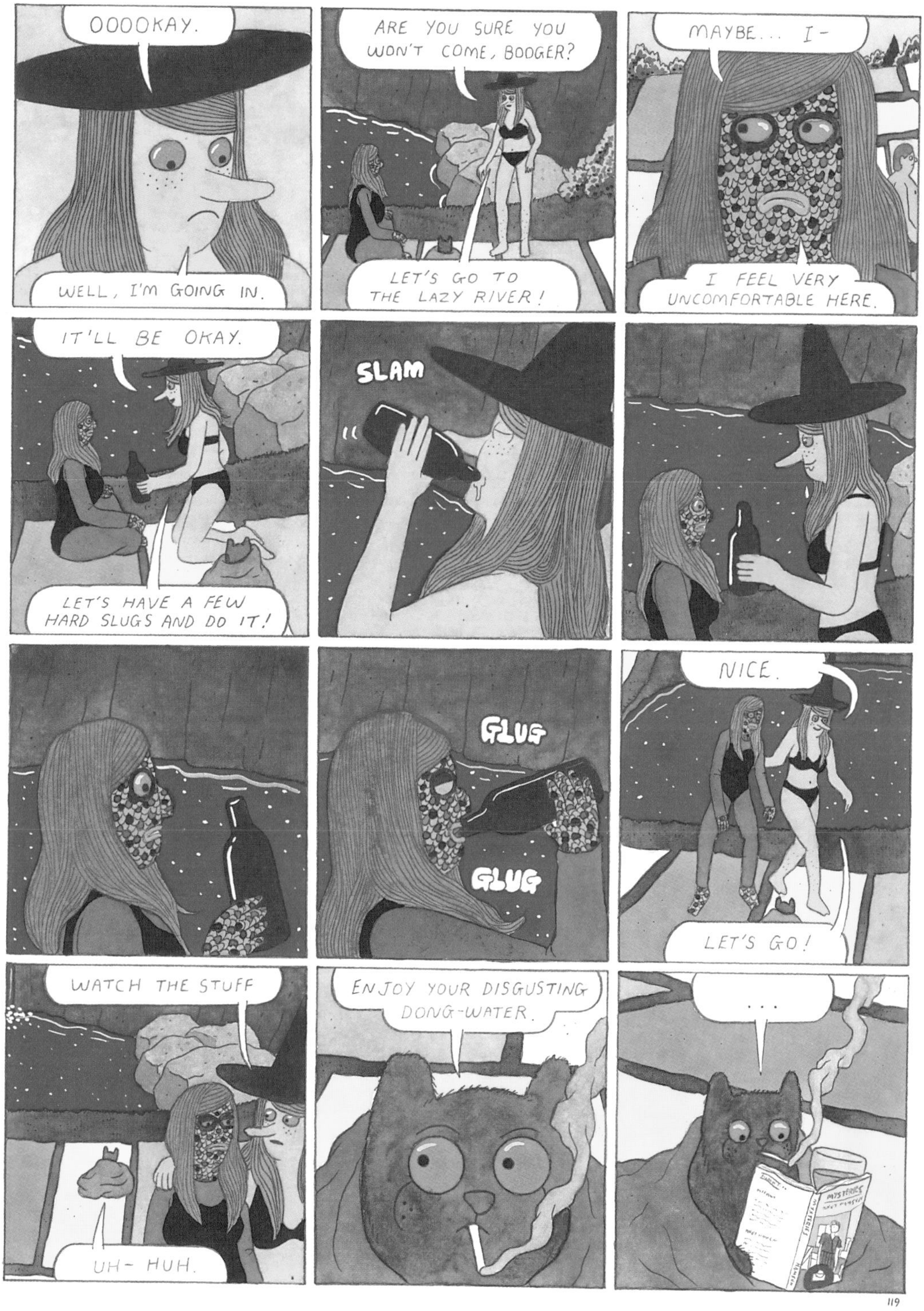
OOOOKAY.
WELL, I'M GOING IN.
ARE YOU SURE YOU WON'T COME, BOOGER?
LET'S GO TO THE LAZY RIVER!
MAYBE... I-
I FEEL VERY UNCOMFORTABLE HERE.
IT'LL BE OKAY.
LET'S HAVE A FEW HARD SLUGS AND DO IT!
SLAM
GLUG
GLUG
NICE.
LET'S GO!
WATCH THE STUFF
UH- HUH.
ENJOY YOUR DISGUSTING DONG-WATER.
...

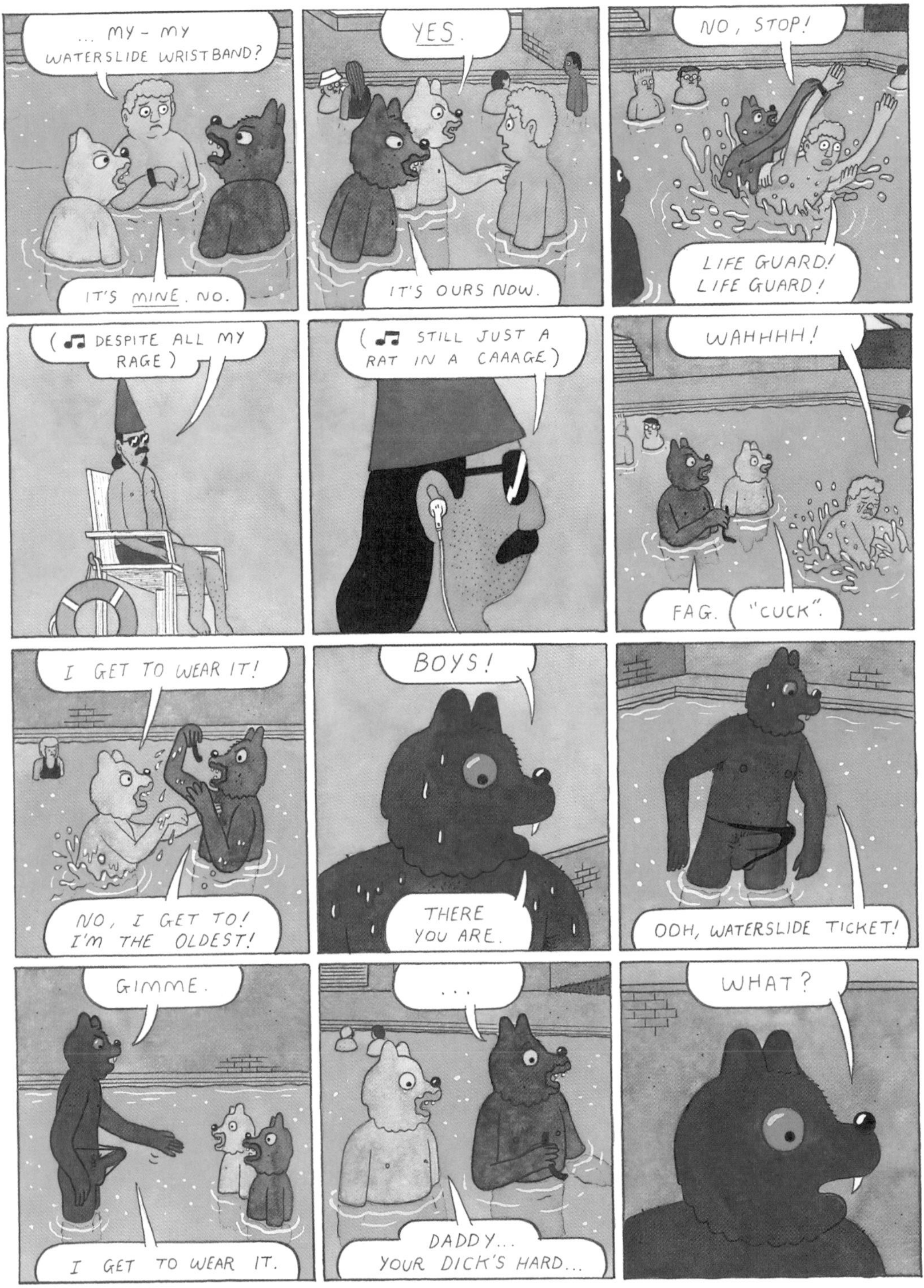
... MY - MY WATERSLIDE WRISTBAND?
IT'S MINE. NO.
YES.
IT'S OURS NOW.
NO, STOP!
LIFE GUARD! LIFE GUARD!
(♫ DESPITE ALL MY RAGE)
(♫ STILL JUST A RAT IN A CAAAGE)
WAHHHH!
FAG.
"CUCK".
I GET TO WEAR IT!
NO, I GET TO! I'M THE OLDEST!
BOYS!
THERE YOU ARE.
OOH, WATERSLIDE TICKET!
GIMME.
I GET TO WEAR IT.
...
DADDY... YOUR DICK'S HARD...
WHAT?

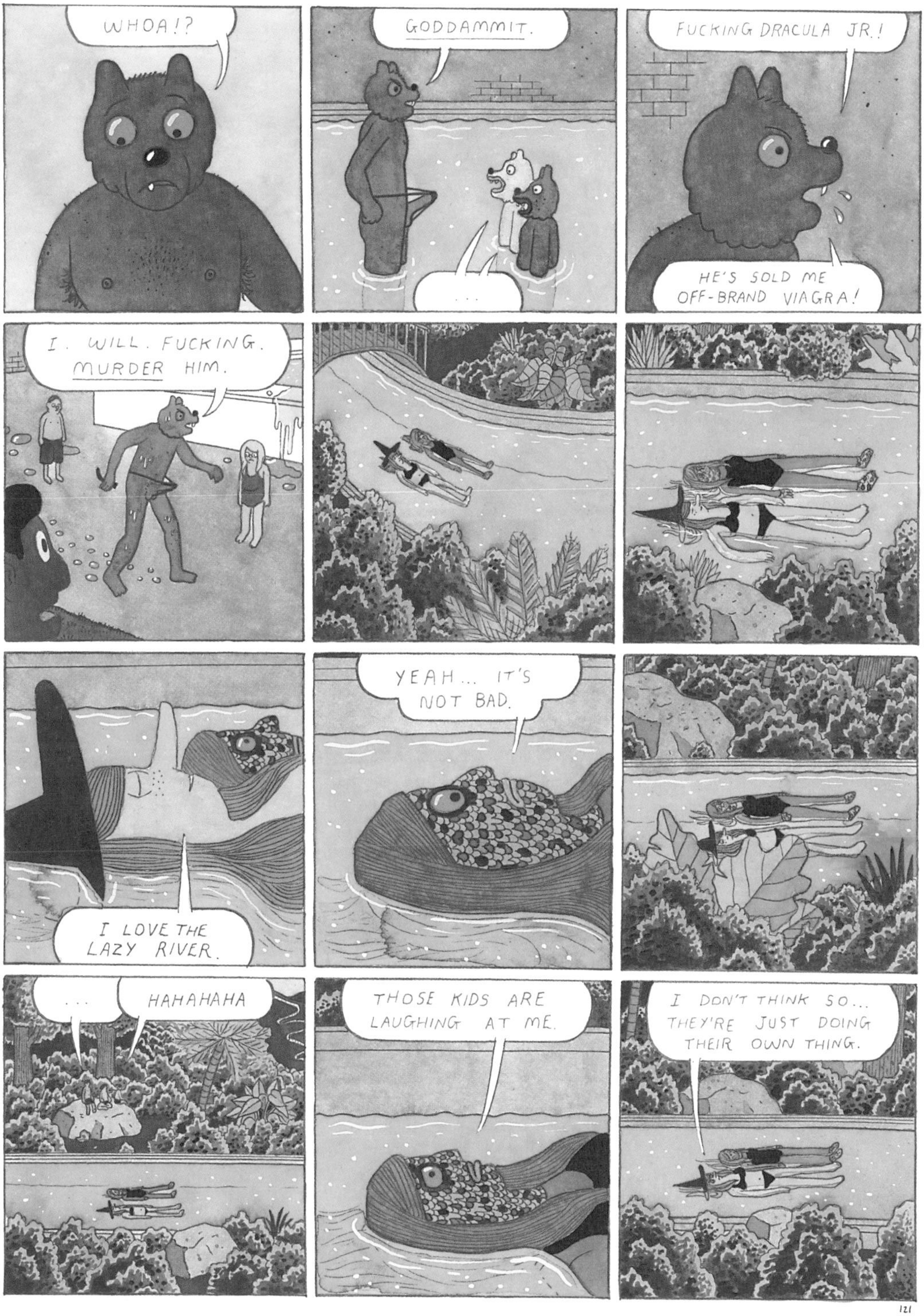
WHOA!?
GODDAMMIT.
...
FUCKING DRACULA JR.!
HE'S SOLD ME OFF-BRAND VIAGRA!
I. WILL. FUCKING. MURDER HIM.
I LOVE THE LAZY RIVER.
YEAH... IT'S NOT BAD.
...
HAHAHAHA
THOSE KIDS ARE LAUGHING AT ME.
I DON'T THINK SO... THEY'RE JUST DOING THEIR OWN THING.

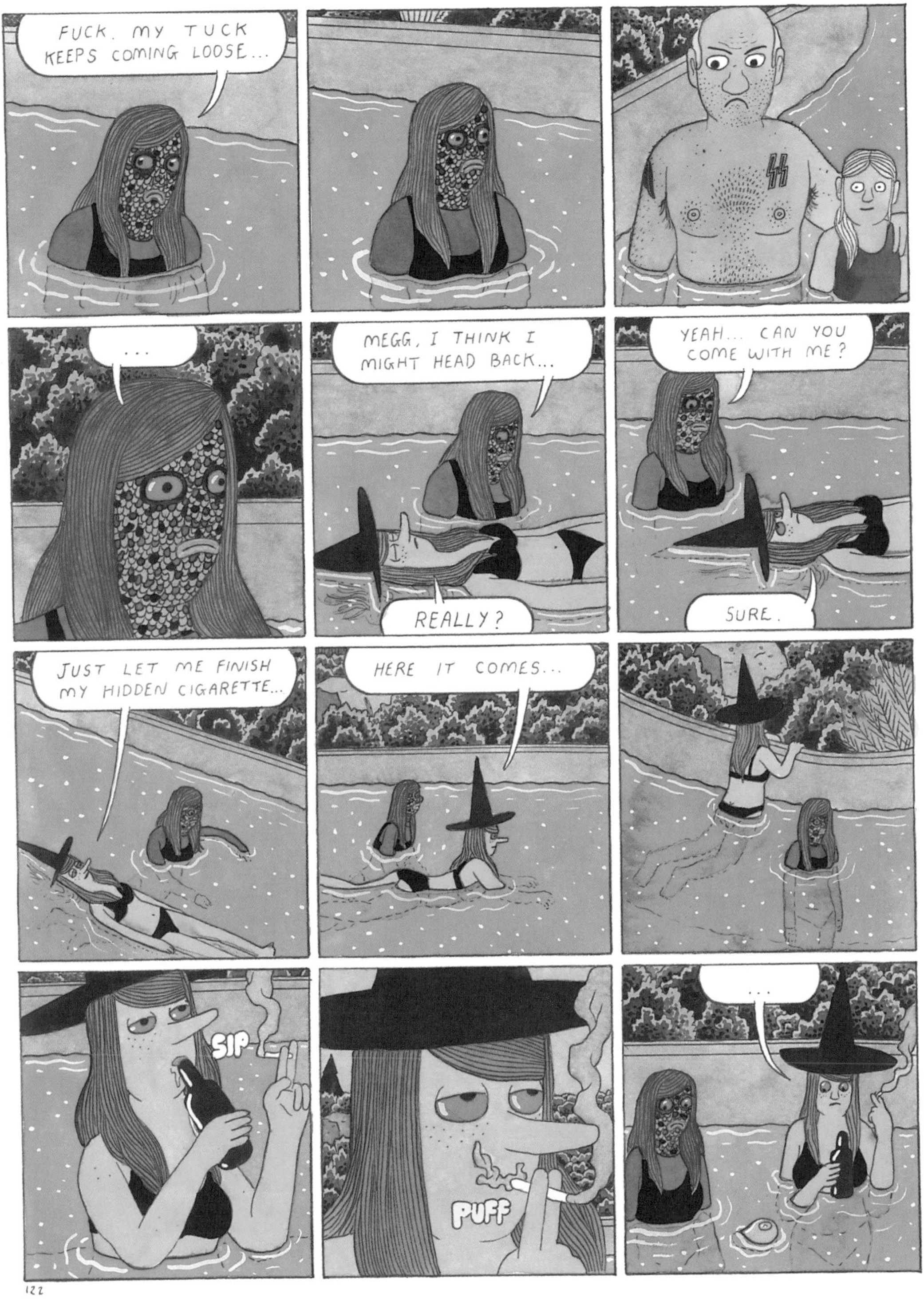
FUCK. MY TUCK KEEPS COMING LOOSE...
...
MEGG, I THINK I MIGHT HEAD BACK...
REALLY?
YEAH... CAN YOU COME WITH ME?
SURE.
JUST LET ME FINISH MY HIDDEN CIGARETTE...
HERE IT COMES...
SIP
PUFF
...

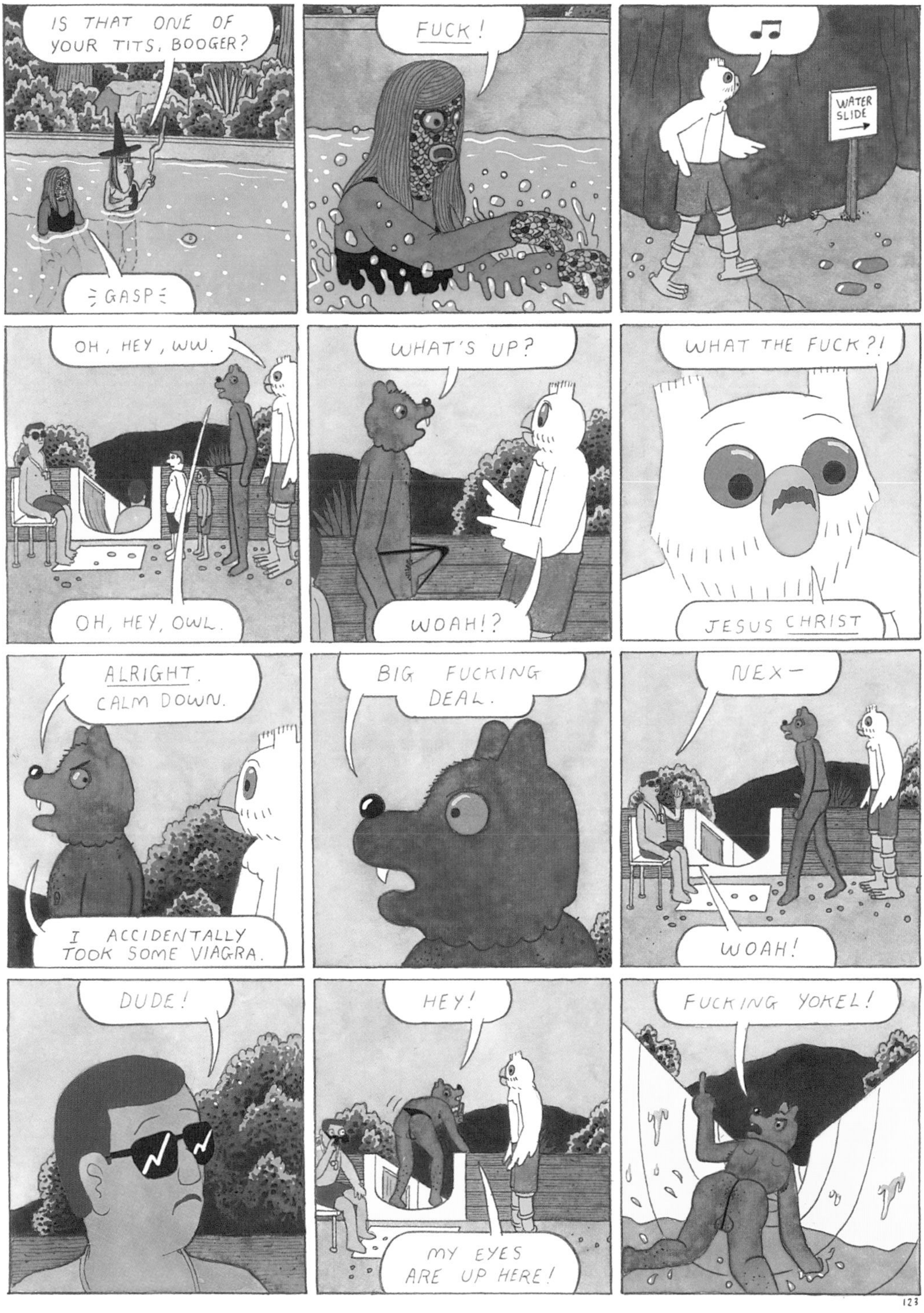
IS THAT ONE OF YOUR TITS, BOOGER?
GASP
FUCK!
♫
WATER SLIDE
OH, HEY, WW.
OH, HEY, OWL.
WHAT'S UP?
WOAH!?
WHAT THE FUCK?!
JESUS CHRIST
ALRIGHT. CALM DOWN.
I ACCIDENTALLY TOOK SOME VIAGRA.
BIG FUCKING DEAL.
NEX–
WOAH!
DUDE!
HEY!
MY EYES ARE UP HERE!
FUCKING YOKEL!

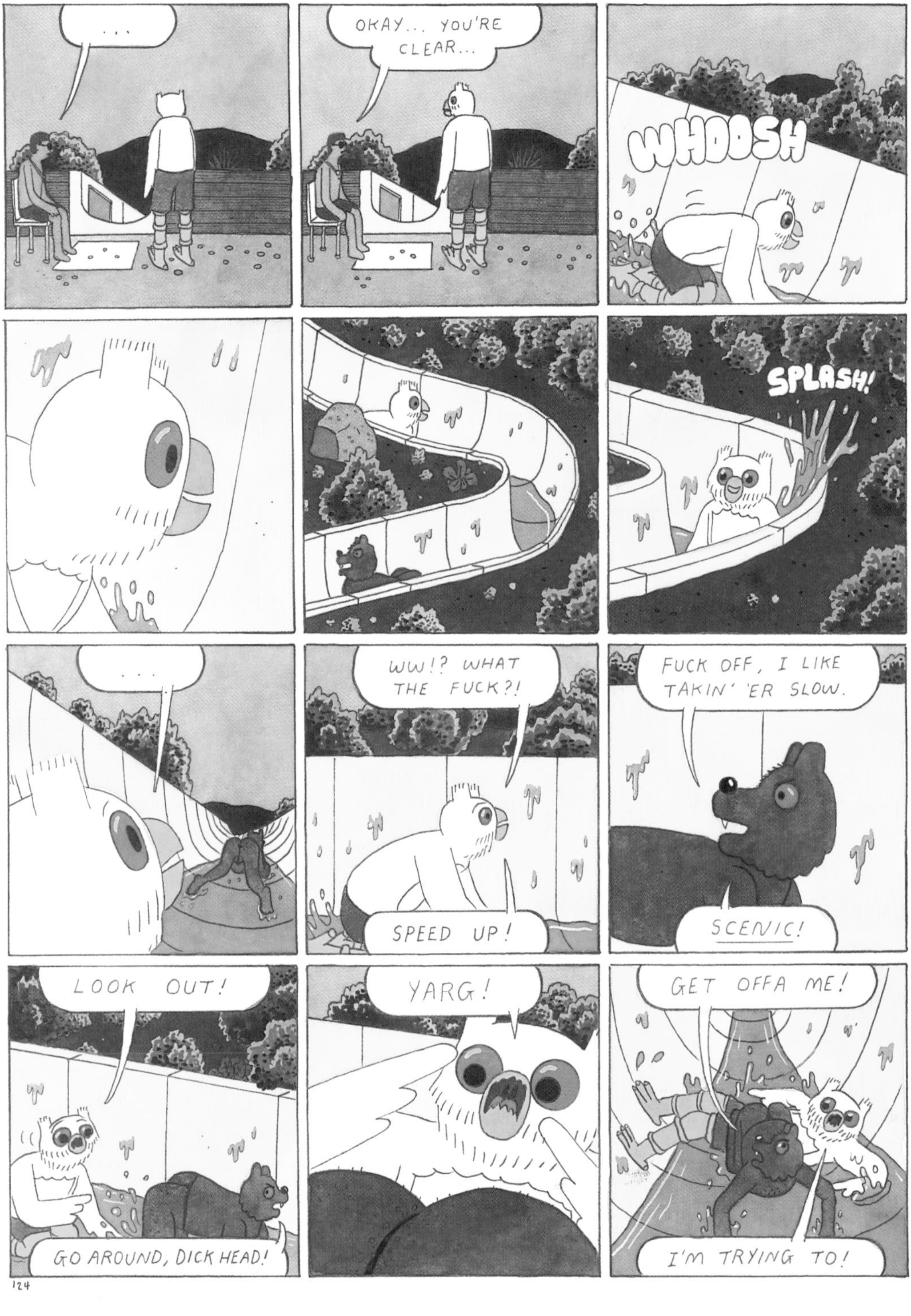
. . .
OKAY... YOU'RE CLEAR...
WHOOSH
SPLASH!
. . .
WW!? WHAT THE FUCK?!
SPEED UP!
FUCK OFF, I LIKE TAKIN' 'ER SLOW.
SCENIC!
LOOK OUT!
GO AROUND, DICK HEAD!
YARG!
GET OFFA ME!
I'M TRYING TO!

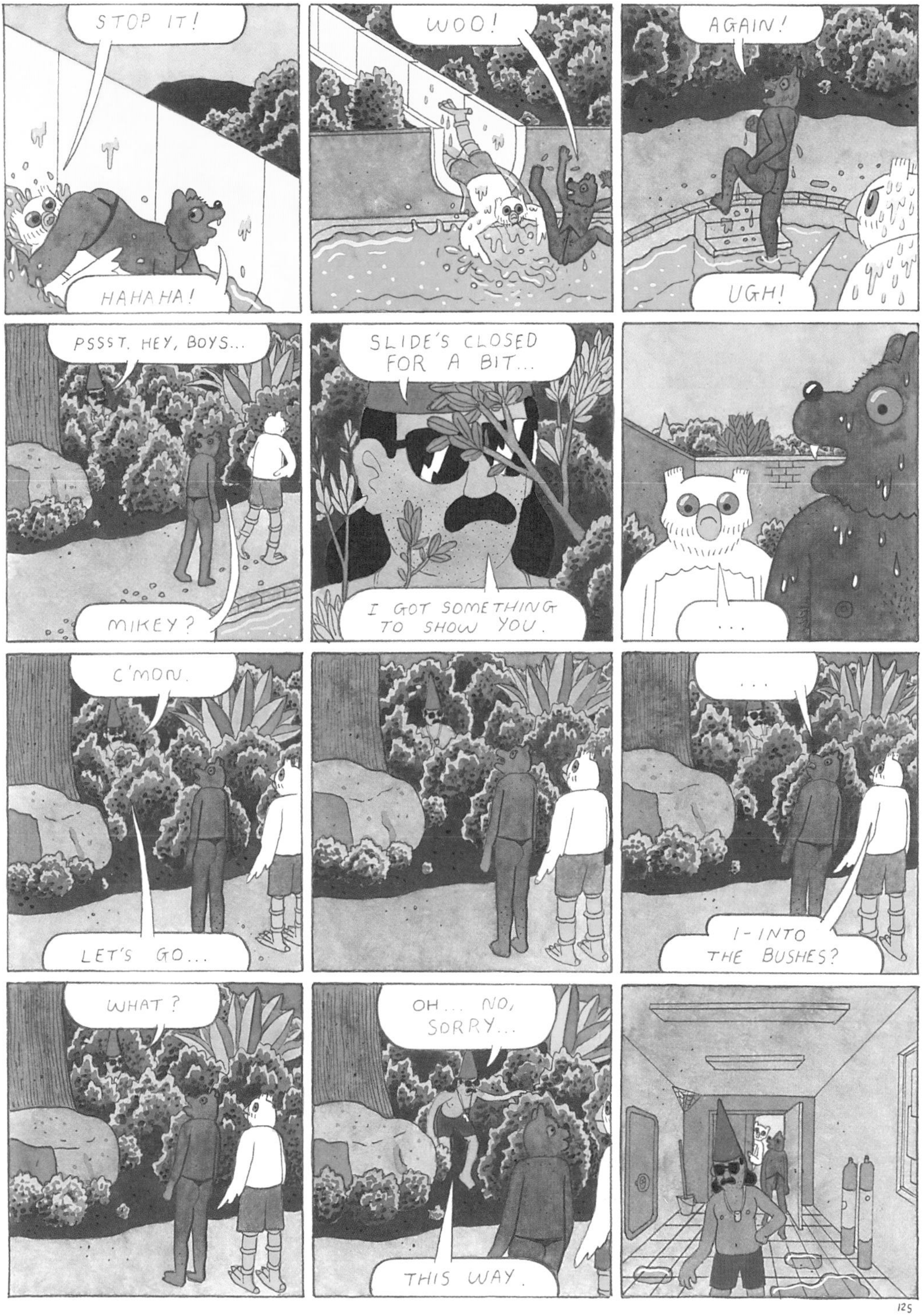
STOP IT!
HAHAHA!
WOO!
AGAIN!
UGH!
PSSST. HEY, BOYS...
MIKEY?
SLIDE'S CLOSED FOR A BIT...
I GOT SOMETHING TO SHOW YOU.
...
C'MON.
LET'S GO...
...
I- INTO THE BUSHES?
WHAT?
OH... NO, SORRY...
THIS WAY.

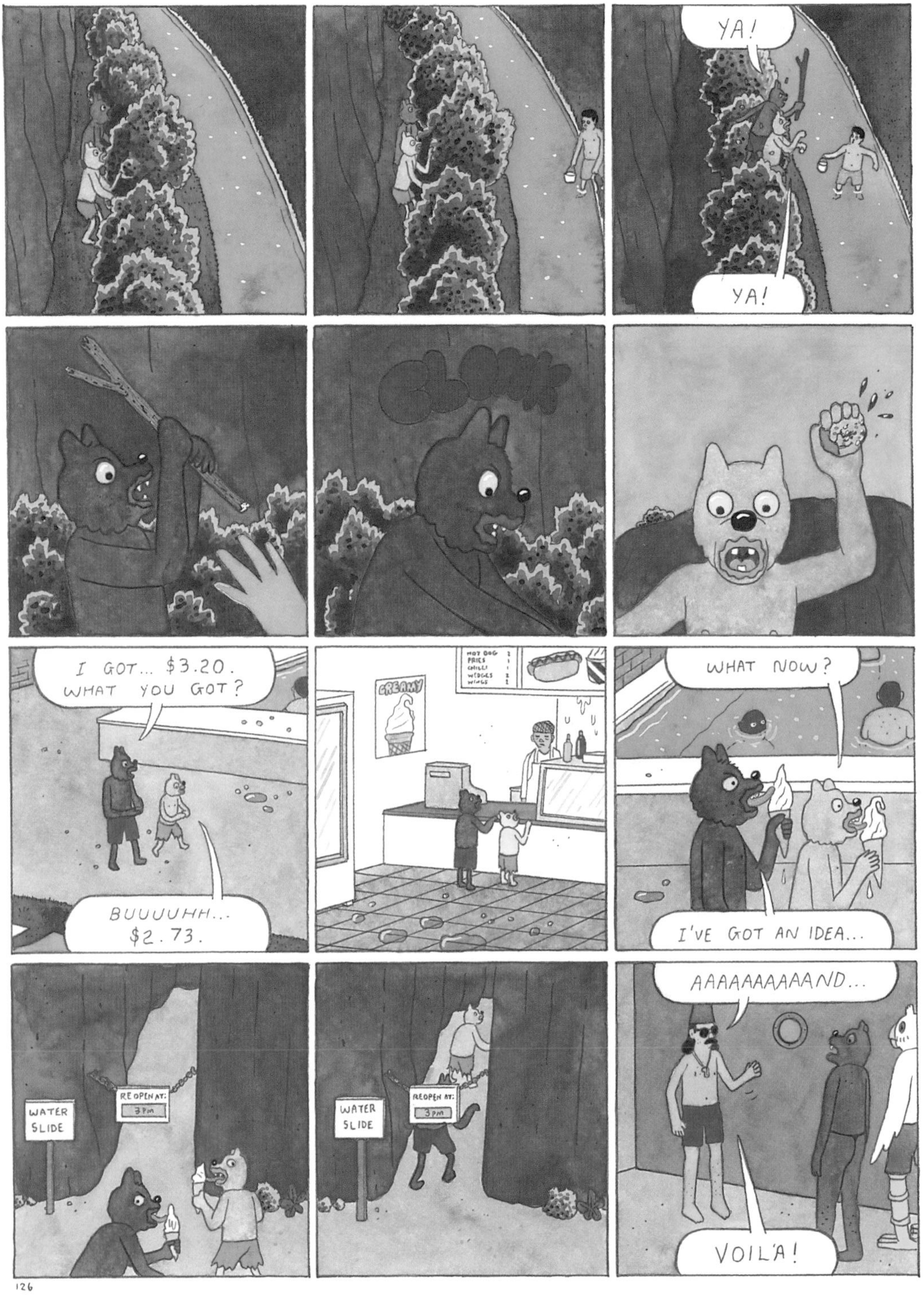
YA!
YA!
CLONK
I GOT... $3.20. WHAT YOU GOT?
BUUUUHH... $2.73.
HOT DOG 2
FRIES 1
CHILLI 1
WEDGES 2
WINGS 2
CREAMY
WHAT NOW?
I'VE GOT AN IDEA...
WATER SLIDE
REOPEN AT: 3PM
WATER SLIDE
REOPEN AT: 3PM
AAAAAAAAAAND...
VOILÀ!

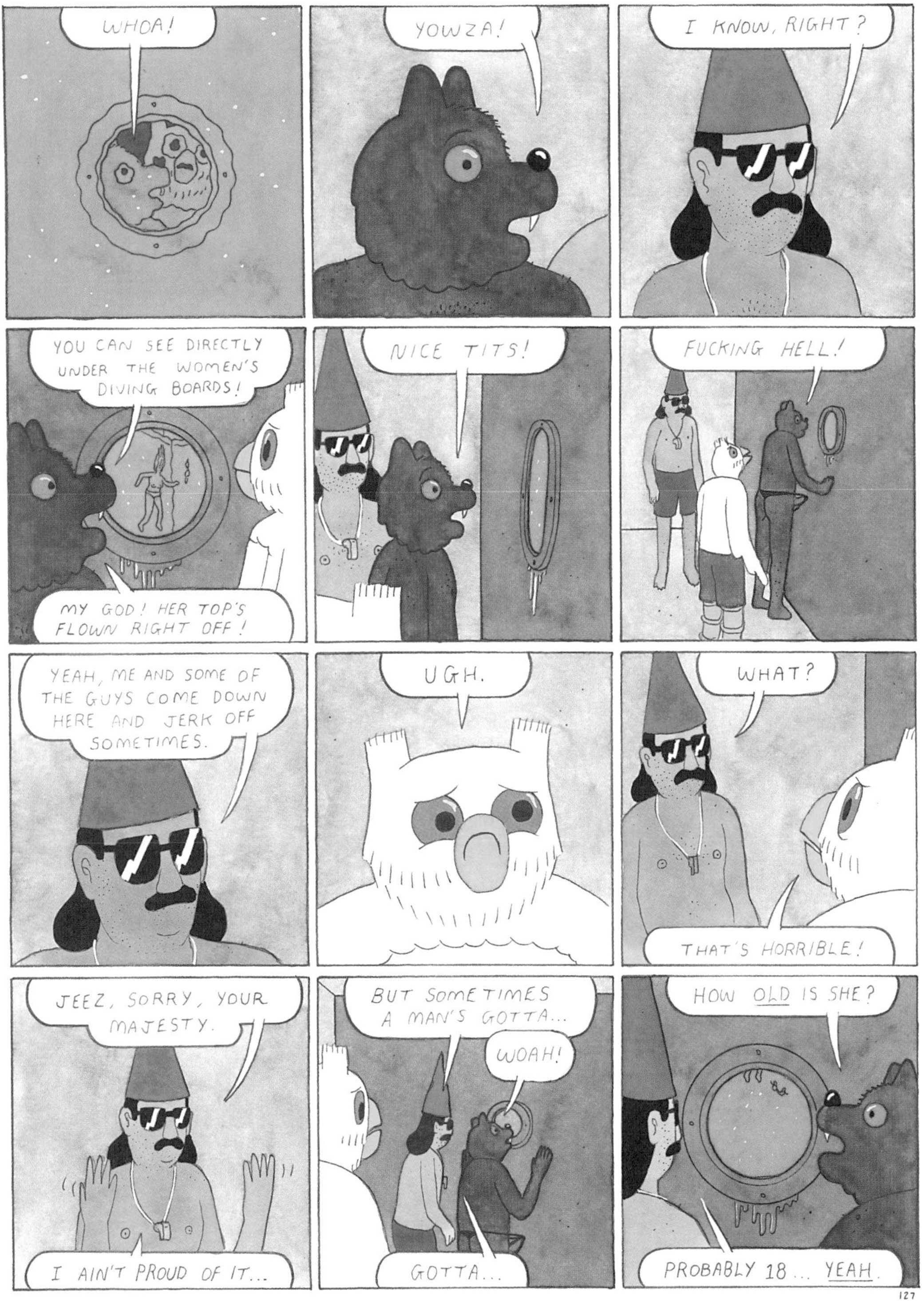
WHOA!
YOWZA!
I KNOW, RIGHT?
YOU CAN SEE DIRECTLY UNDER THE WOMEN'S DIVING BOARDS!
MY GOD! HER TOP'S FLOWN RIGHT OFF!
NICE TITS!
FUCKING HELL!
YEAH, ME AND SOME OF THE GUYS COME DOWN HERE AND JERK OFF SOMETIMES.
UGH.
WHAT?
THAT'S HORRIBLE!
JEEZ, SORRY, YOUR MAJESTY.
I AIN'T PROUD OF IT...
BUT SOMETIMES A MAN'S GOTTA...
WOAH!
GOTTA...
HOW OLD IS SHE?
PROBABLY 18... YEAH.

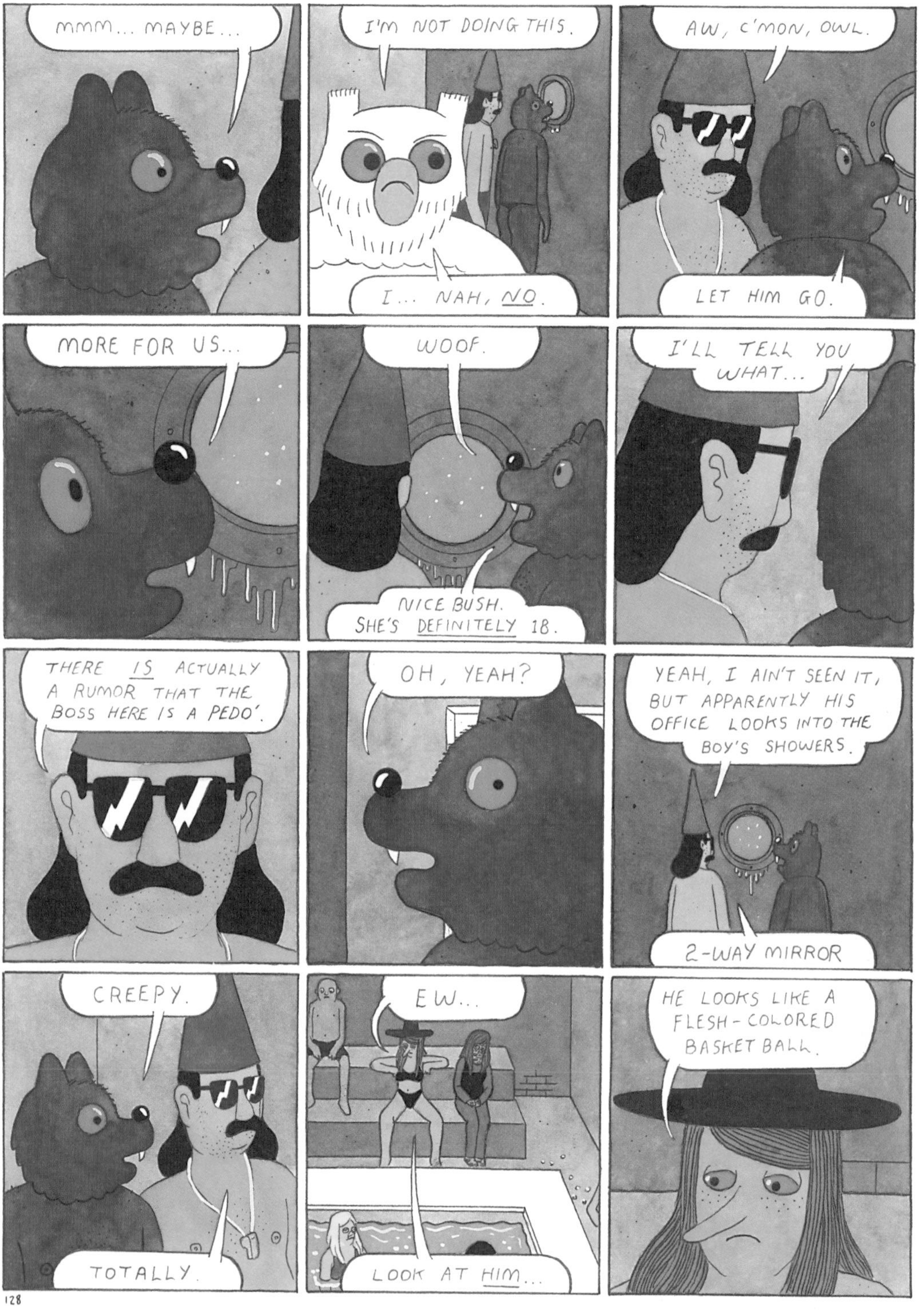
MMM... MAYBE...
I'M NOT DOING THIS.
I... NAH, NO.
AW, C'MON, OWL.
LET HIM GO.
MORE FOR US...
WOOF.
NICE BUSH. SHE'S DEFINITELY 18.
I'LL TELL YOU WHAT...
THERE IS ACTUALLY A RUMOR THAT THE BOSS HERE IS A PEDO'.
OH, YEAH?
YEAH, I AIN'T SEEN IT, BUT APPARENTLY HIS OFFICE LOOKS INTO THE BOY'S SHOWERS.
2-WAY MIRROR
CREEPY.
TOTALLY.
EW...
LOOK AT HIM...
HE LOOKS LIKE A FLESH-COLORED BASKETBALL.

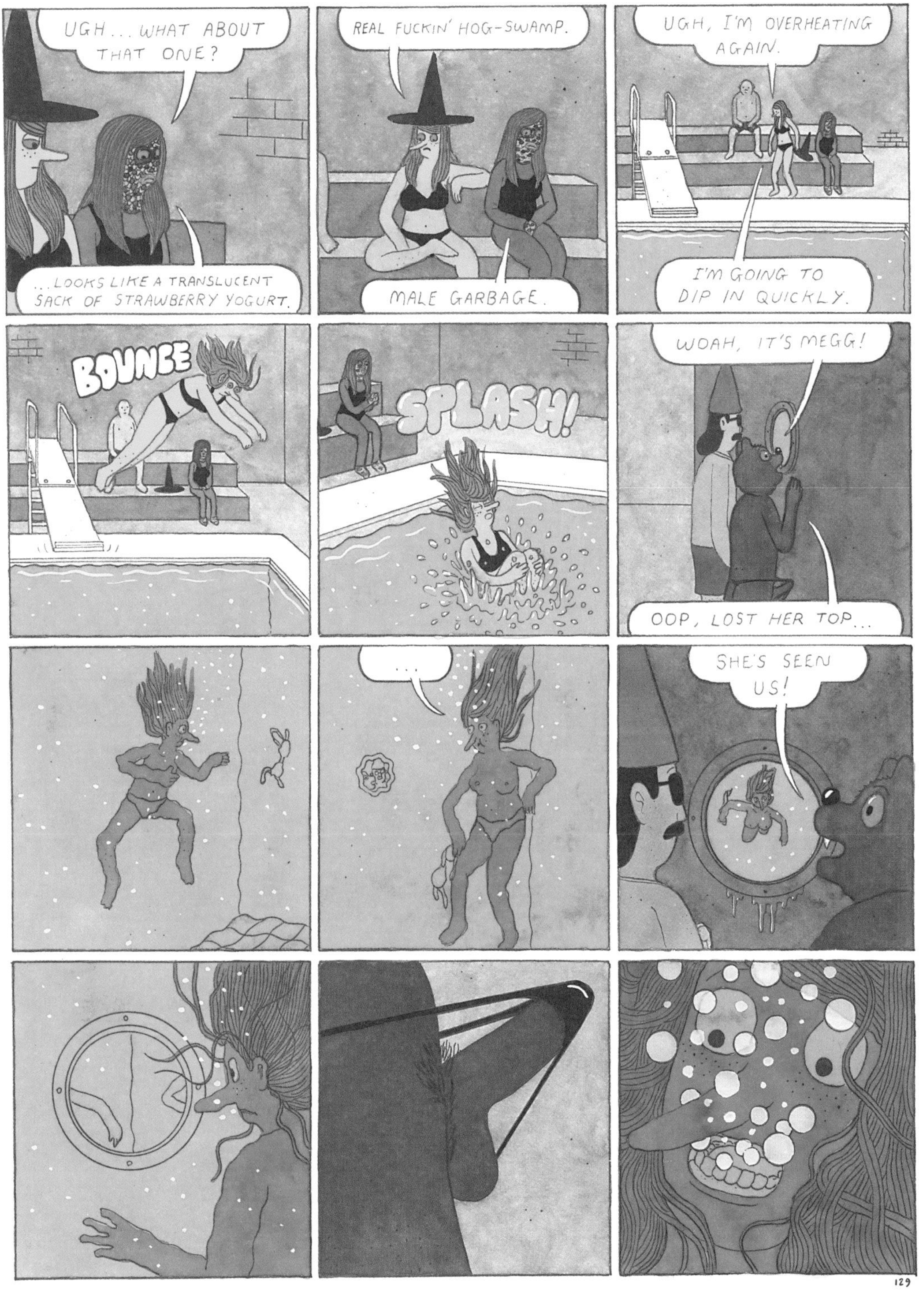
UGH... WHAT ABOUT THAT ONE?
...LOOKS LIKE A TRANSLUCENT SACK OF STRAWBERRY YOGURT.
REAL FUCKIN' HOG-SWAMP.
MALE GARBAGE.
UGH, I'M OVERHEATING AGAIN.
I'M GOING TO DIP IN QUICKLY.
BOUNCE
SPLASH!
WOAH, IT'S MEGG!
OOP, LOST HER TOP...
...
SHE'S SEEN US!

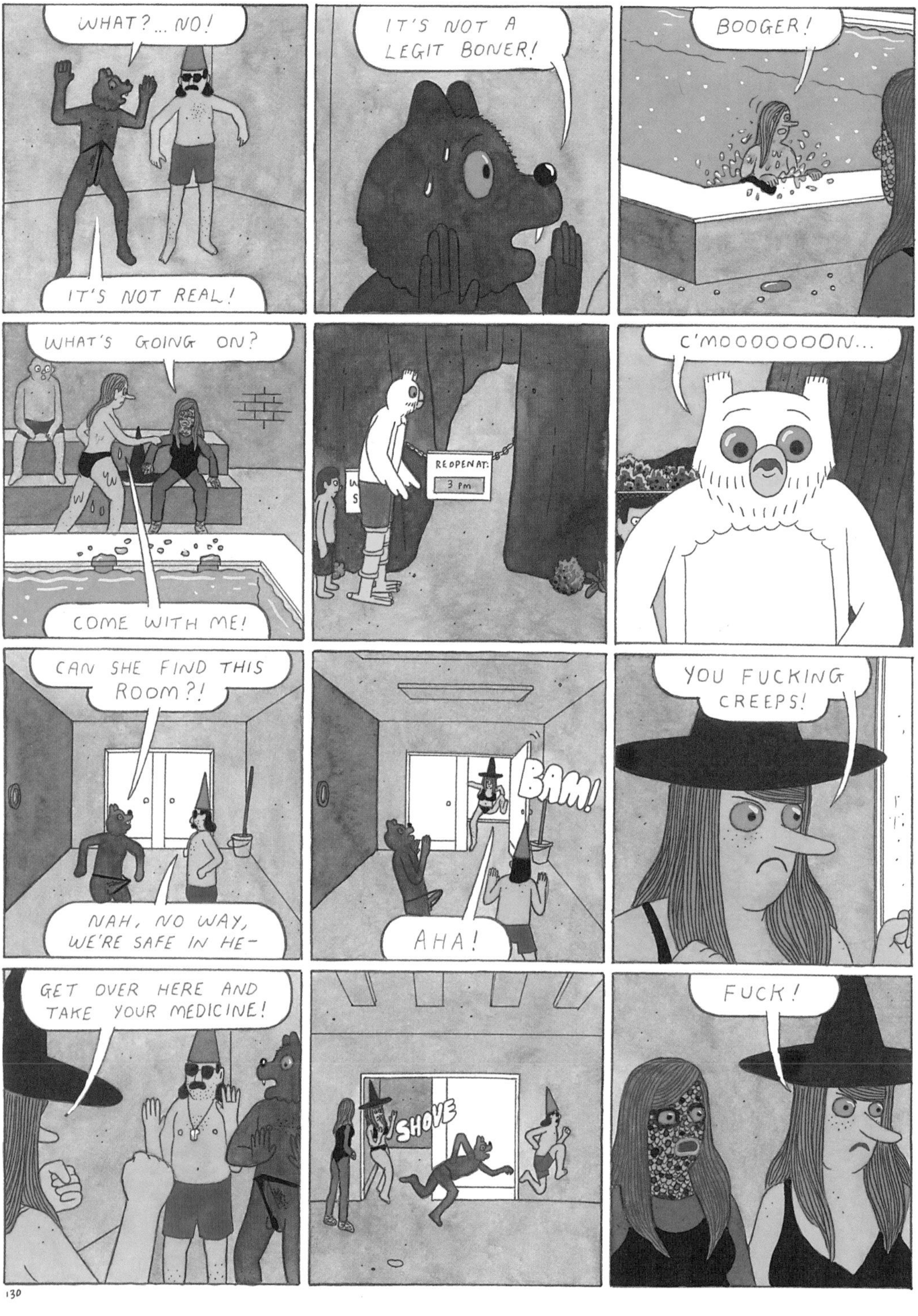

WHAT?... NO!
IT'S NOT REAL!
IT'S NOT A LEGIT BONER!
BOOGER!
WHAT'S GOING ON?
COME WITH ME!
REOPEN AT:
3 PM
C'MOOOOOOOON...
CAN SHE FIND THIS ROOM?!
NAH, NO WAY, WE'RE SAFE IN HE-
BAM!
AHA!
YOU FUCKING CREEPS!
GET OVER HERE AND TAKE YOUR MEDICINE!
SHOVE
FUCK!

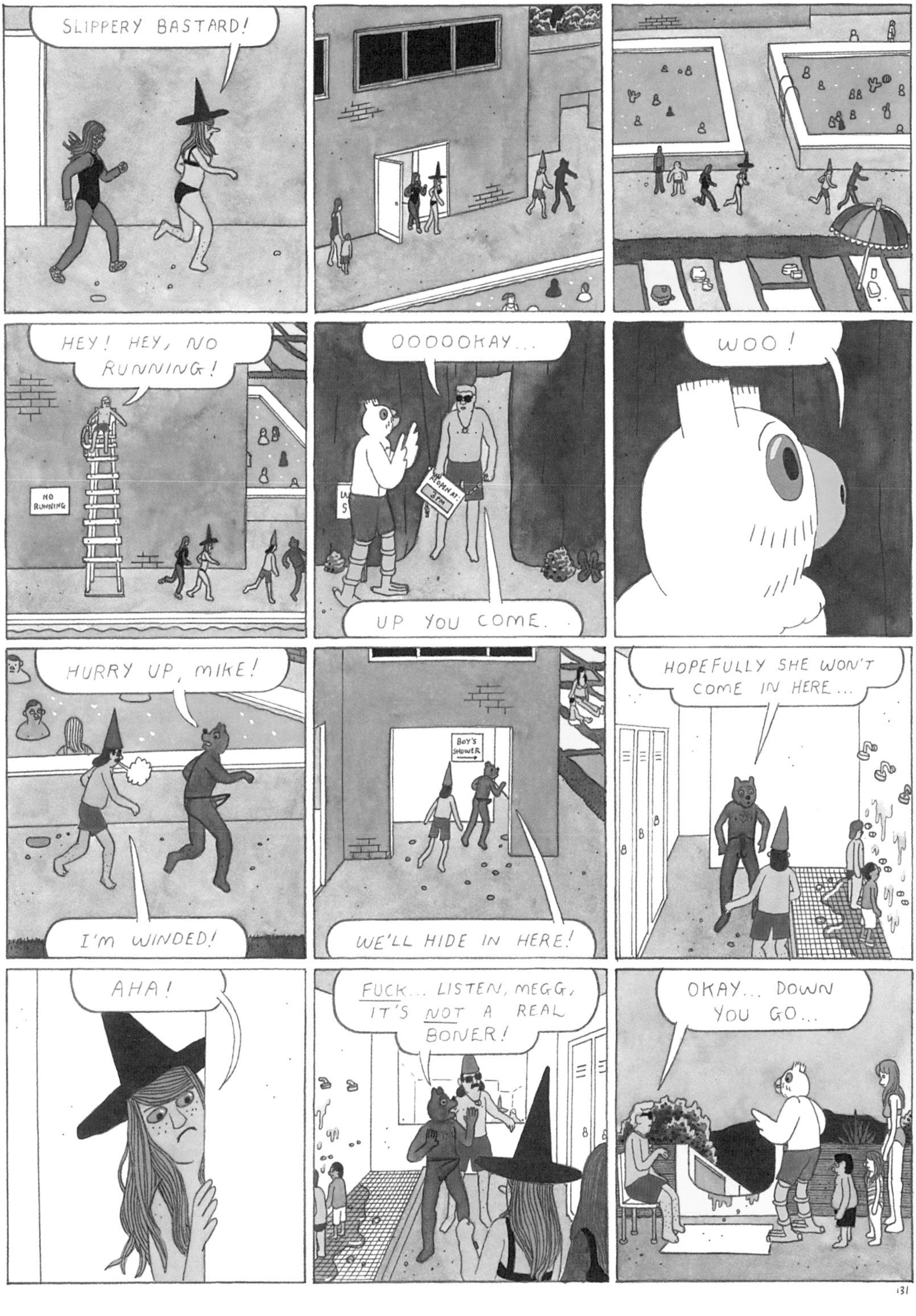
SLIPPERY BASTARD!
HEY! HEY, NO RUNNING!
NO RUNNING
OOOOOKAY...
REOPEN AT: 3PM
UP YOU COME.
WOO!
HURRY UP, MIKE!
I'M WINDED!
BOY'S SHOWER
WE'LL HIDE IN HERE!
HOPEFULLY SHE WON'T COME IN HERE...
AHA!
FUCK... LISTEN, MEGG, IT'S NOT A REAL BONER!
OKAY... DOWN YOU GO...

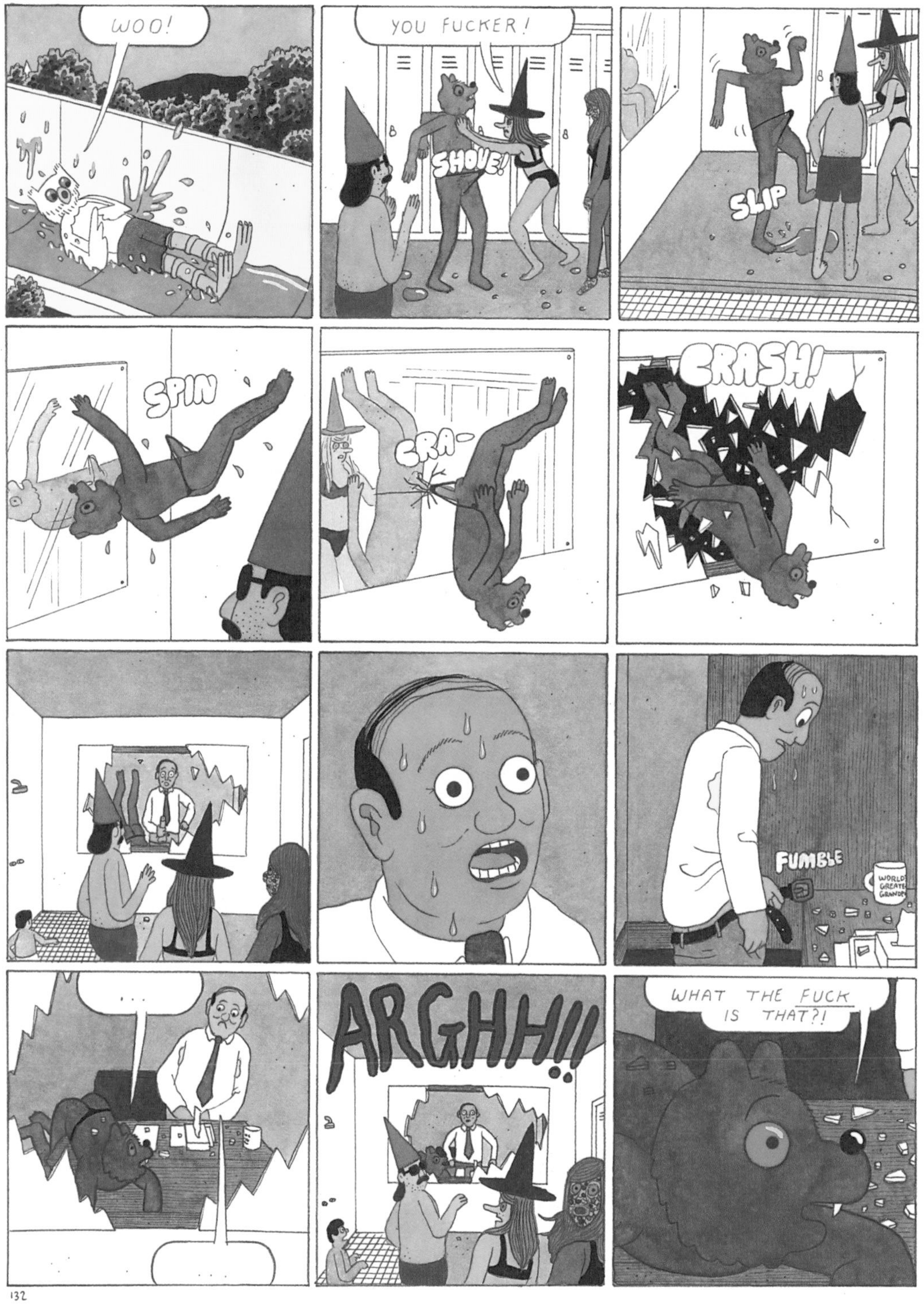
WOO!
YOU FUCKER!
SHOVE!
SLIP
SPIN
CRA-
CRASH!
FUMBLE
WORLD'S GREATE GRANDP
. . .
. . .
ARGHH!!
WHAT THE FUCK IS THAT?!

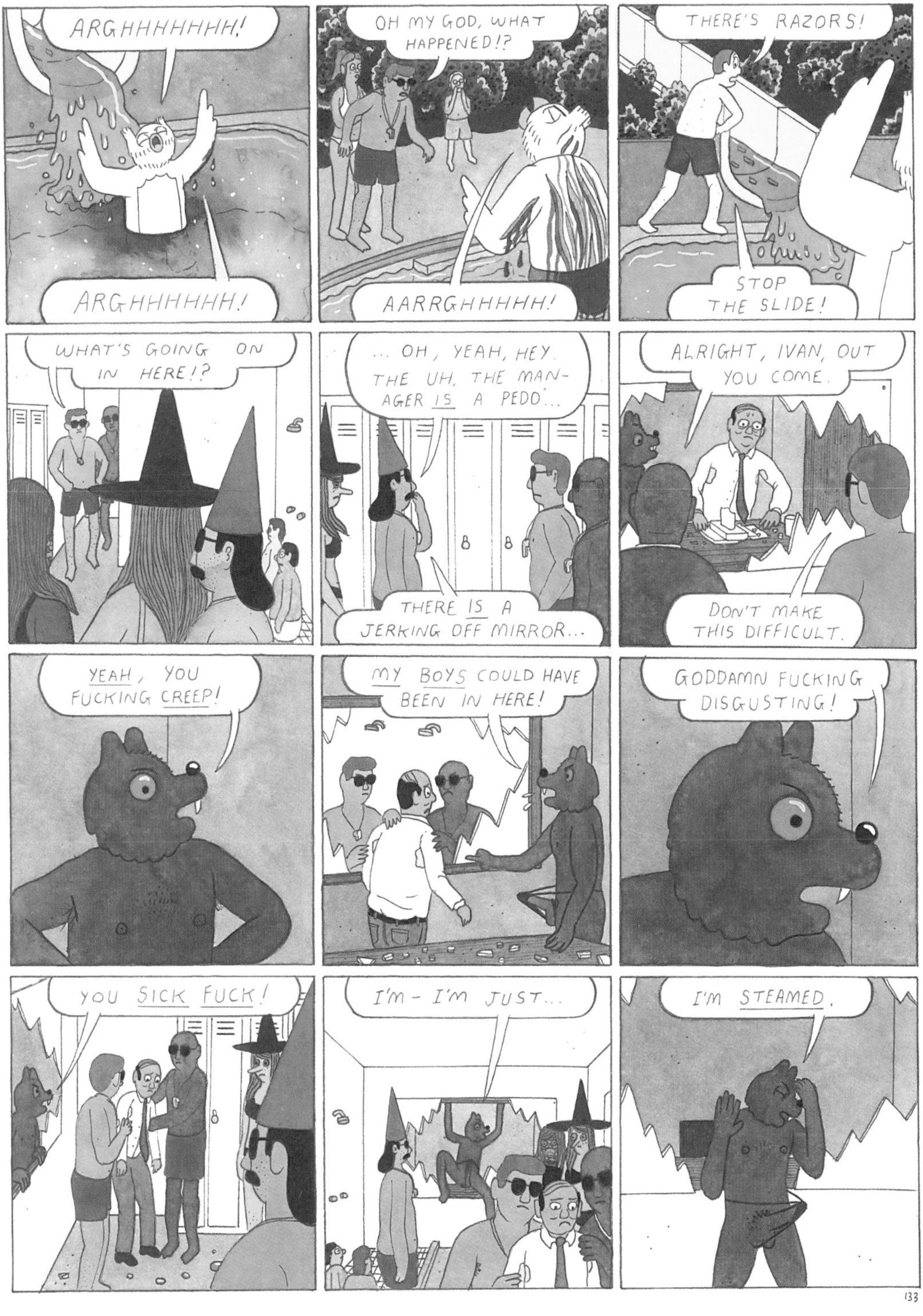
ARGHHHHHHH!
ARGHHHHHHH!
OH MY GOD, WHAT HAPPENED!?
AARRGHHHHH!
THERE'S RAZORS!
STOP THE SLIDE!
WHAT'S GOING ON IN HERE!?
... OH, YEAH, HEY. THE UH, THE MANAGER IS A PEDO...
THERE IS A JERKING OFF MIRROR...
ALRIGHT, IVAN, OUT YOU COME.
DON'T MAKE THIS DIFFICULT.
YEAH, YOU FUCKING CREEP!
MY BOYS COULD HAVE BEEN IN HERE!
GODDAMN FUCKING DISGUSTING!
YOU SICK FUCK!
I'M - I'M JUST...
I'M STEAMED.

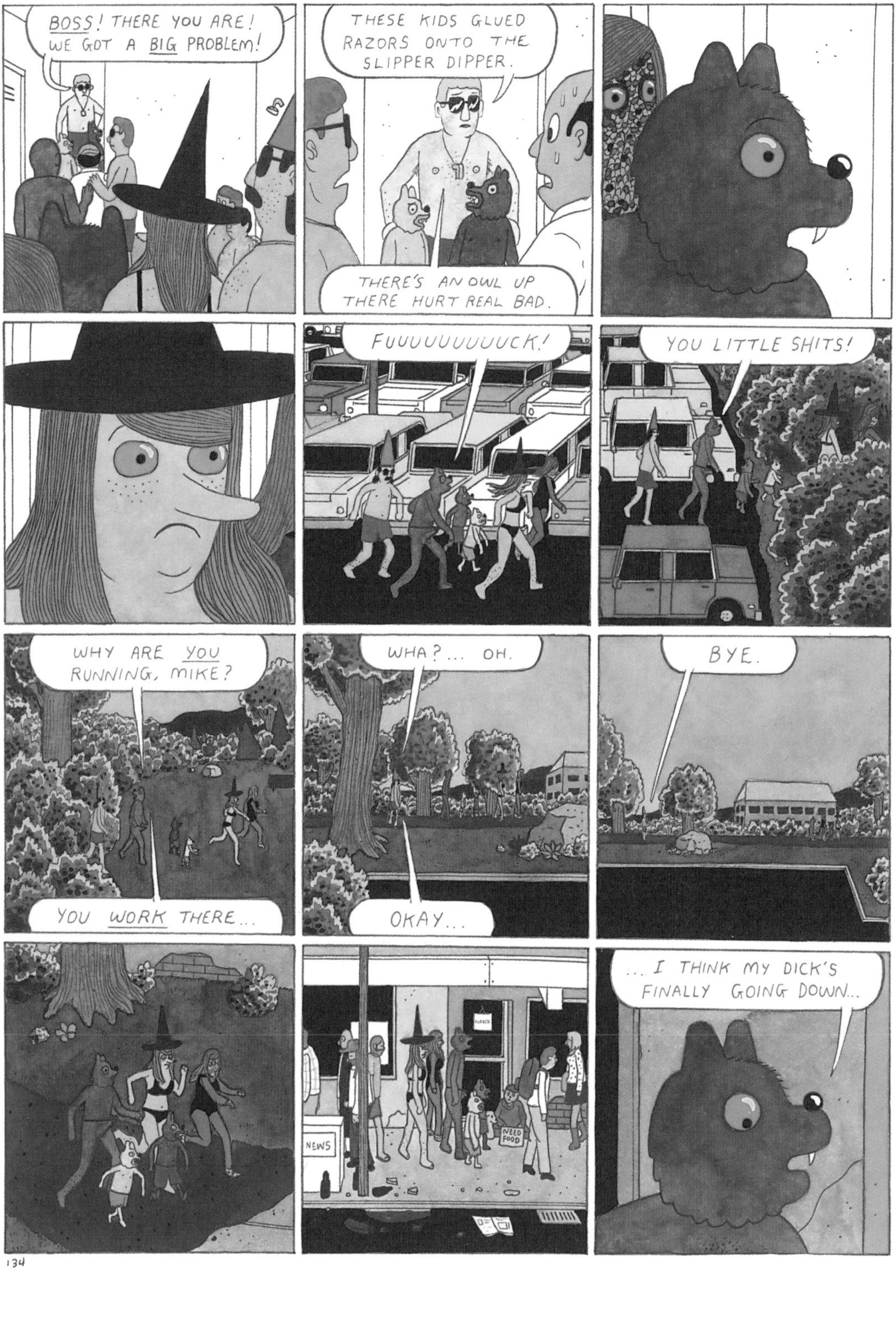
BOSS! THERE YOU ARE! WE GOT A BIG PROBLEM!
THESE KIDS GLUED RAZORS ONTO THE SLIPPER DIPPER.
THERE'S AN OWL UP THERE HURT REAL BAD.
FUUUUUUUUUCK!
YOU LITTLE SHITS!
WHY ARE YOU RUNNING, MIKE?
YOU WORK THERE...
WHA?... OH.
OKAY...
BYE.
NEWS
NEED FOOD
...I THINK MY DICK'S FINALLY GOING DOWN...

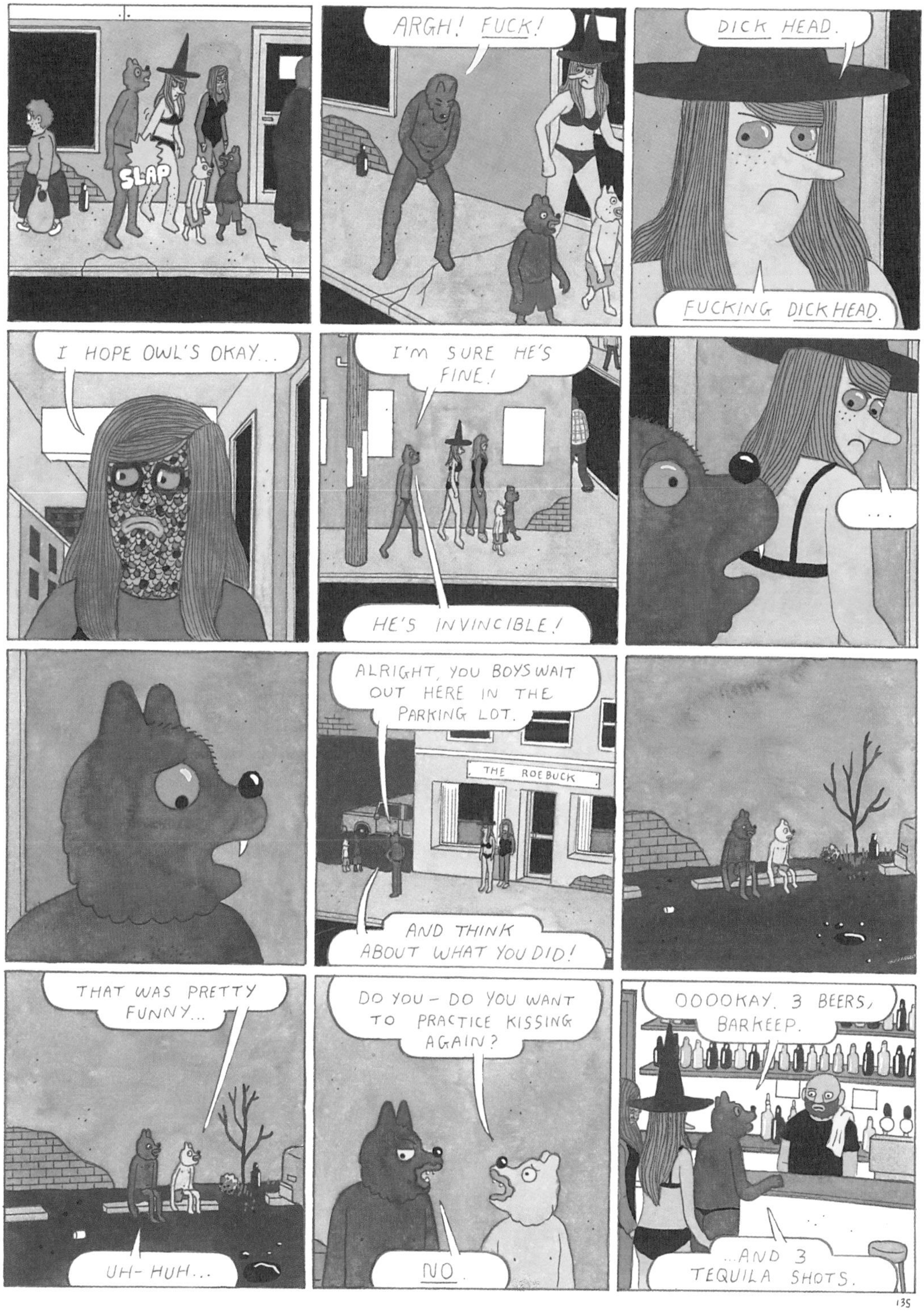
SLAP
ARGH! FUCK!
DICK HEAD.
FUCKING DICKHEAD.
I HOPE OWL'S OKAY...
I'M SURE HE'S FINE!
HE'S INVINCIBLE!
...
ALRIGHT, YOU BOYS WAIT OUT HERE IN THE PARKING LOT.
THE ROEBUCK
AND THINK ABOUT WHAT YOU DID!
THAT WAS PRETTY FUNNY...
UH-HUH...
DO YOU - DO YOU WANT TO PRACTICE KISSING AGAIN?
NO.
OOOOKAY. 3 BEERS, BARKEEP.
...AND 3 TEQUILA SHOTS.

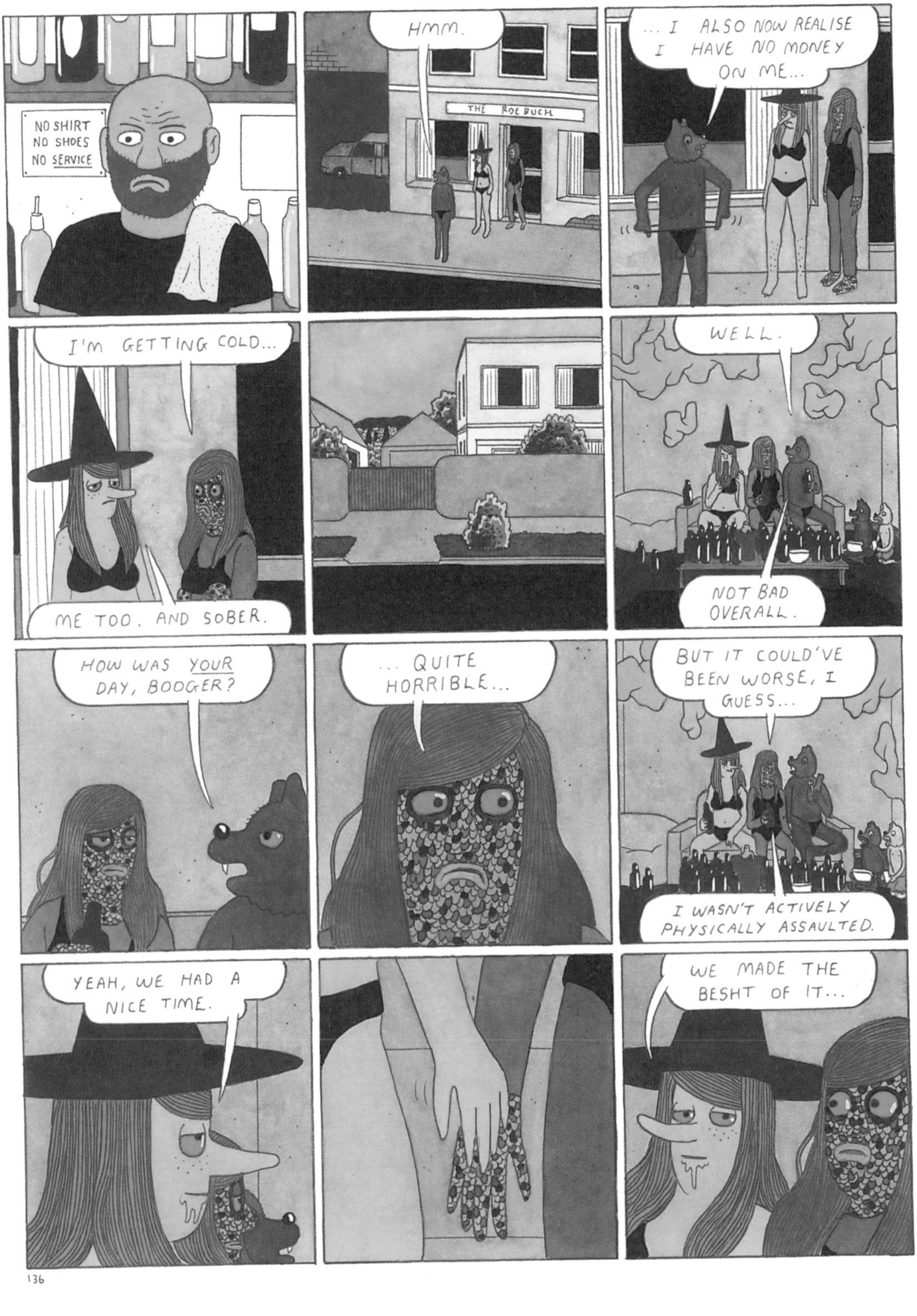
NO SHIRT
NO SHOES
NO SERVICE
HMM.
THE ROEBUCK
... I ALSO NOW REALISE I HAVE NO MONEY ON ME...
I'M GETTING COLD...
ME TOO. AND SOBER.
WELL.
NOT BAD OVERALL.
HOW WAS YOUR DAY, BOOGER?
... QUITE HORRIBLE...
BUT IT COULD'VE BEEN WORSE, I GUESS...
I WASN'T ACTIVELY PHYSICALLY ASSAULTED.
YEAH, WE HAD A NICE TIME.
WE MADE THE BESHT OF IT...

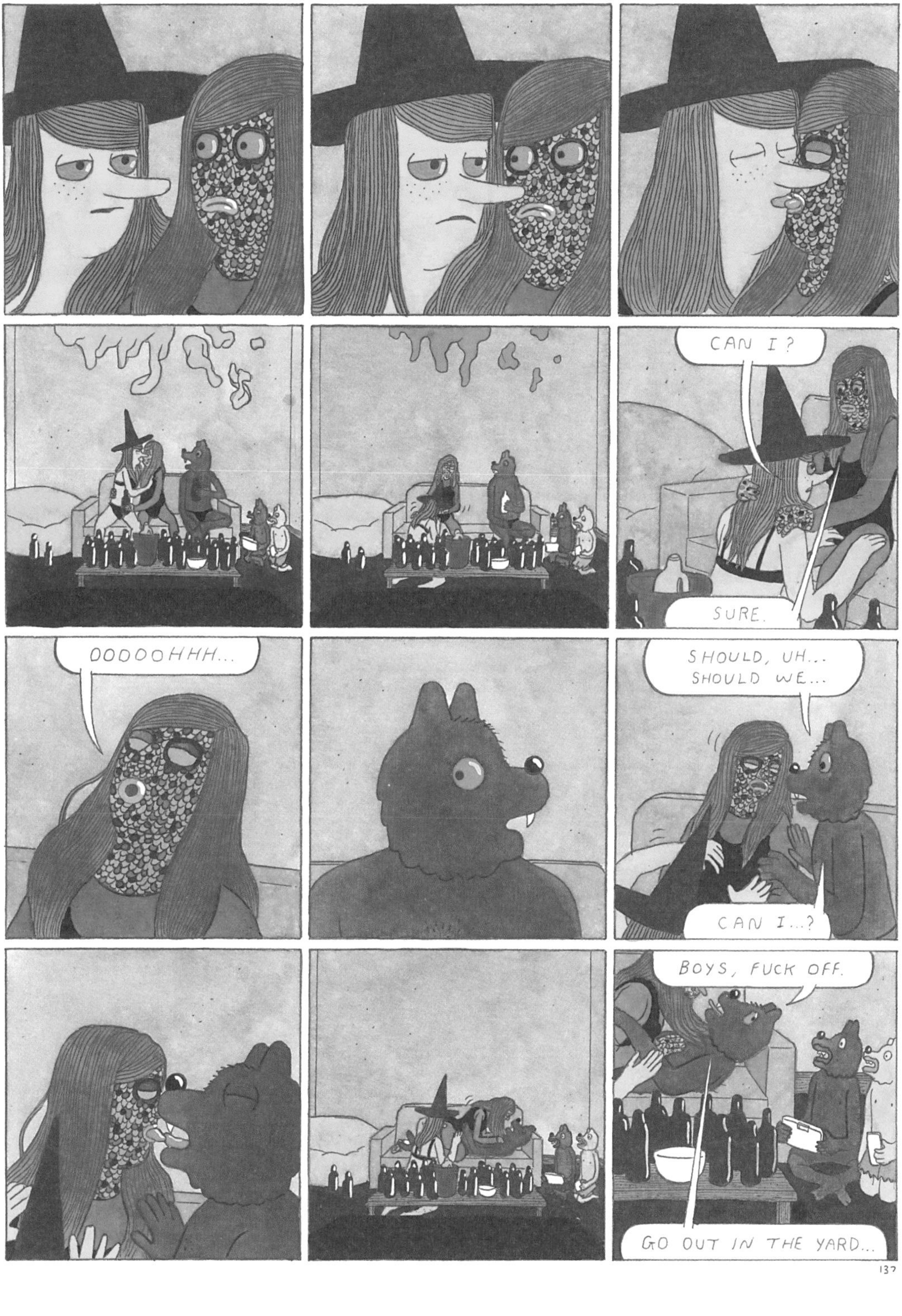
CAN I?
SURE.
OOOOOHHH...
SHOULD, UH...
SHOULD WE...
CAN I...?
BOYS, FUCK OFF.
GO OUT IN THE YARD...

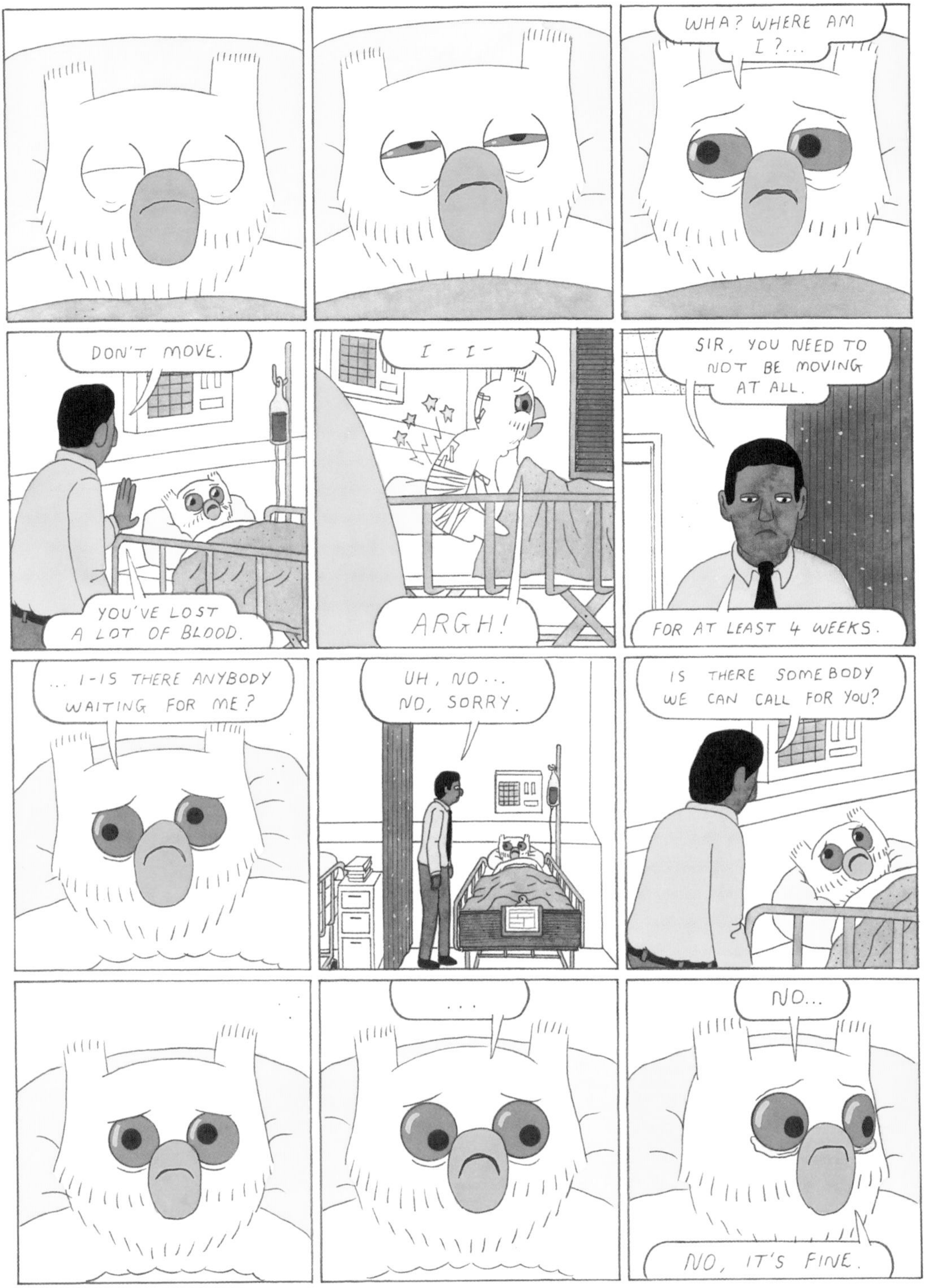
WHA? WHERE AM I?...
DON'T MOVE.
YOU'VE LOST A LOT OF BLOOD.
I - I -
ARGH!
SIR, YOU NEED TO NOT BE MOVING AT ALL.
FOR AT LEAST 4 WEEKS.
... I-IS THERE ANYBODY WAITING FOR ME?
UH, NO... NO, SORRY.
IS THERE SOMEBODY WE CAN CALL FOR YOU?
...
NO...
NO, IT'S FINE.

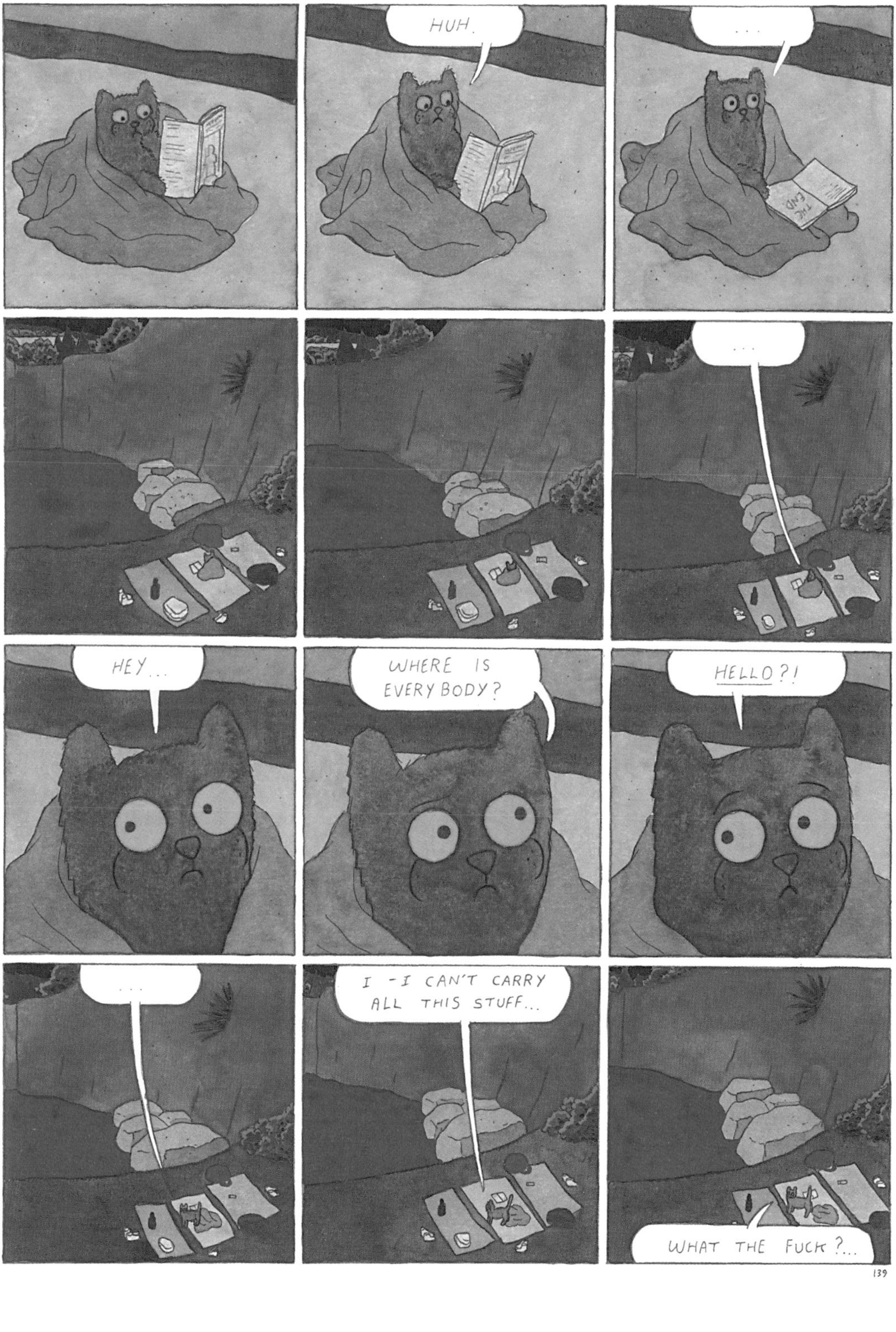
HUH.
...
THE END
...
HEY...
WHERE IS EVERYBODY?
HELLO?!
...
I -I CAN'T CARRY ALL THIS STUFF...
WHAT THE FUCK?...

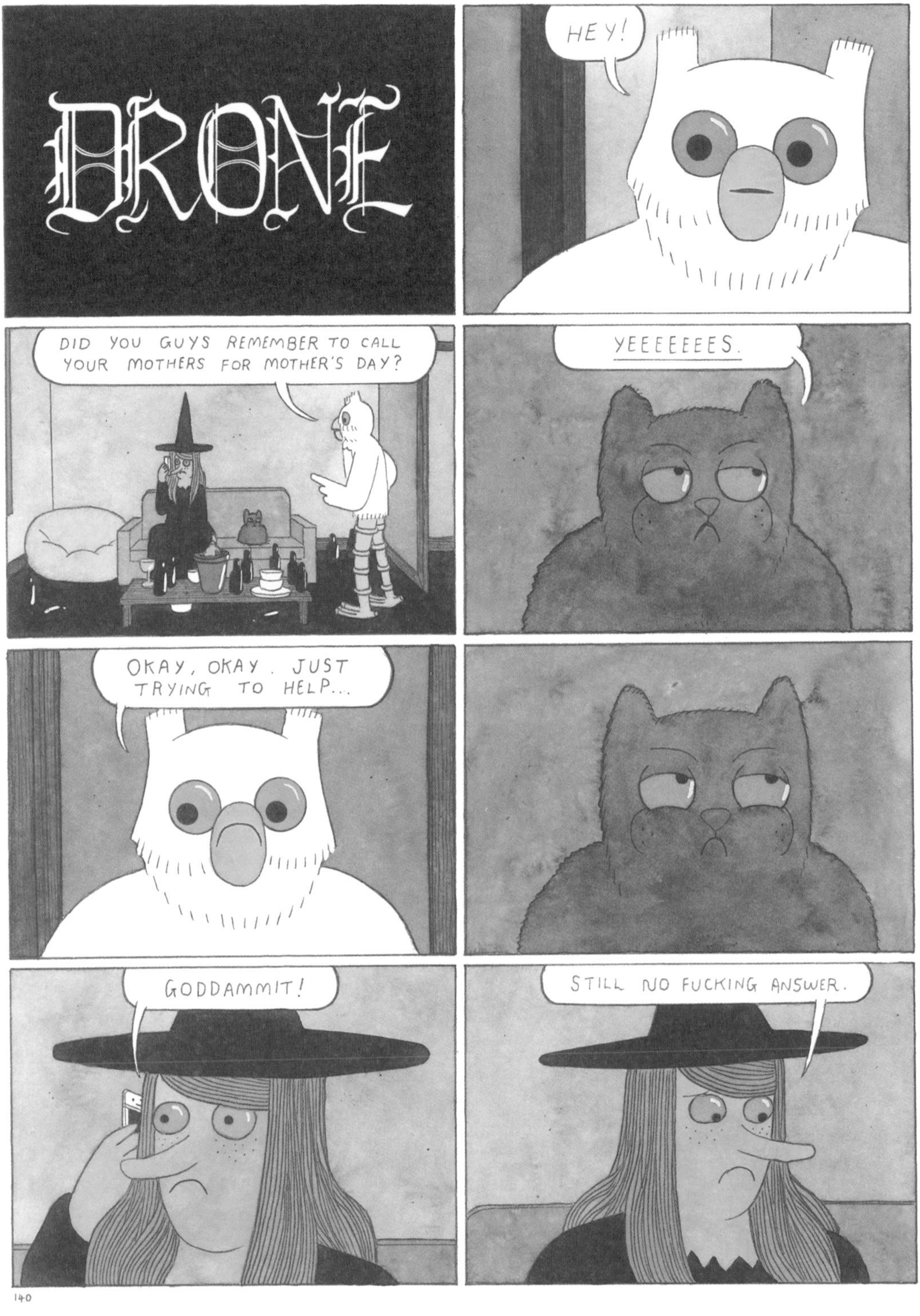
DRONE
HEY!
DID YOU GUYS REMEMBER TO CALL YOUR MOTHERS FOR MOTHER'S DAY?
YEEEEEEES.
OKAY, OKAY. JUST TRYING TO HELP...
GODDAMMIT!
STILL NO FUCKING ANSWER.

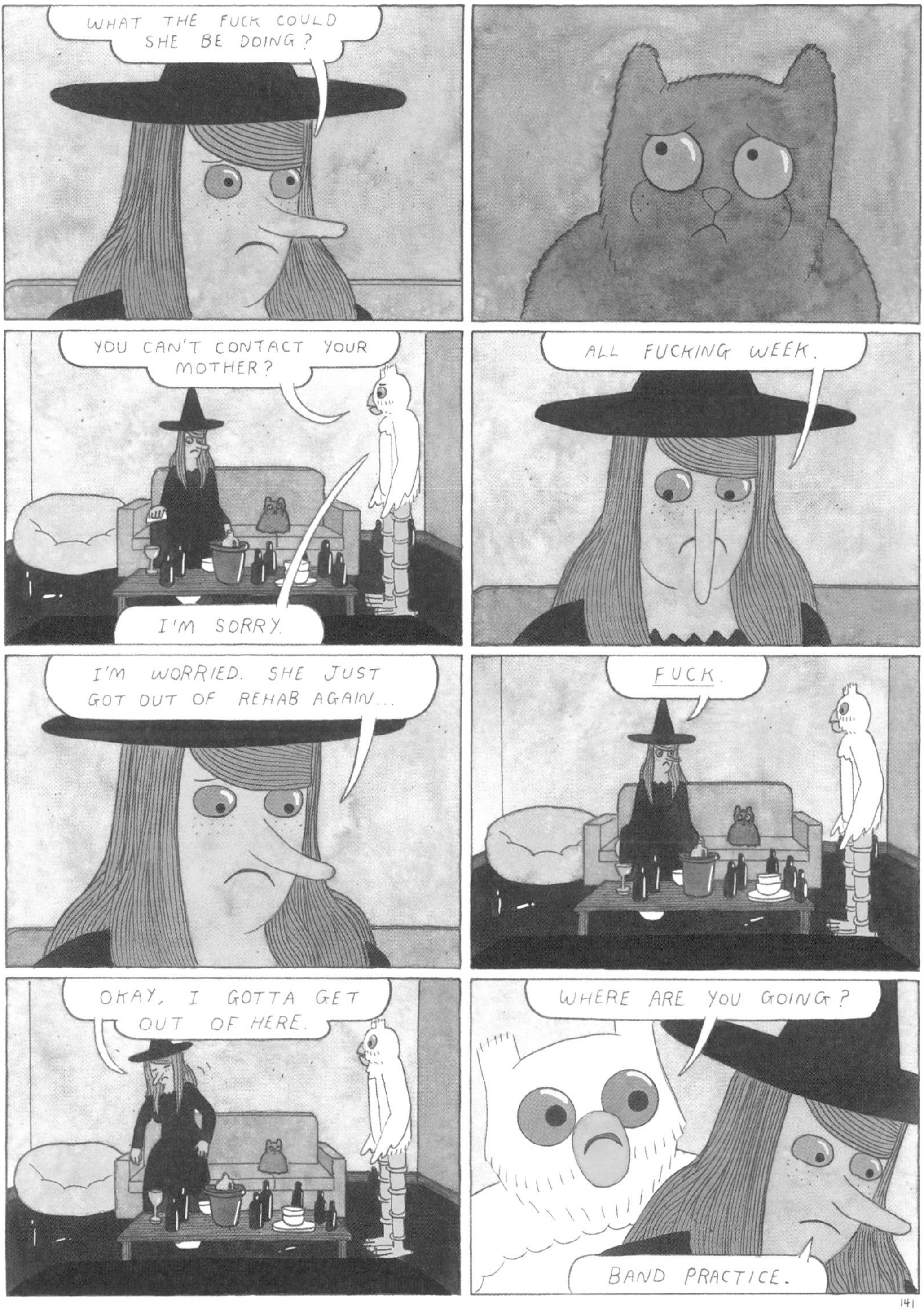
WHAT THE FUCK COULD SHE BE DOING?
YOU CAN'T CONTACT YOUR MOTHER?
I'M SORRY.
ALL FUCKING WEEK.
I'M WORRIED. SHE JUST GOT OUT OF REHAB AGAIN...
FUCK.
OKAY, I GOTTA GET OUT OF HERE.
WHERE ARE YOU GOING?
BAND PRACTICE.

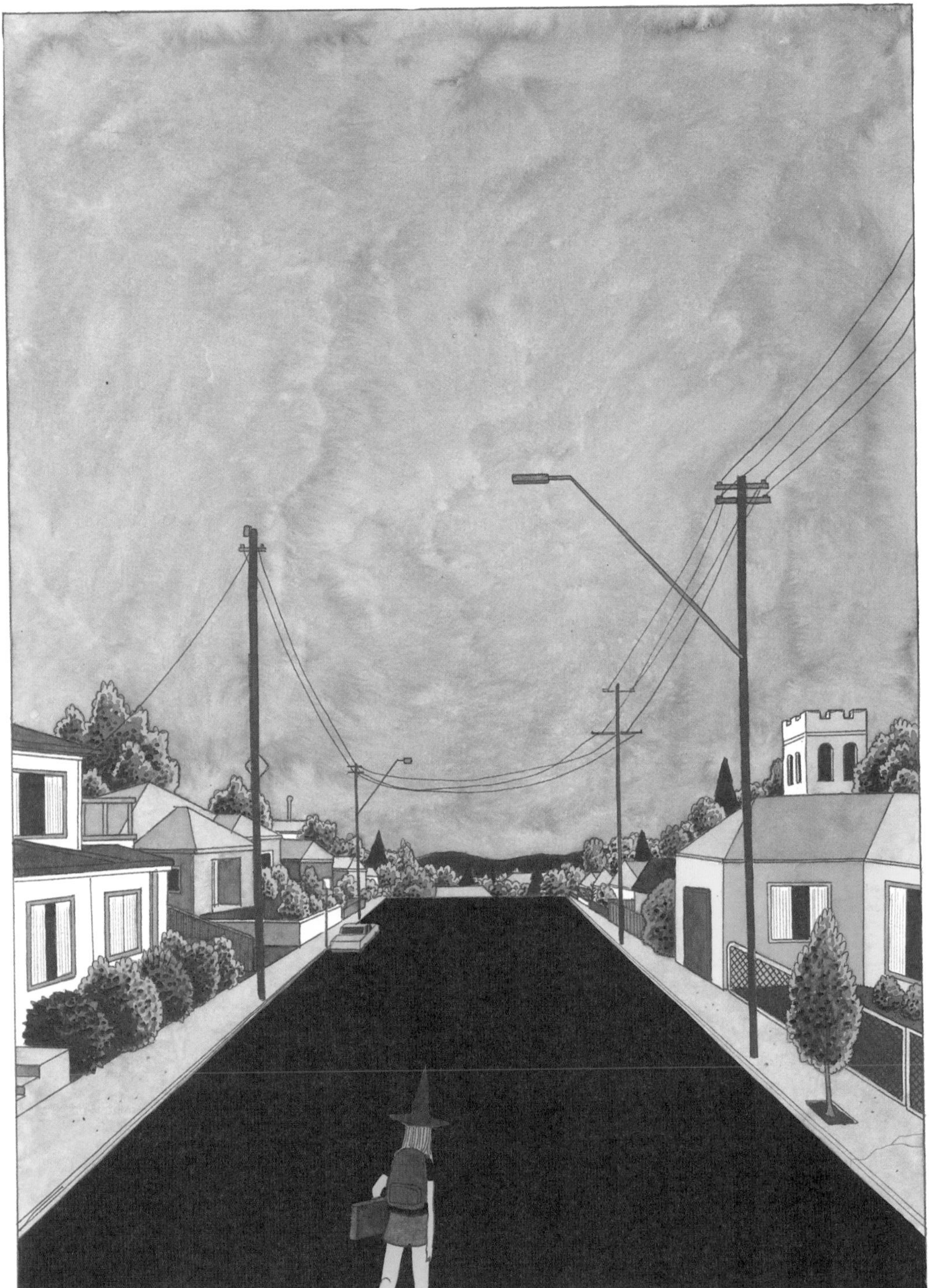

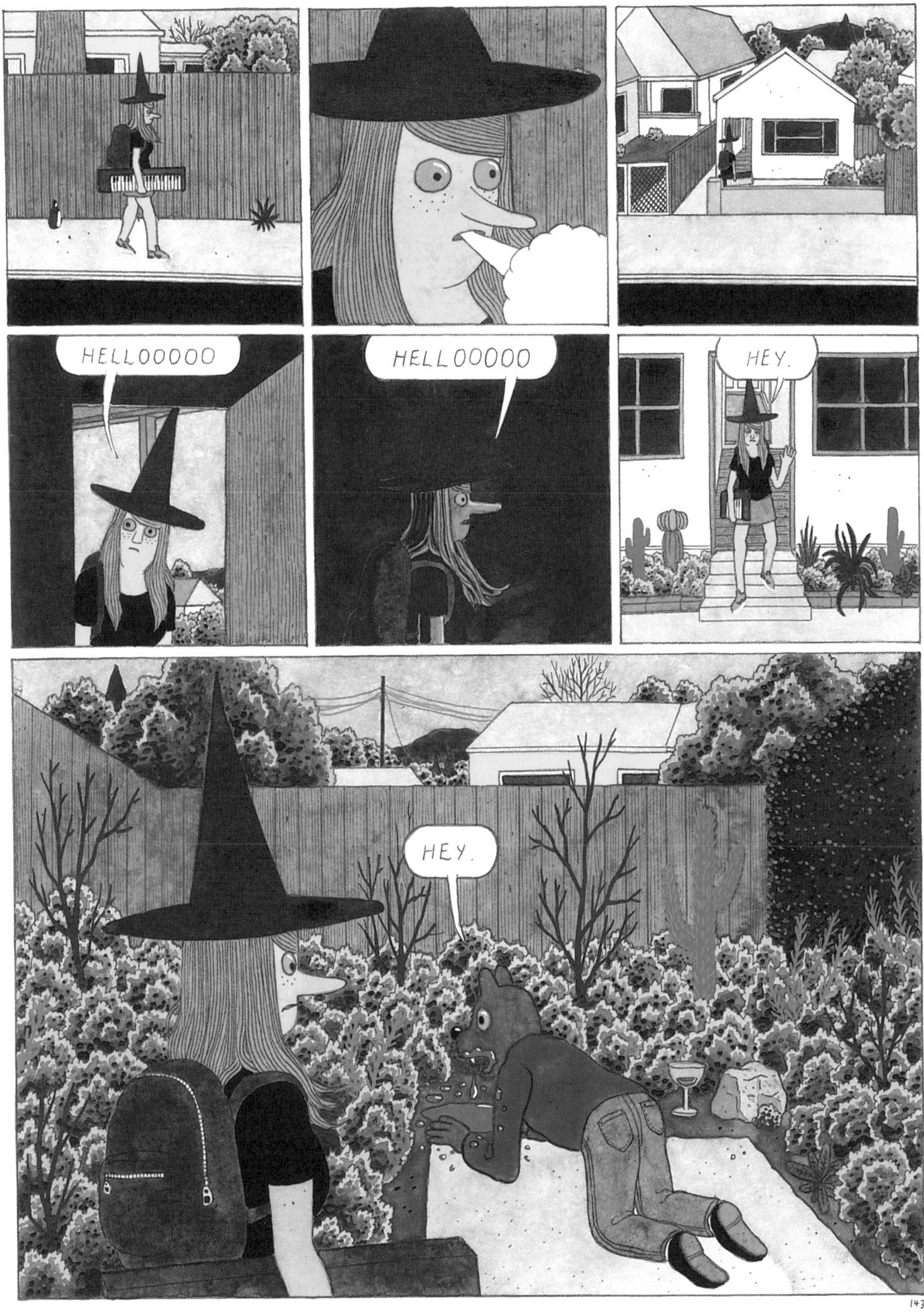
HELLOOOOO
HELLOOOOO
HEY.
HEY.

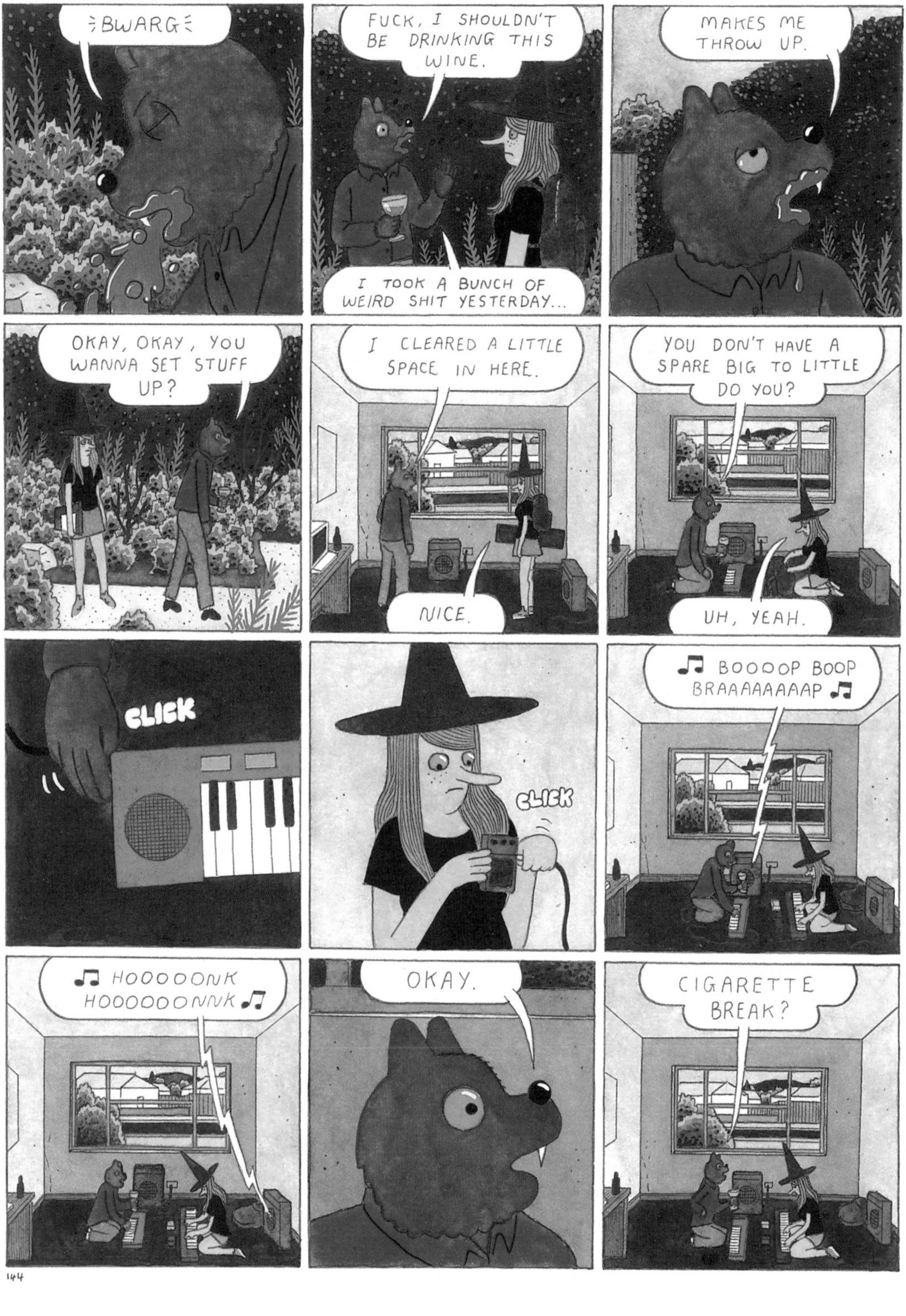
BWARG
FUCK, I SHOULDN'T BE DRINKING THIS WINE.
I TOOK A BUNCH OF WEIRD SHIT YESTERDAY...
MAKES ME THROW UP.
OKAY, OKAY, YOU WANNA SET STUFF UP?
I CLEARED A LITTLE SPACE IN HERE.
NICE.
YOU DON'T HAVE A SPARE BIG TO LITTLE DO YOU?
UH, YEAH.
CLICK
CLICK
BOOOOP BOOP BRAAAAAAAAP
HOOOOONK HOOOOOONNK
OKAY.
CIGARETTE BREAK?

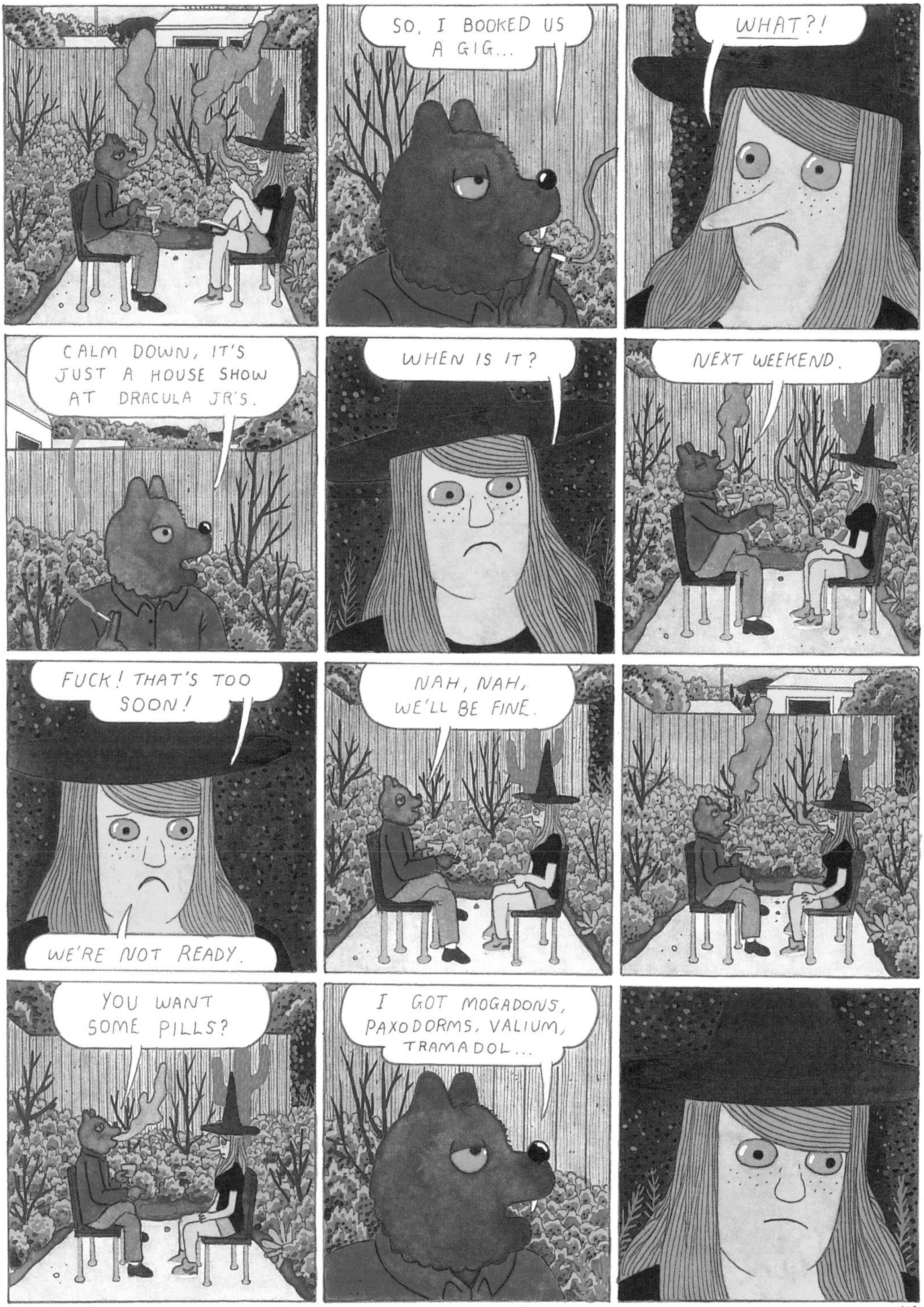
SO, I BOOKED US A GIG...
WHAT?!
CALM DOWN, IT'S JUST A HOUSE SHOW AT DRACULA JR'S.
WHEN IS IT?
NEXT WEEKEND.
FUCK! THAT'S TOO SOON!
WE'RE NOT READY.
NAH, NAH, WE'LL BE FINE.
YOU WANT SOME PILLS?
I GOT MOGADONS, PAXODORMS, VALIUM, TRAMADOL...

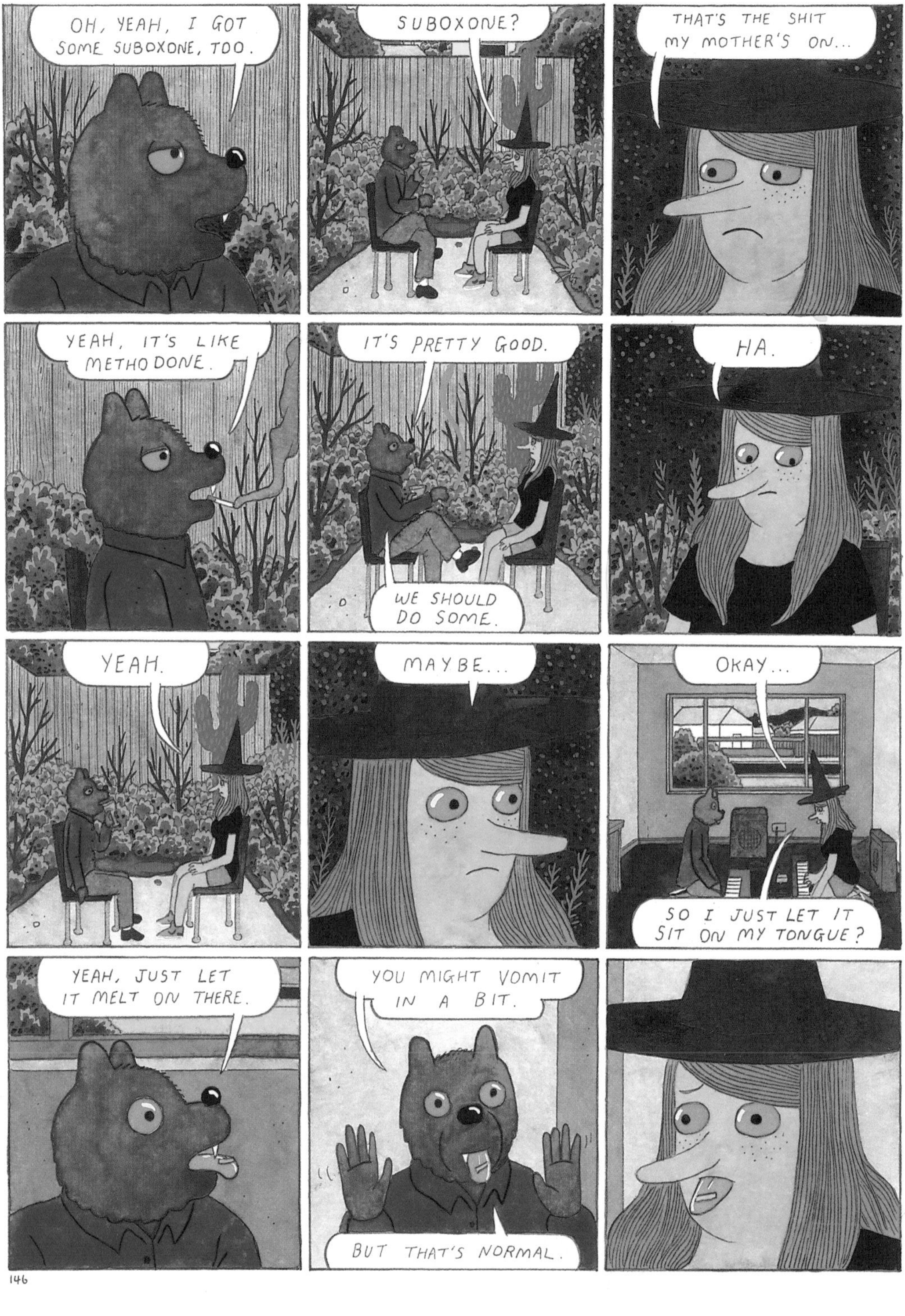
OH, YEAH, I GOT SOME SUBOXONE, TOO.
SUBOXONE?
THAT'S THE SHIT MY MOTHER'S ON...
YEAH, IT'S LIKE METHODONE.
IT'S PRETTY GOOD.
WE SHOULD DO SOME.
HA.
YEAH.
MAYBE...
OKAY...
SO I JUST LET IT SIT ON MY TONGUE?
YEAH, JUST LET IT MELT ON THERE.
YOU MIGHT VOMIT IN A BIT.
BUT THAT'S NORMAL.

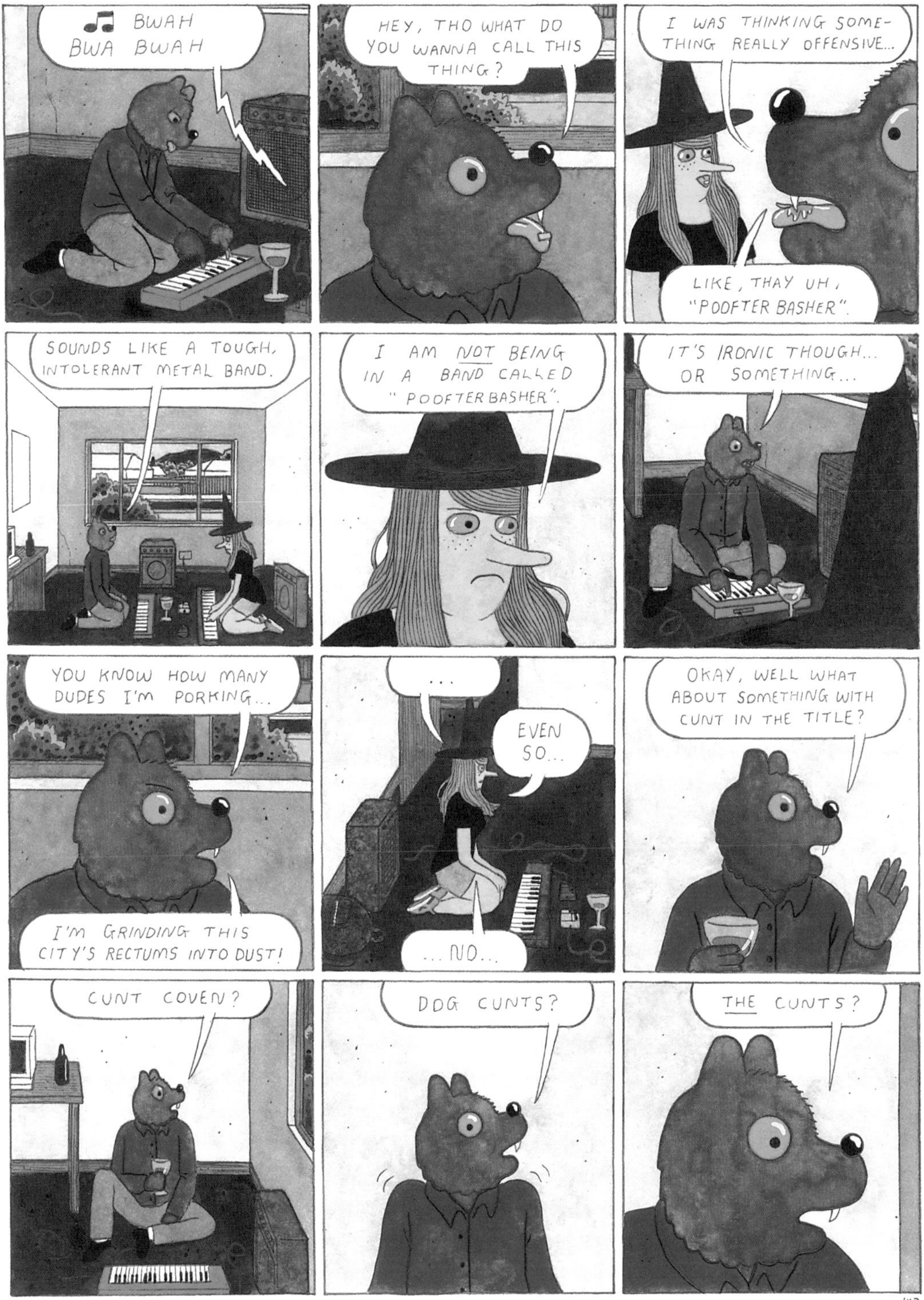
BWAH BWA BWAH
HEY, THO WHAT DO YOU WANNA CALL THIS THING?
I WAS THINKING SOME-THING REALLY OFFENSIVE...
LIKE, THAY UH, "POOFTER BASHER".
SOUNDS LIKE A TOUGH, INTOLERANT METAL BAND.
I AM NOT BEING IN A BAND CALLED "POOFTER BASHER".
IT'S IRONIC THOUGH... OR SOMETHING...
YOU KNOW HOW MANY DUDES I'M PORKING...
I'M GRINDING THIS CITY'S RECTUMS INTO DUST!
...
EVEN SO...
...NO...
OKAY, WELL WHAT ABOUT SOMETHING WITH CUNT IN THE TITLE?
CUNT COVEN?
DOG CUNTS?
THE CUNTS?

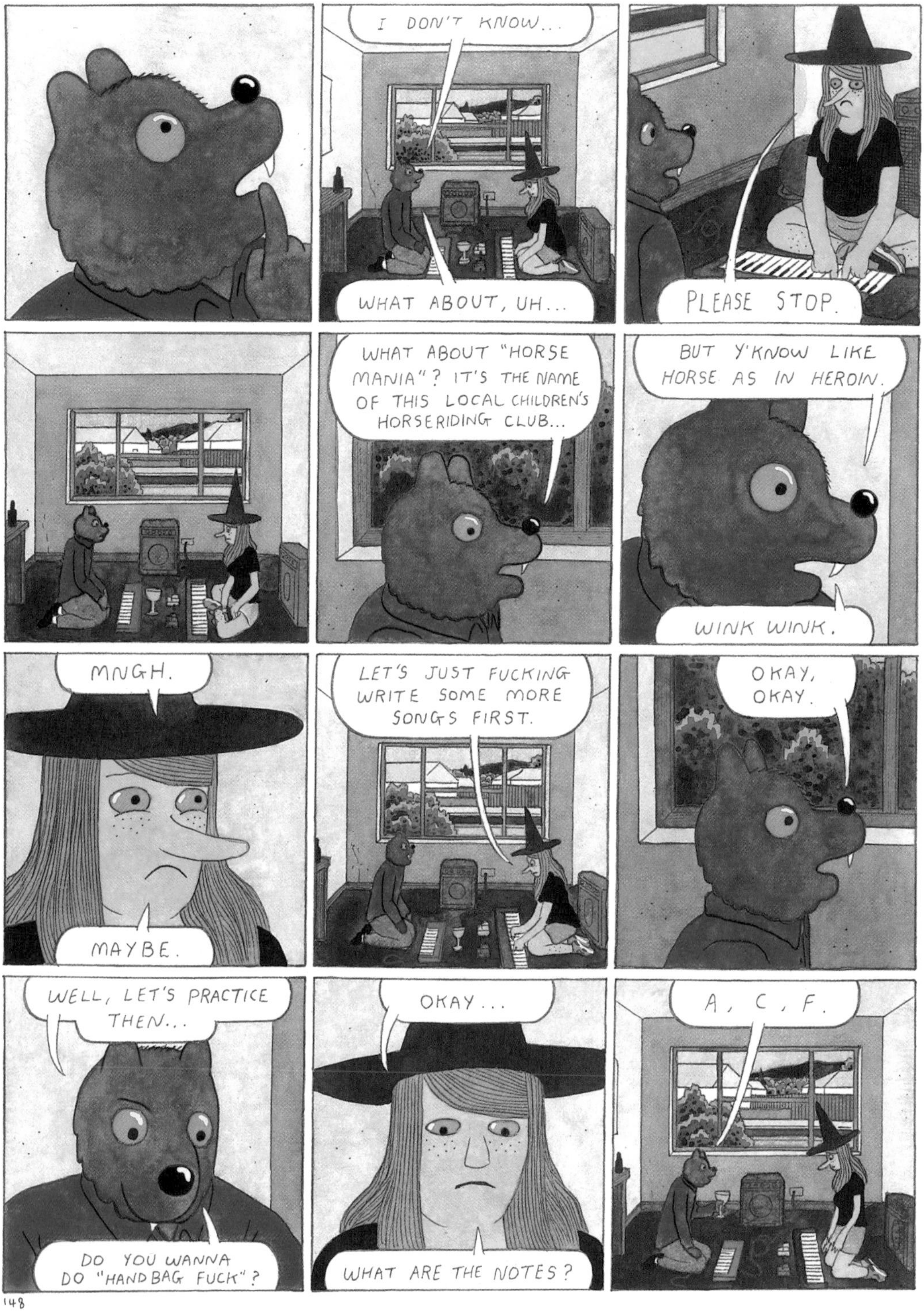
I DON'T KNOW...
WHAT ABOUT, UH...
PLEASE STOP.
WHAT ABOUT "HORSE MANIA"? IT'S THE NAME OF THIS LOCAL CHILDREN'S HORSERIDING CLUB...
BUT Y'KNOW LIKE HORSE AS IN HEROIN.
WINK WINK.
MNGH.
MAYBE.
LET'S JUST FUCKING WRITE SOME MORE SONGS FIRST.
OKAY, OKAY.
WELL, LET'S PRACTICE THEN...
DO YOU WANNA DO "HANDBAG FUCK"?
OKAY...
WHAT ARE THE NOTES?
A, C, F.

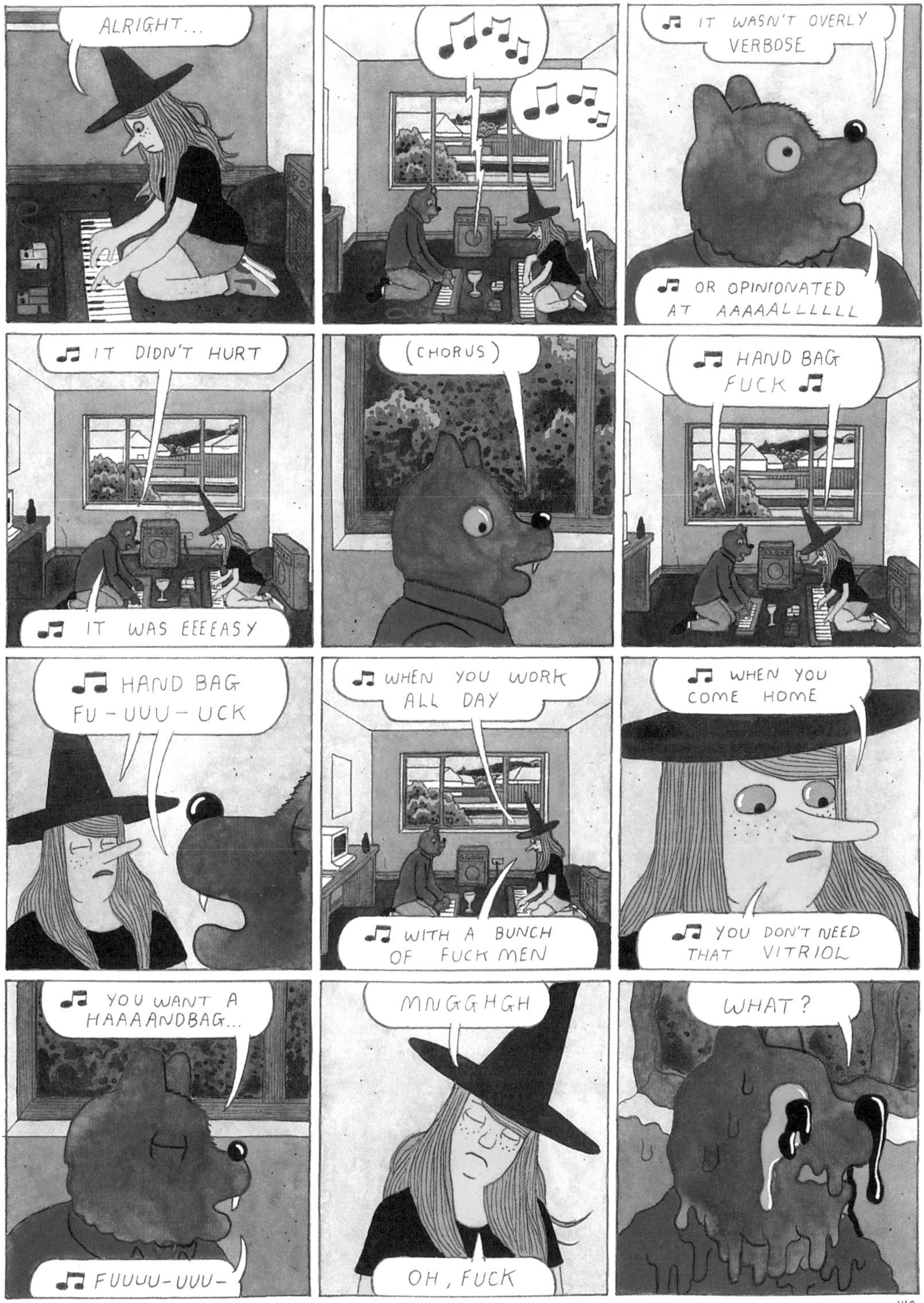
ALRIGHT...
♫ IT WASN'T OVERLY VERBOSE
♫ OR OPINIONATED AT AAAAALLLLLL
♫ IT DIDN'T HURT
♫ IT WAS EEEEASY
(CHORUS)
♫ HAND BAG FUCK ♫
♫ HAND BAG FU-UUU-UCK
♫ WHEN YOU WORK ALL DAY
♫ WITH A BUNCH OF FUCK MEN
♫ WHEN YOU COME HOME
♫ YOU DON'T NEED THAT VITRIOL
♫ YOU WANT A HAAAANDBAG...
♫ FUUUU-UUU-
MNGGHGH
OH, FUCK
WHAT?

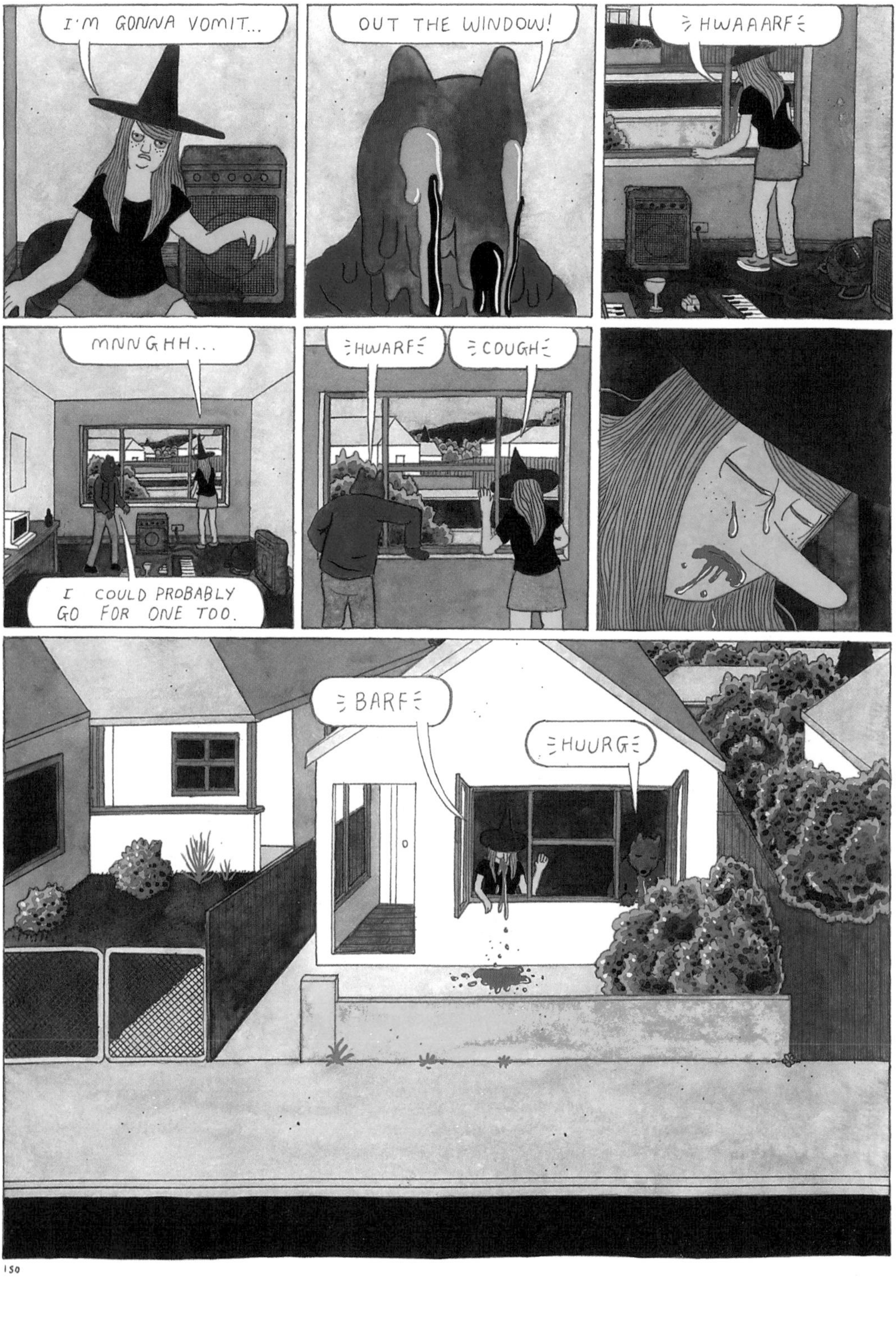
I'M GONNA VOMIT...
OUT THE WINDOW!
HWAAARF
MNNGHH...
I COULD PROBABLY GO FOR ONE TOO.
HWARF
COUGH
BARF
HUURG

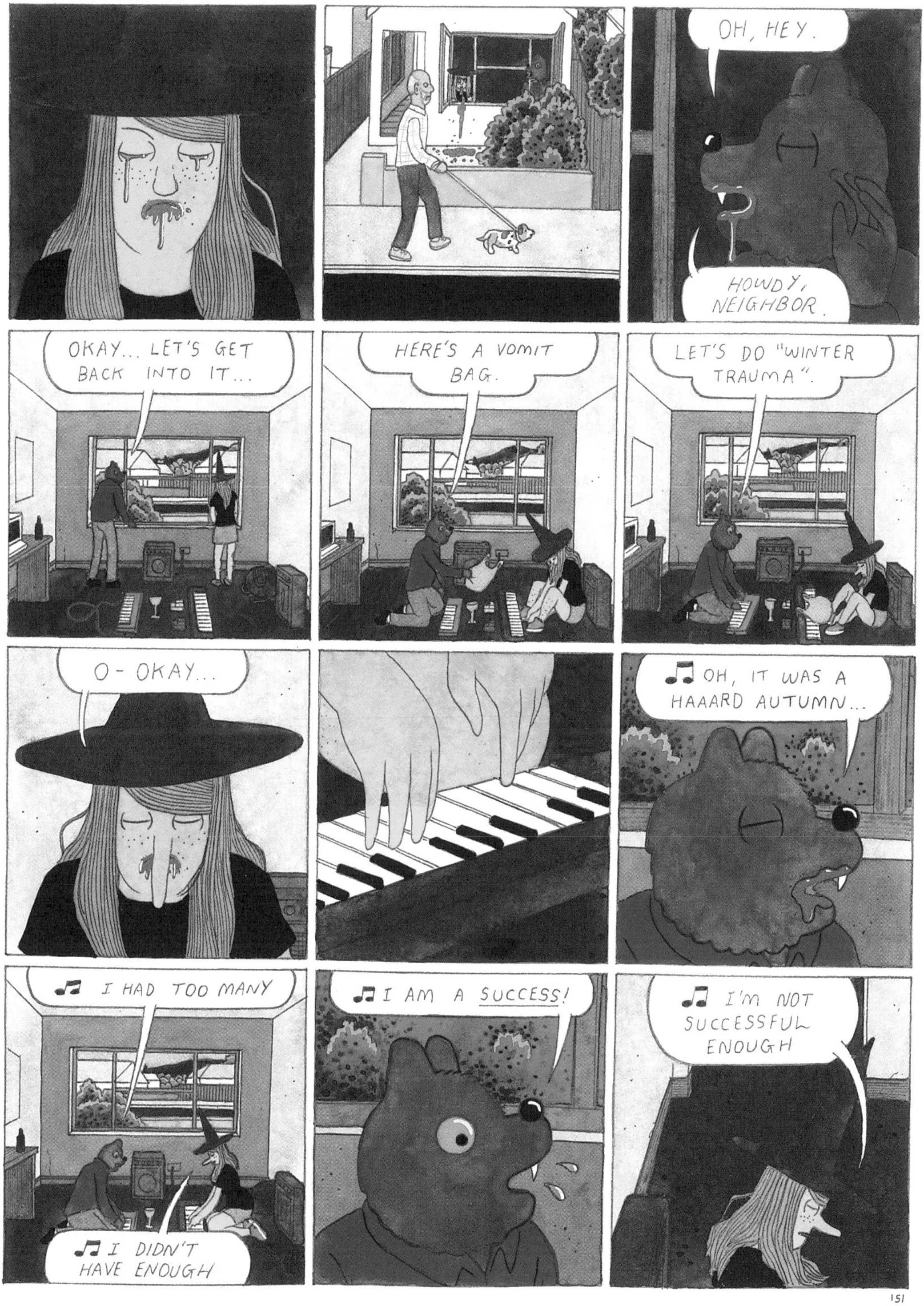
OH, HEY.
HOWDY, NEIGHBOR.
OKAY... LET'S GET BACK INTO IT...
HERE'S A VOMIT BAG.
LET'S DO "WINTER TRAUMA".
O-OKAY...
♫ OH, IT WAS A HAAARD AUTUMN...
♫ I HAD TOO MANY
♫ I DIDN'T HAVE ENOUGH
♫ I AM A SUCCESS!
♫ I'M NOT SUCCESSFUL ENOUGH

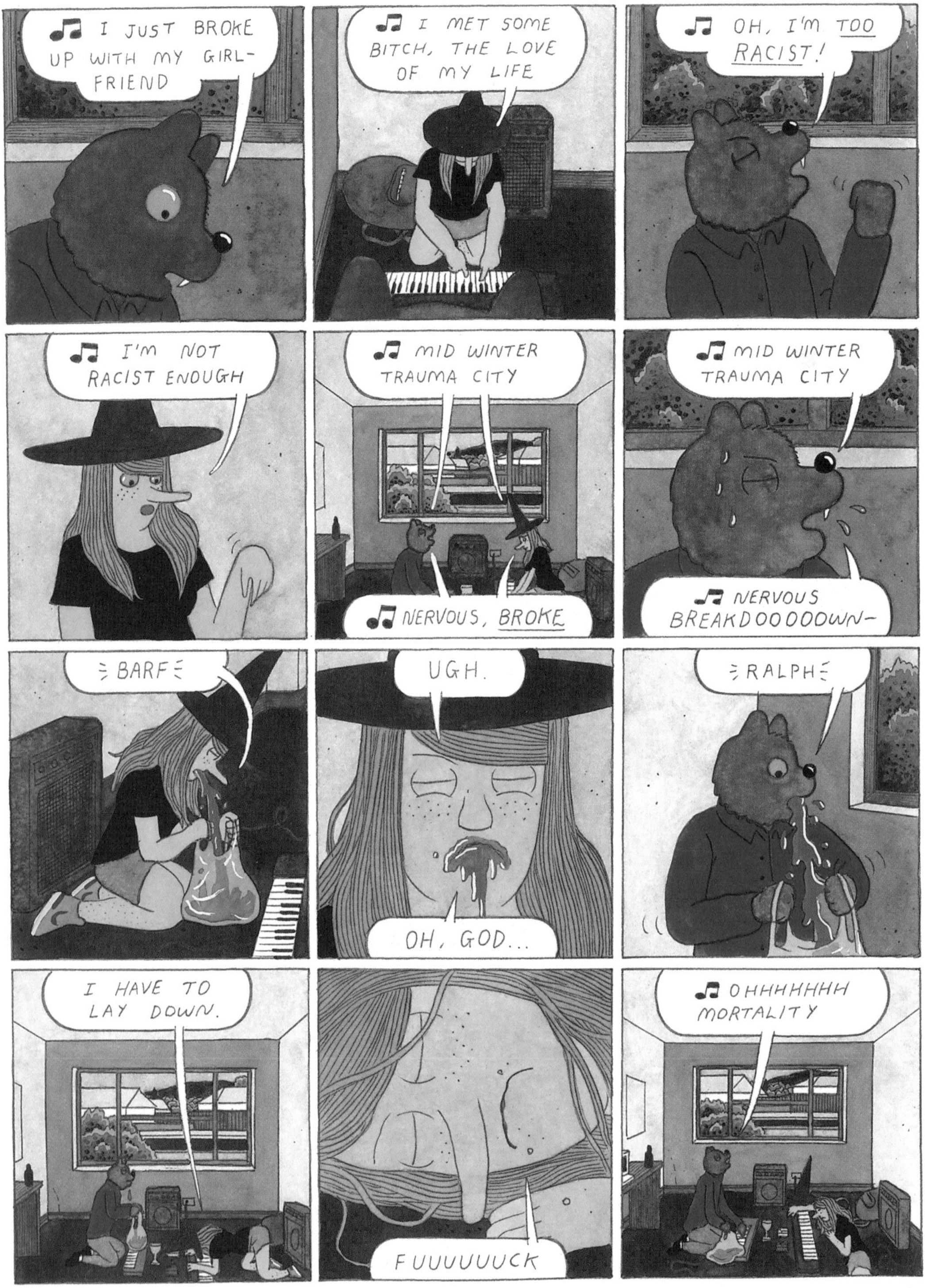
♫ I JUST BROKE UP WITH MY GIRL-FRIEND
♫ I MET SOME BITCH, THE LOVE OF MY LIFE
♫ OH, I'M TOO RACIST!
♫ I'M NOT RACIST ENOUGH
♫ MID WINTER TRAUMA CITY
♫ NERVOUS, BROKE
♫ MID WINTER TRAUMA CITY
♫ NERVOUS BREAKDOOOOOWN-
BARF
UGH.
OH, GOD...
RALPH
I HAVE TO LAY DOWN.
FUUUUUUCK
♫ OHHHHHHH MORTALITY

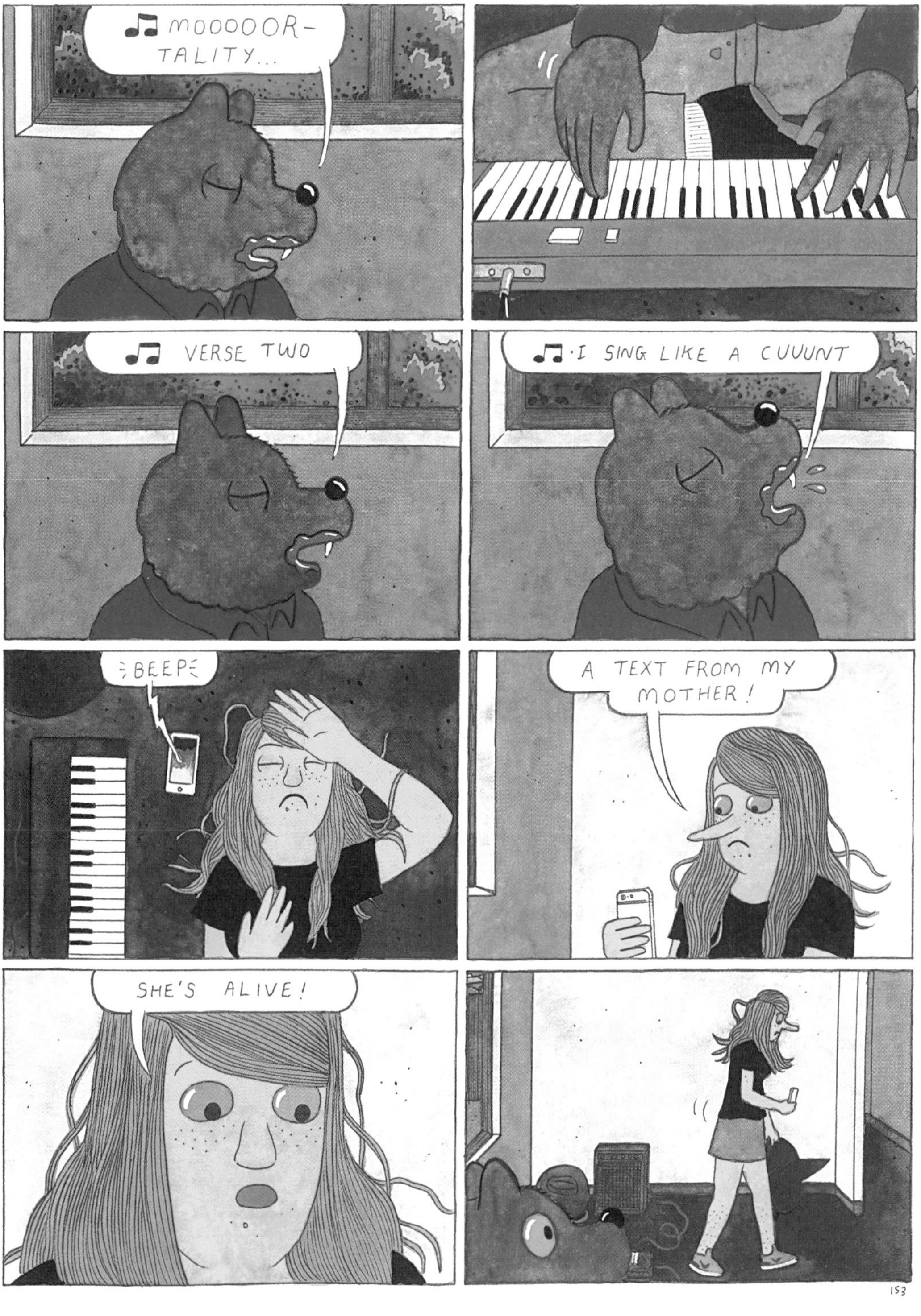
♫ MOOOOOR-TALITY...
♫ VERSE TWO
♫ · I SING LIKE A CUUUNT
BEEP
A TEXT FROM MY MOTHER!
SHE'S ALIVE!

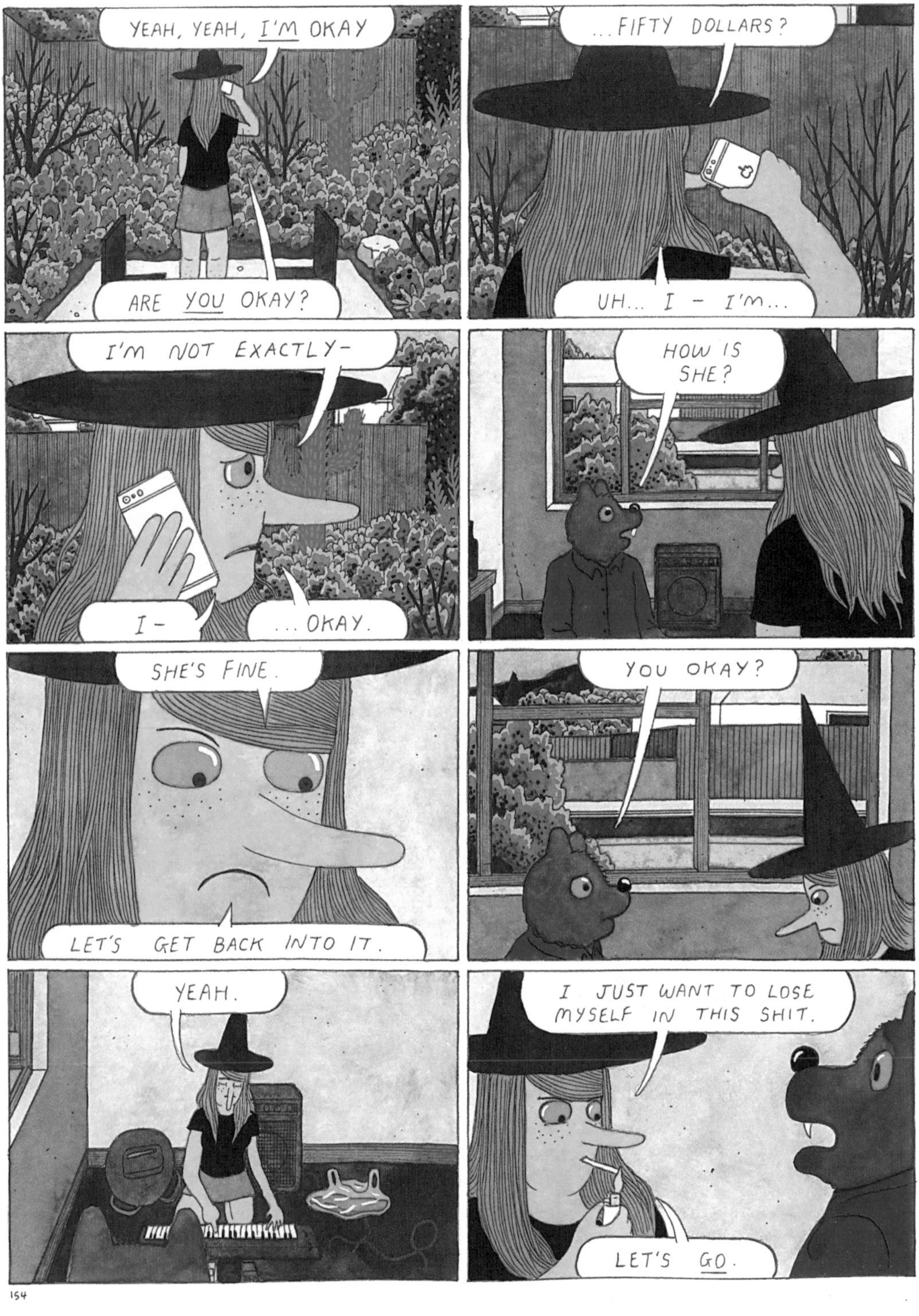
YEAH, YEAH, I'M OKAY
ARE YOU OKAY?
...FIFTY DOLLARS?
UH... I - I'M...
I'M NOT EXACTLY-
I-
...OKAY.
HOW IS SHE?
SHE'S FINE.
LET'S GET BACK INTO IT.
YOU OKAY?
YEAH.
I JUST WANT TO LOSE MYSELF IN THIS SHIT.
LET'S GO.

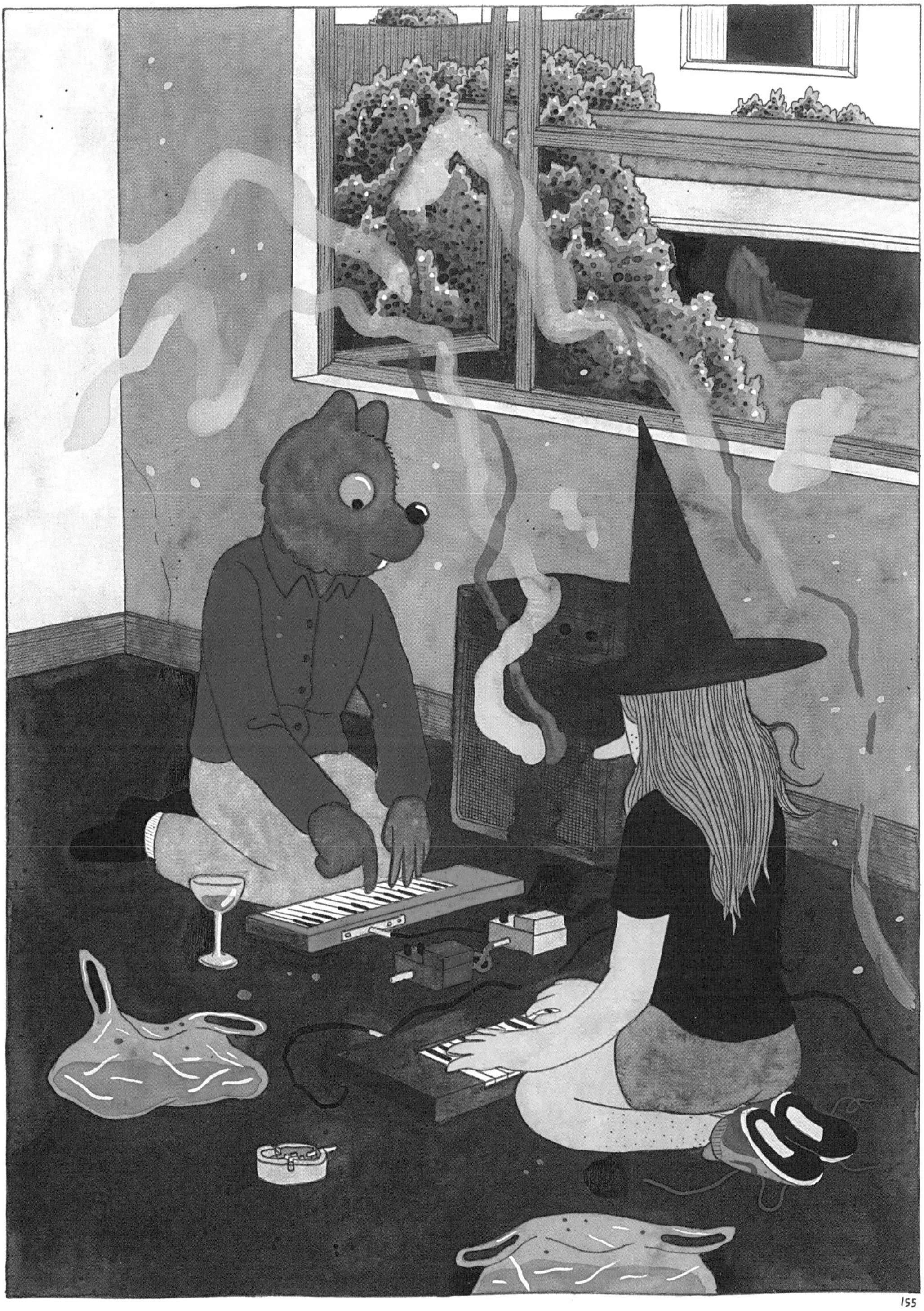

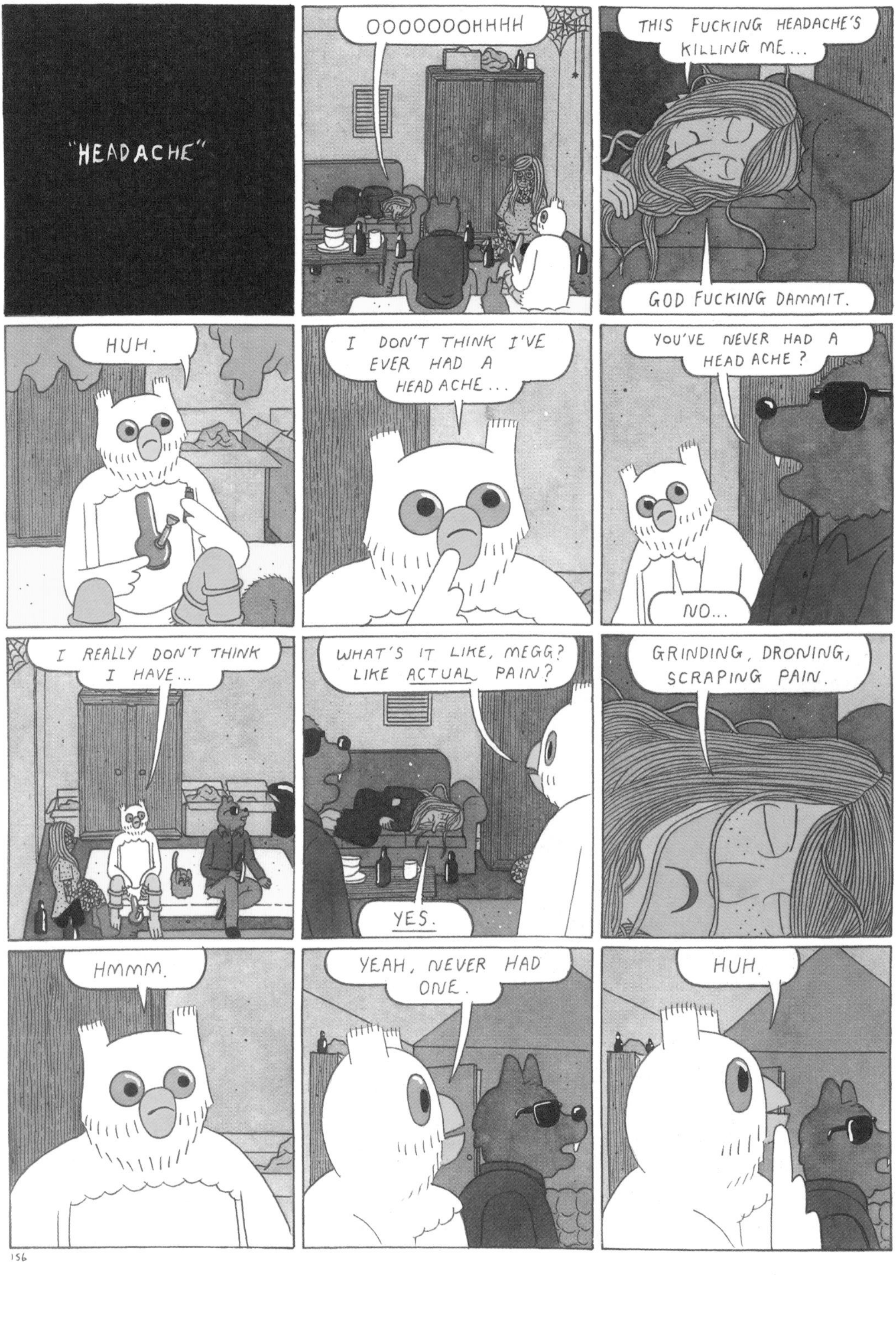

"HEADACHE"
OOOOOOOHHHH
THIS FUCKING HEADACHE'S KILLING ME...
GOD FUCKING DAMMIT.
HUH.
I DON'T THINK I'VE EVER HAD A HEADACHE...
YOU'VE NEVER HAD A HEADACHE?
NO...
I REALLY DON'T THINK I HAVE...
WHAT'S IT LIKE, MEGG? LIKE ACTUAL PAIN?
YES.
GRINDING, DRONING, SCRAPING PAIN.
HMMM.
YEAH, NEVER HAD ONE.
HUH.

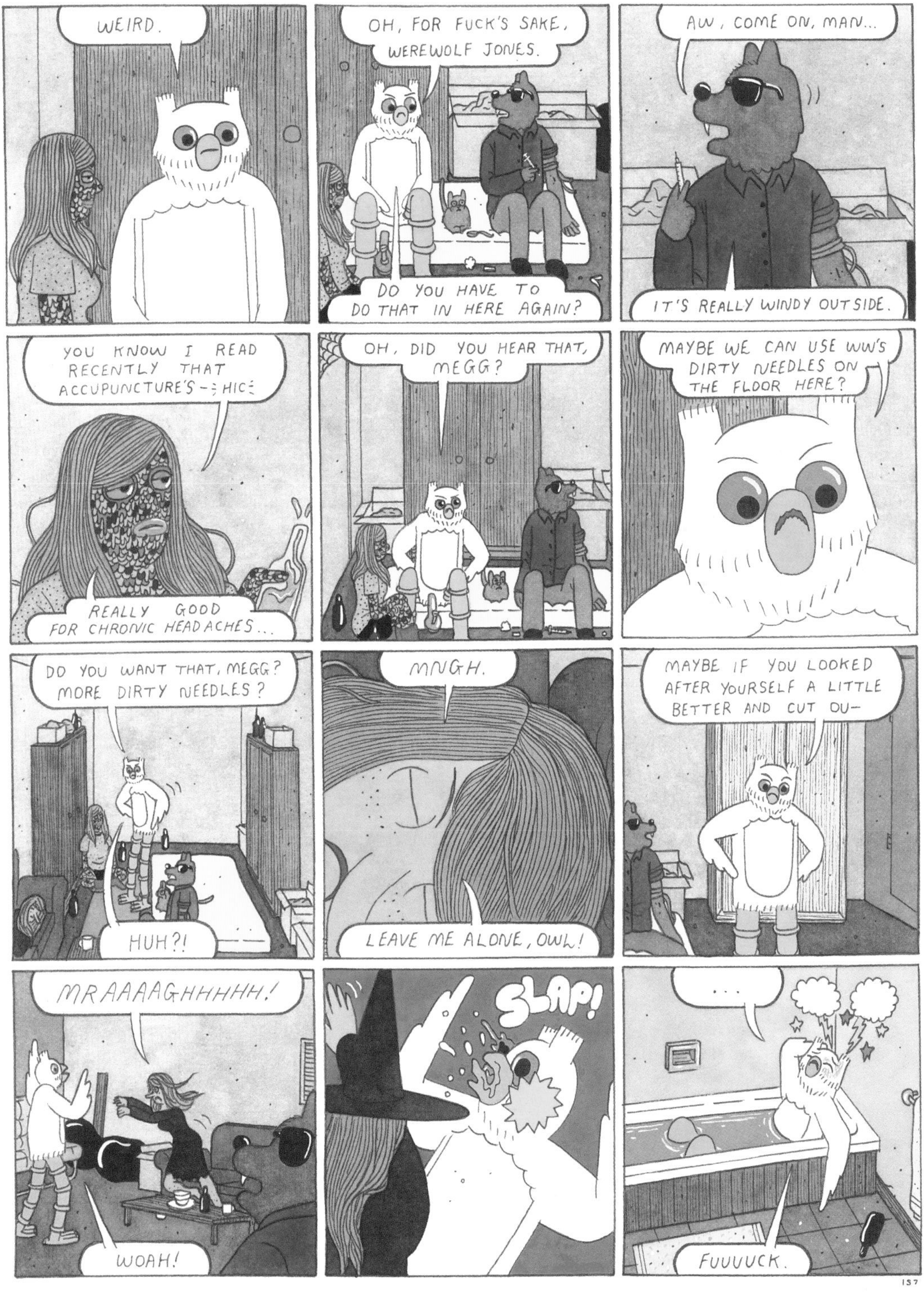
WEIRD.
OH, FOR FUCK'S SAKE, WEREWOLF JONES.
DO YOU HAVE TO DO THAT IN HERE AGAIN?
AW, COME ON, MAN...
IT'S REALLY WINDY OUTSIDE.
YOU KNOW I READ RECENTLY THAT ACCUPUNCTURE'S –HIC–
REALLY GOOD FOR CHRONIC HEADACHES...
OH, DID YOU HEAR THAT, MEGG?
MAYBE WE CAN USE WW'S DIRTY NEEDLES ON THE FLOOR HERE?
DO YOU WANT THAT, MEGG? MORE DIRTY NEEDLES?
HUH?!
MNGH.
LEAVE ME ALONE, OWL!
MAYBE IF YOU LOOKED AFTER YOURSELF A LITTLE BETTER AND CUT OU–
MRAAAAGHHHHH!
WOAH!
SLAP!
...
FUUUUCK.

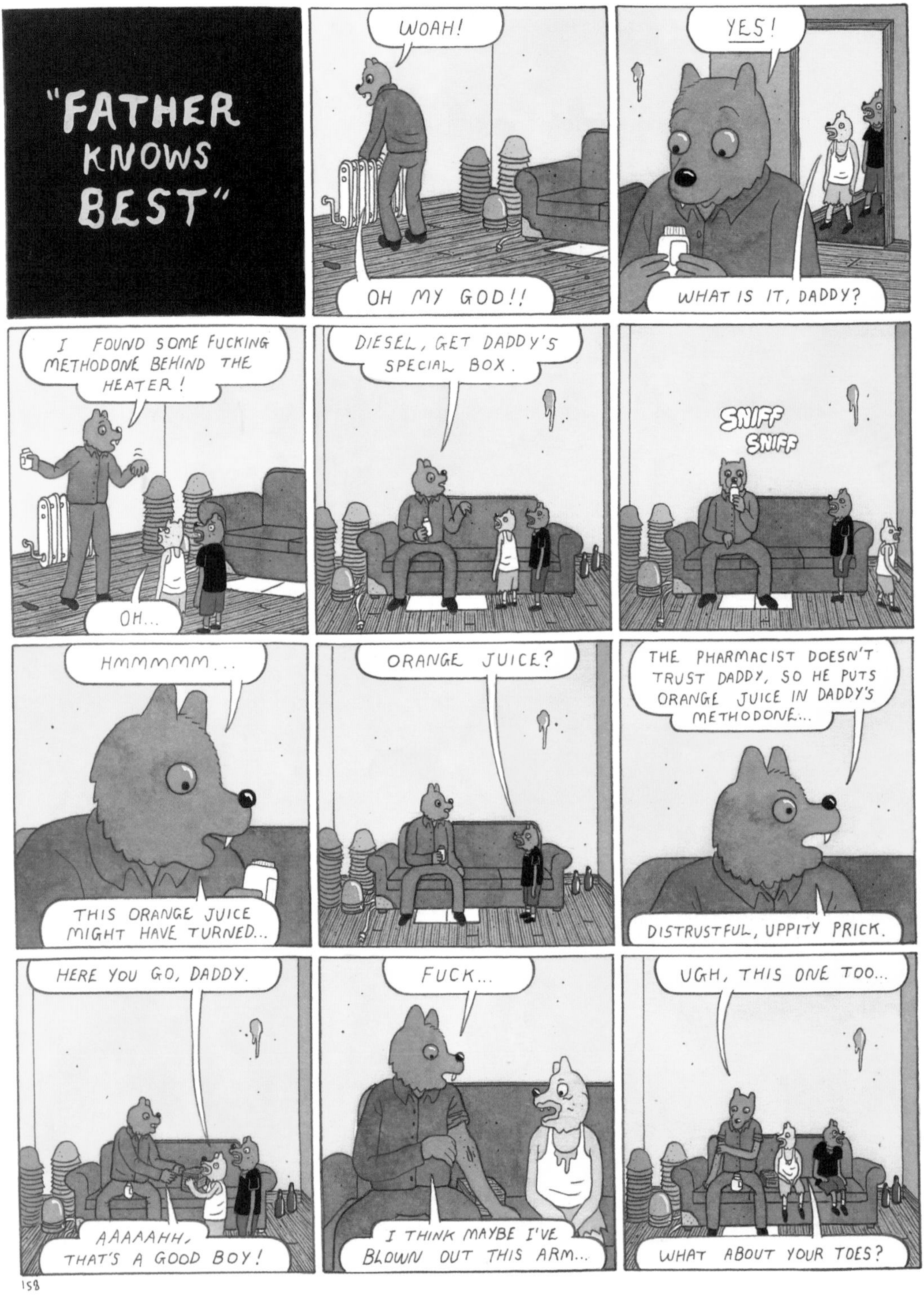
"FATHER KNOWS BEST"
WOAH!
OH MY GOD!!
YES!
WHAT IS IT, DADDY?
I FOUND SOME FUCKING METHODONE BEHIND THE HEATER!
OH...
DIESEL, GET DADDY'S SPECIAL BOX.
SNIFF
SNIFF
HMMMMMM...
THIS ORANGE JUICE MIGHT HAVE TURNED...
ORANGE JUICE?
THE PHARMACIST DOESN'T TRUST DADDY, SO HE PUTS ORANGE JUICE IN DADDY'S METHODONE...
DISTRUSTFUL, UPPITY PRICK.
HERE YOU GO, DADDY.
AAAAAHH, THAT'S A GOOD BOY!
FUCK...
I THINK MAYBE I'VE BLOWN OUT THIS ARM...
UGH, THIS ONE TOO...
WHAT ABOUT YOUR TOES?

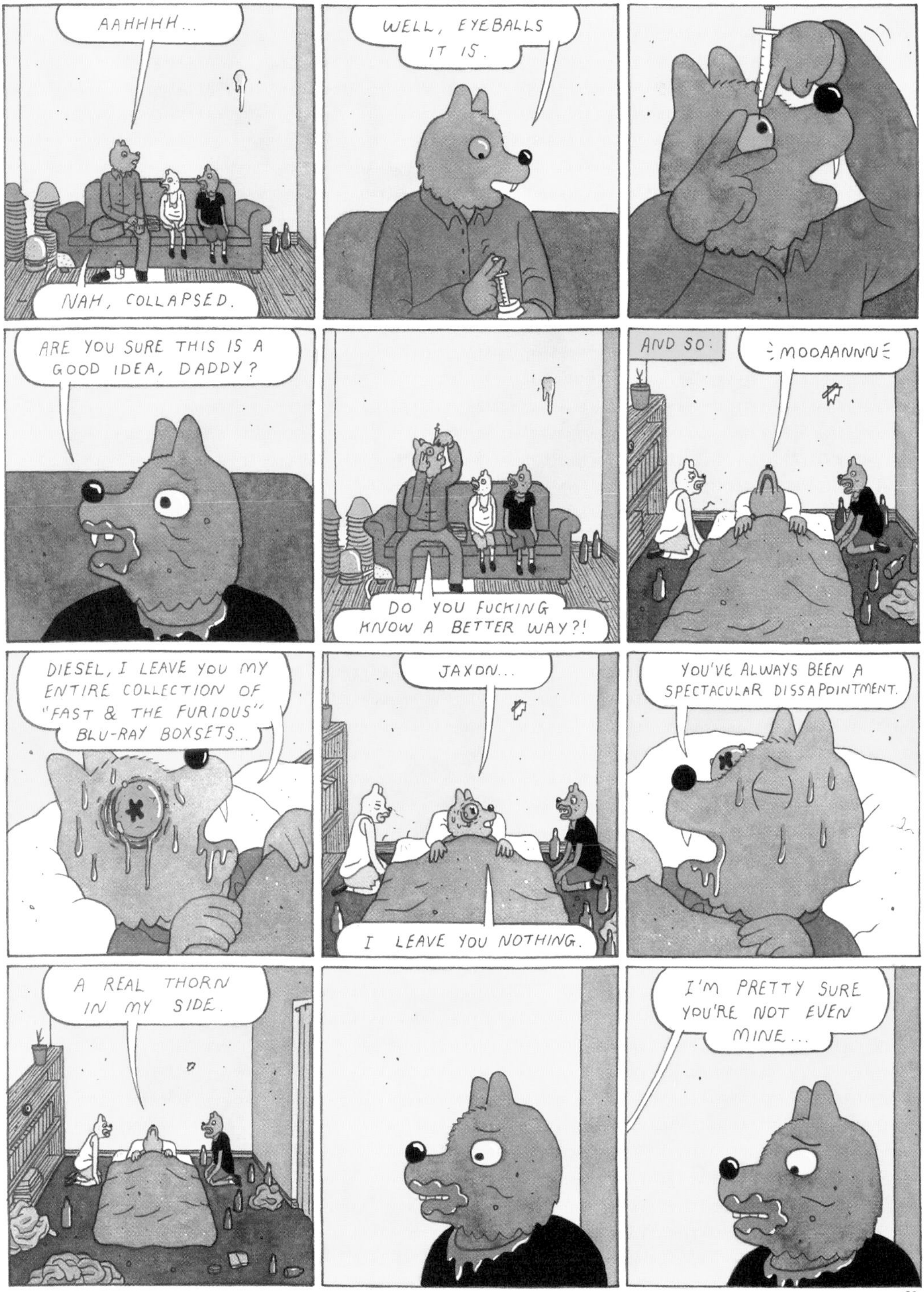
AAHHHH...
NAH, COLLAPSED.
WELL, EYEBALLS IT IS.
ARE YOU SURE THIS IS A GOOD IDEA, DADDY?
DO YOU FUCKING KNOW A BETTER WAY?!
AND SO:
MOOAANNN
DIESEL, I LEAVE YOU MY ENTIRE COLLECTION OF "FAST & THE FURIOUS" BLU-RAY BOXSETS...
JAXON...
I LEAVE YOU NOTHING.
YOU'VE ALWAYS BEEN A SPECTACULAR DISSAPOINTMENT.
A REAL THORN IN MY SIDE.
I'M PRETTY SURE YOU'RE NOT EVEN MINE...

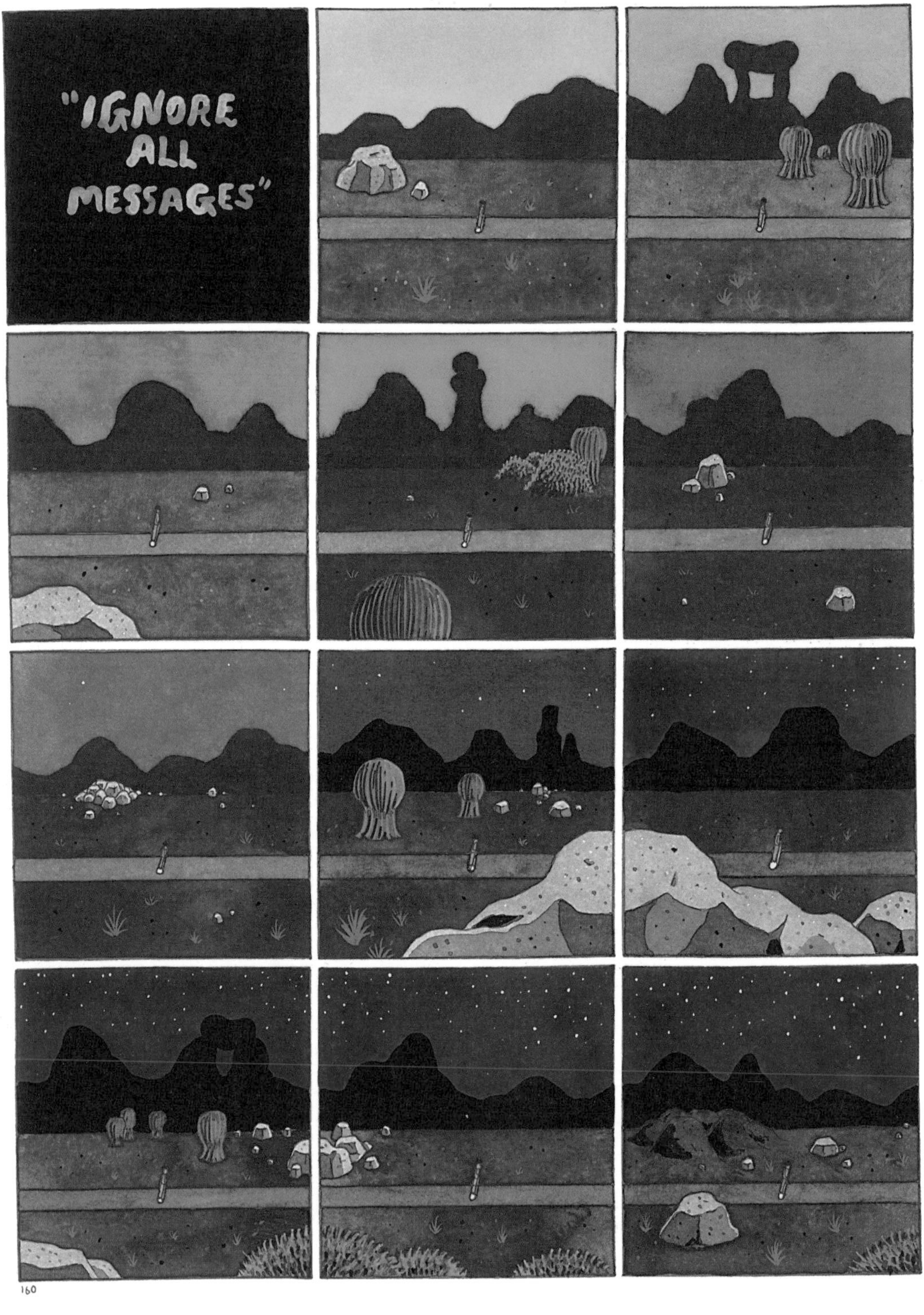
"IGNORE ALL MESSAGES"

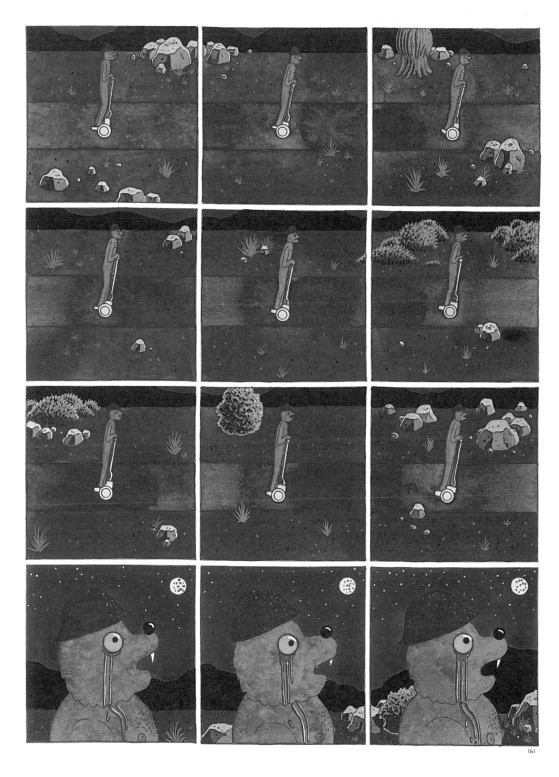

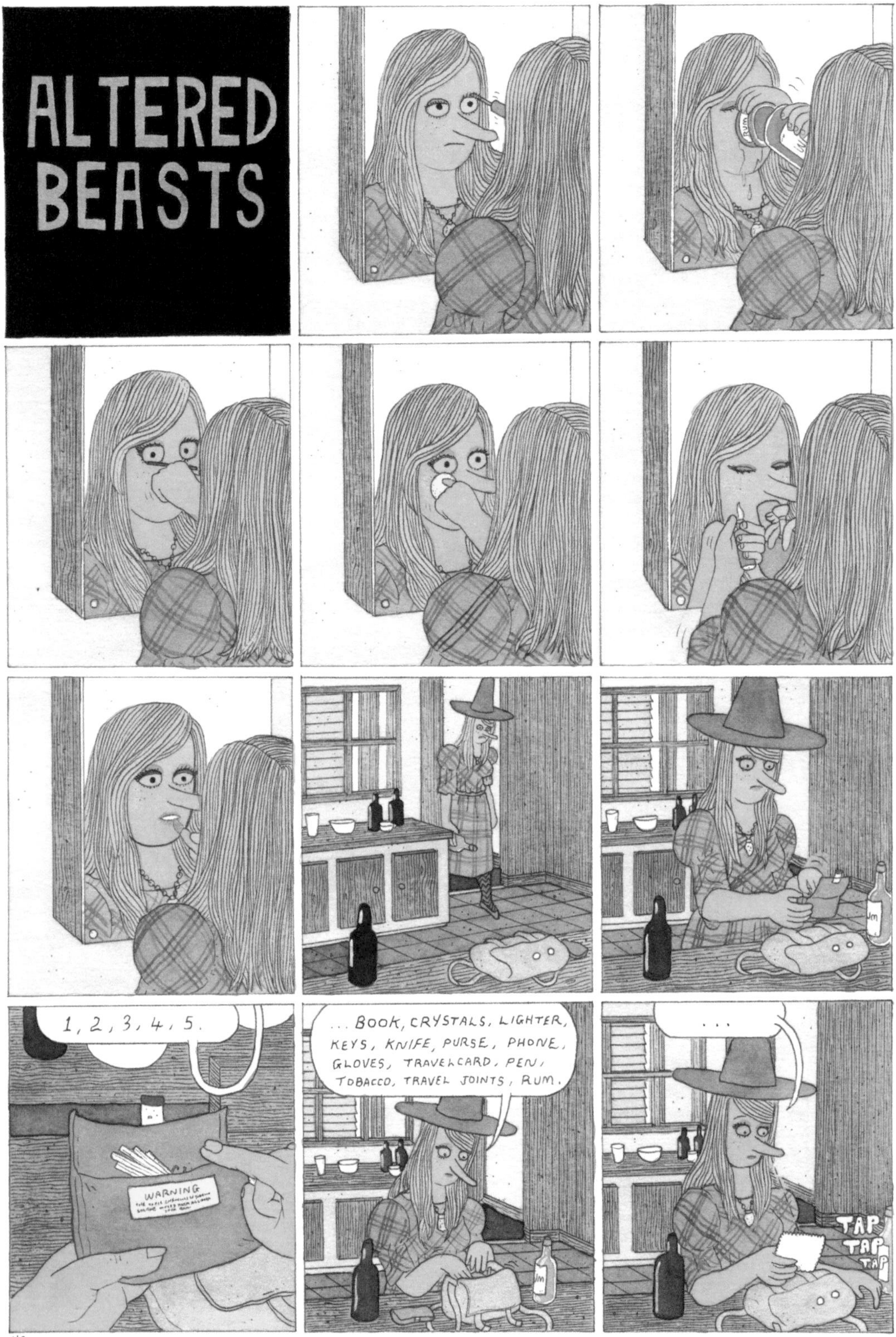
ALTERED BEASTS
Rum
WARNING
1, 2, 3, 4, 5.
...BOOK, CRYSTALS, LIGHTER, KEYS, KNIFE, PURSE, PHONE, GLOVES, TRAVELCARD, PEN, TOBACCO, TRAVEL JOINTS, RUM.
...
TAP TAP TAP

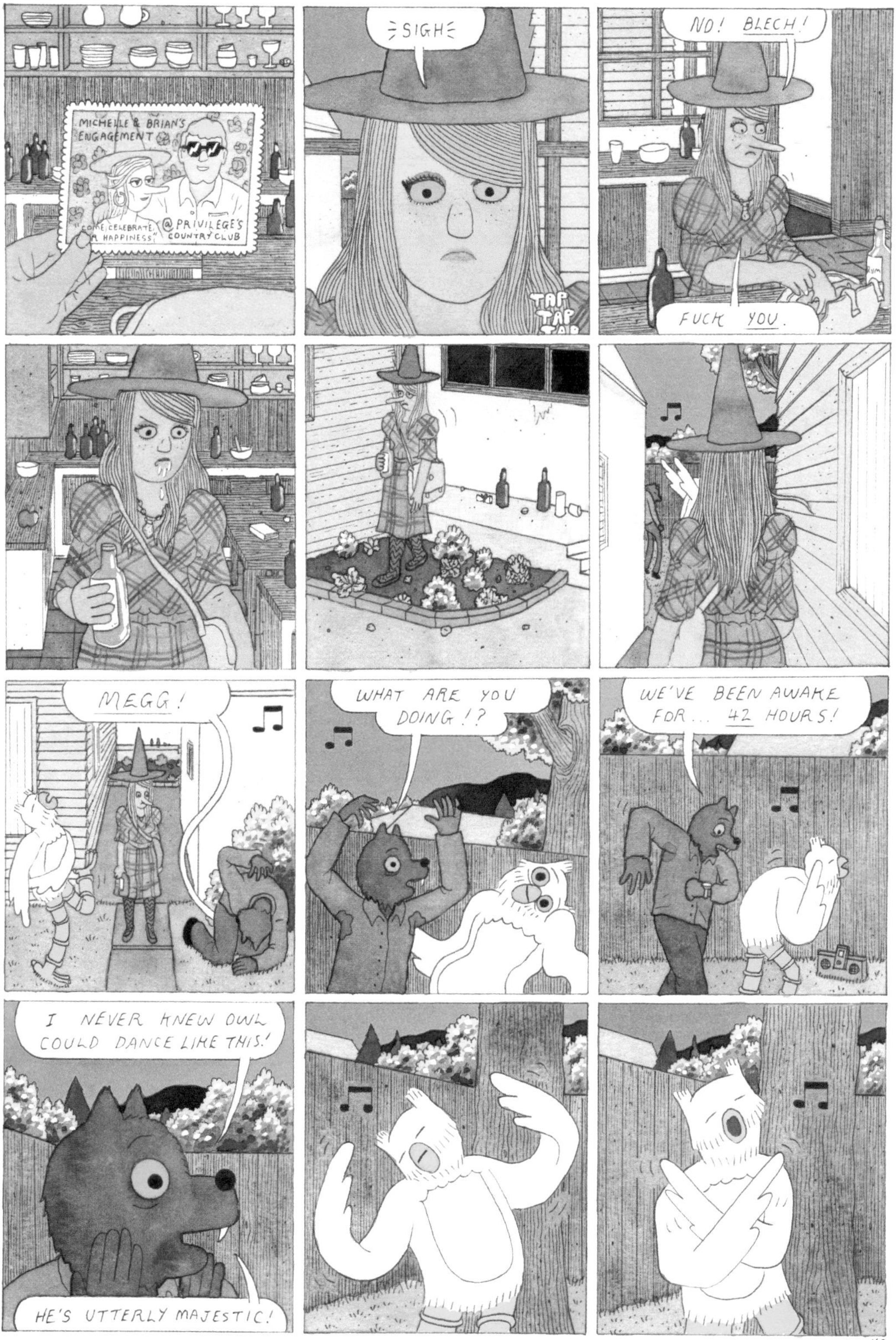
MICHELLE & BRIAN'S ENGAGEMENT
"COME CELEBRATE A HAPPINESS"
@ PRIVILEGE'S COUNTRY CLUB
SIGH
TAP TAP TAP
NO! BLECH!
FUCK YOU.
MEGG!
WHAT ARE YOU DOING!?
WE'VE BEEN AWAKE FOR... 42 HOURS!
I NEVER KNEW OWL COULD DANCE LIKE THIS!
HE'S UTTERLY MAJESTIC!

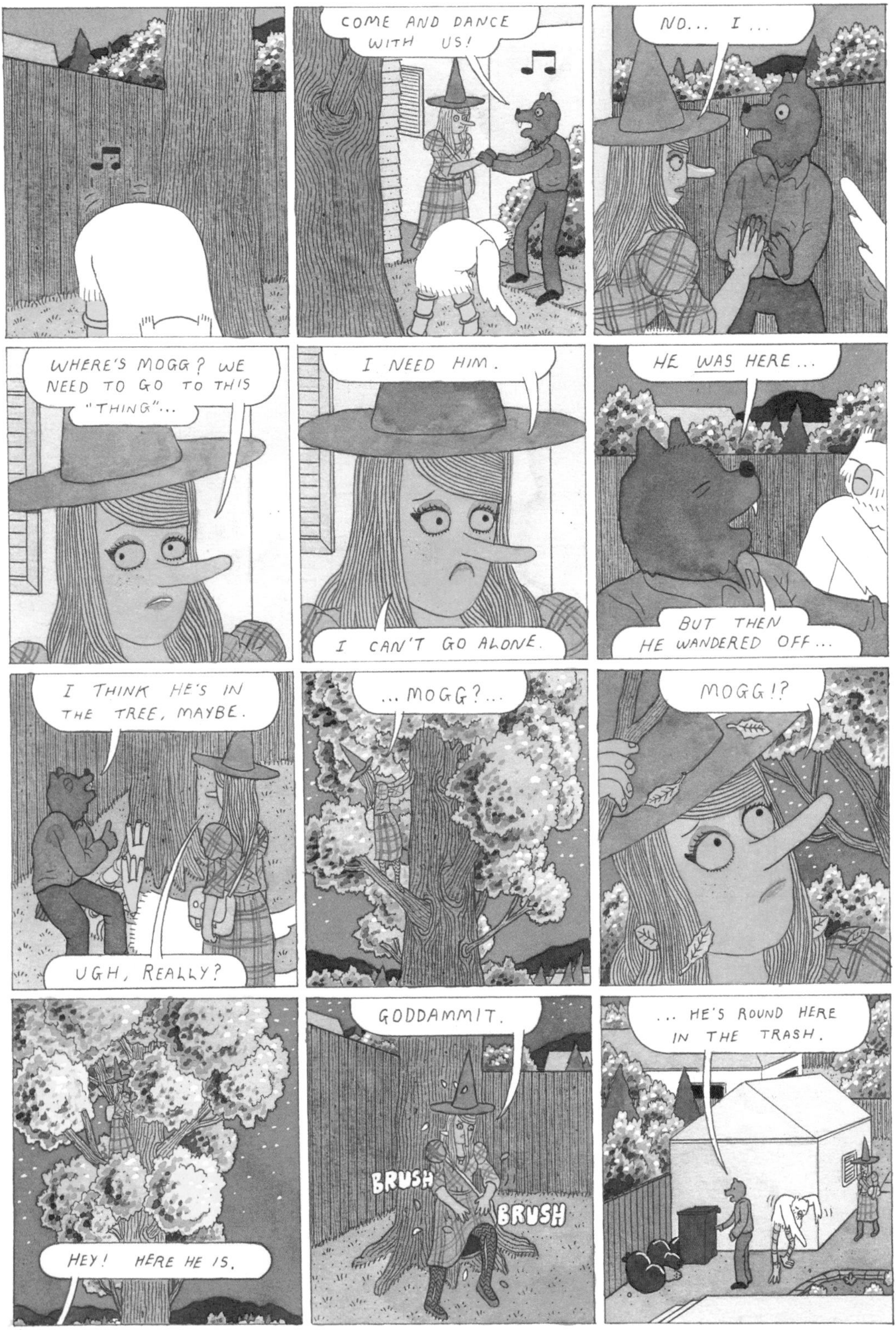
COME AND DANCE WITH US!
NO... I ...
WHERE'S MOGG? WE NEED TO GO TO THIS "THING"...
I NEED HIM.
I CAN'T GO ALONE.
HE WAS HERE...
BUT THEN HE WANDERED OFF...
I THINK HE'S IN THE TREE, MAYBE.
UGH, REALLY?
...MOGG?...
MOGG!?
HEY! HERE HE IS.
GODDAMMIT.
BRUSH
BRUSH
... HE'S ROUND HERE IN THE TRASH.

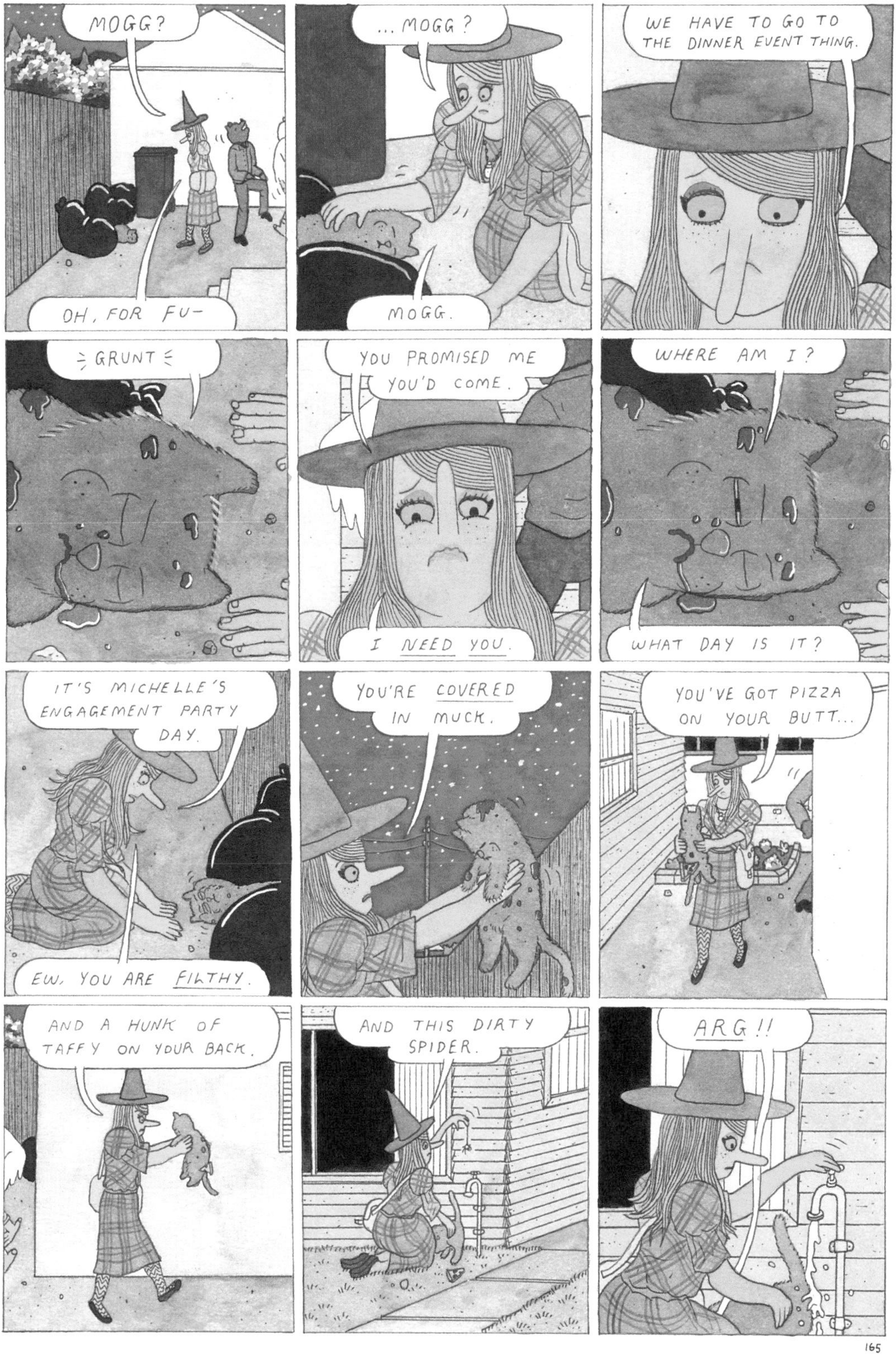
MOGG?
OH, FOR FU-
...MOGG?
MOGG.
WE HAVE TO GO TO THE DINNER EVENT THING.
GRUNT
YOU PROMISED ME YOU'D COME.
I NEED YOU.
WHERE AM I?
WHAT DAY IS IT?
IT'S MICHELLE'S ENGAGEMENT PARTY DAY.
EW, YOU ARE FILTHY.
YOU'RE COVERED IN MUCK.
YOU'VE GOT PIZZA ON YOUR BUTT...
AND A HUNK OF TAFFY ON YOUR BACK.
AND THIS DIRTY SPIDER.
ARG!!

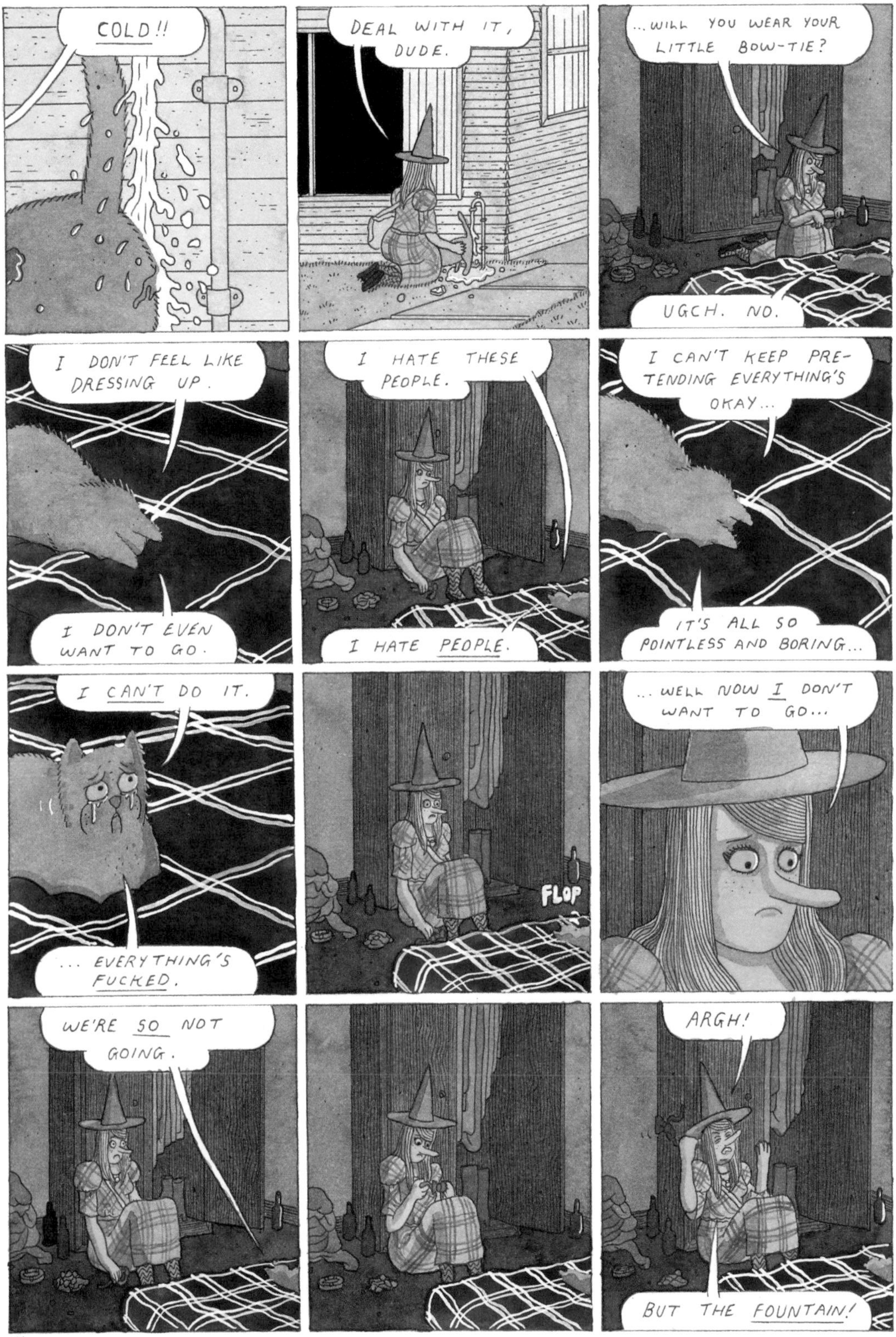
COLD!!
DEAL WITH IT, DUDE.
...WILL YOU WEAR YOUR LITTLE BOW-TIE?
UGCH. NO.
I DON'T FEEL LIKE DRESSING UP.
I DON'T EVEN WANT TO GO.
I HATE THESE PEOPLE.
I HATE PEOPLE.
I CAN'T KEEP PRETENDING EVERYTHING'S OKAY...
IT'S ALL SO POINTLESS AND BORING...
I CAN'T DO IT.
... EVERYTHING'S FUCKED.
FLOP
...WELL NOW I DON'T WANT TO GO...
WE'RE SO NOT GOING.
ARGH!
BUT THE FOUNTAIN!

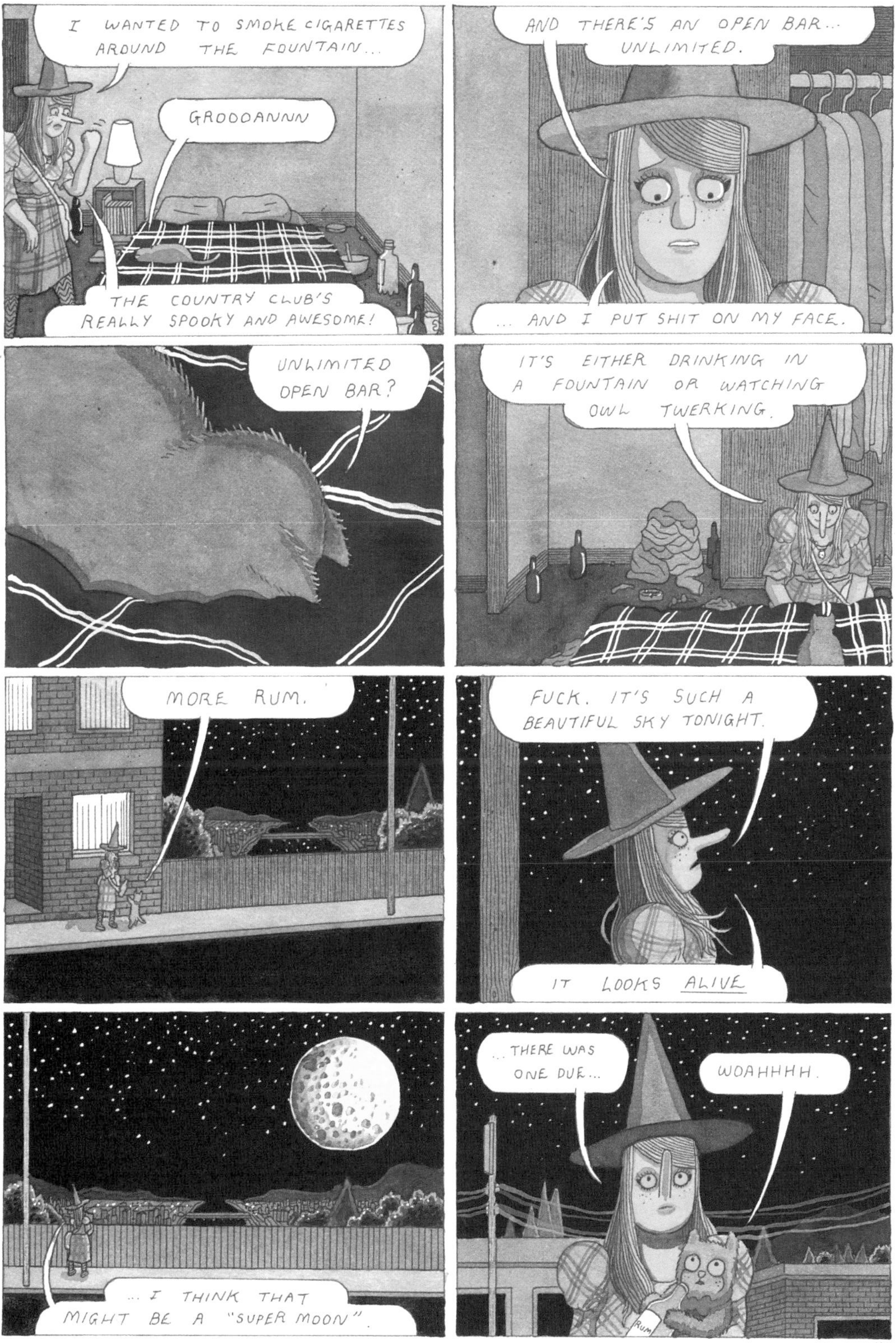
I WANTED TO SMOKE CIGARETTES AROUND THE FOUNTAIN...
GRODOANNN
THE COUNTRY CLUB'S REALLY SPOOKY AND AWESOME!
AND THERE'S AN OPEN BAR... UNLIMITED.
... AND I PUT SHIT ON MY FACE.
UNLIMITED OPEN BAR?
IT'S EITHER DRINKING IN A FOUNTAIN OR WATCHING OWL TWERKING.
MORE RUM.
FUCK. IT'S SUCH A BEAUTIFUL SKY TONIGHT.
IT LOOKS ALIVE
... I THINK THAT MIGHT BE A "SUPER MOON".
...THERE WAS ONE DUE...
WOAHHHH.
RUM

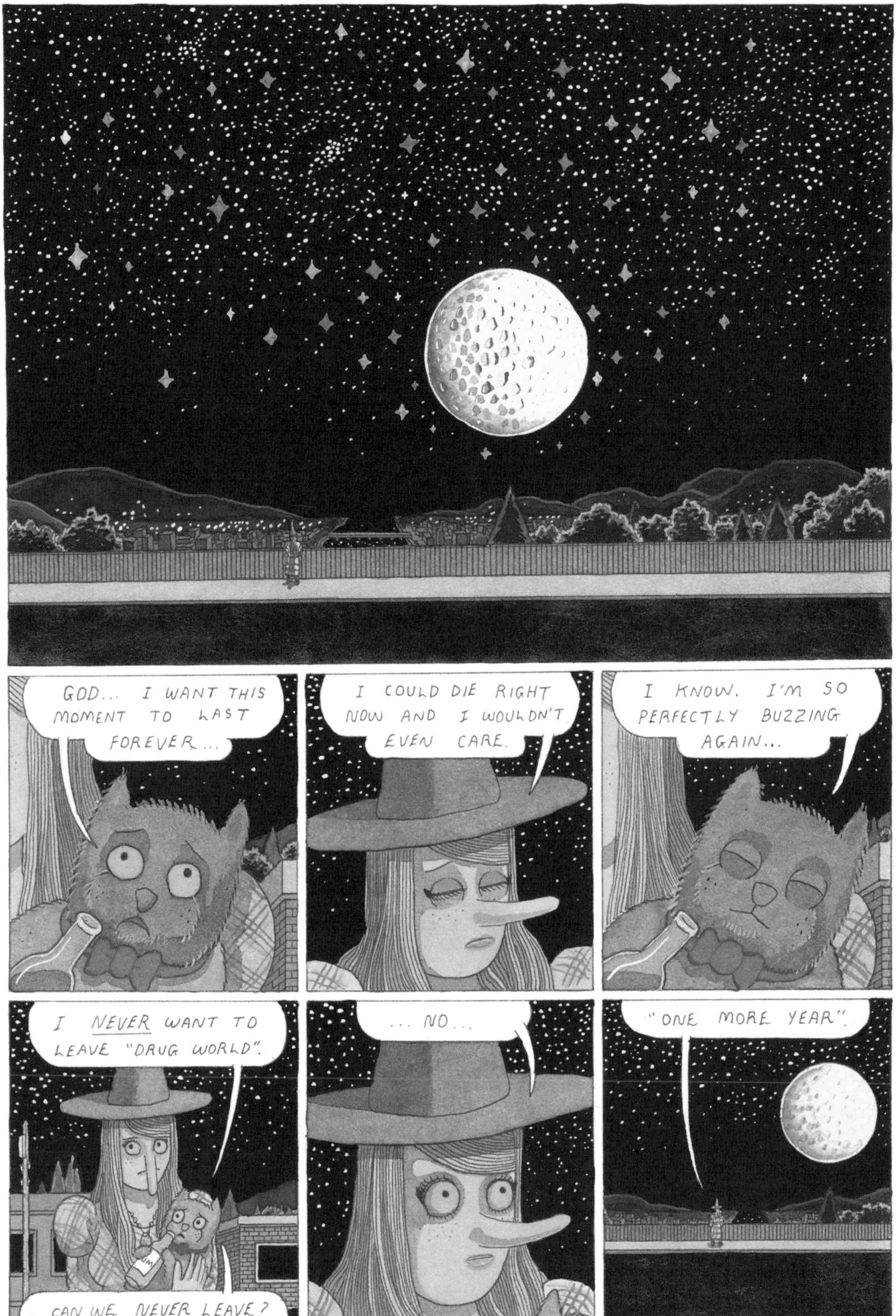
GOD... I WANT THIS MOMENT TO LAST FOREVER...
I COULD DIE RIGHT NOW AND I WOULDN'T EVEN CARE.
I KNOW. I'M SO PERFECTLY BUZZING AGAIN...
I NEVER WANT TO LEAVE "DRUG WORLD".
...CAN WE NEVER LEAVE?
...NO...
"ONE MORE YEAR".

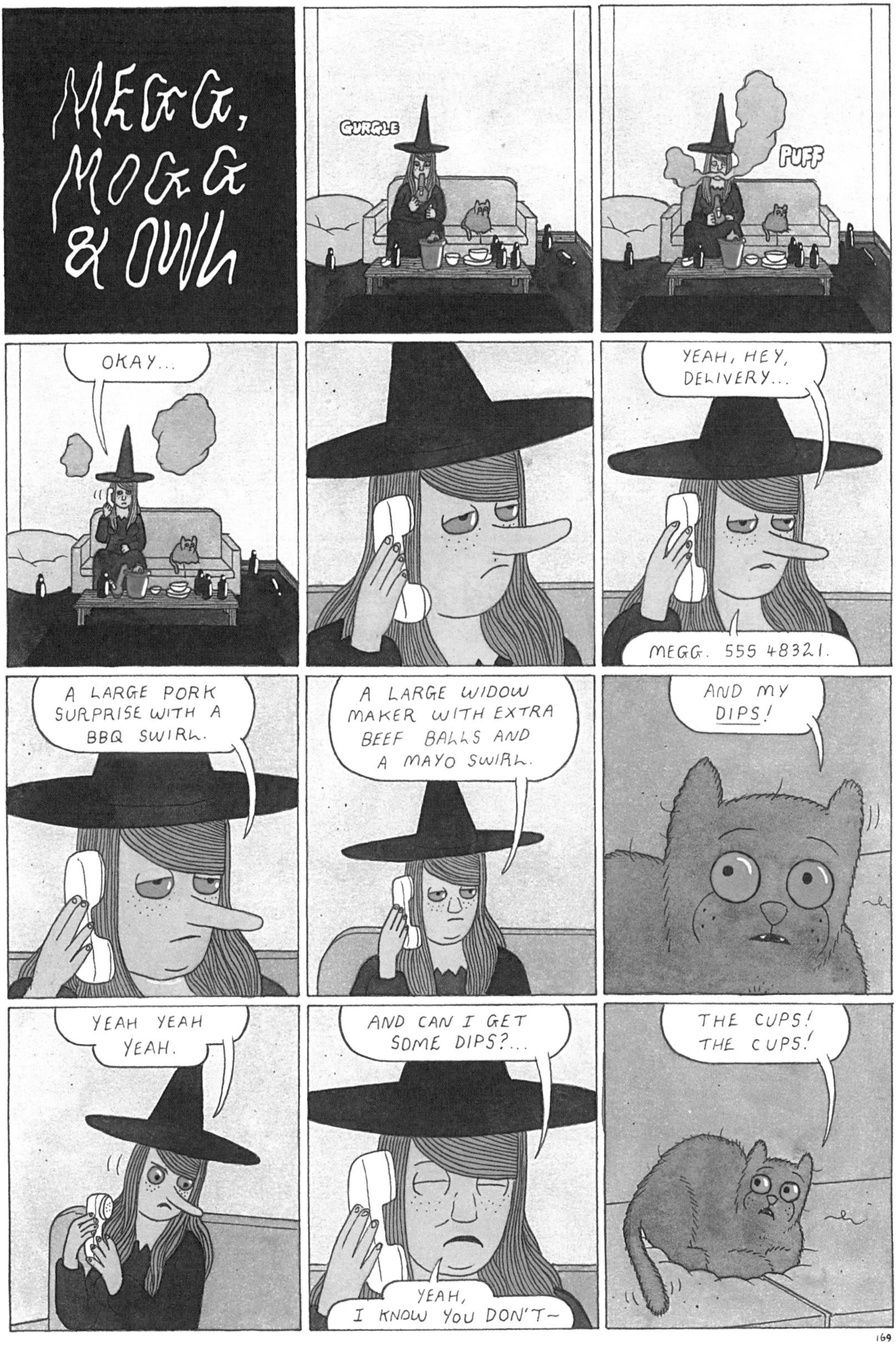
MEGG, MOGG & OWL
GURGLE
PUFF
OKAY...
YEAH, HEY, DELIVERY...
MEGG. 555 48321.
A LARGE PORK SURPRISE WITH A BBQ SWIRL.
A LARGE WIDOW MAKER WITH EXTRA BEEF BALLS AND A MAYO SWIRL.
AND MY DIPS!
YEAH YEAH YEAH.
AND CAN I GET SOME DIPS?...
YEAH, I KNOW YOU DON'T–
THE CUPS! THE CUPS!

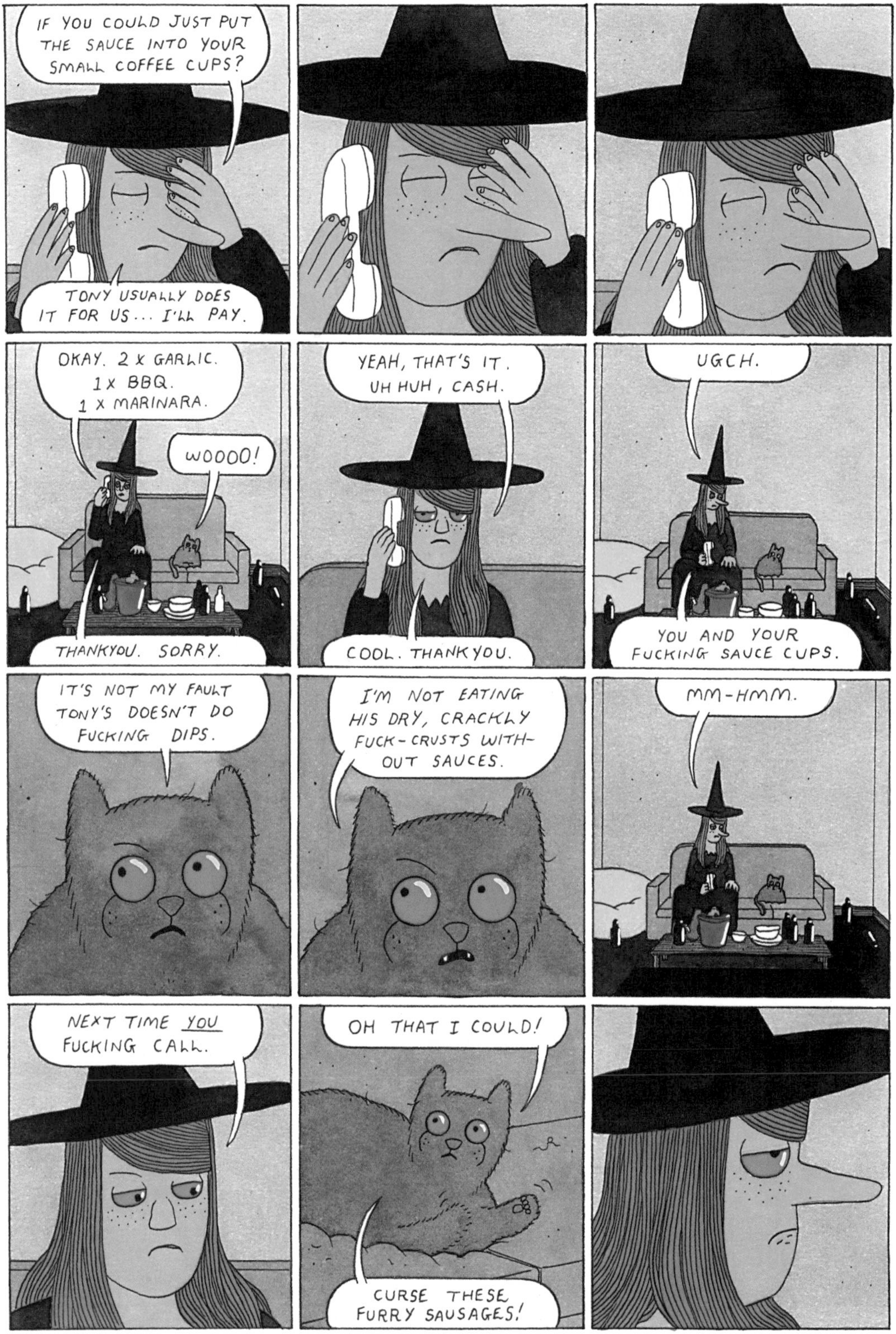
IF YOU COULD JUST PUT THE SAUCE INTO YOUR SMALL COFFEE CUPS?
TONY USUALLY DOES IT FOR US... I'LL PAY.
OKAY. 2 X GARLIC. 1 X BBQ. 1 X MARINARA.
WOOOO!
THANKYOU. SORRY.
YEAH, THAT'S IT. UH HUH, CASH.
COOL. THANKYOU.
UGCH.
YOU AND YOUR FUCKING SAUCE CUPS.
IT'S NOT MY FAULT TONY'S DOESN'T DO FUCKING DIPS.
I'M NOT EATING HIS DRY, CRACKLY FUCK-CRUSTS WITH-OUT SAUCES.
MM-HMM.
NEXT TIME YOU FUCKING CALL.
OH THAT I COULD!
CURSE THESE FURRY SAUSAGES!

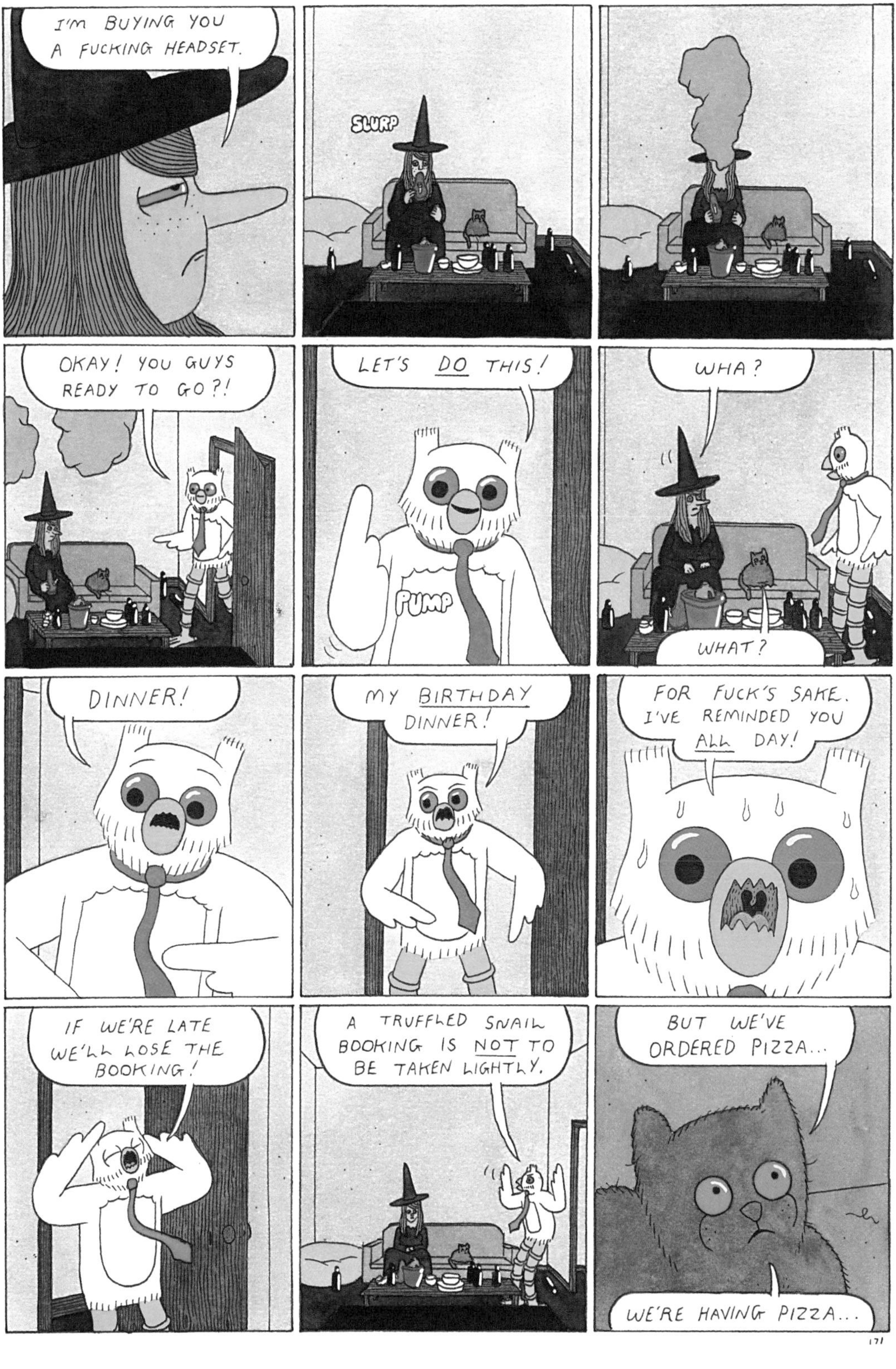
I'M BUYING YOU A FUCKING HEADSET.
SLURP
OKAY! YOU GUYS READY TO GO?!
PUMP
LET'S DO THIS!
WHA?
WHAT?
DINNER!
MY BIRTHDAY DINNER!
FOR FUCK'S SAKE. I'VE REMINDED YOU ALL DAY!
IF WE'RE LATE WE'LL LOSE THE BOOKING!
A TRUFFLED SNAIL BOOKING IS NOT TO BE TAKEN LIGHTLY.
BUT WE'VE ORDERED PIZZA...
WE'RE HAVING PIZZA...

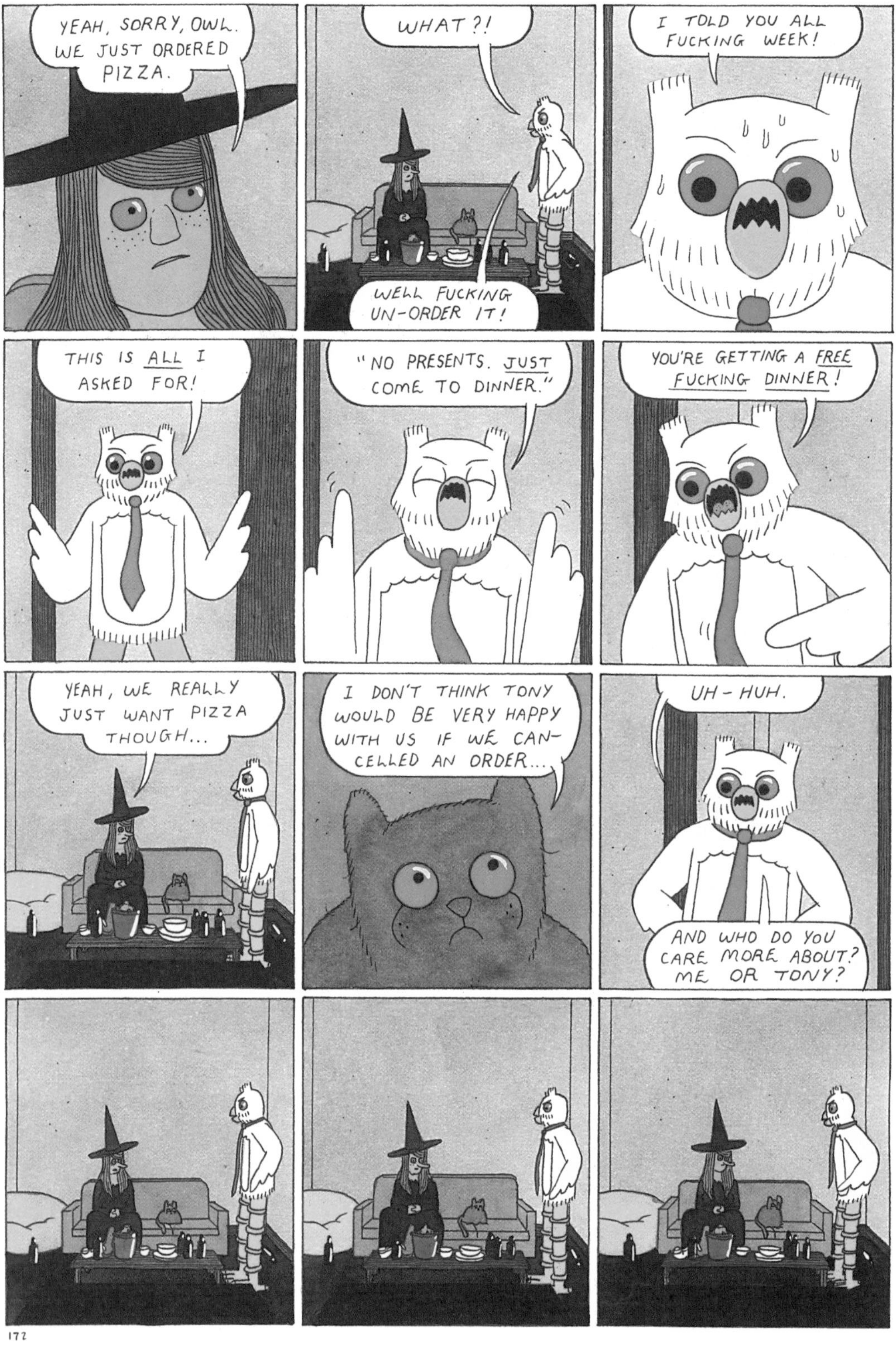
YEAH, SORRY, OWL. WE JUST ORDERED PIZZA.
WHAT?!
WELL FUCKING UN-ORDER IT!
I TOLD YOU ALL FUCKING WEEK!
THIS IS ALL I ASKED FOR!
"NO PRESENTS. JUST COME TO DINNER."
YOU'RE GETTING A FREE FUCKING DINNER!
YEAH, WE REALLY JUST WANT PIZZA THOUGH...
I DON'T THINK TONY WOULD BE VERY HAPPY WITH US IF WE CAN-CELLED AN ORDER...
UH-HUH.
AND WHO DO YOU CARE MORE ABOUT? ME OR TONY?

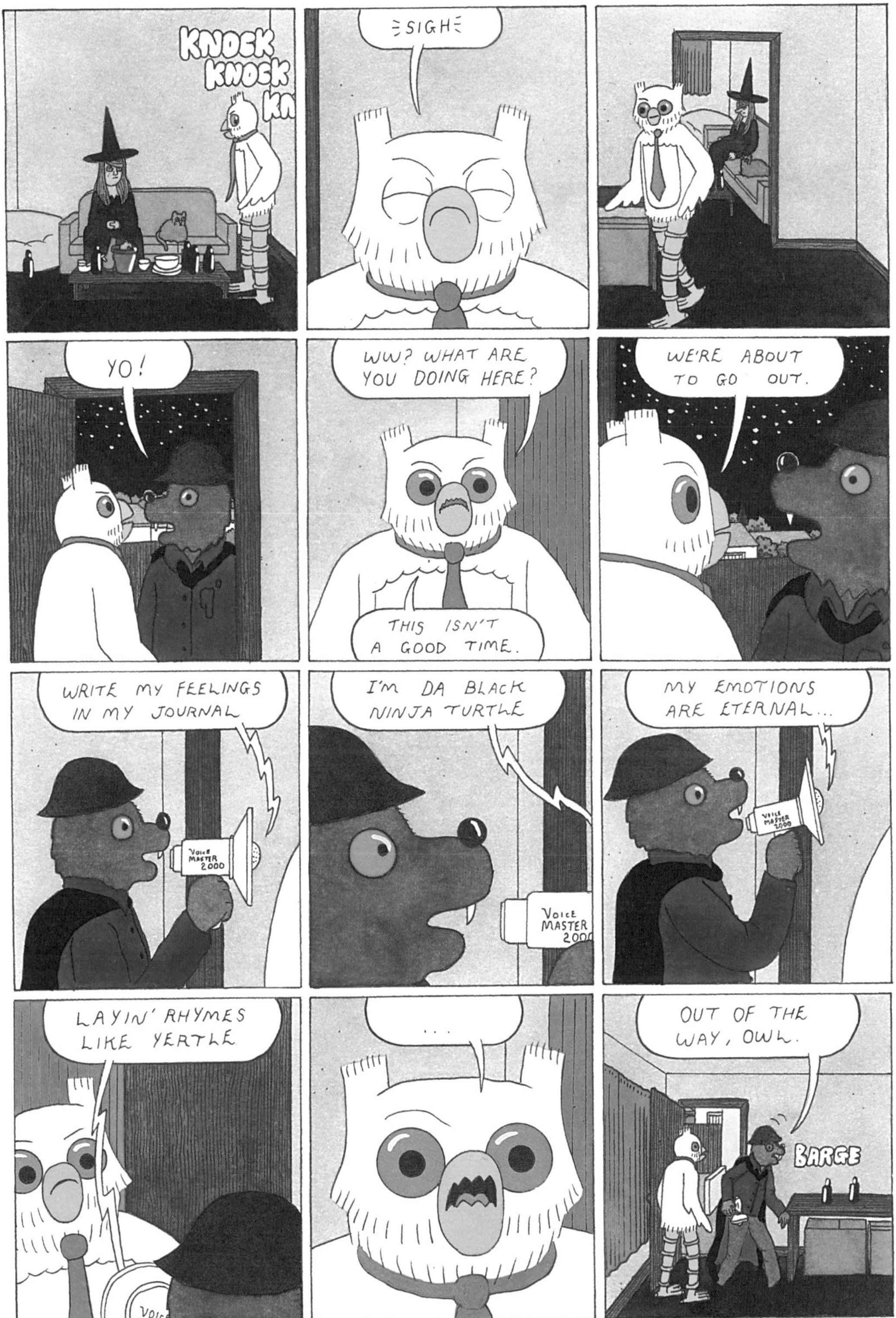
KNOCK KNOCK KN
SIGH
YO!
WW? WHAT ARE YOU DOING HERE?
THIS ISN'T A GOOD TIME.
WE'RE ABOUT TO GO OUT.
WRITE MY FEELINGS IN MY JOURNAL
VOICE MASTER 2000
I'M DA BLACK NINJA TURTLE
MY EMOTIONS ARE ETERNAL...
LAYIN' RHYMES LIKE YERTLE
...
OUT OF THE WAY, OWL.
BARGE

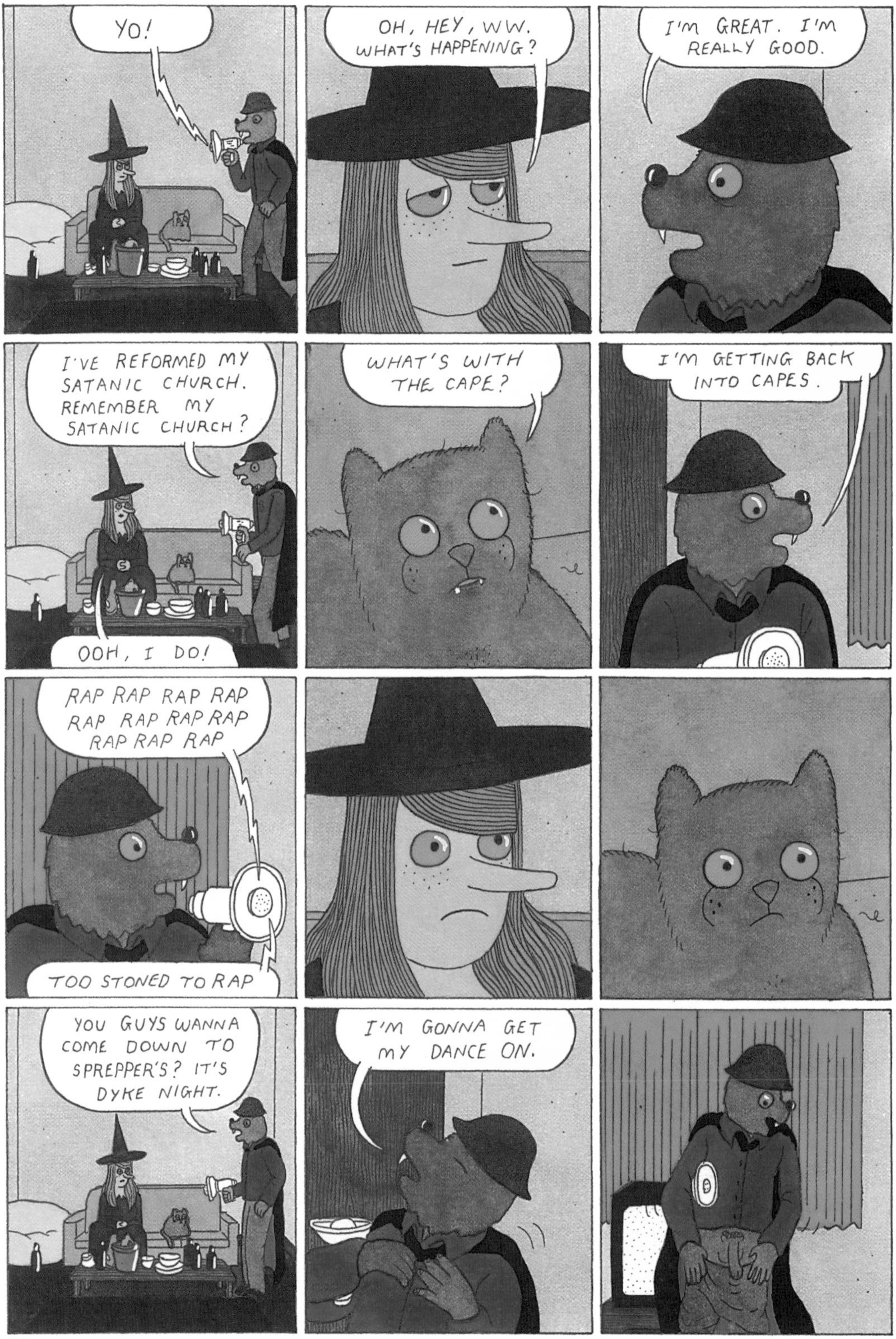
YO!
OH, HEY, WW. WHAT'S HAPPENING?
I'M GREAT. I'M REALLY GOOD.
I'VE REFORMED MY SATANIC CHURCH. REMEMBER MY SATANIC CHURCH?
OOH, I DO!
WHAT'S WITH THE CAPE?
I'M GETTING BACK INTO CAPES.
RAP RAP RAP RAP RAP RAP RAP RAP RAP RAP RAP
TOO STONED TO RAP
YOU GUYS WANNA COME DOWN TO SPREPPER'S? IT'S DYKE NIGHT.
I'M GONNA GET MY DANCE ON.

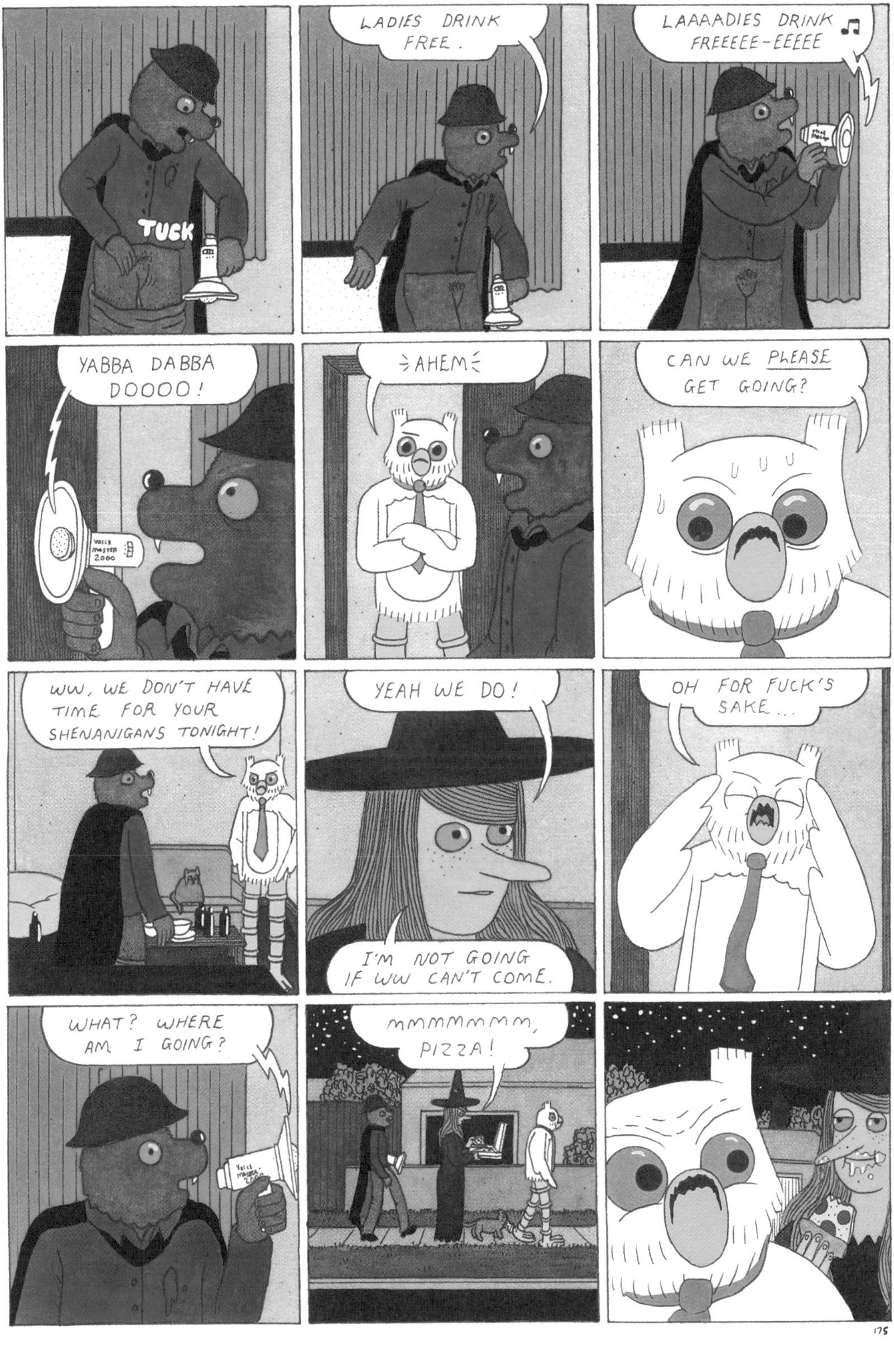
TUCK
LADIES DRINK FREE.
LAAAADIES DRINK FREEEEE-EEEEE
YABBA DABBA DOOOO!
VOICE MASTER 2000
AHEM
CAN WE PLEASE GET GOING?
WW, WE DON'T HAVE TIME FOR YOUR SHENANIGANS TONIGHT!
YEAH WE DO!
I'M NOT GOING IF WW CAN'T COME.
OH FOR FUCK'S SAKE...
WHAT? WHERE AM I GOING?
MMMMMMM, PIZZA!

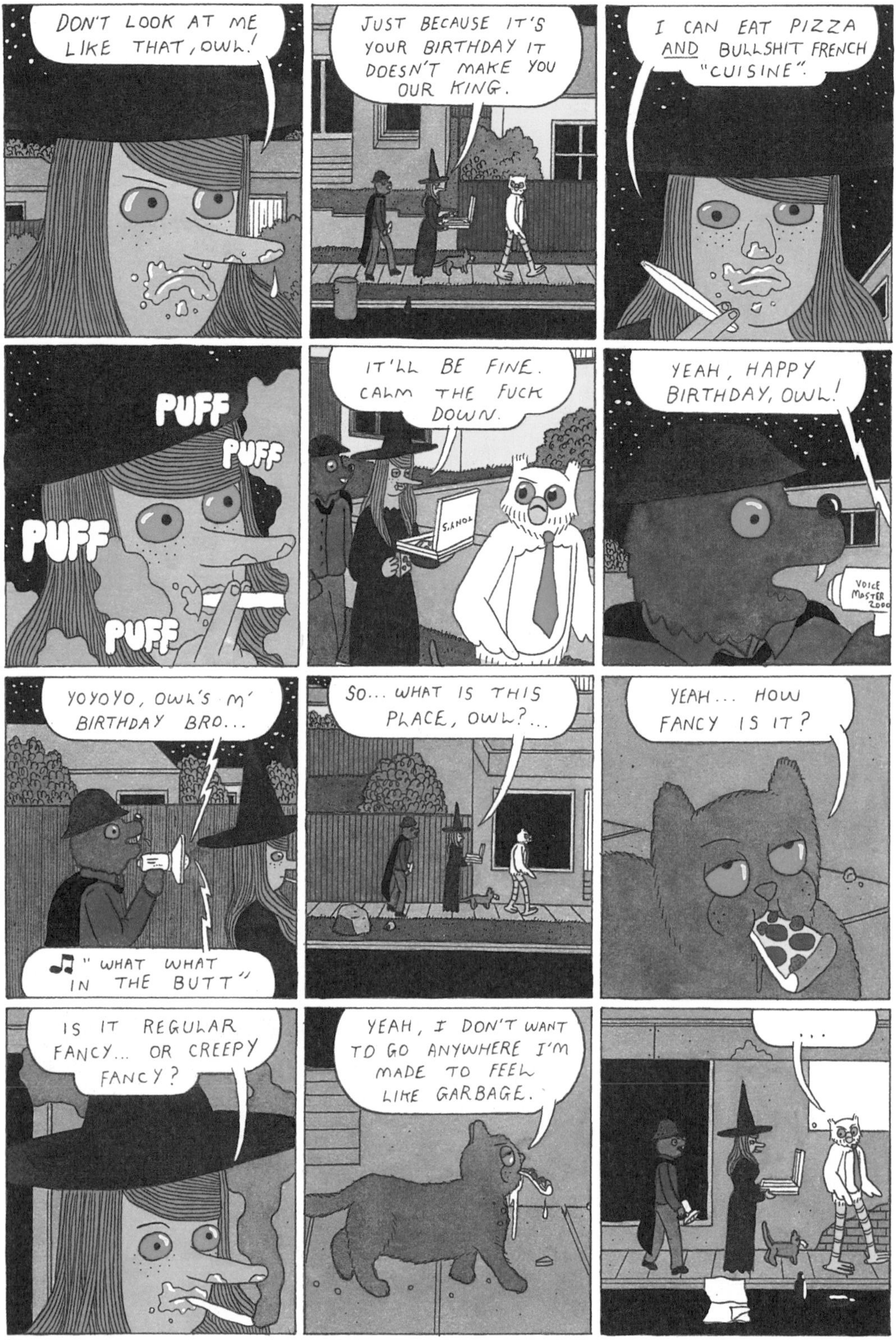
DON'T LOOK AT ME LIKE THAT, OWL!
JUST BECAUSE IT'S YOUR BIRTHDAY IT DOESN'T MAKE YOU OUR KING.
I CAN EAT PIZZA AND BULLSHIT FRENCH "CUISINE".
PUFF
PUFF
PUFF
PUFF
IT'LL BE FINE. CALM THE FUCK DOWN.
S.ANOL
YEAH, HAPPY BIRTHDAY, OWL!
VOICE MASTER 2000
YOYOYO, OWL'S M' BIRTHDAY BRO...
"WHAT WHAT IN THE BUTT"
SO... WHAT IS THIS PLACE, OWL?...
YEAH... HOW FANCY IS IT?
IS IT REGULAR FANCY... OR CREEPY FANCY?
YEAH, I DON'T WANT TO GO ANYWHERE I'M MADE TO FEEL LIKE GARBAGE.
...

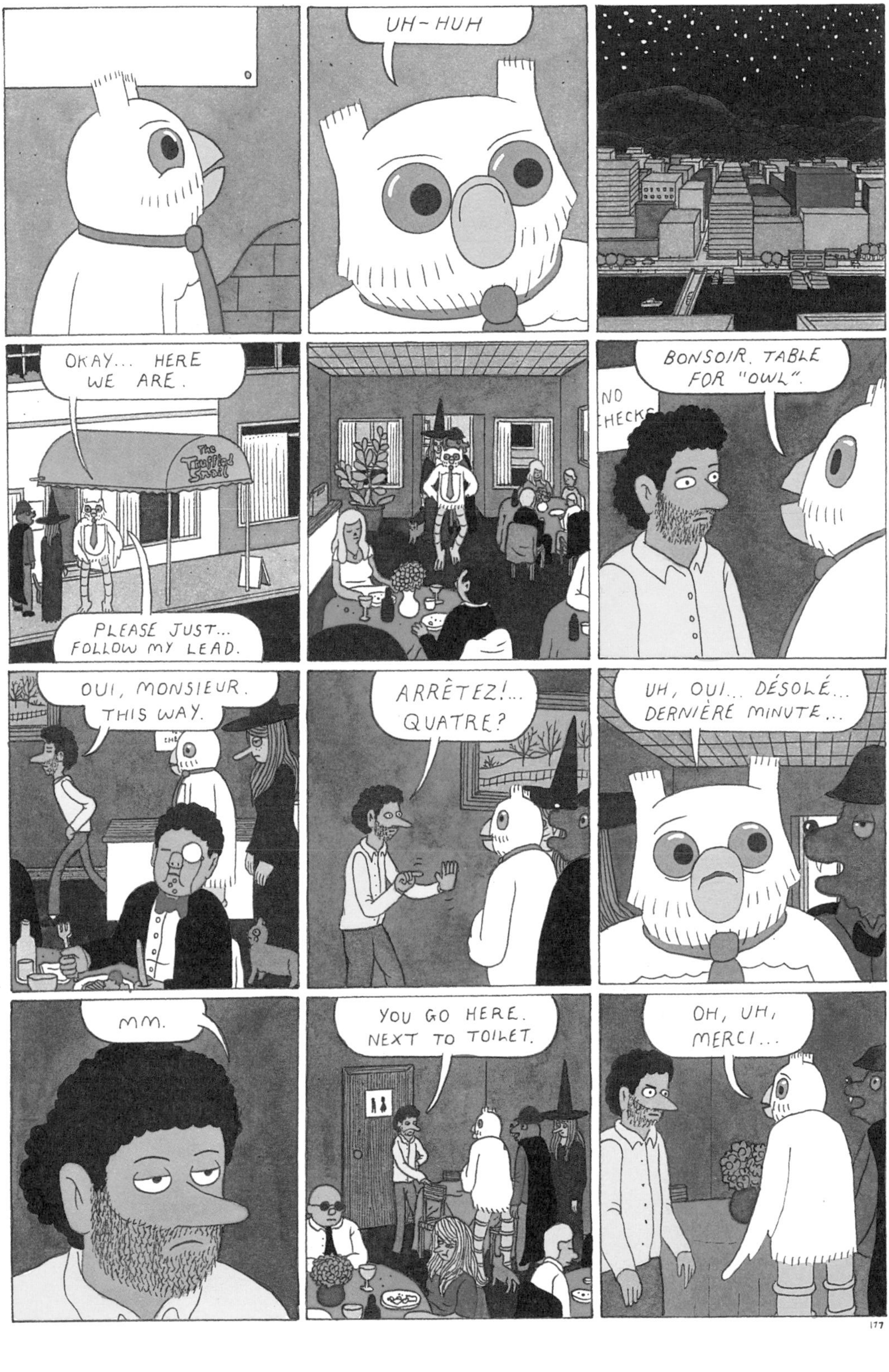
UH-HUH
OKAY... HERE WE ARE.
The Truffled Snail
PLEASE JUST... FOLLOW MY LEAD.
NO CHECKS
BONSOIR. TABLE FOR "OWL".
OUI, MONSIEUR. THIS WAY.
ARRÊTEZ!... QUATRE?
UH, OUI... DÉSOLÉ... DERNIÈRE MINUTE...
MM.
YOU GO HERE. NEXT TO TOILET.
OH, UH, MERCI...

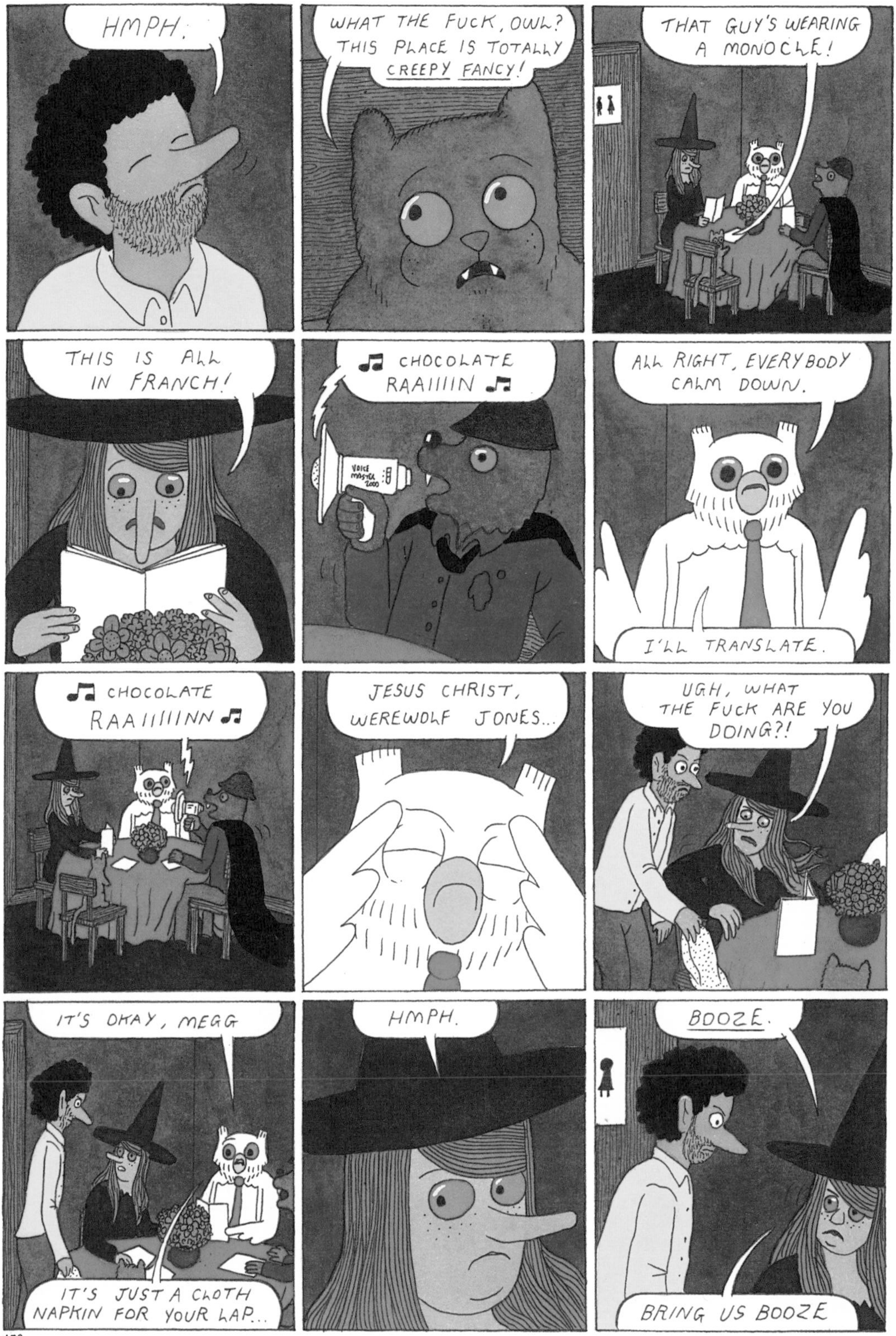
HMPH.
WHAT THE FUCK, OWL? THIS PLACE IS TOTALLY CREEPY FANCY!
THAT GUY'S WEARING A MONOCLE!
THIS IS ALL IN FRANCH!
♫ CHOCOLATE RAAIIIIN ♫
VOICE MASTER 2000
ALL RIGHT, EVERYBODY CALM DOWN.
I'LL TRANSLATE.
♫ CHOCOLATE RAAIIIIINN ♫
JESUS CHRIST, WEREWOLF JONES...
UGH, WHAT THE FUCK ARE YOU DOING?!
IT'S OKAY, MEGG
IT'S JUST A CLOTH NAPKIN FOR YOUR LAP...
HMPH.
BOOZE.
BRING US BOOZE

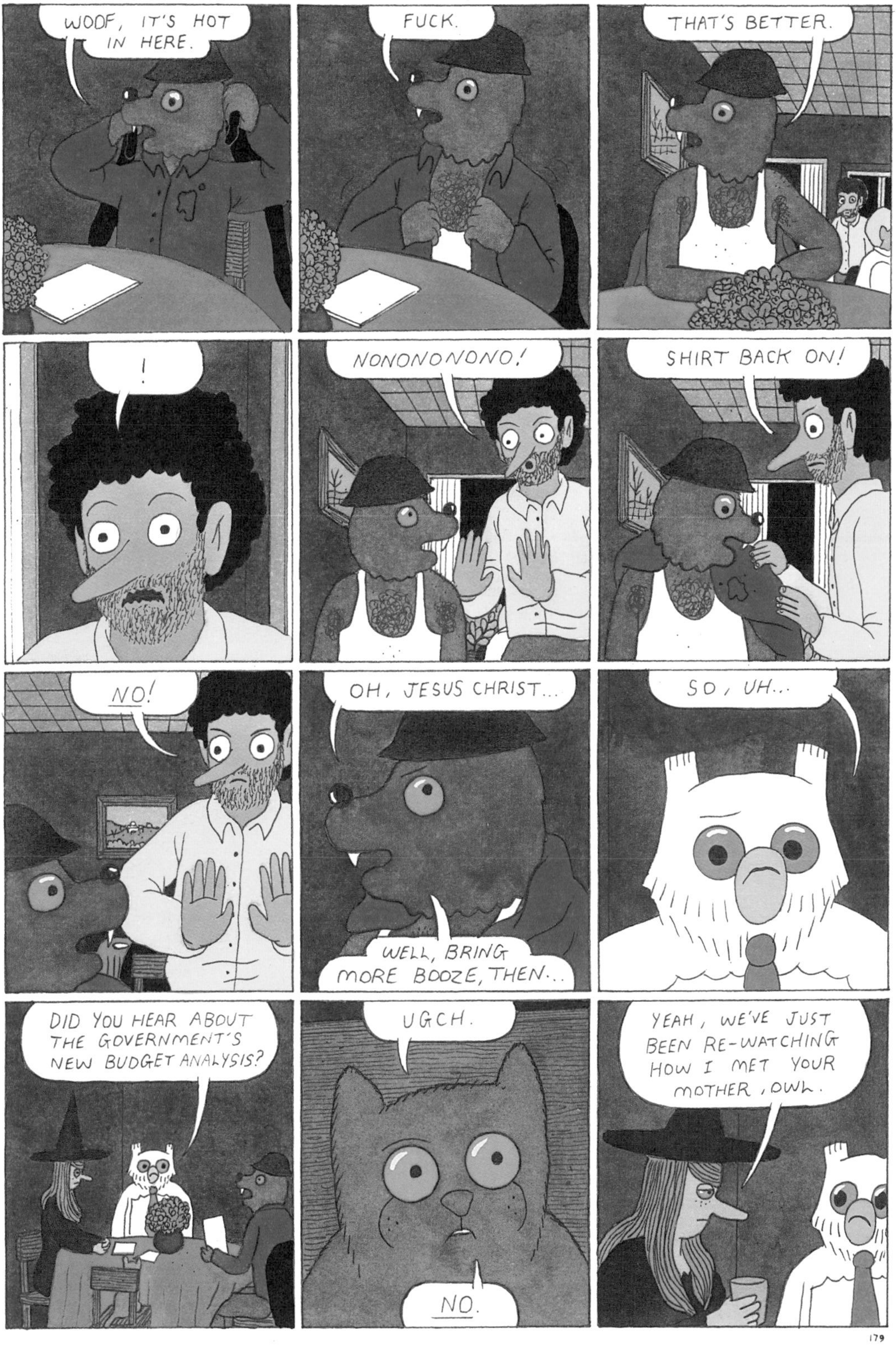
WOOF, IT'S HOT IN HERE.
FUCK.
THAT'S BETTER.
!
NONONONONO!
SHIRT BACK ON!
NO!
OH, JESUS CHRIST...
WELL, BRING MORE BOOZE, THEN...
SO, UH...
DID YOU HEAR ABOUT THE GOVERNMENT'S NEW BUDGET ANALYSIS?
UGCH.
NO.
YEAH, WE'VE JUST BEEN RE-WATCHING HOW I MET YOUR MOTHER, OWL.

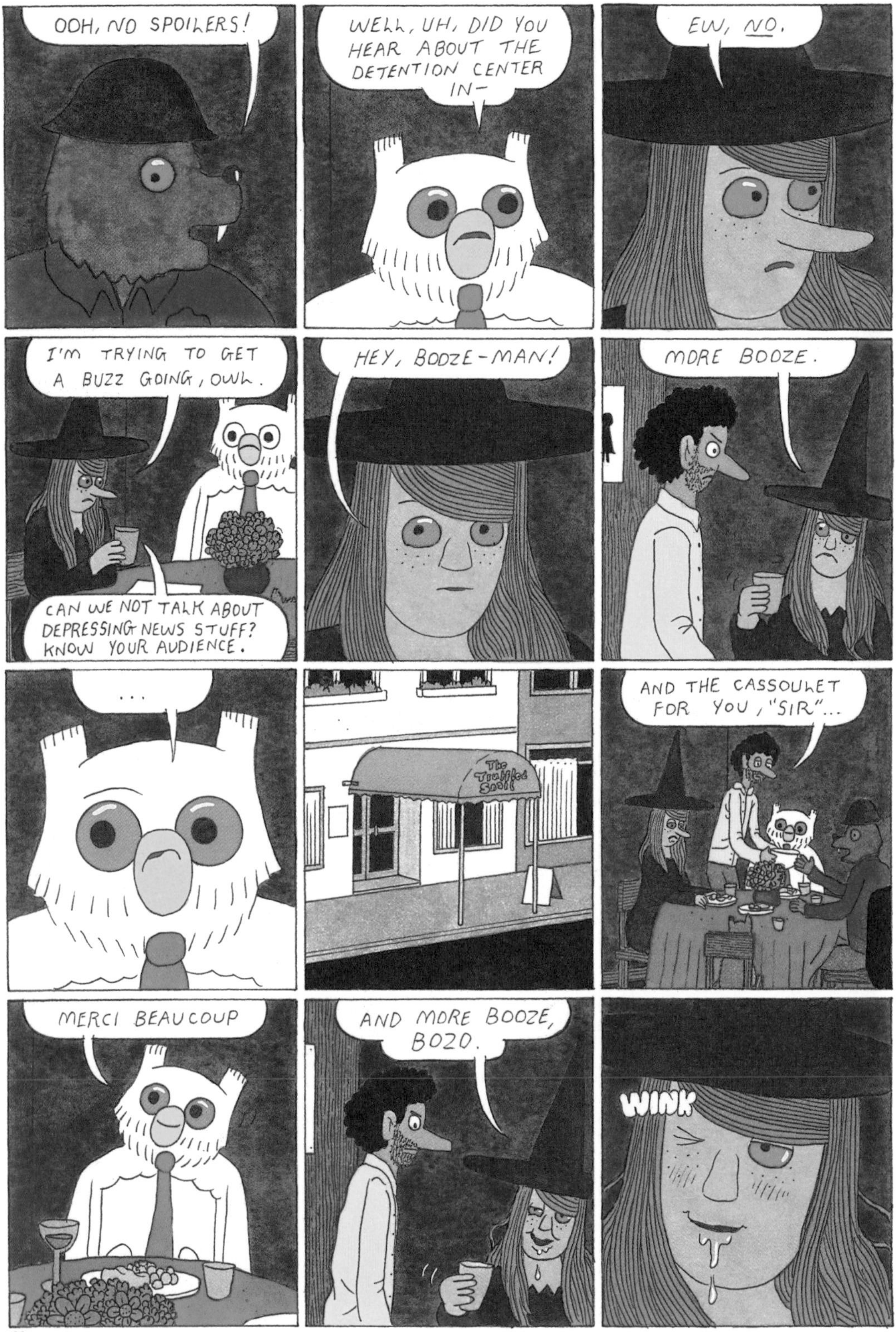
OOH, NO SPOILERS!
WELL, UH, DID YOU HEAR ABOUT THE DETENTION CENTER IN—
EW, NO.
I'M TRYING TO GET A BUZZ GOING, OWL.
CAN WE NOT TALK ABOUT DEPRESSING NEWS STUFF? KNOW YOUR AUDIENCE.
HEY, BOOZE-MAN!
MORE BOOZE.
...
The Truffled Snail
AND THE CASSOULET FOR YOU, "SIR"...
MERCI BEAUCOUP
AND MORE BOOZE, BOZO.
WINK

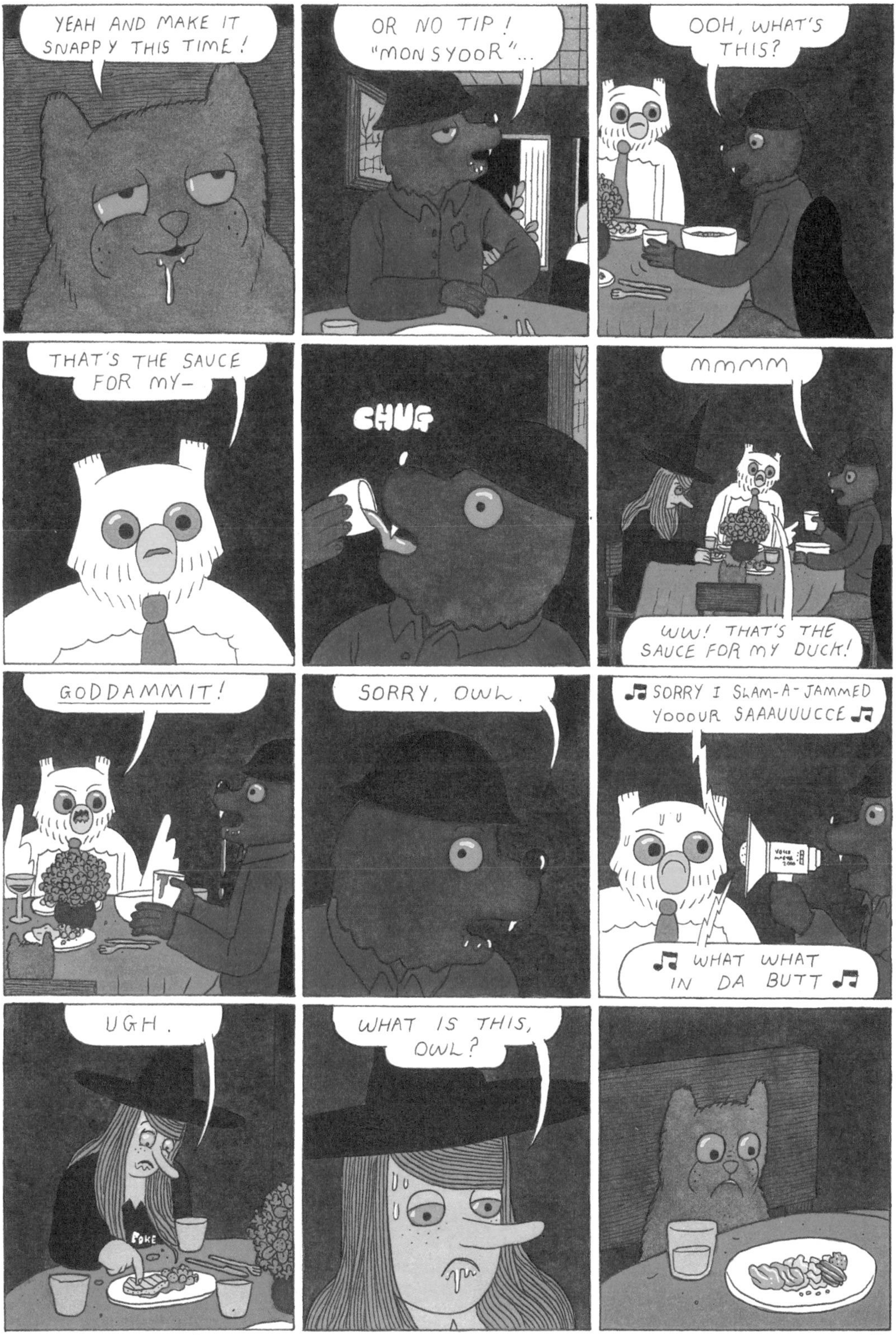
YEAH AND MAKE IT SNAPPY THIS TIME!
OR NO TIP! "MONSYOOR"...
OOH, WHAT'S THIS?
THAT'S THE SAUCE FOR MY-
CHUG
MMMM
WW! THAT'S THE SAUCE FOR MY DUCK!
GODDAMMIT!
SORRY, OWL.
SORRY I SLAM-A-JAMMED YOOOUR SAAAUUUCCE
WHAT WHAT IN DA BUTT
UGH.
WHAT IS THIS, OWL?

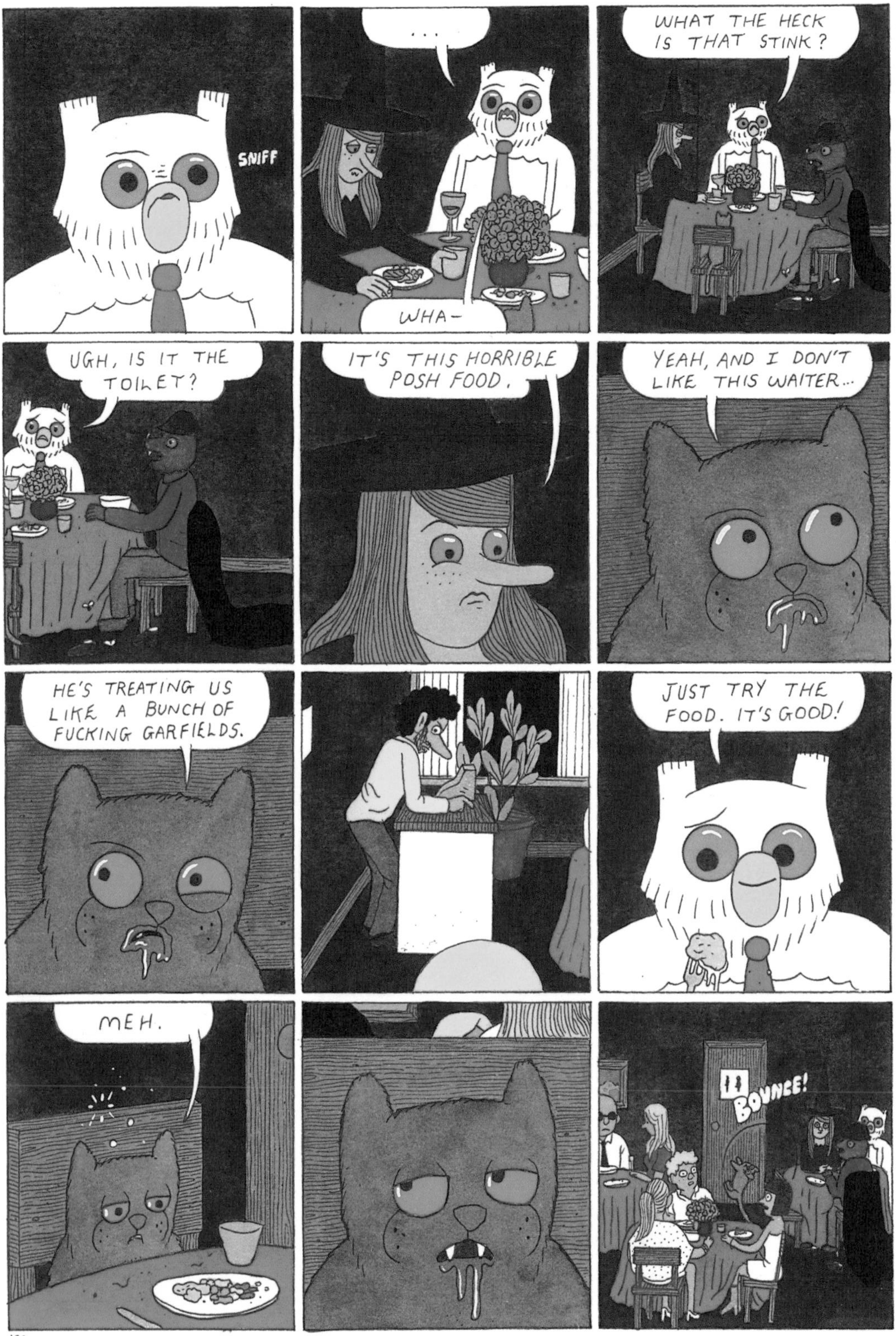
SNIFF
...
WHA-
WHAT THE HECK IS THAT STINK?
UGH, IS IT THE TOILET?
IT'S THIS HORRIBLE POSH FOOD.
YEAH, AND I DON'T LIKE THIS WAITER...
HE'S TREATING US LIKE A BUNCH OF FUCKING GARFIELDS.
JUST TRY THE FOOD. IT'S GOOD!
MEH.
BOUNCE!

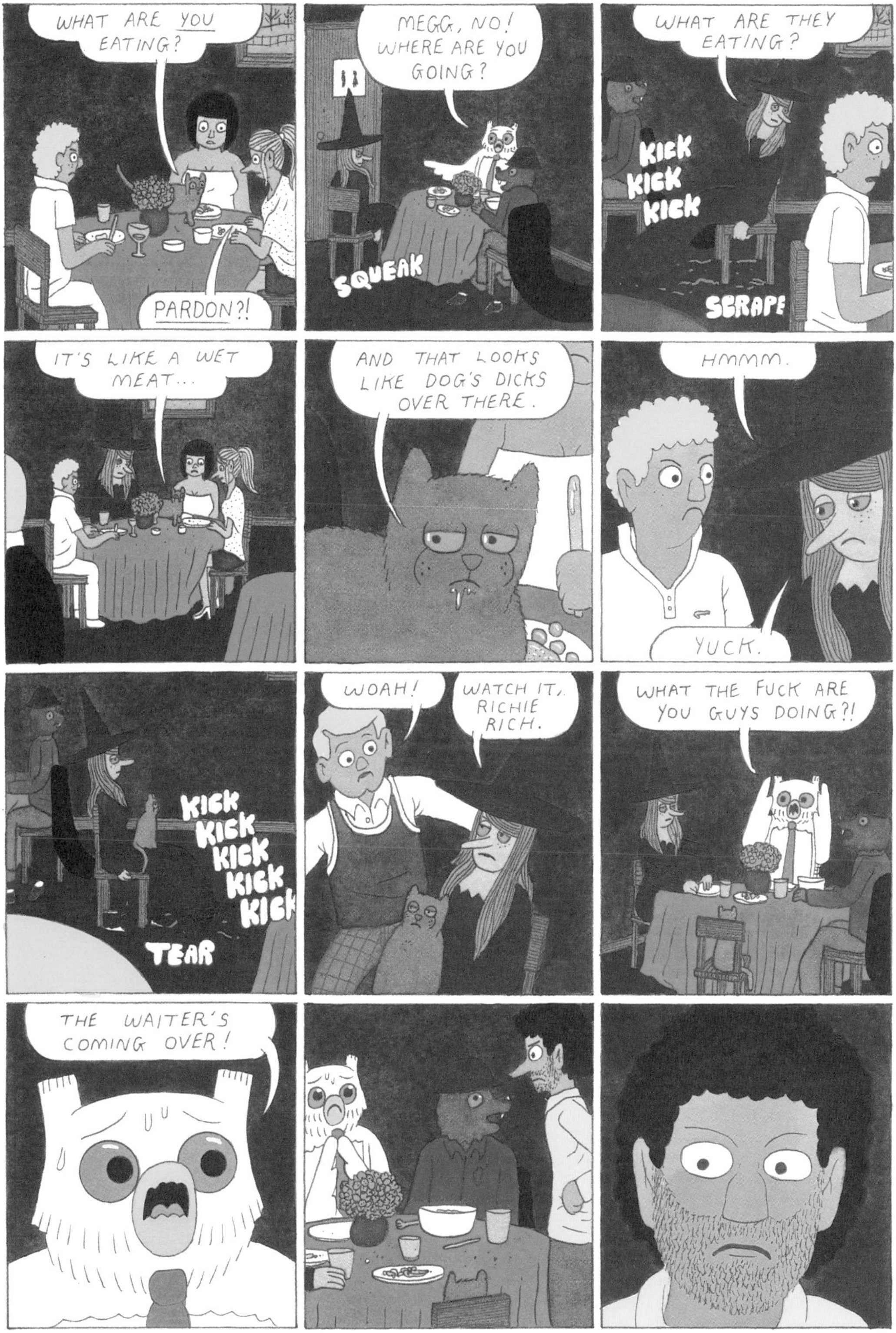
WHAT ARE YOU EATING?
PARDON?!
MEGG, NO! WHERE ARE YOU GOING?
SQUEAK
WHAT ARE THEY EATING?
KICK KICK KICK
SCRAPE
IT'S LIKE A WET MEAT...
AND THAT LOOKS LIKE DOG'S DICKS OVER THERE.
HMMM.
YUCK.
KICK KICK KICK KICK KICK
TEAR
WOAH!
WATCH IT, RICHIE RICH.
WHAT THE FUCK ARE YOU GUYS DOING?!
THE WAITER'S COMING OVER!

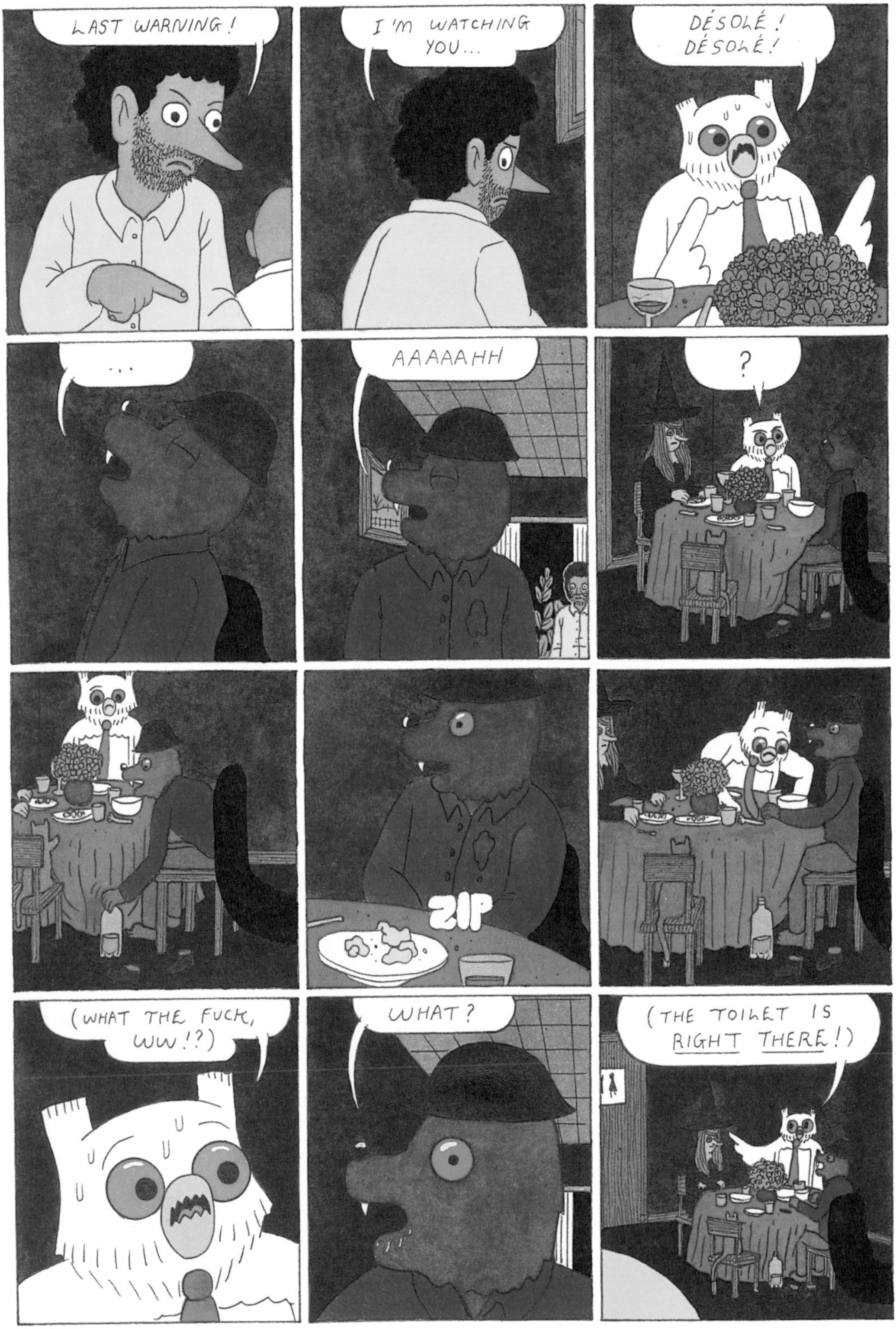
LAST WARNING!
I'M WATCHING YOU...
DÉSOLÉ! DÉSOLÉ!
...
AAAAAHH
?
ZIP
(WHAT THE FUCK, WW!?)
WHAT?
(THE TOILET IS RIGHT THERE!)

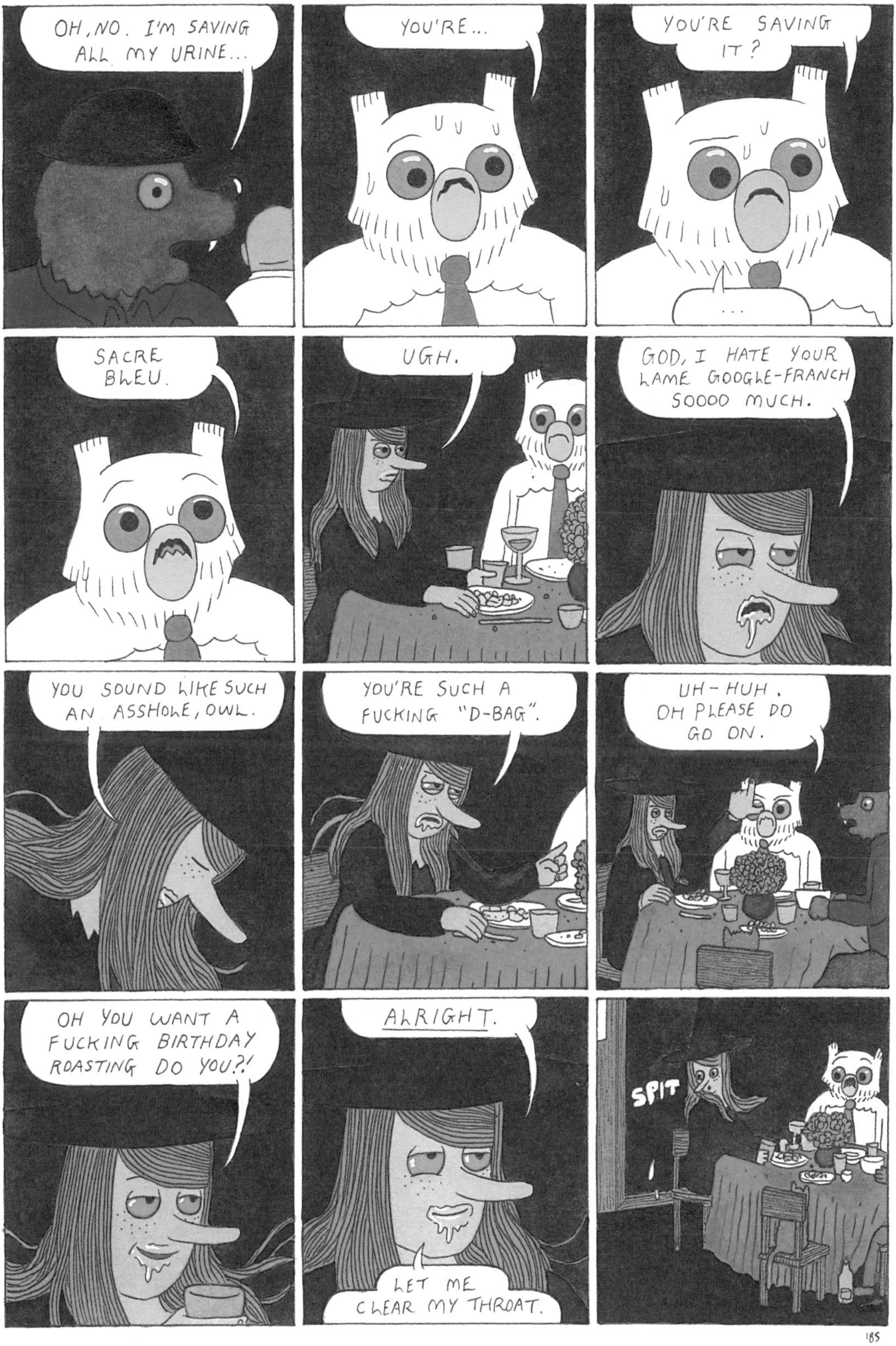
OH, NO. I'M SAVING ALL MY URINE...
YOU'RE...
YOU'RE SAVING IT?
...
SACRE BLEU.
UGH.
GOD, I HATE YOUR LAME GOOGLE-FRANCH SOOOO MUCH.
YOU SOUND LIKE SUCH AN ASSHOLE, OWL.
YOU'RE SUCH A FUCKING "D-BAG".
UH-HUH. OH PLEASE DO GO ON.
OH YOU WANT A FUCKING BIRTHDAY ROASTING DO YOU?!
ALRIGHT.
LET ME CLEAR MY THROAT.
SPIT

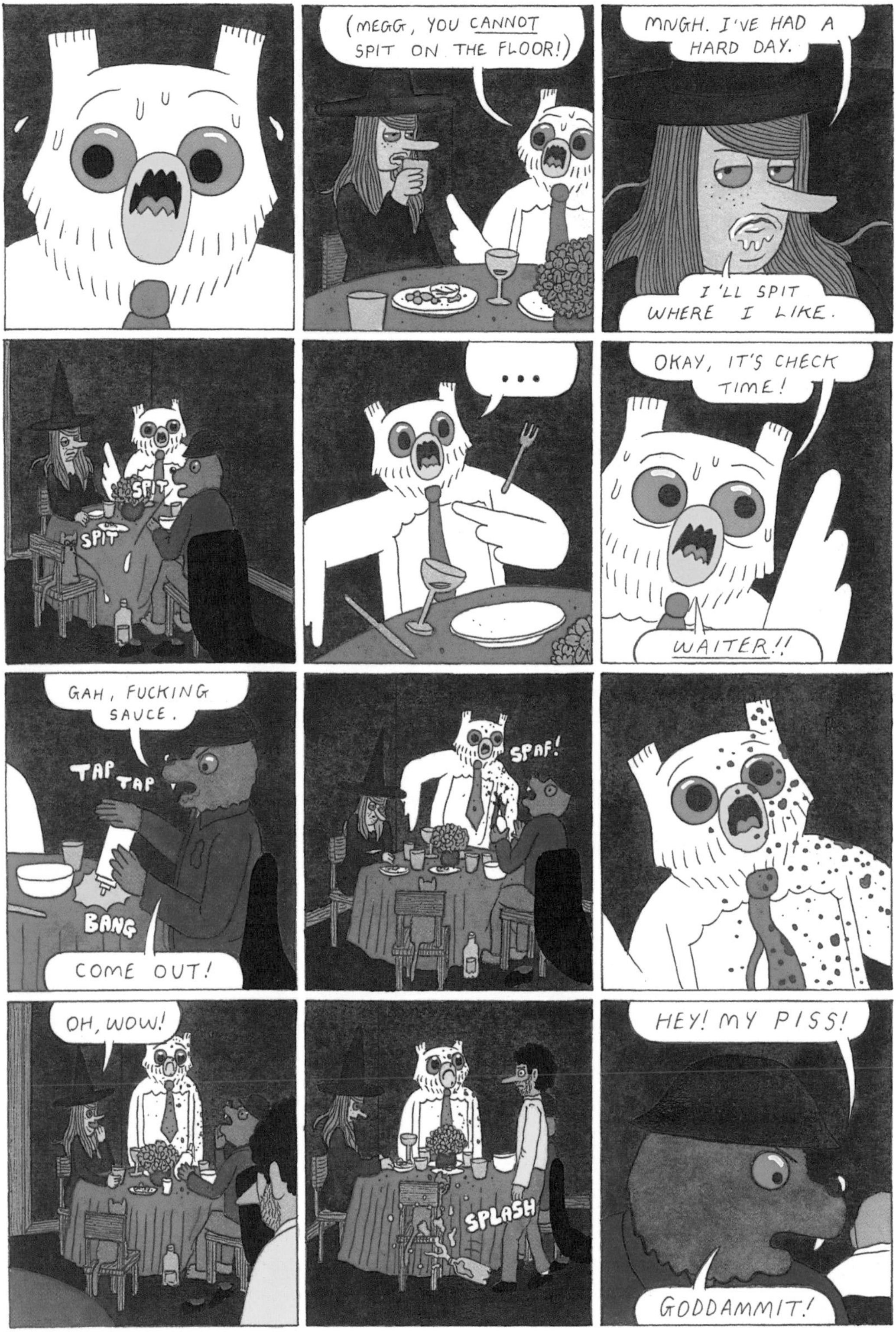
(MEGG, YOU CANNOT SPIT ON THE FLOOR!)
MNGH. I'VE HAD A HARD DAY.
I'LL SPIT WHERE I LIKE.
SPIT
SPIT
...
OKAY, IT'S CHECK TIME!
WAITER!!
GAH, FUCKING SAUCE.
TAP TAP
BANG
COME OUT!
SPAF!
OH, WOW!
SPLASH
HEY! MY PISS!
GODDAMMIT!

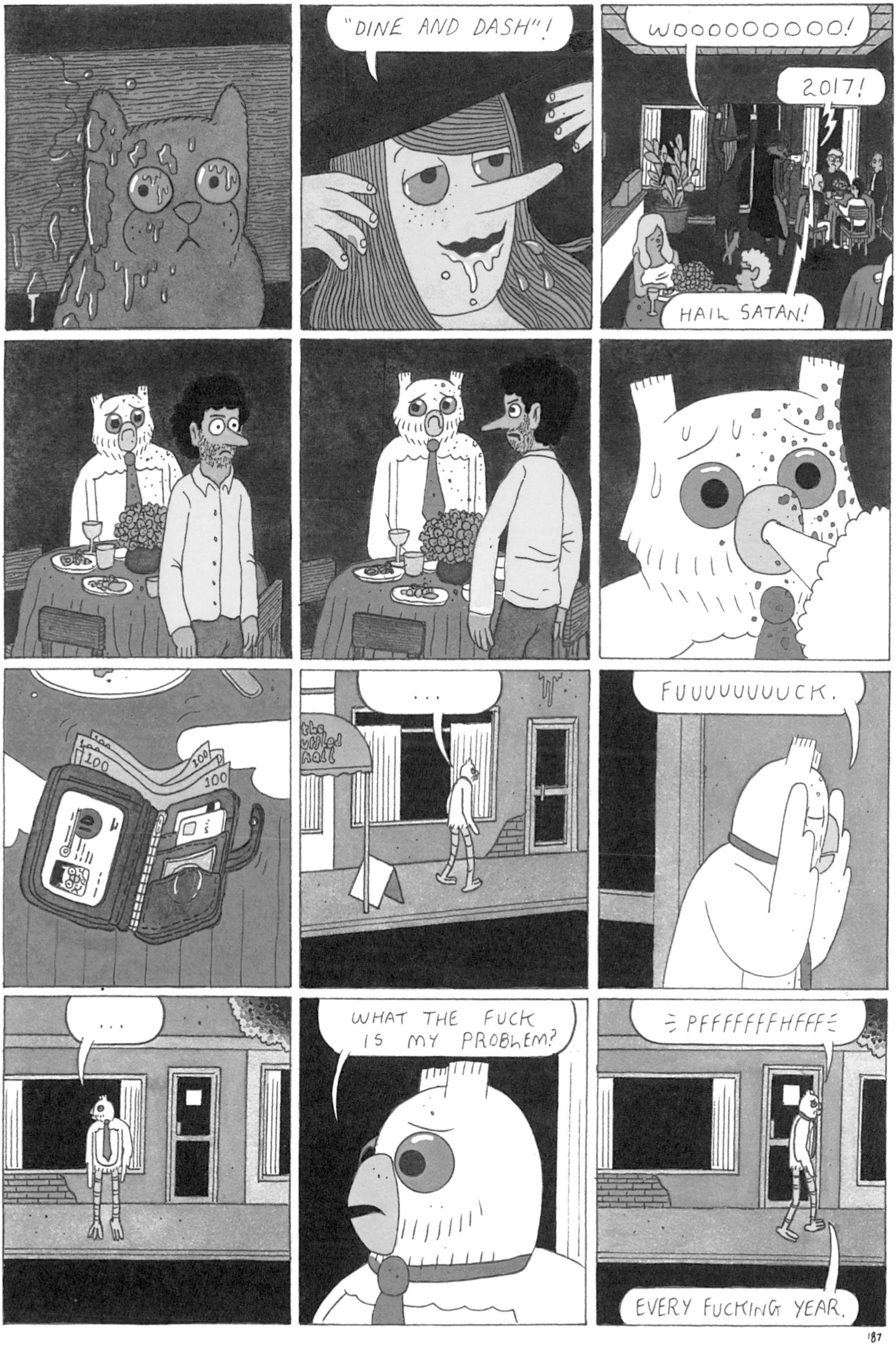
"DINE AND DASH"!
WOOOOOOOOO!
2017!
HAIL SATAN!
the ruffled snail
...
FUUUUUUUUCK.
...
WHAT THE FUCK IS MY PROBLEM?
PFFFFFFFHFFF
EVERY FUCKING YEAR.

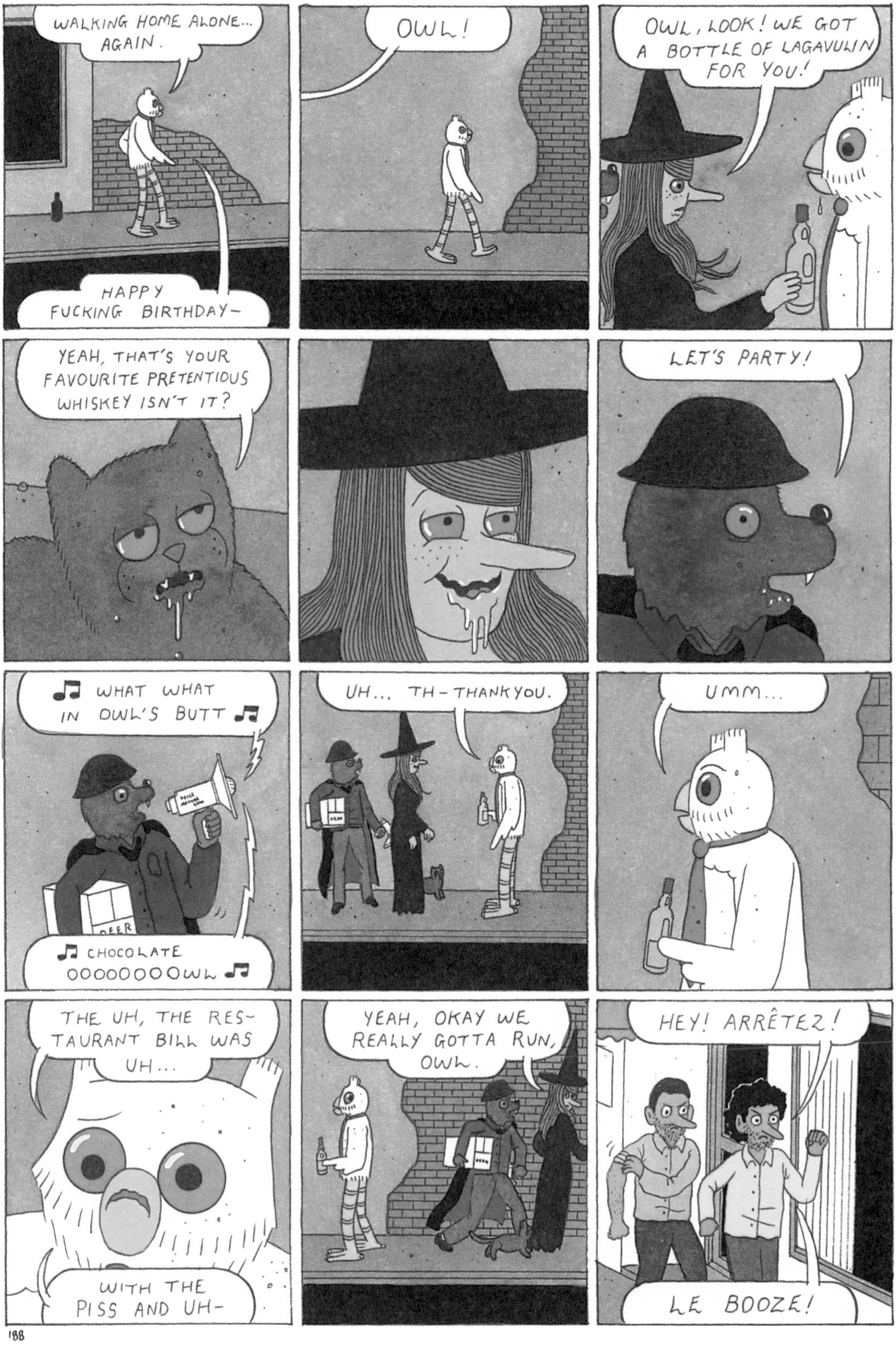
WALKING HOME ALONE... AGAIN.
HAPPY FUCKING BIRTHDAY-
OWL!
OWL, LOOK! WE GOT A BOTTLE OF LAGAVULIN FOR YOU!
YEAH, THAT'S YOUR FAVOURITE PRETENTIOUS WHISKEY ISN'T IT?
LET'S PARTY!
♫ WHAT WHAT IN OWL'S BUTT ♫
DEER
♫ CHOCOLATE OOOOOOOOWL ♫
UH... TH-THANKYOU.
UMM...
THE UH, THE RES-TAURANT BILL WAS UH...
WITH THE PISS AND UH-
YEAH, OKAY WE REALLY GOTTA RUN, OWL.
HEY! ARRÊTEZ!
LE BOOZE!

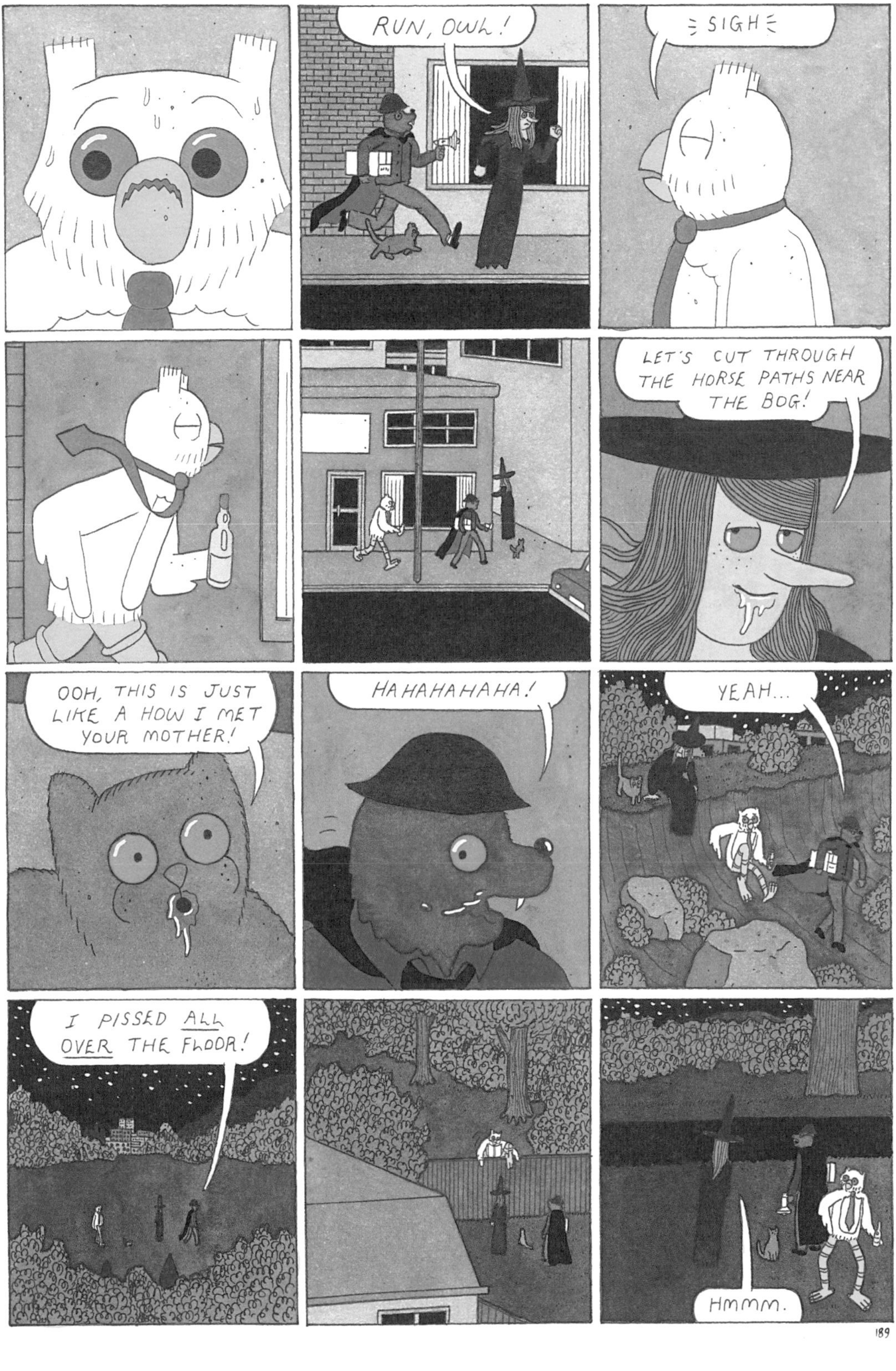
RUN, OWL!
≡ SIGH ≡
LET'S CUT THROUGH THE HORSE PATHS NEAR THE BOG!
OOH, THIS IS JUST LIKE A HOW I MET YOUR MOTHER!
HAHAHAHAHA!
YEAH...
I PISSED ALL OVER THE FLOOR!
HMMM.

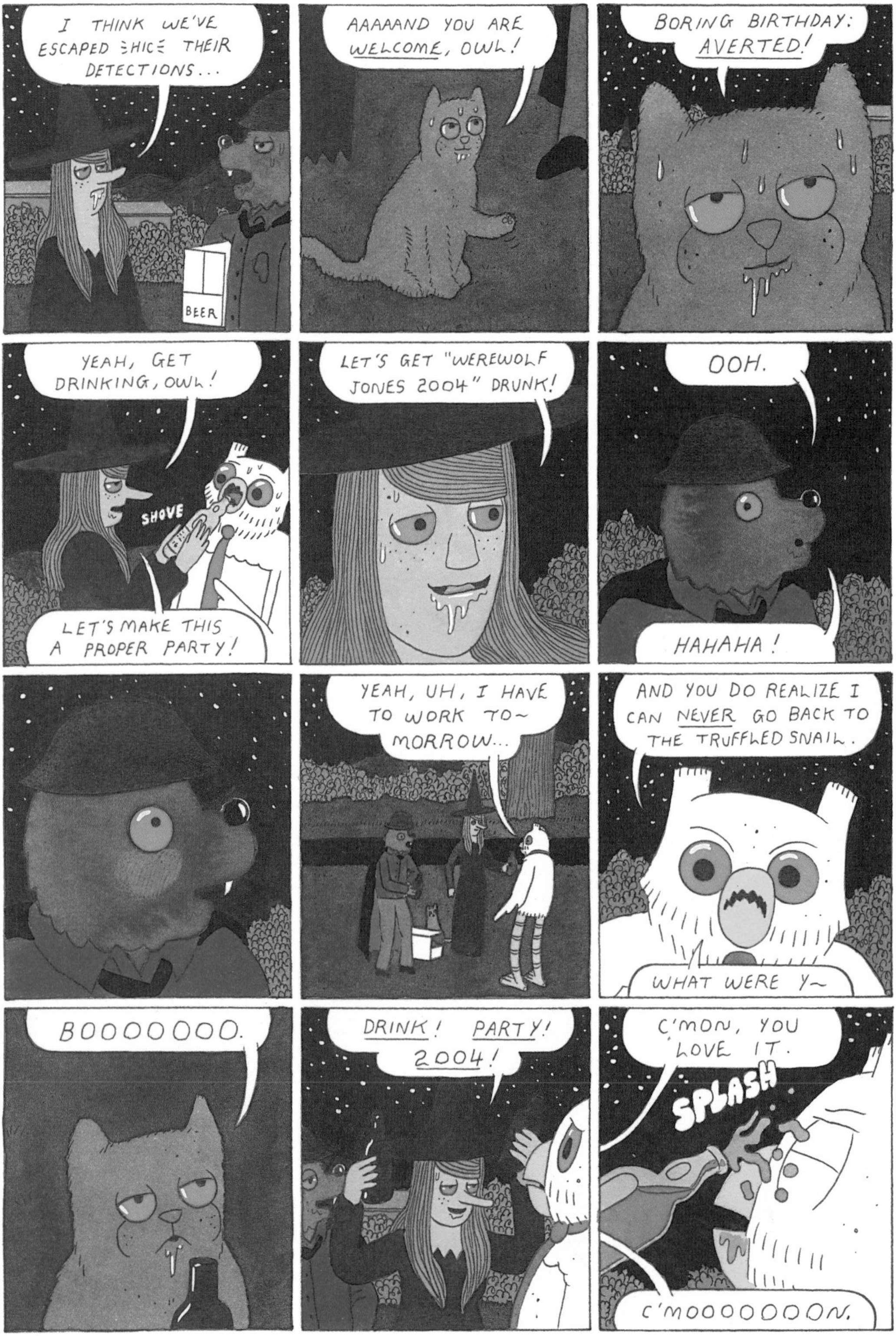
I THINK WE'VE ESCAPED *HIC* THEIR DETECTIONS...
BEER
AAAAAND YOU ARE WELCOME, OWL!
BORING BIRTHDAY: AVERTED!
YEAH, GET DRINKING, OWL!
SHOVE
LET'S MAKE THIS A PROPER PARTY!
LET'S GET "WEREWOLF JONES 2004" DRUNK!
OOH.
HAHAHA!
YEAH, UH, I HAVE TO WORK TO-MORROW...
AND YOU DO REALIZE I CAN NEVER GO BACK TO THE TRUFFLED SNAIL.
WHAT WERE Y~
BOOOOOOO.
DRINK! PARTY! 2004!
C'MON, YOU LOVE IT.
SPLASH
C'MOOOOOOOON.

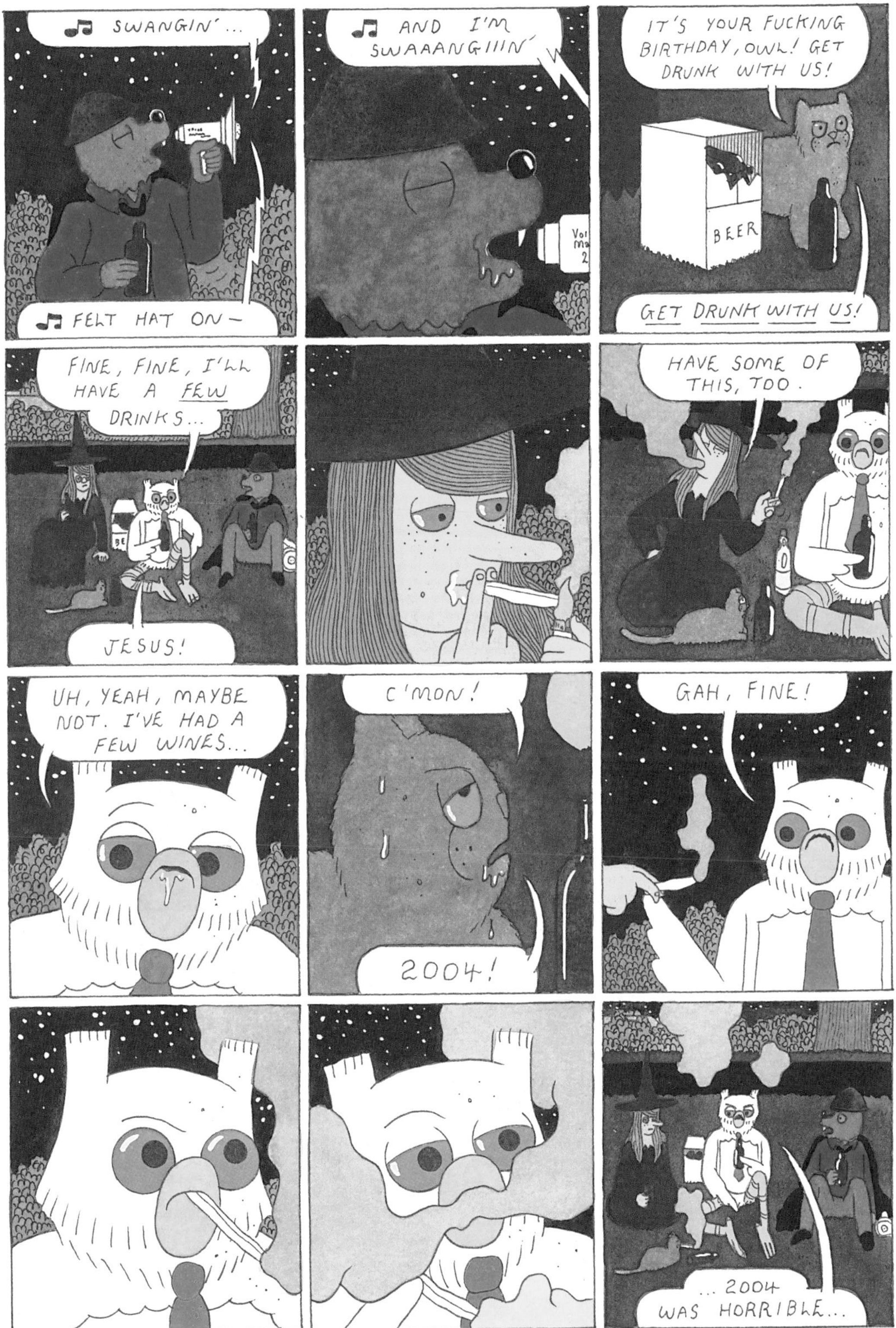
♫ SWANGIN'...
♫ FELT HAT ON—
♫ AND I'M SWAAAANGIIIN'
IT'S YOUR FUCKING BIRTHDAY, OWL! GET DRUNK WITH US!
BEER
GET DRUNK WITH US!
FINE, FINE, I'LL HAVE A FEW DRINKS...
JESUS!
HAVE SOME OF THIS, TOO.
UH, YEAH, MAYBE NOT. I'VE HAD A FEW WINES...
C'MON!
2004!
GAH, FINE!
...2004 WAS HORRIBLE...

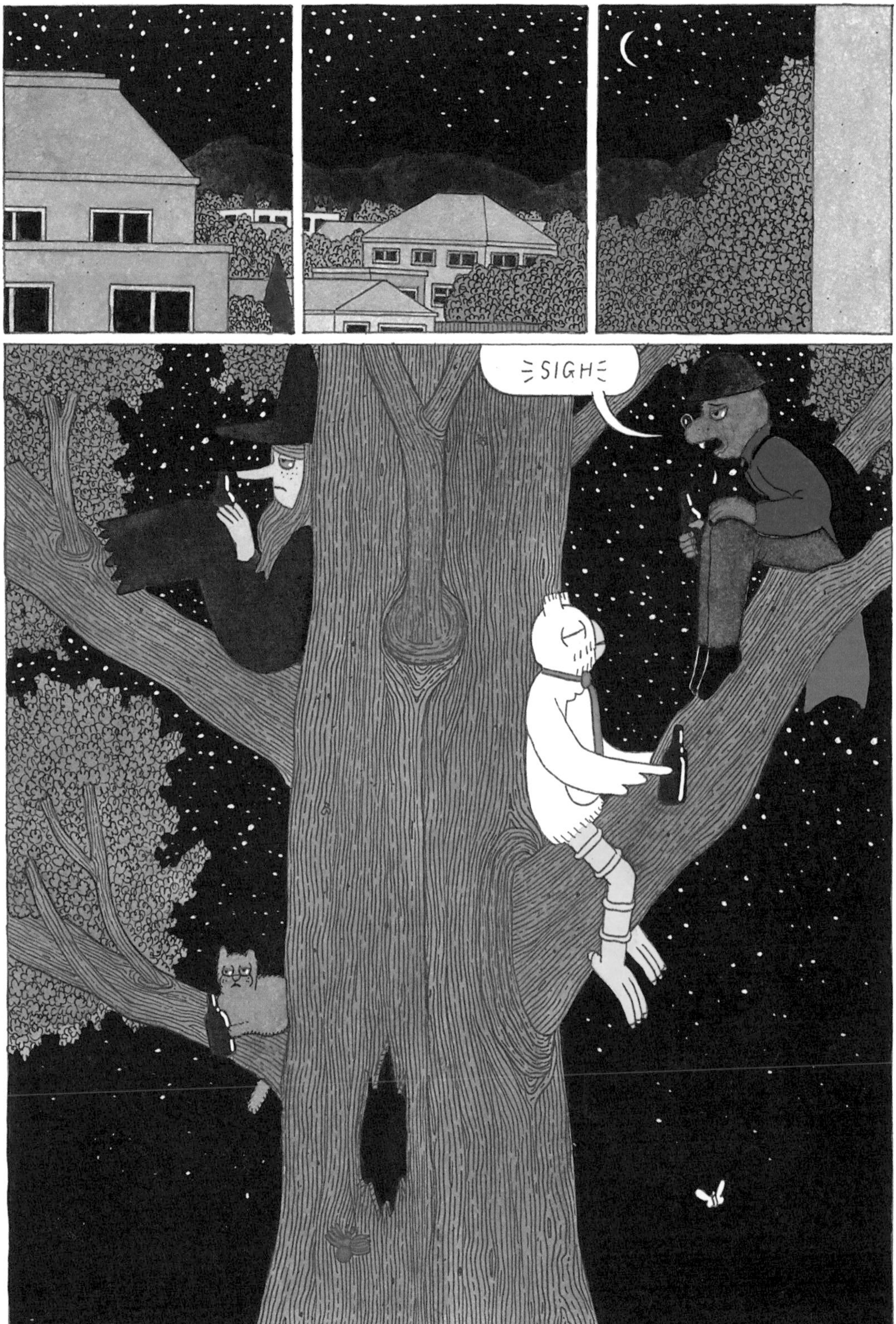
SIGH

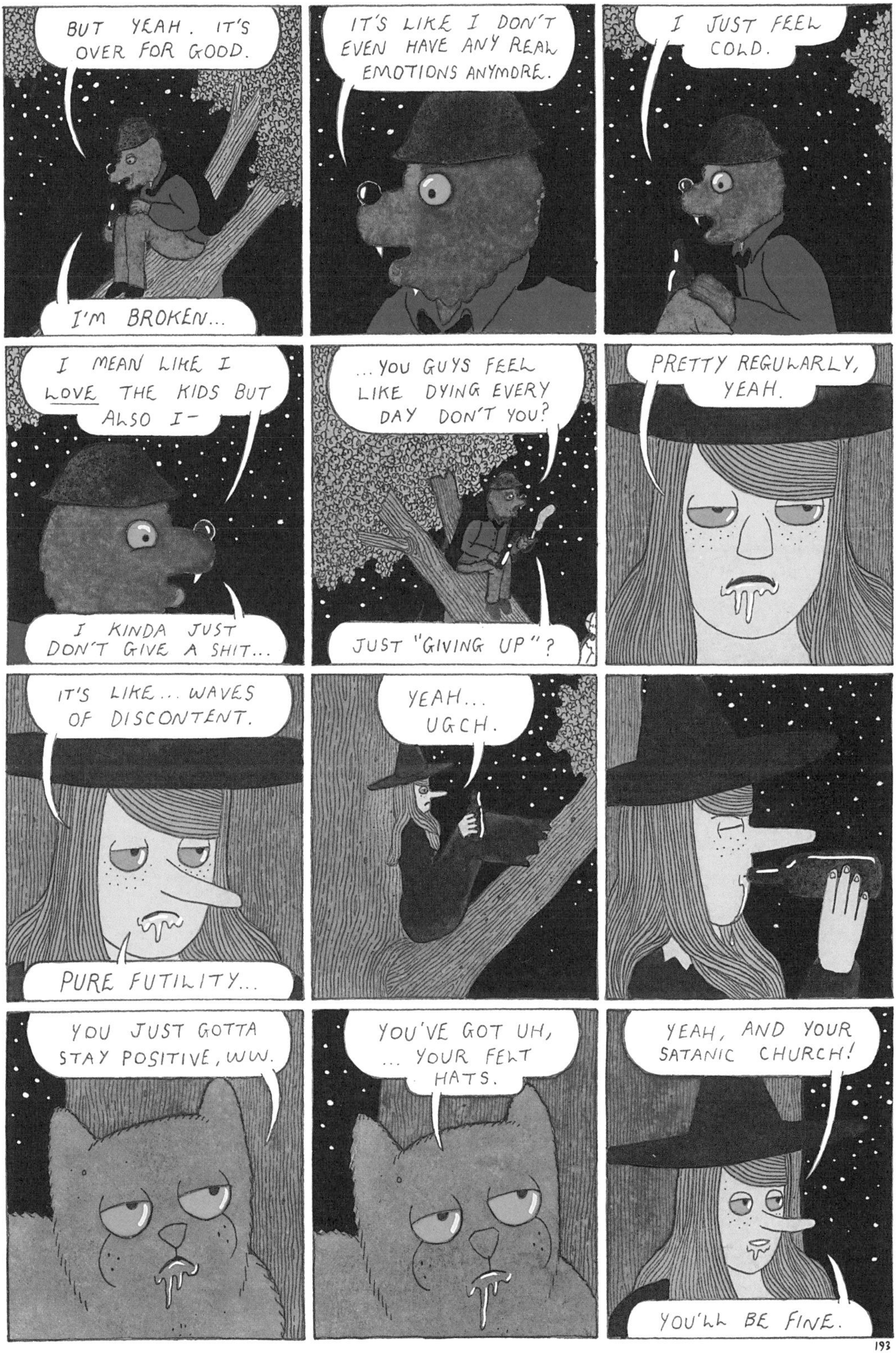

BUT YEAH. IT'S OVER FOR GOOD.
I'M BROKEN...
IT'S LIKE I DON'T EVEN HAVE ANY REAL EMOTIONS ANYMORE.
I JUST FEEL COLD.
I MEAN LIKE I LOVE THE KIDS BUT ALSO I-
I KINDA JUST DON'T GIVE A SHIT...
...YOU GUYS FEEL LIKE DYING EVERY DAY DON'T YOU?
JUST "GIVING UP"?
PRETTY REGULARLY, YEAH.
IT'S LIKE... WAVES OF DISCONTENT.
PURE FUTILITY...
YEAH... UGCH.
YOU JUST GOTTA STAY POSITIVE, WW.
YOU'VE GOT UH, ... YOUR FELT HATS.
YEAH, AND YOUR SATANIC CHURCH!
YOU'LL BE FINE.

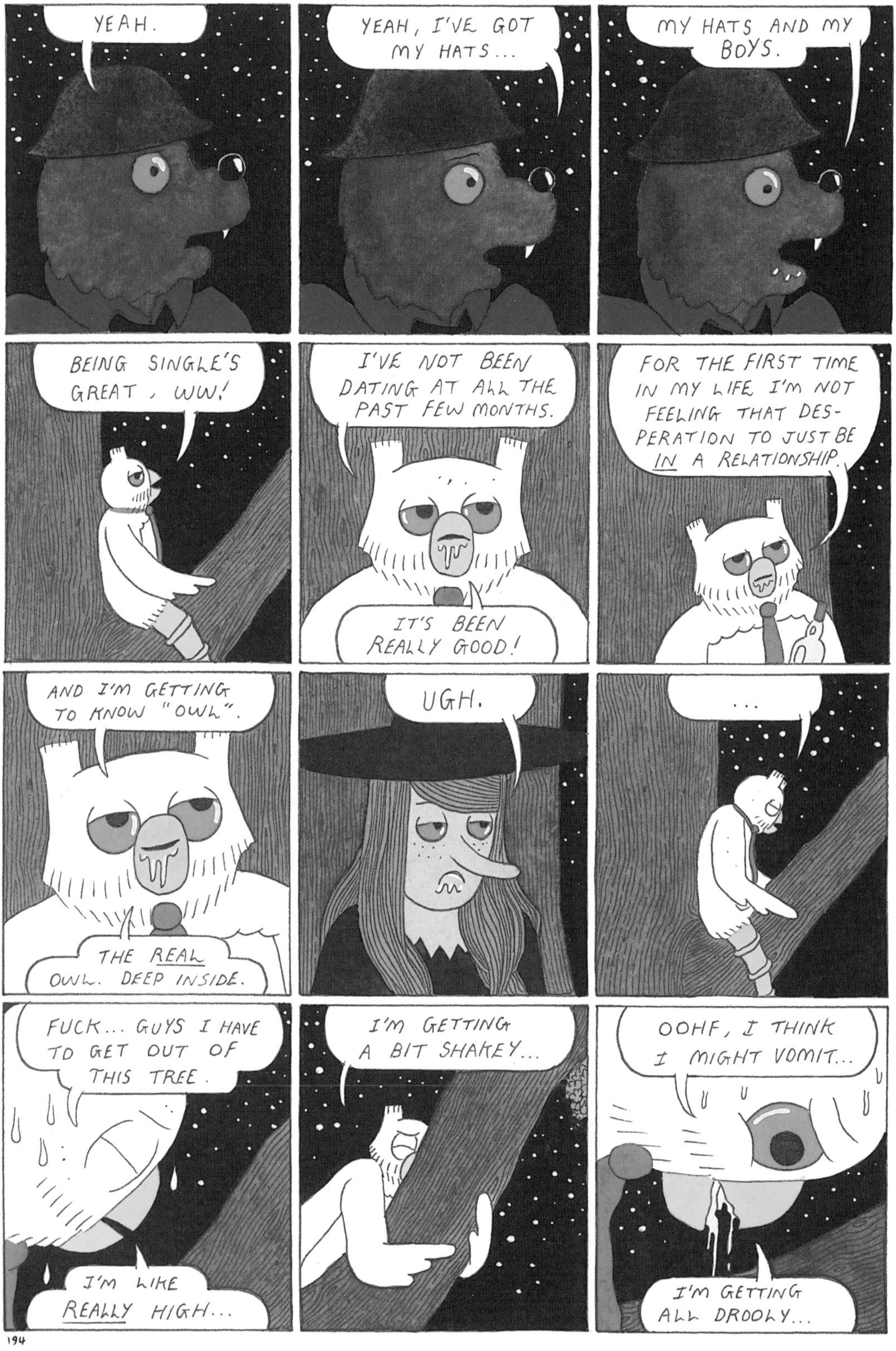

YEAH.
YEAH, I'VE GOT MY HATS...
MY HATS AND MY BOYS.
BEING SINGLE'S GREAT, WW!
I'VE NOT BEEN DATING AT ALL THE PAST FEW MONTHS.
IT'S BEEN REALLY GOOD!
FOR THE FIRST TIME IN MY LIFE I'M NOT FEELING THAT DES-PERATION TO JUST BE IN A RELATIONSHIP.
AND I'M GETTING TO KNOW "OWL".
THE REAL OWL. DEEP INSIDE.
UGH.
...
FUCK... GUYS I HAVE TO GET OUT OF THIS TREE.
I'M LIKE REALLY HIGH...
I'M GETTING A BIT SHAKEY...
OOHF, I THINK I MIGHT VOMIT...
I'M GETTING ALL DROOLY...

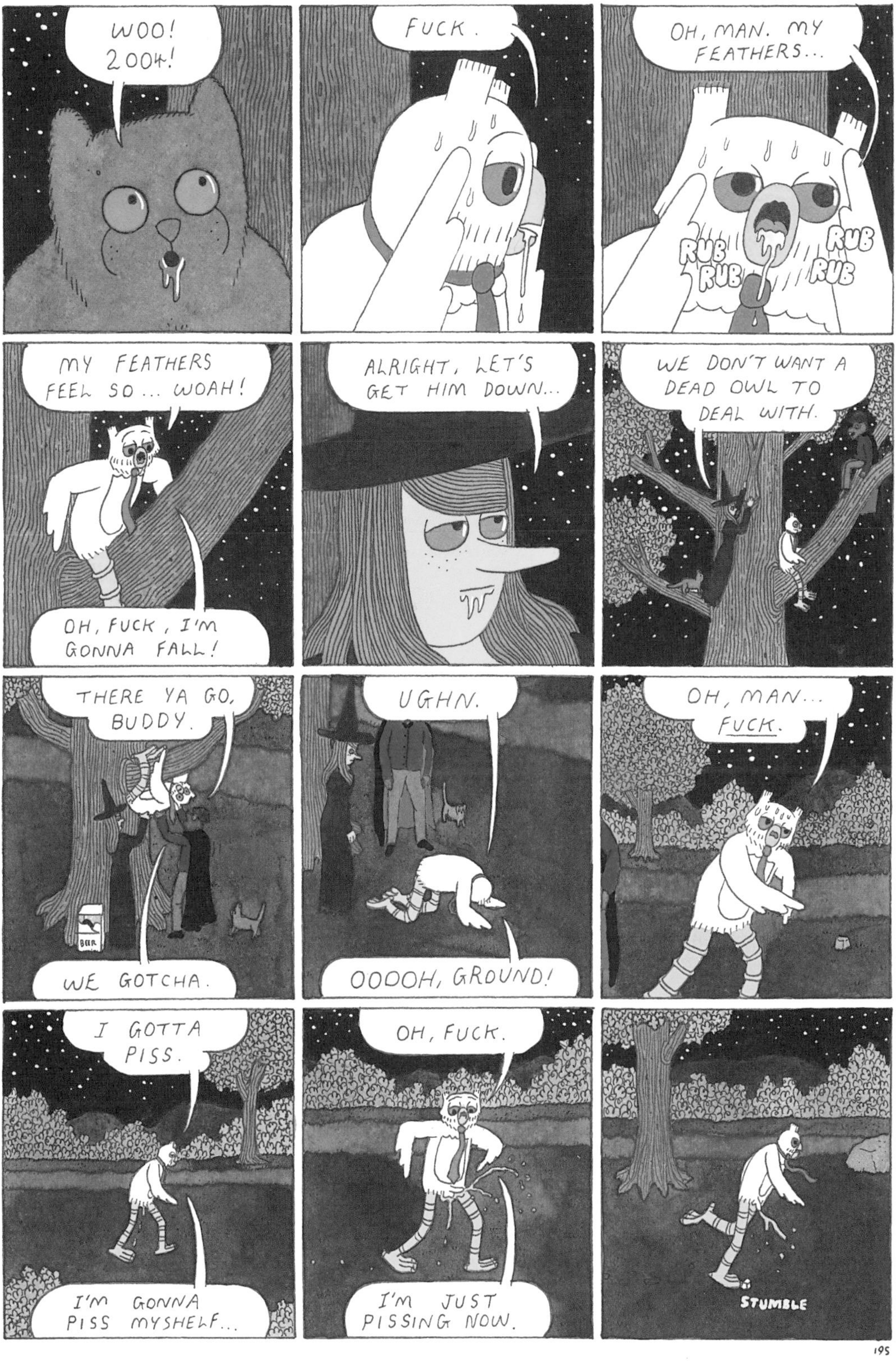
WOO! 2004!
FUCK.
OH, MAN. MY FEATHERS...
RUB RUB RUB RUB
MY FEATHERS FEEL SO... WOAH!
OH, FUCK, I'M GONNA FALL!
ALRIGHT, LET'S GET HIM DOWN...
WE DON'T WANT A DEAD OWL TO DEAL WITH.
THERE YA GO, BUDDY.
BEER
WE GOTCHA.
UGHN.
OOOOH, GROUND!
OH, MAN... FUCK.
I GOTTA PISS.
I'M GONNA PISS MYSHELF...
OH, FUCK.
I'M JUST PISSING NOW.
STUMBLE

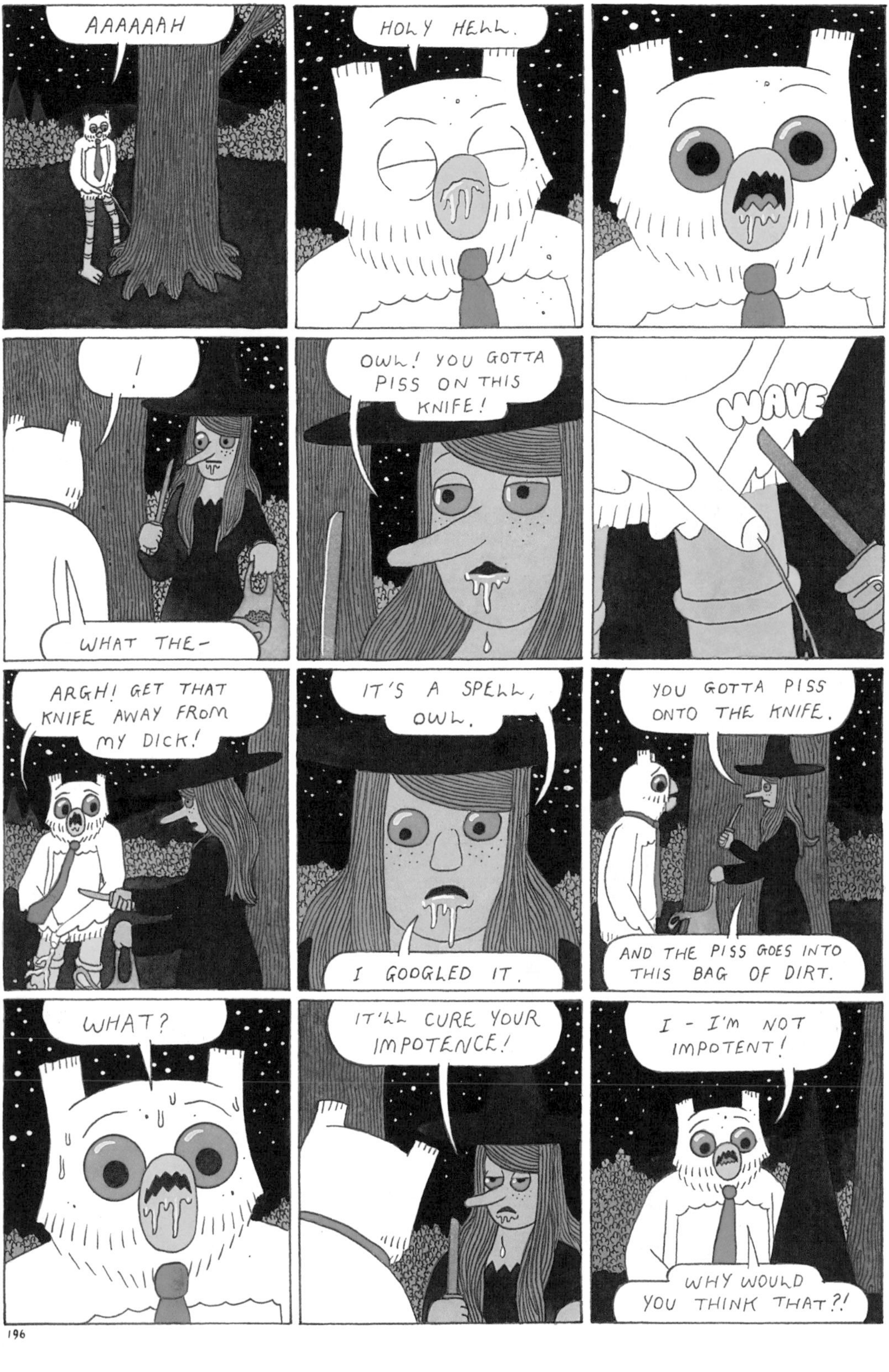
AAAAAAH
HOLY HELL.
!
WHAT THE-
OWL! YOU GOTTA PISS ON THIS KNIFE!
WAVE
ARGH! GET THAT KNIFE AWAY FROM MY DICK!
IT'S A SPELL, OWL.
I GOOGLED IT.
YOU GOTTA PISS ONTO THE KNIFE.
AND THE PISS GOES INTO THIS BAG OF DIRT.
WHAT?
IT'LL CURE YOUR IMPOTENCE!
I - I'M NOT IMPOTENT!
WHY WOULD YOU THINK THAT?!

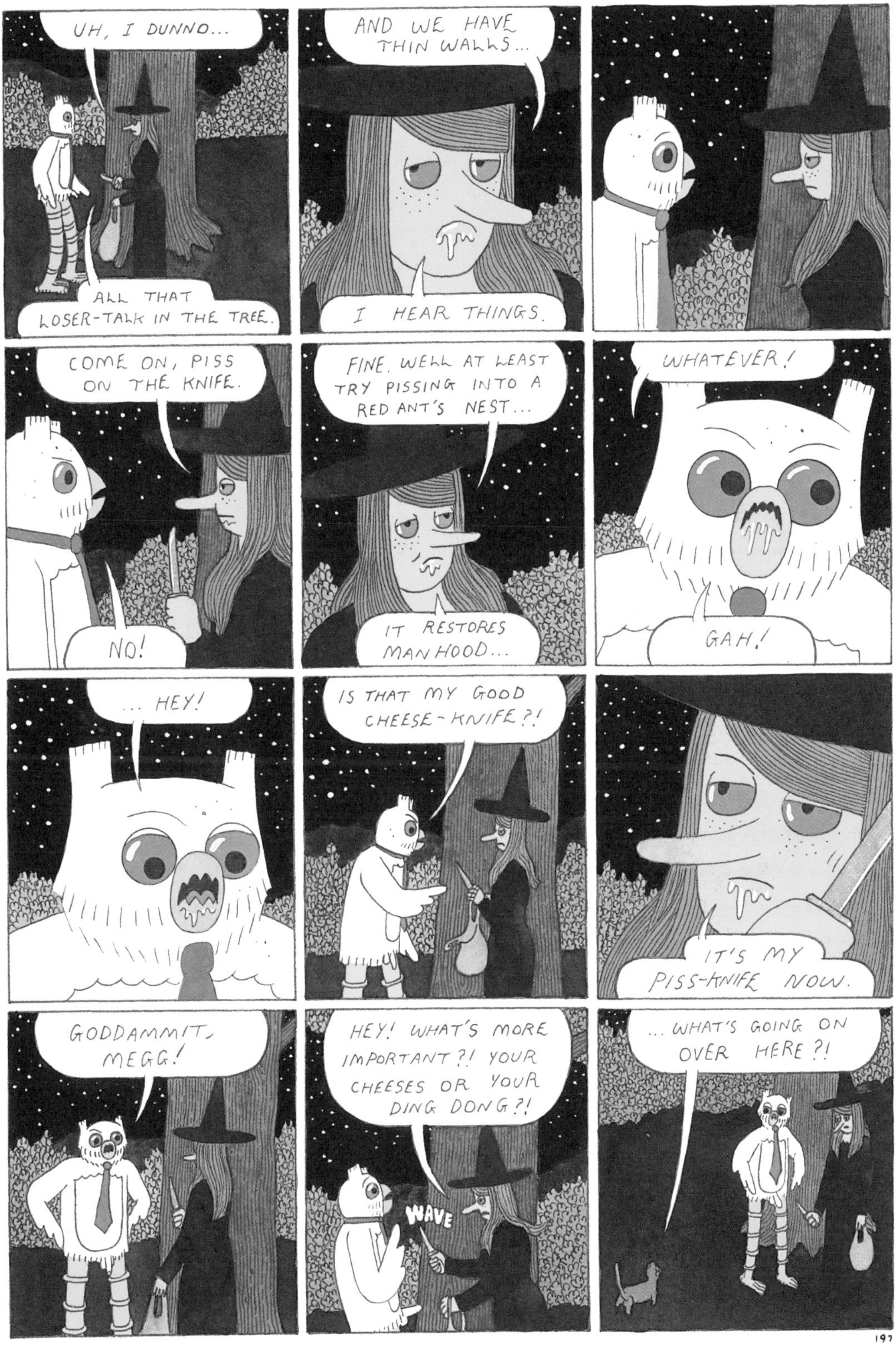
UH, I DUNNO...
ALL THAT LOSER-TALK IN THE TREE.
AND WE HAVE THIN WALLS...
I HEAR THINGS.
COME ON, PISS ON THE KNIFE.
NO!
FINE. WELL AT LEAST TRY PISSING INTO A RED ANT'S NEST...
IT RESTORES MANHOOD...
WHATEVER!
GAH!
... HEY!
IS THAT MY GOOD CHEESE-KNIFE?!
IT'S MY PISS-KNIFE NOW.
GODDAMMIT, MEGG!
HEY! WHAT'S MORE IMPORTANT?! YOUR CHEESES OR YOUR DING DONG?!
WAVE
... WHAT'S GOING ON OVER HERE?!

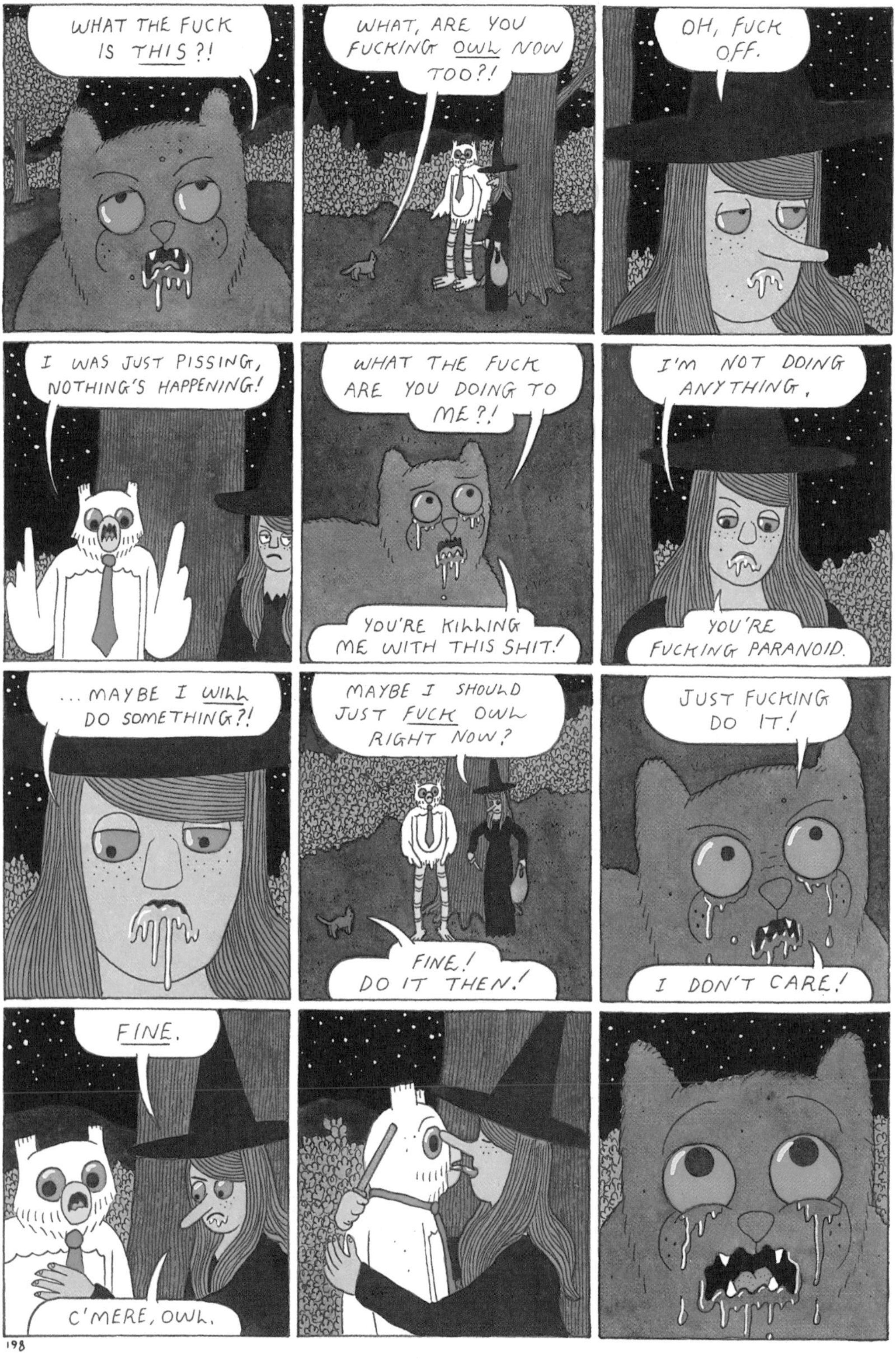
WHAT THE FUCK IS THIS?!
WHAT, ARE YOU FUCKING OWL NOW TOO?!
OH, FUCK OFF.
I WAS JUST PISSING, NOTHING'S HAPPENING!
WHAT THE FUCK ARE YOU DOING TO ME?!
YOU'RE KILLING ME WITH THIS SHIT!
I'M NOT DOING ANYTHING.
YOU'RE FUCKING PARANOID.
...MAYBE I WILL DO SOMETHING?!
MAYBE I SHOULD JUST FUCK OWL RIGHT NOW?
FINE! DO IT THEN!
JUST FUCKING DO IT!
I DON'T CARE!
FINE.
C'MERE, OWL.

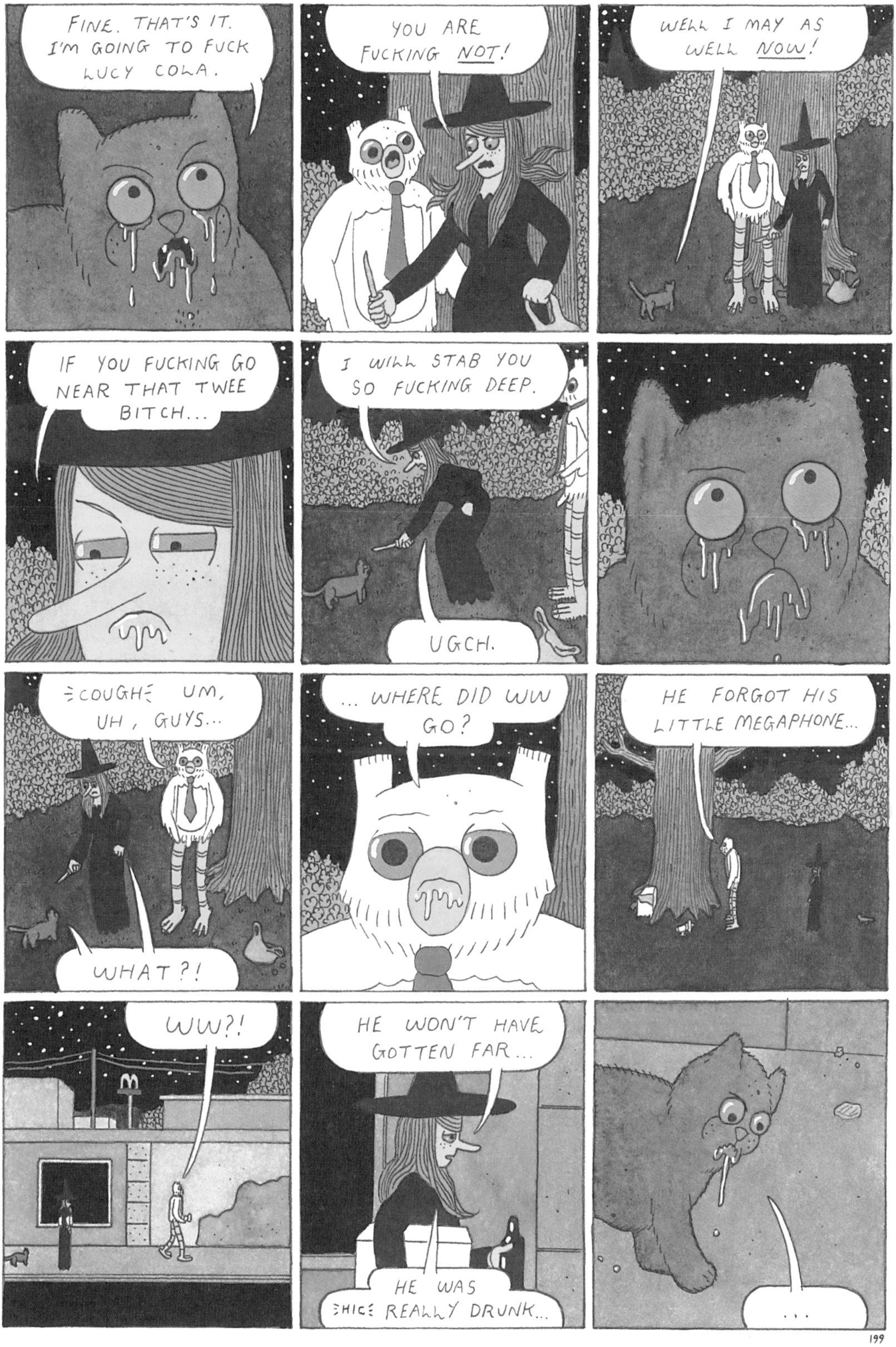
FINE. THAT'S IT. I'M GOING TO FUCK LUCY COLA.
YOU ARE FUCKING NOT!
WELL I MAY AS WELL NOW!
IF YOU FUCKING GO NEAR THAT TWEE BITCH...
I WILL STAB YOU SO FUCKING DEEP.
UGCH.
≡COUGH≡ UM, UH, GUYS...
WHAT?!
... WHERE DID WW GO?
HE FORGOT HIS LITTLE MEGAPHONE...
WW?!
HE WON'T HAVE GOTTEN FAR...
HE WAS ≡HIC≡ REALLY DRUNK...
...

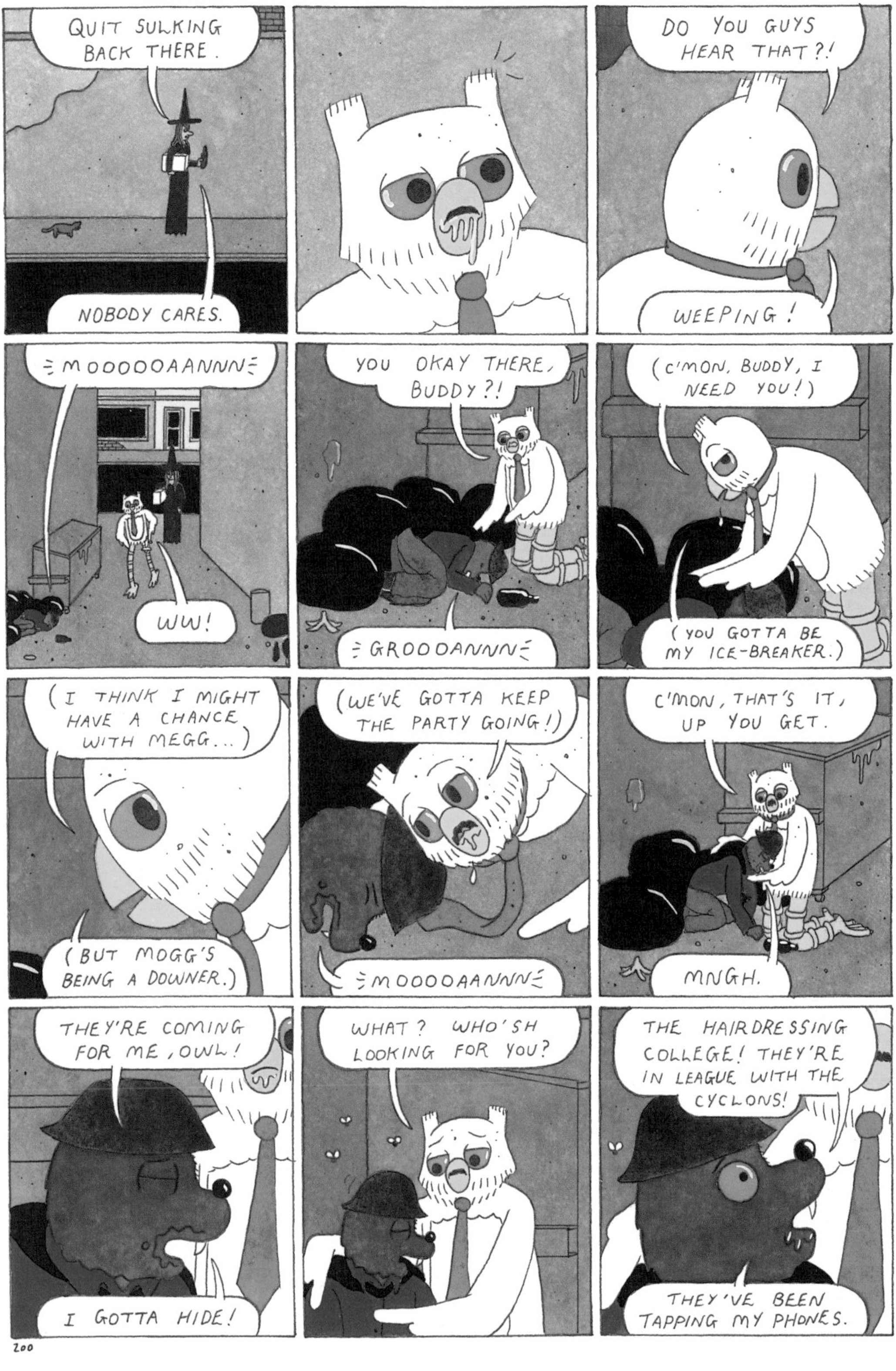
QUIT SULKING BACK THERE.
NOBODY CARES.
DO YOU GUYS HEAR THAT?!
WEEPING!
MOOOOOAANNN
UU!
YOU OKAY THERE, BUDDY?!
GROOOANNN
(C'MON, BUDDY, I NEED YOU!)
(YOU GOTTA BE MY ICE-BREAKER.)
(I THINK I MIGHT HAVE A CHANCE WITH MEGG...)
(BUT MOGG'S BEING A DOWNER.)
(WE'VE GOTTA KEEP THE PARTY GOING!)
MOOOOAANNN
C'MON, THAT'S IT, UP YOU GET.
MNGH.
THEY'RE COMING FOR ME, OWL!
I GOTTA HIDE!
WHAT? WHO'SH LOOKING FOR YOU?
THE HAIRDRESSING COLLEGE! THEY'RE IN LEAGUE WITH THE CYCLONS!
THEY'VE BEEN TAPPING MY PHONES.

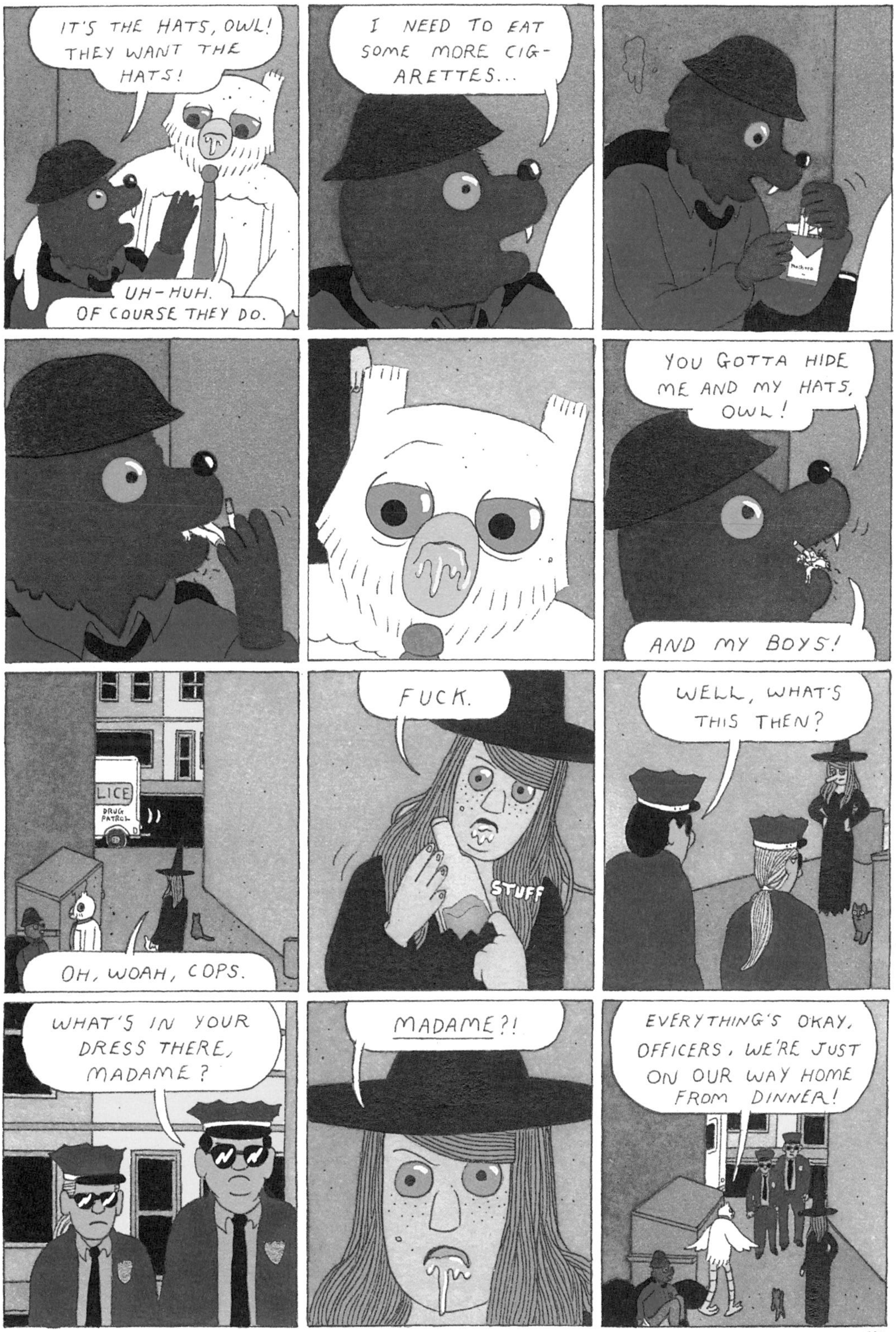
IT'S THE HATS, OWL! THEY WANT THE HATS!
UH-HUH. OF COURSE THEY DO.
I NEED TO EAT SOME MORE CIG-ARETTES...
YOU GOTTA HIDE ME AND MY HATS, OWL!
AND MY BOYS!
LICE
DRUG PATROL
OH, WOAH, COPS.
FUCK.
STUFF
WELL, WHAT'S THIS THEN?
WHAT'S IN YOUR DRESS THERE, MADAME?
MADAME?!
EVERYTHING'S OKAY, OFFICERS, WE'RE JUST ON OUR WAY HOME FROM DINNER!

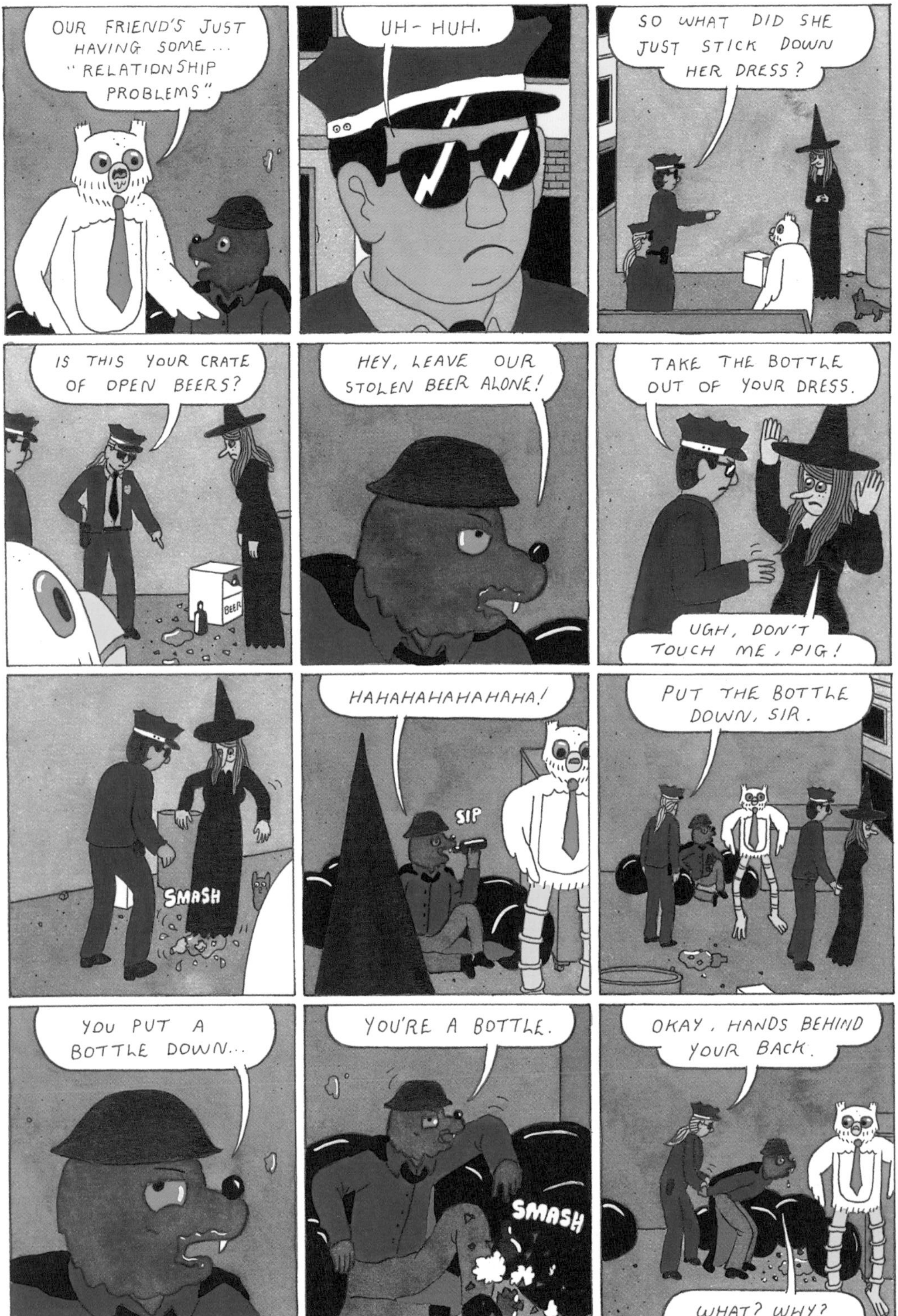
OUR FRIEND'S JUST HAVING SOME... "RELATIONSHIP PROBLEMS".
UH-HUH.
SO WHAT DID SHE JUST STICK DOWN HER DRESS?
IS THIS YOUR CRATE OF OPEN BEERS?
BEER
HEY, LEAVE OUR STOLEN BEER ALONE!
TAKE THE BOTTLE OUT OF YOUR DRESS.
UGH, DON'T TOUCH ME, PIG!
SMASH
HAHAHAHAHAHAHA!
SIP
PUT THE BOTTLE DOWN, SIR.
YOU PUT A BOTTLE DOWN...
YOU'RE A BOTTLE.
SMASH
OKAY, HANDS BEHIND YOUR BACK.
WHAT? WHY?

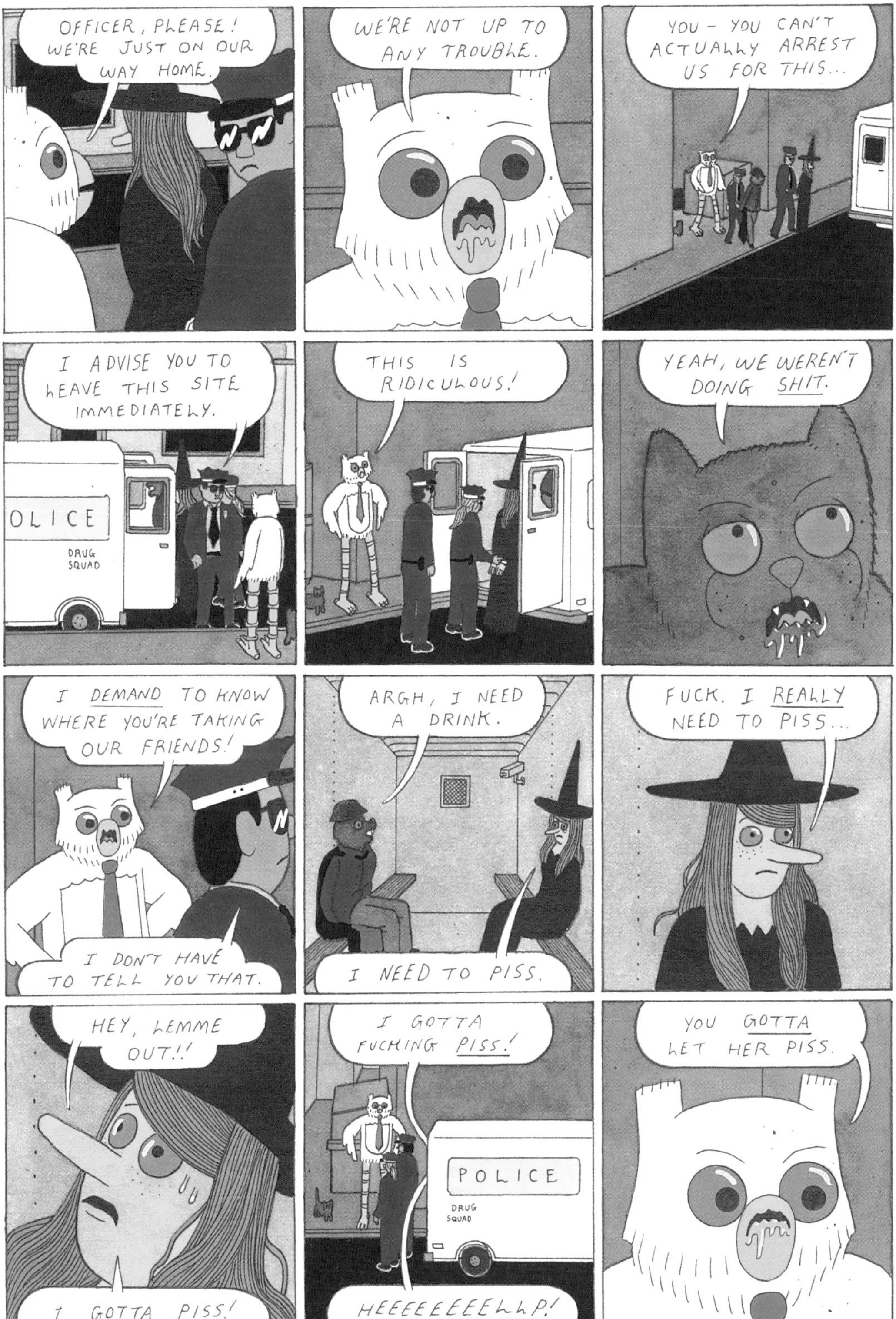
OFFICER, PLEASE! WE'RE JUST ON OUR WAY HOME.
WE'RE NOT UP TO ANY TROUBLE.
YOU - YOU CAN'T ACTUALLY ARREST US FOR THIS...
I ADVISE YOU TO LEAVE THIS SITE IMMEDIATELY.
OLICE
DRUG SQUAD
THIS IS RIDICULOUS!
YEAH, WE WEREN'T DOING SHIT.
I DEMAND TO KNOW WHERE YOU'RE TAKING OUR FRIENDS!
I DON'T HAVE TO TELL YOU THAT.
ARGH, I NEED A DRINK.
I NEED TO PISS.
FUCK. I REALLY NEED TO PISS...
HEY, LEMME OUT!!
I GOTTA PISS!
I GOTTA FUCKING PISS!
POLICE
DRUG SQUAD
HEEEEEEEELLP!
YOU GOTTA LET HER PISS.

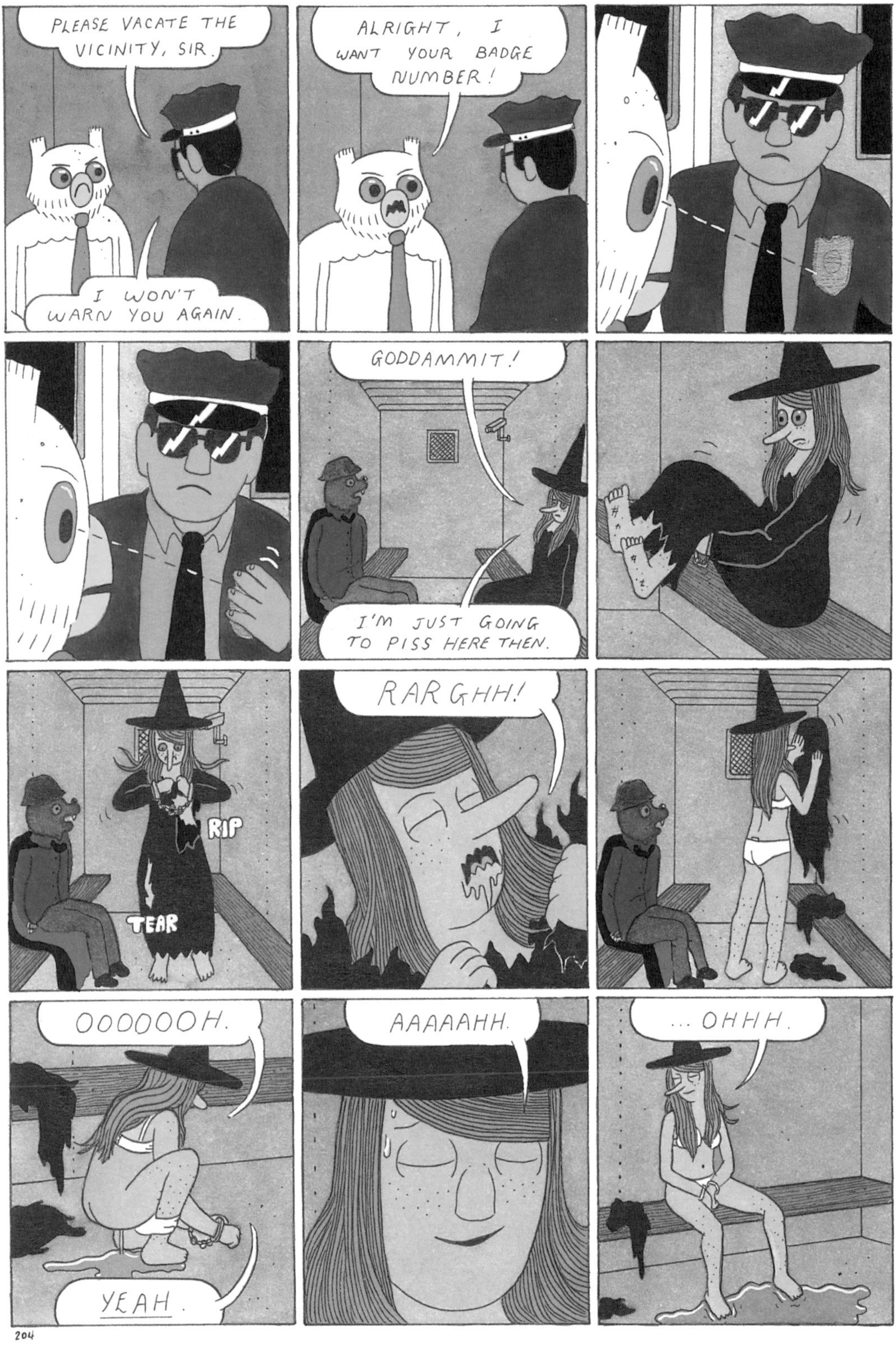
PLEASE VACATE THE VICINITY, SIR.
I WON'T WARN YOU AGAIN.
ALRIGHT, I WANT YOUR BADGE NUMBER!
GODDAMMIT!
I'M JUST GOING TO PISS HERE THEN.
RIP
TEAR
RARGHH!
OOOOOOH.
YEAH.
AAAAAHH.
... OHHH.

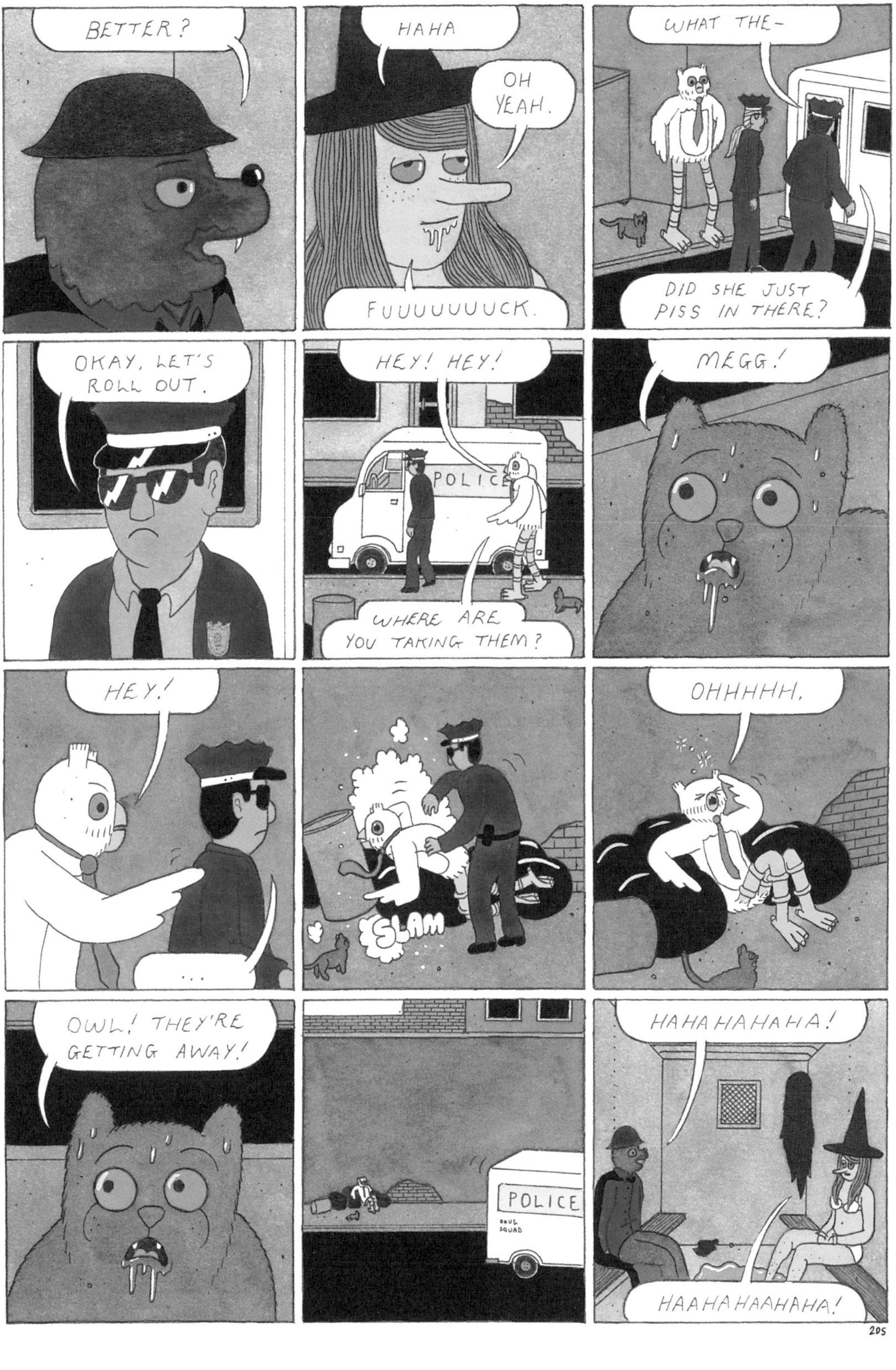
BETTER?
HAHA
OH YEAH.
FUUUUUUUCK.
WHAT THE-
DID SHE JUST PISS IN THERE?
OKAY, LET'S ROLL OUT.
HEY! HEY!
POLICE
WHERE ARE YOU TAKING THEM?
MEGG!
HEY!
...
SLAM
OHHHHH.
OWL! THEY'RE GETTING AWAY!
POLICE
DRUG SQUAD
HAHAHAHAHA!
HAAHAHAAHAHA!

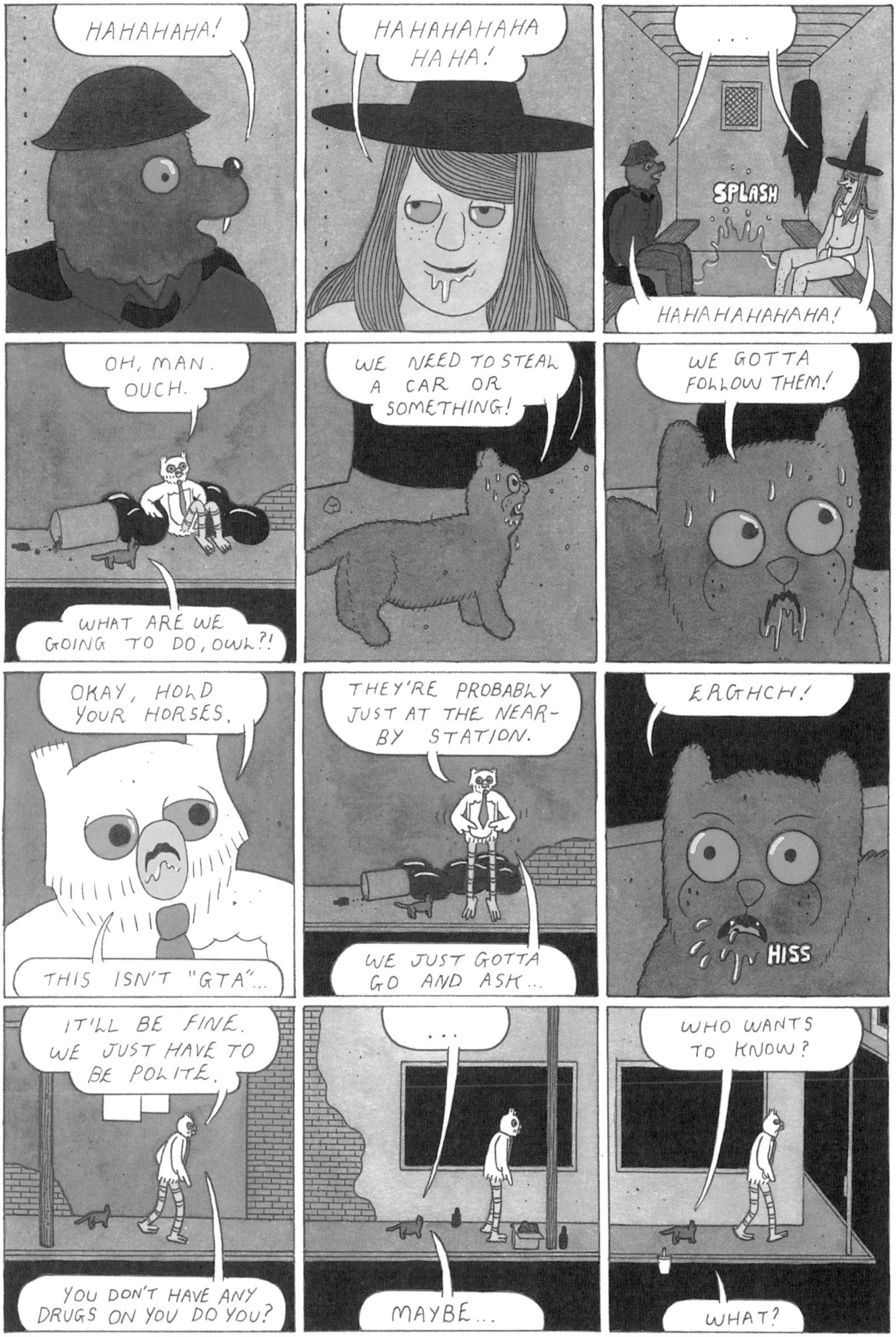
HAHAHAHA!
HAHAHAHAHA HAHA!
...
SPLASH
HAHAHAHAHAHA!
OH, MAN. OUCH.
WHAT ARE WE GOING TO DO, OWL?!
WE NEED TO STEAL A CAR OR SOMETHING!
WE GOTTA FOLLOW THEM!
OKAY, HOLD YOUR HORSES.
THIS ISN'T "GTA"...
THEY'RE PROBABLY JUST AT THE NEAR-BY STATION.
WE JUST GOTTA GO AND ASK...
ERGHCH!
HISS
IT'LL BE FINE. WE JUST HAVE TO BE POLITE.
YOU DON'T HAVE ANY DRUGS ON YOU DO YOU?
...
MAYBE...
WHO WANTS TO KNOW?
WHAT?

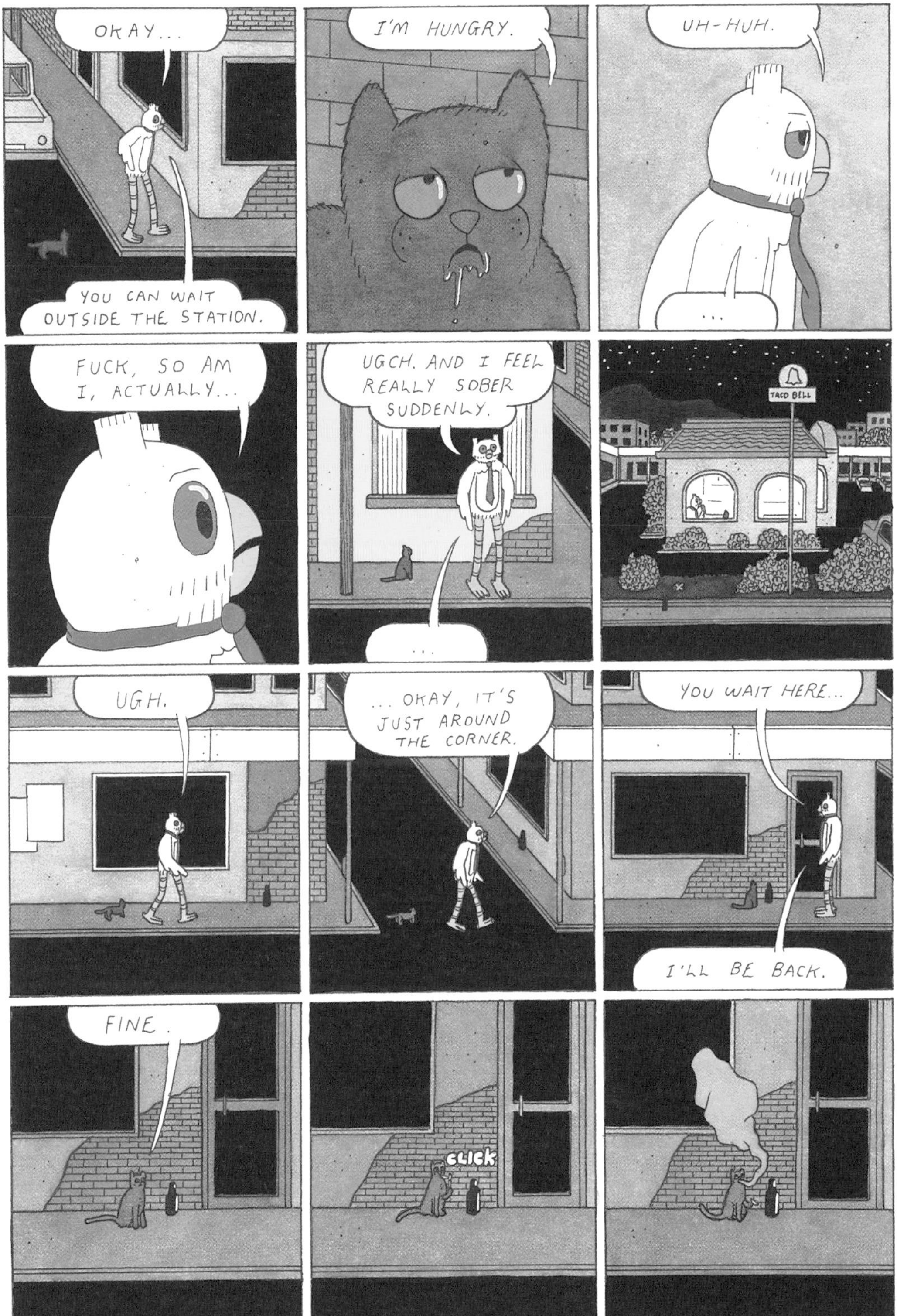
OKAY...
YOU CAN WAIT OUTSIDE THE STATION.
I'M HUNGRY.
UH-HUH.
...
FUCK, SO AM I, ACTUALLY...
UGCH. AND I FEEL REALLY SOBER SUDDENLY.
...
TACO BELL
UGH.
...OKAY, IT'S JUST AROUND THE CORNER.
YOU WAIT HERE...
I'LL BE BACK.
FINE.
CLICK

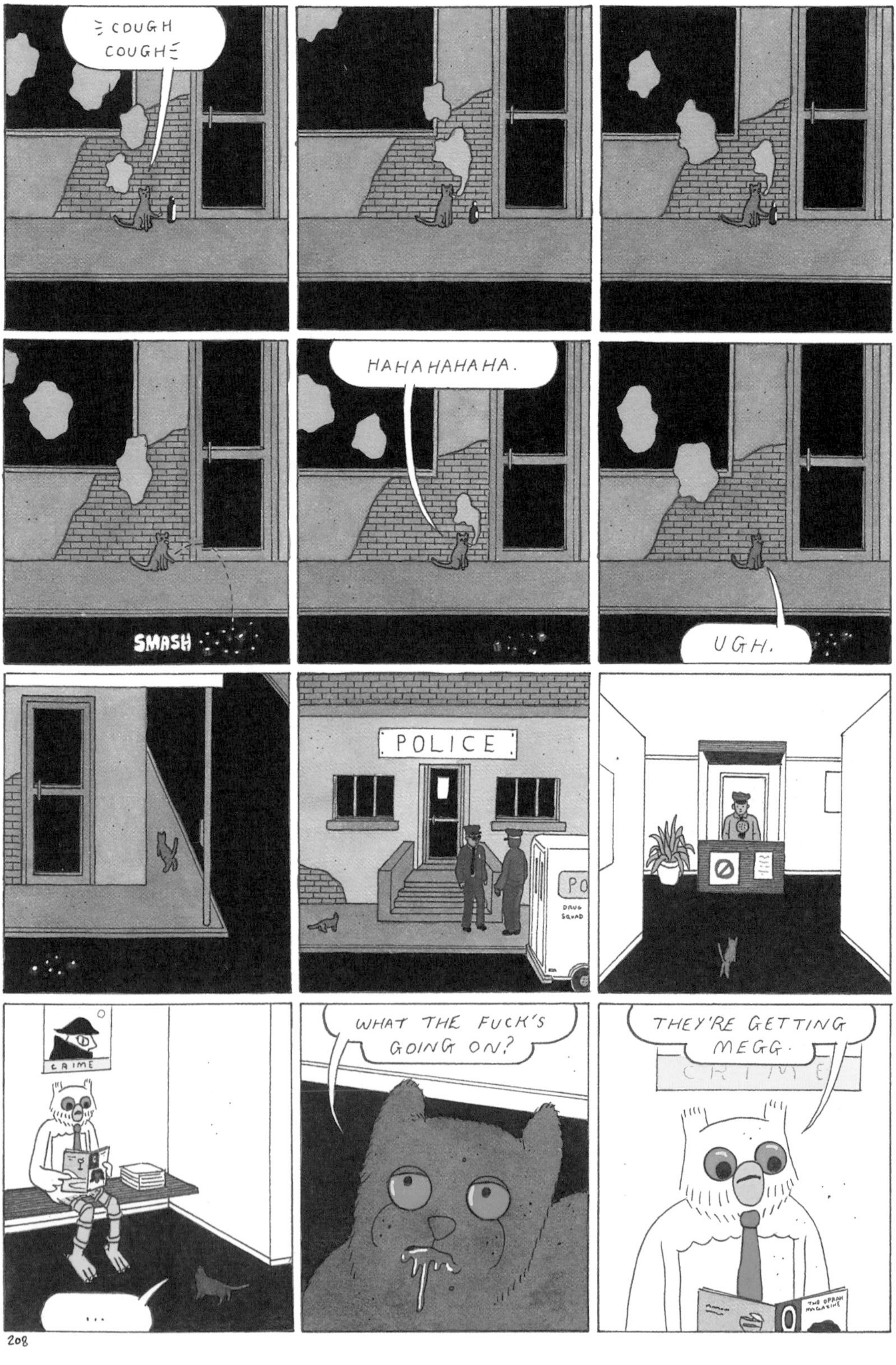
COUGH COUGH
HAHAHAHAHA.
SMASH
UGH.
POLICE
CRIME
...
WHAT THE FUCK'S GOING ON?
THEY'RE GETTING MEGG.

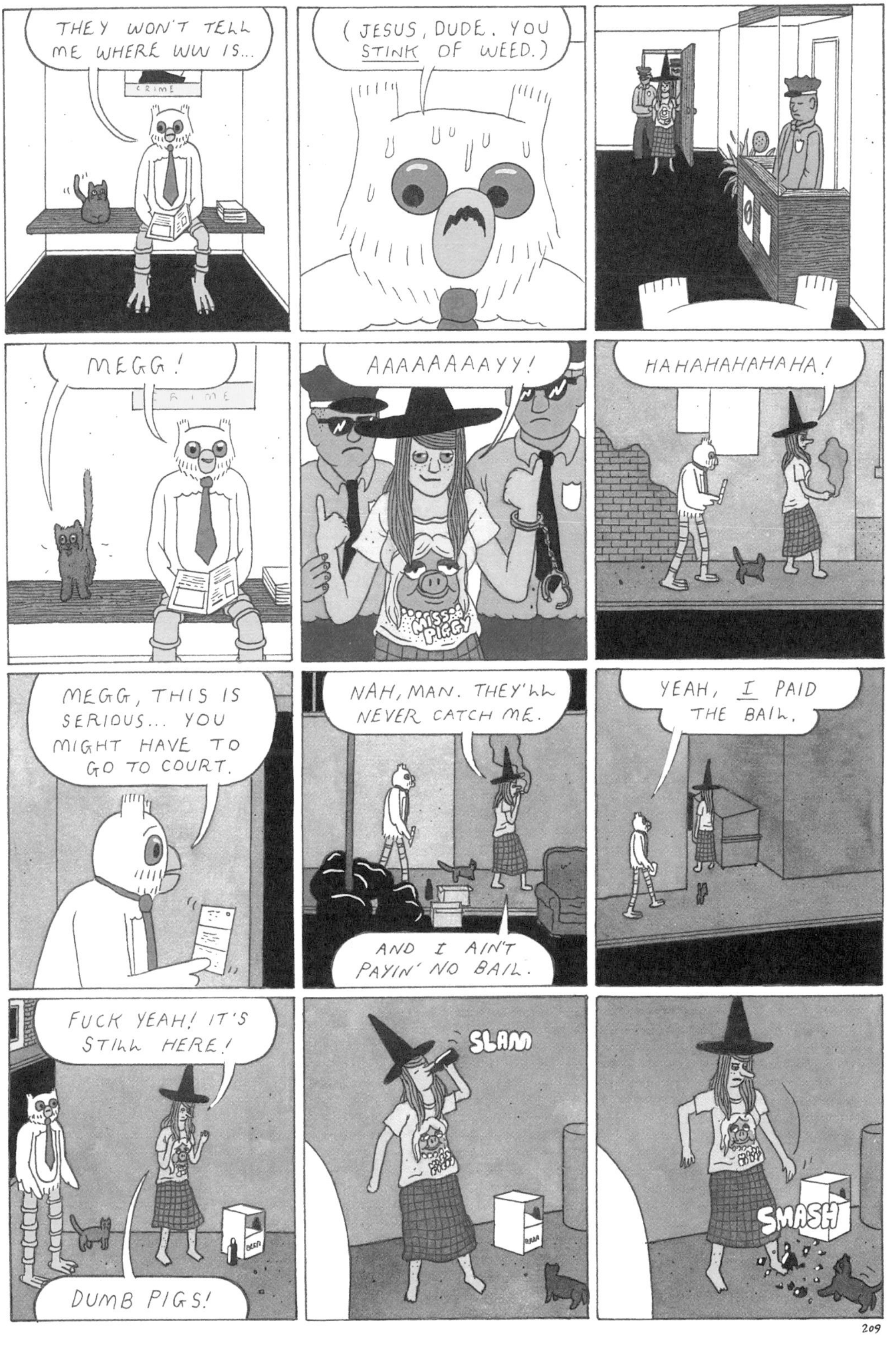
THEY WON'T TELL ME WHERE WW IS...
CRIME
(JESUS, DUDE. YOU STINK OF WEED.)
MEGG!
CRIME
AAAAAAAAYY!
MISS PIGGY
HAHAHAHAHAHA!
MEGG, THIS IS SERIOUS... YOU MIGHT HAVE TO GO TO COURT.
NAH, MAN. THEY'LL NEVER CATCH ME.
AND I AIN'T PAYIN' NO BAIL.
YEAH, I PAID THE BAIL.
FUCK YEAH! IT'S STILL HERE!
DUMB PIGS!
SLAM
SMASH

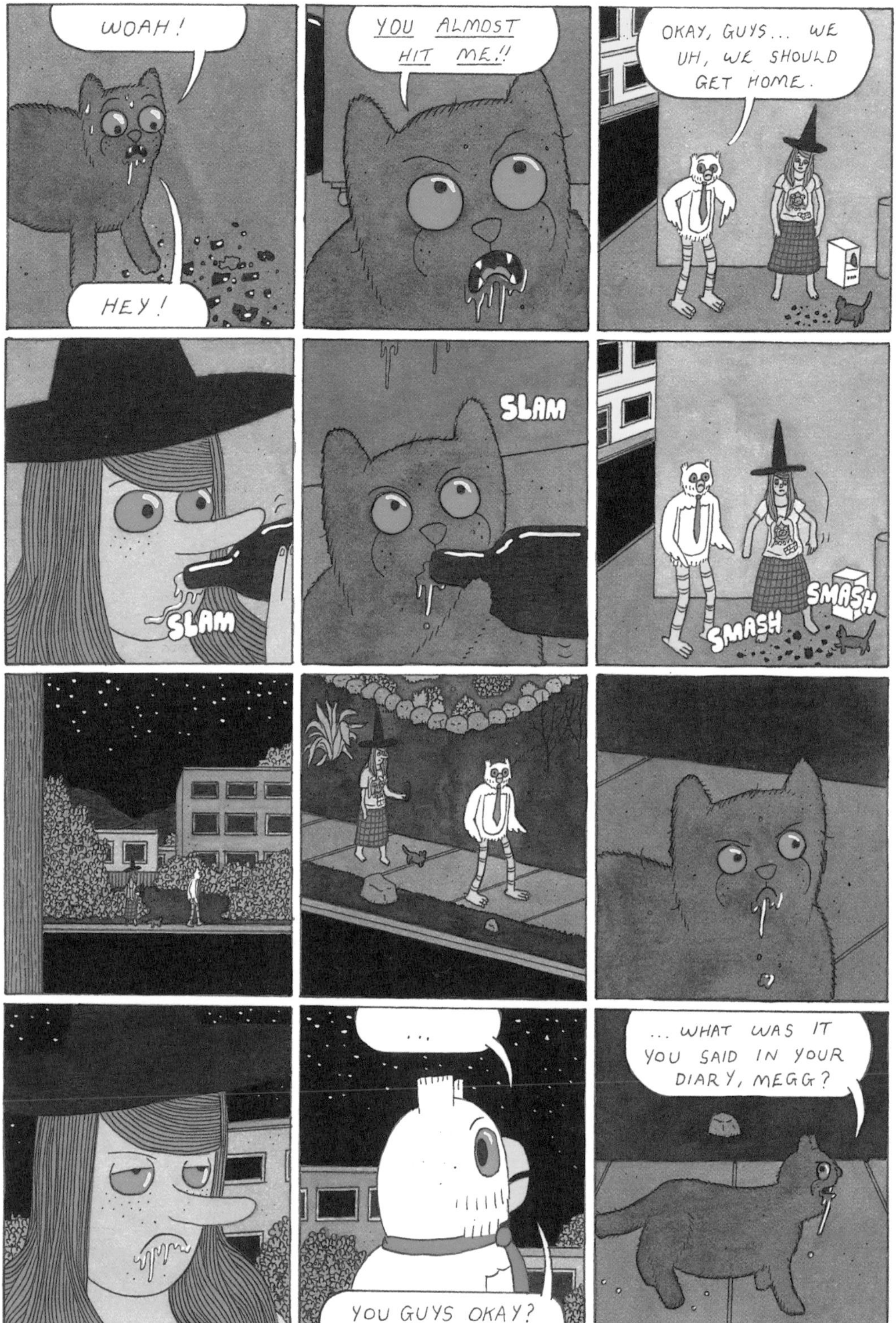
WOAH!
HEY!
YOU ALMOST HIT ME.!!
OKAY, GUYS... WE UH, WE SHOULD GET HOME.
SLAM
SLAM
SMASH
SMASH
...
YOU GUYS OKAY?
...WHAT WAS IT YOU SAID IN YOUR DIARY, MEGG?

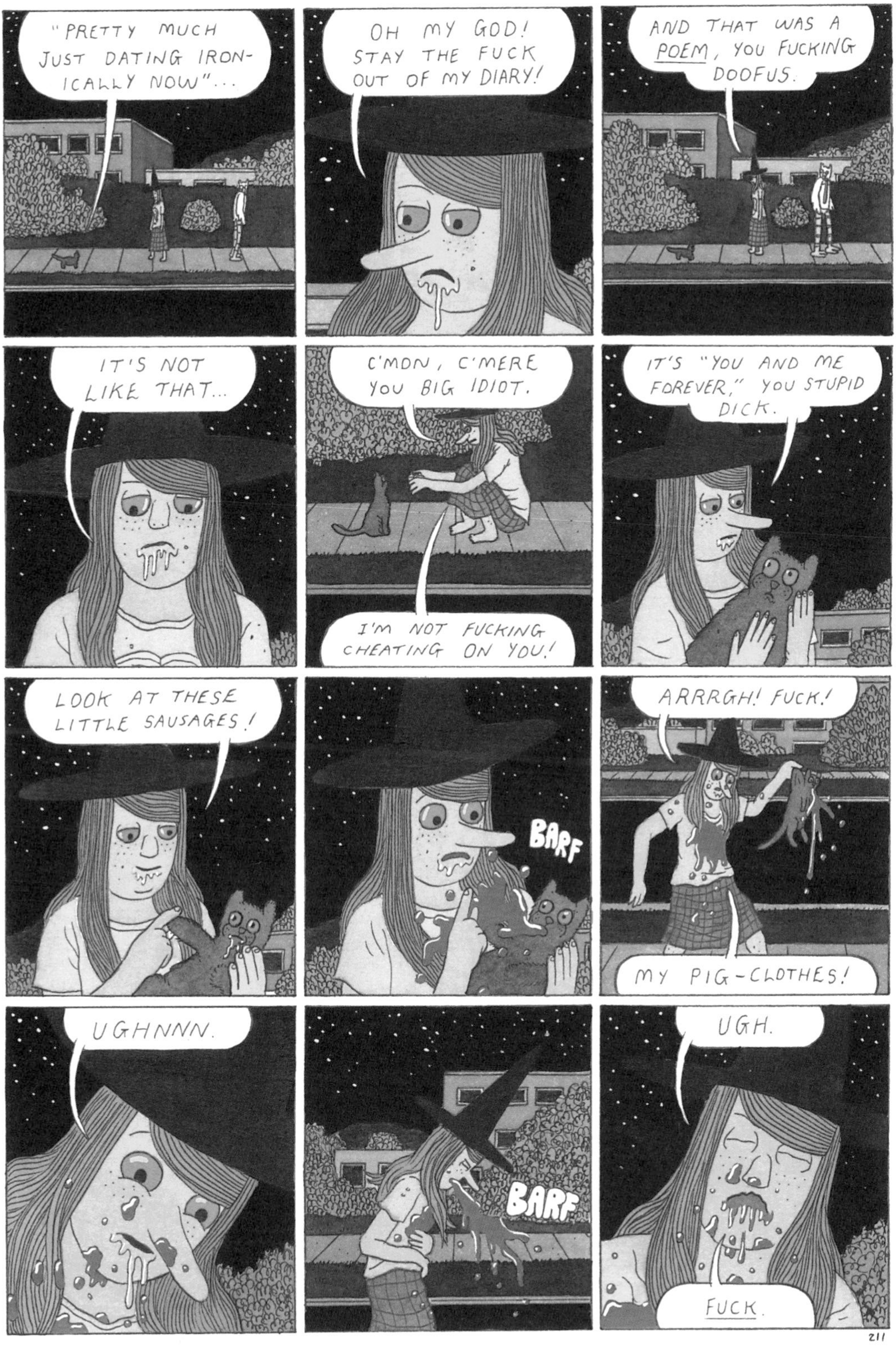
"PRETTY MUCH JUST DATING IRON-ICALLY NOW"...
OH MY GOD! STAY THE FUCK OUT OF MY DIARY!
AND THAT WAS A POEM, YOU FUCKING DOOFUS.
IT'S NOT LIKE THAT...
C'MON, C'MERE YOU BIG IDIOT.
I'M NOT FUCKING CHEATING ON YOU!
IT'S "YOU AND ME FOREVER," YOU STUPID DICK.
LOOK AT THESE LITTLE SAUSAGES!
BARF
ARRRGH! FUCK!
MY PIG-CLOTHES!
UGHNNN.
BARF
UGH.
FUCK.

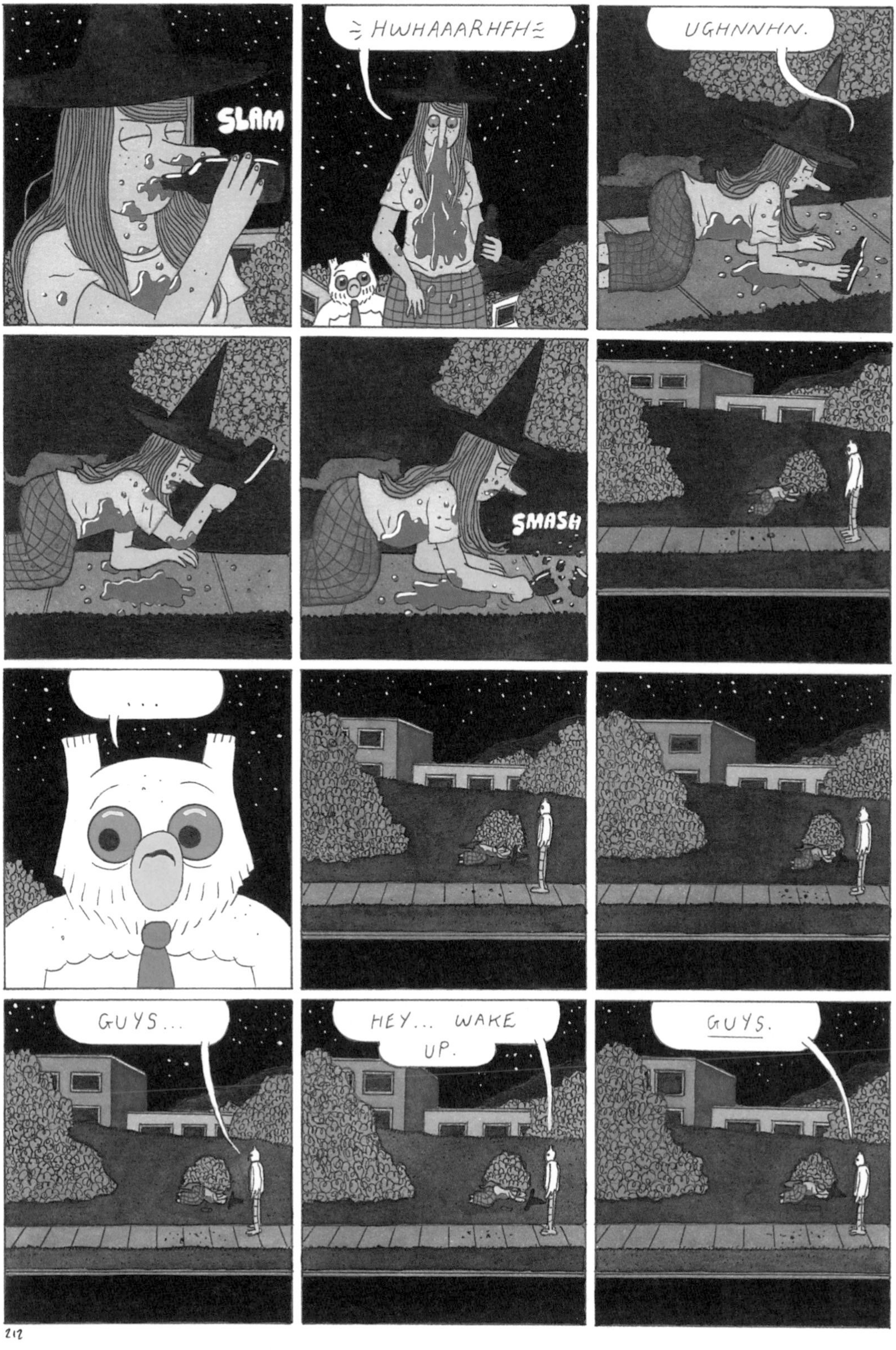
SLAM
≈HWHAAARHFH≈
UGHNNHN.
SMASH
...
GUYS...
HEY... WAKE UP.
GUYS.

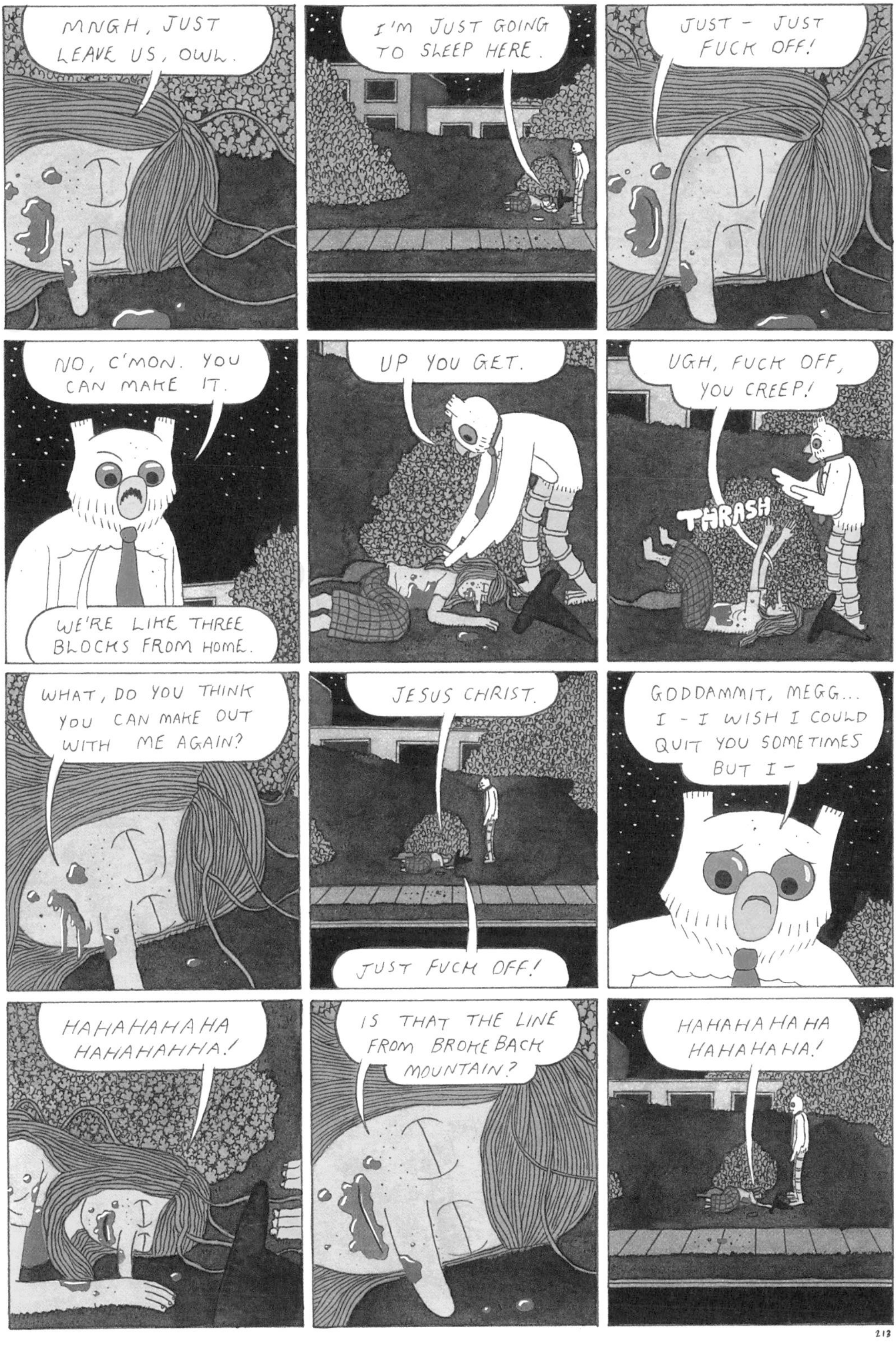
MNGH, JUST LEAVE US, OWL.
I'M JUST GOING TO SLEEP HERE.
JUST - JUST FUCK OFF!
NO, C'MON. YOU CAN MAKE IT.
WE'RE LIKE THREE BLOCKS FROM HOME.
UP YOU GET.
UGH, FUCK OFF, YOU CREEP!
THRASH
WHAT, DO YOU THINK YOU CAN MAKE OUT WITH ME AGAIN?
JESUS CHRIST.
JUST FUCK OFF!
GODDAMMIT, MEGG... I - I WISH I COULD QUIT YOU SOMETIMES BUT I -
HAHAHAHAHA HAHAHAHHA!
IS THAT THE LINE FROM BROKEBACK MOUNTAIN?
HAHAHAHAHA HAHAHAHA!

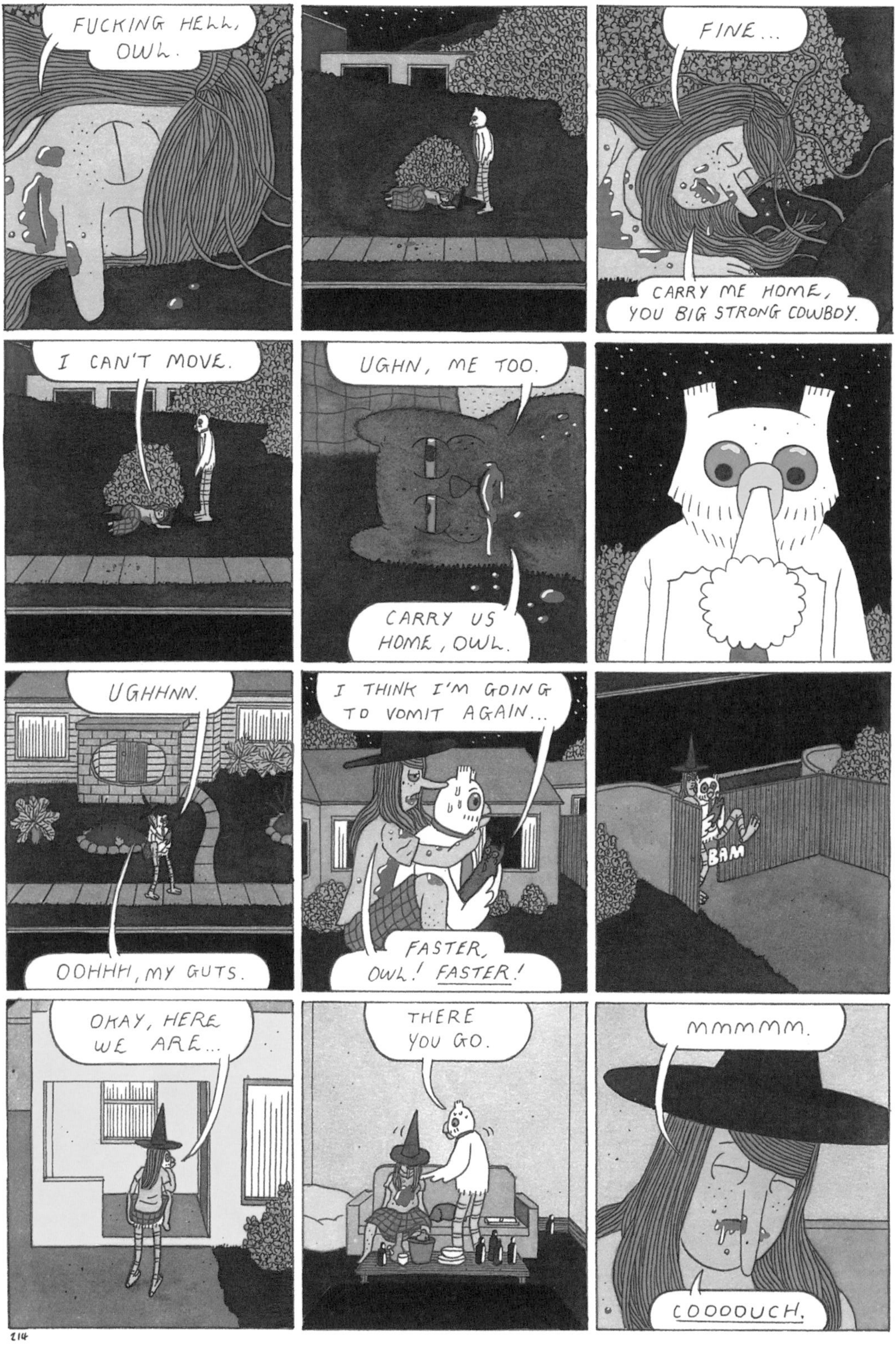
FUCKING HELL, OWL.
FINE...
CARRY ME HOME, YOU BIG STRONG COWBOY.
I CAN'T MOVE.
UGHN, ME TOO.
CARRY US HOME, OWL.
UGHHNN.
OOHHH, MY GUTS.
I THINK I'M GOING TO VOMIT AGAIN...
FASTER, OWL! FASTER!
BAM
OKAY, HERE WE ARE...
THERE YOU GO.
MMMMM.
COOOOUCH.

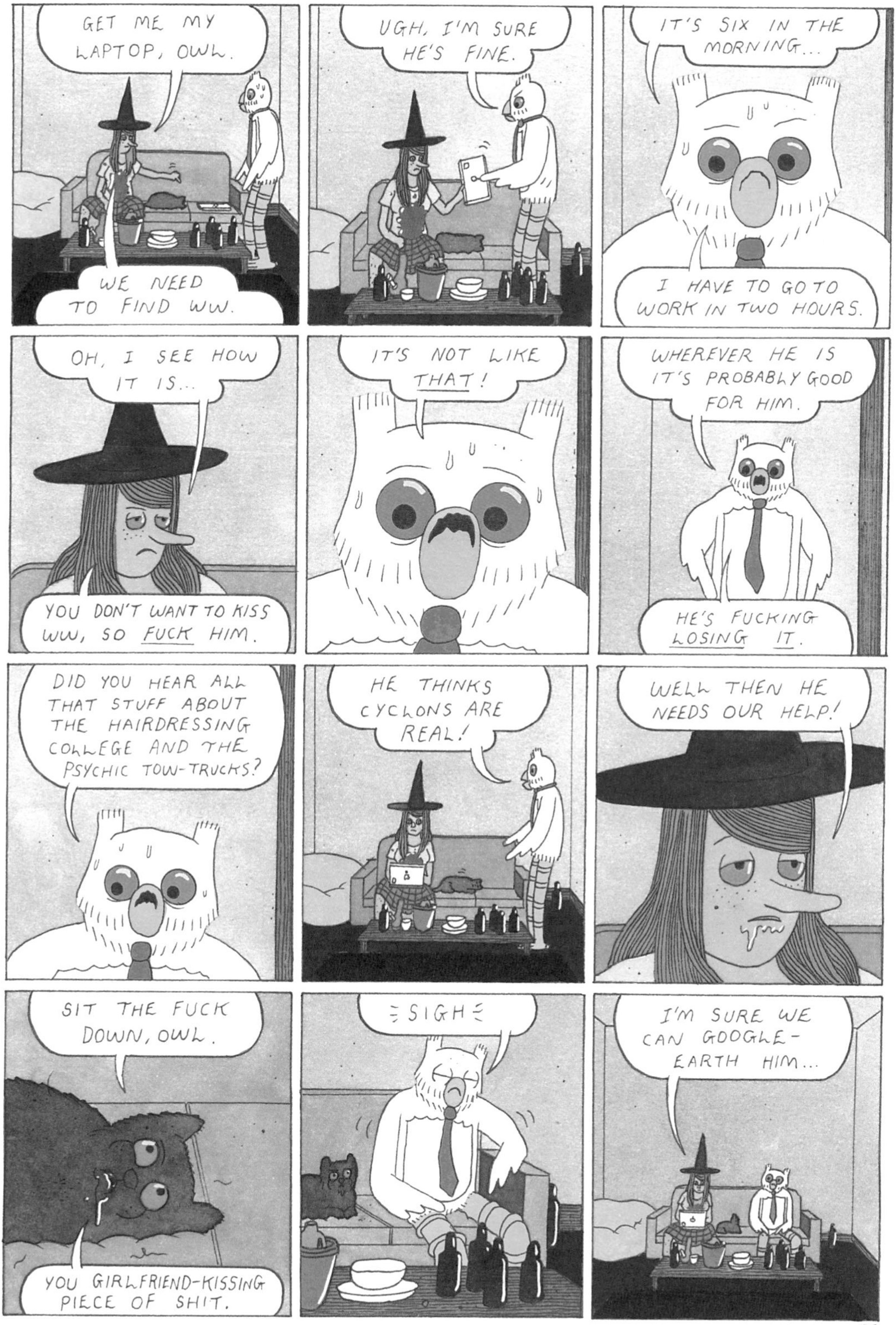
GET ME MY LAPTOP, OWL.
WE NEED TO FIND WW.
UGH, I'M SURE HE'S FINE.
IT'S SIX IN THE MORNING...
I HAVE TO GO TO WORK IN TWO HOURS.
OH, I SEE HOW IT IS...
YOU DON'T WANT TO KISS WW, SO FUCK HIM.
IT'S NOT LIKE THAT!
WHEREVER HE IS IT'S PROBABLY GOOD FOR HIM.
HE'S FUCKING LOSING IT.
DID YOU HEAR ALL THAT STUFF ABOUT THE HAIRDRESSING COLLEGE AND THE PSYCHIC TOW-TRUCKS?
HE THINKS CYLONS ARE REAL!
WELL THEN HE NEEDS OUR HELP!
SIT THE FUCK DOWN, OWL.
YOU GIRLFRIEND-KISSING PIECE OF SHIT.
SIGH
I'M SURE WE CAN GOOGLE-EARTH HIM...

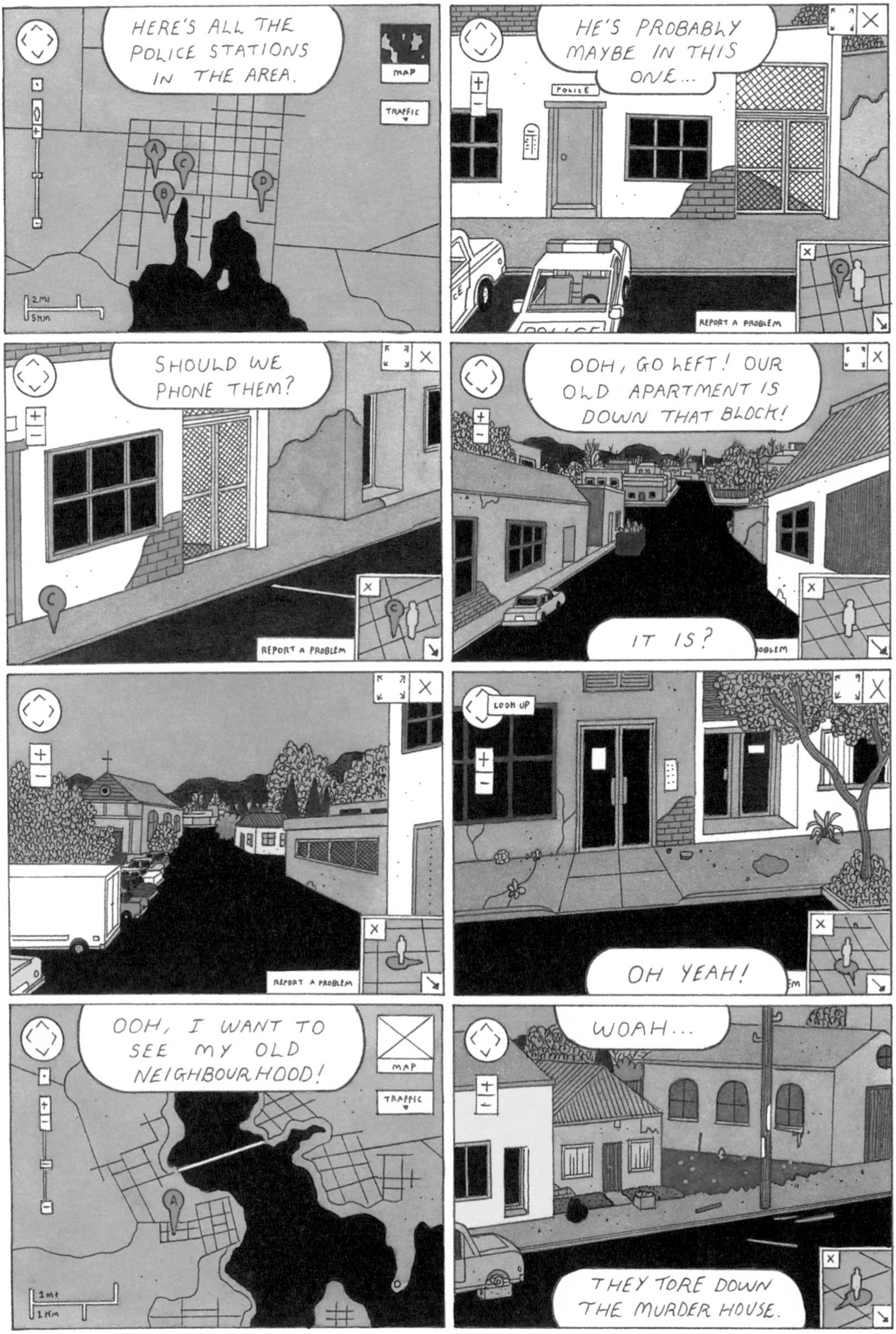
HERE'S ALL THE POLICE STATIONS IN THE AREA.
MAP
TRAFFIC
2MI
5KM
HE'S PROBABLY MAYBE IN THIS ONE...
POLICE
REPORT A PROBLEM
SHOULD WE PHONE THEM?
REPORT A PROBLEM
OOH, GO LEFT! OUR OLD APARTMENT IS DOWN THAT BLOCK!
IT IS?
REPORT A PROBLEM
LOOK UP
OH YEAH!
OOH, I WANT TO SEE MY OLD NEIGHBOURHOOD!
MAP
TRAFFIC
1MI
1KM
WOAH...
THEY TORE DOWN THE MURDER HOUSE.

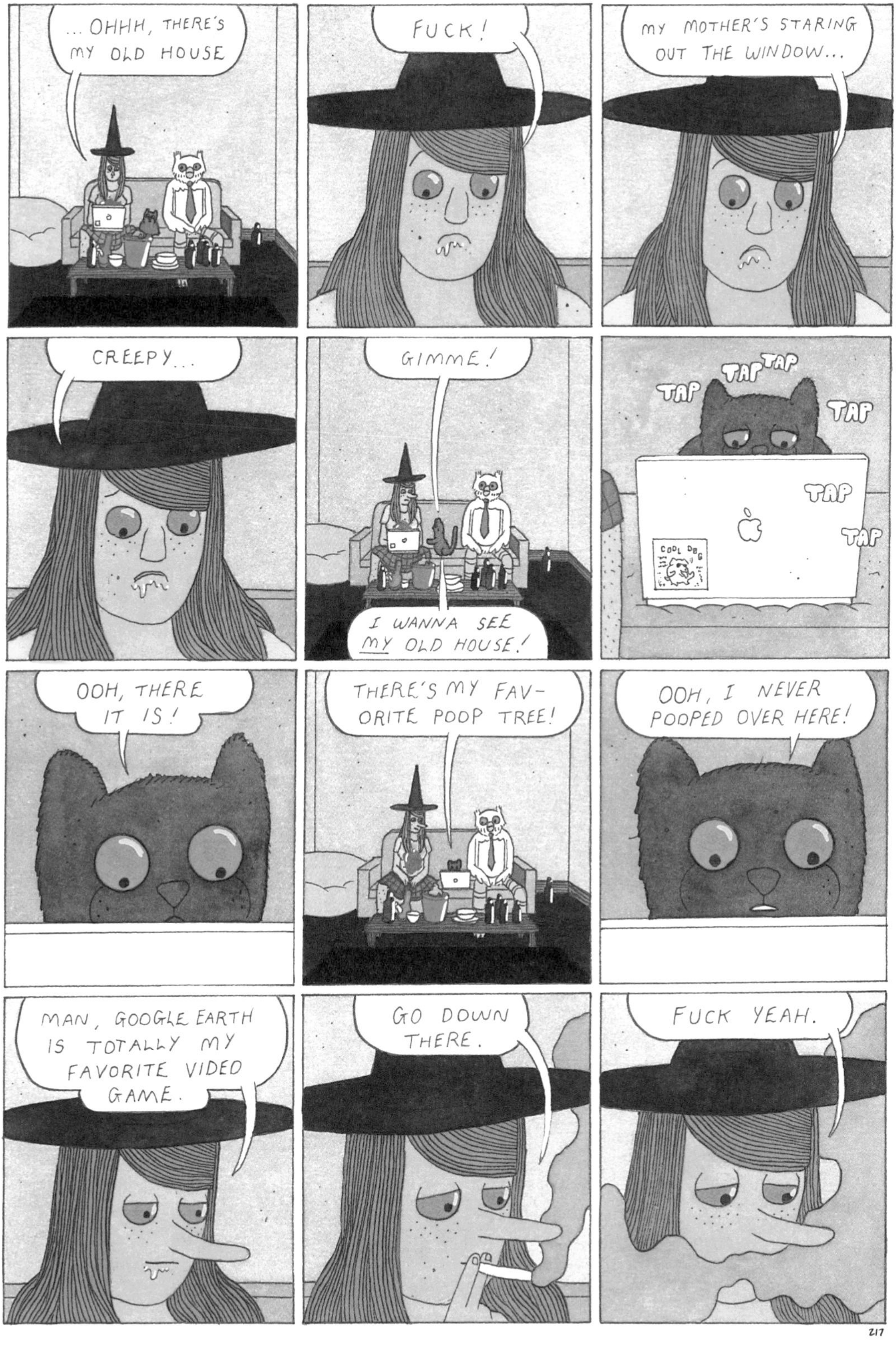
...OHHH, THERE'S MY OLD HOUSE
FUCK!
MY MOTHER'S STARING OUT THE WINDOW...
CREEPY...
GIMME!
I WANNA SEE MY OLD HOUSE!
TAP TAP TAP TAP TAP TAP
COOL DOG
OOH, THERE IT IS!
THERE'S MY FAVORITE POOP TREE!
OOH, I NEVER POOPED OVER HERE!
MAN, GOOGLE EARTH IS TOTALLY MY FAVORITE VIDEO GAME.
GO DOWN THERE.
FUCK YEAH.

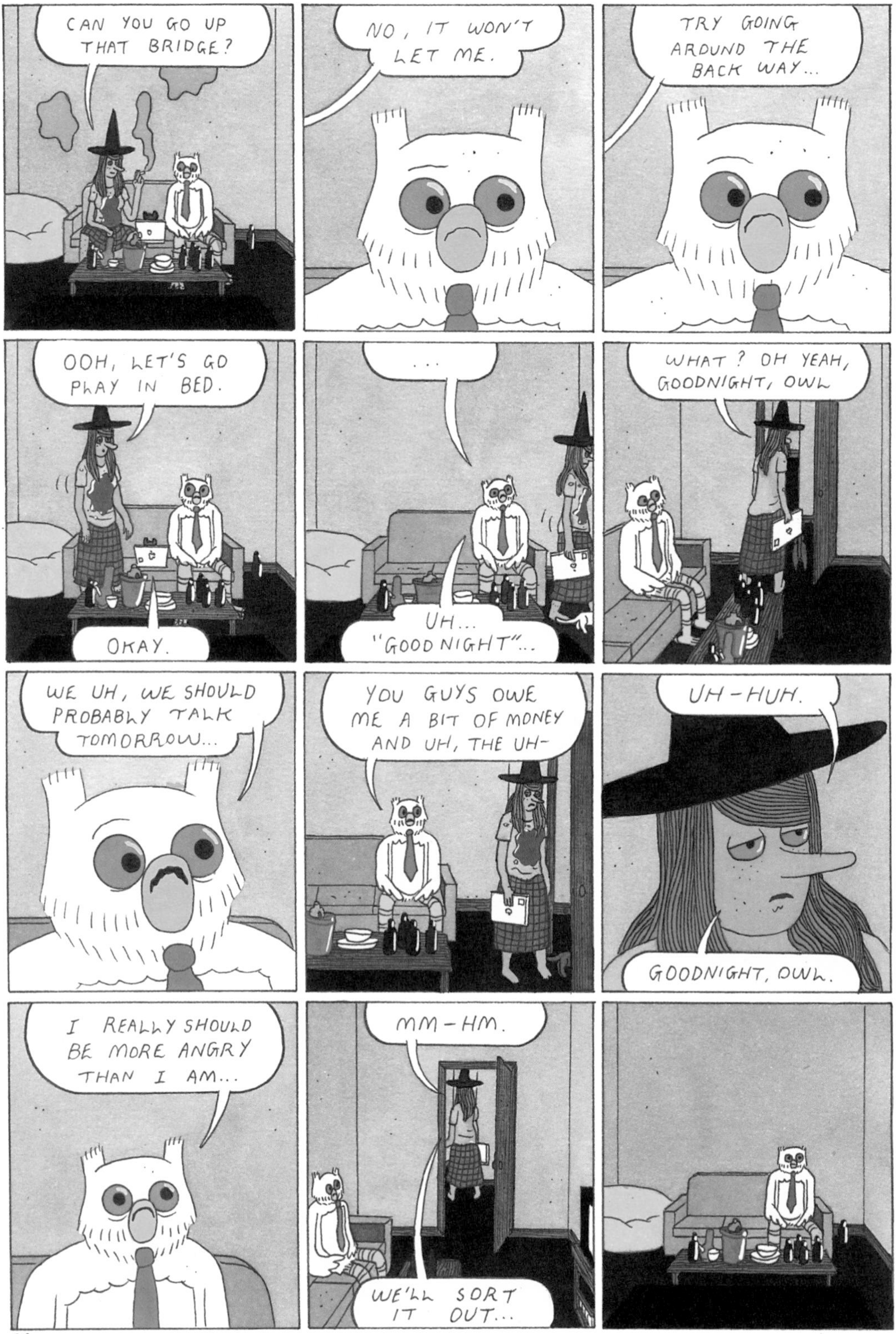
CAN YOU GO UP THAT BRIDGE?
NO, IT WON'T LET ME.
TRY GOING AROUND THE BACK WAY...
OOH, LET'S GO PLAY IN BED.
OKAY.
...
UH... "GOOD NIGHT"...
WHAT? OH YEAH, GOODNIGHT, OWL
WE UH, WE SHOULD PROBABLY TALK TOMORROW...
YOU GUYS OWE ME A BIT OF MONEY AND UH, THE UH-
UH-HUH.
GOODNIGHT, OWL.
I REALLY SHOULD BE MORE ANGRY THAN I AM...
MM-HM.
WE'LL SORT IT OUT...

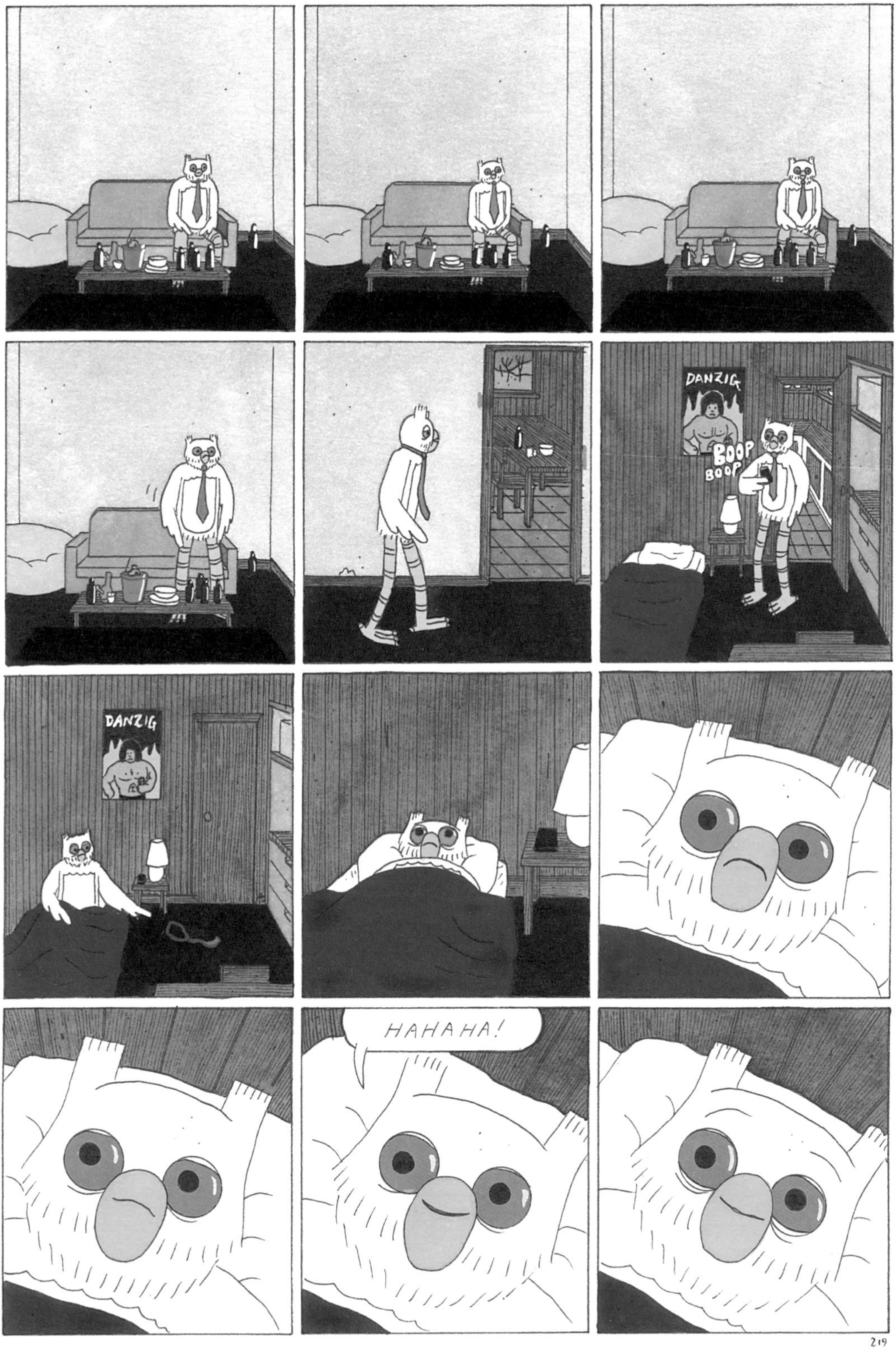
DANZIG
BOOP
BOOP
DANZIG
HAHAHA!

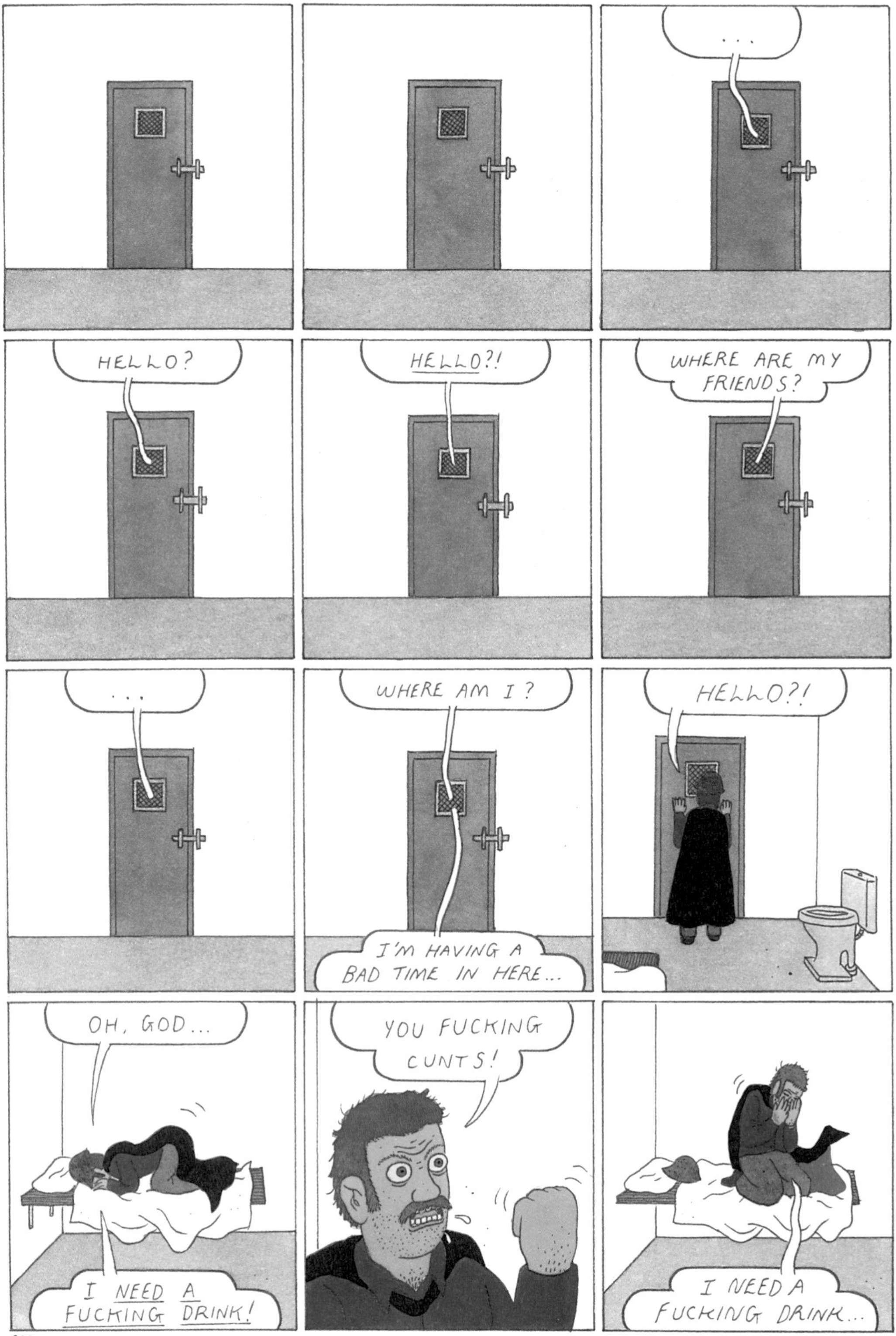
. . .
HELLO?
HELLO?!
WHERE ARE MY FRIENDS?
. . .
WHERE AM I?
I'M HAVING A BAD TIME IN HERE...
HELLO?!
OH, GOD...
I NEED A FUCKING DRINK!
YOU FUCKING CUNTS!
I NEED A FUCKING DRINK...

(THE END.)

CREDITS:

WRITTEN & DRAWN 2013-2017 BY SIMON HANSELMANN IN:

EAGLEMONT, VICTORIA.
BRUNSWICK EAST, VICTORIA.
PARIS, FRANCE.
BACK OF A CAR, SPAIN.
BEACON HILL, SEATTLE.
FANTAGRAPHICS OFFICE, SEATTLE.

JUNIOR WRITING ASSISTANT ON "RAM RAIDS", "BOSTON CLANGER" & "WORST BEHAVIOUR": HTML FLOWERS.

BACKGROUND COLOR ASSISTANTS ON "JOBS", "OWL'S DATE", "HIGH SCHOOL" & "ALTERED BEASTS": MARC PEARSON & LASHNA TUSCHEWSKI.

HORSE MANIA LYRICS BY KARL VON BAMBERGER & SIMON HANSELMANN, 2007 & 2014.

THANK YOU: JACQ COHEN, HTML FLOWERS, ALESSANDRA STERNFIELD, GARY GROTH, ERIC REYNOLDS, PAUL BARESH, KEELI McCARTHY, NICK GAZIN, KARL VON BAMBERGER, ELIZABETH ROSE JAMES, MACK PAULY, MARC PEARSON, LASHNA TUSCHEWSKI, ALVIN BUENAVENTURA, DYLAN DOCKSTADER, KEN PARILLE, MICHAEL DEFORGE, PATRICK KYLE, COREY RUFFIN, ALEXIS BEAUCLAIR, SAMMY STEIN, JOE KESSLER, SIMON HACKING, TOMMY OLDHAM, STEPHANE BEAUJEAN, MISMA TWINS, CESAR SANCHEZ, EL TIO BERNI, CHARLES BURNS, DAN CLOWES, PHILIP HUSTON, FRANK SANTORO, LARRY REID, LEON SADLER, AWAZU KIYOSHI, JAAKKO PALLUSVUO, JASON T. MILES, RAIGHNE HOGAN, NOAH VAN SCIVER, ANNA HAIFISCH, JIM HEMMINGFIELD.

PORTIONS OF THIS COLLECTION PREVIOUSLY APPEARED AS/IN: "LIFE ZONE", PUBLISHED BY SPACE FACE BOOKS, 2013. "WORST BEHAVIOUR", PUBLISHED BY PIGEON PRESS, 2015. "DOME", PUBLISHED BY LAGON REVUE & BREAKDOWN PRESS, 2016. ON VICE.COM & IN SELF-PUBLISHED MINI'S.

ALSO AVAILABLE FROM FANTAGRAPHICS BOOKS:

FORTHCOMING (STILL): MEGG'S COVEN. BAD GATEWAY.

WEBSITES OF INTEREST:
WWW.FANTAGRAPHICS.COM
(ON INSTAGRAM): @SIMON.HANSELMANN
MEGGANDMOGG.BIGCARTEL.COM

FB

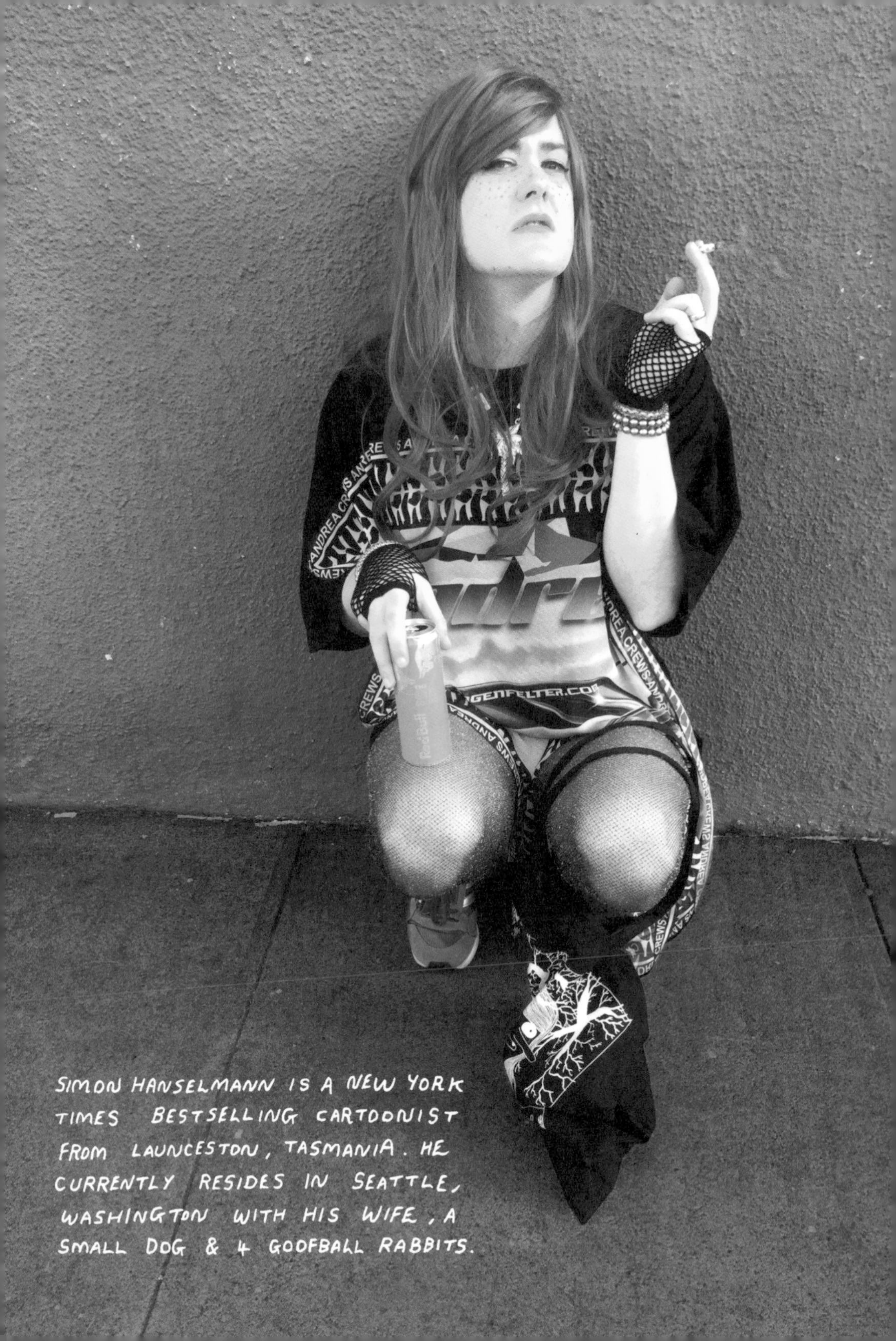
ANDREA CREWS

SIMON HANSELMANN IS A NEW YORK TIMES BESTSELLING CARTOONIST FROM LAUNCESTON, TASMANIA. HE CURRENTLY RESIDES IN SEATTLE, WASHINGTON WITH HIS WIFE, A SMALL DOG & 4 GOOFBALL RABBITS.

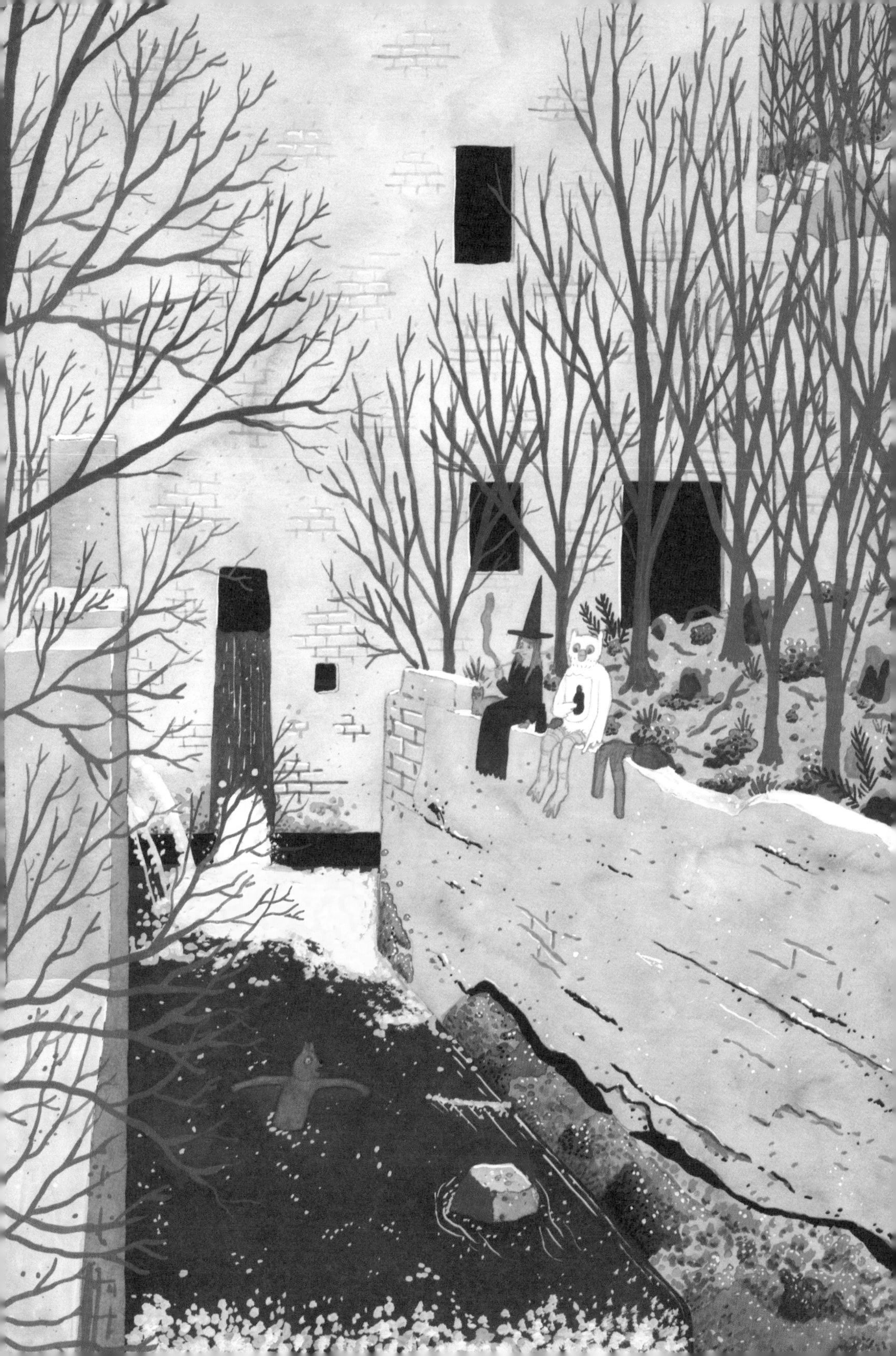

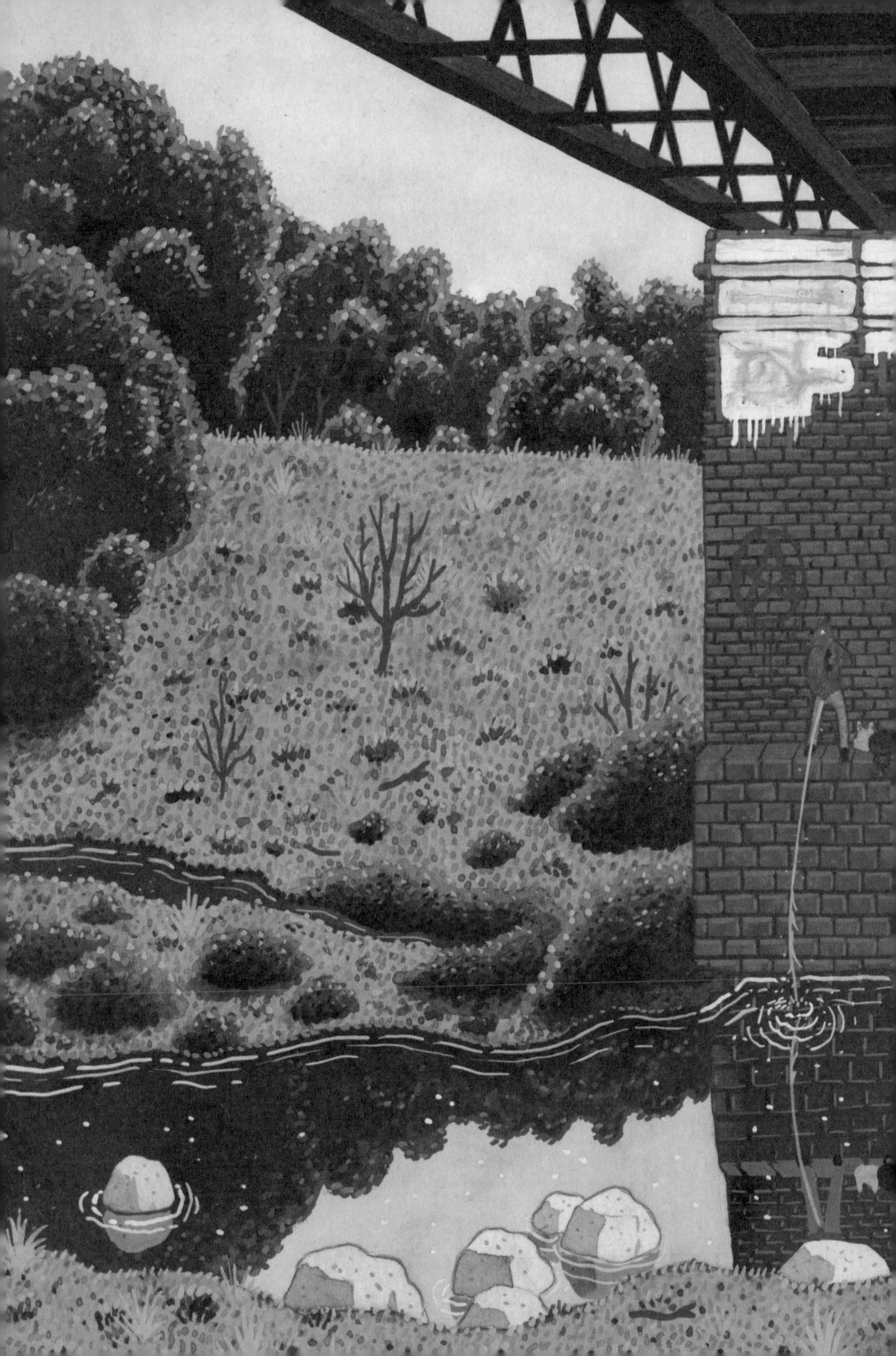